Single Parent Families: Diversity, Myths and Realities

The *Marriage & Family Review* series:

- *Cults and the Family*, edited by Florence Kaslow and Marvin B. Sussman
- *Alternatives to Traditional Family Living*, edited by Harriet Gross and Marvin B. Sussman
- *Intermarriage in the United States*, edited by Gary A. Crester and Joseph J. Leon
- *Family Systems and Inheritance Patterns*, edited by Judith N. Cates and Marvin B. Sussman
- *The Ties that Bind: Men's and Women's Social Networks*, edited by Laura Lein and Marvin B. Sussman
- *Social Stress and the Family: Advances and Developments in Family Stress Theory and Research*, edited by Hamilton I. McCubbin, Marvin B. Sussman, and Joan M. Patterson
- *Human Sexuality and the Family*, edited by James W. Maddock, Gerhard Neubeck, and Marvin B. Sussman
- *Obesity and the Family*, edited by David J. Kallen and Marvin B. Sussman
- *Women and the Family*, edited by Beth B. Hess and Marvin B. Sussman
- *Personal Computers and the Family*, edited by Marvin B. Sussman
- *Pets and the Family*, edited by Marvin B. Sussman
- *Families and the Energy Transition*, edited by John Byrne, David A. Schulz, and Marvin B. Sussman
- *Men's Changing Roles in the Family*, edited by Robert A. Lewis and Marvin B. Sussman
- *The Charybdis Complex: Redemption of Rejected Marriage and Family Journal Articles*, edited by Marvin B. Sussman
- *Families and the Prospect of Nuclear Attack/Holocaust*, edited by Teresa D. Marciano and Marvin B. Sussman
- *Family Medicine: The Maturing of a Discipline*, edited by William J. Doherty, Charles E. Christianson, and Marvin B. Sussman
- *Childhood Disability and Family Systems*, edited by Michael Ferrari and Marvin B. Sussman
- *Alternative Health Maintenance and Healing Systems for Families*, edited by Doris Y. Wilkinson and Marvin B. Sussman
- *Deviance and the Family*, edited by Frank E. Hagan and Marvin B. Sussman
- *Transitions to Parenthood*, edited by Rob Palkovitz and Marvin B. Sussman
- *AIDS and Families: Report of the AIDS Task Force Groves Conference on Marriage and the Family*, edited by Eleanor D. Macklin
- *Museum Visits and Activities for Family Life Enrichment*, edited by Barbara H. Butler and Marvin B. Sussman
- *Cross-Cultural Perspectives on Families, Work, and Change*, edited by Katja Boh, Giovanni Sgritta, and Marvin B. Sussman
- *Homosexuality and Family Relations*, edited by Frederick W. Bozett and Marvin B. Sussman

- *Families in Community Settings: Interdisciplinary Perspectives*, edited by Donald G. Unger and Marvin B. Sussman
- *Corporations, Businesses, and Families*, edited by Roma S. Hanks and Marvin B. Sussman
- *Families: Intergenerational and Generational Connections*, edited by Susan K. Pfeifer and Marvin B. Sussman
- *Wider Families: New Traditional Family Forms*, edited by Teresa D. Marciano and Marvin B. Sussman
- *Publishing in Journals on the Family: A Survey and Guide for Scholars, Practitioners, and Students*, edited by Roma S. Hanks, Linda Matocha, and Marvin B. Sussman
- *Publishing in Journals on the Family: Essays on Publishing*, edited by Roma S. Hanks, Linda Matocha, and Marvin B. Sussman
- *American Families and the Future: Analyses of Possible Destinies*, edited by Barbara H. Settles, Daniel E. Hanks III, and Marvin B. Sussman
- *Families on the Move: Migration, Immigration, Emigration, and Mobility*, edited by Barbara H. Settles, Daniel E. Hanks III, and Marvin B. Sussman
- *Single Parent Families: Diversity, Myths and Realities*, edited by Shirley M. H. Hanson, Marsha L. Heims, Doris J. Julian, and Marvin B. Sussman

Single Parent Families: Diversity, Myths and Realities

Shirley M. H. Hanson
Marsha L. Heims
Doris J. Julian
Marvin B. Sussman
Editors

The Haworth Press, Inc.
New York • London • Norwood (Australia)

Single Parent Families: Diversity, Myths and Realities has also been published as *Marriage & Family Review,* Volume 20, Numbers 1/2 and Volume 20, Numbers 3/4 1995.

The Haworth Press, Inc., 10 Alice Street, Binghamton, NY 13904-1580 USA

Library of Congress Cataloging-in-Publication Data

Single parent families : diversity, myths and realities / Shirley Hanson . . . [et al.], editors.
p. cm.
"Has also been published as Marriage & family review, v. 20, no. 1/2 and v. 20, no. 3/4, 1995"–T.p. verso.
Includes bibliographical references and index.
ISBN 1-56024-688-X (acid-free paper)
1. Single parents–United States. I. Hanson, Shirley.
HQ759.915.S19 1995
306.85'6–dc20

94-14154
CIP

INDEXING & ABSTRACTING

Contributions to this publication are selectively indexed or abstracted in print, electronic, online, or CD-ROM version(s) of the reference tools and information services listed below. This list is current as of the copyright date of this publication. See the end of this section for additional notes.

- ***Abstracts in Social Gerontology: Current Literature on Aging,*** National Council on the Aging, Library, 409 Third Street SW, 2nd Floor, Washington, DC 20024
- ***Abstracts of Research in Pastoral Care & Counseling,*** Loyola College, 7135 Minstrel Way, Suite 101, Columbia, MD 21045
- ***Academic Abstracts/CD-ROM,*** EBSCO Publishing, P.O. Box 2250, Peabody, MA 01960-7250
- ***AGRICOLA Database,*** National Agricultural Library, 10301 Baltimore Boulevard, Room 002, Beltsville, MD 20705
- ***Applied Social Sciences Index & Abstracts (ASSIA) (Online: ASSI via Data-Star) (CDRom: ASSIA Plus),*** Bowker-Saur Limited, Maypole House, Maypole Road, East Grinstead, West Sussex RH19 1HH, England
- ***Current Contents/Social & Behavioral Sciences,*** Institute for Scientific Information, 3501 Market Street, Philadelphia, PA 19104-3302
- ***Family Life Educator "Abstracts Section",*** ETR Associates, P.O. Box 1830, Santa Cruz, CA 95061-1830
- ***Family Violence & Sexual Assault Bulletin,*** Family Violence & Sexual Assault Institute, 1310 Clinic Drive, Tyler, TX 75701
- ***Guide to Social Science & Religion in Periodical Literature,*** National Periodical Library, P.O. Box 3278, Clearwater, FL 34630
- ***Index to Periodical Articles Related to Law,*** University of Texas, 727 East 26th Street, Austin, TX 78705
- ***Inventory of Marriage and Family Literature (online and hard copy),*** National Council on Family Relations, 3989 Central Avenue NE, Suite 550, Minneapolis, MN 55421

(continued)

- ***PASCAL International Bibliography T205: Sciences de l'information Documentation,*** INIST/CNRS-Service Gestion des Documents Primaires, 2, allee du Parc de Brabois, F-54514 Vandoeuvre-les-Nancy, Cedex, France
- ***Periodical Abstracts, Research I (general & basic reference indexing & abstracting data-base from University Microfilms International (UMI), 300 North Zeeb Road, PO Box 1346, Ann Arbor, MI 48106-1346),*** UMI Data Courier, P.O. Box 32770, Louisville, KY 40232-2770
- ***Periodical Abstracts, Research II (broad coverage indexing & abstracting data-base from University Microfilms International (UMI), 300 North Zeeb Road, PO Box 1346, Ann Arbor, MI 48106-1346),*** UMI Data Courier, P.O. Box 32770, Louisville, KY 40232-2770
- ***Psychological Abstracts (PsycINFO),*** American Psychological Association, P.O. Box 91600, Washington, DC 20090-1600
- ***Sage Family Studies Abstracts (SFSA),*** Sage Publications, Inc., 2455 Teller Road, Newbury Park, CA 91320
- ***Social Planning/Policy & Development Abstracts (SOPODA),*** Sociological Abstracts, Inc., P.O. Box 22206, San Diego, CA 92192-0206
- ***Social Sciences Index,*** The H.W. Wilson Company, 950 University Avenue, Bronx, NY 10452
- ***Social Work Abstracts,*** National Association of Social Workers, 750 First Street NW, 8th Floor, Washington, DC 20002
- ***Sociological Abstracts (SA),*** Sociological Abstracts, Inc., P.O. Box 22206, San Diego, CA 92192-0206
- ***Special Educational Needs Abstracts,*** Carfax Information Systems, P.O. Box 25, Abingdon, Oxfordshire OX14 3UE, United Kingdom
- ***Studies on Women Abstracts,*** Carfax Publishing Company, P.O. Box 25, Abingdon, Oxfordshire OX14 3UE, United Kingdom

(continued)

SPECIAL BIBLIOGRAPHIC NOTES

related to special journal issues (separates) and indexing/abstracting

- ❑ indexing/abstracting services in this list will also cover material in the "separate" that is co-published simultaneously with Haworth's special thematic journal issue or DocuSerial. Indexing/abstracting usually covers material at the article/chapter level.
- ❑ monographic co-editions are intended for either non-subscribers or libraries which intend to purchase a second copy for their circulating collections.
- ❑ monographic co-editions are reported to all jobbers/wholesalers/approval plans. The source journal is listed as the "series" to assist the prevention of duplicate purchasing in the same manner utilized for books-in-series.
- ❑ to facilitate user/access services all indexing/abstracting services are encouraged to utilize the co-indexing entry note indicated at the bottom of the first page of each article/chapter/contribution.
- ❑ this is intended to assist a library user of any reference tool (whether print, electronic, online, or CD-ROM) to locate the monographic version if the library has purchased this version but not a subscription to the source journal.
- ❑ individual articles/chapters in any Haworth publication are also available through the Haworth Document Delivery Services (HDDS).

Single Parent Families: Diversity, Myths and Realities

CONTENTS

∞ ALL HAWORTH BOOKS AND JOURNALS ARE PRINTED ON CERTIFIED ACID-FREE PAPER

ABOUT THE EDITORS

Shirley M. H. Hanson, PhD, RN, PMHNP, FAAN, is Professor in the Department of Family Nursing at Oregon Health Sciences University in Portland. Her research interests include families and health, single parent families, fatherhood, and child/adolescent/family mental health and therapy. Dr. Hanson practices as a child, marriage, and family therapist and has authored/co-edited many articles and chapters in books and journals, including *Dimensions of Fatherhood* (1985), *Fatherhood and Families in Cultural Context* (1991), and *Family Assessment and Intervention* (1991). She is an editorial board member/reviewer for *Nursing Research, Western Journal of Nursing Research,* and *Advances in Nursing Science.* Dr. Hanson is a Fellow of the American Academy of Nursing.

Marsha L. Heims, EdD, is Associate Professor in the Department of Family Nursing at Oregon Health Sciences University in Portland. A Registered Nurse, the focus of her career has been the health of children and families and the education of nurses. Her research interests include family nursing and nursing education. Dr. Heims is a member of the American Nurses Association, the National League for Nursing, the National Council on Family Relations, and the American Education Research Association. She has co-authored articles on nursing education and family nursing in the *Journal of Nursing Education* and *Family Relations.*

Doris Moor Julian, EdD, is Associate Professor of Family Nursing in the Department of Family Nursing at the Oregon Health Sciences University in Portland. Her previous experience includes serving as Research Associate with the Mental Retardation Nurse Training Project in Seattle, Washington. Her research interests include family nursing, disability, single or primary parenting, and adult learning. She was elected Fellow in the American Association on Mental Retardation in 1990 for contributions to the field.

Marvin B. Sussman, PhD, is UNIDEL Professor of Human Behavior Emeritus at the College of Human Resources, University of Delaware, and member of the CORE Faculty of Union Graduate School, Union Institute, Cincinnati, Ohio. A member of many professional organizations, he was awarded the 1980 Ernest W. Burgess Award of the National Council on Family Relations. In 1983, he was elected to the prestigious academy of Groves for scholarly contributions to the field, and in 1984 was awarded a life-long membership for services to the Groves Conference on Marriage and the Family. Dr. Sussman received the Distinguished Family Scholar Award of the Society for the Study of Social Problems (1985) and the Lee Founders Award (1992).

Preface

Major changes are taking place in western families exerting dramatic influences on family life, which in turn impact the way professionals interact with families. This compendium includes the work of a multidisciplinary team of scholars from across North America for the purpose of bringing together the latest information available regarding a wide variety of single parent families. The purpose of this volume is to present a synthesis of the demographic, theoretical and research data that resulted from this endeavor. Each contributor to this volume included a brief introduction, demographics, a synthesis of the literature, and implications of that material for their specific kind of single parent family. The volume includes the following topics pertinent to single parent families: general economics; poverty; homelessness; legal dimensions; single custodial/noncustodial mother/fatherhood following divorce; never married teen single parenthood (fathers and mothers); single parenting by grandparents; adoptive parents; widows/widowers; and finally single parents in families of disabled children. In conclusion, a synthesis of major themes across the different single parent family structures is presented, accompanied by implications for research, practice, education, and social policy.

There are four issues and two parts in volume 20: Part I contains issues 1/2 (chapters 1-13) and Part II under separate cover contains issues 3/4 (chapters 14-25). A separate hardbound book which includes all 25 chapters is also available. A glossary of terms is included in both parts. An index is included in the book. Biographical sketches for contributors are located in their respective double issue, and all contributors' information appear in the book.

The overall format for this volume is as follows. Part I includes the following:

[Haworth co-indexing entry note]: "Preface." Hanson, Shirley M. H. and Marsha L. Heims. Co-published simultaneously in *Marriage & Family Review* (The Haworth Press, Inc.) Vol. 20, No. 1/2 and Vol. 20, No. 3/4, 1995, pp. xvii-xviii; and: *Single Parent Families: Diversity, Myths and Realities* (ed: Shirley M. H. Hanson et al.) The Haworth Press, Inc., 1995, pp. xvii-xviii. Multiple copies of this article/chapter may be purchased from The Haworth Document Delivery Center [1-800-3-HAWORTH; 9:00 a.m. - 5:00 p.m. (EST)].

- a detailed overview of all the chapters with implications for research, practice, education and social policy,
- a conceptualization of single parents in the context of wider families,
- a conceptualization of single parenting,
- changing demographic and socioeconomic characteristics,
- economics of single parenthood,
- poverty and single mother families,
- homeless single mother headed families,
- the law and single parenthood,
- single divorced mothers with custody,
- single divorced fathers with custody,
- noncustodial divorced mothers,
- noncustodial divorced fathers, and
- emergent issues regarding noncustodial parents.

Part II includes

- never married single teen mothers,
- never married single teen fathers,
- single parenting by grandparents,
- single parenting by adoptive parents,
- single parenting in families with children with disabilities,
- single parent widows,
- single parent widowers,
- an annotated bibliography on single parent families,
- an annotated video/filmography on single parent families,
- an annotated resource list of organizations for single parent families,
- a theoretical synthesis concerning the state of the science regarding single parent families, and
- a commentary and dialogue about single parent families changing from a stereotype to an archetype.

In summary, this two year project produced a state of the art volume on single parent families. We hope that you find it useful, readable and challenging in your future work with all families. Please let us know your response to this endeavor.

Thank you and best wishes,
Shirley M. H. Hanson
Marsha L. Heims
Doris J. Julian
Marvin B. Sussman

Shirley M. H. Hanson
Marsha L. Heims

Acknowledgements

The co-editors would like to acknowledge the many people who have contributed to this special volume on single parents and single parent families. First of all, we would like to thank all the authors of the manuscripts in this volume for their excellence, scholarliness and perseverance. Second, we would like to thank our colleagues for their assistance in critiquing the manuscripts; they are: Linda Wheeler, Kathleen Tice and Jane Kirschling. Furthermore, we would not have been able to do this without the conscientious and excellent assistance of our support person, Virginia Nufer. We have enjoyed working with all of you and with each other. We also want to acknowledge the support of our respective families as we completed this project. Thank you all.

Shirley M. H. Hanson
Marsha L. Heims
Doris J. Julian
Marvin B. Sussman

Chapter 1

Single Parent Families: Present and Future Perspectives

Shirley M. H. Hanson
Marsha L. Heims
Doris J. Julian
Marvin B. Sussman

SUMMARY. Major changes are taking place in American and Canadian families exerting dramatic influences on family life and the professional of nursing. This was a recently completed project involving a multidisciplinary team of scholars from across North America that brought together the latest information available on a wide variety of single parent families. The purpose of this chapter is to present a synthesis of the demographic, theoretical and research literature that resulted from this project. Following a brief introduction, the authors summarize the changing demographics of single parent families, and present a synthesis of the research literature on the following topics pertinent to single parent families: economics, poverty, homelessness; legal dimensions; single custodial/noncustodial mother/fatherhood following divorce; never married teen single parenthood (fathers and mothers); single parenting by grandparents, adoptive parents; widows/widowers; and finally single parents in families of disabled children. In conclusion, a synthesis of major themes across all these different single parent family structures is given as well as implications for research, practice, education, and social policy.

KEYWORDS. Single parent families, Family futures, Research, Practice

---

[Haworth co-indexing entry note]: "Single Parent Families: Present and Future Perspectives." Hanson, Shirley M. H. et al. Co-published simultaneously in *Marriage & Family Review* (The Haworth Press, Inc.) Vol. 20, No. 1/2, 1995, pp. 1-25; and: *Single Parent Families: Diversity, Myths and Realities* (ed: Shirley M. H. Hanson et al.) The Haworth Press, Inc., 1995, pp. 1-25. Multiple copies of this article/chapter may be purchased from The Haworth Document Delivery Center [1-800-3-HAWORTH; 9:00 a.m. - 5:00 p.m. (EST)].

Major changes have taken place in American families exerting dramatic influences on family life in the United States. Increases in marriage, divorce, and remarriage are among the more notable of these trends (U.S. Bureau of the Census, 1992), but age at first marriage, labor force participation of women, and delays and declines in childbearing are also evident. These individual and collective developments, in the span of just one generation, have altered the structure, process and function of American families. As compared with twenty years ago, an increase percentage of today's families are smaller, more likely to be maintained by a single parent, to have multiple wage earners, to require child care assistance, or to contain step children (U.S. Bureau of the Census, 1989). Individual and family life courses involve many more important transitions today as people openly form, dissolve and restructure households and families.

The litany of statistics regarding marriage and divorce over the last 25 years has been described many times. Beginning in the latter half of the 1960s, marriage, divorce and remarriage rates started on a course that profoundly influenced family living in the United States (U.S. Bureau of the Census, 1992). More recently, the first marriage rates have begun to fall, while divorce rates have leveled off. The remarriage rate initially rose in response to rising divorce rates, but ultimately they declined similarly to that of first marriage rates. High rates of separation and divorce, as well as larger numbers of never-married women having children, resulted in significant numbers and proportions of adults and children experiencing life in single parent families. Their status was often socially and economically deprived, requiring assistance from several societal sectors. It is estimated that almost half of children today will spend time in a one parent family (Zill, 1988; Bumpass, 1990). These trends, although reported as American, may be similar in other complex societies and may be global.

The literature on single parent families has grown in conjunction with these trends of more single parents, more divorce and more parents who have never been married. Most notable was the first special issue of a major family journal on this topic in the January 1986 *Family Relations* (Hanson & Sporakowski, 1986). This former work was well received but the material is now outdated. It seemed timely and appropriate that another special issue be devoted to the expansion of knowledge and research on single parent families. That opportunity came when Marvin Sussman, on behalf of the journal *Marriage & Family Review* asked us to put together a special issue on parenting. We decided that a refocus on single parents was needed.

The purpose of these special issues was to bring together a collection of original articles written by experts in their respective fields to reflect the current state of knowledge about single parent families (Hanson, Heims, Julian & Sussman, 1995). In addition it was important to know what the issues and challenges are in relation to these families in the United States and North America. Our goal was to analyze the literature and empirical research regarding single parent families and parenting and consider what was useful to advance our theoretical understanding, clinical practice, research and education of this growing group of families. We incorporated a special focus on primary parenting within single parent families. Part of our goal was to explore the territory beyond the definition of single parent which uses marital or couple status as the defining characteristic. Our aims were to explore individual parents as primary caretakers, irrespective of the marital/couple status.

This volume examines a broad scope of subjects focusing on single/lone/one parent families where there is a person who is primarily responsible for parenting the children. We intended to present the many ways that one variety of family structure, the single parent family, is operationalized in society today. This volume is written by and intended for multidisciplinary family professionals such as family social scientists, sociologists, psychologists, health care professionals, social workers, therapists, clinicians, educators, makers of family policy and other researchers, practitioners and educators working in the family field. The overall goal of this special volume is a synthesis of theory, practice, and research on single parent families and primary parenting.

Preparing this special issue was an interesting process. First we explored a title in relation to the purpose. We asked ourselves: who are "single parents," "families" and "primary parents." Is there such a thing as a real single parent since it takes two biological parents to create a child? Does single mean more or less? And subsequently, more or less of what? What does primary parenting really imply and is the meaning of the word similar to psychological parent? We know there is nothing single about being in a single parent family as this is about mothers, fathers, children, grandparents, friends, lovers and partners. We are not talking about less, but more: more people, more relationships, more myths, more stereotypes, and more problems. We are talking about less congruency between policies/resources and actual family needs, less availability of health care, and a deficit of thinking and acceptance on the part of large segments of the general public and of policy makers.

Part of our deliberations involved the ever-important definitions, thus setting the parameters for our discussion. Here are a few definitions to start; for others we refer the reader to the glossary at the end of the volume.

> Family: Two or more persons who are joined together by bonds of sharing and emotional closeness and who identify themselves as being part of the family. (Friedman, 1992, p. 9)

> Primary parenting: One parent who assumes major physical and psychological care of the child(ren). In American culture, this is usually the mother, but this practice is shifting with new family configurations where fathers, grandparents, foster, or adoptive parents also fulfill the primary nurturing role. This definition crosses socioeconomic status, financial, structural, gender, age, and generational boundaries.

A recent article in *The Oregonian*, the major newspaper in Portland, Oregon, described the changing definitions and ideas about families. Sidney Callahan, a Professor of Psychology at New York's Mercy College stated that "Amid a variety of misuses of the word 'family,' we can discern dimensions" (April 10, 1993, p. C9). Some of these dimensions are: a shared intentional desire to be a unit, and support and nurturance of members. The author continued by stating that "Most crucially, families share irreversible bonds and a particular history, usually engendered by blood and/or permanent legal commitments. Around this core that defines features of family existence, other kinds of kin and caring may emerge. While a family is a real thing, a "group fact" that has to be reckoned with, our concept of a family may need to be flexibly defined. In new approaches advocating that we bend logic, we understand that sometimes the boundaries of things may be impossible to delineate precisely" (p. C9). This article is an example of many current descriptions of family that represent the broader definitions of family that are useful to family professionals in their decisions about who are single parent families and how to work with them.

Subsequent to determining the general focus on the single parent, we continued the development of this volume by seeking a wide variety of perspectives. Experts in various fields around the USA and Canada were asked to contribute. Many types of professionals and perspectives were considered as people were contacted. Next, a formal call for abstracts was published. All potential contributors were given a broad outline from which to write in order to promote internal consistency of the volume. In addition, an extensive review of the literature was conducted by the co-editors of this volume. One of the purposes of the special volume was to synthesize this wide review of literature form and knowledge.

In the following summary we present an overview of the articles in this special volume. These summaries follow the sequence of the articles.

Following the summary and overview, themes and implications are discussed.

The first manuscript in this special volume was written by sociologist Teresa Donati (Donati, 1995) from Fairleigh Dickinson University in New Jersey. Dr. Donati authored the paper "Single Parents and Wider Families in the New Context of Legitimacy" wherein she describes the social support of single parents going beyond blood lines and traditional policy and societal definitions. A whole special volume devoted to this notion of wider families appears in another special volume of *Marriage & Family Review* entitled "Wider Families: New Traditional Family Forms" and published by The Haworth Press, Inc. in 1991 (Marciano & Sussman, 1991). Dr. Donati argues that the norms of legitimacy currently used by society to define family members are no longer valid or desirable. She considers that the contracts between wider family members may be more short lived than those defined by blood kin. The definition of family could be a shifting alliance depending on the needs of the family. Single parents find the resources they need at the time and place that they need them. The notion of wider families does not ignore some of these family realities, but rather maintains that families exist as social constructions, co-existing with traditionally defined families and frequently overlapping with them in expressing family-like behaviors (Marciano & Sussman, 1991, p. 2). Donati uses the concept of wider families to challenge existing social perceptions of appropriate or functional families through her discussion of how wider families (1) go beyond traditional policy and societal definitions and beyond blood and traditional kin lines, (2) expand the norms of legitimacy, and (3) reflect changing alliances to reflect social constructions.

The next manuscript (Horowitz, 1995) was written by nurse academician June Horowitz at Boston College and coauthor of the book *Parenting reassessed: A nursing perspective* (Prentice-Hall, 1982). Dr. Horowitz provides a framework for the examination of the parenting process which is not tied to a particular family structure or type. "Parenting is the process undertaken with the goal of 'ferrying' children from conception and birth through developmental challenges and life events" to what she called "interdependent functioning" or adulthood. The essential components of parenting that are discussed are: tasks, roles, rules, resources, relationships, and communication. She then bridges the gap between this broader conceptualization of parenting in general to parenting in single parent families. She considers the idea that children in single parent families are not automatically at risk but rather that we need to identify the ingredients needed for adequate or "good enough" parenting. The examination of these ingredients for adequate parenting provide a useful framework for the evaluation of the effectiveness of the many forms of single parent families. She provides the framework and a summary figure for the components of parenting and the related effective characteristics, all towards the goal of the adequate or "good enough parents." Finally, she challenges stereotypical as well as naive thinking in relation to risks, difficulties and challenges with regard to single parents and their children.

The next manuscript was developed by Family Demographer Suzanne Bianchi from the U.S. Bureau of the Census in Washington, D.C. (Bianchi, 1995). She describes the demographic and socioeconomic characteristics of single parent families and how they have changed dramatically during the past three decades. More specifically she outlines the increase in single parent families and examines specific issues pertaining to different structures caused by divorce and unmarried parents. For example, during the 1980s the rate of increase in father-child families was greater than mother-child families although only 3 percent of all children resided with lone fathers. She focuses on never-married mother-child families since this group represents the largest increase in single parent families in the USA today. There are higher proportions of never-married mothers in the black than the white community. Finally she makes the point that single parent families remain disadvantaged relative to two parent families in economic status, health and housing conditions. Furthermore, children living with never-married mothers are the most disadvantaged group of children in single parent families. She projects that one-half of children born in the 1980s will spend some time living in a one-parent situation. Among these children as much as one-third of the time they spend in a mother-child family will be in their grandparents home or living in a household which includes their mother's cohabitating partner. Bianchi believes that our picture of life with a single parent is being enhanced by better methods of data collection and analyses.

Mark Lino, a family economist from the Family Economics Research Group in the U.S. Dept. of Agriculture, wrote the next manuscript on the economics of single parenthood (Lino, 1995). He suggests since there is dramatic increase in numbers of single parent families and the involvement of so many children, that the economic situation in these families is of great importance. He analyzes the trends in the economic status of single parent households over time. He differentiates between single parent families and single parent households. Dr. Lino then explores the economics of becoming a single parent and surviving in this status. At particular economic risk are the increasing numbers of out-of-wedlock mothers who have a lower likelihood of receiving child support. He questions their standard of living and its adequacy for nutrition and health care.

He includes discussions of income, expenditures, assets and liabilities of single parent household budgets–how much money is possessed and how it is spent. He also presents a section regarding the impact on children in single parent families. He concludes that a greater number of single parents are living in wider household situations in order to survive, and calls for more investigation of this phenomenon. Research is also needed on the economic trends for single parent fathers. Given fluctuating economic conditions, periodic research will be needed to assess the contemporary status of single parents, and future or societal implications.

The next manuscript written by a Professor of Social Work, Gary Bowen, at the University of North Carolina at Chapel Hill, along with graduate students Laura Desimone and Jennifer McKay, focused on poverty and female headed households with dependent children from a macroeconomic point of view (Bowen, Desimone, & McKay, 1995). This article examines how recent changes in the economic structure of the U.S. may hinder the successful transition of many single mothers with dependent children from poverty toward welfare independence and economic self-sufficiency, regardless of how motivated they are to seek employment or to receive additional educational and occupational training. Further, the basic theme is that single mothers in poverty increasingly find themselves in a "catch 22" situation. They earn just enough to be disqualified for public assistance but not enough to provide for a minimum level of subsistence. This problem exists partially due to the fact that neither public assistance nor the low-paying jobs that women have provide funds sufficient for subsistence. The authors conclude that single mothers in poverty face an insufficient supply of jobs that pay well enough to move them toward economic self-sufficiency and out of poverty. They recommend that the federal government adopt public policies that counteract the effects of these adverse macroeconomics and more clearly reflect the context of social and economic realities. Historically, efforts to reduce poverty in single mother households have typically taken an individual approach, often focusing on the values, motives, attitudes, and abilities of single mothers. Interventions from this perspective centered on "fixing" the individual. This article focused on structural shifts in the economy within the context of a residual social welfare system upon which most single mother households depend. Here intervention is directed toward the greater environment of the individual. Any comprehensive change effort to reduce the level of poverty in single mother households must address both the individual and situational sides of the equation with an aim of increasing the fit between family needs, family abilities, employability, resources, supports and opportunities in the greater community. Recommendations for public policy include a combination of economic, social welfare, and nonwelfare family policy initiatives.

In a manuscript by Marcia Steinbock, an attorney and a faculty member of the criminal justice program at The Richard Stockton College of New Jersey, homeless female-headed families are presented as relationships at risk (Steinbock, 1995). Homeless single parent families who are already fragmented, are being further disintegrated by a myriad of well-meaning federal, state, and local policies which, ironically promote the destruction of family integrity. This manuscript describes national policies and laws in the areas of Aid to Families with Dependent Child (AFDC), domestic violence, and foster care. She distinguishes the enormous discrepancies which exist between policy goals and the reality of program implementation. She concludes that overall these policies compound the inherent stress that homelessness has on the parenting capabilities of single parents. Additionally, she describes the effects of homelessness on children, largely due to the poverty into which they are born. The disqualification of poor women from public assistance forces them into the labor market, thereby removing adequate health care and child care protection for their children. She also addresses the relationship between foster care, homelessness and substance abuse. She believes the focus needs to be on ameliorating poverty and recommends supporting the emergent trend from an incrementalist emergency mentality to a more comprehensive preventative strategy. She stresses the importance of professionals understanding the macro-level policy issues which account for many of the problems and risks at the micro-level of female-headed families.

The manuscript written by Lynda Henley Walters, a family social scientist and Carla Rae Abshire both from the University of Georgia, addresses single parenthood and the law (Walters & Abshire, 1995). The authors first examine the legal context in which laws affecting single parents have been developed and are applied, and some of the myths about women and biases against women in courts. Following comments on the historical development of domestic relations law and child custody, attention is given to factors that affect custody decisions. There are highly complex issues involving married, formerly-married, and never-married parents. Child support issues are reviewed with attention to reasons for modification and termination and to efforts to enforce support obligations. Third, tax law developments for single parents are also briefly reviewed. Finally, noting that many single-mother families fall below the poverty threshold and considering that welfare statutes and regulations may have the most direct effect of any laws on poor, never-married, single-mother families, the role of courts in shaping welfare policy is covered. The theme of the paper is that although law reform efforts have resulted in a gender-neutral statutory framework for divorce, in practice, women continue to be disadvantaged by the courts. The authors conclude that in this time of evolving family forms and merging sex roles, it is easy to be distracted from serious, ongoing problems of the vast majority of single parent families who are women. Their lives are shaped by unrecognized myths and stereotypes while in reality they are poor, and often educationally unprepared to work for an adequate wage. They still believe that they should be at home to care for children. To better serve single parent families, this country must address the issue of equality. When we understand what is meant by equality, we will be better able to educate children of the future to assume the variety of roles that are required to function in any kind of future family structure including single parent families. Henley Walters and Abshire recommend the promotion of the "best interests of child and of parents."

Linda Ladd and Anisa Zvonkovic, family social scientists from Oregon State University Extension Service, write on "Single Mothers with Custody Following Divorce." This paper is a comprehensive review of the literature on this topic. They address single parents over the life course, adult relationships for single parents, ongoing family relationships, social support networks, divorce adjustment, custodial arrangements, parent/child relationships, financial resources, public policy, educational programs and strengths/limitations of research. Scientists have traditionally perceived divorce as creating a deficit family form. Drs. Ladd and Zvonkovic call for a broader perspective in which single custodial mothers are part of a family structure which is growing and adapting to ongoing transitions. They challenge researchers to explore and critique strengths as well as weaknesses in variant family forms.

Geoffrey Greif, Professor of Social Work at the University of Maryland, writes on "Single Fathers with Custody Following Separation and Divorce" (Greif, 1995). He states that the literature on single fathers, a population that was virtually unstudied until the 1970s, shows this lifestyle to be a viable one. In recent years the notion that the children's best interests can be served primarily by mothers has been questioned. With the initiation and growth of the women's movement and alterations in custody and support laws to sex neutral criteria, mothers no longer have preferential status as appointed custodial parents. Also, women are increasingly choosing careers over parenting, allowing for more men to become actively involved parents. These factors account for much of the growth in single parent fatherhood. Greif reviews the literature of single fathers in both English and non-English speaking countries summarizing the data from the perspective of the internal and external functioning of male headed single parent families. Areas of difficulties for these fathers are balancing work and child care, reestablishing a social life, and interacting with the court system. Fathers who choose the role tend to have an easier time than those who are forced into it. This article provides an overview of custody after divorce and discusses the policy, practice, education and research implications that the literature raises.

Catalina Herrerías, social worker and social service director from Philadelphia, examines noncustodial mothers following divorce (Herrerías, 1995). Dr. Herrerías explores the many contextual and circumstantial variables involved in the process of mothers becoming the noncustodial parents for their children. This is accomplished through the literature and an analysis of a large descriptive study which examines the processes, problems and outcomes of women becoming noncustodial parents/mothers. The processes are emphasized, rather than viewing this as an event with defined boundaries, and Herrerías discusses how mothers may move in and out of the noncustodial role over time. Relationships between noncustodial mothers and their children are explored pursuant to relinquishment. Research on noncustodial mothers reveals that most were reared in predominantly intact households with both biological parents, but with a history that reflects family problems with serious personal consequences involving trust issues, communications, interactions with intimate partners and managing significant relationships. Research also revealed an overall theme of general societal disapproval regarding maternal custody relinquishment, and this negatively affected the mother's self perceptions. The implications of culture for the relationships between the children and their mothers/parents is also explored for families over the life cycle. The author summarizes the personal, social, economic and policy factors in the decision of mothers to become a noncustodial parent. In response to the research and to current conditions, Dr. Herrerías recommends an approach to custody that involves compulsory mediation and more uniform, enforced child support provisions. This would achieve more informed and workable custody conditions, accessible mental health services for noncustodial mothers, support groups for this population, and nurturing professionals than are now available.

In the next manuscript, Greer Litton Fox and Priscilla White Blanton from the Department of Child and Family studies at the University of Tennessee, explore the contours of noncustodial fathering as shaped by changing demographic patterns and shifts in legal frameworks defining parenting rights and obligations (Litton Fox & White Blanton, 1995). Research was examined on the nature of fathering by men who are removed from the customary father role of the maritally intact co-resident family, and placed in a noncustodial father status. Their review of literature covers historic trends, current statistics, and data limitations. The bulk of this synthesis is organized around custody dispositions, visitation, support awards and compliance. The authors address the issues pertaining to parenting of children by noncustodial fathers. Finally, they conclude by proposing appropriate strategies for psychoeducational and therapeutic interventions for men and their families who are confronted with the challenge to renegotiate relationships following divorce. Post-divorce responses and reactions of noncustodial fathers use gender and power as crucial concepts in both familial and broader sociocultural contexts. They conclude that to avoid "father bashing" in society today, we must understand the ways in which men respond to changes precipitated by divorce. This is done by studying their situation in broader social context in which they operate.

Continuing with this theme, the myths and common conceptions of the noncustodial parent are further explored by Joyce Arditti, a faculty member in Family and Child Development at the Virginia Polytechnic Institute and State University (Arditti, 1995). She reviews the literature and presents the noncustodial parents, which usually presents the noncustodial father as a nonsupportive parent and refers to the noncustodial mother negatively. Her review includes research on the societal images about noncustodial fathers and mothers, and common stereotypes about these parents that are not clearly supported by the research. She also addresses the legitimacy issues for noncustodial parents, a concern in discussions of parenting in other-than-two parent situations. Dr. Arditti conceptualizes noncustodial parenting and suggests a more progressive and constructive one of parenthood. The focus is the quality of the parent-child relationships in nonresidential parenting, rather than one that operates from a deficit model. She compares and contrasts the myths regarding noncustodial mothers with noncustodial fathers and concludes that research on noncustodial parents is to fully understand divorcing parents in order to modify the stereotype of the deadbeat parent. She recommends that research, practice and education utilize interactions and methodologies that are sensitive to diversity and process. These two major themes emerged from the review of literature.

Loretta Prater in the Department of Human Ecology at the University of Tennessee at Chattanooga, discusses the never married biological teen mother as head of household (Prater, 1995). The transition to parenthood can be a challenge for persons of any age, considering the fact that most people do not experience anticipatory socialization for parenting. However, the reality of parenthood with its many demands can be a culturally shocking experience for teenage parents. The changes of adolescence occurring concurrently with parenting can create the need to assume multiple complex roles. Then, adding the job of household manager and single parenthood, a lifelong struggle for survival becomes a reality. Dr. Prater's analysis of the literature focuses on the dynamics of never married female parents who are teenage heads of households. She invokes three theoretical models; deficit, decision-making, and subjective utilities. Finally, her synthesis includes model intra- and interrelationships, demographic patterns of teenage mothers, and recommendations for research implications.

Sociologist William Marsiglio from University of Florida, examines young biological fathers who live apart from their children (Marsiglio, 1995). It has only been in the past decade that researchers, clinicians and policy makers began to investigate the role of adolescent fathers. Focus is both on young men who make serious commitments to their partners and children, and the large percent of young fathers who never experience this kind of family responsibility. Because the concept single parent, when applied to teenage fathers, typically implies that they are not living with their children, Dr. Marsiglio primarily addresses issues relevant to nonresidential adolescent/young adult fathers who fathered a child with another adolescent. Marsiglio describes a conceptual model, developed from his own prior work, to depict how a series of interrelated factors affect pregnant/parenting adolescents and their partners. The model indicates that social structure and cultural values/norms play an important role in shaping the macro and micro context within which young men experience aspects of their paternity, and alter their lifestyle in response to becoming a father. These factors affect young fathers through their association with particular social policies/programs and the flow of financial and social supports from significant others. In turn, young fathers' responses to a pregnancy, birth and their future life and well being, in addition to the well being of their partners and children, can be affected by the interrelationship of these micro and macro phenomena. The author challenges researchers to examine these phenomena, suggesting identity and commitment theories. In summary, he believes that future policies intended to increase paternal involvement, especially among nonresidential fathers, will continue to be fraught with political and legal controversy, as the debate over the balancing of mothers' and fathers' rights takes center stage. So the major policy challenge of the future will be to intensify efforts to increase nonresidential fathers' commitments to their children while being sensitive to young mothers' parental rights and needs.

Grandparents are the subject of the manuscript by Linda Burton

(Human Development and Sociology at Pennsylvania State University), Peggye Dilworth-Anderson (Child Development and Family Relations at University of North Carolina), and Cynthia Merriwether-deVries (Penn State). Burton and her co-authors examine the context in which grandparents become surrogate parents (Burton, Dilworth-Anderson, & Merriwether-deVries, 1995). Conditions of the overall population, that is aging, and that of young parents, that is joblessness, single parent households and chronic illnesses of children and parents, have contributed to the increasing number of grandparents in the role of surrogate parent. The authors provide a conceptual discussion of three contextual factors that may influence the surrogate parenting role of grandparents in contemporary American society; temporal, developmental and ethnicity/race. The authors employ an historical and ethnically diverse perspective as they examine the grandparent in contemporary society. Ethnicity and development often exert profound effects upon the process of aging and parenthood for many adults, which is often excluded from the research analysis. Many grandparents find themselves assuming the role of parent with little advance notice. Also problematic can be the individual grandparent's circumstances, which dictate if they experience the role of parent with a sense of accomplishment or one of insufficiency. The instrumental and expressive aspects of the grandparenting roles are presented from the temporal, developmental, and ethnicity/racial context. Recommendations for research are abundant as this is an underresearched topic. The authors suggest that researchers, practitioners, educators and social policy makers utilize the conceptualizations of grandparenting discussed in this manuscript to propose future work with grandparents as surrogate and single parents.

Joan Shireman, a Professor of Social Work at Portland State University, reviews the literature regarding single parent adoptions and indicates that such adoptions offer good homes for young children and for older ones with special needs (Shireman, 1995). There is minimal literature on transracial single parent adoptions. In general, adoption is considered to be a good way to establish a permanent home for children whose birth parents have demonstrated an inability to care for them. The adoptive home, legally sanctioned the approval of society, and the loving and caring of adoptive parents, offers the best hope for children whose parents cannot care for them. Dr. Shireman points out that there has been controversy regarding adoption by single parents. In this article the literature regarding single parent adoption is reviewed and its interpretation enriched by references to personal accounts of single men and women who have adopted. Dr. Shireman's research forms these stories. The processes of adoption for single parents and the characteristics of single parents and adopted children are examined. The main stress in single parent adoptive homes is economic. Adoption subsidies are important in strengthening these placements. Single parent adoptions now comprise between 12 and 15% of all nonrelative adoptions. Single parents are still considered marginal by adopting agencies and almost always receive special needs children or hard to place ones. It is surprising that the agencies will place these high risk children with parents whom they label marginal or high risk. In such instances agency functionaries may be willing to place "risk children" with single parents because they have difficulties in obtaining intact couples to adopt them. Such a pragmatic stance may cover the desire of such officials to rid single parents as adopters by giving them children who are likely to require institutionalization regardless of the loving and caring they receive. However, Shireman's conclusions are optimistic. She says troubled older children tend to adapt better with a single parent because the relationship is focused on one parent, rather than two parents. From the standpoint of the large numbers of children needing permanent family placement, the growing willingness of single parents to adopt, opens doors for a richer family life for parent and child. Thus, adoptive parents deserve the support of agencies and society. Overall, Dr. Shireman concludes that single parent adoptions look more like than unlike same race or two parent adoptions.

Four academics from Utah State University coauthor the next manuscript: Glenna Boyce, family social scientist; Brent Miller, family social scientist; Karl White, psychologist; and Michael Godfrey, family social scientist (Boyce, Miller, White, & Godfrey, 1995). They analyze the research literature on single parent families of children with disabilities in order to understand stress and adaptation in these families. First, an historical overview of the assumptions and directions of previous research provides the base for understanding the problems and concerns of these families. Second, the stress of single parents who are rearing children with disabilities are presented. Third, the research studies are reviewed in relation to their sample characteristics and measures. Fourth, the research findings across studies are examined under the categories of stress, resources, and adaptation. They found that single mothers of children with disabilities often were younger, had less education, and lower incomes than mothers who have partners. The authors suggested that other factors need to be considered in future research and in provision of services there needs to be understanding of the interplay between stress, adaptation, and family coping. They concluded that single mothers' positive adaptation to the specific challenges of having a child with disabilities is a reasonable expectation provided they have services built upon family strengths and competencies.

The next two manuscripts address single parents who have been widowed. Nurse faculty Kathleen Gass-Sternas from Rutgers University focuses on widows as single mothers and provides an extensive review of the literature and a critique of current research on widows as single mothers (Gass-Sternas, 1995). She compares the recent incidence of single parents as less the result of widowhood and more because of divorce or never marrying. Widows have higher incomes compared to other categories of single parents. Also they experience fewer social sanctions. Gass-Sternas reviews the various theoretical approaches to widowhood. She examines the stressors, appraisal of bereavement, ways of coping, grieving processes, resources and health of widows in four types of single widow parent families. She writes about four categories of single parent widows. These are: (1) young widows who are raising young children, (2) widows who are caring for a physically or mentally handicapped child, (3) independent older widows with one or more healthy children, and (4) dependent, ill, older widows with a healthy child in the home. She points out the lack of information on various cultural groups, citing that most research studies are conducted on caucasian or white populations.

Jane Burgess, Professor Emeritus in Sociology from the University of Wisconsin in Waukesha, focused on widowers (Burgess, 1995). Much of her writing and research focused on widowers as single parents. Her paper describes the interactions of the newly widowed man and his children as both adjust to the reality of their new lives. She uses both role theory and ecological perspectives to examine (1) how the widower handles new stresses, seeks guidance and adopts to his new parenting roles, (2) how he copes with his own feelings and needs, and (3) how he adapts to changes occurring outside the family, such as the workplace. She also discusses implications for professionals and recommendations for further study. Historically, cultural values and expectations have determined parental roles. Recently changing expectations about the role of women has created concomitant changes in the role of men, with men participating increasingly with parenting their children. Men have always cared for children under certain circumstances, because of the high maternity mortality in past centuries. Widowed fathers were the original custodial fathers, however, when men had custody of their children, they were not seen as being capable of providing primary care for them, and often were pressured into remarriage or enrolling a relative to become a substitute mother. In either case, men were seldom identified as being the primary parent. The numbers of widowers serving as primary parents has remained steady despite the increase in population. For widowers who assisted their wives in the rearing of children assuming full responsibility is less difficult. That is, in general fathers who share in nurturing their children before the death of the mother, tend to do better in providing social and emotional care for their children. The age of children, when their mother dies, greatly influences the development of reciprocal interaction between children and fathers. Younger children seem to accept the change more readily than older children. Widowers who receive voluntary assistance with child care from family friends or neighbors find less stress in performing their roles as fully responsible parents. A final section discusses implications for professionals and recommendations for further study.

Three manuscripts deal with resources for scholars, clinicians, educators and policy makers working with families who have single or primary parents. The first is a bookshelf by Dr. Ben Schlesinger, Faculty of Social Work at the University of Toronto, Canada (Schlesinger, 1995). He wrote a previous bookshelf on single parent families for the January, 1986, vol. 35, no. 1 issue of *Family Relations*, which covered the years 1978-1985. The current one is an update and includes some overlap with the first. Ben Schlesinger developed a summary and annotated bibliography containing 125 entries of books and special editions of journals related to the topic of single parent families. The entries cover the 1980 to 1990 period, and include cross-cultural, ethnic and international citations. The references are arranged generally according to the existing literature and the chapter titles in the overall volume, thus assisting the reader to find further relevant literature. Information regarding general sources and methods of access are included. This bookshelf will be useful for researchers, clinicians and educators.

The second manuscript is a filmography, written by Dr. Lee Kimmons, Department of Human Resources at the University of Hawaii (Kimmons, 1995). The purpose of Lee Kimmons' filmography/videography is to increase readers awareness of recent film titles dealing with some aspect of single parenting. Most titles selected are for short educational films, but a few dramatic lengthy releases now available are included. Dr. Kimmons found that videotape dominate the market. The titles are grouped in the following categories: (1) general interest, (2) teenage single parenting, (3) children in single parent families, (4) single parents, and (5) theatrical releases. Dr. Kimmons also gives the addresses and telephone numbers of the distributors with each title and recommends appropriate audience levels, by age, for the films.

The third manuscript is a resource guide to national and community agencies written by Dr. Doris Julian, Professor Emeritus at the Oregon

Health Sciences University School of Nursing in Portland, Oregon (Julian, 1995). National and community resources for single parent families and primary parenting are summarized and annotated. She provides a full description of types of agencies and formalized resources and guides for professionals from multiple disciplines as they interact with primary parents and their families. Many resources are also of value to parents in general.

This volume ends with two unique manuscripts. First, Marilyn Ihinger-Tallman, sociologist at Washington State University, was asked to review all the manuscripts and synthesize the material (Ihinger-Tallman, 1995). Further, she was asked to build on her earlier similar work on single parent families published in the journal *Family Relations* (Hanson & Sporokowski, 1986). She brings together the multiple factors that impact single parent families and effect their quality of life and well-being. In doing so, she identifies influential variables at three levels–institutional, interpersonal and individual, and then presents a model that includes the most salient determinants of an emotionally healthy and satisfying life for single parents and their families. The factors that promote or decrease this process were grouped into sets of variables that fit into the three analytic levels of individual personality characteristics, interactional networks and institutions in the environment. Dr. Ihinger-Tallman weaves the concept of temporality over the levels to reflect the importance of process and transition in the lives of single parents and their families.

Finally, the volume ends with a commentary by Kris Jeter, the analytic essay editor for *Marriage & Family Review.* The article incorporates ideas stemming from anthropology, archaeology, art, history, literature, research methodology, religion, sociology and psychology. The author explores the question: "Is there something or someone vitally missing in a single parent family?" Historically, the family has always been challenged, but throughout all of its changes, a continuity of care emerges. By relating stories based on Hesiod as well as Hebrew/Christian scriptures, Dr. Jeter proposes a schematic to help elevate typical views of the single parent family from that of a stereotype of victimization to one of responsible archetype. She ends by discussing a program in New York called *Mama Said* where special work is done with single mothers to elevate their quality of life through the use of time-honored lessons of female wisdom handed down through the centuries. ". . . choice by responsible adults to bear and rear children alone is an ancient tradition and worthy of praise today in the light of its time-honored integrity."

CONCLUSIONS

In conclusion, much has been written on single parenting but myths and gaps continue to exist. For example, treating single mothers and welfare mothers interchangeably continues and the role of economics is underplayed. There are gaps in our knowledge about fathers from culturally and ethnically diverse backgrounds, especially black men. Although Burton writes about grandparents as single parents, there is little known about grandfathers. Gaps that remain unfilled even in this volume include some focus on the single parented child(ren), and gay and lesbian (homosexual) single parents. Certainly there are gaps in our knowledge about healthy single parent families and single parents who are ethnically diverse. The editors acknowledge that we were unable to cover every important category of information regarding this topic.

The editors and authors in this volume attempted to grasp what it means to parent within these families. The chapters described commonly known as well as new categories of single parent families. We described the diversity as well as the numerous risks/issues: risks of stereotypical thinking and the issues of viability. As we defined, redefined, described and categorized, we continually asked ourselves: what are the critical issues? We remembered the old saying "the more we change, the more we stay the same." Our history reflects that the American people are not as different as one may think. Therefore, to review the history of the single parent family and single parenting is as important an activity as the review of current practice. In closing, the editors provide an overview of implications for research, practice, social policy, welfare and education as a guide for the future work on single parent families and primary parenting.

Implications for Research

1. Research needs to differentiate groups of single parents in order to reduce confounding variables. At least we need an indepth description of the population. This is critical in order to establish risk factors and correlations.

2. Extensive indepth qualitative research is needed to gain an understanding of the conditions and variables for the many types of single parent families and primary parents.

3. There is a need to define and describe what is a family. Collecting life stories of the experiences of single adults beginning in their childhood is a robust technique to collect such data. Such definitions and descriptive clarity would immediately reduce the pathological myth of single parents. Researchers could then examine the many different types of families with

many different and similar needs. How similar and different are these families as they deal with different types of helpers and facilitators in their quest for livelihood?

4. Related to the above item is correcting the paucity of research on family/organizational linkages. The concern is how families relate to large scale bureaucracies and who represents the best interests of the family individual and the whole. A related issue is the role of the kin network and wider family in such relationships. Of particular concern is how "non-traditional" families utilize "like family" members in dealing with bureaucracies and as social supports.

5. Researchers should explore the emergent family life cycles for single parents and primary parents. For example, intergenerational boundaries and cycles of parenthood are being blurred for grandparents as they provide primary parenting for their grandchildren and greatgrandchildren.

6. We are in need of research that challenges current myths that exist regarding single parent characteristics and practices. Important foci are legal, economic and parenting concerns.

7. Research is suggested on the type of parenting that occurs between parents and children. The relationship needs to be conceptualized and studied as a phenomenon irrespective of the marital or coupled structure of the family. Structure is not the only legitimate referent for determining or attributing parental characteristics.

8. There is a need to reconceptualize the special issues of single parent families and the issues that they share and differ with dual parent families. This process of delineating and defining variables for studies with families is important for future research.

9. The meaning of single parenthood to holders of this role over the life course is a high priority research activity. How do single parents think and feel at various stages of the life course? Do their perceptions of reality, interpersonal and interorganizational relationships, and economic and social needs remain constant or change over time of a life span? The objective would be to illuminate the complexity and variability of the single parent role over the life course.

10. Given the demographic predictions of a major increase in the incidence of births by unmarried mothers in the 21st century, far beyond the current 30% estimate, a new paradigm for practice is now required. The old structure does not work to change the myths, ideologies, economic and social status of this kind of single parent. A new non-pathological paradigm, based on self-esteem, empowerment, nurturance and caring is one of the highest needs and objectives of the family scholar. Developing and testing this new paradigm is priority.

11. Sources and bases of stigmatization and stereotyping of "singleness" requires systematic investigation. The most maligned and stereotyped is the black single teenage mother on welfare, although most other types of singles are also viewed through the welfare lens. Why is there a persistence of this myth? What is an alternative and how can it be promulgated and enhanced?

Implications for Practice

1. We must continue to ask ourselves and the families with whom we interact: In whose best interest are we acting? Which questions are we asking that should be continued to be asked?

2. All family practitioners should question their own practices and actions with single parents and their families. What messages are being sent and are these the intended messages? What messages do single parents perceive they are receiving? An answer requires research using a conceptual framework which uses communication theory.

3. Practitioners need to develop and compile a comprehensive prevention strategy, rather than an incrementalist emergency one. For example, after determining the impact of working poverty on society, consider options for action.

4. Consider how the viability of a family is defined by family researchers and groups of practitioners and policy makers. Determine appropriate interventions after examining the impact of these definitions on single parents, single parent families and primary parents.

5. In view of the changing roles of women and men in relation to primary parenting, ask: What assistance can be given to both genders of single parents? Practitioners often conceptualize mothering as a verb and not a noun. Mothering is not gender specific to females and males can also learn how to nurture children. We are just beginning to do so in increasing numbers. What support can they expect and receive when taking on this unfamiliar role?

6. Recognize that all families expect and deserve legitimacy for their "alternate" forms, because these families are real. These varietal forms need to be viewed as constituting a significant portion of mainstream family life in America. Practitioners need to educate others on these points and act politically when relevant.

7. Develop sensitivity and competence when working with the special and individual needs of single parents, primary parents and single parent families. Their needs and values vary widely so they cannot be viewed as one homogenous population.

8. Practitioners should become knowledgeable of the many resources that exist for single parents and single parent families. Through multidisci-

plinary coalitions, practitioners can cooperate to increase awareness and accessibility to resources for scholars, researchers, policy makers and other practitioners.

9. Challenge the use of the deficit model for single parent families, and offer more affirmative models. There are many paths to a high quality and satisfying life.

10. Single parent families have many of the same issues and experiences as dual parent families. Practitioners often address only the unique issues of these families, but forget the legitimacy of general overall parental issues that all families have in common.

Implications for Social Policy and Social Welfare

1. Federalize and standardize Aid to Families with Dependent Children (AFDC).

2. Increase the minimum wage and reduce the inequities between men and women regarding pay and jobs. Labor market discrimination persists as lower wages and occupational segregation.

3. Promote programs that include both training and placements. That is, do not train people for jobs that do not exist, and include placement in jobs that provide adequate salaries. Also, promote elimination of jobs that are extremely low paying without benefits, as these perpetuate problem of the working poor.

4. Allow asset accumulation for the poor, so they can build their own safety net. Many policies now prohibit the poor from saving, requiring them to use *all* of their assets before being eligible for *any* assistance. Disallowing any asset accumulation decreases their ability to sustain living requirements when extra expenses arrive.

5. Support efforts to modify family policy to reflect both dual and single parent families as legitimate structures. That is, move beyond using the two parent family as the benchmark or gold standard against which all other families are judged.

6. Advocate and take action on the interpretations of law and legitimacy for single parents, primary parents and single parent families.

7. Work to expose the incongruencies between stated policy goals and people's actual needs and conditions. Many policies are counterproductive to their stated goals. For example, work to resolve the paradox of financial independence and welfare for single mothers. The United States has a large set of cumbersome laws and policies that do not reflect current realities of single parent families in this economy.

Implications for Education

1. Conduct discussions about families, including definitions that go beyond simple marital structures.
2. Discuss and hold seminars on definitions of single parent and primary parenting with many intra- and inter-disciplinary colleagues and students.
3. Explore metaphors for parenting. Metaphors are a useful way to characterize and explore the many meanings of a given activity. For example, one metaphor for single parenting is the MAP, or "multiple approaches to parenting." Conceptualize an airplane runway being approached from any number of directions and modes. Then think that there are many ways to land as a single parent!

CONCLUSION

In conclusion, we the editors and contributors present this volume to you the readers. It was constructed by a multidisciplinary group of authors, and then reviewed by the co-editors and external reviewers. Our overall goal was to provide a comprehensive and thought-provoking volume on single parents and single parent families. Now discover your own, new thoughts, perspectives and practices as you examine the themes, perspectives, changes and implications for practice, research, education and policy.

BIBLIOGRAPHY

Ahlburg, D. A., & DeVita, C. J. (1992). New realities of the American family. *Population Bulletin, 47*(2), 1-42.

Arditti, J. A. (1995). Noncustodial parents: Emergent issues of diversity and process. *Marriage & Family Review, 20*(1/2), 283-304.

Bianchi, S. M. (1995). The changing demographic and socioeconomic characteristics of single parent families. *Marriage & Family Review, 20*(1/2), 71-97.

Bianchi, S. M. (1990). American's children: Mixed prospects. *Population Bulletin, 45*(1), 1-43.

Bowen, G. L., Desimone, L. M., McKay, J. K. (1995). Poverty and the single mother family: A macroeconomic perspective. *Marriage & Family Review, 20*(1/2), 115-142.

Boyce, G. C., White, K., Miller, B. C. & Godfrey, M. K. (1995). Single parenting in families of children with disabilities. *Marriage & Family Review, 20*(3/4), 389-409.

Bumpass, L. L. (1990). What is happening to the family? Interactions between demographic and institutional change. *Demography, 27*, 483-498.

Burgess, J. (1995). Widowers as single fathers. *Marriage & Family Review, 20*(3/4), 447-461.

Burton, L. M., Dilworth-Anderson, P., & Merriwether-deVries, C. (1995). Context and Surrogate Parenting Among Contemporary Grandparents. *Marriage & Family Review, 20*(3/4), 349-366.

Callahan, S. (1993, April 10). Definition of what constitutes "family" may need to be rethought. *Oregonian*, p. C9.

Cherlin, A., & Furstenberg, F. F. (1982, Fall). *The shape of the American family in the year 2000*. Washington, DC: American Council of Life Insurance.

Children's Defense Fund. (1990). *Children 1990: A report card, briefing book and action primer*. Washington, DC: Children's Defense Fund.

Coontz, S. (1992). *The way we never were. American families and the Nostalgia trap*. New York: Basic Books.

Dail, P. W., & Jewson, R. H. (Eds.). (1986). *In praise of fifty years: The Groves Conference on the conservation of Marriage & Family*. Lake Hills, IA: Graphic Publishing Co.

Doherty, W. J. (1992). Private lives, public values: The new pluralism. *Psychology Today, 25*(3).

Donati, T. D. (1995). Single parents and wider families in the new context of legitimacy. *Marriage & Family Review, 20*(1/2), 27-42.

Family Service America. (1987). *The state of families: Work and family* (pp. 1-95). Milwaukee, WI: Family Service America.

Friedman, M. M. (1992). *Family nursing: Theory and practice*. (3rd ed.). Norwalk, CT: Appleton & Lange.

Gass-Sternas, K. A. (1995). Single parent widows: Stressors, appraisal, coping, resources, grieving responses, and health. *Marriage & Family Review, 20*(3/4), 411-445.

Glick, P. C. (1988). Fifty years of family demography: A record of social change. *Journal of Marriage and the Family, 50*, 861-873.

Greif, G. L. (1995). Single fathers with custody following separation and divorce. *Marriage & Family Review, 20*(1/2), 213-231.

Hanson, S. M. H. & Sporakowski, M. (Eds.) (1986). The single parent family. *Family Relations, 35*(1), pp. 1-224.

Hanson, S. M. H., Heims, M. L., Julian, D. J. & Sussman, M. B. (1995). Single parent families: Present and future perspectives. *Marriage & Family Review, 20*(1/2), 1-25.

Hareven, T. (1982). American families in transition: Historical perspectives on change. In F. Walsh (Ed.), *Normal family process* (pp. 446-465). New York: Guilford.

Herrerías, C. (1995). Noncustodial mothers following divorce. *Marriage & Family Review, 20*(1/2), 233-255.

Horowitz, J. A. (1995). A conceptualization of parenting: Examining the single parent family. *Marriage & Family Review, 20*(1/2), 43-70.

Ihinger-Tallman, M. (1995). Quality of life and well-being of single parent families: Disparate voices or a long overdue chorus? *Marriage & Family Review, 20*(3/4), 513-532.

Jeter, K. (1995). From stereotype to archetype: Single parent families. *Marriage & Family Review, 20*(3/4), 533-550.

Julian, D. (1995). Resources for single parent families. *Marriage & Family Review, 20*(3/4), 499-512.

Kimmons, L. C. (1995). Video/filmography on single parenting. *Marriage & Family Review, 20*(3/4), 483-498.

Kirkendall, L. A., & Gravatt, A. E. (Eds.). (1984). *Marriage and the family in the year 2020.* New York: Prometheus Books.

Kissman, K., & Allen, J. A. (1993). *Single parent families.* Newbury Park, CA: Sage.

Ladd, L. D. & Zvonkovic, A. (1995). Single mothers with custody following divorce. *Marriage & Family Review, 20*(1/2), 189-211.

Levine, M. O., Carey, W. B., Crocker, A. L., & Gross, R. T. (1983). Traditional and alternative family life styles. In M. O. Levine, W. B. Carey, A. L., Crocker, & R. T. Gross (Eds.). *Developmental-behavioral pediatrics* (pp. 193-208). Philadelphia: W. B. Saunders.

Lino, M. (1995). The economics of single parenthood: Past research and future directions. *Marriage & Family Review, 20*(1/2), 99-114.

Litton Fox, G. & White Blanton, P. (1995). Noncustodial fathers following divorce. *Marriage & Family Review, 20*(1/2), 257-282.

Marciano, T. D., & Sussman, M. B. (1991). *Wider families: New traditional family forms.* New York: The Haworth Press, Inc.

Marciano, T. D., & Sussman, M. B. (1991). Wider families: New traditional forms. *Marriage & Family Review, 17*(1/2).

Marciano, T. D., & Sussman, M. B. (1991). Wider families: An overview. In T. D. Marciano & M. B. Sussman, *Wider families: New traditional family forms.* New York: The Haworth Press, Inc.

Marsiglio, W. (1995). Young nonresident biological fathers. *Marriage & Family Review, 20*(3/4), 325-348.

Masnick, G., & Bane, M. (1980). *The nation's families: 1960-1990.* Boston: Auburn House.

National Council on Family Relations. (1990). *2001: Preparing families for the future.* Minneapolis, MN: Author.

Norton, A. J., & Glick, P. C. (1986). One parent families: A social and economic profile. *Family Relations, 35*, 9-17.

Norton, A. J., & Moorman, J. E. (1987). Current trends in marriage and divorce among American Women. *Journal of Marriage and the Family, 49*, 483-497.

Popenoe, D. (1989). The family transformed. *Family Affairs*, 2(2-3), 1-15.

Prater, L. (1995). Never married biological teen mother headed household. *Marriage & Family Review, 20*(3/4), 305-324.

Public Health Service, U.S. Department of Health and Human Services. (1990). *Healthy people 2000: National health promotion and disease prevention objectives*. Washington, DC: Government Printing Office (017-001-00473-1).

Scanzoni, J. (1983). *Shaping tomorrow's family: Theory and policy for the 21st century*. Beverly Hills, CA: Sage.

Schlesinger, B. (1995). Single parent families: A bookshelf. *Marriage & Family Review, 20*(3/4), 463-482.

Schneider, J. A. (1986). Rewriting the SES: Demographic patterns and divorcing families. *Social Science and Medicine, 23*, 211-222.

Seward, R. R. (1978). *The American family: A demographic history*. Beverly Hills, CA: Sage.

Shireman, J. F. (1995). Adoptions by single parents. *Marriage & Family Review, 20*(3/4), 367-388.

Smith, R. M. (Ed.). (1990, Winter/Spring). The 21st century family: Who we will be, how we will live. *Newsweek*, pp. 1-108.

Spanier, G. B. (1986). The changing American family: Demographic trends and prospects. In P. W. Dail & R. H. Jewson (Eds.). *In pause of fifty years: The Groves Conference on the conservation of marriage & family*. Lake Hills, IA: Graphic Publications.

Spanier, G. B. (1989). Bequeathing family continuity. *Journal of Marriage and the Family, 50*, 3-13.

Sprey, J. (1988). Current theorizing on the family: An appraisal. *Journal of Marriage and the Family, 50*, 875-890.

Steinbock, M. R. (1995). Homeless female-headed families: Relationships at risk. *Marriage & Family Review, 20*(1/2), 143-159.

U.S. Bureau of the Census. (1989a). Current population reports, Series P-25, No. 1018. *Projections of the population of the United States, by age, sex, and race: 1988 to 2080*. Washington, DC: U.S. Government Printing Office.

U.S. Bureau of the Census. (1989b). Current Population Reports, Series P-23, No. 162. *Studies in marriage and the family: Singleness in America; Single parents and their children; Married-couple families with children*. Washington, DC: U.S. Government Printing Office.

U.S. Bureau of the Census. (1992). Current Population Reports, Series P-23, No. 181, *Households, families, and children: A 30-year perspective*. Washington, DC: U.S. Government Printing Office.

U.S. Bureau of the Census. (1992). Current Population Reports, Series P-20, No. 468, *Marital status and living arrangements: March, 1992*. Washington, DC: U.S. Government Printing Office.

U.S. Bureau of the Census. (1992). Current Population Reports, Series P-23, No. 180, *Marriage, Divorce, and Remarriage in the 1990's*. Washington, DC: U.S. Government Printing Office.

Walters, L. H., & Abshire, C. R. (1995). Single Parenthood and the Law. *Marriage & Family Review, 20*(1/2), 161-188.

Whitehead, B. D. (1992). A new familism? *Family Affairs, 5*(1-2), 1-5.

Zill, N. (1988). Behavior, achievement, and health problems among children in stepfamilies: Findings from a National Survey of Child Health. In E. M. Hetherington & J. Arasteh (Eds.). *The impact of divorce, single parenting and stepparenting* (pp. 325-368). Hillsdale, NJ: Lawrence Erlbaum.

Zigler, E., & Black, K. B. (1989). America's family support movement: Strengths and limitations. *American Journal of Orthopsychiatry*, *59*, 6-19.

Chapter 2

Single Parents and Wider Families in the New Context of Legitimacy

Teresa Donati

SUMMARY. The term "single parents" implies discrete entities in isolation, who by the adjective "single" are implied to be different from–and indeed deviant in regard to–parents in general. This paper looks at the location of single parents, who are overwhelmingly female, in the context of wider families, which are families formed or joined to fill needs arising from the single parent lifestyle. The role of these wider families is made possible and necessary by the specific economic and social conditions of women, and by changed views of "legitimate birth" which have shown a marked shift from findings of the early 1960s. Policy implications include recognition and support of networks which become "families" wider than those offered by kin or marriage.

KEYWORDS. Single parents, Context, Single mothers, Wider families, Legitimacy

INTRODUCTION

The term "single parents" implies discrete entities in isolation, who by the adjective "single" are implied to be different from–and indeed deviant

---

Teresa Donati is affiliated with the Department of Sociology, T39A, Fairleigh Dickinson University, 1000 River Road, Teaneck, NJ 07666.

[Haworth co-indexing entry note]: "Single Parents and Wider Families in the New Context of Legitimacy." Donati, Teresa. Co-published simultaneously in *Marriage & Family Review* (The Haworth Press, Inc.) Vol. 20, No. 1/2, 1995, pp. 27-42; and: *Single Parent Families: Diversity, Myths and Realities* (ed: Shirley M. H. Hanson et al.) The Haworth Press, Inc., 1995, pp. 27-42. Multiple copies of this article/chapter may be purchased from The Haworth Document Delivery Center [1-800-3-HAWORTH; 9:00 a.m. - 5:00 p.m. (EST)].

in regard to–parents in general. Yet the number of single parents has grown, and continues to grow, and affects women–single mothers–far more than it affects men. Biological families may or may not be available to help the single childrearer in the many demands on time and money. Kin networks are not necessarily dependable nor willing to share childrearing tasks, and so others, who are not biological or marital kin, but who are willing and able to assume one or more "family" functions, may come to fill these needs. These are "wider families," which tend to give task support and emotional support. The preponderance of women single parents makes it likely and often economically necessary to find in wider families what a more affluent male might find in a hired housekeeper, a female or male companion, or a biological family that tends to see single men parents as more needful of their time and support. There is furthermore, as a result of differential socialization by sex, a greater likelihood for women to turn to family and wider family; Gilligan (1982) has demonstrated these differences wherein males separate, and females affiliate, with family and friendship groups as part of sex role development.

Concurrent with this is the shift in attitudes toward "legitimate birth" that has occurred since the early 1960s. The stigma that affected both mother and child has now been greatly attenuated both socially and in law. Without this stigma, more open participation in social and economic activities are possible. Furthermore the reduction of stigma is economically and emotionally very necessary. The result can be varieties of wider families that are the links to lifestyle similars and to the larger community. Wider families and their connection to single parents and the new views of legitimacy are treated successively below.

WIDER FAMILIES

The term "wider families" was developed (Marciano, 1988) and elaborated (Marciano and Sussman, 1991) to describe families formed to meet changing lifestyle needs. They are formed willingly and noncoercively. They are at once similar to and different from, biological and marital families. They are similar in that bonds of affiliation and obligation evolve; they fill needs of time, emotion, and economy that other institutions, as Bogan (1991) demonstrates, cannot be matched by other social institutions. But wider families also differ from traditional families in significant ways. First, they are choice-based, and therefore legally voluntary from their inception, and legally and ritualistically voluntary in member departure; this therefore excludes religious orders, military life, and coercive, fear-based, restricted-exit groups such as the tragic and cautionary "family" of Branch Davidian.

Second, wider families' longevity may vary from any brief time to a lifetime. Just as people enter and leave or outgrow given lifestyles, so they may form, enter, and leave wider families which emerged from those lifestyles. With single parents, for example, children do not remain young forever; the needs of young children, in terms of time, attention, schedule and developmental concerns, shift as the children enter their teen years, and then adulthood. Just as healthy biological families adapt to these changes, so the existence and forms of wider families change. It remains to be studied in detail, as so many aspects of wider family must be studied, but wider families may be adaptations to maladaptive kin groups. It is perhaps symptomatic of some of the maladaptation of biological families, that single parents often find respect for their own adulthood and parenthood among similars, and struggle with their own "child" status in their biological families. Connected to this absence of necessary longevity, the wider family only voluntarily, if at all, shows the property, contract, and inheritance characteristics of traditional families.

Finally, and logically proceeding from these other characteristics, the wider family may coexist with, replace, or countervail the traditional family. Wider families, which fill lifestyle needs, are "familial" in their task, lifestyle, and support aspects. If traditional family is insufficient in numbers, time available, or support; wider families may be more consciously, intentionally formed. Again, many more studies are needed to explore the varieties of wider family emergence, continuation, and demise.

HISTORICAL USES OF THE TERM "FAMILY"

Given these comparisons and wider family characteristics, the term "family" becomes a guide to research rather than a fixed set of definitions. Thus while we may assume that modern urban society, with its greater anonymity, freedom, fluidity of possibilities, is the "reason" for wider families, they seem to have existed in other times and places. Some of the historical and literary precursors have already been cited (Marciano, 1988), with new examples arising as one examines contemporary texts and those from the past. Two historical examples can be drawn, respectively, from the family of ancient Rome, and from the Christian scriptures.

Dixon (1992) notes that in ancient Rome the term "familia" denoted "slaves and freed slaves attached to a married couple," who often married or cohabited, "and even [grouped] in kinlike clusters for such purposes as funeral commemoration" (1992, p. 2). Dixon's term is "reciprocal obligations," and her description has many elements of wider family formation. Furthermore, in elaborating on Roman adoption practices–where typically an adult male was adopted to continue a childless family's line–social and legal obligations to the adoptee's biological family continued (1992, p. 112). Finally, friends as well as children were named as heirs, and the special role of friends easily echoes the wider family idea (Dixon, 1992, pp. 114-115):

> Friends could thus take the place of children in the sense that their attentions and affections would ease the later part of life. . . .

Today, individuals with aging or retired parents, especially where parents live in adult or retirement communities, often find those parents in new, voluntary connections of love, support and sharing with their lifestyle similars, coexisting with kin ties. In fact, many an adult child has reported relief on finding one or both parents so involved, especially where geographical distance or character conflicts make visiting those parents an infrequent occurrence.

And another modern "echo" of this is the single parent, whose own parents and other kin may be emotionally or geographically distant. Family studies of kin reaction to single parents' finding emotional and other support alternatives in wider families, would be a wonderful study for family systems theorists. This author's own as-yet unpublished observations of the phenomenon show a range of kin reactions in these cases, ranging from apparent envy of the single parent who has "broken free," to cynical dismissal of the single parent's choices as further evidence of her "craziness" or "willfulness." Even in the latter case, however, there are elements of resentment at the freedom exercised by the single parent. Whether this is more of a family system or gender dynamic, remains to be studied.

Returning to the historical perspective, a second example can be drawn from Christian scriptures. In the Gospel of Mark (3: 31-35), an incident is reported where Jesus evidently has been neglecting his filial and familial obligations, or perhaps has embarrassed his family by his public messages:

> His mother and brothers now arrived and, standing outside, sent in a message asking for him. A crowd was sitting round him at the time the message was passed to him, 'Your mother and brothers and sisters are outside asking for you.' And looking round at those sitting in a circle about him, he said, 'Here are my mother and my brothers. Anyone who does the will of God, that person is my brother and sister and mother.'

For all its religious significance to Christian believers, this Bible story is indeed "great literature" in that it touches upon enduring themes.

Modern reflections of this include the college student who finds greater warmth and receptivity among housemates than kin, for his or her aspirations and dreams, the daughter or son who find themselves loved and valued and helped by friends and neighbors and their families rather than being criticized or demeaned. They have found "new" parents, brothers, and sisters. Among contemporary single parent families, an inquiry into who are a child's "aunts" and "uncles," especially but not necessarily confined to urban areas, often reveals the transformation of friends and neighbors into wider family networks.

For Jesus in the gospel story, then, and for innumerable individuals today, families are created out of the ways we live, in ways wider than kin or marriage may provide, and which support our work as well as our needs for sympathetic response and help in meeting obligations to self, children, and community. African-American communities have long used fictive kin to establish broad bases of love, monetary help, and the exchange of goods and services where biological or marital families could not provide these (Stack, 1974; Collins, 1990). Indeed we must wonder whether the public concern over "family values" might not be a form of criticism for racial and gender-based phenomena. If more women are single parents, and if many African-American women are single parents, surely they are in "families," but are not in that normative ideal of the two-parent (read: man present) family.

BIOLOGICAL FAMILIES TO WIDER FAMILIES: EMERGENCE

Some recent evidence that biological family availability to its members is greater than has been thought, is found in Kolata's (1993) report on families' aid to their elderly. In a national sample of 12,000 Americans conducted for the National Institute on Aging, it was found that for people in their 50s, between 30 and 40 percent helped aging parents financially and in other ways. The study is interpreted as refuting the idea of scattered families and abandoned elderly. There are, however, some warnings and policy implications in the study: first, more people in their 50s were thinking of retiring than had been found in previous studies of this age group, and with retirement comes geographic mobility and perhaps reduced economic resources; second, the very high number of younger Americans who are and who will remain childless, invites the question of who will help them as they have helped their parents? Third, there is the fact that even allowing for elderly who do not need help of any sort, the numbers of middle-aged children helping their parents physically and financially is not a majority. And last, there is the matter of age itself: many adult children help aging parents despite experiencing considerable emotional upset in dealing with those parents. Age, fear, loneliness, generational norms, illness and pain, and general cantankerousness, all are possible reasons for "difficult" parents. If anything, keeping one's own emotional equilibrium while dealing with aging parents requires more alternative networking that would provide comfort not available from one's biological progenitors. In fact, there are numbers of support groups that have arisen for adult children caring for aging parents, as this author's ongoing research in the area has shown. Churches and hospitals have sponsored such groups which in turn often serve, as a whole, or in parts, as "wider families" for some or all members. This is particularly the case where the main helper for the aging parent is herself a single parent whose time and resources are already strained.

If anything, then, this study of aid to the elderly shows a greater likelihood of more types of wider families to emerge as the demographic picture of the United States continues to change. With the large number of single parents already in the population, and the likelihood that the pattern will continue and grow, "family values" must inevitably be expressed through and include wider families. "Family values" may not include having another parent present, but certainly it does include a concern for one's kin, and a desire to maintain family in either kin or wider form.

Given America's high geographical mobility patterns, and the fact that contacts with kin are often a product of chance (the job one finds, the spouse one marries) and geography, wider family contact tends to be more frequent and immediate than biological family contact. Family traditionalists forget that the family with adult children looks and acts differently from the family with young children, and, surprise, the wider family looks more like the adult-child biological family. Children are incidental to the wider family, in the sense that the presence of children is only one reason why wider families form; they may form for a purpose such as unemployment support, or training groups, and may expand their tasks to include child help for members who happen to have children. Single parents in wider families are in "adult child" families in that sense. Again, from the author's unpublished research to date, "family values" are powerfully expressed in wider families insofar as they include being there during times of need, and supporting members in specific tasks as well as sharing affection. Given all of these considerations, it is very likely that the "family of the future" will be determined by choice, in wider forms, for that preponderant part of our lives in which we are adults.

SINGLE PARENTS AND LEGITIMACY

All of the above is posited on a contemporary ethos, i.e., that single parenthood, however it was achieved, does not carry the stigmas and burdens it once did. The only traditionally unstigmatized single parents seem to be widows or widowers. The divorced bore social disapprobation for their marital fate though not the children's legitimacy; the never-married were stigmatized for immorality. Single parents could not lay claim to community connections so openly, irrespective of their marital status, sexual preferences, or "legitimacy" of their children, unless the whole notion of legitimacy changed. Any significant change in single parenting certainly must include the economic conditions and sex role changes linked to the phenomenon; but there must also be a consideration of world views, on the premise that changes in what things mean, create changes in how life is lived and how life can be lived. The changed view of "legitimacy" is the key to today's view of single parents and their lives. While the majority of single parents at any given time may be formerly married and widowed, gay single parents, and never-married heterosexual single parents, the changed view must at least in part depend on a changed view of marriage, conception, and the child. All single parents, however, are affected by these changes. Thus an examination of shifting meanings, with an emphasis on new attitudes toward legitimacy, must be explored.

Consider how different the term "single parent" is, compared to the terms "unwed mother," or "divorced mother." As noted earlier, the term "single parent," like the term "cohabitation," is a sanitized concept, i.e., it has removed elements of onus and shame from a lifestyle description. This shift from negative to neutral-positive terminology resulted from the prevalence of divorce among the middle class/affluent. Education, which remains a major avenue of mobility to and stability in the more affluent sectors of a class structure, raises consciousness, expectations, and the sense of personal efficacy. It provides more extensive resources for understanding and defining situations, including one's own life situation. Economic, social, and intellectual resources can be mustered to defend, and even advocate, positions that formerly were socially questionable–such as divorce, or unmarried parenthood. Education, however much its insufficiencies are bemoaned, extends our exposure to ways of thinking, and varieties of words and ideas, that confer power to make new definitions out of new understandings.

Power to name one's own situation was claimed by a variety of lifestyle groups as the Sixties progressed into the Seventies. "Black is beautiful," "Woman Power," the Liberation movements (Black, Women's, Gay) used the power of definition to shape perception. Assertions of freedom took precedence over the respectability of conforming.

These developments were supported by reference groups, the groups against which we measure how well we are doing in our statuses; these are the groups that confirm or deny our "success" in our status performances, including those of spouse and worker. Through the 1960s, as the romanticized version of marriage, home and children unraveled, there were ever more people in the reference groups of the more affluent who had gone through divorce, and who were raising children alone. The group Parents Without Partners, one of the earliest single-parent social and support networks in the country, symbolized an important definitional and reference group shift, emphasizing the parental reality and ignoring the divorce or widowhood that had created the members' single parent status.

Older notions of shame were also transformed by the birth control pill, which removed the most common "punishment" of pregnancy from extramarital sex. The musical *Hair* connected nudity to freedom, the body's nakedness to an openness to the New Age of Aquarius. The young, now present in vast numbers on college campuses, created and found new definitional contexts for their ideals and their physical and intellectual desires.

This same generation experienced what was called the "female marriage squeeze," in which the number of marriageable women exceeded the number of men in socially acceptable partner categories. Thus, the plentiful numbers of young women looking for older men, found a shortage of such men in the cohorts born before the Baby Boom. Eventually, same-age and older-female marriages have become more acceptable, but men had many more marital options among women their own age and younger, than women had. Marriage itself was a questionable condition, and the Women's Liberation Movement had promoted employment for women as a key to their economic and social freedom. Sex barriers had fallen in the formerly all-male colleges and universities, and women saw careers as the path to self-fulfillment, so that early marriage became less important than educational preparation for the professions and business. And marriage was less likely because of that same shortage of socially acceptable (i.e., older) marriage partners (Guttentag and Secord, 1983). These authors also argue that such conditions of low sex ratios, where women outnumber men, provide ideal conditions for women's movements, in part also because women feel poorly treated by the scarcer eligible men.

The ideals of the Sixties also included a condemnation of blaming victims for their plight. Poverty was a structural condition, not a personal failure, and the lifestyles of the poor–nonmarital unions, unwed parenthood, unemployment–were adaptive outcomes to necessity rather than weakness of character or moral deficiency. Judging others, whether for their poverty, parental situation, sexual behavior, or work habits, contradicted the ethic of self-expression which, in the idiom of the time, was stated as "Do your own thing." The ability to do one's own thing, however, was greatly facilitated by education and affluence, so that middle classes benefited greatly from the freedom ethic and the resources to explore that freedom with relative impunity.

For educated women with middle class incomes, then, the demographic and social conditions of the past twenty years have increased the likelihood of never marrying, have reduced the duration of marriage, with divorce rates moving upward and remarriage rates moving downward (Glick, 1984). Additionally, so many women have been on their own for so long, that the experience of freedom and self-direction, without answerability to or interference from a cohabiting partner or spouse, make singlehood (especially postmarital singlehood) a condition of release rather than an interim state until the next marriage.

The social climate for the notion of "legitimacy" has also substantially changed in the past two decades, and this, perhaps more than any other single thread of change, has created new understandings of the term "single parent." The Principle of Legitimacy, that every child must have a socially recognized father, was stated by anthropologist Bronislaw Malinowski (1930). Whether biological, adoptive, or socially defined (as with the mother's brother in matrilineage), a child's status placement in a society was based on the existence of a social father; he alone, in effect, conferred on the child the right to be born at all.

This point cannot be emphasized enough: that the burden of illegitimacy placed on children signified that they did not have a cultural or social right to exist. Since children are innocent victims of parental sexual activity, their stigmatized existence as "illegitimate" served as powerful incentives for pregnant brides to marry as quickly as possible, not to mention enriching the then-illegal abortionists and endangering the lives of or actually killing pregnant girls and women. A nurse who had trained at Bellevue Hospital in New York City in the 1950s told this author that on the maternity ward which served so many in the Harlem community, innumerable birth certificates were stamped "O.O.W." signifying, "Out Of Wedlock."

The imprint of stigma at birth would, presumably, be different if most of a population were born "illegitimately." Goode (1961) tested just this notion: that if just about everyone were born out of wedlock, it would cease to have negative or shameful meanings and consequences. He did his study in Caribbean society, and found that the principle of legitimacy held fast. His indicator was that when a woman did marry, only the children she had by her now-legal husband remained in the household, and children by nonmarital unions were sent to grandparents or other relatives or friends in the countryside.

This study, published just as the Sixties began to unfold, is a wonderful illustration of the fact that sheer numbers alone do not change anything. But once the context of meanings changes, those "illegitimate" children now become simply, "children of single parents." Since approximately one-third of all children in the U.S. will at some point at least, live with one parent, the reinforcement of this "new legitimacy" occurs via reference group confirmation: women everywhere find their similars raising children alone. (For summaries of the data, see Gill, Glazer and Thernstrom, 1992). Perhaps another indicator of the meanings shift is found in the terminologies now used to describe women who have children without having legal husbands: they are "single parents," or if they are a young, poor sample, they may be called "unmarried mothers." The scholarly literature, public figures' oratorical references, and The New York Times' reporting, however, no longer mentions "illegitimate children."

Part of the force for changing legitimacy norms was the media visibility of the more outrageous alternative lifestyles of the 1960s. Imagine the horror of "traditional" Sixties parents reading of young unmarried women having babies under the open sky while friends or fellow communards danced around them, where the babies ware named for berries, animals, celestial bodies, or mythological figures, and where parents had no plans for marriage, job, or other acceptable pattern of parenthood. As such relatively rare occurrences took on exaggerated probability for Sixties parents, who saw demonstrations and civil upset at every turn, even rebellious adolescents at home seemed less fearsome and threatening. And over time, as education and job plans proceeded together with unmarried cohabitation, where no children were born, parents could at least sigh with relief that their children were "mature and sensible," and begin to see the prevalent pattern of cohabitation as "normal." The extremes of behavior in the culture of the Sixties, then, broadened the notion of what was acceptable at the center: the "normal" widened to include more possibilities, and behaviors that had been normatively marginal were now "mainstream" (Marciano, 1975). Thus: the more "radical" or "outrageous" the possibilities at the margins, the wider the latitude that tends to develop in the mainstream.

This was true also for the notion of legitimacy. If parenthood remained a desirable and self-fulfilling avenue, rediscovered by Baby Boomers who had delayed pregnancy or who had never married, and if money and resources were sufficient, why was marriage a necessary condition of parenthood? Technology had entered the reproductive arena in a new way, permitting women to select fathers for their children without knowing or touching that father. Sperm banks offer lists of genetic and achievement characteristics so that a woman may try not only for a healthy baby but also one whose genes seem to carry musical or scientific ability, or certain eye and hair color. Thus can an unmarried woman select an "ideal father" for her baby. And if it is wrong to condemn the poor who become parents without marrying, why is it right to condemn the middle-class woman whose income and career prospects enable her to give a child love and social advantages? The old controls, fears, dependencies, and stigmas that had surrounded the notion of legitimacy had ceased to be rational.

LEGITIMACY AND RATIONALITY

Malinowski (1930), and the Functionalist theorists in sociology, explained legitimacy norms in terms of social order and property inheritance in a patriarchal and patrilineal society (Davis, 1949). The weakest family bond–and in a patriarchy, the weakest community bond–is between father and child. Social norms take the place of direct physical indicators (pregnancy, lactation), to define the father's meaning and role in the child's life.

As long as access to desired resources is indeed tightly controlled by a selected few, rules defining "legitimate" existence become the conditions of life for everyone. But one of the changes that undermined the old "legitimacy" was its increasing irrationality. If, for example, legitimacy governed women's behavior so that, to inherit, and to have her child inherit, it had to be "legitimate," it behooved her to marry with as much social advantage as possible, since her economic well-being and that of her children, depended on their having a man's name, and therefore a legal right to inherit his property.

It became obvious, in the closer examination of poverty, that "legitimacy" only makes sense if a man's presence in some way was economically or socially beneficial to the woman and children, and to the man himself. If the man's presence was a constant reminder of his unemployment, if he could not meet the breadwinner expectations placed upon men for reasons of racism and poor opportunity structures, it was not rational for him to remain in the household. Liebow's (1967) classic study of Black streetcorner men offered just such an analysis of the men's behavior. Without diminishing the helpfulness and sharing that can be provided by another adult in the household, the presence of a biological father who had no property, title, or special knowledge to transmit, whose presence compounded his embitterment and perhaps family arguments, was not rational. It was far more rational for the man to give or send money when he had it for his children, and to experience their visits and praise on such occasions. Under low opportunity conditions, the men as well as the women could optimize outcomes for themselves and their children.

This is not to say that then, and today, there are not substantial numbers of people who see "fatherless children," born in or out of wedlock, as causes and signs of the intractable moral deficiencies of the poor. In general, however, if anyone is condemned today it is the mother, for her promiscuity, lack of forethought, or lack of self-control. The father may be blamed as an afterthought, but the contraceptive burden, despite its greater physical ease and accessibility for men, remains on the woman. This is compounded where single parents cannot provide for children in ways that are deemed minimally necessary and acceptable. Thus, "welfare mothers" still experience stigma, because by having children they are unable to support with jobs, they demonstrate social and personal irresponsibility, and "fail" their young. It is a bitter irony that those who condemn are frequently benefitted by the welfare system they disparage. Welfare mothers are paid very low wages indeed to do the work that childrearing institutions would charge much more to do. The hidden tax savings from welfare families, rather than from public orphanages, would be eye-opening to those outraged by welfare. And as all mothers who have "stayed home" know, without income and status of her own, the welfare mother is not considered to be doing special work in the rearing of children. Only the paid labor market seems able to confer the notion that the work done is worth something. It remains the case, however, that the most economically frugal way to raise children is to let them live with their own families, with subsistence provision via welfare payments (Marciano, 1986).

That issue of responsibility is, however, skirted by the employed woman who seeks parenthood on her own. Her own education, job, and medical benefits, change the perception of her as a parent. The Murphy Brown controversy notwithstanding, women who opt for single parenthood claim for themselves definitions of courage, love, and self-actualization. With divorce rates so high, and with so much distrust of chance encounters in this age of AIDS, grandparents can look at their single-parented grandchildren as bonuses, rather than as burdens. With changes in the legal system, children can claim inheritances irrespective of their parents' marital status. But most importantly, the creation of status remains, for most people, a matter of achievement rather than ascription: it is the education we get, the things we do, not the name we inherit, that governs the life chances we have.

In terms of rationality, then, the most rational thing grandparents and all other family members can do, is to maximize opportunities for a child, "legitimate" or not, to be cared for, well-educated, and launched on a good job or career. By providing monetary and emotional resources, grandparents thus obtain emotional gratifications, serving in turn as adult resources for employed single mothers.

One intriguing contrast appears to exist between never-married single mothers and post-divorce single mothers in this author's research. There is thus far an observed greater likelihood to admire, however grudgingly, the never-married woman who chooses to bear a child, and far less admiration for the divorced woman who is raising her children with occasional "help" from their father. Several possible reasons present themselves: that the divorced woman parent is a "discarded" woman (never mind who left whom); and that divorced single parents presumably made their child-bearing choices under putatively permanent conditions, and "failed" to make it work. This continuing reference to divorce as "failed marriage," equates wedlock with an examination which a person could "pass." The view persists despite the fact that a "successful" marriage is not necessarily a happy one; if success is measured simply by endurance, then to remain married is to succeed. And if the first measure of successful marriage were the happiness of the partners, we must wonder how many enduring, unsuccessful marriages must exist in the country and in the world. We have not yet come to the point of redefining divorce so that it is viewed as a solution rather than a problem; but if and when such a definitional change occurred, it will be interesting to hear, "We solved our marital problems by divorcing."

Meanwhile, divorced single parents seem to be viewed as "rejects," especially where divorce was at the behest of one party rather than by mutual agreement, and especially where the departing partner had already found another love. By contrast, and as yet not fully explored, a latent consequence of never-married parenthood is that, despite the constraints on time that children create, such a parent is not viewed as a victim or as a rejected partner. This "higher status" never-married, especially affluent, single parent appears to have other advantages: there is no network of "other couples," which the married tend to form, who will withdraw rather than taking sides, or who will opt for the first-remarried partner (which is more likely to be the husband). Never-married single parents have their single networks, as well as their biological families and married connections; for singles, who tend to have little contact with marital networks and children's lives, the new baby in the network is a rare, exotic, part of a friend's life choices. In married networks, children are common, and one's own children command first attention and priority. Much qualitative study is needed to discover all the dimensions of contrast and similarity between never-married and postmarital single parents.

It is very likely that where legitimacy norms are no longer rational, and alternatives are available, more children will be born to the unmarried. This issue was explored in terms of the former Soviet Union (David, Fisher, and Marciano, 1978), examining the question of legitimacy where the state was "father" to all children born within it. It was found that the state's "father" role was relatively constant, but that the responsibility for economic support by biological fathers, varied according to policy shifts by the government. Perceived underpopulation, due to the long-term shortage of men after World War II, affected whether men could or could not be compelled to pay for children they had fathered. However, children were not "illegitimate," and the mother was granted all care and maternal allowances granted any other mother. The government did this to encourage the birthrate without appearing to encourage promiscuity.

Last, there is the question of how single mothers are faring when their life-chances and options are relatively few: and this is the connection between employment and parenthood. It may validate one's status as a woman or man to have a child; but after the euphoria of birth, there is the reality of how well one can live. Those who have worked with young unmarried mothers in poor areas frequently witness the pressure placed upon the young women to have sex, and then to have a baby rather than an abortion. If anything, changed attitudes toward legitimacy have worked in favor of pressure and against abortion, since the young woman–or girl–cannot claim to be at risk for a unique, shaming unwed motherhood. The weight of numbers that changed middle-class definitions of cohabitation and single parenthood, do not necessarily serve the young in poor populations. Campaigns to promote responsible fatherhood among the young men have been sporadic and not noticeably successful. In both the young women's and men's cases, campaigns to prevent early pregnancy can only work if alternative sources of validation, love, and affirmation are available. The same conditions which limit educational opportunities and hopes, make children one of the few ways to gain standing, respect, and love. This is true for men as well as for women, however much economic duty to children is ignored by men.

Where, then, does this leave us on social policy? Perhaps the wider family should itself be recognized, and become part of the social policy options available. If social policy is law and action taken to solve social problems, and if wider families are adaptive responses to family needs not met in traditional ways, then they are already solutions, or "grass roots" social policy actions.

WIDER FAMILY AS SOCIAL POLICY

Support groups, both independent and existing under the aegis of various social agencies, abound in this country. But the isolation of young, poor single parents can only be overcome by finding them, and then providing ways to invite them into support networks that will be, in however broad or limited a sense, a wider family to them.

Since the root cause of poverty is lack of money, (which is so obvious as to go unnoticed), and since we may yet see a new Keynsian commitment to putting money into poor communities to stimulate economic life, an ideal first program would be the neighborhood canvas. Individuals would be hired to go to every house, and ring every doorbell, and ask every person they see, about who lives in the neighborhood. Churches and schools can be enlisted, along with existing community centers, to promote trust of the neighborhood canvas project and its workers. Thus can the isolated young single parent be identified and contacted.

With contact and follow-up, the parents can be invited by the social agency to bring their children to a "get-acquainted" group where children are supervised by adults who, being together, come to know each other. Once a pattern of meeting times is established, and the meetings regularly attended, that setting can be the first "home" of the "wider family." Once this is established, wider and perhaps deeper connections will emerge from those contacts. Agencies can make contact with and provide health agency speakers for nutrition and general preventive medical and dental care; schools and libraries can be invited to give story sessions for children which would also provide personnel to encourage young mothers to continue their education. Telephone trees and "listen to a friend" networks can be encouraged.

For those helped in this way, and indeed for all social classes, given our mobility and the chanciness of satisfactory kin families, the bloodlines of the future will no doubt be far more in our hearts and minds than in our genes.

REFERENCES

Bogan, Beth (1991). "Economics of the Wider Family," in T.D. Marciano and M.B. Sussman, Eds. *Wider Families; New Traditional Family Forms*. New York: The Haworth Press, Inc.

Collins, Patricia Hill (1990). *Black Feminist Thought*. New York: Routledge Kegan Paul.

David, Deborah, Wesley Fisher and Teresa D. Marciano (1978). "Illegitimacy Norms Reconsidered: The Case of State Socialism." Paper presented at the Annual Meetings of the Society for the Study of Social Problems, San Francisco, September 2.

Davis, Kingsley (1949). *Human Society*. New York: Macmillan.

Dixon, Suzanne (1992). *The Roman Family*. Baltimore: Johns Hopkins Press.

Gill, Richard T., Nathan Glazer and Stephan A. Thernstrom (1992). *Our Changing Population*. Englewood Cliffs NJ: Prentice-Hall.

Gilligan, Carol (1982). *In A Different Voice*. Cambridge: Harvard University Press.

Glick, P. C. (1984). American Household Structure in Transition. *Family Planning Perspectives*. 16, 205-211.

Goode, William J. (1961). "Illegitimacy, Anomie, and Cultural Penetration," *American Sociological Review* 26:4 (Dec.): 910-925.

Guttentag, Marcia and Paul F. Secord (1983). *Too Many Women? The Sex Ratio Question*. Beverly Hills, CA: Sage Publications.

Kolata, Gina (1993). "Family Aid to Elderly is Very Strong, Study Shows." *The New York Times*. May 3: A16.

Liebow, Elliot (1967). *Tally's Corner: A Study of Negro Streetcorner Men*. Boston: Little, Brown.

Malinowski, Bronislaw (1930). "Parenthood–The Basis of Social Structure," in V.F. Calverton and S.D. Schmalhusen, *The New Generation*. New York: Macauley.

Marciano, T. D. (1986). Why did poverty feminize when women have always been poor? *Proteus* 3:2 (Fall) 33-41.

Marciano, Teresa Donati (1988). "Families Wider Than Kin Or Marriage." *Family Science Review* 1:2 (May), pp. 115-124.

________ (1991). "A Postscript on Wider Families: Traditional Family Assumptions and Cautionary Notes," in T.D. Marciano and M.B. Sussman, Eds., *Wider Families: New Traditional Family Forms*. New York: The Haworth Press, Inc.

Marciano, Teresa D. (1975). "Variant Family Forms in a World Perspective." *The Family Coordinator* 24:4, pp. 407-420.

Marciano, Teresa D. and Marvin B. Sussman (1991). "Wider Families: An Overview," in T.D. Marciano and M.B. Sussman, Eds. *Wider Families: New Traditional Family Forms*. New York: The Haworth Press, Inc.

Stack, Carol (1974). *All Our Kin: Strategies for Survival in a Black Community*. New York: Harper & Row.

Chapter 3

A Conceptualization of Parenting: Examining the Single Parent Family

June Andrews Horowitz

SUMMARY. The purpose of this paper is to provide a framework for examining the parenting process. Tasks, roles, rules, communication, resources, and relationships are described as essential components of parenting. The conceptualization of parenting is not tied to a particular family structure or type. Rather, parenting is examined as a process undertaken with the goal of ferrying children from conception and birth through developmental challenges and life events to adulthood. As a bridge between the conceptualization of parenting and its application to single parent families, questions are raised concerning what it takes to parent adequately. Notions of the successful or "good enough" parent are derived from facets of the conceptual framework. The challenge of providing adequate parenting for single parent families is presented. Single parent families are not described as automatic "at risk" situations for children. However, identification of the ingredients needed for adequate parenting provides a useful framework for evaluation of the effectiveness of single parent families in the many forms and situations considered in the other papers in this special volume of *Marriage & Family Review.*

June Andrews Horowitz is affiliated with the Department of Psychiatric-Mental Health Nursing, School of Nursing, Boston College, Chestnut Hill, MA 02167.

[Haworth co-indexing entry note]: "A Conceptualization of Parenting: Examining the Single Parent Family." Horowitz, June Andrews. Co-published simultaneously in *Marriage & Family Review* (The Haworth Press, Inc.) Vol. 20, No. 1/2, 1995, pp. 43-70; and: *Single Parent Families: Diversity, Myths and Realities* (ed: Shirley M. H. Hanson et al.) The Haworth Press, Inc., 1995, pp. 43-70. Multiple copies of this article/chapter may be purchased from The Haworth Document Delivery Center [1-800-3-HAWORTH; 9:00 a.m. - 5:00 p.m. (EST)].

KEYWORDS. Conceptualization, Parenting, Examining, Single parent family, Framework

INTRODUCTION

This paper presents a conceptualization of parenting. Tasks, roles, rules, communication, resources, and relationships are examined as critical facets of parenting. This framework provides a basis for evaluation of single parent families' functioning. Because there is great diversity in structural composition and context among single parent families, it is impossible to apply a simple criterion for measurement of success; rather, careful assessment of the dimensions of effective parenting is required in order to understand and identify both strengths and difficulties.

PARENTING DEFINED

Parenting is the primary domain of families. Families have existed for thousands of years as the fundamental social unit. Yet families evolve to meet changing conditions in a given place and time. The contemporary family is a dynamic system; its pattern is changing at a rapid rate within the context of social crises that mark the latter portion of the twentieth century.

For many years, definitions of the ideal American family have been shaped by norms that emphasized traditional sex role stereotypes, two parent family structures, and membership in the majority racial group and middle or upper social classes. *Normal* families were equated with two parent (that is, mothers and fathers), white, middle to upper class families. During the 1950s and 1960s, media portrayals of families such as "Leave It to Beaver," "The Donna Reed Show," and "Father Knows Best" shaped our image of the normal family. Minority and poor families were virtually ignored. Single parent families were called "broken families" and by implication their members were also seen as deficient.

Greater diversity in lifestyles and household structures emerged during the 1960s and 1970s as a manifestation of the dramatic social change that was taking place. Stable norms of American family life were altered in the face of assassinations of political leaders, the Civil Rights and Women's Movements, and the Viet Nam War and its protest (Horowitz, 1992). Old values and expectations were shaken and the definition of "family" was changed forever. When a broader perspective is taken, concerns about ideals and norms fade in the face of issues of survival of family members, wherein parenting then focuses on provision of resources necessary to sustain life of the members.

Definitions of family have also moved beyond the traditional criteria for nuclear families that include legal marriage, kinship bonds based on biological and marital connections, and the presence of children (or plans to have children in the future). The concept of "wider families" reflects such change. The term wider families refers to types of social organizations that do not conform to all of the conditions applied to traditionally-defined families (Marciano, 1991; Marciano & Sussman, 1991). These family structures may form without legal marriage, may or may not involve procreation of children, and are not bound by the age groupings found in traditional families. Wider families emerge from people's lifestyles as voluntary social systems that are unstructured, not rule- or time-bound, independent of required kin or biological connections. Wider families fill needs of their members through support, availability, and bonds of affection and emotion. When defining parenting, diverse meanings of family must be appreciated.

Parenting is a process composed of tasks, roles, rules, communication, resources, and relationships (Horowitz, Hughes & Perdue, 1982). Parenting is dynamic, multifaceted, and complex. Individuals, families, and institutions fulfill parenting functions such as nurturing and nourishing a child, and creating an environment in which children can learn skills needed for social participation and acceptance of personal responsibility. Parenting "involves the skillful and creative use of knowledge, experience, and technique" (p. 2).

Despite the complexity and importance of parenting, people typically receive little or no formal preparation for becoming parents and inadequate support for carrying out the job (LeMasters & DeFrain, 1989). There is no formal discipline devoted to the study and teaching of parenting. Clinicians and social scientists from a variety of disciplines have attempted to link childrearing practices, parental attitudes and traits, and family characteristics to a host of outcomes concerning children's development and functioning. Because assumptions, methodological flaws, biases in interpretation, and the complexity of the phenomena plague researchers in this area, current knowledge is in its infancy (Amato & Keith, 1991; Blechman, 1982; Herbert, 1986; Macklin, 1980). For example, much of the early literature concerning single parenting was rooted in the assumption that children of single parents were automatically at risk for some form of deviance ranging from weakened gender or "sex role" identity, to poor self-esteem, to social deviancy. Causal inferences often were made from statistical correlations between family structure and children's traits and behaviors; while there may have been such associations, the role of intervening factors such as poverty were too frequently overlooked. In addition, the personal and social perspectives of the researchers and clinicians have influenced questions asked, interpretation of data, and treatment provided. The importance of understanding the factors involved in single parenting and family members' well-being challenges social scientists to build on the existing knowledge base, uncover variable interactions, explicate conditions of change, and examine long-term consequences (Amato & Keith, 1991; Ihinger-Tallman, 1986).

THE GOALS OF PARENTING

Parenting ranks among the most important functions in society. The goals of parenting are to nurture, protect, and promote the successful journey of children from birth to adequate adult/lifetime functioning or simply to reach age 21. The social context of this developmental journey requires transmission of cultural heritage from parents to their children (Herbert, 1986; Horowitz, Hughes & Perdue, 1982; Lidz, 1968). To do their job well, parents must imbue children with an understanding of values and norms, and assist them to develop the skills and resources needed to navigate successfully through adulthood. Ultimately, parenting is the process that ensures continuation of human society. Herbert (1986) extends this theme and raises a caution in his description of parenting:

> Parents, as 'agents' of society, exerting social influence and control on an impressionable, malleable child, bear an awesome responsibility. The very processes which help the child adapt to social life can, under certain circumstances, contribute to the development of deviant, dysfunctional modes of behaviour. (p. 318)

While it is also important to acknowledge that the child is not a tabula rasa but rather an active participant who brings a great deal to the parent-child relationship, Herbert's point is that parents carry the responsibility for supporting the child through the many developmental and situational challenges of childhood and adolescence within the social environment. In addition, social norms concerning desired behavior can sometimes conflict with the best interests of the child.

Thus, the social fabric that supports parenting critically affects outcomes. Families perpetuate the species by producing and raising children; however, families' biological functions can only be fulfilled when the social system in which the family exists supports its aims. In addition, social conditions influence access to economic resources and development of psychological bonds within families (Ackerman, 1958).

COMPONENTS OF THE PARENTING PROCESS

Tasks

Successful parenting involves fulfillment of two types of major tasks: managing the environment and maintaining relationships among family members. Research concerning behavior within small groups has shown that these two functions tend to interfere with each other and are more easily performed by separate individuals, the group's environmental and social-emotional task specialists (Bales & Slater, 1955). Parsons (1955) extended these ideas to analysis of the American family by proposing a model of task differentiation: the husband-father was seen as the instrumental task specialist whose primary activities revolved around the world of employment and outside systems; and the wife-mother was seen as the expressive task specialist whose primary activities involved childbearing and childrearing, and meeting the affective needs of the family members. Cross-cultural support for this model of task differentiation was also demonstrated (Zelditch, 1955).

However, there is evidence that the division of task categories is not completely gender specific nor static. In a study of middle class married couples more than 25 years ago, Levinger (1968) found that one spouse typically took responsibility for carrying out a variety of household tasks. However, in the social-emotional realm, there was far less contrast between wives' and husbands' task performance. Levinger concluded that social-emotional performance may be mutual rather than specialized. The entrance of women to the workforce in increasingly large numbers during the period of childrearing has led to shifts in the activities associated with mothering and fathering. In one study it was shown that after new mothers returned to work, fathers' involvement and comfort with their babies increased considerably (Hall, 1992). However, a caution must be voiced: despite some shifts in activities when both parents are engaged in paid labor, women still bear the major responsibility for domestic and childrearing tasks (O'Neill, 1985; Sands & Nuccio, 1989).

The concept of parenting together involves sharing task responsibilities.

"Basic to the partnership of shared responsibility is an agreement to equitably divide the job responsibilities of childrearing" (Ehrensaft, 1990, p. 57). Parents can do this by assigning specific areas of task specialization or by being interchangeable, in other words, to carry out all the parental tasks when "on duty" or "in charge." If sharing task responsibilities within families becomes increasingly normative, the image of parenting will be reshaped.

A host of age-specific tasks are involved in providing for children's physical needs such as feeding, bathing, dressing, and providing safety. Daily caretaking, however, extends beyond physical care to the arenas of nurturance, play, empathy, attachment, and emotionality (Ehrensaft, 1990). Parents vary in the psychological capacities they bring to these activities. Tasks also shift with the development of the child. Many parents lament that as soon as things seem to be going smoothly, their child enters a new phase and they have to develop a new set of parenting skills. Parents with more than one child also have to be adept at a variety of age-related activities that could range from diapering, to helping with homework, to providing support during relationship conflicts, to assisting in school and career choices. The sheer magnitude, diversity, and unending nature of parenting tasks can strain the most devoted parent. "Parenting, with all its joys and pains, has always been hard" (Horowitz, Hughes, & Perdue, p. 9).

For single parents, division of labor is usually a moot point because the "primary parent," that is, the person who takes the major responsibility for parenting, has little choice but to carry out the necessary tasks alone or with only limited help from others. Overload is the most serious issue regarding tasks for single parents. Single mothers have reported more daily hassles related to family and work related tasks than their two parent counterparts (Compas & Williams, 1990).

The range of parental tasks is enormous. While a complete list of parenting activities is impossible to create given the uniqueness of each parent and child, the following categorization of parenting tasks can serve as a useful summary:

1. provide safety;
2. meet basic physical needs;
3. assist children to reach developmental milestones;
4. model problem solving and coping strategies;
5. teach skills necessary for survival, including academic and occupational achievement;
6. promote self-esteem and a positive identity;
7. encourage a sense of personal values, meaning in life, and altruism;
8. transmit the culture.

Roles

Another component of parenting is role. A role is a set of socially endorsed behaviors; it involves tasks but is greater than any single activity because it also refers to a position in an interaction system involving prestige, status, power, and responsibility. "In a well-organized family, the major roles have been identified, assigned, and performed with some degree of competence. When this does not occur, the family may be said to be disorganized to a certain extent" (LeMasters & DeFrain, 1989, pp. 72-73).

In the past, gender determined family roles (Parsons, 1964). As described above in relation to task differentiation, traditionally mothers have had the primary responsibility for childrearing and household maintenance. The role of women was synonymous with mothering. Women who did not parent or who occupied parental *and* employment roles were viewed as exceptions to the norm. Male roles were more varied but centered on the work world outside of the family. Fathering was also a valued role but different from and secondary to the mother's role within the family. Fathers were expected to provide material resources for the family.

Today's parents are balancing multiple roles. The majority of mothers now work outside the home during their children's early years. Employed mothers must obtain help to manage their childrearing tasks; however, their role responsibility as mothers remains in addition to their employment role. Many fathers have expanded their parenting realm to include more caretaking activities than in past generations; yet, for many women, the primary role responsibility remains their's and fathers are praised when they "help" with childcare and household management. One woman, exhausted from juggling her two full-time jobs as mother and school teacher said, "My husband really tries to help. He even babysits sometimes on the weekend so I can get some things done." This woman's comments illustrate that she believes it is her role to provide childcare all the time even though she and her husband both work outside the home. When her husband participates, it is considered help and babysitting even though he is her partner and he is parenting.

Employed mothers often experience role strain as they struggle to carry out two jobs; however, the context for role performance and the salience of role domains may influence the distress experienced (Simon, 1992; Thoits, 1991; Woods, 1985). In a study of women's multiple roles and mental health (Woods, 1985), nontraditional "sex role" norms were found to have a protective effect on the mental health of women who were spouse, employee, and mother. When women maintain traditional expectations that mothers must be fully in charge of their children's development while also having responsibilities in their employment role, role strain is likely to result. Hall (1992) found that among dual-career couples, women experienced greater role strain than their male partners following the birth of their first child as a function of concerns about others' expectations, awareness of unmet household needs, feelings of guilt, and denial of their own needs. However, Simon (1992) found that mothers and fathers were both vulnerable to the strain of combining the roles of parent and worker under conditions of high parental commitment.

The nature of the mother's work may also influence her parenting role and her children. Rogers, Parcel, and Menaghan (1991) assessed the impact of mothers' sense of mastery and maternal working conditions on mothers' perceptions of children's behavior problems as they studied the transmission of social control across generations. They discovered, in their sample, that maternal mastery was related to fewer reported behavior problems among children. The nature of the work also was related to perception of children's behavior: lower involvement with people and greater involvement with things, as well as less physical activity, were related significantly to increased levels of perceived problems. Recent changes in marital status and family composition, including both departure or addition of a father figure in the home, were associated with reports of problems; strong home environments were associated with perceptions of positive child behaviors. This study goes beyond asking the simple question of whether mothers' working is good or bad for children by exploring employment related factors that may shape the way that working parents carry out their parenting roles.

In contrast to other industrialized nations, the United States provides few supports for employed parents. The trend toward dual career or two paycheck parents necessitates changes in social policy concerning parental leave and day care. Moreover, the inadequacy of social policy has fueled the "economic plight of mother-headed single-parent families: low wages, dependence on welfare, and difficulties surrounding child support" (Sands & Nuccio, 1989, p. 25). Employment systems also have done too little to create more flexibility in the parameters of employment such as flextime and on site day care. Collins (1986) provides a thoughtful analysis of the consequences of women's changing roles in American society. "As more women enter the work force, particularly women with young children, it is clear that there are inevitable consequences . . . as both male and female roles evolve, pressure will be extended for fundamental changes in both governmental policy and the workplace" (p. 337).

Generational Boundaries

Parenting roles are also differentiated by generational boundaries (Horowitz, Hughes, & Perdue, 1982; Minuchin & Fishman, 1981). Clear generational boundaries involve role reciprocity among family members; that is, specific distinctions between marital, parent-child, and sibling subsystems. Members are allied more closely within their own generation than across generations, with the parents fulfilling the executive control function. Problems with generational boundaries have been identified. Diffuse generational boundaries refer to vague or unclear alliances which blur the differences between generations. Breached generational boundaries refer to an alliance between members across generations against a member within the peer generation of one of the coalition partners, e.g., a parent and child against the other parent (Clements & Buchanan, 1982).

Generational role boundaries also involve making the needs of children a priority. Interference with the aims of parenting results when parents' roles are unclear because their needs have been given precedence over their children's needs. For example, couples from differing religious backgrounds sometimes wish to perform parallel lifecycle rituals for their children and decide to keep the plan a secret from each other's extended families so that each side will assume that only their own religious tradition is being practiced. When asked about the purpose and meaning of such a plan, these couples frequently cite the wish to please their own parents and to avoid conflicts within the extended families. The important question in these instances is: whose needs are being served? As couples consider the long-term consequences of attempting to maintain this secret and explaining their actions to growing children, they often wonder about what is truly best for the children. This example illustrates blurring of role responsibility and need fulfillment between the grandparents', parents', and children's generations.

The importance of role boundaries is also highlighted when there is conflict between parents. When children become involved in parental conflicts, they tend to experience a greater degree of manifest emotional disturbance than children in families that provide at least some shelter from parental tensions (Spiegel, 1968). Numerous studies have demonstrated that parental conflict contributes to a stressful and insecure home environment for children, negative psychological adjustment of children, and deteriorations in parent-child relationships in both single and two parent families (Amato, 1986; Amato & Keith, 1991; Emery, 1982; Hetherington, Clingempeel, Anderson, Deal, Hagan, Hollier, & Lindner, 1992; Hetherington, Cox, & Cox, 1982, Johnston, Kline, & Tschann,

1989; Maccoby, 1992; Maccoby & Martin, 1983; Wallerstein & Kelly, 1980).

Subsystem Boundaries

Boundaries between subsystems also allow for growth of members. For example, parents who always intervene to settle sibling conflicts rob children of opportunities to develop skills in negotiation, assertiveness, and cooperation. Chronic disrespect for boundaries results in decreased autonomy and possibly enmeshment (Roberts, 1982). Blurring of role boundaries within single parent families frequently occurs due to the introduction of partners of the parents (other than a noncustodial parent), use of a variety of child care providers, allocation of parental roles to one or more of the children, and the role overload experienced by many custodial parents (Westcot & Dries, 1990).

In summary, there are several important dimensions of parental roles to consider: differences and similarities in maternal and paternal roles; changes in traditional sex roles that affect parenting; increasing participation of mothers in the work force; and the importance of maintenance of generational boundaries. Several themes identified by LeMasters and DeFrain (1989) influence contemporary parental roles and merit attention:

1. the role is ambiguous and poorly delimited;
2. there is no margin for error;
3. parents cannot quit;
4. parents have responsibility with only limited authority;
5. parents are judged by professionals, not peers;
6. there is no new model for parents to follow as traditional methods are bypassed;
7. today's parents are expected to "do it better" than in past generations;
8. parenting is a one-way street without reciprocity in responsibility;
9. parental responsibility is total;
10. each child brings unique needs and abilities;
11. parents typically have little training for the role;
12. there is no gradual transition to the parenting role; and
13. increases in divorce and geographic mobility weaken support systems such as assistance from grandparents.

Rules

A third essential component of parenting is rules. Rules structure family roles and specify acceptable behavior and task designation. Rules are the glue that parents use to operationalize their respective family jobs and to teach children about expectations within and outside the family. Daily decisions are facilitated by rules by spelling out who can do what to whom under what conditions. Children learn about structure and limits through rule enforcement. Rules are most functional when there is a balance between consistency and flexibility in the face of special circumstances or changing conditions.

The family's communication style will influence the formulation and execution of rules. Clear and open communication generally leads to explicit rules that are understood by the family members. In contrast, unclear and unspoken expectations and having many family secrets lead to confusion about rules and/or covert rules. Three key questions about family rules can be asked (Horowitz, Hughes, & Perdue, 1982):

1. Who makes the family rules? Do parents take responsibility for establishing rules while allowing for age appropriate input from the children?
2. Are the rules stated clearly in terms of expectations and consequences?
3. Is allowance made to shift rules in responses to changes in the family, its members, or the situation?

While there is no easy or universal formula for establishing family rules, experts have attempted to describe parental styles associated with making functional rules. Two major dimensions with orthogonal axes can be described: warm-hostile and autonomy-control (Herbert, 1986). Consideration of these dimensions can be helpful in analysis of parent-child transactions. Rules may be established with reference to some point along the autonomy-control continuum. Certain behaviors, conditions, and ages of children could call for restrictive rules; for example, rules governing safety around cars or swimming areas typically need to be very specific and restrictive when children are young or unpredictable in their ability to manage potentially dangerous situations. In other situations, greater permissiveness may be appropriate; for example, autonomy can be fostered by allowing children to make choices regarding play or recreational activities during a vacation. The warm-hostile dimension calls for a different interpretation. Rule enforcement requires firmness and clarity; however, rejection and hostility pose threats to the child's well-being. Concern, warmth, and love should characterize rule enforcement even when the child's behavior needs to be corrected.

These dimensions are also embedded in categories of parenting styles labelled as authoritarian, permissive, and authoritative (Baumrind, 1971).

Authoritarian parents typically are highly controlling and lack warmth in their interactions. Permissive parents are noncontrolling, nondemanding, and warm in their interactions. Extremes in either of these types are thought to result in problematic child behaviors. Authoritative parents are controlling and demanding, but also warm, receptive, and rational in relations with children. This style of parenting is thought to encourage the most self-reliant, self-controlled, explorative, and content children. It should be noted that interpretations of parenting styles are culturally bound. The American ideals of individual development and autonomy affect our perspective; in other societies, social norms may point to variations in styles of rule enforcement.

Consistency over time, and consistency between parents and between parents and other providers, is another important aspect of rules. Although some flexibility in family rules in light of new needs, abilities, and special circumstances is desired, constantly shifting expectations and contingencies confuse children and lead to behavior problems. Also, consistency among parents and others who care for the children is critical (Herbert, 1986). When children receive mixed messages about what constitutes acceptable behavior, they become confused and anxious. In this instance, they are likely to test limits constantly to find out what is truly expected and tolerated. Conflicts between parents and/or other providers will surface when consistency is lacking.

Clarity of rules in relation to generational boundaries is also necessary. It is the responsibility of parents to establish and enforce the rules. While children's views may be solicited, it is not up to the children to decide on the rules. Parents who abdicate this responsibility, create parentified children or poorly socialized children. For example, children of alcoholic families often cope by assuming parental responsibility for managing many aspects of the family or by engaging in unsanctioned behavior to get needed attention (Seixas & Youcha, 1985). Sooner or later, the children pay the price for such parental abdication of responsibility.

Today's parents recognize that there is no universal set of rules that can be easily and perfectly applied in their own families. The individuality of family members, variants in developmental stages, family structure, and specific situations must shape the way the parents establish and execute rules. Because life circumstances often force single parent families to learn how to adapt, rigid rules may be abandoned in favor of more flexibility. In a study of single and two parent families with handicapped children, McCubbin (1989) found that relationship rules in single parent families were more flexible and adaptable in response to stress than in two parent families. In addition, single parents who are able to function well in the executive role may create clear rules because rules do not have to be negotiated with another parent in the home. "In summary, we may say that rules that are covert and indiscernible or overt but excessively rigid often result in problematic family patterns. Overt rules that are flexible enough to shift with the family changes are more likely to facilitate growth and reduce tension" (Horowitz, Hughes, & Perdue, 1982, p. 132).

Communication

A fourth essential component of parenting is communication. Effective communication is the foundation of clear and consistent rules that have been examined above. Communication is the medium of exchange within families and occurs in three forms (Horowitz, 1990). Verbal communication is the transmission of information through spoken and written words. Words are symbols for ideas and share meaning through a specific language system.

Nonverbal communication includes all messages sent that are not words. Nonverbal communication takes many forms: gestures, body language, appearance, eye and facial expressions, and vocalizations or paralanguage. The five senses are the channels of nonverbal communication. Because nonverbal communication does not always reflect the sender's conscious intent and is subject to personalized meanings, nonverbal communication is especially open to misinterpretation (Blondis & Jackson, 1982).

Metacommunication refers to a message about the message. Metacommunication is the relationship aspect of communication. It involves reading between the lines of the message's content to its nuances and meaning. Metacommunication captures the idea that one cannot *not* communicate (Watzlawick, P., Beavin, J. H. & Jackson, D. D., 1967). Incongruence between the manifest content and metacommunication makes communication difficult to interpret and leaves the receiver confused. Confusing communication between parents and children is particularly problematic. "Trust is diminished and the child's emergent self-concept can be compromised. The child will not learn to trust personal reactions and interpretations and may find communicating a risky enterprise" (Horowitz, 1990, p. 72). Parents can be more effective in their communication by: (1) firmly and clearly stating the message, (2) clarifying and qualifying the message, (3) seeking feedback, and (4) being receptive to feedback (Brown, 1978; Horowitz, 1990; Satir, 1983).

Within single parent families, particular communication issues arise. When there is a custodial parent and contact exists with the non-custodial parent, or when both parents share custody, there is a risk that communication about expectations and rules can be conflicting. Parents in different households may communicate opposing messages to children leading to confusion. In addition, parents may try to communicate to former partners through the children. Both of these communication difficulties are likely to lead to conflict with negative consequences for the children, as noted during the earlier discussion of role boundaries.

Resources

Resources, another essential component of parenting, are the means and assets required to fulfill the goals of parenting. Finances, social support, and time and energy are discussed because of their critical influences on parenting effectiveness. Ask any parent about what it takes to raise a child today and you will hear a litany of resources with money usually topping the list. When resources are inadequate, it is nearly impossible to do a good job of parenting. In an insightful analysis of four decades of research concerning the influences of single parent household structure on children, Blechman (1982) concluded that risk to children has not been adequately demonstrated; the failure to give appropriate weight to the influence of mediating factors render the results of many studies inconclusive. The question can be raised: are children from one parent families automatically at risk for problems or are child outcomes subject to a host of intervening factors that happen to be frequently associated with single parent households? The adequacy of families' resources is an important factor in successful parenting.

Finances. Financial resources are crucial to effective parenting. Poverty severely limits parents' ability to nurture their children in many ways. Poverty has been associated with a variety of difficulties among children, including poor school performance, delinquency, and poor self-concept, as well as parenting problems including poor housing, lack of safety, neglect and abuse (Blechman, 1982; Horowitz, Hughes, & Perdue, 1981; LeMasters & DeFrain, 1989; Mulroy, 1990).

The negative consequences of poverty do not mean that many low income parents are not striving to obtain the needed resources to raise their children or that many parents and children from poor families do not possess many strengths. Clearly, problems experienced by affluent families have demonstrated that wealth alone is no guarantee of positive outcomes. However, clearly parents are helped in their job by material, psychological, social, and educational resources that are less accessible to the poor. The impact of poverty on children is emphatically stated by Keniston and the Carnegie Council on Children (1977):

> The single most important factor that stacks the deck against tens of millions of American children is poverty. Other things being equal, the best way to ensure that a child has a fair chance at the satisfactions and fulfillments of adult life is to ensure that the child is born into a family with a decent income. (p. 83)

Poverty also affects parents' ability to obtain other resources for their children. Adequate housing, education, and child care are directly tied to parents' income. Lack of financial resources also may have less obvious effects on parenting. To illustrate, in reference to a finding that authoritative parenting carried out by divorced mothers was not associated the same positive child outcomes that were found in two parent families, Maccoby (1992) pointed to the "harsh economic realities of the single-mother situation" (p. 235) as a possible explanation. Inadequate finances cause most single parent mothers to spend more hours away from the house in order to work. As a result, these mothers may be less available to their children despite the quality of their interactions when they are at home.

The failure in America's social policy regarding the financial welfare of its families fuels ongoing problems for our children. "Whether the country cares enough about the welfare of its children to make radical changes in the social system remains a moot question" (Horowitz, Hughes, & Perdue, p. 170).

Social Support. Social support is another resource that has received a great deal of attention in the research literature. The social support system generally refers to the set of people in the person's social network who can provide instrumental and/or emotional aid. Structural aspects of the support system are important; for example, its size, density, accessibility, stability, and reliability. Functional properties of the system include the perceived adequacy and amount of aid received.

Many researchers have proposed that social support functions as a buffer against the negative health consequences of stress (Norbeck, 1988). However, conceptual confusion and overly positive definitions and measurements of social support have plagued research. Thoits (1982) cautions against premature closure concerning the question of the role of social support. The stressful aspects of a parent's support network should be considered in relation to the helpful support that the parent receives. In a study of social support and single parent functioning, Norbeck and Sheiner (1982) found that for their sample of single mothers, the absence of a close friend and the lack of availability of people to call on for practical help were related to problems in parenting. Having emotional support and opportunity to get assistance in carrying out parenting tasks, as well as minimal stress associated with one's social network, are likely to be positive factors in parenting success.

Time. Many contemporary parents find time to be an important but scarce resource. Dual career parents are now the norm across social classes; balancing employment and family roles leaves too little time and/or energy for recreation and pleasant activities. Single parents who have to do it all are likely to feel an even greater pressure to be very efficient each day. Working parents have tried to use the notion of quality time to balance the many hours spent away from children. While it is important for parents to designate some special time to spend with their children, the idea of quality time only works if it is not reduced to mere minutes a day and an occasional weekend outing! Although there is no known minimum amount of time that children must spend with parents, experience with children suggests that it is beneficial for parents to spend time with children engaging in the tasks of daily living, participating in activities and special events, and focusing on their unique needs.

In summary, parents require adequate resources to carry out their job. Economic status affects many other resources such as the quality of the educational system and housing that are available (Gelles, 1989; Mulroy, 1990). Social support can also be a valuable resource to parents in terms of both emotional and functional support. However, support systems can also increase stress if demands or conflicts are extensive. Lastly, time is a scarce commodity in many families; too little time adds to parents' stress and certainly can have a negative impact on their relationships with their children.

Relationships

The sixth and final essential component of parenting is relationships. The parent-child relationship is the thread that weaves the very fabric of the parenting process. The importance of relatedness within the family is stated eloquently by Bowlby (1980): "Intimate attachments to other human beings are the hub around which a person's life revolves . . . From these intimate attachments a person draws his strength and enjoyment of life and, through what he contributes, he gives strength and enjoyment to others (p. 442)." The quality of the parent-child relationship will have a dramatic impact on the child. Rubin's (1967; 1984) model of maternal role attainment places attachment to the child-to-be and formation of a maternal identity as interdependent parts of the same process. Upon arrival of the baby, the mother's attachment to the infant is critical to her identity as a parent. Thus the importance of connectedness of the mother and child can be traced from pregnancy and birth.

Although paternal role attainment and father-infant attachment have received less attention, their importance should not be overlooked.

Sherwin (1987) reported changes experienced by fathers during their partners' pregnancies and suggested that fathers-to-be need to receive support from health care providers during their own transition to the parental role. Highly intimate father-child bonds were also uncovered in Ehrensaft's (1990) examination of couples who shared parenting. These fathers were described as hungering for intimacy; becoming "maternal" with their children fulfilled a need for connectedness and emotional closeness. Too often, socialization for males has devalued relational needs and abilities; however, the opportunity to parent a child awakened these fathers' quest for intimacy. Their experience of fatherhood was not very different from traditional motherhood, an experience of "being" a parent rather than just "doing" it.

Brazelton (1985) identified very early infancy as the most critical period for establishing a trusting, secure relationship. The parent-infant relationship provides a safe haven, a holding environment, that assists the baby to cope with the stresses of everyday living and unfolding developmental challenges (Brazelton, 1985; Winnicott, 1987). During this period, the parent must be sensitive to the emerging and changing needs and capacities of the infant. As the parent tunes in and adjusts to the infant's responses, a rewarding dialogue develops, and the interaction increasingly becomes reciprocal. Once a secure attachment is established during this period, the primary caretaking parent is better able to share the baby with another provider if return to employment is planned.

Variations in family structure necessitate adaptation in the patterns of relationships. Regardless of the family type, attachment to and nurturance from a primary parent remain as critical elements in successful parenting. Certainly, children have the capacity to bond with *more* than one primary parent; however, they do not have the capacity to thrive without at least one secure relationship. In single parent families, different relationship patterns may surface. Issues arise concerning the relative intensity of relationships between primary or custodial parents and children, maintenance of the relationship between children and noncustodial parents, the effect of single parent structure and divorce on sibling relationships, the meaning and influence of intermittent and transient relationships, such as a grandparent as a temporary primary parent, and development of new attachments in "blended" or remarried families.

The research literature provides beginning insights. For example, divorce has been associated with a decrease in quantity and quality of contact between children and noncustodial parents (Amato, 1988; Furstenburg & Nord, 1985). Findings from an extensive study (Hetherington et al., 1992) of adolescents from two parent (nondivorced), single parent (divorced), and remarried families over a 2-year period demonstrated a relationship between children's difficulties in adjustment and having experienced parents' marital transitions. Also, elevated levels of acting out behavior were present for both boys and girls from divorced families, and few changes in children's adjustment were seen over time. Bayrakal and Kope (1990) compared a clinical sample of "only children" in single parent families, labelled "minimal families," to a matched control group. A greater degree of disturbance was found among the adolescents from the minimal families. The researchers attributed this finding, in part, to the relationships of the mothers and children; these relationships were "either minimal or lacked depth and consistency" (p. 5). Amato and Keith's (1991) meta-analysis concerning divorce and well-being of children found that family conflict was associated with lower levels of well-being from children across family types. Friedemann and Andrews (1990) found that in their sample of single and two parent families, supportive relationships among adult caretakers and between children and adults appeared to provide a protective function reducing behavioral problems among single parent children.

In examining parent-child relationships, the theme of balance can serve as a useful lens. Research and treatment literature offer descriptions of relationship extremes associated with pathological outcomes. Labels used to describe extremes in relationship patterns include: pseudo-mutuality, schism, skew, enmeshment, estrangement, rigidity, disengagement, dysfunctional, and undifferentiated family ego mass. Terms used to capture healthy relatedness imply balance without stagnation, connectedness *and* personal differentiation and growth. Examples of such terms are: stability, flexibility, adaptability, individuation, reciprocity, balanced, and clear generational boundaries (Bell & Vogel, 1968; Clements & Buchanan, 1982).

Lastly, parents also have a role in providing opportunities for relationships beyond the family. As children broaden their social network to include more people outside the nuclear family, it is important that parents are comfortable sharing their children with others. Particularly during the school years and adolescence, children turn to their peers for advice, approval, and companionship. For parents who require their children to meet their own needs for esteem and love, and who may be insecure about the solidity of their relationship, their children's movement beyond the family boundaries can be threatening.

Many see attachment as basic and natural to the parent-child relationship. However, it does not develop so naturally for some. Personal and situational deficits can damage parents' ability to bond with and nurture their children. In addition, dramatic events during the twentieth century have shaken the belief that parental love and care for children is part of the natural order (Kagan, 1984). Reaffirmation of the importance of strong, nurturing, caring parent-child relationships is fundamental to any analysis of parenting.

The next section examines the challenge of parenting for single parents through discussion of the adequacy of parenting. Notions of the successful parent or "good enough" parent are derived from facets of a conceptual framework.

"Good Enough Parenting": Challenges for Single Parent Families

> If the inherited potential is to have a chance to become actual in the sense of manifesting itself in the individual's person, then the environmental provision must be adequate. It is convenient to use a phrase like "good-enough mothering" to convey an unidealized view of maternal function. . . . (Winnicott, 1987, p. 90)

> The good enough parent will always be aware that conceiving and bearing a child and bringing it into this world are the most wondrous events in the lives of parents. The more they (parent and child) can enjoy together . . . the happier their lives will be. (Bettelheim, 1987, p. 377)

Notions of good enough parents are fundamental to examination of single parenting. Social scientists and clinicians may hold some concept of parenting adequacy, and, perhaps, even assume that it can be applied impartially to assessments and judgments of parents. Yet a study of health professionals' assessments of the parenting potential of pregnant women raised questions about consistency and subjectivity of ratings (Sommerfield & Hughes, 1987). When the person is a single parent, the risk may be even greater that a legacy of stereotypes and values about what a good enough parent *should* be will influence judgment. Clearly, it is critically important to clarify the facets that contribute to successful parenting.

In this paper, parenting has been described in relation to the following dimensions: tasks, roles, rules, communication, resources, and relationships. Description of each dimension provides a basis for evaluation of the adequacy of the parenting in a particular situation. When parents are single, special considerations are merited. Clinicians and social scientists may ask: "How does single parent status affect each of the components of parenting?"

SINGLE PARENT FAMILIES: THE DEMOGRAPHIC PROFILE & PARENTING OUTCOMES

United States census data (Bureau of the Census, 1992) underscore the importance of this question. Of all households with their own children, 74% are classified as "married couple" (two parent) and 26% as one parent. When factors of race are considered, the picture becomes more dramatic: 78% of White children live in two parent families and 22% live in one parent families; 43% of Black/African American children live in two parent families and 57% live in one parent families; and 69% of Hispanic children live in two parent families and 31% live in one parent families. A large proportion of children, and a majority among Black/African American children, live in single parent homes.

Income data demonstrate that poverty is a serious problem for the majority of single parent families. In 1991 dollars, the median incomes for two parent, mother only, and father only families were $42,514, $13,012, and $24,171 respectively. Among mother only households, 53.4% were classified as below poverty in contrast to 10.4% of two parent and 21.5% of father only households (DaNavas & Welniak, 1992; Saluter, 1993). Single parent mothers who were never married were also younger, less educated, and poorer than divorced and separated mothers (Lester, 1991; Saluter, 1993).

Based on data reported from the National Center of Health Statistics (1991) concerning family structure and child health, strong relationships have been uncovered between family type and all the indicators of children's emotional well-being. Problems in school performance, including repeating a grade, difficulties requiring a parent-teacher conference, and school suspensions or expulsions were about twice as common for children from single parent families, with children from homes with never married mothers exhibiting the highest rates of problems. Children from two parent families had the lowest scores on measures of behavioral problems, and were the least likely to have seen a therapist or counselor during the past year.

IMPLICATIONS FOR PRACTICE AND SOCIAL POLICY

What do these statistics tell us about parenting in single parent families? To address this question, it is useful to consider the specific context and abilities of particular parents. The model proposed in this paper and depicted in Figure 1 directs a review of how single parents carry out the

FIGURE 1. Critical Components and Characteristics of Effective Parenting

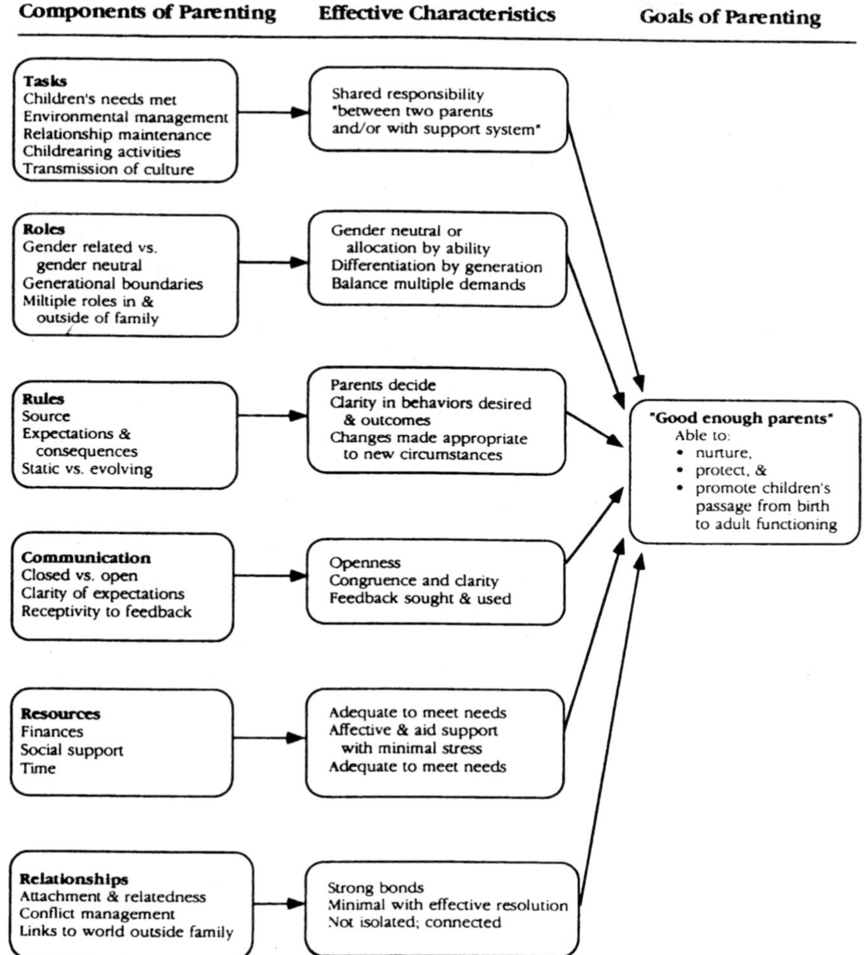

multiple tasks and parental roles. By evaluating the roles, rules, communication, availability and use of resources, and quality of relationships, strategies could be developed to prevent or mediate potential problems. For example, single parents are faced with the dilemma of fulfilling instrumental and expressive parenting roles, balancing employment and parenting roles (or conversely dealing with lack of employment and very scarce financial resources), and having adequate time, energy, and skill to carry out all the tasks of parenting for the child or children. Even single parents who work outside the home frequently face financial problems because of a number of factors including inadequate child care support from a former spouse, never being married and receiving little or no financial support from the other parent, low paying employment, and limited education or job skills so that better paying jobs are an impossibility.

Without adequate resources, single parents are at risk for failing to carry out essential parenting tasks and roles. "The documented high risk of abuse and maltreatment in single-parent households demands the development of treatment and policy programs that can support single parents and protect their children" (Gelles, 1989, p. 500). Given the high incidence of poverty among single parent families, particularly when the family is headed by a single mother, economic resources are the most essential to be addressed. When there are adequate finances, single parents can purchase assistance to carry out parental tasks and roles. Serious problems in the other parenting components may be less likely to develop when parents are not highly stressed with financial worries, have the power to obtain concrete support, and are available to address concerns with the children as they occur. With adequate finances, single parents could also obtain and utilize treatment if problems developed with the children. Single parents who are fighting to feed, clothe, and shelter children will have great difficulty attending to children's emotional, social, and academic needs. Tougher enforcement procedures are imperative. Sands and Nuccio (1989) have provided an insightful critique concerning the alienation, isolation, and economic struggle faced by single parent women in U. S. society.

> The authors' view of mother heads of families through a 'gender lens' finds a misappropriation of the problems caused by sexism, racism, and classism onto the casualties of social and economic oppression–women. Mother-headed families are not, by definition, a problem, although they do suffer from poverty. As long as mother-headed families are defined as Other, their socioeconomic status is likely to remain marginal. (p. 38)

The necessity for changes in social policy in the United States is dramatically apparent, and cannot be overemphasized.

Strategies must address the adequacy of all forms of resources. For example, an important question is: who in the support network can contribute to this family and what institutional supports can be tapped? Psychotherapeutic intervention can be implemented when problems in relation to rules, communication, and/or relationships are present. Single parents also face challenges in relation to negotiating rules and relationships after a parental separation or divorce. For example, confusion and stress result when children are not sure when they will see the noncustodial parent or when tensions between the parents are played out in the parent-child relationships whether or not the parents share custody. The parents need to remember that their relationship continues even when the marriage (or nonmarital intimate relationship) between the partners has ended. Division of tasks, sharing and flexible definitions of roles, clarity of rules and communication, adequate and appropriate allocation of resources, and promotion of stable supportive relationships with the children provide the best bet for successful parenting.

CONCLUSION

A conceptualization of the parenting process assists us to evaluate the success of any parent's efforts. Such an analysis also provides directions for intervention when difficulties surface. For single parents to be good enough parents, their parenting must embody, at the very least, a modicum of each of the components described in this paper and depicted in Figure 1. The challenges are many. It is not helpful or accurate to assume that children from single parent families are automatically at risk for problems; however, it is naive to overlook the many factors that do make it difficult for single parents to do a good job of parenting. Many struggle to overcome incredible obstacles and manage to be very competent parents. Others cannot do an adequate job and the children bear this burden. Clinicians, educators, researchers, and policy makers have a responsibility to recognize the challenges faced by single parents and work for social change that will foster successful parenting for the sake of the children.

REFERENCES

Ackerman, N. W. (1958). *The psychodynamics of family life: Diagnosis and treatment of family relationships*. New York: Basic Books.

Amato, P. R. (1986). Marital conflict, the parent-child relationship, and child self-esteem. *Family Relations, 35*, 103-110.

Amato, P. R. (1987). Family process in one-parent, stepparent, and intact families: The child's point of view. *Journal of Marriage and the Family, 49*, 327-337.

Amato, P. R. (1988). Long-term implications of parental divorce for adult self-concept. *Journal of Family Issues, 9*, 201-213.

Amato, P. R. & Keith, B. (1991). Parental divorce and the well-being of children: A meta-analysis. *Psychological Bulletin, 110*, 26-46.

Bales, R. F. & Slater, P. E. (1955). Differentiation in small decision-making groups. In T. Parsons & R. F. Bales (Eds.), *Family, socialization, and interaction process*. New York: The Free Press.

Baumrind, D. (1971). Current patterns of parental authority. *Psychological Developmental Monographs, 4* (1, part 2), 1-103.

Bayrakal, S. & Kope, T. M. (1990). Dysfunction in the single-parent and only-child family. *Adolescence, 15* (97), 3-7.

Bell, N. W. & Vogel, E. F. (Eds.). (1968). *A modern introduction to the family*. New York: The Free Press.

Bettelheim, B. (1987). *A good enough parent: A book on childrearing*. New York: Vintage Books.

Blechman, E. A. (1982). Are children with one parent at psychological risk? A methodological review. *Journal of Marriage and the Family, 44*, 179-195.

Blondis, M. N. & Jackson, B. E. (1982). *Nonverbal communication with parents: Back to the human touch* (2nd ed.). New York: John Wiley & Sons.

Bowlby, J. (1980). *Attachment and loss, Vol. III: Loss: Sadness and depression*. New York: Basic Books, Inc.

Brazelton, T. B. (1985). *Working and caring*. Menlo Park, CA: Addison-Wesley Pub. Co.

Brown, S. L. (1978). Functions, tasks, and stresses of parenting: Implications for guidance. In L. E. Arnold (Ed.), *Helping parents help their children* (pp. 22-340). New York: Brunner/Mazel, Pub.

Bureau of the Census, (1992). Statistical brief: Housing of single-parent families (SB/91-15). Washington, DC: US Dept. of Commerce, Economics and Statistics Administration.

Clements, I. W. & Buchanan, D. M. (Eds.). (1982). *Family therapy: A nursing perspective*. New York: John Wiley & Sons.

Collins, C. (1986). Combining employment with motherhood. In J. Griffith-Kenney (Ed.), *Contemporary women's health: A nursing advocacy approach* (pp. 324-338). Menlo Park, CA: Addison-Wesley Pub., Co.

Compas, B. E. & Williams, R. A. (1990). Stress, coping, and adjustment in mothers and young adolescents in single- and two-parent families. *American Journal of Community Psychology, 18*, 525-545.

DaNavas, C. & Welniak, E. J. (1992). Money income of households, families, and persons in the United States: 1991. U.S. Bureau of the Census, *Current Population Reports* (Series P-60, No. 180).

Ehrensaft, D. (1990). *Parenting together: Men and women sharing the care of their children*. Urbana, IL: Univ. of Illinois Press.

Emery, R. E. (1982). Interparental conflict and the children of discord and divorce. *Psychological Bulletin, 92*, 310-330.

Freidemann, M. L. & Andrews, M. (1990). Family support and child adjustment in single-parent families. *Issues in Comprehensive Pediatric Nursing, 13*, 289-301.

Furstenburg, F. F., Jr. & Nord, C. W. (1985). Parenting apart: Patterns of childrearing after marital disruption. *Journal of Marriage and the Family, 47*, 893-904.

Gelles, R. J. (1989). Child abuse and violence in single-parent families: Parent absence and economic deprivation. *American Journal of Orthopsychiatry, 59*, 492-501.

Hall, W. A. (1992). Comparison of the experience of women and men in dual-career families following the birth of their first infant. *Image: Journal of Nursing Scholarship, 24*, 33-38.

Herbert, M. (1986). The pathology of human behavior. In W. Sluckin & M. Herbert (Eds.), *Parental behaviour* (pp. 316-345). Oxford, UK: Basil Blackwell, Ltd.

Hetherington, E. M., Clingempeel, W. G., Anderson, E. R., Deal, J. E., Hagan, M. S. Hollier, E. A. & Lindner, M. S. (1992). Coping with marital transitions: A family systems perspective. *Monographs of the Society for Research in Child Development, 57* (2-3, Serial No. 227).

Hetherington, E. M., Cox, M., & Cox, R. (1982). Effects of divorce on parents and children. In M. Lamb (Ed.), *Nontraditional families* (pp. 233-288). Hillsdale, NJ: Erlbaum.

Horowitz, J. A. (1990). Nurse-client relationship. In C. L. Edelman & C. L. Mandle (Eds.), *Health promotion throughout the lifespan* (pp. 65-83). St. Louis: The C.V. Mosby Co.

Horowitz, J. A. (1992, June). Balancing women's multiple roles: The quest to "get a life." *Alpha Chi News, 14*, 3-4.

Horowitz, J. A., Hughes, C. B., & Perdue, B. J. (1982). *Parenting reassessed: A nursing perspective.* Englewood Cliffs, NJ: Prentice-Hall, Inc.

Ihinger-Tallman, M. (1986). Member adjustment in single parent families: Theory building. *Family Relations, 35*, 215-221.

Johnston, J. R., Kline, M., & Tschann, J. M. (1989). Ongoing postdivorce conflict: Effects on children of joint custody and frequent access. *American Journal of Orthopsychiatry, 59*, 576-592.

Kagan, J. (1984). *The nature of the child.* New York: Basic Books Inc.

Keniston, K. & the Carnegie Council on Children (1977). *All our children: The American family under pressure.* New York: Harcourt Brace Jovanovich.

LeMasters, E. E. & DeFrain, J. (1989). *Parents in contemporary America: A sympathetic view* (5th ed.). Belmont, CA: Wadsworth Pub. Co.

Lester, G. H. (1991). Child support and alimony: 1989. U.S. Bureau of the Census, *Current Population Reports* (Series P-60, No. 173).

Levinger, G. (1968). Task and social behavior in marriage. In N. W. Bell & E. F. Vogel (Eds.), *A modern introduction to the family* (pp. 355-367). New York: The Free Press.

Lidz, T. (1968). *The person: His development throughout the life cycle.* London: Basic Books.

Maccoby, E. (1992). Commentary: Family structure and children's adjustment; Is quality of parenting the major mediator? *Monographs of the Society for Research in Child Development, 57*, 23-238 (2-3, Serial No. 227).

Maccoby, E. & Martin, J. A. (1983). Socialization in the context of the family: Parent-child interaction. In E. M. Hetherington (Ed.), *Handbook of child psychology, Vol. IV: Socialization, personality, and social development* (pp. 1-101). New York: Wiley.

Macklin, E. D. (1980). Nontraditional family forms: A decade of research. *Journal of Marriage and the Family, 42*, 175-192.

Marciano, T. D. (1991). A postscript on wider families: Traditional family assumptions and cautionary notes. *Marriage & Family Review, 17*, 159-171.

Marciano, T. D. & Sussman, M. B. (1991). Wider families: An overview. *Marriage & Family Review, 17*, 1-8.

McCubbin, M. A. (1989). Family stress and family strengths: A comparison of single- and two-parent families with handicapped children. *Research in Nursing & Health, 12*, 101-110.

Minuchin, S. & Fishman, H. C. (1981). *Family therapy techniques*. Cambridge, MA: Harvard Univ. Press.

Mulroy, E. (1990). Single-parent families and the housing crisis: Implications for macropractice. *Social Work, 53*, 542-546.

National Center of Health Statistics. (1991). New from NCHS. *American Journal of Public Health, 81*, 1526-1528.

Norbeck, J. S. (1988). Social support. In J. J. Fitzpatrick, R. L. Taunton, & J. Q. Benoliel (Eds.), *Annual review of nursing research, Vol. 6* (pp. 85-109). New York: Springer Pub. Co.

Norbeck, J. S. & Sheiner, M. (1982). Sources of social support related to single-parent functioning. *Research in Nursing and Health, 5*, 3-12.

O'Neill, J. (1985). Role differentiation and the gender gap in wage rates. In L. Larwood, A. H. Stromberg, & B. A. Gutek (Eds.), *Women and work: Annual review* (Vol. 1, pp. 50-75). Beverly Hills, CA: Sage.

Parsons, T. (1955). The American family. In T. Parsons & R. F. Bales (Eds.), *Family, socialization, and interaction process*. New York: The Free Press.

Parsons, T. (1964). *Social structure and personality*. New York: The Free Press.

Roberts, F. (1982). Enmeshment. In I. W. Clements & D. M. Buchanan (Eds.), *Family therapy: A nursing perspective* (pp. 134-138). New York: John Wiley & Sons.

Rogers, S. J., Parcel, T. L., & Menaghan, E. G. (1991). The effects of maternal working conditions and mastery on child behavior problems: Studying the intergenerational transmission of social control. *Journal of Health and Social Behavior, 32*, 145-164.

Rubin, R. (1967). Attainment of the maternal role. *Nursing Research, 16*, 237-246.

Rubin, R. (1984). *Maternal identity and the maternal experience*. New York: Springer Pub. Co.

Saluter, A. F. (1993). Marital status and living arrangements: March 1992. U.S. Bureau of the Census, *Current Population Reports* (Series P-20, No. 468).

Sands, R. G. & Nuccio, K. E. (1989). Mother-headed single-parent families: A feminist perspective. *Affilia, 4* (3), 25-41.

Satir, V. (1983). *Conjoint family therapy* (rev. ed.). Palo Alto, CA: Science and Behavior Books.

Seixas, J. S. & Youcha, G. (1985). *Children of alcoholism: A survivor's manual.* New York: Crowne Publishers.

Sherwin, L. N. (1987). *Psychosocial dimensions of the pregnant family.* New York: Springer Pub. Co.

Simon, R. W. (1992). Parental role strains, salience of parental identity and gender differences in psychological distress. *Journal of Health and Social Behavior, 33*, 25-35.

Sommerfeld, D. P. & Hughes, J. R. (1987). Do health professionals agree on the parenting potential of pregnant women? *Soc. Sci. Med., 24*, 285-288.

Spiegel, J. P. (1968). The resolution of role conflict within the family. In N. W. Bell & E. F. Vogel (Eds.), *A modern introduction to the family* (pp. 391-411). New York: The Free Press.

Thoits, P. A. (1982). Conceptual, methodological, and theoretical problems in studying social support as a buffer against life stress. *Journal of Health and Social Behavior, 23*, 145-159.

Thoits, P. A. (1991). On merging identity theory and stress research. *Social Psychology Quarterly, 54*, 101-113.

Wallerstein, J. S. & Kelly, J. S. (1980). *Surviving the breakup: How children and parents cope with divorce.* London: Grant McIntyre.

Watzlawick, P., Beavin, J. H. & Jackson, D. D. (1967). *Pragmatics of human communication: A study of interactional patterns, pathologies and paradoxes.* New York: W. W. Norton & Co.

Westcot, M. E. & Dries, R. (1990). Has family therapy adapted to the single parent family? *The American Journal of Family Therapy, 18*, 363-372.

Winnicott, D. W. (1987). *Babies and their mothers.* Menlo Park, CA: Addison-Wesley Pub. Co.

Woods, N. F. (1985). Employment, family roles, and mental ill health in young married women. *Nursing Research, 34*, 4-9.

Zelditch, M. (1955). Role differentiation in the nuclear family. In T. Parsons & R. F. Bales (Eds.), *Family, socialization, and interaction process.* New York: The Free Press.

GLOSSARY

Communication: the medium of information exchange within families; occurs in three forms.

Verbal communication–transmission of information through spoken and written words.

Nonverbal communication–all messages sent that are not words.

Metacommunication–messages about the message; the relationship aspect of communication.

Parenting: a process undertaken to support children through developmental challenges and life events from conception and birth to adult functioning. Tasks, roles, rules, communication, resources, and relationships are essential components of parenting.

Parenting styles:

Authoritative parents–highly controlling and lacking in warmth in interactions.

Permissive parents–noncontrolling, nondemanding, and warm in interactions.

Authoritative parents–controlling and demanding but warm and receptive in interactions.

Primary parent: the person who carries out the major parenting responsibilities for the family.

Relationships: interpersonal connections among family members.

Resources: the means and assets required to fulfill the goals of parenting. Essential resources include: finances, social support, and time.

Roles: a set of socially endorsed behaviors involving responsibilities, authority, and status within the family and other social systems including employment and school systems.

Rules: regulations developed within families that specify acceptable behavior and task allocation.

Tasks: activities involving instrumental functions, i.e., management of the environment, and expressive functions, i.e., maintenance of relationships among family members, within the family.

Wider families: social organizations that do not conform to all of the conditions applied to traditionally-defined families; these structures may form without legal marriage, may or may not involve procreation of children, are voluntary and unstructured, are not rule- or time-bound, are independent of required kin or biological connections, and are not bound by the age groupings found in traditional families.

Chapter 4

The Changing Demographic and Socioeconomic Characteristics of Single Parent Families

Suzanne M. Bianchi

SUMMARY. The demographic and socioeconomic characteristics of single parent families have changed dramatically during the past three decades. The increase in single parent families, which was particularly great during the late 1960s and 1970s, slowed in the 1980s. Whereas the increase in divorce fueled the growth in one-parent families in the 1960s and 1970s, delayed marriage and child-bearing outside marriage contributed far more to growth in mother-child families during the 1980s than did marital disruption.

During the 1980s, father-child families increased faster than mother-child families. By 1990, almost one in five single parent families was maintained by a father, although only 3 percent of all children lived in this type of household.

Single parenting on the part of unmarried mothers is much higher within the black than white community and racial differences were as large or larger at the beginning of the 1990s as a generation earlier. Whereas two-thirds of white children currently live with both biological parents, only one-quarter of black children do so.

Suzanne M. Bianchi is affiliated with the Housing and Household Economic Statistics Division, U.S. Bureau of the Census, Iverson Room 302, Washington, DC 20233-3300.

[Haworth co-indexing entry note]: "The Changing Demographic and Socioeconomic Characteristics of Single Parent Families." Bianchi, Suzanne M. Co-published simultaneously in *Marriage & Family Review* (The Haworth Press, Inc.) Vol. 20, No. 1/2, 1995, pp. 71-97; and: *Single Parent Families: Diversity, Myths and Realities* (ed: Shirley M. H. Hanson et al.) The Haworth Press, Inc., 1995, pp. 71-97. Multiple copies of this article/chapter may be purchased from The Haworth Document Delivery Center [1-800-3-HAWORTH; 9:00 a.m. - 5:00 p.m. (EST)].

Single parent families remain disadvantaged relative to two-parent families in economic status, health, and housing conditions and children living with a never-married mother are the most economically disadvantaged group of children in single parent families.

Projections are that one-half of children born in the 1980s will spend some time living in a one-parent situation. The picture of life with a single parent is being enhanced by new data collection and analyses of extended family living arrangements and the role of cohabitation. Among children born in the 1980s, it is estimated that as much as one-third of the time they will spend in a mother-child family will be in their grandparents home or living in a household which includes their mother's cohabiting partner.

KEYWORDS. Single parents, Mother-child families

Almost any discussion of the situation of children in the United States begins by noting that dramatic changes have occurred in the American family and soon focuses on the rise in single-parent households. Today, almost four of every ten children in the U.S. are either currently living in a single parent family or have in the past spent time living with one parent. In 1992, for example, 27 percent of children were living with only one parent and another 11 percent of all children were living with one biological parent and a step-parent (Saluter, 1993: xii; Norton and Miller, 1992: p. 12). This latter group of children had presumably spent time living in a one-parent situation prior to their parent's current marriage. Projections are that one-half of children born today will spend time living apart from one or both biological parents.

The purpose of this paper is to describe the increase in single parent families and examine the demographic and socioeconomic characteristics which differentiate types of single parent families from each other and from two-parent families. The two main sources of time series data on single parent families in the United States are the Census of Population, which provides a snapshot of living arrangements every ten years, and the March supplement to the Current Population Survey (CPS), which provides annual estimates of family living arrangements. This paper begins with a brief discussion of the family concepts embodied in the Census and CPS.

A second section of the paper assesses the growth in single-parent households during the post-World War II period, a period of great change and shifting composition of the population in single parent families. The third section of the paper focuses on components of the increase in single parent families–factors such as divorce and childbearing outside marriage. Research on the relative importance of each component is reviewed and racial differences are highlighted.

A fourth section of the paper discusses the limits of the cross-sectional counts of single parent families and reviews the evidence on "life time experience" in single parent families. That is, what is known about how many children spend all or part of childhood in a single parent family? Is single-parent living transitory or is it a relatively permanent feature of children's lives?

A fifth section of the paper provides a demographic and socioeconomic overview of single parent families and offers comparisons with the situation in two-parent families. A final section summarizes the overall statistics on single parent families.

WHAT IS A SINGLE PARENT FAMILY IN THE CENSUS AND CPS?

Decennial census and CPS data provide the historical record on changes in family living arrangements in the U.S. but accurately assessing growth in one-parent families with these data requires attention to the family concepts used. In the Census and CPS, data are collected on persons who reside together in a housing unit and the relationship of all persons living at a particular address are keyed to a "reference person" or "householder," the person (or one of the persons) in whose name the housing unit is owned or rented. The outcome is that "family" becomes restricted to members who live together. A family, by Census Bureau definition, "is a group of two persons or more (one of whom is the householder) related by birth, marriage, or adoption *and residing together*" (Rawlings, 1992: B-2). Thus, for example, Census and CPS data are adequate for tracking the increase in single mothers who live with dependent children but are not particularly well-suited to the study of family ties that cross households, such as those between children and their absent fathers.[1]

Until recently, the Census Bureau made no distinction in data collection among step, adoptive, or biological family ties. Hence, it is also difficult to use Census or March CPS data to assess change in the proportion of children currently in two-parent families who at some point probably experienced single-parent living. Because the chances of spending one or more years in a one-parent family have been changing for adults and children, it is necessary to go to sources other than the March CPS or the

Census to gain a more complete picture of how family living arrangements have changed in recent decades.

The definition of a family which requires blood, marriage, or adoptive ties affects the classification of families as one- or two-parent. Unless a cohabiting couple with children report themselves as married, the family will be coded in the decennial census and CPS as a one-parent family, either father-child or mother-child depending on which adult is identified as the householder. One of the trends that will be discussed in this chapter is the increase in single parent families that are formed because a child is born to an unmarried mother. Using the 1987-88 National Survey of Families and Households (NSFH) in which cohabitation histories were obtained, Bumpass and Sweet (1989) have shown that approximately one-quarter of nonmarital births are to cohabiting couples. These children are born into two-parent families with unmarried biological parents not lone-parent families.

The Census Bureau has recognized that more than one family (depending on how family is defined) may live within a household and has developed and used the concept of a "subfamily" in its publications. Subfamilies, by definition, are either married couples (with or without children) or parent-child groups who live in someone else's household. Subfamilies can either be "related" to the householder or "unrelated" if they are not relatives of the person identified as the householder.

Subfamilies–how they are counted and how they are tallied–become particularly important in discussing how many single parent families there are in the U.S. because single parents with a dependent child may, with some frequency, live in the household of another person. Whether subfamilies are included or excluded from the count of one-parent families affects trends in the number of such families. In March of 1991, for example, the Census Bureau counted almost 10.1 million one-parent family groups in the United States but only 8.0 million one-parent family households (Rawlings, 1992: p. 9). The count of family groups includes family households plus related and unrelated subfamilies. The 2.1 million difference in the two counts of one-parent families is explained by the 1.6 million parent-child subfamily groups living in a relative's home and the one-half million parent-child subfamilies in households in which they were not related to the householder.

In the early 1980s, changes in field and data processing procedures improved the Census Bureau's ability to identify subfamilies and, therefore, recent counts of family groups are more complete. Due to these changes, caution is warranted in comparing the growth of one-parent family groups in the 1980s to earlier decades. Some of the apparent growth in one-parent subfamilies in the 1980s is a result of methodological improvements and earlier growth in subfamilies was probably understated. Hence, even though the Bureau's family group data are more inclusive of all types of single-parent situations, in the next section changes in the number of single parent families are assessed using data on single-parents who maintain their own household. Comparison of growth in the 1980s to earlier decades with this time series is much less affected by methodological changes in data collection.

GROWTH IN ONE-PARENT FAMILIES

Sweet and Bumpass (1987: pp. 362, 372) provide evidence that the number of one-parent families changed little between 1940 and 1950. The number of mother-child families increased by 6 percent but this was more than counter-balanced by a decline in the number of father-child families. Similarly, Hernandez (1993a: p. 65) shows that the number of children living in one-parent families increased by 1 million during the 1940s but the proportion of all children in one-parent situations actually declined by a percentage point (from 9 to 8 percent).

The picture for subsequent decades is much different, as evidenced in Table 1 which shows decennial census data on one-parent households and Figure 1 which graphs annual March CPS data. The number of one-parent households increased by 43 percent in the 1950s, rising from 1.5 to almost 2.2 million.

Growth accelerated in the latter half of the 1960s and 1970s. During the 1960s, the number of households headed by a single-parent increased to 3.5 million, a 57 percent increase. By 1980, the number of single parent families stood at 5.9 million, which represented an increase of 71 percent during the 1970s. The rate of increase slowed significantly during the 1980s, although the number of one-parent families continued to increase. According to the 1990 Census, there were 7.4 million households maintained by a lone parent, an increase of only 26 percent over the decade.

Table 1 disaggregates these figures by whether the single parent was male or female and shows trends for whites and blacks. The increase is dominated by the growth in mother-child families because the number of these families is so much greater than the number of father-child families.[2] However, during the 1980s, as the growth in mother-child families slowed significantly, the increase in father-child families accounted for more than one-third of the overall growth in the number of one-parent families. The proportion of one-parent family households maintained by a father declined between 1950 and 1970 (from 18 to 12 percent), changed little

TABLE 1. Growth in One-Parent Family Households with Own Children Under Age 18: 1950-90 (Numbers in Thousands)

						Percent Change			
	1950	1960	1970	1980	1990	1950s	1960s	1970s	1980s
TOTAL									
One Parent	1,531	2,191	3,428	5,871	7,383	43.1	56.5	71.3	25.8
Mother-child	1,256	1,891	3,007	5,062	6,028	50.6	59.0	68.4	19.1
Father-child	275	300	421	809	1,355	9.1	40.3	92.1	67.4
Two-Parent	18,316	23,470	24,545	24,265	23,495	28.1	4.6	–1.1	–3.2
WHITE									
One Parent	1,200	1,638	2,382	3,760	4,579	36.5	45.4	57.9	21.8
Mother-child	971	1,394	2,058	3,166	3,608	43.6	47.6	53.8	14.0
Father-child	229	244	324	594	971	6.6	32.8	83.3	63.5
Two-Parent	16,990	21,625	22,268	20,997	19,777	27.3	3.0	–5.7	–5.8
BLACK									
One Parent	331	552	989	1,727	2,127	66.8	79.2	74.6	23.2
Mother-child	285	497	901	1,568	1,897	74.4	81.3	74.0	21.0
Father-child	46	55	88	159	230	19.6	60.0	80.7	44.7
Two-Parent	1,326	1,845	1,951	1,950	1,780	39.1	5.7	–0.1	–8.7

Note: Data for 1950 and 1960 are for nonwhites. Percent change = (Year 2 – Year 1)/Year 1 * 100.

SOURCE: U.S. Bureau of the Census, 1955: Table 4; 1964: Table 188, 1973: Table 54; 1983: Table 46; 1993: Tables 38 and 40.

FIGURE 1. Growth in the Number of Mother-Child and Father-Child Families: 1951-1991

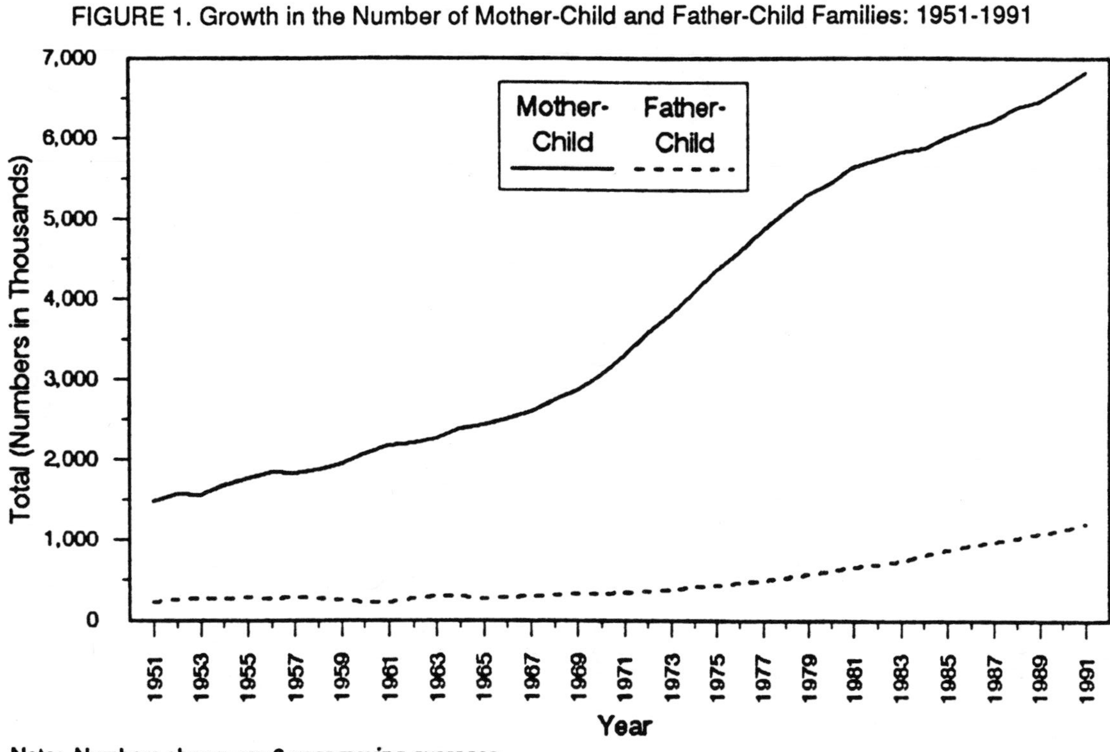

Note: Numbers shown are 3-year moving averages
Source: Unpublished data, Bureau of the Census

during the 1970s, but increased from 13 to 18 percent between 1980 and 1990.[3] Despite growth in the number of father-only families, only a small percentage (around 3 percent) of all children lived only with their father in the early 1990s (Saluter, 1993: p. 21).

During the past four decades, growth in the number of single parent families has been dramatic for both blacks and whites: a 280 percent increase among whites (from 1.2 to 4.6 million) and a 543 percent increase for blacks (from around 300,000 to 2.1 million). Both blacks and whites experienced an accelerated growth in one-parent families during the 1970s and both have experienced a sizable decline in the rate of growth in the 1980s. During the 1980s, father-child families grew faster than mother-child families among both races, although the increase in father-child families accounted for only 18 percent of the net increase in black, one-parent families but 46 percent of the net increase in white, one-parent families.

Despite overall similarity of trends, racial differences remain extremely large. The overwhelming majority of white children live with two parents and almost two-thirds are currently being raised by both biological parents. Only around one-quarter of black children live with both biological parents and the majority (54 percent in 1992) live in mother-child families (Bianchi, 1990: p. 12; Saluter, 1993: p. 23).

Time series data do not exist for other racial and ethnic groups, although there is information with which to chart growth in single-parenting among the Hispanic population as a whole. In general, trends are intermediate between the black and white population. For example, as enumerated in the decennial census, about 23 percent of Hispanic compared with 14 percent of non-Hispanic white and 49 percent of black households with children were mother-child situations in 1990 (U.S. Bureau of the Census, 1993). (See Figure 2.)

Bean and Tienda (1987: pp. 191-194), using 1980 Census data, show considerable variation among Hispanic sub-groups in the likelihood of single-parenting. Puerto Rican family living arrangements are similar to those of black families whereas Cuban families are similar to white families, and other Hispanic subgroups, such as Mexican Americans, are intermediate between Puerto Ricans and Cubans.

The 1990 Census provides further perspective on racial variation in single parenthood. Single parent families made up 30 percent of Native American but only 11 percent of Asian and Pacific Islander households with children (U.S. Bureau of the Census, 1993: Table 40). The percentage of households with children that included two parents (step, biological, and/or adoptive) was highest for Asians (86 percent), followed by non-His-

FIGURE 2. Percent of Households with Children Under 18, Which Were Two-Parent or Mother-Child Families in 1990, Selected Racial and Ethnic Groups

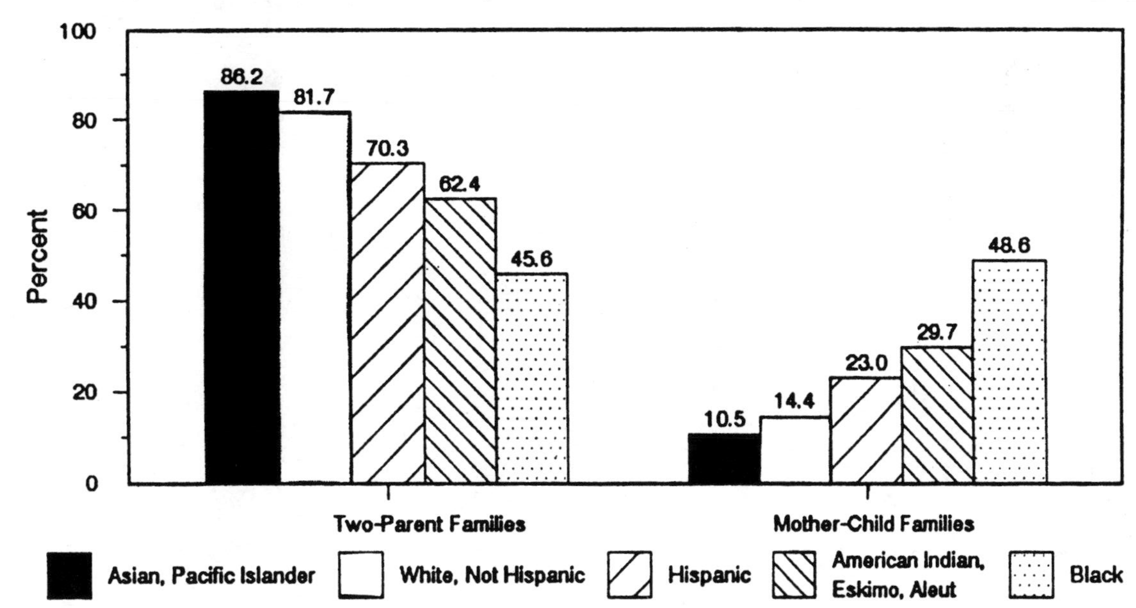

Note: Persons of Hispanic Ethnicity may be of any race
Source: U.S. Bureau of the Census, 1993: table 40

panic whites (82 percent), Hispanics (70 percent), Native Americans (62 percent), and finally, blacks (46 percent).

In sum, trends reveal that in addition to the large increases in the number of single parent families, racial differences in the family experiences of children remain large. Not only has growth in single parent families been substantial, there has been a change in the path to single-parenthood. Increasingly, mother-child families are formed by a birth to an unmarried mother rather than because married parents divorce. This is the topic of the next section and later in the paper the economic significance of this increase in never-married, single mothers is discussed.

COMPONENTS OF GROWTH IN MOTHER-CHILD FAMILIES

Several studies attempt to quantify the importance of various behavioral components of the increase in mother-child families, the vast majority of single parent families (Cutright, 1974; Cooney, 1979; Garfinkel and McLanahan, 1986; Ross and Sawhill, 1975; Smith and Cutright, 1985; Wojtkiewicz, McLanahan, and Garfinkel, 1990). By far the most common path to single-parenting is for a woman to marry, have one or more children, experience a marital disruption (divorce, separation, or death of spouse), and then raise dependent children on her own. Another path to single parenting, one that is becoming more common, especially among blacks, is for an unmarried woman to have a child and raise that child on her own.

The proportion of female family householders with dependent children who were divorced increased during the 1960s and 1970s. The divorce rate reached an all-time high in 1981 but has since leveled off, even declined slightly (National Center for Health Statistics, 1992: p. 4). Since 1980, growth in the number of divorced mothers has been quite modest and the proportion of female family householders who are divorced has declined a bit. In 1992, the proportion of children in single parent families who were with a divorced parent was 37 percent, a drop from 42 percent in 1983 (Saluter, 1991: p. 6; 1993: p. 29).

As shown in Table 2, the proportion of female family householders who had never married rose steadily from 4 to 31 percent between 1960 and 1992. The number of never-married, female family householders with dependents tripled in both the 1960s and 1970s and more than doubled during the 1980s. Between 1983 and 1992, the proportion of children in single parent homes with a never-married parent rose 10 percentage points to 34 percent (Saluter, 1991: p. 6; Saluter, 1993: p. 29).

Evident in Table 2 are the large racial differences in marital status of

TABLE 2. Change in the Marital Status of Female Family Householders with Children Under Age 18,1960 to 1992 (Numbers in Thousands)

	Total		White		Black	
	1960	1992	1960	1992	1960	1992
Total, Female Family	1,891	7,043	1,394	4,488	497	2,335
Householders	100.0%	100.0%	100.0%	100.0%	100.0%	100.0%
Never Married	4.4	30.6	1.9	18.4	11.5	54.7
Divorced	26.2	40.6	30.6	50.7	13.7	21.0
Separated	24.0	19.8	17.9	21.1	41.2	18.1
Spouse Absent	13.4	3.3	14.7	3.3	9.5	2.2
Widowed	32.0	5.8	34.9	6.5	24.0	3.9

Note: 1960 decennial census data for nonwhites and 1992 March CPS data.
SOURCE: U.S. Bureau of the Census, 1964: Table 6; Rawlings, 1993: Table 9.

single mothers. In 1992, 55 percent of black single mothers had never married, a 43 percentage point increase from 1960 when 12 percent of black mother-child families were maintained by a never-married mother. Although the proportion of white single mothers who had never married increased from 2 to 18 percent, the majority of white single mothers (51 percent) in 1992 were divorced mothers with young children.[4] Whereas one in five white children in mother-child families lived with a never married parent and one-half with a divorced parent by the early 1990s, the reverse was true of black children (Saluter, 1993: pp. 33, 37). One-half lived with a never-married parent and one-fifth lived with a divorced parent.

The figures shown in Table 2 may overstate the growth in never-married, one-parent families because cohabitation is not taken into account but the racial differences are unlikely to be any narrower after consideration of cohabitation. Bumpass and Sweet (1989: Table 4) have shown that about one-quarter of all births to unmarried women are to a cohabiting couple but this percentage is actually lower for blacks (18 percent) than for whites (29 percent).

Wojtkiewicz, Garfinkel and McLanahan (1990: Table 3) show that, during the 1950s the most important behavioral shifts resulting in more mother-only families among whites were the overall rise in fertility of the Baby Boom years (which increased the likelihood that a formerly married woman had children at the time of a marital disruption) and an increase in the propensity of a married woman to form an independent household after her marriage dissolved. In the 1960s and 1970s, the overwhelming behavioral factor in the growth in white mother-only families was the increase in marital disruption.

The picture for blacks is similar to whites but the behavioral components involved in the growth of black mother-only families are more diverse. During the 1950s, the increased fertility of the Baby Boom years left more women with children when a marriage dissolved. During the 1960s and 1970s, however, marital disruption was not the overwhelming component of growth for blacks that it was for whites. In addition to marital disruption, the large increase in the proportion of black women who remained unmarried, the increase in the likelihood of childbearing outside marriage (which was a more important factor in the 1960s than the 1970s), and an increase in living independently, (again more so in the 1950s and 1960s than in the 1970s), all played a role in the growth of black mother-child families (Garfinkel and McLanahan, 1986: pp. 53-54; Wojtkiewicz et al., 1990: pp. 26-27).

Table 3 presents indicators of the racial differences in marriage which in part produce the dramatic racial gap in single parenting. Cherlin (1992) notes that during the first part of this century, blacks married at younger ages than white women but this reversed after World War II. As can be seen in Table 3, black women are much less likely to marry in their twenties than white women. Among women 20 to 24 years of age, the proportion never married has increased for both races but has risen from 44 to 80 percent among blacks compared with an increase from 35 to 63 percent among whites. The gap between whites and blacks, which was 9 percentage points in 1970 was twice as large in 1992. Even more striking, among women in their late twenties, over 70 percent of white women have married but only 40 percent of black women have ever married.

First marriages of black women more often dissolve. Data from the 1988 National Survey of Family Growth (NSFG), shown in Table 3, indicate that among marriages formed in the latter half of the 1960s, the percentage which had disrupted by 1988 was 62 percent among blacks and 47 percent among whites, a differential of 15 percentage points. A similarly large percentage point gap between blacks and whites characterized marriages formed in the late 1970s and early 1980s.

Table 3 also shows that the percentage who subsequently remarry after a first marriage ends was far lower among blacks than among whites. Racial differences in the percent remarried by 1988 were around 30 percentage points for those whose marriage ended in the early 1970s or early 1980s (37 percentage points among those experiencing disruption in the late 1970s). The racial differentials result both because black women have a lower probability of ever remarrying and because black women who

TABLE 3. Racial Differences in Marital Behavior, Selected Indicators

	Black	White	Difference (B–W)
Percent of Women, Age 20-24, Who Have Never Married			
1970	43.5	34.6	8.9
1980	68.5	47.2	21.3
1992	80.3	62.7	17.6
Percent of Women, Age 25-29, Who Have Never Married			
1970	18.8	9.2	9.6
1980	37.2	18.3	18.9
1992	60.4	28.5	31.9
Percent of First Marriages Disrupted by 1988 Married In:			
1965-69	61.7	47.0	14.7
1970-74	55.8	46.2	9.6
1975-79	50.4	34.6	15.8
1980-84	38.1	22.9	15.2
Percent Remarried by 1988 Marital Disruption In:			
1965-69	81.2	91.0	–9.8
1970-74	59.0	87.5	–28.5
1975-79	32.3	69.5	–37.2
1980-84	19.7	51.4	–31.7
Percent of Women, Age 15-44, Currently Married and Living with Spouse			
1970	42.0	61.0	–19.0
1980	30.0	55.0	–25.0
1992	26.3	54.1	–27.8

SOURCE: Saluter, 1993: Table 1; Farley and Bianchi, 1991: Table 1; London, 1991; Tables 3 and 4.

subsequently remarry spend more years between marriages than do white women (Castro-Martin and Bumpass, 1989; Espenshade, 1985; Cherlin, 1992).

At any given point in time, the proportion of women currently married is much lower for blacks than whites. Among women of childbearing age, roughly age 15 to 44, the proportion married declined significantly for both races between 1970 and 1992. But whereas around one-quarter of black women were married and living with a spouse, almost one-half of white women in this age range were living with a husband in 1992. As Cherlin (1992) points out, a much smaller proportion of a black than a white woman's adult life is spent living with a spouse and this difference is greater than a generation ago.

In terms of childbearing, black women have reduced the total number of children they bear as have white women but they start and stop having children at much earlier ages, on average, than white women. Although black women are delaying marriage, they have continued to have children at relatively early ages. White women, on the other hand, have more often postponed both entry into marriage and first births (Cherlin, 1992).

Nonetheless, as shown in Table 4, birth rates for white, unmarried women rose dramatically during the 1980s whereas rates for black women declined during the 1970s and early 1980s but then increased during the latter half of the 1980s. Despite the greater increase among whites, birth rates for black unmarried women were almost three times higher than for white women in 1990.

Among both races the proportion of births that are to unmarried women has risen not only because birth rates to unmarried women have increased but because there has been a decline in fertility within marriage and because women spend more of their childbearing years unmarried, and hence "at risk" of a birth outside marriage. Black women spend so many years unmarried during their childbearing years, that the chances that they have one or more children while unmarried is extremely high.

The proportion of children born to unmarried mothers has risen for both races but, during the 1980s, a 45 percentage point differential separated the two racial groups. In 1990, almost two-thirds of black births compared with 20 percent of white births were to an unmarried mother. As a consequence, 54 percent of black children but 18 percent of white children lived in mother-child households in 1992. Thirty-one percent of black children lived with a never-married mother in 1992 compared with only 4 percent of white children.

LIFETIME EXPERIENCE OF SINGLE-PARENT SITUATIONS

March CPS and Census data provide snapshots of living arrangements but do not give a perspective on lifetime probabilities of experiencing single-parent living. Retrospective marital and fertility histories of women have provided evidence on the likelihood that a child born in a given year

TABLE 4. Racial Differences in Childbearing Outside Marriage, Selected Indicators

	Black	White	Difference (B–W)
Birth Rates per 1000 Unmarried Women			
1970	95.5	13.9	81.6
1980	82.9	17.6	65.3
1985	79.0	21.8	57.2
1990	93.9	31.8	62.1
Birth Rates per 1000 Unmarried Teenagers			
1970	96.9	10.9	86.0
1980	89.2	16.2	73.0
1985	89.3	20.3	69.0
1990	110.1	29.5	80.6
Percent of Total Births Which Are to Unmarried Mothers			
1970	35.0	6.0	29.0
1980	55.0	11.0	44.0
1985	60.1	14.5	45.6
1990	65.2	20.1	45.1
Percent of Children Who Live in Mother-Child Households			
1970	29.5	7.8	21.7
1980	43.9	13.5	30.4
1992	54.0	17.6	36.4
Percent of Children Who Live with a Never-Married Mother			
1992	30.8	3.8	27.0

SOURCE: Farley and Bianchi, 1991: Table 1; Lugaila, 1992: Tables 4 and 5; National Center for Health Statistics, 1982: Table 15; 1987: Table 16; Saluter, 1993: Table 6; Ventura and Martin, 1993: Tables 17 and 18.

will spend time in a single parent family (Bumpass and Rindfuss, 1979; Bumpass, 1984; Bumpass and Sweet, 1989; Bumpass and Raley, 1993). Bumpass and Raley (1993) estimate that "about half" (p. 9) of children born in the early 1980s will spend time in a single parent family before age 18. Similarly, by age 35, about half of the mothers of these children will have become a single parent.[5]

Racial differences are extremely large and a single-parent situation does not seem to be a transitory state for the majority of black children. Among blacks, 80 percent of children are projected to spend time living in a single parent family compared with 36 percent among white children. Only 23 percent of black children are projected to exit from a single parent family within 5 years and only 35 percent within 10 years compared with 44 percent and 61 percent, respectively, among non-Hispanic white children (Bumpass and Sweet, 1989).

Bumpass and Raley (1993) show that estimates of how many children enter a single parent family because of a nonmarital birth and projections of how much time children will spend in single parent families are affected by whether cohabitation is taken into account. For example, if only married couples are defined as two-parent families, as is the case in the birth registration, CPS, and decennial census data relied on in previous sections of this paper, close to one-half of the entries into single parent families were due to a nonmarital birth for the cohort of children born in the early 1980s (and for their mothers). On the other hand, if cohabiting couples are included with married couples in the count of two-parent families, around one-third of the women and children who entered a single-parent situation did so because of a birth outside of a union. However, because cohabiting unions are less stable than marital unions, the likelihood that a child will eventually spend time in a single-parent situation remains higher for children born into a two-parent, cohabiting union than for those born into a marital union.

Estimates of how long children remain in a single-parent situation are also affected by whether cohabiting couples are counted as two-parent or one-parent families. For the cohort of children born during the early 1980s, the estimated average length of time spent in a single parent family is 6.9 years if only married couples are considered two-parent families but 3.7 years if cohabiting couples are counted as two-parent rather than one-parent situations (Bumpass and Raley, 1993). (The comparable estimates for their mothers are 6.6 versus 3.6 years as a single parent, on average.) Under the marital definition, the length of time in single parent families has increased over time whereas the average duration in one-parent situations has been shrinking under the broader definition of unions which includes cohabitation.

Finally, in addition to the role of unmarried partners, Bumpass and Raley (1993) and Ghosh, Easterlin, and Macunovich (1993) note the importance of the role of grandparents in assisting single parent families (see chapter by Burton this volume). Bumpass and Raley (1993) estimate that 16 percent of the cohort of children born in the early 1980s will spend some time living in a grandparent(s) home. Among single mothers, almost one-third will live at some point in their parents' (their child's grandparents') home and the average length of that stay is estimated to be almost 2 years. Perhaps as much as one-third of the time single parents spend outside a marital union is spent either living with a cohabiting partner or living in a (grand)parent's home.

THE HEALTH AND WELL-BEING OF CHILDREN IN ONE-PARENT FAMILIES

Although single parents make adjustments, such as living in their parents' household to ease the financial strain that comes with raising children alone, it is still the case that children who grow up in one-parent families are economically disadvantaged compared with those who remain in two-parent families. McLanahan and Booth's (1989) literature review concludes that children in single parent families are disadvantaged psychologically and educationally as well and that negative consequences carry into adulthood.

Table 5 presents selected indicators of the demographic and socioeconomic condition of children in single parent families compared with those in two-parent families. Two caveats are in order. First, because cohabiting partners are not defined as family members in the CPS data shown in the Table, the family income and poverty figures for children living with single-parents do not include income from unmarried partners of their mother (or father). The income of relatives, such as grandparents, is included.

An upper-bound area on the percentage of children who may be living with a parent and his or her unmarried partner is shown in Table 5. In 1992, 15 percent of children in mother-child and 37 percent of those in father-child situations had at least one nonrelative living in the household.

Secondly, these data do not control for the fact that individuals who end up in a one-parent family because of marital disruption (or a birth outside marriage) may be disadvantaged economically relative to individuals in stable two-parent families even before single parenting begins. For example, longitudinal data show that, on average, children who experience parental marital disruption have family income levels *prior to the disruption* that are only 80 percent of those of children who remain in intact families (Bianchi and McArthur, 1991) and that poverty precedes marital disruption for one-third of poor mother-child families that are formed in a given year (Hernandez, 1993b).

As can be seen in Table 5, the median family income of mother-child families was only 31 percent that of two-parent families in 1991. Mother-

TABLE 5. Selected Demographic and Socioeconomic Characteristics of Children in Two-Parent and One-Parent Families

	Two Parent	Mother Child	Father Child
DEMOGRAPHIC CHARACTERISTICS			
Mean Number of Siblings	1.49	1.39	0.94
Median Age of Parent	37.6	33.1	36.8
Percent with Adults Other than			
Parents in Household	17.2	39.8	56.7
Nonrelatives in Household	1.4	15.1	37.1
Percent with Parent Who Is			
High School Graduate	85.4	69.3	75.8
College Graduate	26.4	7.6	13.6
ECONOMIC STATUS			
Employment Status of Parent			
Percent Employed	85.4	52.0	78.4
Percent Employed Full-time	78.3	29.3	69.6
Median Family Income (1991$)	$42,514	$13,012	$24,171
Ratio One/Two Parent (*100)	100.0	30.6	56.9
Income per Family Member	$11,668	$5,506	$10,040
Ratio One/Two Parent (*100)	100.0	47.2	86.0
Percent Below Poverty (1991)	10.4	53.4	21.5

SOURCE: DaNavas and Welniak, 1992: Table 18; Saluter, 1993: Table 6.

only families are smaller, on average, than two-parent families. Hence, income per family member in these families was about one-half that in two-parent families. Half of children living in a mother-only family resided in poverty in 1991, a fraction far higher than for children in either father-only or two-parent families.

Children in father-child families were better off financially than those in mother-child families but still were less well-off than those in two-parent families. Family income in father-only families was only 57 percent of that in two-parent families with children, although income per family member was 86 percent as high as for married couples because of the relatively small households maintained by a father. The poverty rate in father-only families, 22 percent, was twice as high as in two-parent families.

These differential poverty rates for children in mother-child, father-child, and two-parent families result, in part, from differences in the age, education, and labor force participation of their parents. Children in mother-child families have the youngest parents and are less likely to have a parent who has completed high school. On average, they are only half as likely as children in father-child families and one-third as likely as children in two-parent families to live with a college-educated parent.

Whereas 85 percent of children in two-parent families and 78 percent of children in father-child families live with an employed parent, only 52 percent of children in mother-child families live with a mother who is employed. Even more striking differences emerge if the statistic cited is the percentage of children in families where at least one parent is employed full-time: 78 percent for two-parent families and 70 percent in father-child families but only 29 percent in mother-child families. Interestingly, the proportion of children in two-parent families with two earners (48 percent) (data not shown) is higher than the proportion in mother-child families with one full-time worker. Given this, it is not surprising that the gap in the income of two-parent and mother-child families has been increasing (Bianchi, 1990; Lichter and Eggebeen, 1993).

Data comparing the housing situation of two-parent and one-parent families with children (not distinguished by sex of parent) are available from the Census Bureau's American Housing Survey (Grall, 1992). One-parent households are no more crowded (in terms of persons per room) than married couple households but they do reside in smaller housing units (in terms of square footage per person). Far fewer single parents are owners and when they do own the value of their home is significantly less than that of two-parent families. Finally, the economic burden of housing is higher for single parents, accounting for 31 percent of their income, on average, compared with 20 percent for two-parent families.

Not surprisingly, given the poverty statistics, selected indicators of participation in public assistance programs indicate far higher recipiency of cash welfare, food stamps, and living in publicly assisted housing among single parent families (Grall, 1992; DaNavas and Welniak, 1992). Mother-child families are, on average, less likely to be covered by health insurance than two-parent families although there is an interesting reversal when the population is divided into poverty and nonpoverty segments. Primarily because of the availability of Medicaid benefits for mothers who receive Aid for Families with Dependent Children (AFDC), children in poor mother-child families are actually more likely than children in poor, two-parent families to be covered by health insurance (Lugaila, 1992: p. 52).

Children not living with both biological parents are also at risk of negative health, psychological, and educational outcomes. Controlling for the lower socioeconomic status of single parent families, Dawson (1991a) found that children from disrupted marriages (though not children living with a never-married mother) had a risk of accident or injury 20 to 30 percent greater than children in in-tact families. Children in single parent families had a greater risk of asthma and their overall health vulnerability score was elevated when compared with children living with both biological parents.

In addition, around 12 percent of children with both biological parents had repeated a grade in school compared with 16 percent of children from disrupted marriages and 20 percent of children with a never-married mother (Dawson, 1991a). Children in single parent families (and step-parent situations) were more likely to have been suspended or expelled from school or to have required a nonroutine parent-teacher conference. Differences among children were most pronounced on indicators of psychological functioning and behavioral problems, with children in single parent and step-parent families having a much higher incidence of past or present difficulty than children living with both biological parents (Dawson, 1991a; 1991b).

Table 6 shows differences among children in mother-child families by the marital status of their mother, and begins to make apparent why the shift toward never-married, mother-child families is so problematic for the material well-being of children. Never married mothers are young and less well-educated than divorced mothers because unmarried childbearing often occurs before young women finish high school (Hofferth and Moore, 1979). In 1992, only 59 percent of children with a never-married mother lived with a high school graduate compared with 82 percent of those with a divorced mother.

Only 38 percent of children with a never-married mother lived with a parent who was employed compared with 70 percent of those with a divorced mother. The median family income in never-married, mother-child families was only one-half that available to children living with a divorced mother in 1991.

In addition to their own low levels of education and employment, never-married mothers' ability to garner income from the father of their children is much lower than among women who are formerly married. According to April 1989 CPS data, three-quarters of divorced women with own children under 21 have an agreement or court award of child support from the absent father compared with around one-half of separated mothers and only one-quarter of never-married mothers. Approximately 18 percent of never-married mothers received at least some child support in 1989 compared with 38 percent of separated mothers and 59 percent of divorced mothers. The average annual amount received by never-married

TABLE 6. Selected Demographic and Socioeconomic Differences Among Children Living with a Divorced, Separated, or Never-Married Mother

	Divorced	Separated	Never Married
AGE OF MOTHER			
Percent Under Age 25	3.6	9.3	30.1
Median Age	36.0	34.0	28.5
PRESENCE OF ADULTS OTHER THAN MOTHER IN THE HOUSEHOLD			
Percent with Additional Adults	38.1	33.0	44.9
Percent with Nonrelative Adults	18.0	10.0	15.7
EDUCATION OF MOTHER			
Percent High School Graduate	81.7	66.4	59.1
Percent College Graduate	12.6	7.0	2.9
EMPLOYMENT/INCOME OF MOTHER			
Percent with Employed Mother	68.9	47.2	37.6
Median Family Income (1991$)	$17,503	$10,053	$8,609
Percent Below Poverty in 1991	36.6	64.3	66.1
CHILD SUPPORT IN 1989			
(1) Percent of Mothers with Award	76.8	47.9	23.9
(2) Percent with Award Who Receive	77.0	79.7	73.2
(3) Percent Receiving [(1) * (2)]	59.1	38.2	17.5
Mean Annual Amount per Recipient	$3,322	$3,060	$1,888

Note: Separated includes a small number of women with spouse absent for reasons other than marital discord. Age, education and employment status of mother are as of March 1992. The denominator for the percentage in (2) under child support is those who have an award (or agreement) and were supposed to receive support in 1989.

SOURCE: Saluter, 1993: Table 6; Lester, 1991: Table C.

mothers was considerably lower than for divorced or separated mothers who received support.

Not surprisingly, a child's likelihood of living below the poverty level was much higher if that child lived with a never-married mother than with a divorced mother. Two-thirds of children with a never-married mother were in poverty in 1991 compared with a little over one-third of children living with a divorced mother. Children with a separated mother also had a high probability of residing in poverty, comparable to the percentage among children with a never-married mother.

As noted previously, black children tend to live with never-married or separated mothers whereas white children more often live with divorced mothers. Although economic differentials by marital status of mother are not as great among black as for white children in mother-child families, black children with a never-married mother have a poverty rate one-third higher and an average family income about 60 percent that of children with a divorced mother (Saluter, 1993: p. 37). Hence, not only do black children have a higher risk of living in a mother-child family but the types of single parent families in which they grow up tend to be the most disadvantaged among single-parent groups.

CONCLUSION

The purpose of this paper has been to chart the growth in single parent families, examine the demographic components of that growth, and elaborate the socioeconomic circumstances of single parents and their children. Growth in single parent families, which was very rapid during the 1970s, slowed in the 1980s. Since the early 1980s, the divorce rate has declined somewhat but the percentage of children born to an unmarried mother has continued to increase. Hence, recent growth in mother-child families has in large part been an increase in families with a never-married mother.

A noteworthy trend of the 1980s was the faster growth of father-child than mother-child families, particularly among whites. By 1990, almost one in five single parent families was maintained by a father, although only 3 percent of all children lived in this type of household.

The educational, economic, and housing situation of single parents and their children is less advantaged than for those in two-parent families. Children with a never-married mother are worse off economically than children with a divorced mother, who in turn are less well-off than children in father-child families, and much less advantaged than children in two-parent families.

The shift toward more single parenting has occurred among both blacks and whites but racial differences in the living arrangements of children are as large or larger today than a generation ago. It is now more common for a black child to be growing up in a mother-child than in a two-parent family. Given the close tie between family living arrangements and economic security, the life chances of the average black child born today are likely to continue to be much lower than for the average white child.

Projections are that perhaps as many as one-half of children born in the 1980s will spend some time living in a one-parent situation. Recent data highlight the significance of cohabitation–whether children living with a parent and the parent's unmarried partner are classified as one-parent or two-parent families–for estimates of how much time children spend in one-parent families and for assessing the economic well-being of children. The role of grandparents is also receiving more attention as entry into single-parenting more often results from a birth outside marriage, a birth which frequently occurs to a young woman still living in her parent(s)' home (Bumpass and Raley, 1993: pp. 15-16).

Will the trends of the past continue into the future? Although it appears as if the rise in divorce has halted, there is little evidence of a dramatic decline in divorce. Rather the divorce rate hovers at a level much higher than three decades ago. Hence, it is reasonable to expect that a sizable portion of children will continue to experience a parental divorce before they reach age 18.

The postponement of marriage, and to a lesser extent, the increase in birth rates to unmarried women have been the more significant components of growth in one-parent families in recent years. Whether these trends have run their course is uncertain. With two-thirds of black births already occurring to unmarried women, unless marriage is foregone by all black women, a limit to the growth in never-married motherhood among the black population may soon be reached. Among whites, unmarried childbearing was not the major source of growth in single parent families before 1980, and the much slower rate of increase in single-parenting during the 1980s suggests that small, incremental increases in the number of single parent families may characterize the 1990s rather than the dramatic growth that characterized earlier decades.

Whatever the future holds, an awareness of the diversity of the paths to single parenting and of the likely economic circumstances that accompany those divergent paths is a necessary first-step in recognizing the needs of the children and adults who spend time in various one-parent situations. The overview of single parent families provided in the foregoing pages, along with other recent analyses of extended family living arrangements, the role of cohabitation, and the interrelationship between family compositional change and economic well-being, hopefully help to increase understanding of the living arrangements of single parents, their social and economic needs, and, ultimately, the policies and services required to adequately meet those needs.

AUTHOR NOTE

The views expressed are those of the author and do not necessarily reflect those of the Bureau of the Census. The author wishes to thank Andrea Walter for assistance with the figures, Robert Grimes, Steve Rawlings, and Arlene Saluter for help in locating data used in the paper, and Donald Hernandez, Larry Long, Steve Rawlings, and the editors of the volume for comments on an earlier version of the manuscript.

NOTES

1. There are exceptions to this generalization, of course. For example, in even-numbered years, information on absent fathers' payment of court-ordered child support is collected in the April CPS. However, the data are collected by asking custodial mothers (and beginning in 1992) custodial fathers how much they receive rather than directly assessing how much absent parents pay.

2. March CPS estimates of mother-child family households were about the same as decennial census counts in 1950 and 1970, 200,000 higher in 1960, 400,000 higher in 1980, and 600,000 higher in 1990. Therefore, the estimated percent increase in this type of household in the CPS is higher than for the decennial census in the 1950s (65 versus 51 percent), lower in the 1960s (42 versus 59 percent), higher in the 1970s (83 versus 68 percent) but about the same during the 1980s (21 versus 19 percent).

3. March CPS estimates show a similar trend as the Census, in fact a higher percent increase in father-child families in the 1980s, but the 1990 March CPS estimate of the number of father-child family households was about 200,000 lower than the Census. Father-child families accounted for 15 percent of all single-parent families in the March 1990 CPS (Rawlings, 1991).

4. The percentage of single mothers reported to be separated was around 20 percent in 1960 and 1992 for whites but there was a 23 percentage point decline for blacks (from 41 to 18 percent). It is possible that some of this decline is artifact. Black unmarried women in 1960 may have been less likely to report that they had never married and more likely to report themselves separated than in 1990 because childbearing outside marriage was less socially acceptable, and certainly less common, in 1960. If this is the case, the increase in black never-married mothers may be overstated. Even if all the decline in the percentage separated is a reporting change, the increase in never-married parents would still be 20 percentage points but changes by race would appear more similar.

5. Bumpass and colleagues obtain fairly consistent estimates over several data sets and also take cohabitation into account in recent estimates. Higher estimates, ranging from 55 to 74 percent, can be found in Hernandez, 1993: 71; Hofferth, 1985; Norton and Glick, 1986.

REFERENCES

Bean, F.D. and M. Tienda. (1992). *The Hispanic population of the United States.* New York: Russell Sage Foundation, 1992.

Bianchi, Suzanne M. (1990). America's children: Mixed prospects. *Population Bulletin, 45:1.* Washington, DC: Population Reference Bureau.

Bianchi, S.M. and E. McArthur. (1991). Family disruption and economic hardship: The short-run picture for children. U.S. Bureau of the Census, *Current Population Reports*, Series P-70, No. 23.

Bumpass, L.L. (1984). Children and marital disruption: A replication and update. *Demography, 21:1*, 71-82.

Bumpass, L. and R.K. Raley. (1993). Trends in the duration of single-parent families. Paper presented at the annual meeting of the Population Association of America, Cincinnati, OH.

Bumpass, L. and R. Rindfuss. (1979). Children's experience of divorce. *American Journal of Sociology, 85*: 49-65.

Bumpass, L.L. and J.A. Sweet. (1989). Children's experience in single-parent families: Implications of cohabitation and marital transitions. *Family Planning Perspectives, 21:6*, 256-260.

Castro-Martin, T. and L. Bumpass. (1989). Recent trends in marital disruption. *Demography, 26:1*, 37-51.

Cherlin, A. (1992). *Marriage, Divorce, Remarriage: Revised and Expanded Edition.* Cambridge, MA: Harvard University Press.

Cooney, R.S. (1979). Demographic components of growth in white, black, and Puerto Rican female-headed families: A comparison of the Cutright and Ross/ Sawhill methodologies. *Social Science Research, 8*, 144-158.

Cutright, P. (1974). Components of change in the number of female family heads aged 15-44: United States, 1940-70, *Journal of Marriage and the Family, 36*, 714-721.

DaNavas, C. and E.J. Welniak, Jr. (1992). Money income of households, families, and persons in the United States: 1991. U.S. Bureau of the Census, *Current Population Reports*, Series P-60, No. 180.

Dawson, D.A. (1991a). Family structure and children's health and well-being: Data from the 1988 National Health Interview Survey on child health. *Journal of Marriage and the Family, 53:3*, 573-584.

Dawson, D.A. (1991b). Family structure and children's health: United States, 1988. National Center for Health Statistics, *Vital and Health Statistics*, Series 10, No. 178.

Espenshade, T.J. (1985). Marriage trends in America: Estimates, implications, and underlying causes. *Population and Development Review, 11*, 193-245.

Farley, R. and S.M. Bianchi. (1991). The growing racial difference in marriage and family patterns. In R. Staples (Ed.) *The black family: Essays and studies.* 4th Edition. Belmont, CA: Wadsworth.

Garfinkel, I. and S.S. McLanahan. (1986). *Single mothers and their children.* Washington, DC: The Urban Institute.

Ghosh, S., R.A. Easterlin, and D.J. Macunovich. (1993). How badly have single parents done?: Trends in economic status of single parents since 1964. Paper presented at the annual meeting of the Population Association of America, Cincinnati, OH.

Grall, T.S. (1992). Housing characteristics of one-parent households: 1989. U.S. Bureau of the Census, *Current Housing Reports*, Series H121/92-2.

Hernandez, D. (1993a). *America's children: Resources from family, government, and the economy*. New York: Russell Sage Foundation.

Hernandez, D. (1993b). When households continue, discontinue, and form. U.S. Bureau of the Census, *Current Population Reports*, Series P-23, No. 179.

Hofferth, S.L. and K.A. Moore. (1979). Early childbearing and later economic well-being. *American Sociological Review*, *44:5*, 784-815.

Hofferth, S.L. (1985). Updating children's life course. *Journal of Marriage and the Family*, *47*, 93-111.

Lester, G.H. Child support and alimony: 1989. U.S. Bureau of the Census, *Current Population Reports*, Series P-60, No. 173.

Lichter, D.T. and D.J. Eggebeen. (1993). Rich kids, poor kids: Changing income inequality among American children. *Social Forces*, *71:3*, 761-780.

London, K.A. (1991). Cohabitation, marriage, marital dissolution, and remarriage: United States, 1988. National Center for Health Statistics, *Advance Data*, No. 194.

Lugaila, Terry. (1992). Households, families, and children: A chartbook. U.S. Bureau of the Census, *Current Population Reports*, P23-181.

McLanahan, S. and K. Booth. (1989). Mother-only families: problems, prospects, and politics. *Journal of Marriage and the Family*, *51:3*, 557-580.

National Center for Health Statistics. (1982). Advance report of final natality statistics, 1985. *Monthly Vital Statistics Report*, *31, 8*, Supplement.

National Center for Health Statistics. (1987). Advance report of final natality statistics, 1985. *Monthly Vital Statistics Report*, *36, 4*, Supplement.

National Center for Health Statistics. (1992). Annual summary of births, marriages, divorces, and deaths: United States, 1991. *Monthly Vital Statistics Report*, *40:13*.

Norton, A.J. and P.C. Glick. (1986). One parent families: A social and economic profile. *Family Relations*, *35:1*, 9-17.

Norton, A.J. and L.F. Miller. (1992). Marriage, divorce, and remarriage in the 1990s. U.S. Bureau of the Census, *Current Population Reports*, P23-180.

Rawlings, S.W. (1991). Household and family characteristics: March 1990. U.S. Bureau of the Census, *Current Population Reports*, Series P-20, No. 450.

Rawlings, S.W. (1992). Household and family characteristics: March 1991. U.S. Bureau of the Census, *Current Population Reports*, Series P-20, No. 458.

Rawlings, S.W. (1993). Household and family characteristics: March 1992. U.S. Bureau of the Census, *Current Population Reports*, Series P-20, No. 4__.

Ross, H.L. and I.V. Sawhill. (1975). *Time of transition: The growth of families headed by women*. Washington, DC: The Urban Institute.

Saluter, A.F. (1991). Marital and status and living arrangements: March 1990. U.S. Bureau of the Census. *Current Population Reports*. Series P-20, No. 450.

Saluter, A.F. (1993). Marital and status and living arrangements: March 1992. U.S. Bureau of the Census. *Current Population Reports*, Series P20-468.

Smith, H.L. and P. Cutright. (1985). Components of change in the number of female family heads ages 15 to 44, update and reanalysis: United States, 1940 to 1983. *Social Science Research, 14*, 226-250.

Sweet J.A. and L.L. Bumpass. (1987). *American families and households*. New York: Russell Sage Foundation.

U.S. Bureau of the Census. (1955). *Census of Population: 1950*, Vol. IV, Part 2, Chapter A. *General Characteristics of Families.*

U.S. Bureau of the Census. (1964a). *Census of Population: 1960*, Vol. 1, Part 1. *U.S. Summary.*

U.S. Bureau of the Census. (1964b). *Census of Population: 1960*, Vol. 2, *Families*, PC(2)-4A.

U.S. Bureau of the Census. (1973). *Census of Population: 1970*, Vol. 1, Part 1. *U.S. Summary.*

U.S. Bureau of the Census. (1974). *Census of Population: 1970*, Vol. 2, *Family Composition*, PC(2)-4A.

U.S. Bureau of the Census. (1983). *Census of Population: 1980*, Vol. 1, Chapter B, Part 1. *General Population Characteristics, U.S. Summary*, PC80-1-B1.

U.S. Bureau of the Census. (1984). *Census of Population: 1980*, Vol. 1, Chapter D, *U.S. Summary*, PC80-1-D1.

U.S. Bureau of the Census. (1993). *Census of Population: 1990*, Vol. 1, *General Population Characteristics, U.S. Summary.*

Ventura, S.J. and J.A. Martin. (1993). Advance report of final natality statistics, 1990. National Center for Health Statistics, *Monthly Vital Statistics Report, 41:9*, Supplement.

Wojtkiewicz, R.A., S.S. McLanahan, and I. Garfinkel. (1990). The growth of families headed by women: 1950-1980. *Demography, 27:1*, 19-30.

Chapter 5

The Economics of Single Parenthood: Past Research and Future Directions

Mark Lino

SUMMARY. An increasing proportion of children in the United States are residing with a single parent. The economic status of single-parent situations is therefore of great importance. This paper reviews the literature on the economics of single parenthood. Research on the economics of becoming a single parent is first reviewed. Studies on the income, expenditures, and assets and liabilities of single-parent situations are then addressed. Possible future research directions are discussed in the final section.

KEYWORDS. Economics, Income, Expenditures, Single parent families

One of the most dramatic changes in American family life during the past 20 years has been the growth in the number of single parents and their children. In 1970, 13% of all family groups with children under age 18 (3.8 million) were single-parent situations. By 1991, 29% of all family groups with children under age 18 (10.1 million) were single-parent situations (U.S. Bureau of the Census, 1992a). Single parents with children, as

---

Mark Lino is affiliated with the U.S. Department of Agriculture, Agricultural Research Service, Family Economics Research Group.

[Haworth co-indexing entry note]: "The Economics of Single Parenthood: Past Research and Future Directions." Lino, Mark. Co-published simultaneously in *Marriage & Family Review* (The Haworth Press, Inc.) Vol. 20, No. 1/2, 1995, pp. 99-114; and: *Single Parent Families: Diversity, Myths and Realities* (ed: Shirley M. H. Hanson et al.) The Haworth Press, Inc., 1995, pp. 99-114. Multiple copies of this article/chapter may be purchased from The Haworth Document Delivery Center [1-800-3-HAWORTH; 9:00 a.m. - 5:00 p.m. (EST)].

a proportion of all family groups, are expected to continue increasing in the future (Martin & Bumpass, 1989). Although single parenthood may be viewed as transitional, given that most people marry or remarry (Saluter, 1989), it is estimated that more than half of all children will live, at some time in their lives, with only one parent. For children, average time spent in a single-parent situation is 6 years (Bumpass, 1984).

Because so many children are likely, for a period of time, to reside with one parent, the economic status of single-parent situations is of primary concern. This article reviews the literature on the economic status of single parents and their children. First, studies on the economics of becoming a single parent are examined. Studies on the income, income sources, and expenditures of these households are then addressed. Research on the assets and liabilities of single parents are also discussed. When possible, trends in the economic status of single-parent households over time are analyzed. The last section of this paper summarizes what is known about the economic status of single parents and their children–and what is not known–for future research directions. Before turning to the literature review, two points need to be made.

First, although the terms single parent families and single-parent situations are often used interchangeably in the literature, there are differences. A single parent family is typically composed of a parent with his or her children who reside in a housing unit they own or rent; single-parent situations include those single parents sharing others' homes (U.S. Bureau of the Census, 1992a). Most studies, however, do not distinguish between the two. This will be discussed further in the final section of the paper.

Second, because other papers in this special volume of *Marriage & Family Review* examine the socio-demographic characteristics of single parents and their children (see chapters by Bianchi and Bowen), this chapter discusses these characteristics only as they relate to the economic status of single-parent situations. To profile single-parent situations in brief: in 1991, 86% were maintained by the mother, 79% owned or rented their own home, 65% were white, and the median age of parents was 35 to 38 (depending on sex of the parent) (U.S. Bureau of the Census, 1992a).

ECONOMICS OF BECOMING A SINGLE PARENT

Single parenthood basically occurs as a result of divorce or separation, births to never-married women, or death of a spouse. In 1991, 60% of single-parent situations resulted from divorce or separation, 34% from births to never-married women, and 6% from death of a spouse (U.S. Bureau of the Census, 1992a). Of these various paths to single parenthood, the economic ramifications of divorce or separation have been most extensively examined.

One of the most widely cited studies on the economic consequences of divorce or separation was conducted by Weitzman (1981). This study was based on interview data of 228 divorced men and women in Los Angeles County who had been divorced for approximately 1 year in 1978. One year after divorce, women who had been married less than 10 years had incomes between 29% and 71% of their pre-divorce household income. Comparable incomes of men 1 year after divorce were between 74% and 78% of their pre-divorce household income. Women in the highest household income group before divorce experienced the largest drop in household income after marital dissolution. Their post-divorce income, however, remained the highest of all women in the sample. Since total household income does not adjust for different family needs, Weitzman derived an income-to-needs standard (from the Bureau of Labor Statistics' lower standard budget for an urban family of four) to measure economic well-being. On average, women experienced a 73% decline and men experienced a 42% rise in their economic well-being, as measured by this standard, 1 year after marital dissolution. Although the Weitzman study is often cited, it has also been criticized for its geographically-specific sample.

Weiss (1984), Duncan and Hoffman (1985), and Stirling (1989) examined the economic consequences of divorce using nationally representative data from the Panel Study of Income Dynamics. Weiss (1984) studied mothers who were divorced or separated between 1969 and 1974. For women in upper income families prior to divorce or separation, household income in real terms 1 year after marital dissolution was approximately one-half that reported in the last year of marriage. For women in middle income families, this income was about two-thirds of what it had been, and for women in lower income families, income was about three-fourths of that in the last year of marriage. Family income in real terms for these newly created families maintained by females remained at this lower level over a 5-year observation period. Mother's earnings became a more important source of household income after marital dissolution for all income groups.

Duncan and Hoffman (1985), using an income-to-needs standard derived from U.S. poverty thresholds, found the economic consequences of divorce or separation for women with children to be less severe than found in earlier studies. Economic consequences, however, were still negative. For women who did not remarry, the income-to-needs standard declined to 87% of its pre-divorce or separation level 1 year after marital dissolution and rose to 94% of its pre-divorce or separation level by the fifth year after marital dissolution. In addition, families that experienced a marital dissolution were found to have a lower pre-divorce or separation income than families that did not. This further compounded the adverse economic impact of single parenthood.

As the last year of marriage may be associated with a downward trend in economic status, Stirling (1989) argued that measuring post-divorce income in relation to family income during this last year may yield biased results. Therefore, Stirling developed an income-to-needs ratio standard using average income during the last 3 years of marriage. This standard declined 30% for women the first year after divorce and fluctuated 2% to 4% each year in the 4 succeeding years.

McLindon (1987), Wishik (1986), and Rowe and Morrow (1988) examined the economic consequences of divorce or separation using regional samples. Their results were similar to those of previous studies; divorce or separation had negative economic consequences for women who retained primary physical care of children.

Rather than examine the economic consequences of divorce or separation on women, Bianchi and McArthur (1991) examined the short-term economic effects of marital dissolution on children, using the 1984 Panel of the Survey of Income and Program Participation. Children in households where the father departed experienced a 23% drop in average family income in real terms over a 32-month observation period. Those children who remained with two parents had an 8% increase in average household income in real terms, and those in households where the mother remarried or reconciled with the father had a 115% increase. The increase in real income of the latter group was due to the addition of another earner to the family. An income-to-needs standard derived from U.S. poverty thresholds, measured a 13% decline in economic well-being over the 32-month period for children in households where the father departed, compared with a 7% increase for children in households where the parents stayed together and a 90% increase for those where a "father" entered the household. This decline in real income and in the income-to-needs standard for children in households where the father departed was not the result of a decrease in mothers' labor force participation. In fact, there was an increase in labor force participation by women after marital dissolution.

The economics of situations caused by widowhood or births to never-married women have received less attention than situations caused by divorce or separation (for more on widows and never-married mothers, see chapters by Gass and Prater in this special volume). Duncan and Morgan (1976) examined changes in economic status among wives who became widowed between 1967 and 1973 using the Panel Study of Income Dynamics. Of those who were nonpoor in 1967 (before the death of their spouse), 24% were poor in 1973 (after the death of their spouse). These figures include women both with and without dependent children.

INCOME AND INCOME SOURCES OF SINGLE PARENTS

Single parent families maintained by mothers typically have the lowest income of all family groups. The 1991 Current Population Survey showed that average before-tax family income for single mothers with children under age 18 was $17,747; for single fathers, $30,445; and for married-couple families with children, $48,737. Adjusting for family size, per capita family income for single mothers with children under age 18 was $5,506; for single fathers, $10,040; and for married-couple families with children, $11,668 (U.S. Bureau of the Census, 1992b).

A substantial percentage of single parent families fall below the U.S. poverty threshold for their family size. Poverty thresholds for 1991 were $8,865 for a two-person family, $10,860 for a three-person family, and $13,924 for a four-person family (U.S. Department of Agriculture, 1992). In 1991, 47% of all families composed of single mothers with children under age 18 were in poverty, compared with 20% of their male counterparts and 8% of married-couple families with children under age 18 (U.S. Bureau of the Census, 1992c). The poverty rate of single mothers and their children over the 1980s was relatively constant but always well above the rates of families maintained by single fathers and married couples.

Money income does not include the value of noncash benefits such as food stamps, Medicaid, public housing, and employer-provided fringe benefits. When taxes and noncash benefits were taken into consideration, the median effective family income of single mothers in 1990 increased from 34% to 45% that of married couples with children (U.S. Bureau of the Census, 1991). Generally, transfer programs raise the effective income of families maintained by mothers and taxes reduce that of married couples. Accounting for various transfer programs also reduced the percentage of families maintained by mothers in poverty, although a significant percentage, at least 32%, still were poor.

Garfinkel and McLanahan (1986) undertook one of the few studies that examined the income and income sources of single parent families by marital status. They looked separately at white and black families with children maintained by mothers using data from the 1983 Current Population Survey. For white families, those maintained by widows had the highest income and those maintained by never-married women, the lowest income–less than half that of widows ($17,799 vs. $7,812). Earnings of white widows accounted for 29% of total household income–a lower percentage than for divorced women (69%), separated women (60%), and never-married women (58%). Public assistance accounted for the second largest share of income for white families maintained by never-married mothers, with 53% receiving such assistance.

For black families maintained by mothers, there was less dispersion in income by marital status. Families maintained by divorced women had the highest income, and those maintained by separated women the lowest ($11,187 vs. $8,221). Earnings of divorced, separated, and never-married black mothers composed the bulk of household income. Social Security was the major source of household income for widowed single parents. As with white families, public assistance accounted for the second largest share of income for black families maintained by never-married mothers, with 59% receiving such assistance.

Garfinkel and McLanahan concluded that the low income level of single parent families maintained by mothers reflects the low earnings of women in general. They hypothesized that women receive lower earnings because they have less education and job experience and because of market discrimination. In addition, they speculate that female single parents are hindered in working outside the home because of child-care problems.

The overall income of single parent families has also declined in real terms over the years. Using Current Population Survey data, Danziger and Gottschalk (1986) examined the real income of single parent families maintained by mothers. Over the 1973 to 1984 period, this income fell 8% for white, 9% for black, and 13% for Hispanic single parent families. A decline in cash transfer payments accounted for some of this decrease.

Employment Status

A recent study on the employment status of single parents was done by Rawlings (1989) using the Current Population Survey. For all children under age 18 living with a single parent in 1988, 46% of parents were employed full time at the time of the survey, 9% part time, 8% were unemployed, and 37% were not in the labor force (unemployed persons are those actively looking for work, whereas those not actively looking are considered not in the labor force). Because such a large percentage of single parents were not in the labor force, the average income of their families is reduced.

Using 1979 Current Population Survey data, Beller and Graham (1985) examined factors affecting the labor force participation of divorced and separated women with children. The longer the time these women had been divorced or separated and the greater the amount of public assistance and child support payments received, the less likely these women were to be in the labor force, all else equal; presence of young children also reduced this probability. The greater the educational level and age of these women, the more likely they were to be in the labor force. Divorced and separated black women and those of Hispanic origin were also less likely than white women to be in the labor force.

To measure the work constraint of child care, a special 1982 Census Bureau survey asked nonemployed mothers with preschool children if they would look for work if child care were available to them at a reasonable cost (O'Connell & Bloom, 1987). Not surprisingly, many mothers with young children said they would. This was especially true for unmarried and never-married mothers. For unmarried mothers in 1982, 59% were in the labor force and 17% stated they would look for work if reasonably priced child care were available, resulting in a potential labor force participation rate of 76% for this group. For never-married mothers, 50% were in the labor force and 24% stated they would look for work if reasonably priced child care were available, resulting in a potential labor force participation rate of 74%. Although these potential labor force participation rates may not be realized even if reasonably priced child care were available, it does suggest that child care is a labor force constraint for many single mothers.

Child Support

Child support is the income source of single parent families that has received the most research attention. Periodic supplements to the Current Population Survey have tracked child support over time as a source of income for families maintained by mothers. In the most recent study (Lester, 1991), among women with children from an absent father, 50% were awarded and due child support in 1989, 42% had not been awarded child support, and 8% were awarded but not due child support that year (this support was due in a following year). Of the women not awarded child support, 64% desired it but the father was deemed unable to pay, could not be located, or the mother did not pursue it even though it was wanted; 22% stated they did not want any child support; and 14% either had a final agreement pending or had made other financial arrangements. Of the women due child support, 51% reported receiving the full amount awarded, 24% received less than the full amount, and 25% did not receive any support at all.

For single mothers being paid child support, the mean amount received in 1989 was $2,995, accounting for 19% of their before-tax household income. The mean amount of child support received by never-married mothers being paid such support was $1,888, which accounted for 20% of their before-tax income. Never-married mothers, however, were less likely to receive child support than divorced or separated women. Difficulties in establishing paternity and lower incomes of fathers in these situations probably are contributing factors. In real terms, child support payments received did not change much from 1981 to 1989, averaging $2,898 (in 1989 dollars) in 1981 and $2,995 in 1989. The percentage of women due child support payments, who received them, slightly increased from 72% in 1981 to 75% in 1989.

Studies have examined factors affecting receipt of child support income. Teachman (1991) used data from the National Longitudinal Study of the High School Class of 1972 to do this. The higher the father's income and amount of child support due, his being remarried, having a voluntary support agreement, and his visiting children at least as often as stipulated in the divorce agreement, the more likely child support payments were made, all else equal. The longer the time since divorce and the farther away a father lived from his children, the less likely child support payments were made. Peterson and Nord (1990) found similar results using the 1984 Survey of Income and Program Participation. Also, single mothers who were black, had less than a high school education, or were never married, were less likely to receive child support of any amount, all else equal.

EXPENDITURES OF SINGLE PARENTS

Research on expenditures of single parent families typically has used the Consumer Expenditure Survey. This survey collects data on expenditures and major socioeconomic and demographic characteristics of a sample of approximately 20,000 households weighted to the population. Using 1990 Consumer Expenditure Survey data, total expenses of single parent families averaged $19,230 (U.S. Department of Labor, 1991). Of this total, 36% went for housing, 18% for food, 14% for transportation, 8% for clothing, 6% for personal insurance and pensions (including Social Security taxes), 5% for entertainment, 3% for health care, and 10% for other expenses (education, personal care items, and miscellaneous goods and services). Although housing consumed slightly more than one-third of the total outlay of single parent families, only 35% were homeowners.

Total expenditures of single parent families were approximately half those of married couples with children; the latter group had total expenses averaging $38,999 in 1990 (U.S. Department of Labor, 1991). Married couples with children allocated a smaller proportion of their expenses to housing than single parent families, although 76% were homeowners. Boyle (1989) found per capita expenditures of single parent families also to be less than those of married couples with children. The average family size of married couples with children was four and that of single parent families, three.

Lino (1989a) examined the total expenditures of single parent families by sex, age, and race of the parent as well as family size using the 1984-85 Consumer Expenditure Survey. Families maintained by male single parents had higher total expenses than those maintained by female single parents ($24,626 vs. $15,022) with housing and transportation composing the major shares for both groups. Families with a single parent over age 40 had higher total expenses than those with a single parent under age 30 ($20,086 vs. $9,565); those with a single parent age 30 to 40 had total expenses between these two amounts. Housing accounted for a larger share of expenses in families with a parent under age 30. However, only 12% of these families were homeowners, compared with 69% of families with a single parent over age 40. White single parent families had higher total expenses than nonwhite families ($18,739 vs. $9,991) with nonwhite families allocating nearly 40% of their expenses to housing. Transportation accounted for only 11% of total expenses in nonwhite families as 56% did not own an automobile. For many groups of single parent families, total expenditures exceeded after-tax income, which probably indicates these families went into debt to cover their expenses.

In another study, Lino (1989b) analyzed the expenditures of single parent families by marital status. Total expenditures of single parent families maintained by a widowed parent amounted to $22,071; those by a divorced or separated parent, $16,426; and those by a never-married parent, $7,741. Families maintained by a widowed and divorced or separated parent each allocated 35% of total expenses to housing, with 75% of the widowed group and 51% of the divorced/separated group being homeowners. Families maintained by a never-married parent allocated 40% of their total expenses to housing with 10% being homeowners. Examining expenditures of single parent families over the 1980s, Lino (1991) found the total expenses of these families increased 3% in real terms from 1980 to 1989, with housing slightly increasing and food decreasing as a budgetary share.

Of the individual expenses of single parent families, housing has received the most attention. Grall (1992) used the 1989 American Housing Survey to examine the housing status of single parents and their children. Thirty-five percent of single-parent households owned a home, compared with 74% of married couples with children. Single parents resided in smaller living quarters than married couples with children whether they owned a home or not. For single-parent households, the median size of owned living quarters was 1,646 square feet and that of rented units, 1,202 square feet; for married couples with children, the median size of owned living quarters was 1,914 square feet and that of rented units, 1,342 square feet.

Using data from the 1988 Survey of Income and Program Participation, Fronczek and Savage (1991) studied the affordability of home ownership for single mothers with children. Overall, 87% of these families (including current homeowners) could not afford to purchase a median-priced home in the region where they lived. Among single mothers with children who rented a home, 97% could not afford to purchase a median-priced home in the region where they lived.

Horton and Hafstrom (1985) examined factors affecting selected expenditures of single parent families maintained by mothers using data from the 1972-73 Consumer Expenditure Survey. Family income had a positive effect on all expenditures, all else equal. Nonblack (white and other races) families spent more on shelter, less on food at home, and less on clothing than black families. The older the single mother, the more was spent on food. Lino (1990) expanded on the Horton and Hafstrom study by including single parent families maintained by fathers in the analysis and using the 1984-85 Consumer Expenditure Survey. Single parent families maintained by fathers did not have different expenditure patterns than families maintained by mothers for housing, transportation, and food, all else equal. Families maintained by fathers spent less on clothing than those maintained by mothers.

In addition to looking at changes in income after marital dissolution, Weiss (1984) examined changes in housing and food expenditures for women divorced or separated between 1969 and 1974 using the Panel Study of Income Dynamics. Women with children in lower and middle income families prior to marital dissolution experienced no reduction in housing expenses in real terms within 5 years. For single mothers in higher income families prior to marital breakup, real housing expenses declined sharply in the year following divorce or separation and continued at this reduced level over the next 5 years. Regardless of income, housing expenses consumed a larger percentage of income after divorce or separation than before. For all three income groups, food expenditures in real terms declined the year following marital dissolution and continued at this reduced level.

For employed single mothers child care can be a large expense. Using data from the 1988 Survey of Income and Program Participation, O'Connell and Bachu (1992) examined child care arrangements and weekly child care costs. Among employed single mothers, 39% made payments for some type of child care. The large percentage of employed mothers without child care expenses had care provided by relatives and others at no charge. For employed single mothers with the expense, the mean weekly child care cost was $47, which accounted for 10% of their monthly family income. These women worked an average of 39 hours per week in the labor force.

ASSETS AND LIABILITIES OF SINGLE PARENTS

Given the low income levels of single parent families, little research has focused on their assets. Kennickell and Shack-Marquez (1992) examined the financial and nonfinancial assets and liabilities of households, including those maintained by unmarried persons under age 55 with children, using data from the 1989 Survey of Consumer Finances. This survey contains information from approximately 3,100 households weighted to the population.

Sixty-eight percent of these single parent families owned some type of financial asset (checking, savings, money market, and retirement accounts; certificates of deposit; stocks; bonds; trusts; and other). The most common financial asset owned was a checking account, held by 55% of these families. The median value of their financial assets was approximately $3,000. By comparison, among married couples under age 55 with children, the median value of financial assets was approximately $11,000.

Regarding nonfinancial assets (principal residence, vehicles, business, investment real estate, and other), 72% of single parent families reported owning one or more such assets. A vehicle was the most common nonfinancial asset held (owned by 65% of families). The median value of nonfinancial assets held by single parent families was approximately $23,000; for their married counterparts the median value of nonfinancial assets was $86,000.

Seventy percent of single parent families were in debt (home mortgage, investment real estate, home equity lines of credit, credit cards, car loans, and other). Median debt was approximately $7,000 for these households. For their married counterparts, the median amount of debt carried was $31,000. Credit card debt was the most common individual liability of single parent families, carried by 33%. From 1983 to 1989, the real value (in 1989 dollars) of financial assets held by families maintained by unmarried persons under age 55 with children increased by approximately

$1,000, their nonfinancial assets decreased by $16,000, and their liabilities remained nearly constant.

Another study by Canner and Luckett (1991) used data from the 1989 Survey of Consumer Finances to examine payment of household debt. Among all marital status groups, families maintained by divorced or separated persons had the highest rate of payment difficulties. Of indebted families maintained by divorced or separated persons, 27% experienced payment difficulties (such difficulties being defined as having missed or been late in debt payments in the preceding year).

CONCLUSION

This review of the literature on the economics of single parenthood shows the negative economic impact associated with such a status. Family income of single parent families maintained by mothers, who account for most single parents, is usually the lowest of all household groups. In addition, single mothers often face child care constraints that hinder their labor force participation, and they do not always receive the full amount of child support due. For most single parent families, total expenditures consumed a large part of their income. For some, total expenditures exceeded income with debt a likely result. Housing accounted for the largest share of total expenses for these families, although most were renters. The low home ownership rate among single parent families contributed to their lower level of assets.

Although many economic aspects of single parenthood have been researched, there are others that need further study. One major area that has only recently received attention concerns the distinction between single parent families and single-parent situations. As stated at the beginning, although most studies have used these terms interchangeably, there are differences between the two (single parent families are typically parents who live in a housing unit they own or rent with their children, whereas single parent family situations include those single parents and their children who share others' homes). For many of the studies reviewed, it is difficult to determine whether just one or both types of living arrangements of single parents and their children are included.

Because a large percentage of single parents and their children are residing in the homes of others, 21% in 1991 (U.S. Bureau of the Census, 1992a), the two groups need to be identified separately in research. The economic status of each type of single-parent living arrangement should then be assessed. For those residing with others, the economic status of single parents and their children may be enhanced by additional sources of income or reduced by expenditures for other household members. In addition, the number of never-married mothers is increasing. Research needs to more closely examine the economic implications of births to these women. Single parenthood probably has the most adverse economic effects on never-married women as they are typically younger, less educated, and have a lower likelihood of receiving child support.

Future research should also focus on single parent families maintained by fathers, who account for an increasing number of single-parent situations. The economic consequences of single parenthood for fathers has not been extensively researched. Do single fathers with primary physical care of children experience a decline in economic status after marital dissolution similar to that of mothers? Also, do single fathers receive child support and how does it compare with that awarded their female counterparts?

Although the economics of divorce have been widely researched in the past, periodic research in this area would be useful given changing economic conditions. As more women enter the labor force, the economic condition of women after marital dissolution may improve. However, limited job opportunities and a shortage of affordable child care can hinder labor force participation by women. These and other factors affecting the economic consequences of marital dissolution over time need to be investigated.

Research on expenditures of single parent families has focused on major budgetary components. This research usually has not determined whether these expenses ensure an adequate standard of living. For example, does the amount allocated to food expenses in single parent families provide a nutritionally adequate diet? Similarly, do the health care expenses of these families ensure basic medical care? Given the low level of assets in single parent families, the implications for these parents' retirement years also needs to be analyzed. Will these people be able to retire at a traditional age or will they have to work in the labor force beyond this to meet their expenses?

These are just some of the issues concerning the economics of single parenthood that need to be addressed in future research. As long as single-parent situations account for a large segment of American households with children, and their economic status remains relatively poor, research must continue to focus on these families.

REFERENCES

Beller, A. H. & Graham, J. W. (1985). Variations in economic well-being of divorced women and their children: The role of child support income. In M. David & T. Smeeding (Eds.), *Horizontal equity, uncertainty, and measures of well-being, NBER studies in income and wealth* (No. 50, pp. 471-509). Chicago, IL: University of Chicago Press.

Bianchi, S. & McArthur, E. (1991). *Family disruption and economic hardship: The short-run picture for children*. (Current Population Reports Series P-70, 23). U.S. Bureau of the Census. Washington, DC: U.S. Government Printing Office.

Boyle, M. (1989). Spending patterns and income of single and married parents. *Monthly Labor Review, 112*(3), 37-41.

Bumpass, L. L. (1984). Children and marital disruption: A replication and update. *Demography, 21*(1), 71-82.

Canner, G. B. & Luckett, C. A. (1991). Payment of household debts. *Federal Reserve Bulletin, 77*, 218-229.

Danziger, S. & Gottschalk, P. (1986). Families with children have fared worst. *Challenge, 29*(2), 40-47.

Duncan, G. J. & Morgan, J. N. (1976). Introduction, overview, summary, and conclusions. In G. J. Duncan and J. N. Morgan (Eds.), *Five thousand American families–Patterns of economic progress* (Vol. IV, pp. 1-22). Ann Arbor, MI: The University of Michigan, Survey Research Center, Institute for Social Research.

Duncan, G. J. & Hoffman, S. D. (1985). A reconsideration of the economic consequences of marital dissolution. *Demography, 22*, 485-497.

Fronczek, P. J. & Savage, H. A. (1991). *Who can afford to buy a house?* (Current Housing Reports H121/91-1). U.S. Bureau of the Census. Washington, DC: U.S. Government Printing Office.

Garfinkel, I. and McLanahan, S. S. (1986). Single mothers and their children. Washington, DC: The Urban Institute.

Grall, T. S. (1992). *Housing characteristics of one-parent households, 1989*. (Current Housing Reports H121/92-2). U.S. Department of Housing and Urban Development and U.S. Bureau of the Census. Washington, DC: U.S. Government Printing Office.

Horton, S. E. & Hafstrom, J. L. (1985). Income elasticities for selected consumption categories: Comparison of single female-headed and two-parent families. *Home Economics Research Journal, 13*, 292-303.

Kennickell, A. & Shack-Marquez, J. (1992). Changes in family finances from 1983 to 1989: Evidence from the Survey of Consumer Finances. *Federal Reserve Bulletin, 78*(1), 1-18.

Lester, G. H. (1991). *Child support and alimony: 1989*. (Current Population Reports Series P-60, 173). U.S. Bureau of the Census. Washington, DC: U.S. Government Printing Office.

Lino, M. (1991). Changes in income and expenditures for families with children in the 1980s. In J. Bauer (Ed.), *Family economic well-being in the next century: Challenges, changes, continuity* (pp. 159-166). Proceedings of the 1991 pre-conference workshop of the Family Economics-Home Management Section of the American Home Economics Association.

Lino, M. (1990). Factors affecting expenditures of single-parent households. *Home Economics Research Journal, 18*, 191-201.

Lino, M. (1989a). Financial status of single-parent households. *Family Economics Review, 2*(1), 2-7.

Lino, M. (1989b). Financial status of single-parent households headed by a never-married, divorced/separated or widowed parent. In R. Walker (Ed.), *Families in transition: Structural changes and effects on family life* (pp. 151-160). Proceedings of the 1989 pre-conference workshop of the Family Economics-Home Management Section of the American Home Economics Association.

Martin, T. C. & Bumpass, L. L. (1989). Recent trends in marital disruption. *Demography, 26*, 37-51.

McLindon, J. B. (1987). Separate but unequal: The economic disaster of divorce for women and children. *Family Law Quarterly, XXI*, 351-405.

O'Connell, M. & Bachu, A. (1992). Who's Minding the Kids? Child Care Arrangements: Fall 1988. (Current Population Reports Series P70-30). U.S. Bureau of the Census. Washington, DC: U.S. Government Printing Office.

O'Connell, M. & Bloom, D. E. (1987). *Juggling Jobs and Babies: America's Child Care Challenge*. Issue Number 12, Population Trends and Public Policy. Population Reference Bureau, Inc.

Peterson, J. L. & Nord, C. W. (1990). The regular receipt of child support: A multistep process. *Journal of Marriage and the Family, 52*, 539-551.

Rawlings, S. W. (1989). *Single parents and their children*. (Current Population Reports Series P-23, 162). U.S. Bureau of the Census. Washington, DC: U.S. Government Printing Office.

Rowe, B. R. & Morrow, A. M. (1988). The economic consequences of divorce in Oregon after ten or more years of marriage. *Willamette Law Review, 24*, 463-484.

Saluter, A. F. (1989). *Changes in American family life*. (Current Population Reports Series P-23, 163). U.S. Bureau of the Census. Washington, DC: U.S. Government Printing Office.

Stirling, K. J. (1989). Women who remain divorced: The long-term economic consequences. *Social Science Quarterly, 70*, 549-561.

Teachman, J. D. (1991). Who pays? Receipt of child support in the United States. *Journal of Marriage and the Family, 53*, 759-772.

U.S. Bureau of the Census. (1992a). *Household and family characteristics: March 1991*. (Current Population Reports Series P-20, 458). Washington, DC: U.S. Government Printing Office.

U.S. Bureau of the Census. (1992b). *Money income of households, families, and persons in the United States: 1991*. (Current Population Reports Series P-60, 180). Washington, DC: U.S. Government Printing Office.

U.S. Bureau of the Census. (1992c). *Poverty in the United States: 1991*. (Current Population Reports Series P-60, 181). Washington, DC: U.S. Government Printing Office.

U.S. Bureau of the Census. (1991). Measuring the effects of benefits and taxes on income and poverty: 1990. (Current Population Reports Series P-60, 176-RD). Washington, DC: U.S. Government Printing Office.

U.S. Department of Agriculture, Family Economics Research Group. (1992). Poverty Thresholds. *Family Economics Review, 5*(3), 36.
U.S. Department of Labor, Bureau of Labor Statistics. (1991). Consumer Expenditures in 1990. *News* 91-607.
Weiss, R. S. (1984). The impact of marital dissolution on income and consumption in single-parent households. *Journal of Marriage and the Family, 46*, 115-127.
Weitzman, L. J. (1981). The economics of divorce: Social and economic consequences of property, alimony, and child support awards. *UCLA Law Review, 28*, 1181-1268.
Wishik, H. R. (1986). Economics of divorce: An exploratory study. *Family Law Quarterly*, XX (1), 79-103.

Chapter 6

Poverty and the Single Mother Family: A Macroeconomic Perspective

Gary L. Bowen
Laura M. Desimone
Jennifer K. McKay

SUMMARY. This article examines how recent changes in the structure of the U.S. economy have contributed to the impoverishment of single mother families. The impacts of the disappearance of the manufacturing sector, the concurrent growth in service-oriented industries, the decline in real wages, and the polarization of the income distribution are considered in the context of recent social welfare reforms that have focused on the employability and employment of low-income single mothers. These policies have encouraged single mothers to move toward welfare independence, but they have not ensured that these women can attain economic self-sufficiency through employment. The authors offer public policy recommendations for responding to shifts in the economy, for helping single mothers move beyond the grasp of poverty, and for providing an

---

Gary L. Bowen is Professor and Co-Chair of the Doctoral Program, School of Social Work, University of North Carolina at Chapel Hill, 223 E. Franklin St., CB #3550, Chapel Hill, NC 27599-3550. Laura M. Desimone is a graduate student in the PhD program in public policy analysis at the University of North Carolina at Chapel Hill. Jennifer K. McKay is a 1993 graduate of the Master of Public Administration Program at the University of North Carolina at Chapel Hill.

[Haworth co-indexing entry note]: "Poverty and the Single Mother Family: A Macroeconomic Perspective." Bowen, Gary L., Laura M. Desimone, and Jennifer K. McKay. Co-published simultaneously in *Marriage & Family Review* (The Haworth Press, Inc.) Vol. 20, No. 1/2, 1995, pp. 115-142; and: *Single Parent Families: Diversity, Myths and Realities* (ed: Shirley M. H. Hanson et al.) The Haworth Press, Inc., 1995, pp. 115-142. Multiple copies of this article/chapter may be purchased from The Haworth Document Delivery Center [1-800-3-HAWORTH; 9:00 a.m. - 5:00 p.m. (EST)].

adequate safety net for those who have difficulty being absorbed into the labor market.

KEYWORDS. Single parent families, Single mothers, poverty, AFDC

The number of single mother families with children has doubled since 1970, significantly outpacing the growth of all other household patterns in this nation (Ahlburg & De Vita, 1992; Rodgers, 1990). Unfortunately, they are among the families in the United States most severely mired in poverty. Although only one in eight families (11.6%) was headed by female householders with children under 18 years old in 1990, nearly one-half (48.3%) of all families who were poor in 1990 fit this profile (U.S. Bureau of the Census, 1991).

The rate of poverty for female headed households with children under 18 years (44.5%) is approximately six times greater than the rate for married-couple families with children under 18 years (7.8%), and more than twice the rate for such families headed by male householders (18.8%) (U.S. Bureau of the Census, 1991). This disproportionate representation of single mother families among the poor has been described as the "feminization of poverty" (cf. Besharov, 1989; Rodgers, 1990).

The rate of poverty is even higher in Black and Hispanic-origin families with a female householder and children under 18 years. While nearly two-fifths (37.9%) of White families with female householders and children under 18 years fell below the poverty threshold, the corresponding rate for Black families and Hispanic-origin families was 56.1% and 58.2%, respectively.

The level of economic distress faced by many single mothers and their children today incurs not only direct financial costs to society, but also indirect costs, which include a waste of human capital, a loss of national income, and a loss of tax revenues. These costs place a drag on the U.S. economy, and greatly restrict this nation's competitiveness in the world economy. They also erode the foundation for effective role performance as a parent, and limit the ability of children to achieve their full developmental potential (Barber & Eccles, 1992; Marshall, 1991; Morrison, 1991; National Center for Health Statistics, 1990). According to Marshall (1991), former Secretary of Labor in the Carter Administration, "Except for some inspiring exceptions, poor families are not very efficient learning and nurturing systems" (p. 22).

These economic and social costs have moved both sides of the political spectrum to join together to develop reforms for reducing poverty and welfare dependency through paid employment (Hagen, 1992; Harris, 1991). Yet, as concluded by Jones (1992), "Motivating a person to look for work when it is not likely he or she will find a job [or a "good" job] is tantamount to blaming the victim" (p. 360).

Assuming a neostructuralist orientation (Neenan & Bowen, 1991), this chapter examines how recent changes in the structure of the economy in the United States may hinder the successful transition of many single mothers with dependent children from poverty toward welfare independence and economic self-sufficiency, regardless of how motivated they are to seek employment or to receive additional education and occupational training. The emphasis is on "good" jobs, jobs that pay a decent wage and that provide some degree of intrinsic satisfaction and opportunity for single mothers to move away from poverty and toward welfare independence and economic self-sufficiency. The basic theme of the article is that single mothers in poverty may increasingly find themselves in a "catch 22" situation: they may earn just enough from employment to move them beyond the income threshold necessary to qualify or to continue to qualify for means-tested public assistance, but not enough to provide for an adequate level of subsistence or to free them from the grasp of poverty.

The residual social welfare system that has been institutionalized in the United States, including recent welfare reforms and other public efforts to assist low-income families, serves as an important context for this macroeconomic analysis. According to Jones, (1992), "the welfare system is based on the "least eligibility doctrine," which states that benefit levels cannot exceed the wages of the worst-paid worker" (p. 360). This system was recently described by the U.S. General Accounting Office (1988) as "a paradoxical network of programs that aims to provide sufficient benefits to meet basic needs, yet these benefits must be so low that the poor have a clear interest in leaving the system" (p. 20).

Based on the analysis, recommendations for public policy are suggested for responding to the economic struggles and dilemmas of single mothers. These recommendations include a combination of economic, social welfare, and nonwelfare family policy initiatives.

DEFINITIONS

Work and employment are used interchangeably in the present review to refer to employment that results in wages. Although Jones (1992) makes a convincing argument for replacing the "paid work ethic" with a "work ethic" that includes child care and child rearing by caretakers as work, this issue is beyond the scope of the present review (cf. Davidson & Gaitz, 1974).

The "official" definition of poverty, a definition developed in 1965 by Molly Orshansky who was a researcher in the Social Security Administration, is used in this review. The formula, which is adjusted annually for inflation, defines poverty as three times the annual cash income required to meet minimum daily nutritional standards. Adjusted for family size, the official poverty level in 1992 was $13,950 for a family of four, $11,570 for a family of three, and $9,190 for a family of two. Although this measure of poverty has been criticized by both policy makers and economists alike for not reflecting current economic realities, the formula has remained unchanged (Winnick, 1988).

THE SOCIAL WELFARE CONTEXT

Given both the actual and the relative proportion of single mother families below the poverty line, it is not surprising that a high proportion of these families with related children under 18 years of age received some form of means-tested assistance from government programs in 1990. Single mothers and their children are the single largest group receiving welfare assistance (Rodgers, 1990). According to Rodgers (1990), "Female family heads and their dependents constitute over 80 percent of all AFDC (Aid to Families with Dependent Children) recipients, over half of all Food Stamp households, almost half of the recipients of free or reduced-price school meals, 55 percent of the households receiving Medicaid, and well over half of the non-aged residents of public housing" (p. 15).

Approximately two-thirds (68.6%) of persons in single mother households with related children under 18 years received some form of means-tested government assistance in 1990; more than nine out of ten (93.7%) of those below the poverty line received some form of public assistance, including cash assistance and noncash benefits, such as food stamps, medicaid, and subsidized housing (U.S. Bureau of the Census, 1991). More than two-thirds (69.5%) of persons in single mother households with related children under 18 years and who lived below the poverty line received means-tested cash assistance in 1990 (U.S. Bureau of the Census, 1991).

A number of individual, situational, and contextual factors have been associated with poverty and welfare dependency among single mother families (Bane & Ellwood, 1983; Garfinkel & McLanahan, 1986; Goodwin, 1983). Yet, consistent with the Protestant work ethic that links salvation to working hard, and within the context in which the majority of mothers with preschool children in the United States are employed for pay

(Hayes, Palmer, & Zaslow, 1990; Jones, 1992), public policies for reducing poverty and welfare dependency since the 1960s have focused largely on encouraging poor mothers to work (Hagen, 1992; Joesch, 1991). This emphasis on work now even extends to single mothers with preschool children, provided that child care is available (Hagen, 1992). According to Harris (1991), "the formula seems so simple–if the poor could only work, or work more, they would no longer be poor" (p. 492).

In general, recent welfare reforms and efforts to assist low-income families, such as the Family Support Act (FSA) of 1988 and the Child Care and Development Block Grant Act of 1990, have largely focused on increasing the employability and employment of low-income mothers through education and occupational training, expanding subsidies for child care assistance to support employment or preparation for employment, and increasing incentives to exit the welfare system (Bowen & Neenan, 1992; Meyers & van Leuwen, 1992; Wolf & Sonenstein, 1991). These policies have received bipartisan support from both liberals and conservatives because of their dual focus on both reducing welfare rolls and moving welfare recipients into jobs (Harris, 1991).

Yet, while recent initiatives to reform welfare and to assist low-income families that focus on education, training, and child care are essential components of any comprehensive plan to improve the economic future of single mother families (Hagen, 1992), they have largely neglected broader structural barriers to employment that restrict the economic participation, earnings, and potential of many single mothers. These initiatives, including the FSA of 1988, have given greater attention to helping the individual welfare recipient overcome structural impediments to employment than to developing strategies to remove the barriers themselves (Bowen & Neenan, 1990; Nichols-Casebolt & McClure, 1989).

A problem often cited in reaction to the Job Opportunities and Basic Skills (JOBS) initiative and to the FSA in general is that the programs do not consider the structure of the economy, that is, the availability and nature of jobs (Griffen, 1992; Hagen, 1992; Nichols-Casebolt & McClure, 1989). A report by the National Coalition on Women, Work and Welfare Reform (1986) makes the point succinctly: "A state that focuses on job preparation without job creation is wasting its investment" (p. 22).

In order for workfare to be successful, there needs to be available a sufficient number of jobs that pay adequate wages (Winnick, 1988). No recent reform proposals confront the issues of employment prospects and the changing structure of the labor market (Nichols-Casebolt & McClure, 1989), and the need for labor market policies to be tied directly with any policy directed at reducing the poverty and dependence of poor women

(Kamerman, 1984). This orientation reflects the general tendency of U.S. public policy to see the root causes of poverty as resulting more from deficiencies within the individual rather than from barriers within the larger social system (Mason, Wodarski, & Parham, 1985).

Available research suggests that employment alone is not enough to move a significant number of low-income single mothers out of poverty and welfare dependency and toward economic self-sufficiency (Coalition on Human Needs, 1987; Goodwin, 1983; Harris, 1991). Not only are a high proportion of poor single mothers, including those who receive public assistance, highly motivated to work (Benjamin & Stewart, 1989; Bowen & Neenan, 1992, 1993; Davidson & Gaitz, 1974; Goodwin, 1972), but also a significant proportion either earn or have earned wages from employment (Bowen & Neenan, 1992, 1993; Duncan, 1984; Harris, 1991; Mayo, 1975; Rodgers, 1990; U.S. General Accounting Office, 1992).

Unfortunately, many of the jobs held by these single mothers are marginal in terms of pay, security, benefits, and opportunities for promotion–jobs that hold little immediate promise of either welfare independence or long-term economic self-sufficiency (Bowen & Neenan, 1992, 1993; Coalition on Human Needs, 1987; Goodwin, 1983). Frequent job changes and periods of unemployment are a way of life for many single mothers who pursue paid employment, even in situations in which they are satisfied with their jobs and highly motivated to work (Bowen & Neenan, 1992).

Training and education and the provision of child care are important, but unless "good" jobs also are available, these strategies will do little to end poverty (Gueron, 1987; Nichols-Casebolt & McClure, 1989). Jobs are needed that offer single mothers some security and the opportunity to break free from the tentacles of poverty and welfare dependency and to move toward a greater level of economic self-sufficiency (Easterlin, 1987; Edelman, 1987). As stated by Mayo (1975, p. 9), work and welfare are not "mutually exclusive alternatives," although this has historically been an implicit assumption of the welfare system in the United States.

This chapter will consider an assumption that is more implicit than explicit in this employment focused government response to poverty and welfare dependency among single mothers: that a sufficient number of "good" jobs are available in the American economy for moving single mothers away from poverty and welfare dependency and toward economic self-sufficiency once they receive the necessary education, training, and support services. As concluded by Jones (1992), "trained workers need a market in which they can spend the human capital acquired through training. If jobs are not available, nothing is accomplished, or the trained worker ends up dislodging an untrained worker, which creates another unemployed person who needs either training or a job" (p. 361).

STRUCTURAL CHANGES IN THE U.S. ECONOMY

The U.S. economy has changed drastically over the past 30 years. The disappearance of the manufacturing base has been associated with declining productivity growth and increasing international competition. At the same time that middle class, blue collar jobs were disappearing from the U.S. landscape, the service sector was growing at a phenomenal rate. This surge in the service sector brought both high wage, high skill jobs and low wage, low skill jobs. Yet, because few middle income jobs were created, the income distribution became more bipolar. Caught in this web of change were single mothers–their income levels dropped and, subsequently, their poverty rates increased.

Decline in Productivity Growth and an Increase in International Competitiveness

While the U.S productivity rate remains the world's standard (Carnevale, 1991), U.S. productivity growth has been declining since the 1960s. Low productivity growth in manufacturing has been notable in the steel and copper industries and in transportation equipment (Levitan & Werneke, 1984). The U.S. productivity growth is much lower than that of its competitor nations, such as Japan, Germany, France, and the United Kingdom (Carnevale, 1991; Levitan & Werneke, 1984).

The international differences in productivity growth rates have hurt the United States' position in the world economic market. Indeed, increased competitive pressures have manifested themselves in several ways. Most notably, the competitiveness of U.S. manufacturers has declined. From the end of World War II to the 1960s, the U.S. led the world in the export of manufactured goods. However, by 1970, West Germany had surpassed the U.S. in exports, and by the 1980s exceeded U.S. exports by 22% (Levitan & Werneke, 1984).

Trade imbalance is just one manifestation of America's declining competitiveness. A survey of the American manufacturing sector reveals that entire segments of industry have declined or completely disappeared in this country (Gunn, 1987). Cameras, copiers, video recorders, audio equipment, machine tools, and steel are just a few of the industries that are dead or dying in the United States (Gunn, 1987).

The Changing Face of Industry: A Result of International Competition

To remain afloat in increasingly competitive times, most American corporations have had to rethink their methods of operation. Russell (1989) observes that "American companies have started the huge task of rebuilding themselves from the ground up, erecting a sleek new operating architecture to replace the unwieldy processes of the past" (p. 33). Many companies have been forced by economic constraints either to restructure or to downsize. For the purposes of this chapter, restructuring refers to changes in business practices aimed at making the business more efficient and competitive. On the other hand, companies who downsize eliminate entire functions, instead of restructuring them, in order to stay competitive. The unfortunate result of both of these strategies has been the decline of goods-producing jobs; jobs that are capable of moving single mothers towards economic self-sufficiency.

Restructuring. The nature of production has changed as a result of international competition. In an attempt to reduce costs and raise profits, more firms have moved from labor-intensive to capital-intensive production, replacing people with machines (Leontief, 1986). For example, microprocessor technology has made its way to the factory floor in the form of robots. Because robots can be reprogrammed, they allow the rapid conversion of the machines to produce new models or products. The benefits of using robots rather than people include reductions in work time and vastly improved productivity (Levitan & Werneke, 1984). These benefits accrue mainly to producers in the form of lower production expenditures and to consumers in the form of lower prices.

While advanced technology may relieve workers from many monotonous and labor-intensive jobs, workers may also bear grave costs as firms take advantage of new technology (Kuttner, 1989). According to Roberts (1986), "advancing technology has social and economic costs, including downgrading and displacement of workers and job loss. Too often the progress of technology results in plant shutdowns and more workers jobless or working at lower pay with reduced income" (p. 123).

Optimists claim that "high-tech" production will generate output and employment in excess of the lost output and employment in basic industries. However, there will not be enough jobs created to replace the jobs lost in the declining industries. For example, approximately 521,000 computer specialists were employed in 1982, and the Bureau of Labor Statistics projects employment in these occupations to reach 943,000 by 1995. While this growth looks impressive, it will represent less than 1 percent of total employment in 1995 (Roberts, 1986).

In addition to making technological advances, manufacturers have also lowered wages in an attempt to remain competitive. According to economist William Niskansen, a member of the Council of Economic Advisors in the Reagan Administration, low-skilled production workers in the U.S. are increasingly competing with low-skilled workers in other countries producing similar products. International competition has created a "brake on wage increases at the low end of the pay scale" (Rich, 1992, p. D3). Apparently, low wages in the U.S. are justified by the low wages paid for similar work abroad.

Because of the low-wage strategy that American companies have adopted, real wages, which are wages adjusted for inflation, were lower in 1990 than they were in 1970. In 1989, American wages ranked about 10th among the major industrialized countries (Marshall, 1991). Most of the wage cuts that management has pursued have been for hourly workers. Indeed, the historic gap in hourly wages between U.S. and other major industrial competitors that has favored workers in the U.S. has largely disappeared. Yet, the difference between U.S. and foreign executive pay still remains substantial. America's low wage strategy has only hurt workers, and it has done little to correct our trade imbalance (Mishel and Simon, 1988).

In addition to our low-wage strategy, the adoption of technology-based production methods has also resulted in lower wages for workers. Technology results in unemployment and a shrinking job base for low-skilled workers. Because workers must compete for their jobs with the unemployed, who are willing to work for less, wages are driven down (Kuttner, 1989).

Downsizing. Not only have U.S. manufacturers changed their wage strategies and production methods in response to foreign competition, they have also moved to streamline their operations. Russell says that "the task has the general aim of sharply cutting back on costs to make dramatic and durable improvements in long-term profitability and growth" (p. 34). Streamlining may involve either reducing unnecessary layers of management and staff or cutting back certain "marginal operations." In the case of large corporations, operations are often synonymous with location. Therefore, the decision to eliminate an unprofitable operation is a decision to eliminate the plant in which that unprofitable operation takes place (Russell, 1989).

Plant closings probably represent the most severe form of downsizing. While the decision to close or relocate a facility is a private decision based on economic efficiency, the decision carries with it both social and public costs. Plant closure results in individual financial stress and permanently reduces the employment and tax base in a community. At the same time that community resources are restricted, the demand on local services by displaced employees increases. The potential for a "ripple effect" can make the situation even worse. Plant closure may result in job loss in supplier plants, and the ensuing economic downturn may force the layoff of public employees due to lower tax revenues (Gordus, Jarley, & Ferman, 1981).

From 1979 to 1985, more than 11.5 million workers lost their jobs because of plant closings (Hoffman et al., 1991; Mishel and Simon, 1988). Dislocated workers experience high levels of unemployment, longer-than-average spells of joblessness, and reductions in earnings. In January 1986, the unemployment rate was 5.9%. Yet, blue-collar workers who had lost their jobs at least a year earlier had unemployment rates more than twice as high: 15.3% for men and 13.6% for women (Mishel & Simon, 1988). The rate of unemployment for women may be lower because women are much more likely than men to drop out of the labor force after displacement (Maxwell & D'Amico, 1986).

Dislocated workers experience longer-than-average spells of joblessness after being displaced, especially women. The median time without work for blue-collar males who were dislocated from 1981 to 1984 was 19.7 weeks. However, the length of joblessness was twice as high for blue-collar women–47.7 weeks. While more than one-third (35.2%) of dislocated blue-collar women were without work for more than one year, only about one-fifth of male blue-collar workers remained unemployed for more than one year (Mishel & Simon, 1988).

When dislocated workers find new jobs, these jobs tend to pay less than their previous employment. For blue-collar workers displaced between 1981 and 1984, one-third (33.4%) of males who found new employment were being paid at least 25% less. Among females, 40.6% had earnings reductions which exceeded 25% (Mishel & Simon, 1988). It seems that a combination of dislocation effects and gender discrimination operates to depress the wages of re-employed women.

As a result of restructuring and downsizing, there has been a decline in goods-producing jobs in the United States. Manufacturing employment fell from 34% of all jobs in 1950 to 25.1% in 1959 to 18% in 1989. In addition, the U.S. has created no net additional manufacturing jobs since the late 1960s (Marshall, 1991). The bipolarization of the income distribution and the shrinking middle class is often considered a result of this "deindustrialization" of the American economy, a trend that has been described by the Institute for Southern Studies as a shift from "mills" to "malls" ("Study Says," 1990). As the availability of high paying blue-collar jobs has declined, so has the middle-class lifestyle that those jobs allowed (Winnick, 1988).

The Surge in Services: A Parallel Phenomenon

At the same time that jobs in the manufacturing sector have been disappearing, the service sector has been experiencing tremendous growth. By 1989, more than 75% of America's workers were employed in service and service-related activities (Marshall, 1991; Mishel & Simon, 1988). This represents a 5% increase in just one decade; the service sector's share of employment was 70.5% in 1979. The 12.2 million (net) jobs created between 1979 and 1987 involved a loss of 1.6 million goods-producing jobs and an increase of 13.9 million service sector jobs (Mishel & Simon, 1988). Unfortunately, these service sector jobs are not an adequate substitute for the jobs being lost in the manufacturing sector. Service sector jobs tend to pay low-wages, lack benefits, such as health insurance, and are frequently temporary or part-time in nature.

Low-Paying Jobs. The service sector is characterized by great variation in wages. More specifically, there are both high-paying and low-paying service jobs, but few jobs in between. Critics of service sector job growth must be cautious in condemning such growth merely because the service sector generates low-paying jobs (Marshall, 1991). Indeed, they should carefully examine the various types of service sector job growth before concluding that all growth in the service sector is bad.

Yet, comparing the areas of employment growth or decline from 1950 to 1989 with their average weekly salary makes it evident that growth in the service sector has primarily occurred in low wage jobs. In 1990, average weekly earning in consumer services and retail trade, areas that evidenced the majority of employment growth in the service sector, were $321 and $198, respectively. In contrast, those areas which experienced employment decline, transportation and public utilities and wholesale trade, had the highest average weekly earnings, $510 and $409, respectively. Areas of modest growth, finance, insurance and real estate, paid an average weekly earning of $355 (Marshall, 1991).

The majority of new service sector jobs pay low wages, and women are more likely to be employed in these low-wage jobs. Data from the Survey of Income and Program Participants (SIPP) provide information on the movement of individuals into new jobs. Roughly 43.1% of the women age 25 to 54 who experienced job accessions entered the low-paying, service-producing industries. The majority of these women (82.9%) were paid by the hour, with an average hourly rate of pay of $4.84. The remaining women were paid weekly and had an average weekly pay of $196 (U.S. Bureau of the Census, 1992).

In contrast, only 24.8% of men age 25 to 54 who experienced job accessions entered the low-paying, service-producing industries. Most of these men (64.7%) were paid hourly, with an average wage rate of $6.62. The men who were paid weekly had an average salary of $374. The data from SIPP make it clear that women not only enter low-paying service jobs, but their wages are significantly less than those of men who are entering the same industry (U.S. Bureau of the Census, 1992).

Growth in Part-Time and Temporary Work. As the service sector grows, so do the number of part-time jobs available in this sector. Between 1969 and 1988, part-time employment increased from 15.5% to 17.9% of total employment (Tilly, 1990). However, part-time work is most prevalent in the service sector. In 1987, more than one-third (35.8%) of employment in retail trade was part-time and more than one-fifth (22.3%) of employment in personal and consumer services was part-time. However, only 6.9% of goods-producing jobs were part-time (Mishel & Simon, 1988).

Part-time work is concentrated in low-paying, low-skilled jobs. Part-time workers have less chance of promotion, less job security, less chance of receiving paid benefits, and lower overall status in their place of work (Mishel & Simon, 1988; Tilly, 1990, 1992). In addition, part-time workers earn much less per hour than do full-time workers. In 1987, part-timers had a median hourly wage of $4.42, while full-timers had a median hourly wage of $7.43 (Tilly, 1990).

Involuntary part-time workers, part-time workers who would rather work full-time, accounted for 72% of the growth of part-time work between 1969 and 1988. Part-time employment has expanded not because workers want part-time work, but because employers realize the savings associated with part-time employment. Employing workers part-time allows service sector employers to cut wages and benefits, two of their largest costs (Kingston, 1990; Tilly, 1990).

In addition to part-time work, the number of workers holding temporary positions has also increased in recent years. Temporary and personnel-services workers increased from 0.3% of total employment in 1973 to 0.6% in 1979 to 1.2% in 1989 (Marshall, 1991). Temporary employment grew six times faster than overall employment in the 1970s, and nine times faster than total employment since 1979. Temporary work is like part-time work in that workers are denied benefits, promotions, and access to better jobs (Mishel & Simon, 1988).

Part-time and temporary workers are most likely to be women. In 1988, 26.8% of women worked part-time, while only 11.4% of men worked part-time. Women are 1.5 times more likely to be employed part-time than the average worker. In addition, the female rate of involuntary part-time work (5.6%) is 44% greater than that for men (3.9%) (Tilly, 1990). In 1989, 58% of the personnel service employees in the temporary employment industry were women (Marshall, 1991). Because of its low pay, part-time and temporary employment may be augmenting the occupational discrimination experienced by women (Dex, 1992).

The Changing Income Distribution: The Outcome of Economic Change

The shift from a manufacturing to a service economy has caused blue-collar, middle income wage jobs to be replaced with low wage service jobs. This change has resulted in a decline in real wage and the polarization of the income distribution. Women and single mothers have been hurt worst by these changes, which is documented by their increasing levels of poverty.

Decline in Real Wages. As a result of the industrial shift that has occurred in the economy, real wages for American workers, which are wages adjusted for inflation, have declined. Since 1973, both hourly and weekly earnings have declined. From 1973 to 1979, average hourly earnings fell from $10.08 to $9.65 and average weekly earnings fell from $371.83 to $344.33, declines of 4.3% and 7.4% respectively. Between 1979 and 1987, both hourly and weekly earnings continued to decline. Hourly earnings fell to $8.98, a drop of 6.9%, and weekly earnings fell to $312.50, a drop of 9.2%. By 1987, average weekly wages had fallen to a level that prevailed in the early 1960s (Mishel & Simon, 1988).

Changes have taken place not only in real wages for individuals, but also in real incomes for families. Between 1973 and 1979, the mean real income of families with children declined from $32,206 to $31,138, a change of 3.3%. By 1984, real income had dropped an additional 5.2% to $29,527 (Danziger & Gottschalk, 1986).

Family incomes have not dropped as much as individual incomes because more family members are working now than was the case two decades ago (Danziger & Gottschalk, 1986; Marshall, 1991). Yet, this option is often not available to single mothers with dependent children who must typically shoulder the full responsibility for earning income without the backup support of a second potential wage earner. This attempt to sustain family incomes by increasing the level of employment participation has also meant a decrease in the leisure time enjoyed by family members, including the time devoted to the nurturing of children.

These changes in real wages are reflected in increases in the poverty rate. Between 1973 and 1979, the poverty rate increased slightly, from 11.1% to 11.7%. Yet, by 1987, the poverty rate was 13.5% (Mishel & Simon, 1988). The poverty rate for young families (families with heads under 30) increased from 16% to 30% between 1973 and 1986 (Voydanoff, 1990). In addition, the number of near poor families has increased. In 1973, 3.9% of families had incomes within 25% of the poverty level. By 1979 that rate increased to 4.7%, and declined only slightly to 4.6% by 1987 (Mishel & Simon, 1988).

Inequities in Income and Wealth. The industrial shift in the U.S. has not only resulted in a decline in real wages, but also it has generated a more unequal distribution of income and wealth. Between 1979 and 1986, the distribution of average family incomes became more unequal. For the wealthiest fifth of the population, real incomes increased from $70,260 to $76,300, a gain of $6,040 or 7.9%. On the other hand, the poorest fifth's average family income fell from $8,761 to $8,031, a drop of 8.3% (Marshall, 1991). While the portion of both rich and poor families has been increasing, middle class families have been disappearing. Most of those who left the middle class category have fallen into the lower income brackets, instead of moving up to the higher brackets. Both the industrial shift that has occurred in the U.S. and the increase in part-time work are responsible for the disappearance of the middle class (Winnick, 1988).

The distribution of wealth between U.S. citizens is far more unequal than the distribution of income (Marshall, 1991; Mishel & Simon, 1988; Winnick, 1988). In 1983, more than half of all families (54%) had negative or zero financial assets. While the top 0.5% of wealth holders owned 46.5% of all corporate stock, the bottom 90% owned only 10.7%. Between 1979 and 1989, the average net worth of the top 0.5% of families increased 6.7% while the average net worth of the bottom 90% of families fell by 8.8% (Marshall, 1991).

Financial assets, not income, contribute the most to the economic well-being of the wealthiest families: the top 10% of families owned 86% of financial assets, yet received only 33% of the nation's income (Mishel & Simon, 1988). Wealth, in addition to income, is important because it represents a household's level of economic security. Asset accumulation provides protection from prolonged unemployment and medical emergencies (Mishel & Simon, 1988; Winnick, 1988). Unfortunately, the wealth owned by most working people, equity in their homes or cars, is not easily liquidated and thus does not readily function as a protective net (Mishel & Simon, 1988).

Disparate Impact on Women and Single Mothers

The evidence clearly demonstrates that women and single mothers, especially those from minority racial and ethnic groups, have been hurt worst by the structural changes that have taken place in the U.S. economy. When plants close, women have longer durations of unemployment and lower wages upon re-entry into the labor force. Even though the service sector has emerged with both high and low-paying jobs, women continue to be employed mainly in the low paying jobs, which are often part-time and temporary in nature. As real wages have declined and incomes have become more unequal, low wages, discrimination, and a reliance on wage income have caused women's real wages to drop more than men's wages, and have caused women's poverty rates to increase at a rate much faster than men's.

The mean real income of families with children declined between 1973 and 1984. While this decline was experienced by both two-parent families and female-headed families, the latter fared worst. During this period, the real income of two-parent families with children declined 3.1% while the real income of female-headed families declined 7.8%. The real income of black female-headed families declined more, by 9.4%, and the decline experienced by Hispanic female-headed families, 13.3%, was even worse.

The increases in real income between 1967 and 1973 experienced by all families with children were able to compensate for the decline in real income during 1973-1984 for two-parent families only. Between 1967 and 1984, the mean real income of two-parent families increased 14.1% while it declined 6.5% for female-headed families with children. Thus, female-headed families were better off in 1967 than they were in 1984 (Danziger & Gottschalk, 1986).

The shift in importance from wage to property income has hurt women, especially single mothers whose economic well-being continues to rely on wages. Between 1967 and 1984, the percentage of total income accounted for by mother's earnings increased from 45.8% to 57.3% in white female-headed families with children. However, during the same time period, the percentage of total income accounted for by father's earnings in white two-parent families decreased from 80.2% to 70.4%. Black and Hispanic families experienced similar changes (Danziger & Gottschalk, 1986).

Single mothers have continued to rely on wage income, a source of income that has become less important in recent years in determining total wealth. The median net worth of a white female-headed household in 1984 was $22,500, while the median net worth for a white married couple was twice as high, $54,184. Black female householders had a median net worth of only $671, compared to $13,061 for black married couples (Marshall, 1991; Mishel & Simon, 1988).

Women have consistently earned less than men. Since World War II, the average full-time year-round working woman has earned less than 70 percent of the wages of her male counterpart. This earnings gap is not sufficiently explained by differences in education attainment, work experience, or work commitment (Cherry, 1989; Garfinkel & McLanahan, 1986).

The male-female earning gap also needs to be analyzed by considering the occupational distribution of men and women. The majority of women, 75.4% in 1981, are employed in female-dominated industries (Cherry, 1989). In 1989, women held more than 80% of clerical and administrative support positions, about one-half of sales positions, and more than 60% of service occupations (Marshall, 1991). These female-dominated occupations tend to be lower paying than male-dominated occupations. However, even the differences in occupational distribution between men and women does not adequately explain the earnings gap (Blau & Winkler, 1989; Cherry, 1989).

On the surface, the increase in women's wages from 60.2% of men's wages in 1980 to 66.0% in 1988 appears encouraging for women (Marshall, 1991). However, it is the fall in men's wages and not the rise in women's wages that is the main cause of improvement in the male-female wage gap (Marshall, 1991; Mishel & Simon, 1988). Labor market discrimination persists despite anti-discrimination legislation and improved attitudes about the employment of women (Marshall, 1991). This labor market discrimination takes the form of both lower wages and occupational segregation, and it has detrimental implications for the economic situation of single mothers.

Summary and Discussion

In a recent study, the Coalition on Human Needs (1987) conducted personal interviews with 202 low income people in four locations across the United States to discern their ideas about how to best remedy poverty. Although many opinions were shared by interviewees, "the view that good jobs are the ultimate solution to poverty was shared by whites and blacks, people in small towns and inner cities, homemakers and ex-steelworkers, welfare recipients and the working poor" (p. 1). As concluded by Marian Wright Edelman (1987), "the expansion of employment opportunities is the most effective mechanism for raising family incomes and promoting self-sufficiency" (p. 86).

The preceding analysis suggests that single mothers in poverty face an insufficient supply of "good" jobs. In addition, they face this situation in the context of a welfare system that obligates those who receive public assistance, including those with preschool children, to work or to pursue education or employment training in order to receive their welfare grants. As a consequence, they often get low-wage jobs that lack security, intellectual stimulation, or opportunity; jobs that may reinforce an already fragile self-image (Jones, 1992).

Such a situation has negative implications for the mother and her children. In many cases, they cycle in and out of both poverty and public assistance. Faced with an unresponsive job market, they may experience increased levels of frustration, despair, and hopelessness over time. This may be especially true for those who invest in increasing their human capital through education and job training, but who still remain trapped in jobs that hold little immediate promise of higher levels of economic self-sufficiency.

Our present public policies support mothers neither at home nor at work (Ellwood, 1988). The combined effects of job market problems, the need for females to fill both the dual roles of nurturer and provider, and victimization by an isolating and often counterproductive income support system trap many single mothers in poverty and dependence (Ellwood, 1988). If single mothers are expected to work toward welfare independence and eventual economic self-sufficiency, the federal government needs to adopt public policies that counteract the effects of adverse macroeconomic circumstances. Past efforts at welfare reform have done little, if anything, to promote employment opportunities, improve wages, or take into account the dual role of single parents in a useful way (Ellwood, 1988). Kamerman (1992) and Ellwood (1988) suggest that we move beyond welfare reform to build a non-welfare family policy agenda.

Recommendations to improve jobs and single mothers' access to them need to be considered in the context of economic and social realities. Jones (1992) questions the possibility of providing jobs for all welfare mothers. He views full employment as "an elusive and unreachable policy" (p. 359) in the United States. He argues that structural unemployment caused by a skill or location mismatch between the supply and demand for labor, technological change, and stiff international competition, are reasons that unemployment will remain high (Jones, 1992). Small countries like Sweden, Austria, and Norway have successfully expanded their public sectors, and thus their tax base, to allow full employment, but free market principles in the U.S. discourages large expansions in public sector employment as a viable long-term solution to unemployment (Jones, 1992).

In addition, not everyone agrees that the remedy for single parent poverty is sending mothers into the workforce. For many welfare mothers, the decision to enter the labor force is often one between welfare poverty and wage poverty (Griffen, 1992). It is neither socially nor economically desirable to require single mothers receiving welfare to work outside the home at jobs that do not pay enough to support their families (Jones, 1992). Sherraden (1988) points out that policy makers should consider that mothers who receive AFDC may be needed more at home to care for their children than to look for poverty-wage employment, especially when millions of Americans are already unemployed and looking for work.

Finally, there will always be some single mothers who, because of their young age, poor health, or other extenuating circumstances, are going to rely on the government for economic support. Consequently, despite the movement to establish AFDC as a transitional benefit, and to move welfare mothers into the workforce, changes in AFDC are needed before it will provide a decent income support system for those mothers who are unable to be absorbed in the labor market (Ellwood, 1988; Garfinkel & McLanahan, 1986; Kamerman, 1992; Sarri, 1988).

RECOMMENDATIONS FOR PUBLIC POLICY

The economic situation of single parent mothers results from public policies that influence both their labor market participation, earnings, and potential and their access to an economic safety net (Kamerman, 1992). Yet, current welfare efforts have neither stimulated the supply of "good" jobs that offer single mothers an opportunity to achieve a decent standard of living nor have they provided a safety net for these families. As recently concluded by Harris (1991), "social policy perennially stumbles over how to promote work among the poor and at the same time relieve poor families from their deprivation" (p. 492). The following public policy recommendations are offered as "grist for the mill" for responding to the conditions in the U.S. economy and to the specific needs of poor single mothers.

Economic Initiatives

Develop an Economic Plan for Sustaining Long Term Economic Growth and Viability. In view of evidence of the failure of the economy to promote productivity growth, there is a justification for a more active government role in national industrial policy to channel more resources into productivity growth (Burton, 1986; Heller, 1986). The key to high productivity and competitiveness lies in investment in research and development (Levitan & Werneke, 1984), physical resources (Marshall, 1986), and human resources (Bluestone & Havens, 1986; Burton, 1986; Cohen & Zysman, 1986). For example, Bowen (1990) advocates government subsidies to low income communities to promote economic growth and development and the creation of government initiatives to manufacturing and industrial firms to modernize their facilities so that they may compete more successfully with other industrialized nations.

Increase the Minimum Wage. There is an assumption implicit in the structure of the welfare system in the United States that equates work and welfare independence with economic self-sufficiency (Mayo, 1975, p. 9). However, single mothers who work may remain poor because of low wages, large families, or the combination of the two (Mayo, 1975). A statement by Mayo (1975) nearly twenty years ago remains true today: "The prominence of the 'working poor' in current discussions of poverty and proposals for welfare reform challenges the assumption that full-time employment necessarily means economic self-sufficiency and no need for public assistance" (p. 10).

An important step in promoting welfare independence among single mothers is raising the minimum wage (Edelman, 1987; Ellwood, 1988; Kelly, 1988; Winnick, 1988) so that single mothers working full-time will be able to support their families above the poverty line. Tilly (1990) contends that an equitable increase in the minimum wage would press employers to create more productive and skilled jobs by rendering low wage, low productivity strategies less possible. Legislation that indexes the minimum wage to increases in the cost of living may be a particularly viable strategy for providing single mothers who work with more income stability, especially those who change employers frequently.

Reduce Pay and Job Opportunity Inequities for Women. The argument that wage inequities are a result of human capital differences between men and women has not been supported in the research on wage discrimination (Blau & Winkler, 1989; Cherry, 1989). Pay equity policies and the enforcement of these policies are needed to increase women's earning capacity (Hagen & Davis, 1992; McLanahan, Sorensen & Watson, 1989; Treiman & Hartmann, 1981), as well as overcome gender discrimination (Blau & Winkler, 1989). Much of the disparity between men and women in economic well-being results from the unequal access that women have to better paying jobs and job advancement, and intervention in this area can make the workplace more equitable (Bielby & Baron, 1986).

Social Welfare Initiatives

With economic policies in line to increase productivity growth, improve the minimum wage, and reduce pay and job opportunity inequities for women, the next step is to design social policies that guarantee single mothers who participate in education and training programs access to jobs, provide an adequate safety net for those who are unable to move toward self-sufficiency through employment, and allow single mothers to accrue assets and still receive government support.

Guarantee Jobs for JOBS Participants. Despite the good intentions of the Family Support Act's training and education component, failure to include a job guarantee makes the goals of the legislation unrealistic. It may also result in increased levels of frustration and despair among single mothers who participate in the program but who find themselves unable to find a job or unable to achieve any degree of occupational upward mobility. If the goals of the JOBS program are to be realized, a guaranteed jobs program must be established by the government (Ellwood, 1988; Garfinkel & McLanahan, 1986; Kamerman, 1992; Kelly, 1988).

Federalize and Standardize AFDC. Types of means-tested assistance, like AFDC, food stamps, and medicaid, are generally based on multiples of the poverty level (U.S. Bureau of the Census, 1991). Each state determines its own eligibility requirements and the amount of assistance from government programs within general federal guidelines. The factor with the greatest variability is the needs standard–the dollar amount that a state determines is essential to meet a minimum standard of living in that state for a family of specified size. The family's need is theoretically equal to the difference between the determined needs standard for a family of given size, taking into account allowances for food, clothing, shelter, utilities and other necessities, and the actual income and resources available to the family.

However, states are not required to provide the full amount of this difference, resulting in assistance payments below the needs standard. States have statutory and administrative ceilings on the amount that may be paid, and payment standards may be adjusted periodically by the states based on their fiscal abilities (U.S. Department of Health and Human Services, 1989).

Kamerman (1992) emphasizes the need to federalize the AFDC program and establish a minimum benefit level that, when combined with food stamps, reaches the poverty threshold. Allowing states to continue to set their own benefit levels and to target AFDC for cuts and restrict eligibility will only increase the number of single mother families living below the poverty threshold. Although some conservative scholars, like Charles Murray (1984), blame the social welfare system for increasing single parent household formation and encouraging mothers to remain on welfare, empirical evidence generally refutes the premise that AFDC encourages single families to form and to live on welfare indefinitely (Duncan, 1984; Ellwood & Bane, 1984).

Allow Asset Accumulation. Michael Sherraden (1988) argues that a major blockade in single parents' struggle to become welfare independent is the fact that they cannot collect assets. According to Sherraden (1988), "class limitations begin with limited assets, which in turn limit opportunity structures, which are quickly internalized" (p. 40). He advocates an assets-based social welfare which would make a portion of transfers in the form of assets rather than entirely in the form of income. He believes assets are important because they cushion income shocks, reduce household transaction costs (better neighborhoods and cars cut down on security and repair costs), and give people a more positive outlook and stake in the future.

Nonwelfare Family Policy Initiatives

The package of programs that includes national health insurance, expanded earned income tax credit (EITC), increased child care subsidies, child support enforcement and child support assurance, is designed after the family support model in European and Scandinavian countries (Kamerman, 1984; Kamerman & Kahn, 1978). Despite the success of the family support model, American policy makers have never seriously considered the model as a policy alternative. This is due largely to the model's critique of capitalism and the free market system (Kelly, 1988).

Opponents of this model often contend that even if the U.S. expanded its government sector to provide assistance and security for low-income single parent families the way European and Scandinavian countries do, the larger and more complex U.S. economy would still serve as a barrier (Rodgers, 1990). But Kamerman (1992) claims that this argument has little merit, and that if political and economic leaders in the U.S. can compare the American economy to that of its European counterparts, then it follows that social policy can be compared as well.

Create a Program of National Health Insurance. Single mothers may choose not to enter the labor force because they fear the loss of Medicaid, which is unlikely to be replaced when they take a low wage job (Ellwood, 1988). In the present system, health insurance is tied to employment, and poor single mothers are those most likely to obtain jobs that have little or no health insurance, especially part-time and temporary jobs. Enacting some form of national health insurance would disassociate AFDC from health care and employment, and ensure that those in low wage and low skilled jobs have health care benefits (Kamerman, 1984, 1992; Kamerman & Kahn, 1978). Most advocates of national health insurance suggest building on the present system, adding a national health insurance component into a restructured system, which still would have a strong component of privatized medicine to ensure financial stability and technological excellence.

Expand the Earned Income Tax Credit (EITC), or Establish a Family Allowance. The current dependent tax credit benefits middle and upper income families, not the poor, since their income is generally too low to take advantage of it. Transforming the current dependent tax credit into a universal refundable child tax credit would benefit all families with children, including poor single mothers (Ellwood, 1988; Garfinkel & McLanahan, 1986; Kamerman, 1984, 1992). The objective of universal family allowances is to provide an income supplement for low wage earners and to create a work incentive while protecting the economic well-being of children. A child or family allowance benefit now exists in 67 countries, including every major industrialized country in the world, except the United States (Kamerman, 1984, 1992).

Increase Child Care Subsidies. Child care services are critical for allowing single mothers to enter the labor force and to maintain employment continuity. The lack of affordable, available and accessible child care for single mothers with young children is a major barrier to the successful transition from welfare to work (Bowen & Neenan, 1992, 1993; Ellwood, 1988; Handler & Hasenfeld, 1991; Sarri, 1988; Wilson, 1987). Single mothers need quality child care that is flexible and responsive to work shifts other than the traditional 9-5 time period (Bowen & Neenan, 1992; 1993). New federal funds to increase the supply of subsidized slots for low-income parents, such as from the Child Care and Dependent Block Grant Act of 1990, are a step in the right direction.

Increase Child Support Enforcement. The lack of child support from fathers is considered a major barrier to self-sufficiency for single mothers (Ellwood, 1988; Garfinkel & McLanahan, 1986; Kamerman, 1984, 1992; Sarri, 1988). Only one-third of single parents receive any child support (Ellwood, 1988). In many cases, dollar awards are not adjusted for inflation over time, and mothers are responsible for bringing all actions and court sanctions against fathers who fail to comply with court orders.

Although an important component of the Family Support Act is increased enforcement of child support, more is needed to ensure that fathers accept financial responsibility for their offspring and that the level of child support is adequate. Legislation is needed to ensure that courts order support awards, use an appropriate formula in determining the amount of support, index awards to inflation, and that the government and businesses play an even more active role in collecting payments from parents who are delinquent in their support (Kamerman, 1992).

Establish Child Support Assurance. When the collections from earnings of the absent parent do not reach some minimum level, the government should provide a minimum level of child support (Ellwood, 1988; Garfinkel & McLanahan, 1986; Handler & Hasenfeld, 1991; Kamerman, 1992; Wilson, 1987). This would raise the standard of living and make one of the main sources of support for single parent families a mainstream insurance. The protection system would be more like Social Security than AFDC and would simultaneously reinforce the responsibilities of absent fathers to support their children (Ellwood, 1988). Critics may complain about the expense of this program but it puts single mothers in a much more realistic position to become self-supporting and reduces the need for welfare.

CONCLUSIONS

Efforts to reduce poverty in single mother households have typically taken an individual approach, often focusing on the values, motives, attitudes, and abilities of single mothers. Interventions from this perspective have most often centered on "fixing" the individual. This chapter has assumed a situational perspective, electing to focus on structural shifts in the economy within the context of a residual social welfare system from which a majority of persons in single mother households depend upon for some level of assistance. From this perspective, intervention is directed toward the environment of the individual.

Any comprehensive change effort to reduce the level of poverty in single mother households needs to address both the individual and the situational sides of the equation. The aim is to increase the level of fit between the needs of the family, the abilities of its members, including their level of employability, and the resources, supports and opportunities in the environment.

In solving the poverty equation for single mothers, it is critical that policy makers take into account changing labor market conditions, the potential implausibility of full employment or the availability of a "good" job for each person who wants one, and the need to ensure an adequate safety net for families. It is also critical that policy makers involve single mothers in the policy debate. As recently concluded by Daniel Yankelovich ("An Interview," 1992), "If you include people in the dialogue, they will struggle with hard issues. They will take the responsible positions. If you exclude them, the opposite happens" (p. 14). While neither exhaustive nor necessarily mutually exclusive, it is our hope that the above policy recommendations will help to better frame the debate about the types of interventions that will be necessary to reduce the level of economic distress experienced by single mothers and their children.

REFERENCES

Ahlburg, D.A., & De Vita, C.J. (1992). New realities of the American family. *Population Bulletin, 47*(2) (Washington, D.C.: Population Reference Bureau, Inc.).

An interview with Daniel Yankelovich (1992, Summer). *Family Affairs, 5*(1-2). New York: Institute for American Values.

Bane, M.J., & Ellwood, D.T. (1983). *The dynamics of dependence: The route to self-sufficiency*. Unpublished manuscript prepared for the U.S. Department of Health and Human Services, Washington, D.C.

Barber, B.L., & Eccles, J.S. (1992). Long-term influence of divorce and single parenting on adolescent family- and work-related values, behaviors, and aspirations. *Psychological Bulletin, 111*, 108-126.

Bielby, W.T. & Baron, J.N. (1986). Occupations and labor markets: A critical evaluation. Sex segregation within occupations. *AEA Papers and Proceedings*, 43-47.

Benjamin, L., & Stewart, J.B. (1989). The self-concept of Black and White women: The influences upon its formation of welfare dependency, work effort, family networks, and illnesses. *American Journal of Economics and Sociology, 48*, 165-175.

Besharov, D.J. (1989). Targeting long-term welfare recipients. In P.H. Cottingham & D.T. Ellwood (Eds.), *Welfare policy for the 1990s* (pp. 146-164). Cambridge, MA: Harvard University Press.

Blau, F.D., & Winkler, A.E. (1989). Women in the labor force: An overview. In J. Freeman (Ed.), *Women: A feminist perspective* (pp. 265-286). Mountain View, CA: Mayfield.

Bluestone, B. & Havens, J. (1986). How to cut the deficit and rebuild America. *Challenge, 29*, 22-29.

Bowen, G. (1990). The structural shift in the American economy and homelessness. In Relos (Ed.), *North Carolina homeless families: Issues for the nineties* (pp. 1-5). Paper presented at the North Carolina Conference for Social Services, Raleigh, NC.

Bowen, G.L., & Neenan, P.A. (1990). *Child day care recycling fund experiment*. Chapel Hill, NC: University of North Carolina at Chapel Hill.

Bowen, G.L., & Neenan, P.A. (1992). Child care as an economic incentive for the working poor. *Families in Society, 73*, 295-303.

Bowen, G.L., & Neenan, P.A. (1993). Child day care and the employment of AFDC recipients with preschool children. *Journal of Family and Economic Issues, 14*, 49-68.

Burton, B.F. (1986). Policy options and the changing world of work. In D.F. Burton, Jr. et al. (Eds.), *The jobs challenge: Pressures and possibilities* (pp. 229-264). Cambridge, MA: Ballinger.

Carnevale, A. P. (1991). *America and the new economy*. Alexandria, VA: U.S. Department of Labor.

Cherry, R. (1989). *Discrimination: Its economic impact on blacks, women, and Jews*. Lexington, MA: Lexington Books.

Coalition on Human Needs (1987). *How the poor would remedy poverty.* Washington, DC: Author.

Cohen, S.S., & Zysman, J. (1986). Can America compete? *Challenge, 29,* 56-64.

Danziger, S. & Gottschalk, P. (1986). Families with children have fared worst. *Challenge, 29,* 26-32.

Davidson, C., & Gaitz, C.M. (1974). "Are the poor different?" A comparison of work behavior and attitudes of the urban poor and nonpoor. *Social Problems, 22,* 229-245.

Dex, S. (1992). Women's part-time work in Britain and the United States. In Barbara Warme et al. (Eds.), *Working part-time: risks and opportunities* (pp. 161-174) New York: Praeger.

Duncan, G.J. (1984). *Years of poverty, years of plenty.* Ann Arbor: University of Michigan, Institute for Social Research.

Easterlin, R.A. (1987). The new age structure of poverty in America: Permanent or transient? *Population and Development Review, 13,* 195-208.

Edelman, M.W. (1987). *Families in peril: An agenda for social change.* Cambridge, MA: Harvard University Press.

Ellwood, D.T. (1988). *Poor support: Poverty in the American family.* Basic Books, Inc.

Ellwood, D.T. & Bane, M.J. (1984). *The impact of AFDC on family structure and living arrangements.* Report prepared for the U.S. Department of Health and Human Services under grant no. 92A-82. John F. Kennedy School of Government, Harvard University.

Garfinkel, I. & McLanahan, S. (1986). *Single mothers and their children: A new American dilemma.* Washington, D.C.: Urban Institute Press.

Goodwin, L. (1972). *Do the poor want to work: A social-psychological study of work orientations.* Washington, D.C.: The Brookings Institution.

Goodwin, L. (1983). *Causes and cures of welfare.* Lexington, MA: Lexington Books.

Gordus, J. P., Jarley, P. & Ferman, L.A. (1981). *Plant closing and economic dislocation.* Kalamazoo: W.E. Upjohn Institute for Employment Research.

Griffen, S. (1992). Poor relations: The backlash against welfare recipients. *Dollars & Sense,* (176), 6-8.

Gueron, J.M. (1987). Reforming welfare with work. *Public Welfare, 45*(4), 13-25.

Gunn, T. G. (1987). *Manufacturing for competitive advantage: Becoming a world class manufacturer.* Cambridge, MA: Ballinger.

Hagen, J.L. (1992). Women, work, and welfare: Is there a role for social work? *Social Work, 37*(1), 9-14.

Hagen, J.L., & Davis, L.V. (1992). Working with women: Building a policy and practice agenda. *Social Work, 37,* 495-502.

Handler, J.F. & Hasenfeld, Y. (1991). *The moral construction of poverty: Welfare reform in America.* Newbury Park, CA: Sage Publications, Inc.

Harris, K.M. (1991). Teenage mothers and welfare dependency: Working off welfare. *Journal of Family Issues, 12,* 492-518.

Hayes, C.D., Palmer, J.L., & Zaslow, M.J. (Eds.). (1990). *Who cares for America's children: Child care policy for the 1990s*. Washington, DC: National Academy Press.

Heller, W.W. (1986). Activist government: Key to growth. *Challenge*, *29*, 4-10.

Hoffman, W. S. et al. (1991). Initial impact of plant closings on automobile workers and their families. *Families in Society: The Journal of Contemporary Human Services*, *172*, 103-107.

Joesch, J.M. (1991). The effect of the price of child care on AFDC mothers' paid work behavior. *Family Relations*, *40*, 161-166.

Jones, L. (1992). The full employment myth: Alternative solutions to unemployment. *Social Work*, *37*, 359-364.

Kamerman, S.B. (1984). Women, children, and poverty: Public policies and female-headed families in industrialized countries. *Signs: Journal of Women in Culture and Society*, *10*(21), 249-271.

Kamerman, S.B. (1992, November). *Family income and social policy*. Plenary presentation at the annual conference of the National Council on Family Relations, Orlando, FL.

Kamerman, S.B. & Kahn, A. (eds.) (1978). *Family policy: Government and family in fourteen countries*. New York: Columbia University Press.

Kelly, R.F. (1988). Poverty, the family, and public policy: Historical interpretations and a reflection on the future. In P. Voydanoff & L.C. Majka (Eds.), *Families and economic distress: Coping strategies and social policy* (261-301). Newbury Park, CA: Sage Publications, Inc.

Kingston, P.W. (1990). Illusions and ignorance about the family-responsive workplace. *Journal of Family Issues*, *11*, 438-454.

Kuttner, R. (1989). The changing occupational structure. In D. Stanley Eitzen and Maxine Baca Zinn (Eds.), *The reshaping of America: Social consequences of the changing economy*. (pp. 85-102) Englewood Cliffs, NJ: Prentice Hall.

Leontief, W. (1986). Technological change, employment, the rate of return on capital and wages. In Daniel F. Burton, Jr. et al. (Eds.), *The jobs challenge: Pressure and possibilities* (pp. 47-54). Cambridge, MA: Ballinger.

Levitan, S.A. & Werneke, D. (1984). *Productivity: Problems, prospects, and policies*. Baltimore: Johns Hopkins University Press.

Marshall, R. (1986). Reversing the downtrend in real wages. *Challenge*, *29*, 48-55.

Marshall, R. (1991). *The state of families, 3: Losing direction*. Milwaukee: Family Service America.

Mason, J., Wodarski, J.S., & Parham, T.M.J. (1985). Work and welfare: A reevaluation of AFDC. *Social Work*, *30*, 197-203.

Maxwell, N. L. & D'Amico, R.J. (1986). Employment and wage effects of involuntary job separation: Male and female differences. *American Economics Review*, *76*, 373-377.

Mayo, J. (1975). Work and welfare: *Employment and employability of women in the AFDC program*. Chicago: University of Chicago.

McLanahan, S.S., Sorensen, A. & Watson, D. (1989). Sex differences in poverty, 1950-1980. *Signs: Journal of Women in Culture and Society*, *15*(1).

Meyers, M.K., & van Leuwen, K. (1992). Child care preferences and choices: Are AFDC recipients unique? *Social Work Research & Abstracts, 28*, 28-34.

Mishel, L. and Simon, J. (1988). *The state of working America*. Washington, DC: Economic Policy Institute.

Morrison, P.A. (1991). *Congress and the year 2000: A demographic perspective on future issues*. Santa Monica, CA: RAND.

Murray, C.A. (1984). *Losing ground: American social policy, 1950-1980*. New York: Basic Books.

National Center for Health Statistics (1990, November 16). *Developmental, learning, and emotional problems: Health of our nation's children, United States, 1988*. Advance Data, Vital and Health Statistics, No. 190.

National Coalition on Women, Work and Welfare Reform. (1986). Welfare reform: Who's looking out for the women? *Youth Policy, 8*(10), 22-24.

Neenan, P.A., & Bowen, G.L. (1991). Multimethod assessment of a child care demonstration project for AFDC recipient families: The genesis of an evaluation. *Evaluation Review, 15*, 219-232.

Nichols-Casebolt, A., & McClure, J. (1989). Social work support for welfare reform: The latest surrender in the war on poverty. *Social Work, 34*, 77-80.

Rich, S. (1992, May 12). Wage earners losing ground: Census reports jump in low-paying jobs. *The News and Observer*, p. 1D.

Roberts, M. (1986). A labor agenda for jobs. In Daniel F. Burton, Jr. et al. (Eds.), *The jobs challenge: Pressure and possibilities* (pp. 119-133). Cambridge, MA: Ballinger.

Rodgers, H.R., Jr. (1990). *Poor women, poor families: The economic plight of America's female-headed households* (Rev. Ed.). Armonk, NY: M.E. Sharpe, Inc.

Russell, G. (1989). Corporate restructuring. In D. Stanley Eitzen and Maxine Baca Zinn (Eds.), *The reshaping of America: Social consequences of the changing economy* (pp. 33-36). Englewood Cliffs, NJ: Prentice Hall.

Sarri, R.C. (1988). The impact of federal policy changes on the well-being of poor women and children. In P. Voydanoff & L.C. Majka (Eds.), *Families and economic distress: Coping strategies and social policy* (pp. 209-231). Newbury Park, CA: Sage.

Sherraden, M. (1988). Rethinking social welfare: Toward assets. *Social Policy*, 37-43.

Study says N.C. workplace shifted from 'mills to malls.' (1990, October 23). Raleigh, NC: *The News and Observer*, p. 4D.

Tilly, C. (1990). *Short hours, short shrift: Causes and consequences of part-time work*. Washington, D.C.: Economic Policy Institute.

Tilly, C. (1992). Two faces of part-time work: Good and bad part-time jobs in the U.S. service industries. In Barbara Warme et al. (Eds.), *Working part-time: Risks and opportunities* (pp. 227-238). New York: Praeger.

Treiman, D. & Hartmann, H. (1981). *Equal pay for jobs of equal value*. Washington, DC: National Academy Press.

U.S. Bureau of the Census (1991, August). *Poverty in the United States: 1990.* Current Population Reports P-60, No. 175.

U.S. Bureau of the Census (1992, January). *Job creation during the late 1980's: Dynamic aspects of employment growth.* Current Population Reports P-70, No. 27.

U.S. Department of Health and Human Services. (1989). *Social Security Bulletin: Social Security Programs in the United States.* Washington, D.C.: Social Security Administration.

U.S. General Accounting Office. (1988). *Work and welfare: Analysis of AFDC employment programs in four states* (HRD-88-33FS). Washington, D.C.: Author.

U.S. General Accounting Office (1992). *Poverty trends, 1980-88: Changes in family composition and income sources among the poor* (GAO/PEMD-92-34). Washington, D.C.: Author.

Voydanoff, P. (1990). Economic distress and family relations: A review of the eighties. *Journal of Marriage and the Family, 52*, 1099-1115.

Wilson, W.J. (1987). *The truly disadvantaged: The inner city, the underclass, and public policy.* Chicago: The University of Chicago Press.

Winnick, A.J. (1988). The changing distribution of income and wealth in the United States, 1960-1985: An examination of the movement toward two societies, "Separate and unequal." In P. Voydanoff & L.C. Majka (Eds.), *Families and economic distress: Coping strategies and social policy* (pp. 232-260). Newbury Park, CA: Sage.

Wolf, D.A., & Sonenstein, F.L. (1991). Child-care use among welfare mothers: A dynamic analysis. *Journal of Family Issues, 12*, 519-536.

Chapter 7

Homeless Female-Headed Families: Relationships at Risk

Marcia R. Steinbock

SUMMARY. Homeless female-headed families are affected by national and local policies which impact adversely on the parent-child relationship. The first section of this article examines the ways in which national and state family welfare laws affect the parenting capacities of the single mother. Our legal system's response to domestic violence, the precipitating factor for roughly one-half of homeless women seeking shelter, is addressed in the second section. Once poverty and/or domestic violence catapult the single mother into homelessness, the children are often placed in foster care, especially if the mother has a substance abuse problem. The third section of this article focuses on the foster care system's response to family homelessness and maternal substance abuse, which is to place the children in foster care. Finally, implications for policy development, research and practice are discussed. Multidisciplinary family practitioners need to understand the macro-level policy issues which account for many of the micro-level problems within the female-headed family and which put the family relationships at risk. These professionals will then be in a better position to affect situations that contribute to and relate to the broader view and management of the homeless mother and her parenting capabilities.

Marcia R. Steinbock is affiliated with The Richard Stockton College of New Jersey, Pomona, NJ 08240.

[Haworth co-indexing entry note]: "Homeless Female-Headed Families: Relationships at Risk." Steinbock, Marcia R. Co-published simultaneously in *Marriage & Family Review* (The Haworth Press, Inc.) Vol. 20, No. 1/2, 1995, pp. 143-159; and: *Single Parent Families: Diversity, Myths and Realities* (ed: Shirley M. H. Hanson et al.) The Haworth Press, Inc., 1995, pp. 143-159. Multiple copies of this article/chapter may be purchased from The Haworth Document Delivery Center [1-800-3-HAWORTH; 9:00 a.m. - 5:00 p.m. (EST)].

KEYWORDS. Homeless, Women, Poverty, Family

INTRODUCTION AND BACKGROUND

Poor female-headed families throughout the nation are rapidly falling through the safety net and into homelessness. Although the overall poverty rate for families in 1990 was 7.8%, the poverty rate for female-headed families was 44.5%. The greatest incidence of poverty (56%), was found among African American female-headed households with children under eighteen years of age. These families are living at or below the 1990 poverty level of $10,419 for a family of three (U.S. Census, 1991). Because female-headed families comprise between 70% to 90% of homeless families nationwide (Bassuk, 1990), they are the focus of this article.

Not only are individual women affected by poverty and the subsequent loss of their homes, but their children are adversely affected as well. According to the literature, homeless children have a higher incidence of physical ailments, psychological disturbances, developmental delays and educational underachievement than do housed children. Lack of sufficient quantities and qualities of food for proper nutrition are two of the conditions most frequently documented by researchers (Rafferty & Shinn, 1991). Once homeless, the single-mother faces additional difficulties as her relationship with her child becomes public in the homeless shelter. Mothers lose their roles as nurturers, teachers, negotiators and survival guides to their children (Boxhill & Beaty, 1990). And yet, even these relationships which although less-than perfect are nonetheless parent-child relationships, are being further jeopardized by interconnected national policies resulting in foster placements for the children and the loss of family welfare benefits (Zorza, 1991).

The purpose of this article is to examine the mother-child relationship in the context of family homelessness by focusing on family welfare, domestic violence, foster care and substance abuse policies affecting the homeless mother and her parenting capabilities.

NATIONAL AND STATE FAMILY WELFARE POLICIES

Aid to Families with Dependent Children

Before homelessness became the identified problem of its current magnitude, Congress authorized a monetary entitlements program for the benefit of dependent children. Aid to Families with Dependent Children of

1935 (AFDC) was established during the Great Depression as part of the broad sweeping legislation under the Social Security Act. As an optional federal program, AFDC entitlements are administered by any state that chooses to participate. The explicitly stated policy of the Act is to enable children to remain in their home or in the home of relatives. Direct financial support is provided in order that the family members stabilize their lives and regain self-sufficiency. Yet, homeless shelters throughout the country report that many of their clients are receiving AFDC when they become homeless. Ninety-one percent of the homeless single parent families studied in Massachusetts (Bassuk, Rubin & Lauriat, 1986), 82% of the families studied in Los Angeles, California (Wood, Valdez, Hayashi & Shen, 1990) and 89% of the families in the Atlantic City, New Jersey study (Steinbock, in press) had income below the poverty line, despite the fact that they were receiving AFDC. When AFDC grant levels are 20% to 60% lower than typical urban rental rates (Burghardt & Fabricant, 1989), these families arrive at the shelter when they can no longer afford housing.

Fewer single parent families are qualifying for AFDC, while benefits for those who do qualify are inadequate. Three conditions regarding national welfare policies must be held accountable: the drastic reduction in AFDC grant levels, a punitive approach to families during the application process, and the vast discrepancies among states between their grant and need levels. All three areas will be addressed.

First, policies developed in the 1980s during the Reagan Administration slashed AFDC grants by administrative fiat. Restructuring eligibility determinants resulted in 370,000 to 507,000 families being terminated from AFDC (Burghardt & Fabricant, 1989). The 1990s are seeing a continuation of this policy trend as states are experiencing severe budgetary crises. AFDC benefits are the first to be reduced or held constant because, unlike other entitlement programs, AFDC does not reflect changes in the Consumer Price Index. A second condition which accounts for the increased poverty and resultant homelessness for single mothers is a one-sided Federal policy in which states are sanctioned for AFDC overpayments, but are not sanctioned for denying AFDC to eligible applicants (Casey & Mannix, 1989). As a result, two million eligible children and one million eligible women have AFDC benefits denied or terminated each year because of their alleged failure to adhere to procedural requirements (Bussiere, Freedman & Manning, 1991). Finally, as the third condition, state welfare agencies must determine both their state's economic need standard (the amount of income needed for a family of a given size to live at subsistence level) and their state's AFDC grant level. Even though the law does not even require that the grant level match the need level, it has been necessary for courts to enforce the minimal mandate that states establish a need level. As a result, for those remaining families who qualify for AFDC today, a substantial discrepancy exists between their grant and the income necessary to live, even at the poverty level.

In most states, the need standard exceeds the AFDC grant to such an extent that there is little relationship between the two figures (Solomon, 1991). Maximum AFDC benefits for a three-person family are currently below the need standard in 37 states. Furthermore, 38 states have maximum AFDC benefits which are below 75 percent of the 1990 Census Bureau poverty threshold of $10,419 a year for a family of three (Solomon, 1991). Although cost of living standards vary considerably among the states, the range in welfare benefits cannot be explained by cost of living differences alone. Political pressures for fiscal austerity coupled with the low prioritizing of social welfare programs could explain why states generally are resistant to increasing grant levels. For instance, benefits for a three-person family range from $120 in Mississippi to $891 in Alaska (Solomon, 1991). Although states are now required to reevaluate their need and grant standards at least once every three years, efforts to enforce a narrowing of the gap between these standards have been unsuccessful. On the Federal level, a 1991 bill introduced by Senator Daniel Patrick Moynihan would ensure that AFDC and food stamp benefits in all states be at least equal to 50% of the current poverty level. However, the bill has not been enacted. Until the Federal government legislates a policy providing for more equitable and uniform state benefits, single mothers will continue to slide into homelessness.

Because of these low entitlements as well as our national minimum wage, health care and child care policies, most AFDC mothers cannot afford to leave the welfare system. A single wage earner is not able to support a family on an hourly $5.05 minimum wage job which does not provide medical insurance, but which does create additional costs of transportation and child care. Yet, low wage jobs held predominantly by women are the projected area for employment growth in the 1990s (Hagen, 1992). Economic survival, not behavioral dependency, explains many single mothers' continuation on welfare. For those mothers and their children who do not become homeless while on AFDC, it is because they have learned to survive in spite of these national policies and not because they are superhuman money managers (Edin, 1991). Although the impoverished single mother is forced to choose welfare over a low paying job without benefits, the reality is that neither welfare nor the job can economically sustain the family.

The Family Support Act of 1988

In an effort to assist families in making the transition from welfare to work, The Family Support Act of 1988 (FSA) was enacted as the first major piece of Federal family welfare legislation in decades. One major component is Jobs Opportunities and Basic Skills Training Program (JOBS), a welfare-to-work program administered by the states and modeled after the New Jersey Realizing Economic Achievement Program (REACH). All AFDC recipients with children over the age of 3 years are required to participate. Although the program will be funded to 1.3 million dollars by 1995, it is criticized for being insensitive to the structure of the job market and employment availability. By relying on the private sector for the creation of jobs, program participants cannot be accommodated during recessionary times. An example of program inefficacy is seen in New Jersey. Over one third of the homeless mothers studied in Atlantic City were past participants in the prototype New Jersey REACH program (Steinbock, in press). None, however, had received a sufficient enough educational or employment boost to prevent their homelessness. Despite its good intentions, the available resources and programs are apparently ineffective in preventing homelessness.

Welfare policy further contributes to economic dependence and family instability by promoting a narrow definition of "family." By focusing on the admirable goals of collecting child support payments from the non-supporting father and discouraging the birth of children into poverty, the law creates categories of deserving and undeserving mothers. For example, a second major component of FSA establishes stricter enforcement of child support orders in an effort to remove AFDC recipients from the welfare rolls. States are now required to establish paternity, and automatic wage garnishments to collect support payments will be implemented by 1994. The implicit policy underlying the child support reforms is to promote the traditional two-parent family. However, a child support order can offer little economic assistance when the noncustodial parent is impoverished. In reality, the law often fosters divisive family relationships by pitting family members against one another and disrupting kinship ties (Hagen, 1992). The single, poor mother quickly learns that the only way her children will receive benefits is if their father is invisible. This creates a situation in which a child's relationship with both mother and father is at risk.

State AFDC Enactments

Another example of punitive welfare policy which creates categories of deserving and undeserving mothers is a recent approach to welfare law which could become a trend among the states. In 1992 New Jersey became the first state to pass legislation denying welfare benefits to children born after a family begins receiving AFDC, while at the same time not denying additional benefits to mothers who marry (Family Development Initiative Act, 1992). Subsequently, California was granted a waiver for a similar provision in their state AFDC law (Burke, 1992). Federal policy, by granting the necessary waivers for the New Jersey and California programs to be implemented, has encouraged other states to pass similar laws. For instance, Wisconsin, Michigan, Maryland, Oregon, Virginia and Ohio have been granted waivers for AFDC laws containing various punitive consequences for noncompliance (Burke, 1992). These policies may prompt women to enter into or to remain in destructive relationships in order to be categorized as a deserving mother in what the state recognizes as the only healthy family.

Emergency Assistance for Families

For those single mothers and their children who become homeless, the family may qualify for Emergency Assistance for Families (1982), (EAF), a provision of the AFDC statute. Although not a "homeless" program per se, EAF has become the major stop gap measure to shelter impoverished single parent families when all else fails. Motel or hotel accommodations, homeless shelters, payment of rent arrears to prevent eviction and provision of legal services are ways in which EAF funds can be used. Yet, only 28 states provide some form of shelter for homeless families under this optional program. Although Federal law stipulates that EAF may be given to a family only once during a twelve month period, the length of time that a family may stay in a shelter varies among the states. A 30 day limit on shelter stays has been recommended by the Department of Human Services but has not been implemented by Congress (Bussiere, 1991). Because of the current housing crisis discussed herein, it is critical that EAF shelter stays not be truncated by federal or state laws before significant changes in housing policy occur.

Many of our laws affecting family welfare policy are inadvertently causing single, poor mothers to become homeless. Economically marginal women who are the victims of domestic violence are also becoming homeless in great numbers. The parenting capabilities of these women need to be supported and not sabotaged by our family welfare legislation.

DOMESTIC VIOLENCE

Domestic violence is the precipitating factor for roughly one-half of homeless women and their children seeking shelter in Massachusetts, New

York, Oregon and Pennsylvania (Zorza, 1991). Moreover, it is impoverished women who are more likely to become homeless when they flee their abusers. However, since battered women's shelters are usually excluded from studies of the homeless, there has been an undercount of this population.

Even though judicial remedies for domestic violence have been developed by states within the past decade and forty-nine states have laws authorizing the ex parte eviction of spouse abusers from the home, judges generally do not enforce these provisions because of due process concerns. Furthermore, even when evictions do occur, the inadequate enforcement of protective orders forces women to choose homelessness over continued abuse. Ironically, the court's response frequently is to award custody to the batterer or to put the child in foster care, especially in cases alleging child sexual abuse by the batterer. Because most judges are men, it has been suggested that there is a judicial reluctance to believe that fathers sexually abuse their children (Zorza, 1991).

Federal law processes are beginning to address this concern, but may be missing the point. House Concurrent Resolution 172 (1990) urges states to create a statutory presumption against awarding custody to spouse abusers, which means that the abuser will have an enormous legal burden of proof to overcome before being awarded custody. Additionally, the Violence Against Women Act (1992) is pending before Congress. If passed, the Act would fund state judiciaries for educational programs concerning the impact of domestic violence on children. Research regarding the use of expert testimony in domestic violence prosecutions would also be funded. However, until federal policy protects the victims of spouse abuse and is tougher on spouse abusers, homeless female-headed families with children at risk of foster placement will continue to grow.

FOSTER CARE POLICIES

Background

Placing children in foster care has been the child welfare system's major response to family homelessness and substance abuse when the policy goals of AFDC fail. The conditions of poverty, homelessness and substance abuse are interpreted by state courts as dangerous living conditions and mothers are seen as per se negligent. The number of children in foster care nationwide has risen from 280,000 in 1986 to 430,000 in 1991 (Dugger, 1992). The impact on female-headed families is enormous, since foster care children are predominantly from poor families and poor families are predominantly female-headed (Pelton, 1989).

Inadequate housing was cited as the major reason for 30% of the foster care placements of Black children in five metropolitan areas (Allen, 1991), and an underlying factor in 42% of New Jersey foster placements (Zalkind, 1988). Foster care has also become the most likely alternative for children whose mothers are substance abusers, especially when the family is also homeless. According to the literature, homeless women with children have significantly higher rates of substance abuse than do housed women with dependent children (Robertson, 1991). As a result, the impact of foster care on these children is enormous. For many other children not in foster care, living with their extended family becomes a temporary alternative, as in the Atlantic City sample where 14% of the children were not living with their mothers and siblings at the shelter. These children were clearly at-risk of being removed from whatever fragile support system was currently sheltering them (Steinbock, in press). Moreover, there is a strong likelihood that foster children will become homeless in the future when they reach the age of eighteen and no longer qualify for foster care (Barden, 1990).

Homelessness and substance abuse, the two conditions which threaten family relationships and which most frequently cause the single mother and her children to be separated through foster placements, are now examined.

Policies Affecting Foster Care and Homelessness

Child welfare services are primarily the responsibility of state and local agencies. However, the federal government plays a critical role by providing funds which support an estimated 40% of total child welfare programs, primarily foster care, nationwide (Spar, 1992). The largest federal programs relating to child welfare are authorized under the Social Security Act and are contained in the 1980 Adoption Assistance and Child Welfare Act. Yet, it has been federal housing and homeless assistance programs such as the Cranston-Gonzalez National Affordable Housing Act of 1990 and the Stewart B. McKinney Homeless Assistance Amendments Act of 1990 that have dealt most directly with the linkages between foster care and homelessness. However, in the absence of full congressional funding for these programs, without a solid commitment on the state and local levels and without judicial support, there remains a significant gap between policy goals and benefits. Federal programs are not as effective as they could be due to the fact that funding is below authorized levels and the programs are implemented half-heartedly.

Federal housing policy traditionally favors the more affluent homeowner through subsidy programs. The drafters of the Affordable Housing Act tried to address this problem as they noted that 80% of all federal housing assistance goes as an entitlement to higher income homeowners through the mortgage interest and real estate tax deduction, while concurrently direct subsidies for low income families are funded at levels that serve less than one third of those eligible for benefits (U.S. Code, 1990). Two major provisions of the Act are responsive to these inequities. First, the Act creates a statutory housing preference for homeless families with children in, or at risk of, foster placement and for youth discharged from foster care with no place to return. These families are placed ahead of others on waiting lists for federally funded public housing. Second, the Section 8 Existing Housing Program, which provides rental vouchers to eligible families for private housing, has increased funding authorization to 35 million dollars. Specifically, families who are income eligible and are certified by the local child welfare agency as a family at risk of foster placement because of housing problems, could qualify for rental assistance.

Although well intended, the Affordable Housing Act does not compensate for the 25 billion dollars cut from federal housing programs over the past decade. Nor can it compensate for the 4.5 million affordable rental units lost through demolition or structural conversion (Foscarinis, 1991). Preferential treatment on waiting lists for public housing, therefore, is a pyrrhic victory. Once on the list, a family must wait a minimum of two years, and for families in New York City, the wait is 12 years (Foscarinis, 1992). Similarly, the newly created Section 8 Existing Housing Program is not meeting the overwhelming demand for subsidized private housing because there simply are not enough adequate and affordable rental housing units. Moreover, minorities and families with children are less likely to find landlords who will honor their rental vouchers (Savela, 1991).

Additionally, the Affordable Housing Act also mandates that local governments consult with child welfare agencies to develop housing assistance plans for families who face foster care because of inadequate housing. Although local public housing and child welfare agencies may be in a better position to identify families at risk, the Act gives these agencies too much discretionary power. Well intended programs frequently fall prey to ineptitude on the local level (Rimer, 1991). Finally, the Act provides that family eligibility for either public housing or Section 8 rental assistance should not be affected by the absence of a child from the home due to foster placement. For the single mother, this provision is critical.

Placement of a child in foster care can catapult the women into homelessness if, as a consequence, she disqualifies for AFDC and subsidized housing as well. Yet, a New York state appellate court has already held that shelter allowance for the family cannot continue indefinitely while a child is absent from the home due to a foster placement (Campfield v. Perales, 1991).

The Stewart B. McKinney Homeless Assistance Act of 1987, with special emphasis on families and children, was the first national legislation to address homelessness. Approximately $2.4 billion has been appropriated by the federal government since 1987 to fund state and local McKinney emergency food, shelter, housing, child welfare, health, nutrition, education and job training programs. However, severe deficits still exist among the homeless population in all substantive areas of concern addressed by the Act. Designed essentially as emergency relief, the Act cannot begin to address the intractable causes of homelessness. Moreover, it is not even meeting the demands of emergency relief for which it is intended (Foscarinis, 1991). As a result, family relationships continue to be eroded by these program deficits.

Realizing that foster placements can be prevented by maintaining parents and children together in their own homes through supportive services, Congress passed the Stewart B. McKinney Homeless Assistance Amendments Act of 1990. The Act authorizes the Department of Health and Human Services to make demonstration grants available to state and local child welfare agencies to encourage cooperation between their agencies and local housing programs. Strong coordination of services between housing and child welfare agencies is a policy goal. Indeed, it is far more expensive to keep a child in foster placement, in excess of $20,000 a year (Rimer, 1991), than it is to maintain the child in the family or to make suitable housing available. If funded, the $12.5 million authorization will support projects designed to prevent foster placements because of inadequate housing.

The federal Adoption Assistance and Child Welfare Act of 1980 (AACWA) embodies the federal framework for child welfare policy. Crisis intervention and foster care have been the traditional policy preferences of AACWA, while preventive services, focusing on alternatives to foster care have been underfunded. Repeated attempts to repeal the Act during the Reagan years sent a negative message to the states. Not until 1991 did funding even reach the 1980 level (Allen, 1991).

Despite current program deficits, the AACWA has been used in litigation, in addition to various state laws, in an effort to keep families together. The focus of these lawsuits has been an AACWA provision requiring states to submit a foster care plan to the Department of Health and Human Services providing that "reasonable efforts" are being made to prevent foster care placement. The "reasonable efforts" clause, child advocates argue, creates a state obligation to find suitable housing for a homeless or inadequately housed family in order to maintain family integrity. However, a recent United States Supreme Court case (Suter v. Artist M., 1992) held that the "reasonable efforts" clause does not create an enforceable right under the Act. Individual states may still establish a linkage between housing rights and foster care under state statutes or through broader interpretations of the AACWA. However, a combination of low income housing scarcity, public antipathy toward litigation and the federal judiciary's present interpretation of the Act suggest that this is unlikely. Until the AACWA makes a true policy shift away from foster care and more toward preventive services to maintain the family, the relationships between single mothers and their children will be at risk.

On a more positive note, the Family Preservation Act (1992) and the Child Welfare and Preventive Services Act (1991) are two significant bills being considered by Congress. Both bills would authorize funds for, amongst other programs, intensive family preservation services in the form of crisis intervention in the home and around the clock availability of social workers. An advisory committee to study the "reasonable efforts" requirement would also be established.

Although federal policy is trying to break the linkages between homelessness and foster care, these efforts cannot be effective until more affordable housing becomes available. Moreover, the homeless single mother who is a substance abuser stands little chance of retaining custody of her children, even if she seeks treatment for her addiction. Without a stronger policy shift to preventive services on the part of all federal legislation affecting single mothers and their children, foster placements will continue to tear family relationships asunder.

Policies Affecting Foster Care and Substance Abuse

The literature indicates that homeless women with dependent children have significantly higher rates of substance abuse than do housed women with dependent children (Robertson, 1991). In Los Angeles, for instance, 43% of the homeless mothers reported alcohol and drug usage compared to 30% of the housed mothers (Wood, Valdez, Hayashi, & Shen, 1990). Characteristically, substance abusing homeless mothers do not seek treatment for their problem. For instance, in the Atlantic City sample only 5 women were being treated although 40% answered "yes" when asked if they ever had a problem with substance abuse (Steinbock, in press). Policy responses to the substance abusing mother, ranging from child neglect proceedings to criminal prosecutions, may explain why treatment is not sought. For the poor single mother who is also a substance abuser, these policies determine whether or not she can provide a home for herself and her children.

An estimated 700,000 children nationwide are living with caretakers who are substance abusers. Additionally, the number of crack-exposed children born each year ranges from 325,000 to 375,000 (Bowen, Morris & Rivera, 1990-91). Legal precedents in states throughout the country are establishing maternal drug use as being per se negligent, much as courts have decided that homelessness is, in itself, negligent. Moreover, the presence of cocaine in a newborn infant's urine is generally prima facie evidence of child abuse. The most dramatic example of what happens to these newborns is the increasing number of "boarder babies": children under the age of two who remain unclaimed in hospitals. Child welfare laws in some states will not allow hospitals to release these babies to their mothers unless the hospitals are mandated to do so by local child welfare agencies. New York City, in particular, continues to experience a boarder baby crisis which cannot be absorbed by the foster care system (Bowen, Morris & Rivera, 1990-91).

No one will argue that a mother who is an active substance abuser can adequately care for her children. However, foster care may not be the optimal solution for the mother, the child or the family unit. Both mother and child fare better if they can remain together while the mother is being treated for her substance abuse problem. An example of a sensitive, multivariate approach to child placement evaluation, even when there is an ostensibly apparent case of child neglect, has been developed in Illinois. Assessment of the family by child welfare workers includes infant behavior and medical condition, lifestyle of the caregiver, family support system, environmental stability and the expedient linkage of the family to needed resources. An effort is made to keep the child with the mother whenever possible (Wightman, 1991).

Substance abuse programs that address the needs of women and their children are scarce. Even scarcer are programs that serve the pregnant or impoverished addicted woman. For instance, in New York City, 54% of the drug treatment programs refused to treat pregnant addicted women; 67% refused to treat pregnant addicts on Medicaid; and 87% denied treatment to pregnant women on Medicaid who were addicted to crack. Of those programs that did accept pregnant women, less than half had provisions for prenatal care and only 2 programs provided child care (Smith, 1990). One such program, Odyssey House in New York City, reports that twice as many women complete their residential drug treatment program as do mothers in programs where children are not in residence (Sabol, 1991). Successful treatment programs for addicted women and their children require a multidisciplinary approach including supportive services such as housing, public benefits, counseling and support groups. Both the Family Preservation Act (1992) and the Child Welfare and Preventive Services Act (1991) discussed herein would authorize funds to develop substance abuse treatment programs which would enable mothers to reside with their children.

Substance abuse, in itself, can cause family homelessness through drug-related evictions from public housing. An impoverished single mother risks losing her public housing if she or someone in her family or even an acquaintance is involved in the illegal use of drugs on her premises. A controversial provision of the Cranston-Gonzalez Affordable Housing Act (1990) provides that a public housing tenant may be evicted for any drug related criminal activity engaged in by the tenant, a member of the household or a guest. This has become a troublesome issue for attorneys in Legal Services offices throughout the country who traditionally represent tenants in eviction proceedings. In 1990, the national Legal Services Corporation in Washington, D.C. passed a resolution urging legal services programs not to represent clients in drug-related evictions. Additionally, the Department of Housing and Urban Development (HUD) is pressuring local housing authorities to enforce the national policy. Current legal efforts to defend clients facing eviction include attacks on procedural irregularities promulgated by the local housing authorities. Substantive defenses, such as lack of knowledge on the part of the tenant and lack of consent to the drug usage are also being raised in court cases (Young, 1991). Nobody wants to live in a drug-infested neighborhood. Yet, terminating a lease and creating family homelessness without offering any treatment options is a myopic approach to the problem.

CONCLUSION

Stabilization of the family in the family home is a primary goal of AFDC and child welfare laws. However, the discrepancies which exist between these policy goals and the reality of program implementation is enormous. A national philosophical approach to AFDC developed in the 1980s penalizes the poor single parent under the guise of federalism and the myth of empowerment.

The Family Support Act of 1988, though well-meaning, has been unresponsive, for the most part, to the educational, child care and employment needs of the single mother. Once the single mother and her children become homeless, the often strained relationships are at further risk of dissolution because of the daily survival demands being placed upon the family, which leave little time for relationship building. Moreover, barely one half of the states provide some form of shelter for the homeless family under the Federal Emergency Assistance for Families program.

Domestic violence is clearly disruptive to the mother-child relationship and is a major cause of homelessness for the poor single mother and her children. However, this issue is not yet being adequately addressed by our legal system. Domestic violence laws enacted within the past decade are being emasculated by judges who do not enforce eviction provisions and who are biased toward awarding child custody to the batterer.

Foster care policies continue to disrupt the fragile mother child relationship by characterizing homelessness and substance abuse as neglectful situations requiring foster placement of the children, when these conditions are, in fact, caused by abject poverty. By focusing on foster care as a remedy for these conditions rather than on family preservation as a goal, the major child welfare law (AACWA) is not aimed at ameliorating the conditions of poverty. Moreover, current laws designed to prevent foster placements due to homelessness are inadequately funded and cannot compensate for the lack of affordable housing. However, there is an emerging awareness of the need for interrelated housing and child welfare programs, such as those being supported by the McKinney Act. Hopefully, a policy shift from an incrementalist emergency mentality to a more comprehensive preventive strategy may be developing. The question then becomes, what degree of supportive services are we, as a society, willing to provide for these vulnerable families?

Family practitioners in all disciplines need to be aware of the macro level factors impacting homeless, single mothers and their children. Social workers and other family advocates can support legislation which reflects a humane policy towards women and their families and which concentrates on issues such as housing needs, day care and other supportive services.

Family researchers need to focus their studies more on neglected issues of gender and ethnicity. For instance, homeless battered women are traditionally excluded from homeless studies. Research is also needed on domestic violence laws which exclude gay couples from protection. Homeless single fathers needed to be studied, as well as the disproportionate impact of homelessness on the single African American mother. More research is also needed to document the number of foster placements which are precipitated by family homelessness and substance abuse. Perhaps then our policy makers will better understand the emotional costs to the family and the socio-economic costs to society when children are separated from their primary parent.

Educators need to immerse their students in the realities of single-parent homelessness by requiring, for example, that students volunteer in homeless shelters (Steinbock, 1992). Finally, clinicians in all disciplines who work with single parents need to understand the multiple layers of their clients' lives which may result in their diminished parenting capacity. If these multiple layers are not addressed, or at least acknowledged, the gulf between practitioner and client may be impossible to bridge.

REFERENCES

Adoption Assistance and Child Welfare Act of 1980, 42 U.S.C. 602 et seq. (1980).

Aid to Families with Dependent Children of 1935, 42 U.S.C. 601 (1935).

Allen, M. (1991). Creating a federal legislative framework for child welfare reform. *American Journal of Orthopsychiatry, 61*, 610-623.

Barden, J.C. (1990, October 28). Group says violations pervade capital foster care. *The New York Times*, p. 22.

Bassuk, E.L. (1990). Who are the homeless families? Characteristics of sheltered mothers and children. *Community Mental Health Journal, 26*, 425-434.

Bassuk, E.L., Rubin, L. & Lauriat, A.S. (1986). Characteristics of sheltered homeless families. *American Journal of Public Health, 76*, 1097-1101.

Bowen, J.S., Morris, M. & Rivera, J.M. (1990-91). The boarder baby and foster care crisis in New York City: Problems of policy and poverty. *Journal of Law and Health, 5*, 143-178.

Boxhill, N.A., & Beaty, A.L. (1990). Mother/child interaction among homeless women and their children in a public night shelter in Atlanta, Georgia. *Child and Youth Services, 14*, 49-64.

Burghardt, S. & Fabricant, M. (1989). *Working under the safety net: Policy and practice with the new American poor.* Newbury Park, California: Sage Publications.

Burke, V. (1992). Welfare. *Congressional Research Service*. (Order Code IB87007). Washington, D.C.: The Library of Congress.

Bussiere, A. (1991). New federal legislation addresses problems of homeless families. *Youth Law News*, 6-9.

Bussiere, A., Freedman, H., Manning, D., Mihaly, L. & Morales, J. (1991). Homeless women & children, *Clearinghouse Review*, 431-443.

Campfield v. Perales, 169 A.D. 2d 267 (N.Y.A.D. 1991).

Casey, T. & Mannix, M. (1989). Quality control in public assistance: Victimizing the poor through one-sided accountability. *Clearinghouse Review*, 1381-1389.

Child Welfare and Preventive Services Act of 1991, S.4.

Cranston-Gonzalez National Affordable Housing Act of 1990, 42 U.S.C. 12701 (1990).

Emergency Assistance for Families Act of 1982, 42 U.S.C. 606 (e) (1982).

Dugger, C. (1992, September 8). Troubled children flood ill-prepared care system. *The New York Times*, pp. 1, 7.

Edin, K. (1991). Surviving the welfare system: How AFDC recipients make ends meet in Chicago. *Social Problems, 38*, 462-473.

Family Development Initiative Act of 1992, N.J. Stat. Ann. 44:10-1 (1992).

Family Preservation Act of 1992, H.R. 3603.

Family Support Act of 1988, 42 U.S.C. 602 (1988).

Foscarinis, M. (1991). The politics of homelessness: A call to action. *American Psychologist, 46*, 1232-1238.

Foscarinis, M. (September 8, 1992). "Focus on that 12 year Waiting List for Public Housing," *The New York Times*, Section A, p. 18.

Hagen, J. (1992). Women, work and welfare: Is there a role for social work. *Social Work, 37*, 9-14.

House Concurrent Resolution 172, 101st Congress, 2nd Session (1990).

Pelton, L.H. (1989). *For reasons of poverty.* New York: Praeger.

Rafferty, Y. & Shinn, M. (1991). The impact of homelessness on children. *American Psychologist, 46*, 1171-1176.

Rimer, S. (1991, January 15). Drugs, then bureaucracy, divide mother and children. *The New York Times*, pp. 1, 2.

Robertson, M.J. (1991). Homeless women with children: The role of alcohol and other drug abuse. *American Psychologist, 46*, 1198-1204.

Sabol, B. (1991). The urban child. *Journal of Health Care for the Poor and Underserved, 2*, 59-73.

Savela, E. (1991). Homelessness and the affordable housing shortage: What is to be done. *Law & Equity, 9*, 279-314.

Smith, B.V. (1990). Improving substance abuse treatment for women. *Clearinghouse Review*, 490-492.

Solomon, C.D. (1991). AFDC: Need standards, payment standards and maximum benefits. Congressional Research Service.

Spar, K. (1992). Child welfare: A summary comparison of house and senate bills. *Congressional Research Service* (92-652 EPW). Washington, D.C.: The Library of Congress.

Steinbock, M. (in press). Women and children first: The faces of family homelessness nationwide and in Atlantic City, New Jersey. *Seton Hall Journal of Family Law and Society.*

Steinbock, M. (1992). From the trenched in the Field: Serious Observations on the Lighter Side. *Experiential Education, 17*, 2-3.

Stewart B. McKinney Homeless Assistance Act of 1987, 42 U.S.C. 11431 (1987).

Stewart B. McKinney Homeless Assistance Amendments Act of 1990, 42 U.S.C. 11431 (1990).

Suter v. Artist, M. 112 S.Ct. 1360 (1992).

The Emergency Assistance Act 42 U.S.C. 607.

U.S. Bureau of the Census. (1991). Current population reports, poverty in the United States: 1990.

U.S. Code Congressional and Administrative News. (1990). p. 5763.

Violence Against Women Act of 1992, H.R. 1502.

Wightman, M. (1991). Criteria for placement decisions with cocaine-exposed infants. *Child Welfare, 6*, 653-663.

Wood, D., Valdez, R.B., Hayashi, T. & Shen, A. (1990). Homeless and housed families in Los Angeles: A study comparing demographic, economic and family function characteristics. *American Journal of Public Health, 80*, 1049-1052.

Young, K.Y. (1991). Handling a drug-related eviction from public housing. *Clearinghouse Review*, 793-797.

Zalkind, C. (1988). *Splintered lives: A report on decision making for children in foster care*. Association for Children of New Jersey.

Zorza, J. (1991). Woman battering: A major cause of homelessness. *Clearinghouse Review*, 421-429.

Chapter 8

Single Parenthood and the Law

Lynda Henley Walters
Carla Rae Abshire

SUMMARY. Laws that affect single parents are focused on the continuing relationship of parent and child following the dissolution of marriage; increasingly the same laws are being applied to never-married parents. Although most laws affecting family relationships are state statutes, communication among states and accumulated case law have resulted in similarities in family laws across state jurisdictions. Drawing on social scientists, legal commentators, and appellate opinions, the status of laws and experiences of parents in the areas of child custody, child support, tax law, and court involvement in welfare reform are reviewed. A pervasive theme throughout is gender discrimination, a problem that exists more in the legal environment than in law. It is suggested that if the best interests of children are to be served, it will be necessary to resolve conflicting feelings and beliefs, set aside myths and stereotypes, and promote the development of competence and equality for parents.

KEYWORDS. Single parents, Law, Child custody, Child support, Taxes, Welfare reform

With few exceptions, laws that affect single parents are focused on the continuing relationship of parent and child following the dissolution of

---

Lynda Henley Walters and Carla Rae Abshire are affiliated with the Department of Child and Family Development, The University of Georgia.

[Haworth co-indexing entry note]: "Single Parenthood and the Law." Walters, Lynda Henley, and Carla Rae Abshire. Co-published simultaneously in *Marriage & Family Review* (The Haworth Press, Inc.) Vol. 20, No. 1/2, 1995, pp. 161-188; and: *Single Parent Families: Diversity, Myths and Realities* (ed: Shirley M. H. Hanson et al.) The Haworth Press, Inc., 1995, pp. 161-188. Multiple copies of this article/chapter may be purchased from The Haworth Document Delivery Center [1-800-3-HAWORTH; 9:00 a.m. - 5:00 p.m. (EST)].

marriage; both custodial and noncustodial parents are affected. Although never-married parents come under these laws, most laws were developed with reference to formerly-married single parents. However, with the increase in the number of never-married parents, application of laws will increasingly involve never-married, single parent families.

Most single parents are female (see Bianchi chapter in this volume) who have, historically, faced discrimination in the law (Kanowitz, 1969; "Sex Discrimination," 1950) and in the legal environment (Johnston & Knapp, 1971). Important to the examination of law and single parenthood are the consequences of discrimination. It is true that with the revisions of domestic relations laws in most states, laws have become more gender neutral; however, the legal environment in which laws are applied is not gender neutral. According to Schafran (1988, p. 39), when a woman goes to court she has "three strikes against her: she is a woman, she lacks the resources to retain adequate counsel, and her issues are those with which the legal system would prefer not to deal." Task forces appointed by the supreme courts of both New Jersey and New York (see Schafran, 1987, for overview of these task force reports) have confirmed that although law reform efforts have resulted in a gender-neutral statutory framework for divorce, in practice women continue to be disadvantaged by courts. Indeed, according to Lonsdorf (1989), many women are disadvantaged in negotiations before they ever reach court. Although single fathers also encounter discrimination in courts (McCant, 1987; Weitzman & Dixon, 1979), they do so far less frequently and to less extent than women.

In order to gain perspective on the context in which laws affecting single parents have been developed and are applied, some of the myths about women and biases against women in courts are reviewed. Then, following a brief comment on the historical development of domestic relations law, of child custody, child support, tax, and welfare law are considered. Child custody is reviewed with attention to factors that affect custody decisions; these are highly complex issues involving married, formerly-married, and never-married parents.[1] Child support issues are reviewed with attention to reasons for modification and termination and to efforts to enforce support obligations. Because of importance to single parents, developments in the area of tax law are briefly reviewed. Finally, noting that many single-mother families fall below the poverty threshold and considering that welfare statutes and regulations may have the most direct effect of any laws on poor, never-married, single-mother families, the role of courts in shaping welfare policy is reviewed.

LEGAL CONTEXT OF DECISIONS AFFECTING SINGLE PARENTS

More people who live in female-headed households live below the poverty level than any other group (Harrington, 1984; Lugaila, 1992). In female-headed families, median family income was below the poverty threshold and it was less than 58% of the median income in husband-wife families in 1990 (Lugaila, 1992). Approximately 69% of all mother-only families with children under 18 receive means tested assistance (U.S. Bureau of the Census, 1992).

Considering these data and the social problems associated with poverty, it is readily understandable that single parent families are often thought to represent some form of social pathology. This is not a presumption that has evolved in recent years, but dates back prior to the 17th century when even widows with children, if they received public help, were treated punitively and with concern for the kind of moral influence they might have on a community–and there was more sympathy for widows than for divorced, abandoned, or never-married mothers (Kamerman & Kahn, 1988)! In a system where poverty has historically been considered a moral issue and women have been considered legally incompetent, derogatory myths about single mothers should not be unexpected. Reviews of some of the widely-held myths that, in part, have shaped the legal environment can be found in Mulroy (1988), Weisberg (1982), and the New York Task Force on Women in the Courts ("Report of the New York Task Force," 1987).

Examples of myths include the belief that women who are alone have made themselves undesirable to men–especially if they are divorced. If they have never married but have children, they have what they deserve. When they have sought child support that had been awarded but not paid, they have been told by judges that they were vindictive, money-grubbing, and that they had made their beds and must now lie in them ("Report of the New York Task Force," 1987). It is generally believed that if a woman works hard, she will not be in poverty; if she turns to welfare, she is lazy and therefore unworthy. If families headed by women live in substandard housing in central city neighborhoods, it is because it is their choice–perhaps motivated by fear of the unknown or perhaps by choosing to be with people like themselves. Finally, one of the most powerful myths is that women can improve their situation if they want to and work hard enough.

Biases in Courts

Along with cultural and societal myths, bias toward women in courts is also caused by the fact that women have not always been considered legally competent. Women have been thought to deserve the protection of the law, but not as a constitutional right; furthermore, protection has been defined from a male perspective. When women have lived up to the male image of womanhood, they have been more likely to be protected (Weisberg, 1982). Indeed, the Equal Protection Clause of the Fourteenth Amendment was not thought to apply to women (Ginsberg, 1978; Johnston & Knapp, 1971); however, in 1971 (*Reed v. Reed*) the Supreme Court interpreted the Amendment to apply to both men and women. It was not until 1979 (*Orr v. Orr*) that it was interpreted to apply to gender discrimination in family relationships.

Still, many judges have difficulty overcoming the myths they have long accepted. For example, in September, 1992, the *Atlanta Journal Constitution* carried a full page story about a judge in North Carolina who had put a woman in jail because she could only pay $55 of the $60 court costs when she filed a petition to require her former husband to pay child support. This judge was described by friends as a pillar of the community, "a nice fellow, one of the few who would have stopped to help the woman at the well." It was not until one woman was murdered by a man the judge had found not guilty of beating her and a young reporter took the story of abuse and outrageous treatment in the court to the newspaper, that the judge reexamined his views. To his credit he apologized to two of the women who had been treated poorly in his court and set up a separate court to hear domestic violence cases. This judge appears to differ from many other judges primarily in his willingness to admit his mistake; the local bar was "astonished" that he admitted he was wrong.

In another forum, a blue-ribbon panel reported to the New York state chief judge that "Women are often denied equal justice, equal treatment and equal opportunity" ("Report of the New York Task Force," 1987, p. 17). For example, it is widely known that child support payments are not made at an acceptable rate.[2] Not only are child support awards not paid (a problem of law enforcement rather than law-making or interpretation), the amount of awards is low (see for example, "The First Year Report," 1986). Fathers rarely pay more than one-third of their incomes, and with little scrutiny, what fathers say they can pay is often accepted by courts (Weitzman, 1985; Yee, 1979). Indeed, family courts have been accused of making women feel that attempts to gain support for children from fathers is "vindictive, unimportant or even a joke" ("Report of the New York Task Force," 1987, p. 86).

Men, too, face some biases in courts, especially in terms of child custody. Even with the move away from the maternal preference for custody, many courts still view the best interest of children to be with a mother who is "naturally" better able to nurture them.[3] However, considered case by case, stereotyped gender-based expectations for men appear to be balanced by an inclination for male judges to understand and sympathize with the situation of another male–something that is most unlikely to happen in the response of a male judge to a woman (see Johnston & Knapp, 1971). It would be unwise for a single mother seeking custody to count on the maternal preference. For example, if a woman does not work and stays at home where she can maximize her nurturing function, she and her child usually must live in poverty because it is rare for a court to award enough child and spousal support to relieve her of the need to work. On the other hand, if she seeks employment, the bias of the court shifts to favor the male, especially if he has remarried and the child could live with the father and a mother figure. In other words, the maternal presumption is easily overcome or inapplicable if the mother is employed outside the home (Raymond, 1988). For women seeking custody, the maternal preference is balanced by traditional stereotypes and myths about women and poverty.

PERSPECTIVE ON DOMESTIC RELATIONS LAW

The law of domestic relations as it relates to child custody and child support has changed significantly throughout this century. It was developed from state statutory and common law. In creating statutes and deciding cases, legislatures and courts have reviewed other state laws and have considered decisions in other state courts as precedent for their own actions. These efforts have culminated into what is now viewed as a national tradition of the law of domestic relations (Schuele, 1988-89). There are still differences between and among jurisdictions, but there are also national trends that cut across jurisdictions.

Although the "best interests of the child" has been adopted in the United States as the standard by which custody determinations are made, remnants of the Roman and English common law view of children as chattel were influential on the development of the law, especially as it relates to child support. For example, the notion that children were property of the father gave the father certain rights and responsibilities, including the right to services and custody of his children, which led to the responsibility or duty to support his children. Child support has not always, however, been considered a legally enforceable duty of the parent or right of the child. Whereas child custody has been considered in terms of the best interests of the child, child support has been considered in terms of contract law or in terms of a community's interest in keeping citizens from becoming a public charge (Schuele, 1988-89). Even the child support enforcement program that was initiated in 1950 was motivated primarily out of a desire to keep families from becoming dependents of the state (Anders, 1990; Fleece, 1981-82). As would be expected, laws of custody and laws of support although related, affect single parents differently.

CHILD CUSTODY

Most state statutes give courts considerable discretion in making custody determinations. Many would-be custody battles are settled by agreement of the parties before the case reaches the courtroom (Ellman et al., 1991; Mnookin, 1978), but the court, not the parties, decides whether the agreement is in the child's best interests. Even if the court accepts an agreement made by divorcing parents, it is free to reopen the case if a change in circumstances warrants reconsideration. This rule may be viewed as one which greatly limits parental power (Mnookin, 1978). However, the propensity of courts to rubberstamp these agreements may exacerbate a situation in which one parent has little bargaining power. For example, the parent most emotionally involved with the child (usually the mother) may be willing to accept less child support and other monetary or property awards as a result of threats from the other parent (usually the father) to sue for sole custody (Lonsdorf, 1989; and see, for example, the opinion of the Court in *Garska*, 1981).

With extensive judicial discretion, it is difficult to avoid interjecting personal values and opinions in custody and visitation decisions (Neeley, 1984; Uviller, 1978). These decisions require judgments regarding the characteristics of all persons involved in the case as well as consideration of the facts. As a rule, any circumstance relevant to the best interests of the child is admissible–even past behaviors of parents. Adding to the difficulty of courts to be fair, state statutes that enumerate circumstances relevant to the child's best interests generally do not include the weight to be given to each factor in making the custody determination (Wadlington, Whitebread, & Davis, 1983).

Because of the continuing inclination to view mother-custody as best for children, fathers can be at a disadvantage in obtaining custody and visitation. Weitzman and Dixon (1979) found, however, that by 1977, two-thirds of fathers who requested it were awarded custody in California courts. In contrast, according to Albert and Brodek (1989), courts are insensitive to noncustodial fathers who wish to continue a relationship with their children and to those fathers who are frustrated in their efforts to relate to their children. They report that when one man requested maximum visitation with his children, the judge became exasperated and belittled fathers who seek more time with their children.

Additional influences on custody decisions, including putative fathers, mobility, sexual behavior, religious practices, and race, are reviewed below. Both custodial and noncustodial single parents are considered.

Putative Fathers

A series of Supreme Court cases in the 70s and 80s defined the unwed, or putative, father's relationship with his child as the basis of a *liberty interest*. (A liberty interest is not exactly a right but it is similar in that it has been granted constitutional protection.) This liberty interest is thought to arise from belief in the importance of the family unit; it is primarily a function of relationship rather than biological kinship.

The importance of a putative father's relationship with his child as compared to the importance of biological kinship is addressed in what is known as the Stanley line of cases: *Stanley* (1972), *Quillion* (1978), *Caban* (1979), and *Lehr* (1983). In this line of cases, the United States Supreme Court held that (a) biological kinship provides an opportunity for the putative father to develop a relationship with his child; (b) the nature of the relationship between the putative father and his child may give rise to a liberty interest in the relationship; and (c) the liberty interest gives rise to the constitutionally protected right to assert paternity.

Although decisions in the Stanley line of cases emphasized the importance of the psychological relationship, a more recent case (*Michael H.*, 1989) demonstrates that the liberty interest will not always prevail. In this case, a child was born to a woman who was married to a man other than the biological father, and the plurality opinion was that the notion of a protectable liberty interest growing out of the father-child relationship is irrelevant. Instead, the Court relied on the specific tradition of the marital presumption and held that the rights of a putative father are subordinate to the state's interest in protecting the integrity of the marital unit. Only in one concurring opinion and two dissenting opinions was this father's relationship with his child considered in light of the Stanley line of cases. Thus, in *Michael H.*, the last case decided by the Supreme Court, the Stanley line of cases was essentially ignored and the more conservative position of the marital presumption (which had not been addressed in the previous cases) held.

Although the unwed father may be denied the right to gain custody, to visit, or to stop an adoption proceeding, especially if the mother is married to another man, an illegitimate child is entitled to support from the biological father (*Gomez*, 1973). Thus, the state or the mother (whether or not married to another man; see *Smith v. Cole*, 1989) may bring an action to obtain support for a child. For excellent analyses of this issue see Anders,

1990; Batty, 1990; Kishardt, 1991; Solari, 1989; Sylvain, 1990; and Wintjen, 1990.

Mobility of the Single Custodial Parent

The standards applied to cases involving the relocation of a parent outside the jurisdiction in which a custody decree exists varies by jurisdiction. Requirements in different states range from allowing the custodial parent to move for any reason so long as the noncustodial parent does not prove that the move is adverse to the child's best interest (Minnesota) to requiring the custodial parent to show exceptional circumstances in order to obtain permission to move (New York). In many states, only a challenge by the noncustodial parent will require the custodial parent to provide a reason for moving. In a recent decision (*Seessel*, 1988), the Tennessee Supreme Court ruled that the custodial parent could not move without showing that the move was in the best interest of the child; in this case, problems associated with remarriage, career, and the welfare of the family were ignored (Gooch, 1989).

Indeed, many times the custodial parent's desire/need to move to another state is pitted against the desire to retain custody. This may be particularly true for women because courts tend to be more demanding of sacrifice for the sake of children from mothers and question a woman's pursuit of a career (Ellman et al., 1991; Weitzman & Dixon, 1979). An illustration of the restrictiveness of courts toward women is found in *Lozinak* (1990) where the appellate court forced a mother to choose between retaining custody of her daughter or moving to another state with her new husband. In doing so, the court stated that if the mother were really concerned with the child's best interests, as opposed to her own interests, then she would remain in the initial state. Because women are expected to move with a husband, if a woman remarries, restriction of mobility can create a conflict between two deeply held values: the best interest of her child and commitment to her husband.

In the past, if dissatisfied with a custody decision, a parent could move with a child to another state and bring an action for custody. Although not condoned, "forum shopping," as this practice has been called, was possible because jurisdiction rules have not been applied in custody cases as they have in other cases (Bodenheiner & Neeley-Kvarme, 1979). However, parents are finding this practice less viable today.

To address problems of jurisdiction in custody cases, the Uniform Child Custody Jurisdiction Act (UCCJA) was designed as a model to shift the focus from jurisdiction over the parent to the needs of the child. The purposes were to reduce chaos created by interstate jurisdictional competition and to promote cooperation between jurisdictions, as well as to promote the stable environment that most consider to be in a child's best interests. Through the concept of continuing jurisdiction, the act forbids the modification of a child custody decree in one state when the original decree was issued in another state which still has jurisdiction over the case (Schorsch, 1982). The model act is said to have partially laid aside the confusion created by *Halvey* (1947) in which the Supreme Court held that in order to protect the best interests of the child, a court in one state could modify a custody decree from another state. Although most states have adopted the principles in the UCCJA, the issues are complicated and there are still many problems. For an excellent review of the application of and problems with UCCJA see Coombs (1982).

Sexual Behavior of Custodial Parents

As has been seen, courts tend to be biased in favor of traditional assumptions about family life and the roles of men and women. Such biases may be best illustrated in disputes involving the sexual behavior of parents. It should be noted at the outset that jeopardy to custody because of a nonmarital sexual relationship is a greater problem for women than for men (see Sack, 1992, note 65; and Woods, Been, & Schulman, 1983).

Whether the parent is involved in a nonmarital heterosexual or homosexual relationship, the court may grant custody on the condition that the parent not live with certain persons or even that the parent terminate certain relationships. The court may require that a juvenile authority supervise the parent's behavior, may require a change of the parent's conduct, or may prohibit the parent from participating in overnight stays with certain persons–all of which is done in order to insulate the child from behavior considered inappropriate by the court (Allen, 1985). Although courts at all levels may let their views of appropriate behaviors influence custody decisions, these biases appear to be most prevalent at the trial court level. Sack (1992) has provided a review of West Virginia cases involving sexual behaviors of parents in which lower courts denied custody to mothers (primary caretakers) and appellate courts reversed the decision because the mother's sexual relationship was unrelated to her relationship with the child and her fitness as a parent.

Homosexual parents have a more difficult time than heterosexual parents. Where actual harm to the child is presumed, courts will generally prohibit the custodial parent from overnight visitation with lovers (Ellman et al., 1991). Among other things, this indicates that courts are reluctant to expand the definition of family in visitation and custody disputes to reflect trends in the makeup of the American family. For example, in *Allison D.* (1991), a New York court refused visitation rights to a lesbian ex-partner with the biological mother of the child because the statute in question only applied to biological parents. The biological mother had been artificially inseminated, and the lesbian ex-partner had acted as the child's parent during the relationship; after the relationship was terminated, she had provided financial support for the child. The New York Court of Appeals affirmed the lower court, stating that the ex-partner had no standing to bring a petition for visitation ("Family Law," 1992). (When the issues do not involve custody, courts have not been quite so reluctant to consider homosexual unions a family; see for example, *Braschi*, 1989.)

It is common for courts to worry that a homosexual parent will influence a child's sexual orientation even though the evidence clearly indicates this is not a problem. Courts may be concerned that others will harass a child whose parent is homosexual, or may conclude that a homosexual parent is unacceptable because the behavior is in violation of sodomy statutes. The degree of limitation on personal behavior/freedom of parents varies according to the court's beliefs about and knowledge of sexuality ("Sexual Orientation," 1990).

Cohabitation is another situation in which presumed sexual behavior can cause difficulty with custody decisions. A disgruntled spouse may use the traditional assumptions of the court to manipulate and control the behavior of the other spouse. For example, in *Parrillo* (1989), in response to the mother's motion for modification of custody, the father also filed a petition to modify custody. He did not seek custody of his children, but sought to have the mother cease relations with her boyfriend (Carter, 1991). The custodial parent (mother) had sought modification of a custody decree in order to establish specific times at which the noncustodial parent (father) could visit their children. Apparently, the father had not only refused to pay the amount of child support stipulated in the divorce decree, he had also crashed his car into the mother's boyfriend's car and had threatened the family. The trial court, without specific findings of harm to the children, stated that overnight visitations by the mother's boyfriend were not conducive to the children's well-being, but that if the mother were to marry the boyfriend there would be no issue. The Supreme Court of Rhode Island upheld the trial court's decision to modify the custody provision which, in effect, restrained the mother from having overnight visits with her boyfriend. Not only did this court extend the definition of cohabitation to include sexual relations (Knauerhase, 1989), but also, in effect, it allowed an ex-spouse to control the sexual behavior of the custodial parent (Carter, 1991). This decision forced the custodial parent to choose between two constitutional rights, freedom of association and personal privacy from unwarranted governmental intrusion. Although the United States Supreme Court has expressly provided that the government cannot force an individual to choose between two constitutionally guaranteed rights (*Aptheker*, 1964; Knauerhase, 1989), in custody cases, it is the child's best interests, not the parents interests, that are the issue.

Religious Practices

When religious practices of parents are thought to jeopardize the mental health or physical safety of a child, they can be a determining factor in a custody decision. In *Hadeen* (1980), the mother's religious practices included fasting and spanking until the will of a child is broken. The trial court awarded custody to the father, but, on appeal, the court specifically considered whether the religious practices of the mother constituted reasonable likelihood that the child would be impaired. The appellate court reversed and remanded the case for further consideration by the trial court in order to ensure that the trial court had not put too much weight on the religious factor (Ellman et al., 1991). Justice Dore, dissenting, disagreed with the reversal, stating that the facts of the case indicated that the children were in jeopardy. One compelling incident reported in testimony was of Mrs. Hadeen spanking one child for two hours while her other children held the child down (*In re Marriage of Hadeen*, 1980).

In addition to noting that religion is a thorny issue in custody disputes (see for example, Beschle, 1989; Paul, 1989; and "The Establishment Clause," 1984), it is important to recognize that the religious interests of parents are more often seen as commensurate with the best interests of children–even when children are directly affected and hurt (*Hadeen*, 1990)–than are the relationship interests of parents–even if children are neither directly affected nor hurt (recall *Parrillo*, 1989). In *Hadeen*, the court appeared to be more concerned with protecting Mrs. Hadeen's right to freedom of religious practices than with protecting the best interests of the children. In neither of these cases (*Hadeen* and *Parrillo*) was attention clearly focused on the children. Taken together, the cases seem to say that it is not really the effect on children but the values of courts that ultimately determine the outcome. Contrasting outcomes in *Hadeen* and *Parrillo*, it appears to be more acceptable to discipline a child in a manner that constitutes child abuse than to have relationships with members of the same or opposite sex, regardless of whether the nature of the relationship is known by the children or whether the relationship can be shown to be harmful to the children.

Interracial Relationships

Another issue that has been specifically addressed by courts in custody determinations is interracial relationships. Because of the civil rights movement, issues of race are more protected by equal rights legislation and less vulnerable to biases of the court than issues of moral unfitness and sexual behavior of a parent (Johnston & Knapp, 1971). Race was the issue in a recent case before the United States Supreme Court (*Palmore*, 1984) in which the custodial parent was cohabiting with a member of another race. The Court held that, although actual harm sustained by the child due to prejudices of the community may be an appropriate factor to consider in a custody decision, the potential harm of a mixed-race relationship to the child is not a permissible factor to be considered (Ellman et al., 1991). There is both greater clarity in the law and greater sensitivity on the part of judges for handling issues of race than of sexuality; consider this decision in contrast to those where the focus is on sexuality (e.g., *Allison D.*, 1991, and *Parrillo*, 1989).

Although laws governing the parent-child relationship of single parents are not specific to race or ethnicity, minority parents can be expected to have more difficulty in courts than do white parents–especially if they are poor. Minority, low-income women face the greatest difficulty in our legal system. Their problems may be similar to those of other single parents, but it is more difficult for them to obtain qualified legal representation and they are not received well in courts (Schafran, 1988) even though race *per se* will not be an issue.

Joint Custody

Joint custody arrangements have become increasingly popular. Joint legal custody, as opposed to joint physical custody, generally connotes a situation in which the parents share equal responsibilities in child rearing; it is generally not tied to the amount of time that a child is in the presence of one or the other parent (Mnookin, 1978; Wishnew, 1988). The joint custody arrangement has its roots in concern for the best interests of the child (Wishnew, 1988); however, there are still many arguments for and against joint custody (see Folberg, 1991, and Sack, 1992, for reviews of issues and arguments). Joint custody is necessarily a complex arrangement, and partly because of the individual circumstances in each case, there is little agreement on the best policies to be followed (Kass, 1989).

It is interesting that despite the fact that the success of joint custody arrangements is predicated on the willingness of parents to work together, some jurisdictions allow joint custody over the objection of a parent. Some courts feel so strongly about the importance of both parents being involved with the child(ren) that spousal attitudes toward each other can influence custody decisions. Insistence that both parents have access to a child may be warranted in most cases, but where there is a history of family violence or harassment, a parent's objection to an award of joint custody should not prejudice the court (Keenan, 1985). Although there are cases in which a court has ruled that a parent's good faith objection to joint custody should not prejudice a request for sole custody (see for example, *In re Marriage of Weidner*, 1983), one can imagine a situation in which a battered spouse has no specific proof to present to the court in support of a request for sole custody (see Sack, 1992, pp. 311-316; and see Ashe, 1992, for an interesting discussion of the "bad mother").

Additionally, joint custody arrangements may result in reduction in the allowance or in no allowance for child support. In her essays about child custody, Judge Kass has noted that it is not only unfair but also illogical to place equal financial responsibility on parents who are not equivalent in terms of financial resources (Kass, 1989).

CHILD SUPPORT

Regardless of financial resources, parents have a legal duty during and after marriage to support children below the age of majority (i.e., legal age), including those born outside of wedlock. Post-divorce support of children is intended to maintain the marital standard of living. Amount of support required is based on current needs; therefore, it is modifiable if there has been a change in circumstances that warrants reconsideration.

Almost all states have laws that hold mothers and fathers equally responsible for child support (Ellman et al., 1991; Mnookin, 1978; see also 67A C.J.S., 1978). Likewise, most recent court decisions have interpreted the Fourteenth Amendment or state equal rights amendments to require gender-neutral support statutes ("*Constitutionality of Gender-Based Classifications*," 1982). However, gender neutral statutes that essentially eliminate the father's primary duty to support have received some criticism. Not only does level of living improve for men and get worse for women after divorce (Hoffman & Holmes, 1975; Phillip Morris Family Survey, 1987, p. 11; Weitzman, 1985; see especially Sørensen, 1992), Bregande (1989) has noted that, because the custodial parent bears the primary responsibility for the care of children, earning potential often must be sacrificed whereas the noncustodial parent gains earning potential as a result of not having responsibility for the day-to-day care of children. Because the majority of custodial parents are women, and women generally earn less than men, it is the woman who will, *proportionately*, contribute most to the financial support of children.

It is ironic that, in the face of an established parental duty to support, the early courts looked to the custodial parent's financial stability rather than considering the noncustodial parent's duty to support (Schuele, 1988-89). Today some courts are unwilling to increase child support if the increase would improve the custodial parent's standard of living along with the child's. At the same time, even though a court may be reluctant to award enough support for a mother to stay home or obtain excellent care for children, the same court may question whether a working mother should get and/or retain custody (Raymond, 1988).

Modification of Support

There are a number of circumstances under which modifications are made. Examples include a reduction in the income of the supporting parent (however, this is rarely effective even if the supporting parent has been incarcerated; see *Rohloff*, 1987; *Knights*, 1988; *Koch*, 1990) or either a formal or informal agreement to a reduction (see also 67A C.J.S., 1978 §§51-58; Krause, 1977; Lieberman, 1986).

Ordinarily only modifications of future obligations are allowed, but when a parent has requested that the obligation be reduced and has not been able to pay at the current level, retroactive modifications have been made. The problem is that some noncustodial parents have made reduced payments expecting that if the custodial parent seeks enforcement of the original support obligation, it would be possible to get a retroactive reduction (see for example, *Towne*, 1988). Although it is clearly possible in some cases, retroactive reduction of arrearages in child support are prohibited by federal law if the custodial parent receives funds from Aid to Families with Dependent Children (42 U.S.C.A. §666(a)(9)(c), 1990).

Termination of Support

There are several reasons why support may be terminated before a child reaches the age of majority. In some states if the supporting parent dies, support is terminated, but in some, death does not result in automatic termination: inheritance and life insurance are used to continue support (see *In re North Carolina Inheritance Taxes*, 1981). Another reason for terminating support is the emancipation of the minor child; that is, the child is accorded legal status before reaching the age of majority. Examples include marriage, entry into military service, leaving the parent's home and refusing to follow parent's wishes, or becoming economically independent through employment (see Gottesfeld, 1981, for a discussion of emancipation issues). Adoption by a parent who replaces the supporting parent is also a possible reason for termination of a support obligation.

It is also possible for support obligations to be terminated if visitation by the supporting, noncustodial parent is denied. It is commonly thought that the reason why men refuse to pay child support is that they are denied opportunity to visit their children. Although Weitzman (1985) found no correlation between child support compliance and complaints about visitation, some courts have interpreted visitation and support decrees as mutually dependent contracts. Indeed, according to spring 1990 data, when visitation privileges or joint custody were awarded to fathers, almost 80% of mothers were awarded child support, but when neither visitation privileges nor joint custody were awarded to fathers, only about 30% of mothers were awarded child support (U.S. Bureau of the Census, 1992a). In cases where a child has refused to see the custodial parent, courts have terminated support (*Tyrrell*, 1978; *Cohen*, 1983). Also, in extreme cases, such as concealment of the child by the mother, some courts have refused to make fathers pay unpaid support maintaining that concealment is a waiver of support (*Washington*, 1987) even though the child or spouse has been abused by the father (Clark, 1990; Ellman et al., 1991).

Czapanski (1989) maintained that rules that link child support and visitation and those that do not are inherently biased. When support and visitation are linked, the child and custodial parent's need for financial support may be subordinated to the noncustodial parent's need for a relationship with the child. On the other hand, when the rules are not connected, the noncustodial parent's financial support may be considered more important than the nurturance received from either the custodial or the noncustodial parent. This is a problem because the law is more apt to recognize a tangible contribution such as money than it is to recognize an intangible contribution such as nurturance. Under some partially connecting rules, a noncustodial parent may withhold support payments if the custodial parent interferes with his or her visitation rights, but the custodial parent must have court permission to interfere with the visitation rights of the noncustodial parent even if child support has not been paid (Czapanski, 1989). In other words, this partially connecting rule seems to place the noncustodial parent's right to visit above the child's right to support.

Child Support Enforcement

The problems most common to child support are those associated with enforcement (Krause, 1977; Lieberman, 1986; see also 59 American Jurisprudence, 1987; and 67A C.J.S., 1978 §59-61, 63). Courts have used various civil and criminal remedies to enforce the payment of child support obligations, including contempt of court, income withholding in cases of arrearages, criminal prosecution, income tax refund offsets, guarantees for nonpayment such as bonds and liens, and termination of parental rights (59 American Jurisprudence, 1987 §69; 67A C.J.S., 1978 §§59-61, 63; Ellman et al., 1991). Since the mid-1970s, the federal government has been actively involved in enforcement efforts (Schorsch, 1982).

There are two sides to federal involvement in child support enforcement. Both have grown out of efforts to obtain child support from fathers of children who receive AFDC benefits. The Child Support Enforcement Act (Pub. Law No. 93-647) was passed in 1975 and included establishment of state child support agencies, state and federal parent locator services, and the federal Office of Child Support Enforcement operated by the department of Health and Human Services. This law and its amendments put in place a number of strategies for finding fathers and forcing them to pay child support.

On the negative side of federal involvement, mothers of children who receive AFDC must identify the father of the child, a requirement that only affects poor, unmarried mothers. Drawing on logic of the right of privacy that has developed over the past 50 years, Anders (1990) concluded that this legislation gives the government an unconstitutional right to intrude in the lives of poor, unmarried mothers. The United States Supreme Court agreed in *Shapiro v. Thompson* (1969) indicating that the interest of the state in preserving its fiscal resources did not justify an invasion of the constitutional rights of poor women. Later, when the issue was unannounced home visits by social service personnel to insure that there was no father in the home, the Court took a different position. The visits had been objected to as a violation of fourth amendment protection from unlawful search (a part of the logic of the right of privacy), but were upheld by the majority opinion of the Court (*Wyman v. James*, 1971) with dissents from Justices Douglas, Marshall, and Brennan who pointed out the jeopardy to constitutional rights brought on by acceptance of welfare benefits. To date, this violation of the rights of poor, unmarried mothers to privacy and familial autonomy is a problem that has not been resolved either by statute or Court interpretation.

On the positive side, for a mother who wants to find a father and enforce his payment of child support, resources have been improved. This is especially true in cases where parents no longer live in the same state.

Although all states now have laws to deal with problems of enforcement of support obligations when one parent moves out of the state, getting these laws in place has been a long and frustrating problem for both parents and courts. Initially, when a parent moved out of the jurisdiction of a court, the laws that were used to exercise jurisdiction were those that had been developed to apply to commercial activities. Some courts have been unwilling to extend a long-arm statute that applied to commercial activities to a child support case because, obviously, they address different issues (Hughes, 1979-80). In *Shaffer* (1977) the Court would not exercise jurisdiction (i.e., exercise authority to hear the case) over the nonresident parent who had support obligations because the nature of the ties between that parent, the state, and the precedent for litigation (commercial activities) were not related.

In *Kulko* (1978), the Court agreed that the use of commercial long-arm statutes was not appropriate in child support cases. In this case, the mother moved from New York (the marital domicile of the couple) to California where she later obtained custody of her two children. She subsequently filed a motion to modify child support. The only contacts the child's father had with the state of California were (a) a three-day stay years before at the time the couple was married, (b) the act of buying one child's airline ticket to move in with her mother, and (c) the fact that his children were located in that state. The Supreme Court, citing *Shaffer* (1977), ruled that this was insufficient to warrant the exercise of jurisdiction over the father by the state of California. The Court not only noted that from these acts alone the defendant would not have foreseen being summoned to a California court in order to defend himself, but also noted that his actions neither amounted to personal benefits derived from activities within the state nor caused an effect in California that amounted to criminal activities. Thus, the Court concluded that it would not be fair to require the father to defend himself in California. The Court further stated that the mother could have sought relief through the Uniform Reciprocal Enforcement of Support Act (URESA),[4] which would not require the father to leave the state of New York and would satisfy her needs.

The URESA and later the Revised URESA were designed as models to provide for interstate enforcement of a child support obligation (Schorsch, 1982). The drafters of RURESA sought to reduce the possibility of unnecessary or inappropriate modifications of support decrees by requiring that, among other things, motions to modify be reviewed by the court which delivered the initial support decision. In the Federal Child Support Enforcement Amendments of 1984, Congress required all states to have some form of the RURESA. Although state reciprocal enforcement acts have resulted in improvements over past attempts to use long-arm statutes designed for commercial activities, there are still some problems. In this as well as other parenting issues, courts may find themselves juggling a concern for the best interest of the child with often unacknowledged biases that arise from assumptions about relationships between husbands and wives.

TAX IMPLICATIONS FOR SINGLE PARENTS

Single custodial parents who file federal income tax as single head of household are allowed to take the income tax deduction for a dependent child. However, according to the Internal Revenue Code §152(e) (Title 26 U.S.C.A.), in the past it was possible for a noncustodial parent to claim the dependency tax exemption if more than $1,200 was paid in child support in one year and if the custodial parent did not provide more support in the same calendar year. The Tax Reform Act of 1984 (Public Law No. 98-369, §423(a), 98 Stat. 494, 799) clarified that the parent who has custody for the greater part of the year will be considered to provide more than one-half of a child's support. The major exception to this rule is the case wherein the custodial parent releases the dependency exemption. The release is a specific IRS form which must be signed by the custodial parent and filed with taxes by the noncustodial parent.

The question then arose as to whether a trial court could require a custodial parent to sign the release. The most common situation in which the requirement might be imposed is when the custodial parent earns less income than the noncustodial parent. In such a case, the value of the exemption is presumed to be greater for the noncustodial parent–a fact which would certainly be true if the custodial parent earned so little income that no income tax payments were required. Also, it has been suggested that if the noncustodial parent has the exemption and saves money on taxes, an equivalent amount can be added to child support payments, thus, providing greater benefit to the child; however, if support is not increased, there will be no advantage to the child or mother and the discrepancy between the resources available to the father and the custodial mother will be increased.

Some state courts have focused their attention on the interest of the

Internal Revenue Service in avoiding determination of which parent should be allowed the exemption. In these states, trial courts have been allowed to award the exemption to the noncustodial parent and to require the custodial parent to sign the release.

Additional tax issues that are of interest to a single parent include, for example, tax consequences of property settlements including retirement plans. These issues are complex and highly specific and are not discussed here. Excellent reviews can be found in Hjorth (1990) and Langbein and Wolk (1990).

SOCIAL POLICY AND THE COURTS

In this country, social policy has most often been designed to provide a support system that enables individuals to work and help themselves and/or provides income for those who cannot work. In the 18th and 19th centuries, aid was most generously provided for those who were considered "deserving" or for whom there was hope that they would eventually be able to help themselves. It was not until the late 1960s that the notion that disadvantaged persons had a right to government assistance had gained a significant foothold.[5] Policy and policy rhetoric have vacillated between feelings of responsibility for the less fortunate and expectations that those who receive help should work for it. Nearly all policy decisions have been influenced by feelings about deservedness and potential for independence from assistance–it has just been more obvious at some times than at others. Since the late 1960s, the courts have been participants in the development of policy, primarily through the reform of policy. (See Kamerman & Kahn, 1988, chapter 2, and Sard, 1988, for summaries of the history of the development of AFDC and court involvement).

In the 1960s, government funding to provide legal services for poor people was begun. Until that time they had no way to challenge laws or practices that disadvantaged them or ignored their basic rights (Sard, 1988).

It was through early welfare litigation that the right of those in need to receive aid was legitimated. Welfare had been considered discretionary by the courts as well as by those who designed and administered the laws. Those who dispensed aid decided who would receive it; there was neither guarantee that aid could be obtained nor that the amount of aid received would be similar to others in the same circumstances. In *Goldberg v. Kelly* (1970, p. 262), the Supreme Court, drawing on the position articulated by Reich in 1964 and 1965, said that benefits "are a matter of statutory entitlement for persons qualified to receive them." At about the same time, the Court applied the Equal Protection Clause of the Fourteenth Amendment to rule that states could not require time-limited residency that resulted in denial of aid to families with dependent children (*Shapiro v. Thompson*, 1969), but refused to use the Equal Protection Clause to remove the ceiling from welfare grants so that children in large families would not be disadvantaged.

Unsuccessful attempts have been made to use equal protection to correct racial imbalances in amount of aid paid to recipients (*Jefferson v. Hakney*, 1971). Women and illegitimates have been considered more vulnerable to discrimination and lack of protection, a fact that resulted in a 1979 decision against limiting interpretation of the AFDC-Unemployed Parent program. The Court reiterated that no one group of families could be excluded from needed benefits (*Wescott v. Califano*, 1970).

Although AFDC is a part of the Social Security Act, it is a state-run program. States submit the plan for their program and if it conforms to the terms of the Social Security Act (SSA), it must be approved. States receive 50% or greater federal reimbursement for AFDC expenditures; however, states set the standard of need and the level of benefits (in all states, benefits are set below the poverty line). In other words, most of the control of AFDC is in the states. Because states set the standard of need, they determine eligibility conditions. It was not until 1968, more than 30 years after the passage of the SSA that the Supreme Court ruled that states would have to use eligibility conditions contained in the SSA (*King v. Smith*, 1968); the standard of need in SSA was less restrictive than that used in many states.

The limitations of the Court are clearly seen in the history of AFDC decisions. The Court has been interpreting a federal statute which can be changed by Congress, thus, an interpretation that has developed over years can become irrelevant because of a congressional change. Indeed, in the 1980s, at the initiation of the Executive Branch, Congress successfully placed greater restrictions on eligibility for AFDC. The Court can hold Congress to the basic premises of the act in its current form (see *Heckler v. Turner*, 1985), but it cannot keep Congress from changing the act.

Courts have had the most effect on policy via AFDC through protection of procedures for assuring fairness and promptness. Once welfare benefits were considered an entitlement, or property (see *Goldberg*, 1970), the Due Process clause of the Fourteenth Amendment could be used for protection of "fair hearing" and "reasonable promptness" guarantees of the statute. Prior to that time, there was no point in questioning authority because there was no legal protection for fair hearing rights. Although few recipients of AFDC have taken advantage of the right to a fair hearing, this right is an important ingredient in a social system which rejects arbitrary authority.

The Court has limited itself to procedural protections, refusing to become involved in attempts to use litigation as a strategy to increase benefits (see *Rosado v. Wyman*, 1970). However, when *state* laws contain language about levels of AFDC benefits, state courts have greater leeway than federal courts to make decisions and issue orders that affect state appropriations. If a state is not funding at the level its own law requires, the state court can uphold the language of the law and require compliance (see for example "Massachusetts Coalition," 1987).

The important point here is that when the issue is access to AFDC benefits, single parent, mother-headed families who live in poverty are among those who potentially benefit most from Court involvement in welfare reform. To date, reform has been most successful in requiring the application of due process and equal protection. These protections eliminate the possibility for an administrator of welfare to decide who may or may not receive government support on the basis of personal moral position or bias and they create minimal protection from the myths about the poor that have had their greatest impact on women and children. (Recall, however, the discussion of child support enforcement in which it was pointed out that court involvement has left in place a statutory requirement to identify the father that jeopardizes the rights of poor, unmarried mothers.)

CONCLUSIONS

There are many implications for both practice and policy that can be drawn from this discussion, however, one is particularly important. In this time of evolving family forms and merging sex roles, it is easy to be distracted from serious, ongoing problems of single parent families. We have discovered that fathers can be nurturant and some want custody of children following divorce. Grandparents are asserting their rights to visit and even to have custody of grandchildren. Gay and lesbian persons are seeking ways to fulfill their desire to parent. Foster and adoptive parents push for their rights as psychological parents of children they love and have cared for. All these are important issues and deserve careful thought and study. The fact remains, however, that the vast majority of single parents are women. Their lives are shaped by myths and stereotypes that even they often do not recognize–they hold many of the stereotypes themselves. They are poor, often educationally unprepared to work for an adequate wage, and believe that they should be at home to care for their children. Decisions are made about their lives by people who feel that they should be good mothers and stay home with their children while, at the same time, believing that they should be hard workers and support themselves. The double standard that is held for men and women following divorce is well documented at every step of the legal process.

Although "best interest of the child" has emerged as the dominant guiding principle for law-making and court decisions that affect single parent families, it is our observation that before the interests of children can be well served, it will be necessary to resolve conflicting feelings and beliefs and recognize that we must also promote the best interest of the parent. To maximize the effectiveness of either practice or policy, it will be necessary to set aside myths and stereotypes and address the issue of equality. When we understand what we mean by equality, we will be able–without regard to gender–to educate children to assume the variety of roles that are required to function well as a single parent–or a dual parent. When we start from the assumption that every individual should be prepared to function well in both instrumental and expressive roles, policy and practice will not be so heavily colored by myths and stereotypes. Until we achieve this goal, we can make progress by questioning our assumptions with every decision that is made regarding a single parent family. Not only will such a process improve the conditions of single-mother families, it will enable us to think more constructively and clearly about emerging forms of single parent families.

NOTES

1. The issue of friends or relatives such as grandparents who seek custody is most likely to involve a dispute with the state, a non-family member such as a foster parent, or a putative father. Except for putative father cases, these rarely involve single parent issues. For a review of the legal status of grandparents to obtain custody, see Kotkin (1985).

2. In 1985, approximately 61% of women living with children whose father was absent had an agreement/award to receive child support. Less than one-half received the full amount, and more than one-fourth received nothing. Only about one-fourth of *poor* single mothers received any child support (Kamerman & Kahn, 1988, citing 1985 census data). In 1989-90, 72% of ever-married women and 24% of never-married women had been awarded child support; the same proportion received the awards as had in 1985 (U.S. Bureau of the Census, 1992a).

3. It was not until families moved away from farms and into cities where men could earn enough to support a family that maternal instincts were discovered. Until that time, fathers had a presumed right to custody and services of children.

In 1839 the English Parliament modified fathers' absolute right to custody and provided for mothers to get custody of children who were younger than 7 years of age (Weitzman & Dixon, 1979). Fathers absolute right to custody is well illustrated in *King v. DeManneville* (1804) wherein a judge returned a nursing infant to the French father because he was entitled by law to custody of his child even though his cruelty had driven the mother and children from his home. In contrast, in 1938 (*Tuter v. Tuter*), a judge declared that "there is but a twilight zone between a mother's love and the atmosphere of heaven" (*Tuter*, 1938, p. 205).

4. URESA and the Revised URESA are model processes for conferring jurisdiction over a nonresident in child support cases. When the parent who is obligated to pay support leaves the state in which the support decree was initially obtained, the other parent uses RURESA to register the support award in the state to which the parent moved. It is a five step process that entails establishing that a support decree is in existence and registering the decree with the state of the parent who is obligated to pay. The use of RURESA reduces interstate conflict over jurisdiction and it also ensures that neither parent will have to travel to a distant state to collect or object to a support claim. Once the decree is registered with the foreign state, any motions to modify the existing decree are filed. Additionally, some states may allow the use of URESA for establishing a support order. Either URESA or RURESA has been enacted in some form in all states.

5. Because of the gap between the reality of the lives of poor people and the value placed on helping those in need (in part to insure the development of competent citizens of the state), the notion of a right to have needs met has gained some credibility. Until the 1960s, government aid was considered charity, not a right. However, according to Reich (1964, 1965) some conditions are beyond personal control making it important for some individuals to be able to expect government assistance. It is not a child's fault when the family falls on hard times, and it is in the interest of the state to insure adequate food, shelter, and education of future citizens. The government provides many forms of support for valued, but vulnerable, business interests such as agricultural subsidies, postal services, and savings bank insurance. These sources of security are considered essential and deserved, not charity. If business is entitled to such support, surely support for the poor should be considered essential and as deserved as insurance for savings banks.

When the Supreme Court accepted the logic as presented by Reich (*Goldberg v. Kelly*, 1970) and declared welfare benefits to be a matter of statutory entitlement, welfare recipients gained two subtle, but important, advantages. *First*, they gained potential constitutional rights against the arbitrary actions of welfare agencies, actions that often constituted harassment. *Second*, they gained the right to receive benefits as specified in a statute rather than benefits determined at the discretion of an official whose biases often went unchecked. Entitlement protects the poor from undefined procedures and arbitrary officials. It extends the constitutional rights of due process and equal protection to those whose needs are met less well than many others in society, and does so with minimal moral qualifications (Sard, 1988).

REFERENCES

Albert, J. A., & Brodek, G. A. (1989). *Habeas corpus*–A better remedy in visitation denial cases. *Maine Law Review, 41*, 239-271.

Allen, D. M. (1985). Propriety of provision of custody or visitation order designed to insulate child from parent's extramarital sexual relationships. *American Law Review* (4th), *40*, 812.

Allison D. v. Virginia M., 572 N.E.2d 27 (N.Y. 1991).

59 American Jurisprudence 2d *Parent and child* §§ 14, 23-36, 41-49, 57-60, 69 (1987 and supplements).

Anders, C. (1990). State intervention into the lives of single mothers and their children: Toward a resolution of maternal autonomy and children's needs. *Law and Inequality, 8*, 566-610.

Aptheker v. Secretary of State, 378 U.S. 500 (1964).

Ashe, M. (1992). The "bad mother" in law and literature: A problem of representation. *Hastings Law Journal, 43*, 1017-1037.

Batty, D. L. (1990). *Michael H. v. Gerald D.*: The constitutional rights of putative rights of fathers and a proposal for reform. *Boston College Law Review, 31*, 1173-1207.

Beschle, D. L. (1989). God bless the child? The use of religion as a factor in child custody and adoption proceedings. *Fordham Law Review, 58*, 383-426.

Bodenheimer, B. M., & Neeley-Kvarme, J. (1979). Jurisdiction over child custody and adoption after *Shaffer* and *Kulko*. *University of California at Davis, 12*, 229-253.

Braschi v. Stahl Assocs., 543 N.E.2d 49 (N.Y. 1989).

Bregande, M. (1989). No longer the father's primary duty to support: Legal equality or economic disparity among the sexes? *Saint Louis University Law Journal, 34*, 133-147.

Caban v. Mohammed, 441 U.S. 380 (1979).

Carter, E. L. (1991). *Parrillo v. Parrillo*: Less must be seen of the paramour but in whose best interest? *New England Law Review, 25*, 1223-1250.

Clark, L. M. G. (1990). Wife battery and determinations of custody and access: A comparison of U.S. and Canadian findings. *Ottawa Law Review, 22*, 691-724.

Cohen v. Schnepf, 463 N.Y.S.2d 29 (N.Y. App. 1983).

Constitutionality of gender-based classifications in criminal laws proscribing nonsupport of spouse or child. (1982). *American Law Review* (4th) *14*, 717.

Coombs, R. M. (1982). Interstate child custody: Jurisdiction, recognition, and enforcement. *Minnesota Law Review, 66*, 711-864.

67A Corpus Juris Secundum (C.J.S.) *Parent and child* §§ 49-61, 51-58, 59-61, 63 (1978).

Czapanski, K. (1989). Child support and visitation: Rethinking the connections. *Rutgers Law Journal, 20*, 619-665.

Ellman, I. M., Kurtz, P. M., & Bartlett, K. T. (1991). *Family law: Cases, text, problems* (2nd ed.). Charlottesville, VA: Michie.

Family law–visitation rights–New York Court of Appeals refused to adopt a functional analysis in defining family relationships–*Allison D. v. Virginia M.*, 572 N.E.2d 27 (N.Y. 1991) (1992). *Harvard Law Review, 105*, 941-946.

First Year Report of the New Jersey Supreme Court Task Force on Women in the Courts. (1986). *Women's Rights Law Reporter, 9*, 129-177.

Fleece, S. M. (1981-82). A review of the child support enforcement program. *Journal of Family Law, 20*, 489-521.

Folberg, J. (Ed.). (1991). *Joint custody and shared parenting* (2nd ed.). New York: Guilford.

Garska v. McCoy, 278 S.E.2d 357 (W.Va. 1981).

Ginsberg, R. B. (1978). Women, men and the constitution: Key Supreme Court rulings. In W. L. Hepperle & L. Crites (Eds.), *Women in the courts* (pp. 21-46). Williamsburg, VA: National Center for State Courts (Publication #R0037).

Goldberg v. Kelly, 397 U.S. 254 (1970).

Gomez v. Perez, 409 U.S. 535 (1973).

Gooch, K. S. (1989). Family law–*Seessel v. Seessel*: The burden of proof when a custodial parent wishes to remove a child from a court's jurisdiction. *Memphis State University Law Review, 19*, 265-274.

Gottesfeld, H. J. (1981). The uncertain status of the emancipated minor: Why we need a Uniform Statutory Emancipation of Minors Act (USEMA). (1981). *University of San Francisco Law Review, 15*, 473-507.

Halvey v. Halvey, 330 U.S. 610 (1947).

Harrington, M. (1984). The new American poverty. New York: Penguin.

Heckler v. Turner, 470 U.S. 184 (1985).

Hjorth, R. (1990). The effect of federal tax consequences on amount of property allocated to spouses in state court dissolution proceedings. *Family Law Quarterly, 24*, 247-278.

Hoffman, S. P., & Holmes, J. (1976). Husbands, wives and divorce. In G. Duncan & J. N. Morgan (Eds.), *Five thousand American families–Patterns of economic progress* (Vol. 4). Ann Arbor: Institute for Social Research, University of Michigan.

Hughes, L. (1979-80). Interstate enforcement of support obligations through long arm statutes and URESA. *Journal of Family Law, 18*, 537-563.

In re Marriage of Hadeen, 619 P.2d 374 (Wash App. 1980).

In re Marriage of Weidner, 338 N.W. 2d 351 (Iowa, 1983).

In re North Carolina Inheritance Taxes, 277 S.E.2d 403 (N.C. 1987).

Jefferson v. Hackney, 406 U.S. 535 (1971).

Johnston, J. D., Jr., & Knapp, C. L. (1971). Sex discrimination by law: A study in judicial perspective. *New York University Law Review, 46*, 675-747.

Kamerman, S. B., & Kahn, A. J. (1988). *Mothers alone: Strategies for a time of change*. Dover, MA: Auburn House.

Kanowitz, L. (1969). *Women and the law: The unfinished revolution*. Albuquerque: University of New Mexico Press.

Kass, A. (Winter, 1989). A view from the bench: Children and custody. *American Journal of Family Law, 3*, 301-313.

Keenan, L. R. (1985). Domestic violence and custody litigation: The need for statutory reform. *Hofstra Law Review, 13*, 407-441.

King v. DeManneville, 102 Eng. Rep. 1054 (K.B. 1084).

King v. Smith, 392 U.S. 316 (1968).

Kisthardt, M. K. (1991). Of fatherhood, families and fantasy: The legacy of *Michael H. v. Gerald D. Tulane Law Review, 65*, 585-661.

Knauerhase, E. C. (1989). The sexually active custodial parent: A contradiction in terms? *Parrillo v. Parrillo. Cooley Law Review, 6*, 545.

Knights v. Knights, 71 N.Y.2d 865, 522 N.E.2d 1045, 527 N.Y.S.2d 748 (1988).

Koch v. Williams, 456 N.W.2d 299 (N.D. 1990).

Kotkin, R. (1985). Grandparents versus the state: A constitutional right to custody. *Hofstra Law Review, 13*, 375-406.

Krause, M. D. (1977). *Family law in a nutshell.* St. Paul, MN: West.

Kulko v. Superior Court, 436 U.S. 84 (1978).

Langbein, J., & Wolk, B. (1990). *Pension and employment benefit law.* Westbury, NY: Foundation Press.

Lehr v. Robinson, 463 U.S. 248 (1983).

Lieberman, J. I. (1986). *Child support in America: Practical advice for negotiating and collecting a fair settlement.* New Haven, CT: Yale University Press.

Lonsdorf, B.J. (Winter, 1989). Coercion: A factor affecting women's inferior outcome in divorce. *American Journal of Family Law, 3*, 281-300.

Lozinak v. Lozinak, 569 A.2d 353 (Pa. Super., 1990).

Lugaila, T. (1992). Households, families and children: A 30-year perspective. *Current Population Reports* (Series P-23, No. 181). U. S. Bureau of the Census. Washington, D.C.: U. S. Government Printing Office.

Massachusetts Coalition for the Homeless v. Secretary of Human Services, 400 Mass. 806 (1987).

McCant, J. W. (1987). The cultural contradiction of fathers as nonparents. *Family Law Quarterly, 21*, 127-143.

Michael H. v. Gerald, D., 491 U.S. 110 (1989).

Mnookin, R.H. (1978). *Child, family and state: Problems and materials on children and the law.* Boston: Little, Brown.

Mulroy, E. A. (1988). Introduction. In E. A. Mulroy (Ed.), *Women as single parents: Confronting institutional barriers in the courts, the workplace, and the housing market* (pp. 3-12). Dover, MA: Auburn House.

Neeley, R. (1984). The primary caretaker parent rule: Child custody and the dynamics of greed. *Yale Law and Policy Review, 3*, 168-186.

Orr v. Orr, 440 U.S. 268 (1979).

Palmore v. Sidoti, 466 U.S. 429 (1984).

Parrillo v. Parrillo, 554 A.2d 1043 (R.I. 1989), cert. denied, 110 S. Ct. 364 (1989).

Paul, J.C. (1989). "You get the house. I get the car. You get the kids. I get their souls." The impact of spiritual custody awards on the free exercise rights of custodial parents. *University of Pennsylvania Law Review, 138*, 583-613.

Philip Morris Family Survey. (1987). New York: Louis Harris.

Quillion v. Walcott, 434 U.S. 246 (1978).

Raymond, E. L. (1988). Mother's status as "working mother" as factor in awarding child custody. *American Law Review* (4th), *62*, 259-300.

Reed v. Reed, 404 U.S. 71 (1971).

Reich, C. A. (1964). The new property. *Yale Law Journal*, *73*, 733-787.

Reich, C. A. (1965). Individual rights and social welfare: The emerging legal issues. *Yale Law Journal*, *74*, 1245-1257.

Report of the New York Task Force on Women in the Courts. (1987). *Fordham Urban Law Journal*, *15*, 11-177.

Rohloff v. Rohloff, 411 N.W.2d 484 (Mich. App. 1987).

Rosado v. Wyman, 397 U.S. 397 (1970).

Sack, L. (1992). Women and children first: A feminist analysis of the primary caretaker standard in child custody cases. *Yale Journal of Law and Feminism*, *4*, 291-328.

Sard, B. (1988). The role of the courts in welfare reform. In E. A. Mulroy (Ed.), *Women as single parents: Confronting institutional barriers in the courts, the workplace and the housing market* (pp. 167-202). Dover, MA: Auburn House.

Schafran, L. H. (1987). Documenting gender bias in the courts: The task force approach. *Judicature*, *70*, 280-290.

Schafran, L. H. (1988). Gender bias in the courts. In E. A. Mulroy (Ed.), *Women as single parents: Confronting institutional barriers in the courts, the workplace, and the housing market* (pp. 39-72). Dover, MA: Auburn House.

Schorsch, D. (Ed.). (1982). *Federal regulation of family law.* Charlottesville, VA: Michie.

Schuele, D. (1988-89). Origins and development of the law of parental child support. *Journal of Family Law*, *27*, 807-841.

Seessel v. Seessel, 748 S.W.2d 422 (Tenn. 1988).

Sex discrimination and the constitution. (1950). *Stanford Law Review*, *2*, 691.

Sexual orientation and the law/Harvard Law Review. (1990). Cambridge, MA: Harvard University Press.

Shaffer v. Heitner, 433 U.S. 186 (1977).

Shapiro v. Thompson, 394 U.S. 633 (1969).

Smith v. Cole, 553 S.2d 847 (LA, 1989).

Solari, F. P. (1989). Custody of the illegitimate child. *North Carolina Central Law Journal*, *18*, 18-41.

Sorensen, A. (1992). Estimating the economic consequences of separation and divorce: A cautionary tale from the United States. In L. J. Weitzman & M. Maclean (Eds.), *Economic consequences of divorce: The international perspective* (pp. 263-282). Oxford: Clarendon.

Stanley v. Illinois, 405 U.S. 645 (1972).

Sylvain, J. C. (1990). *Michael H. v. Gerald D.*: The presumption of paternity. *Catholic University Law Review*, *39*, 831-858.

The Establishment Clause and religion in child custody disputes: Factoring religion into the best interests equation. (1984). *Michigan Law Review*, *82*, 1702-1738.

The first year report of the New Jersey Supreme Court Task Force on Women in the Courts–June 1984. (1986). *Women's Rights Law Reporter, 9*, 129-177.
Towne v. Towne, 552 A.2d 404 (Vt. 1988).
Tuter v. Tuter, 120 S.W.2d 203 (Mo. Ct. App. 1938).
Tyrrell v. Tyrrell, 359 So.2d 62 (Fla. App. 1978).
42 U.S.C.A. §666(a)(9)(c) (1990).
U.S. Bureau of the Census. (1992a). Child support and alimony: 1989. *Current Population Reports* (Series P-60, No. 173). Washington, DC: United States Government Printing Office.
U.S. Bureau of the Census. (1992b). Poverty in the United States: 1991. *Current Population Reports* (Series P-60, No. 181). Washington, DC: United States Government Printing Office.
Uviller, R. K. (1978). Father's rights and feminism: The material presumption revisited. *Harvard Women's Law Journal, 1*, 107-130.
Washington ex rel Burton v. Leyser, 196 Cal. App.3d 451 (1987).
Wadlington, W., Whitebread, C. H., & Davis, S. M. (1983). *Cases and materials on children in the legal system*. Mineola, NY: Foundation Press.
Weisberg, D. K. (Ed.). (1989). *Women and the law: A social historical perspective (Vol. 2) Property, family and the legal profession*. Cambridge, MA: Schenkman.
Weitzman, L. (1985). *The divorce revolution: The unexpected social and economic consequences for women and children in America*. NY: The Free Press.
Weitzman, L. J., & Dixon, R. B. (1979). Child custody awards: Legal standards and empirical patterns for child custody, support and visitation after divorce. *University of California at Davis Law Review, 12*, 473-521.
Wescott v. Califano, 443 U.S. 89 (1970).
Wintjen, G. (1990). Make room for daddy: A putative father's rights to his children. *New England Law Review, 24*, 1059-1093.
Wishnew, J. A. (April, 1988). Joint custody agreements. *Trial*, 29-30.
Woods, L., Been, V., & Schulman, J. (1983). Sex and economic discrimination in child custody awards. *Clearinghouse Review, 16*, 1130-1134.
Wyman v. James, 400 U.S. 309 (1971).
Yee, L. M. (1979). What really happens in child support cases: An empirical study of establishment and enforcement of child support orders to Denver District Court. *Denver Law Journal, 57*, 21-68.

Chapter 9

Single Mothers with Custody Following Divorce

Linda D. Ladd
Anisa Zvonkovic

SUMMARY. The experience of being a single mother with custody following divorce is influenced by many variables across several levels of interaction, such as age of mother and child, potential for remarriage, coping skills, social networks and income changes. Cross-sectional studies have examined additional variables such as time since divorce and level of family religiosity and subsequent impact on individual well-being. Whereas most studies took a categorical approach to examining the experience of divorce, a few refreshing studies were based on an ecological systems model. As divorce also involves building a new life, longitudinal research provides the best picture of how divorced women accomplish this task. Long-term research clearly points to the fact that divorce is an event whose impact is individual and very often life long. Researchers have provided valuable information to build meaningful programs of intervention for divorced mothers. Perhaps the biggest challenge is to design flexible programs which can grow and change with the needs of the divorced mother. Future research will be most beneficial when it addresses the divorced mother family as a healthy family unit.

Linda D. Ladd is Assistant Professor at the OSU Extension Service. Anisa Zvonkovic is Assistant Professor with Human Development and Family Sciences, Oregon State University.

[Haworth co-indexing entry note]: "Single Mothers with Custody Following Divorce." Ladd, Linda D., and Anisa Zvonkovic. Co-published simultaneously in *Marriage & Family Review* (The Haworth Press, Inc.) Vol. 20, No. 1/2, 1995, pp. 189-211; and: *Single Parent Families: Diversity, Myths and Realities* (ed: Shirley M. H. Hanson et al.) The Haworth Press, Inc., 1995, pp. 189-211. Multiple copies of this article/chapter may be purchased from The Haworth Document Delivery Center [1-800-3-HAWORTH; 9:00 a.m. - 5:00 p.m. (EST)].

Some research variables, such as social networks and individual adjustment, are more pivotal in influencing the recovery process than others (Bronfenbrenner, 1990). Changes in the family responsibilities, adult relationships, social support and networks, adjustment to divorce, custody arrangements, parent/child relationships and social policy were key variables which were examined over the decade of the 80s. Research studies illuminating how these factors influence the experience of single mothering are critically reviewed in this article. The implications of divorce and new ways of looking at single mothers are discussed.

KEYWORDS. Divorced mothers, Social support, Adjustment

INTRODUCTION

Divorce is best described as an extended transition across time for all family members (Hetherington, Cox, & Cox, 1982). Single parent families experience "changes in family role organization and the pile-up of stressor events which precipitate critical transitions from one stage of development to the next involving processes of destructuration, disorganization and reorganization" (Hill, 1986, p. 28). Macklin (1980) called for viewing divorce as a "process involving the reorganization and redefinition of the family rather than its dissolution . . ." (p. 909). Many of the adults and children in Wallerstein's longitudinal study of divorced families in California were continuing to "negotiate their way through" the effects of the parental divorce from twenty years before (Wallerstein & Blakeslee, 1989, p. xiii).

As an extended transition, divorce interrupts the developmental cycle of the family long before the final decree (Ahrons, 1980). Some important points of transition include: the divorce announcement, the financial discussion, child custody decisions, parent-child visitation schedules, and the future plans of both spouses (Carter & McGoldrick, 1989; Furstenberg & Cherlin, 1991). Each stage of marital breakdown can contain a "point of specialized need" for any member of the family (Norton, 1983, p. 274). For most single divorced parents (75%), this stage leads into the more complex transition of remarriage within five years of their divorce. The divorce outcome will have different meanings for each member of the family (Hetherington, Cox, & Cox, 1982). Connecting meaning of an event to the individual's level of coping will provide additional information for professionals in the field.

ADAPTING TO THE DIVORCE

The purpose of this paper is the exploration of three issues relevant to the extended transition period following a divorce. One issue is the adaptive changes in roles and relationships common to the transition. A second issue is concerned with the significant individual or psychological adjustments that may occur. And, lastly, parent-child relationships are the focus of discussion.

Handling Both Parental Roles

Single parent mothers often lack the "personnel" to fill all of the expected positions in the family, placing extra burdens upon remaining family members (Hill, 1986, p. 28). No aspect of the family remains the same, as rules, routines, patterns, roles, boundaries and more are affected by the divorce (Peck & Manocherian, 1989). When compared with nondivorced parents, divorced parents were found to "encounter many more stresses and difficulties in coping, which were reflected in disturbances in personal and social adjustments and family relations" (Hetherington, Cox & Cox, 1982, p. 285).

The experience of divorce creates new role responsibilities within the family. For the single parent mother, her new role has expanded from daily management of the home and children to include being the major financial provider for the family and handling the emotional and social changes which accompany divorce (Burden, 1986; Wallerstein & Kelly, 1980). Role overload may result when one person adds the management of such routine tasks as eating dinner together, keeping a regular bedtime, and having mother-child time (Hetherington, Cox, & Cox, 1982). On the other hand, Hartmann (1981) provides a different perspective to why some divorced mothers spend less time in household management tasks than married women when she suggests that "in households in which husbands contributed minimally to family work, divorced mothers experience a lifting of the burden of housework" (p. 393). The number of children rather than the absence of a husband had more influence on the additional role strain experienced by Black women (Katz & Piotrkowski, 1983). Have family scientists been too quick to assume that the loss of an adult family member leads to an additional burden for the remaining member?

How do custodial mothers view their expanded roles? Custodial female parents still tend to define themselves in the "context of human relationships and to judge themselves in terms of their ability to care" (McGoldrick, 1989, p. 32). When asked about the advantages and disadvantages of custody, one mother responded: "When you're a mother, there is no such question. You have children and you raise them because you love them" (Luepnitz, 1982, p. 29). Still, single mothers reported having significantly less contact with other adults than did married parents and feeling "walled in" and "trapped" (Hetherington, Cox & Cox, 1982, p. 248).

Time is scarce for the custodial mother. Divorced employed mothers had less time for household tasks, child care, personal care, volunteer work, and recreational activities when compared with divorced unemployed and married employed/unemployed mothers. Yet, there were no differences between four groups of mothers when communication and meeting the emotional needs of children were considered (Sanick & Mauldin, 1986). In contrast, Peters and Haldeman (1987) note that single mothers spent less time with their children than dual parents in conversation, reading, listening, helping with homework, or sharing an outing.

Do single divorced mothers delegate more household tasks to their children? Comparing the work of children in one and two parent families has been difficult. However, the literature indicates that children in single parent families do more shopping and maintenance of the home, yard, car, and pets than children in two parent households (Peters & Haldeman, 1989). Longitudinal data suggest that asking children to assume additional work is most beneficial when these chores fit the ability and development of the child (Wallerstein, 1986; Wallerstein & Blakeslee, 1989). This area will remain unclear until such variables as socioeconomic class and gender are addressed.

ADULT RELATIONSHIPS

Quantity and Quality of Contact Between Ex-Spouses

Most divorced spouses continue to have contact due to their parenting responsibilities. In a white, middle-class sample of parents divorced for over two years, 23% of couples reported weekly contact (Masheter, 1991). Ahrons and Wallisch (1986) found that 85% of their sample of 54 divorced parents continued to have contact one year after divorce. Half of the divorced fathers who maintained bi-monthly visitation also reported sharing major decisions about their children (Ahrons, 1981).

The parental relationship is friendlier when noncustodial parents remain in contact with their children. Masheter (1991) compared the levels of friendliness or hostility as reported by noncustodial parents who had monthly, occasional, weekly and no contact with their children. As level of contact with the child rose, so did experienced friendliness for the ex-spouse. Kelly, Gigy, and Hausman (1986) found that when ex-spouses centered communication around child-focused issues their relationship was more positive. After a difficult first postdivorce year, Goldsmith (1980) found that 95% of parents reported that their feelings changed in a positive direction toward their ex-spouse.

Children, Age and Remarriage

Do custodial mothers have a decreased chance at remarriage? The research findings of the 1980's findings do not show clearly the impact children or age have on the remarriage rates of divorced mothers. Numerous other variables such as availability of men, time for meeting eligible men, and change in the custodial mother's economic status must also be considered in relationship to the mother's remarriage potential.

Being a parent adds a strain to the establishment of a new relationship. Conflict between the children and the new male was identified as being negatively related to the success of that new adult relationship for middle-class, white custodial mothers (Coysh, Johnston, Tschann, Wallerstein, & Kline, 1989). Darling, Davidson and Parish (1989) found that a significant number of mothers had not dated since they had become single (ranging from three to six years previously). Cashion (1982) reports that about 35% of divorced mothers remain single for the remainder of their lives.

How age of the divorced mother will influence her potential for remarriage is unclear. Census data suggests that younger women have an increased tendency to remarry (Glick, 1984). Yet, researchers have found that mothers under the age of 25 had a decreased likelihood of marriage; divorced women over the age of 35 with children were more likely to marry (Furstenberg & Spanier, 1984). Few older divorced mothers were able to build intimate adult relationships with men in Wallerstein's (1986) nonrandom study of white divorced families. Women over age forty remained unmarried ten years postdivorce whereas 50% of the husbands in this study had remarried (Wallerstein & Blakeslee, 1989). These differences underscore the need for researchers to be cautious in drawing conclusions from the findings of nonrandom samples.

SOCIAL SUPPORT AND NETWORKS

The effect of social support and networks on the adjustment of single mothers was widely studied during this past decade. Investigators rarely agreed on how to define social support or what constituted membership in a social group, making a comparison of findings difficult. Research variables have included kin and friendship networks, race, occupation, religious commitment, socioeconomic status, time since divorce and work outside the home (Hughes, 1988).

Social Support Networks Following Divorce

Social participation drops off for mothers after divorce and while it may never return to the pre-divorce level, it recovers from the low social interaction of the first postdivorce year (Milardo, 1987). High levels of involvement with support networks, as Belle (1982) has documented, requires an exchange of support which can also be draining to single mothers short on time, energy, and money. It has been assumed that network participants pull away from the divorced mother. On the other hand, divorced mothers may also pull away from social participation in order to conserve resources.

Family scientists are exploring how control over type of support networks is linked to quality of life. Intriguing research by McLanahan, Wedemeyer and Adelberg (1981) indicates that white, divorced mothers value the ability to control their social support networks according to personal need and sex role orientation. As they moved through the stages of divorce recovery, these mothers defined and re-defined themselves either as "stabilizers" (women who wanted to maintain their pre-divorce role) or "changers" (women who sought a new identity through a career). Divorced white mothers who were doing well psychologically one year after divorce had higher levels of non-kin support and also provided higher levels of support for others during their adjustment process (Leslie & Grady, 1988).

Two factors appear to influence the involvement of kin in the support networks of divorced mothers: attitude toward divorce and needs of the single mother. Contact with former in-laws was maintained when an interpersonal relationship existed and a valued level of reciprocal support was exchanged (Finch & Mason, 1990). When the family disapproved of the divorce or was experiencing high need, they were less likely to help out unless the single parent was also experiencing other negative life events (Kitson, Moir & Mason, 1982). Single mothers involved in a dense kin-filled network experienced a lower quality of life and more conservative attitudes toward women than did women with fewer kin in their networks (Leslie & Grady, 1988). Single divorced mothers in the U.S. often lived with kin because they could not afford to live elsewhere. On the other hand, divorced mothers in Sweden lived farther from their networks because they had access to formal supports such as parental leave, a housing allowance and subsidized child care (Gunnarsson & Cochran, 1990). If American single mothers had the level of support available in Sweden, would adaptation to the changes of divorce be easier?

Cross cultural research indicates that type of social network varies between and within cultural groups. Gunnarsson and Cochran (1990) compared married and divorced mothers from Sweden and the United States and found that the support network of all single mothers was smaller, due to the loss of the ex-spouse relatives, but more active than the network of married mothers. When occupation was considered by these researchers, white-collar single mothers had more network members from work and outside interests than did blue-collar mothers. Anglo-American divorced women retained more prior friendships than Mexican-American divorced women immediately after divorce (Wagner, 1988b). First generation Mexican-American women were isolated from a friend network and remained closer to their extended kin. Over time both third generation Mexican-American and Anglo women reported that their friendship network became more important.

Social support in the Black culture is highly valued. Staples and Johnson (1993) note that divorce is rising among Blacks living in the North and West where Black urbanization has increased. Divorce rates are lower in the South where Blacks continue to be involved in tightly knit communities of extended families, ethnic neighborhoods, and low levels of residential mobility. These authors suggest that "a major strength of Black family life has been its social support system" (Staples & Johnson, 1993, p. 167). Many Black divorced women may adapt more successfully to being single because of greater extended family support, the role of children in the family, and a greater acceptance of single parenthood within the Black culture (Fine & Schwebel, 1988).

Both kin and friend support networks are important to Black divorced mothers. Harriette McAdoo's research with single Black women determined that kin and friends were important to these women who reported feeling closest to and who spent more time with mothers, sisters, and aunts (as cited in Hughes, 1988). Drawing upon the National Survey of Black Americans, Taylor (1986) found that marital status did not predict level of social support received from family. Takai (1981) found that Black single women drew upon kinship support to replace the lost income of their ex-husbands more successfully than did white women (as cited in Fine & Schwebel, 1988). Black mothers are more likely to live in an extended family household while white mothers were more likely to receive money from family members who were not living in the same household (Hofferth, 1984).

There is limited research on how the religious beliefs of the extended family relate to the experience of divorce for the single female. In a case study of divorce in a large extended Jewish family of 45 members, Goldman (1982) concluded that being female and having children mediated the rejection of divorced persons in this family; however, single mothers were invited to fewer family functions than married couples. A small sample of divorced Catholic women differed only in availability of nonfamily members for emotional support; variables such as family concept, family postdivorce interaction, network density and sex role orientation did not reach significance (Dicosta & Nelson, 1988). Catholic Mexican-American women reported that their blue-collar fathers reacted with more criticism, non-support and emotional upset than did the fathers of Anglo women of the same economic subset (Wagner, 1988b). One year after divorce, custodial mothers in a primarily Mormon sample reported having worse relations with their extended family and a less satisfactory financial situation than did the men (Pett, 1982).

ADJUSTMENT TO DIVORCE

Divorce can be viewed as a change of consciousness from "couple to individualist assumptions" (Schwartz, 1987, p. 455). Time is considered essential for adjustment to divorce; researchers suggest that custodial mothers will spend a minimum of three to five years restabilizing their lives (Herz Brown, 1989; Peck & Manocherian, 1989; Wallerstein, 1986; Wallerstein & Kelly, 1980). In the 80s several aspects of divorce adjustment were investigated: the pre/postdivorce connection, attitudes about divorce, psychological well-being and divorce as a growth experience.

The Link Between Pre- and Post-Divorce Adjustment

In a new area of study, researchers in the 1980s have learned that pre-divorce and postdivorce adjustments are positively related. Female respondents in Menaghan's (1985) sample who had divorced since the first data collection were significantly more depressed than those women who remained married. The divorced women in the longitudinal Minnesota Family Health Study sample reported a significant decline in psychological well-being both before and after divorce along with a significant increase in substance use and decrease in income when compared with divorced men (Doherty, Su & Needle, 1989). Custodial mothers reported that external pressures to remain married from workmates and friends, obligations to dependent children and concern about the financial costs of divorce were all negatively correlated with subsequent divorce adjustment (Green, 1983). In both pre- and postdivorce relationships, women reported more trouble handling sexual relationships, finances, and independence than the men reported (Newcomb, 1984).

Conversely, mothers who reported a better level of coping and emotional functioning when they filed for divorce had a more effective level of coping, more gratifying social relationships, less anger and emotional distress and less severe psychological disturbance two years later (Coysh, Johnston, Tschann, Wallerstein, & Kline, 1989). When mothers who were divorced were compared with separated mothers, Dreman, Orr, and Aldor (1990) found that time since separation was positively related to an increasing sense of competence, defined as "feeling in control of both general and specific life areas" (p. 77). Building early supports in for women experiencing divorce may be beneficial in offsetting negative consequences.

The Relationship of Sex-Role Attitudes and Adjustment

Traditional sex-role attitudes have repeatedly been found to be associated with poorer adjustment to divorce (Kurdek & Blisk, 1983). Divorced women holding traditional beliefs reported feeling passive, decreased self-assurance, increased dependency, more shyness and increased conformity following divorce than did men (Thomas, 1982). Nontraditional attitudes about roles of men and women were linked to lower levels of depression for divorced women (Keith & Schafer, 1982). Using a longitudinal design, Bloom and Clement (1984) found that over time women with higher traditional family orientations continued to report poorer adjustment to divorce than less traditional women. Perhaps the mother with traditional values finds it especially difficult to function as head of the household, provider and authority figure, a position she was not trained to assume.

Psychological Well-Being Following Divorce

Studies of how custodial mothers have adjusted psychologically to divorce have identified numerous key variables, such as: level and quality of noncustodial contact with the children; ability of both parents to work through their anger; adaptation of children to the divorce; participation in social activities; involvement in education and professional support groups; development of personal understanding, building an autonomous life; and, involvement in home and family activities (Berman & Turk, 1981; Wallerstein & Blakeslee, 1989). Surviving the first postdivorce year and establishing a separate identity stand out as key elements in the psychological well-being of divorced mothers.

The first year following divorce is the most difficult in terms of emotional crisis (Hetherington, Cox & Cox, 1982; Wallerstein & Kelly, 1980). Levels of depression, hostility and the inability to form intimate contacts were reduced for women who had custody of their children, had not initiated the divorce, lived close to their ex-spouses, and had been involved in therapy during the marriage (Kolevzon & Gottlieb, 1983). Single women who reported the least adjustment to their divorce shared these common features: had longer marriages; did not want the divorce; had fewer children, but more male children; and, had less postdivorce income (Berman, 1985). For 42 women divorced less than one year, adjustment increased when the social networks provided emotional and social integration, as well as reassurance of worth (Daniels-Mohring & Berger, 1984).

Building a new life following divorce is generally considered more difficult than the loss of the marital relationship itself (McKenry & Price, 1991). Hetherington and associates (1982) found that intimacy (valuing the welfare of another, strong attachment and desire to be with another person) was positively correlated with happiness, self-esteem, and feelings of competence for divorced single women in their longitudinal study. All single parents were more depressed, less satisfied with their family lives and had more problems with their children than parents from intact and stepfamily structures (Fine, Donnelly & Voydanoff, 1986). Single mothers with custody who had been divorced between 19 and 36 months did not know whether they wanted to be married "when they [were asked to] picture their lives in five years" (Saul & Scherman, 1983, p. 83). How can educators and clinicians help divorced mothers work through these issues when time and money are scarce?

Studies concerning long term adjustment to divorce are scarce (Hetherington, Cox & Cox, 1982; Wallerstein & Blakeslee, 1989). After six years, 40% of the women reported continued emotional involvement with ex-spouses (Hetherington et al., 1982). Ten year interviews with custodial mothers revealed that at least 60% of single women adapt positively to the challenges of this "second chance" while other women continued to have regrets about the divorce, continued emotional involvement with their ex-spouse, and tremendous anger and bitterness (Wallerstein & Blakeslee, 1989).

Is Divorce a Growth Opportunity?

Most often, professionals consider divorce to be a negative event in the lives of their clients. Conversely, Spanier and Thompson (1989) point out that in their sample of divorced men and women, as many respondents felt relief after divorce as felt distress. From a therapeutic perspective, the experience of divorce could provide men or women with the potential for growth and change (Kaslow & Hyatt, 1982). For example, the single mother could model positive coping within her own household which could benefit extended family members as well as her own family. The post-divorce period can be one of exploration if the individual has the time, energy and money (Kaslow, 1983). Divorce has been seen as a time of development when the divorced mothers had sufficient ability to support themselves and maintain a quality standard of living (Veevers, 1991). While divorce may be an opportunity for growth for many women over time, care must be taken not to weigh the emotional costs of divorce too lightly as the growth aspects of the divorce experience are considered. For example, parenting continues long after the divorce marks the legal end of the marriage.

CUSTODIAL ARRANGEMENTS

Co-Parenting: Friend or Foe?

Custody mediation and joint custody decisions are increasingly common; joint custody has cut court costs and relitigation of custody. Initially, wives expressed reservations about the mediation process and reported higher levels of feeling pressured than did their husbands (Pearson & Thoennes, 1988). Clingempeel and Reppucci (1984) report that research concerning the effects of joint custody is sparse and call for a multilevel-multivariable approach to study the impact of joint custody on families over time.

Satisfaction with joint custody appears to be mixed. Fathers with joint custody and the mothers with sole custody believed that their children and their former husbands were more satisfied with this type of custody living arrangement (Shrier, Simring, Shapiro, Greif, & Lindenthal, 1991). In a study of college-educated, career-oriented parents, Steinman (1981, 1984) found that their commitment to joint custody was influenced by two factors: a strong moral and psychological belief that children needed two parents and, a desire by both parents to pursue a career outside their home. Parents who had felt involved in the mediation process reported being satisfied with joint custody (Pearson & Thoennes, 1988). The most important factor may well be the willingness of both parents to work together to provide a healthy environment for their children.

Special Case: Domestic Violence

Ending domestic violence is one reason behind many divorces. Wallerstein and Blakeslee (1989) found that in families who had experienced domestic violence, the subsequent divorce was considered a move away from a negative situation. In making determinations of custody, courts use a "friendly parent" provision which directs the courts to determine sole custody on the basis of which parent would be more likely to allow frequent and continuing contact with the other parent. When women have survived violent marriages, should the courts allow such contact? Concern for ex-wives who have been victims of domestic violence is expressed by Schulmann and Pitt (1984) who suggest that the friendly parent provision presents a danger to custodial mothers. Single parent mothers who had experienced more verbal and physical aggression were less likely to cope effectively with adjustment to divorce and had more anger, emotional distress and psychological disturbance (Coysh, Johnston, Tschann, Wallerstein, & Kline, 1989). Divorce strains the parent-child relationship, the experience of domestic violence adds a critical factor.

PARENT-CHILD RELATIONSHIPS

Changes in the Parent-Child Relationship

Few children want their parents to divorce. The experience of marital dissolution usually means painful adaptation, crisis and the beginning of a series of family changes (Furstenberg & Cherlin, 1991; Hetherington, Cox & Cox, 1982). Being a single mother has less relationship to the recovery of the child than does the cumulative impact of key psychosocial variables such as poverty, age of the child, loss of a parent, ongoing conflict between parents, and the quality of the parent-child relationship prior to divorce (Ahrons, 1981; Wallerstein & Kelly, 1980).

The first year following divorce custodial mothers reported exhibiting more negative behaviors towards their young sons below the age of twelve (Hetherington, Cox & Cox, 1982; Copeland, 1984). Single mothers and single fathers reported exerting less supervision and control in their families than did two-parent families; time since divorce did not lead to greater control or behavior demands by single mothers (Thomson, McLanahan & Curtin, 1992). The absence of a husband appeared to have less influence on the strain resulting from role demands experienced by Black women than did the number of children in the family (Katz & Piotrkowski, 1983). Wallerstein and Blakeslee (1989) reported that divorced mothers often protect their youngest children from the departure of the father by spending more time with the child, sometimes at the cost of spending less time with older children in the family. In the 15-year summary of divorce-related changes on the lives of women, Wallerstein (1989) notes that "women with young children, especially if they are driven into poverty by divorce, face a Herculean struggle to survive emotionally and physically" (p. 301).

Time since divorce may level out differences in parent-child interaction. By two years after divorce, divorced mothers learned to adapt to problem situations and were demanding more mature behavior from their children; however, divorced mothers never gained as much control as their married counterparts (Hetherington, Cox, & Cox, 1982). In a study comparing married mothers and mothers divorced an average of 2.5 years, Hodges, Buchsbaum, and Tierney (1983) found no differences on time available for children, child rearing, and discipline. Single mothers scored significantly higher on use of authority than did mothers in two parent families (Loveland-Cherry, 1986).

Long-term parent-child relationships have many ups and downs (Wallerstein & Blakeslee, 1989). Wallerstein notes "many older men and women coming out of long-term marriages are alone and unhappy . . . [and] . . . lean on their children, with mixed feelings, for support and companionship ten and fifteen years after divorce" (p. 301). For some families the diminished parenting of the first crisis year continued through the next 15 years. When parents cooperated with each other in raising the children, new lives were built. It is imperative that clinicians and educators helping divorcing parents increase their ability to cooperate in parenting!

Health and the Single Family

Selected factors such as education, employment potential, and socioeconomic level have been identified as being important to the overall health of single families. Communication and social support were related to self-reports of good health in single mother families. Mothers' health self-reports were lower than fathers' self-reports. Children living with female parents reported higher overall health; boys had a higher level of health than girls (Hanson, 1986). Marital status did not discriminate between the personal health practices reported by well-educated, white, single and intact families who were active in support groups and community activities (Loveland-Cherry, 1986). Reports of children's positive self-esteem, physical and psychological health was associated with positive maternal control (Machida & Holloway, 1991).

Link Between Child Abuse and Single Parenthood

Using the Second National Family Violence Survey, Gelles (1989) found no significant differences when he investigated the notion that single mothers living alone were more likely to abuse their children than single mothers living with another adult. Unfortunately, this researcher did not separate divorced mothers from other single mothers. He concluded that "economic deprivation is indeed the reason why single parent mothers, who make up nearly 90% of all single-parent families, are more likely to abuse their children" (Gelles, 1989, p. 497). In that same survey, single fathers were more likely than single mothers to severely abuse their children. The frequency of child abuse was nearly twice as high for both male and female single parents than two-parent families; divorced parents were nearly twice as likely to abuse than other type of single parents (Sack, Mason, & Higgins, 1985). Although this study found no gender differences, being a single parent places the divorced mother at risk for abusing her offspring. Ensuring that single mothers are educated about community resources aimed at reducing the occurrence of child abuse is very important.

LIMITATIONS OF THE RESEARCH

Many interesting and insightful conclusions have been produced by this last decade of research into the experience of divorced mothers with custody of their children. Unfortunately, research methods often limited the usefulness of research results. For example, most family scientists individually defined the term social support for their particular sample rather than adopting a common definition, making a comparison of findings across studies meaningless (Hughes, 1988).

Research findings are most powerful when they are drawn from non-random samples or samples which lacked a comparison group. The following studies are examples of this perspective. Fine, Donnelly and Voydanoff (1986) used a comparison group; Gelles (1989) drew his sample from a national survey. Doherty, Su and Needle (1989) not only used a control group but also gathered their data both before and after divorce, a rare event in the field!

Errors can result when participants are not matched on important variables such as on length of time after divorce, education, income, and age of children (Hughes, 1988). Thomson, McLanahan and Curtin (1992) used only the data from parents to explore the interaction of parents and children. Masheter (1991) used appropriate research methods but was forced to work with a final response rate of 24% of the initial sample.

Few studies examined variables across more than twelve months. Cross-sectional research examines only one episode of a life-changing event. While longitudinal research can be biased by sample loss over time, the 15-year longitudinal work of Wallerstein offers the most time-comprehensive examination of the long-term effects of divorce in the family literature. Family scientists must work to translate these findings into useful services and policy.

SERVICES AND SOCIAL POLICY

Single mothers after divorce benefit from services targeted at their families. Programs, such as The Orientation for Divorcing Parents, focus on increasing the coping abilities of single parents. Such programs increase parents' awareness of healthy ways to work through the divorce by helping parents mobilize existing coping strategies that might be paralyzed due to stress (Buehler, Betz, Ryan, Legg, & Trotter, 1992). Building family strengths through increasing social support is a target of Moncrieff Cochran's Family Cluster program. Using a home visitor approach, this program identifies the strengths of single parents and works to reinforce both resource and social exchange networks. Evaluations reflected that single African-American parents reported increased kin and non-kin support. White single mothers noted a more positive self perception which was associated with an expanding primary network as well as an increased involvement with their children's activities (Hughes, 1988).

Other educational programs specifically target parenting. Parenting After Divorce (PAD) is a structured and directed approach to parenting which focuses on the child's needs and stage of development, co-parenting issues, and the role playing of certain issues (Warren & Amara, 1984). These authors found that parents with high post-divorce stress benefitted the most from the program. However, sound evaluation studies are needed to determine both participant satisfaction and the effectiveness of the program.

The legal system tends to act as if men and women have equal financial opportunity, receive equal pay, and as though child care was readily and cheaply available (Weitzman, 1985). Divorcing women need both legal advice which will help them negotiate a fair divorce and custodial settlement and accurate financial information which will help them manage their money (Luepnitz, 1982). Few single women studied report that they understand how to value a pension fund or how to negotiate division of their spouse's pension (Rowe, 1991). In order to more successfully integrate the demands of work and family, single parent families would benefit from available and affordable child care as well as flexible work schedules (Hamner & Turner, 1985).

A longitudinal comparison of variables over a 25 year period yielded the conclusion that welfare expenditures were only one factor in explaining why the divorce rates increased in the 1980s (Zimmerman, 1991a). This researcher called for the "federal government to assume a larger, more integrative role" in addressing welfare needs (Zimmerman, 1991b, p. 153). Government programs that protect the single parent from poverty and provide treatment programs that work to prevent child abuse are essential (Gelles, 1989). Furthermore, the strict enforcement of the child support payments could also decrease poverty and possibly deter divorce among lower income families. If fathers were required to provide financial support, they might also assume more responsibility for the care of their children (Garfinkel & McLanahan, 1986). Increased child support might also enable the custodial mother to cease to rely on welfare dollars. Providing a monthly government child allowance to all children under the age of 18 could be more beneficial to poor mothers than an increase in the personal exemption for children on the federal income tax (Garfinkel & McLanahan, 1986).

WHERE SHOULD RESEARCHERS COMMIT NEW RESOURCES?

Is a Broader Look at the Effects of Divorce Useful?

The research of the 80s has raised good questions. As one example, little is known about how an individual level of religiosity might affect the experience of divorce and custody. What other variables support the positive adjustment of nontraditional divorced mothers? How do individual values concerning divorce, being a parent, and working outside the home influence the custodial experience? Other important questions are: What about adult sexuality and the single parent's experience, including the effect of sexual abstinence or multiple live-in partners on family adjustment? What about the single female parent who has sufficient financial resources but whose greatest difficulty is her own desire to be back in the marriage?

Researchers need to link up historical work on Western Europe, the United States and Canada with current research on the family in developing countries (Cherlin, 1983). An extant problem may be that resources are not available to conduct on-going projects at several representative sites around the United States. Rarely do we find research which shifts through "successful" divorce experiences for variables which contribute to the adaptations made by the family.

What about a divorce ritual in which the loss of the marriage is acknowledged and partners pledge to treat each other with "civil and ethical behavior in the future" (Veevers, 1991, p. 116)?

Researching the Family System

The family is a system existing in a constant state of interaction and adaptation with other systems and its environment. Bronfenbrenner (1990) calls for a new approach to the study of family and social networks when he identifies the family as the "master builder of network structures" and social networks as being "dynamic processes-in-context" which vary in relation to the needs of the family and the environment (vii). Tracking the broad perspective of how families develop and maintain continuity over time would reduce the negative approach of examining the family as a unit in a state of change (Scanzoni, 1987).

Is It Time to Redefine What Should Be Studied

Is divorce a recycling tool by which individuals can leave a relationship which has either maximized its usefulness or is viewed as being detrimental to growth and development? Consider: "divorce is an intrinsic part of a cultural system that values individual discretion and gratification; the more divorce is used, the more exacting the standards" for remarriage (Furstenberg & Spanier, 1984, p. 53). The family needs to be studied on two levels: the developing adult sexually based relationship and the "influential nonromantic relations among parents/children, sibs, and kin" (Scanzoni, 1987, p. 416).

CONCLUSION

As an acknowledged family form, single parenting by divorced females is well established (Schwartz, 1987). Social scientists who once viewed single divorced mothers as a non-traditional, deficit family form are beginning to consider the strengths and weaknesses of this unique family in relation to other systems and demographic variables. Cashion (1982) in her review of female-headed families in the 70s closed her article by suggesting that poverty, not the number of adult parents, is the "plague" of the single parent family (p. 83). How might family scientists design research to document that divorcing families are transitional families working to create a successful single parent family or enter into a blended family experience?

Family scientists have the responsibility to recast their perspective of the family headed by the single mother with custody from a deficit family model to a family which is growing and changing as it adapts to the experience of divorce in a series of transitions. In this culture, which is awed by science, research data is received with an authority which exceeds the power of its statistics and methods. It is essential that family scientists critique research studies with an eye to how these data will be read by the lay public who may not discriminate between a finding which is statistically meaningful and the fact that many studies with questionable results are published.

REFERENCES

Ahrons, C.R. (1980). Divorce: A crisis of family transition and change. *Family Relations*, *29*, 533-540.

Ahrons, C.R. (1981). The continuing co-parental relationship between divorced spouses. *American Journal of Orthopsychiatry*, *51*, 415-427.

Ahrons, C.R., & Wallisch, L.S. (1986). The relationship between former spouses. In S. Duck & D. Perlman (Eds.), *Close relationships: Development, dynamics, and deterioration* (pp. 269-296). Beverly Hills, CA: Sage.

Belle, D. (1982). *Lives in stress: Women and depression*. Beverly Hills, CA: Sage.

Berman, W.H. (1985). Continued attachment after legal divorce. *Journal of Family Issues*, *6*, 375-392.

Berman, W.H., & Turk, D.C. (1981). Adaptation to divorce: Problems and coping strategies. *Journal of Marriage and the Family*, *43*, 179-189.

Bloom, B.L., & Clement, C. (1984). Marital sex role orientation and adjustment to separation and divorce. *Journal of Divorce*, *73*, 87-98.

Bronfenbrenner, U. (1990). Foreword. In M. Cochran, M. Larner, D. Riley, L. Gunnarsson, & C.R. Henderson, Jr. (Eds.), *Extending families: The social networks of parents and their children* (p. vii). Cambridge, MA: Cambridge University Press.

Buehler, C., Betz, P., Ryan, C.M., Legg, B.H., & Trotter, B.B. (1992). Description and evaluation of the *Orientation for Divorcing Parents*: Implications for postdivorce prevention programs. *Family Relations*, *41*, 154-162.

Burden, D.S. (1986). Single parents and the work setting: The impact of multiple job and homelife responsibilities. *Family Relations*, *35*, 37-43.

Carter, E.A. & McGoldrick, M. (1989). Overview: The changing family life cycle. In E.A. Carter & M. McGoldrick (Eds.), *The Changing Family Life Cycle* (pp. 3-28). Boston: Allyn and Bacon.

Cashion, B.G. (1982). Female headed families: Effects on children and clinical implications. *Journal of Marriage and Family Therapy*, *8*(2), 77-85.

Cherlin, A. (1983). Changing family and household: Contemporary lessons from historical research. *Annual Review of Sociology*, *9*, 51-66.

Clingempeel, W.G. & Reppucci, N.D. (1984). Joint custody after divorce: Major issues and goals for research. In J. Folberg (Ed.), *Joint custody and shared parenting* (pp. 87-110). Association of Family and Conciliation Courts: The Bureau of National Affairs, Inc.

Copeland, A.P. (1984). An early look at divorce: Mother-child interactions in the first post-separation year. *Journal of Divorce*, *8*(2), 17-30.

Coysh, W.S., Johnston, J.R., Tschann, J.M., Wallerstein, J.S., & Kline, M. (1989). Parental postdivorce adjustment in joint and sole physical custody families. *Journal of Family Issues*, *10*, 52-71.

Daniels-Mohring, D. & Berger, M. (1984). Social network changes and the adjustment to divorce. *Journal of Divorce*, *8*(1), 17-32.

Darling C.A., Davidson, J.K., Sr., & Parish, W.E., Jr. (1989). Single parents: Interaction of parenting and sexual issues. *Journal of Sex and Marital Therapy*, *15*, 227-244.

Dicosta, D.M. & Nelson G. (1988). Family and social network factors after divorce in Catholic Italian women and Catholic Anglophone women. *The Journal of Divorce*, *12*, 111-127.

Dreman, S., Orr, E., & Aldor, R. (1990). Sense of competence, time perspective, and state-anxiety of separated versus divorced mothers. *Journal of Orthopsychiatry*, *60*, 77-85.

Doherty, W.J., Su, S., & Needle, R. (1989). Marital disruption and psychological well-being. *Journal of Family Issues*, *10*, 72-85.

Finch, J. & Mason, J. (1990). Divorce, remarriage and family obligations. *The Sociological Review*, *38*, 219-247.

Fine, M.A. & Schwebel, A.I. (1988). An emergent explanation of differing racial reactions to single parenthood. *The Journal of Divorce*, *12*, 1-15.

Fine, M.A., Donnelly, B.W., & Voydanoff, P. (1986). Adjustment and satisfaction of parents. *Journal of Family Issues*, *7*, 393-404.

Furstenberg, F.F., Jr. & Cherlin, A.J. (1991). *Divided families: What happens to children when parents part* (pp. 62-76). Cambridge, MA: Harvard University Press.

Furstenberg, F.F., Jr. & Spanier, G.B. (1984). *Recycling the family: Remarriage after divorce* (pp. 7-86). Beverly Hills, CA: Sage.

Garfinkel, I. & McLanahan, S.S. (1986). *Single mothers and their children: A new American dilemma* (pp. 11-42, 129-188). Washington, D.C.: The Urban Institute Press.

Gelles, R.J. (1989). Child abuse and violence in single-parent families: Parent absence and economic deprivation. *American Journal of Orthopsychiatry*, *59*, 492-501.

Glick, P.C. (1984). Marriage, divorce, and living arrangements: Prospective changes. *Journal of Family Issues*, *5*, 7-26.

Goldman, J. (1982). Can family relationships be maintained after divorce. *The Journal of Divorce*, *5*, 141-158.

Goldsmith, J. (1980). Relationships between former spouses: Descriptive findings. *The Journal of Divorce*, *4*, 1-20.

Green, R.G. (1983). The influence of divorce prediction variables on divorce adjustment: An expansion and test of Lewis' and Spanier's theory of marital quality and marital stability. *The Journal of Divorce*, *7*(1), 67-82.

Gunnarsson, L. & Cochran, M. (1990). The support networks of single parents: Sweden and the United States. In M. Cochran, M. Larner, D. Riley, L. Gunnarsson, & C.R. Henderson, Jr. (Eds.), *Extending families: The social networks of parents and their children* (pp. 105-116). Cambridge, MA: Cambridge University Press.

Hamner, T.J. & Turner, P.H. (1985). *Parenting in contemporary society* (pp. 158-163). Englewood Cliffs, NJ: Prentice-Hall.

Hanson, S.M.H. (1986). Healthy single parent families. *Family Relations*, *35*, 125-132.

Hartmann, H. (1981). The family as the locus of gender, class, and political struggle: The example of housework. *Signs: Journal of Women in Culture and Society*, *6*, 366-394.

Herz Brown, F. (1989). Children and divorce. In E.A. Carter & M. McGoldrick (Eds.). *The changing family life cycle: A framework for family therapy* (pp. 371-398). Boston: Allyn and Bacon.

Hetherington, E.M., Cox, M., & Cox, M. (1982). Effects of divorce on parents and children. In M.E. Lamb (Ed.), *Nontraditional Families*, (pp. 233-288). Hillsdale, NJ: Lawrence Erlbaum.

Hill, R. (1986). Life cycle stages for types of single parent families: Of Family Development Theory. *Family Relations*, *35*, 19-29.

Hodges, W.F., Buchsbaum, H.K., & Tierney, C.W. (1983). Parent-child relationships and adjustment in preschool children in divorced and intact families. *The Journal of Divorce*, *7*(2), 43-58.

Hofferth, S.L. (1984). Kin networks, race, and family structure. *Journal of Marriage and the Family*, *46*, 791-806.

Hughes, R., Jr. (1988). Divorce and social support: A review. *Journal of Divorce*, *11*, 123-145.

Kaslow, F. (1983). Divorce: An evolutionary process of change in the family system. *The Journal of Divorce*, *7*(3), 21-39.

Kaslow, F. & Hyatt, R. (1982). Divorce: A potential growth experience for the extended family. *The Journal of Divorce*, *5*, 115-126.

Katz, M.H. & Piotrkowski, C.S. (1983). Correlates of family role strain among employed black women. *Family Relations*, *32*, 331-339.

Keith, P.M. & Schafer, R.B. (1982). Correlates of depression among single parent employed women. *The Journal of Divorce*, *5*(3), 49-60.

Kelly, J., Gigy, L., & Hausman, S. (1986). Mediated and adversarial divorce: Initial findings from The Divorce and Mediation Project. In J. Folberg & A. Milne (Eds.), *Divorce mediation: Theory and practice* (pp. 453-472). New York: Guilford Press.

Kitson, G.C., Moir, R.N., & Mason, P.R. (1982). Family social support in times of crisis: The special case of divorce. *American Journal of Orthopsychiatry*, *52*, 161-165.

Kolevzon, M.S. & Gottlieb, S.J. (1983). The impact of divorce: A multivariate study. *The Journal of Divorce*, *7*(2), 89-98.

Kurdek, L.A. & Blisk, D. (1983). Dimensions and correlates of mothers' divorce experience. *The Journal of Divorce*, *6*, 1-24.

Leslie, L.A. & Grady, K. (1988). Social support for divorcing mothers: What seems to help? *The Journal of Divorce*, *11*: 147-165.

Loveland-Cherry, C.J. (1986). Personal health practices in single parent and two parent families. *Family Relations*, *35*, 133-139.

Luepnitz, D.A. (1982). *Child custody: A study of families after divorce* (pp. 28-30). Lexington, MA: Lexington Books.

Machida, S. & Holloway, S.D. (1991). The relationship between divorced mothers' perceived control over child rearing and children's post-divorce development. *Family Relations*, *40*, 272-278.

Macklin, E.D. (1980). Nontraditional family forms: A decade of research. *Journal of Marriage and the Family*, *42*, 905-922.

Masheter, C. (1991). Postdivorce relationships between ex-spouses: The roles of attachment and interpersonal conflict. *Journal of Marriage and the Family*, *53*, 103-110.

McGoldrick, M. (1989). Women and the family life cycle. In E.A. Carter & M. McGoldrick (Eds.), *The changing family life cycle: A framework for family therapy* (pp. 29-69). Boston: Allyn and Bacon.

McKenry, P.C. & Price, S.J. (1991). Alternatives for support: Life after divorce–A literature review. *The Journal of Divorce and Remarriage*, *15*, 1-19.

McLanahan, S.S., Wedemeyer, N.V., & Adelberg, T. (1981). Network structure, social support and psychological well-being in the single parent family. *The Journal of Marriage and the Family*, *43*, 601-612.

Menaghan, E.G. (1985). Depressive affect and subsequent divorce. *Journal of Family Issues*, *6*, 295-306.

Milardo, R. M. (1987). Changes in social networks of women and men following divorce: A review. *Journal of Family Issues*, *8*, 78-96.

Norton, A.J. (1983). Family life cycle: 1980. *Journal of Marriage and the Family*, *45*(2), 267-275.

Pearson, J. & Thoennes, N. (1988). Divorce mediation research results. In J. Folberg & A. Milne (Eds.), *Divorce mediation* (pp. 429-452). New York: The Guilford Press.

Peck, J.S. & Manocherian, J.R. (1989). Divorce in the changing family life cycle. In E.A. Carter & M. McGoldrick (Eds.), *The changing family life cycle* (pp. 335-370). Boston, MA: Allyn and Bacon.

Peters, J.M. & Haldeman, V.A. (1987). Time used for household work: A study of school-age children from single-parent, two-parent, one-earner, and two-earner families. *Journal of Family Issues*, *8*, 212-225.

Pett, M. (1982). Predictors of satisfactory social adjustment of divorced, single parents. *The Journal of Divorce*, *5*(3), 1-18.

Rowe, B.R. (1991). The economics of divorce: Findings from seven states. *The Journal of Divorce*, *14*, 5-17.

Sack, W.H., Mason, R., & Higgins, J.E. (1985). The single-parent family and abusive child punishment. *American Journal of Orthopsychiatry, 55*, 252-259.

Sanick, M. M. & Mauldin, T. (1986). Single versus two parent families: A comparison of mothers' time. *Family Relations, 35*: 53-56.

Saul, S.C. & Scherman, A. (1983). Divorce grief and personal adjustment in divorced persons who remarry or remain single. *The Journal of Divorce, 7*(3), 75-85.

Scanzoni, J. (1987). Families in the 1980s: Time to refocus our thinking. *Journal of Family Issues, 8*, 394-421.

Schulmann, J. & Pitt, V. (1984). Second thoughts on joint child custody: Analysis of legislation and its implications for women and children. In J. Folberg (Ed.), *Joint custody and shared parenting* (pp. 209-222). Association of Family and Conciliation Courts: The Bureau of National Affairs, Inc.

Schwartz, P. (1987). The family as a changing institution. *Journal of Family Issues, 8*, 455-459.

Shrier, D.K., Simring, S.K., Shapiro, E.T., Greif, J.B., & Lindenthal, J.J. (1991). Level of satisfaction of fathers and mothers with joint of sole custody arrangements: Results of a questionnaire. *The Journal of Divorce, 14*, 163-169.

Spanier, G. and Thompson, L. (1989). *Parting*. Beverly Hills, CA: Sage.

Staples, R. and Johnson, L.B. (1993). *Black families at the crossroads: Challenges and prospects* (pp. 139-194). San Francisco: Jossey-Bass Publ.

Steinman, S. (1981). The experience of children in a joint-custody arrangement: A report of a study. *American Journal of Orthopsychiatry, 51*(3), 403-414.

Steinman, S. (1984). Joint custody: What we know, what we have yet to learn, and the judicial and legislative implications. In J. Folberg (Ed.), *Joint custody and shared parenting* (pp. 111-127). Association of Family and Conciliation Courts: The Bureau of National Affairs, Inc.

Taylor, R.J. (1986). Receipt of support from family among black American's demographic and familial differences. *Journal of Marriage and the Family, 48*, 67-77.

Thomas, S.P. (1982). After divorce: Personality factors related to the process of adjustment. *The Journal of Divorce, 5*(3), 19-36.

Thomson, E., McLanahan, S.S., & Curtin, R.B. (1992). Family structure, gender, and parental socialization. *Journal of Marriage and the Family, 54*, 368-378.

Veevers, J.E. (1991). Traumas versus stress: A paradigm of positive versus negative divorce outcomes. *The Journal of Divorce, 12*, 99-126.

Wagner, R.M. (1988a). Changes in extended family relationships for Mexican American and Anglo single mothers. *The Journal of Divorce, 12*, 69-87.

Wagner, R.M. (1988b). Changes in the friend network during the first year of single parenthood for Mexican American and Anglo women. *The Journal of Divorce, 12*, 89-109.

Wallerstein, J.S. (1986). Women after divorce: Preliminary report from a ten-year follow-up. *American Journal of Orthopsychiatry, 56*, 65-77.

Wallerstein, J.S. and Blakeslee, S. (1989). *Second chances*. New York: Ticknor & Fields.

Wallerstein, J.S. & Kelly, J. (1980). *Surviving the breakup: How children and parents cope with divorce*. New York: Basic Books.

Warren, N.J. & Amara, I.A. (1984). Education groups for single parents: The Parenting after Divorce program. *The Journal of Divorce*, *8*(2), 79-96.

Weitzman, L. (1985). *The divorce revolution* (pp. 184-261). NY: The Free Press.

Zimmerman, S.L. (1991a). The welfare state and family breakup: The mythical connection. *Family Relations*, *40*, 139-147.

Zimmerman, S.L. (1991b). A response to the comments on "The welfare state and family breakup: The mythical connection." *Family Relations*, *40*, 153-154.

Chapter 10

Single Fathers with Custody Following Separation and Divorce

Geoffrey L. Greif

SUMMARY. After years of neglect by researchers, therapists, and lawmakers, interest in fathering has come to the forefront. One group of fathers, those raising their children alone following separation or divorce, has more than tripled in the period between 1970 and 1990 according to the Census Bureau. The literature on single custodial fathers, a population that was virtually unstudied until the 1970s, is based on both large and small samples. Comparison groups consisting of fathers without custody, fathers in joint custody arrangements, married fathers, widowers, and mothers with custody have been employed to further understand single father families. The research shows this lifestyle to be a viable one despite the role ambiguity associated with it. Particular areas of difficulties for these fathers are balancing work and child care, reestablishing a social life, and interacting with the court system. Fathers who choose the role tend to have an easier time than those who are forced into it. This article provides an overview of the topic and discusses the policy, practice, education, and research implications that the literature raises.

KEYWORDS. Single parent families, Custody, Single fathers, Divorce

---

Geoffrey L. Greif is Associate Professor, School of Social Work, University of Maryland at Baltimore, 525 W. Redwood St., Baltimore, MD 21201.

[Haworth co-indexing entry note]: "Single Fathers with Custody Following Separation and Divorce." Greif, Geoffrey L. Co-published simultaneously in *Marriage & Family Review* (The Haworth Press, Inc.) Vol. 20, No. 1/2, 1995, pp. 213-231; and: *Single Parent Families: Diversity, Myths and Realities* (ed: Shirley M. H. Hanson et al.) The Haworth Press, Inc., 1995, pp. 213-231. Multiple copies of this article/chapter may be purchased from The Haworth Document Delivery Center [1-800-3-HAWORTH; 9:00 a.m. - 5:00 p.m. (EST)].

After years of being on the "backburner" of every researcher's grant application, mental health practitioner's calendar, and social policy expert's agenda, fathering has moved into the forefront. It is not only concern with child support collection, African-American male role models, and working mothers in need of child care that have resulted in this new interest. Something more fundamental is happening. The American family, beset by high rates of divorce and out-of-wedlock births, is in trouble. As people look for ways to correct the problems, attention turns to fathers. Common questions arise: Where is the father? How involved is he with his children? What happens to him after a breakup?

In the search for answers, one group of fathers that has garnered particular attention is the father who is potentially most involved: the single custodial father. Even *Reader's Digest* has shown an interest in how single fathers are portrayed on television (Mitchard, 1992). This attention is not without reason. Recent Census Bureau reports have recognized these men as one of the fastest growing groups of ever married single parents (U.S. Department of Commerce, 1989). Whereas in 1970 there were 393,000 single male head of households raising at least one child under 18 alone, the number tripled to 1,351,000 by 1990. The percentage of single custodial parents who were male increased by approximately one-third during this time period to 13.9%. The vast majority of the children these men were raising had mothers living elsewhere, i.e., the number of widowers fell from 124,000 in 1970 to 89,000 by 1990 (U.S. Department of Commerce, 1990). As expected the number of children in single father-headed homes also increased accordingly, from 748,000 in 1970 to 2,016,000 in 1991 (U.S. Department of Commerce, 1992). It is easy to mark 1970 as the beginning of the growth in these families: between 1960 and 1970 the number of children being raised by fathers grew by only 24,000, less than 4% of single parent families, whereas the numbers increased by more than 50% in the next decade, and by almost another 100% again between 1980 and 1990 (U.S. Department of Commerce, 1991). (The reader is also directed to Bianchi's article in this volume.)

If only from an epidemiological point of view, these fathers would merit discussion. But it is clear they should be discussed for a wealth of other reasons: (1) gaining a better understanding of these fathers holds promise of learning more about fathering in general; (2) with the divorce rate high, father custody remains a viable option for many separating families; (3) practitioners are increasingly being confronted by father-headed families and could benefit from a working knowledge of the psychological tasks they are facing; and (4) family policy issues, such as child support and family leave, have absorbed a great deal of the public's attention. A sub-topic in the consideration of family policy issues is the manner in which these policies are applied to fathers when they gain custody.

This article first reviews the single father research during the 20 year period from 1972 to 1992. Single fatherhood here is defined as a father having sole custody the vast majority of the time, i.e., a minimum of five full days a week on average. In these arrangements, the fathers are performing the bulk of the childrearing and are seen as having to adjust accordingly. The article then examines the policy, practice, education, and research implications of the issues raised in the literature.

How do we account for the increase in fathers with custody? Historical precedent exists for men to be raising children alone, though not necessarily because of separation or divorce. Prior to the early years of the 20th century, complications of child birth and disease claimed the lives of many mothers, often leaving fathers to raise children alone or with the help of extended family (Orthner, Brown, & Ferguson, 1976). Adding to the number of father-headed families during this time was the prevailing legal system in the United States in which men "owned" their children and women had few rights of their own. If a family dissolved and a man wanted custody, he held the chips. It was not until the late 19th century, during the Progressive Era, that children and then women gained legal independence from men. At the same time, with the burgeoning Industrial Revolution, men were increasingly being pulled away from the home and going to work in factories. As a result, the importance of the mother to the family was growing (Greif, 1985a; Hanson, 1988). The spread of Freudian psychology further supported the role of the mother in early child development. What followed were many years of legal presumption favoring the mother.

The presumption that a child's interests are best served by a mother has not been seriously questioned until recently. With the women's movement and alterations in many states' custody and child support laws to sex neutral criteria, mothers no longer have the favored status many believe they once possessed. Such changes make it easier for fathers to gain custody when they seek it and account, along with an exploding divorce rate, for some of the rise in single father-headed families.

Further swelling the numbers are the behaviors of the mothers and fathers themselves. With a job market that is increasingly "female-friendly," mothers have more attractive options for how they wish to define themselves. Thus a mother who chooses to pursue a career may be more willing to relinquish custody in the event of a marital breakup than was her predecessor. The increase in joint custody decisions may also add to the single father phenomenon. If a couple is willing to agree upon joint custody, they are a step closer to sole father custody than if they had originally planned for the mother to have custody. In other words, after opening the door for a shared custody arrangement, it is not difficult to have the arrangement evolve, either following a residential move or a remarriage, to a situation where the father has sole custody. Finally, fathers are more willing to be full-time caretakers than before. If a men's movement is afoot in the United States, one outcome of it may be increased willingness for fathers to explore their relationship with their own father as well as with their children. Taken together, these factors may account for much of the growth in these parenting arrangements.

PREVIOUS RESEARCH

Whenever a body of literature on a certain topic is being reviewed, it is possible to consider it in a number of different ways. Here the decision has been made to review the literature as a series of contributions by authors to particular topics. The literature will be examined for its application to the internal and external worlds of the single father. The internal world is meant to refer to the fathers at home, i.e., the feelings fathers have about their parenting experience and themselves as well as to the tasks related to the maintenance of the home (housekeeping and arranging child care). The external world (which often overlaps with the internal) is meant to refer to the interface between the father and the larger systems–experiences at work, dating, navigating the court system, and the evolving relationship with the mother of the children. To aid in understanding this last relationship, occasional reference will be made to the mother without custody. The relevance her well-being has to the single father family cannot be overestimated.

This review will focus on the experiences of single fathers in the United States. Significant and early research has also occurred in other countries, particularly Great Britain where George and Wilding (1972) studied the case loads of 588 single fathers (referred to as lone fathers) known to Health and Education Departments and the Departments of Health and Social Security. Additional early research in Great Britain includes the work of Murch (1973), Ferri (1973), and Ferri and Robinson (1976). Other countries have followed. Katz (1979), working in Australia, surveyed 409 members of Parents Without Partners (PWP) and Wilson (1988, 1989) surveyed 85 members of the same organization. Brown and Ralph (1988) in Tasmania conducted in-depth interviews with 18 "sole-supporting" fathers. Schlesinger and Todres (1976) and Todres (1978) have touched on single fathers in Canada through the viewpoint of mothers without custody, and Saunders and Melville (1987) offered a comparison of custodial mothers and fathers. Non-English speaking countries have also been concerned with single fathers. For example, Shu (1989) reports on the development of a model for understanding single parents based on interviews with over 600 parents in Taipei, Taiwan, a few of whom were fathers.

United States Research

The first wave of research in the United States was published in the mid 1970s and used small samples. By the mid 1980s, larger samples and more sophisticated statistical packages were being used routinely. Almost every relevant comparison group has been employed at some point in the research: widowers (Gasser & Taylor, 1976); fathers without custody (Gersick, 1979; Rosenthal & Keshet, 1981); married fathers (Stewart, Schwebel, & Fine, 1986); mothers with custody (DeFrain & Eirick, 1981); and mothers without custody (Greif & Pabst, 1988). The sample sizes have ranged from a handful to over 1100. Regardless of when the research was undertaken, one consistent finding seems to have emerged–single father families are a viable lifestyle. None of the research questions whether fathers should be raising children alone. The fathers that have serious concerns with childrearing are a minority ranging from 5% to 25% of the sample. The one exception is a study that examined a particular sub-group–17 fathers who gained custody of a child from a mother who was known to child protective services. In that sample, a small minority was deemed appropriate (Greif & Zuravin, 1989).

The reasons fathers give for gaining custody have shown a shift over time that reflects societal changes. Whereas prior to the 1970s, a mother often had to be proven unfit for a father to gain custody. Thus, initially, fathers are described as gaining custody because of the mothers' voluntarily relinquishing custody because of mental problems, illness, or not wanting the children (Orthner et al., 1976; Rosenthal & Keshet, 1981). One study found fathers seeking custody because of wanting revenge at their wives who had been unfaithful (Gersick, 1979). Later studies, concomitant with the rise in no fault divorce, list issues such as the financial status of the mother in relation to the father, the children choosing the father, and the father wanting to hold on to his family and his home (Chang & Deinard, 1982; Greif, 1985a) as reasons. These issues have also found considerable support in studies of mothers without custody (Greif & Pabst, 1988).

It is rare for these fathers to have custody decided by a court battle–the majority gained custody by mutual agreement (Bartz & Witcher, 1976; Greif & DeMaris, 1989; Rosenthal & Keshet, 1981). (For further discussion of contested custody, see Turner, 1984 and Giles-Sims & Urwin, 1989.)

Role theory is the most common lens applied when considering the theoretical constraints on the fathers. Many researchers approach their subjects with a view towards their fulfilling a role for which there are few role prescriptions (Chang and Deinard, 1982; Gersick, 1979; Hanson, 1981; Mendes, 1976b, Orthner et al., 1976; Greif & Demaris, 1989; Smith & Smith, 1981). The theoretical hypothesis is that the fathers will have difficulty adjusting as a result. As noted, this was not substantiated by the research. In fact, if there is one overriding view presented continually in the research, it is the expectation of a strawman, i.e., a stereotypical view of the father that is almost humorous. Like the greeting cards that currently make fun of men as unfeeling rocks, the fathers are thought to be incompetent and stressed to the breaking point. But perhaps because men continue to be viewed this way in society, it is the theoretical model that best applies.

Demographic Profile

For the most part, as Hanson (1988) has noted in her thorough literature review, the demographic profile of single fathers in the research has been fairly homogenous–white, middle-class, Protestant and Catholic, with a slightly higher than average income and some college education. Mendes (1976b), with nearly a 50% minority proportion out of 32 fathers is the exception regarding racial composition. More recent U.S. studies identify slightly greater variations in race and class. Bowen's (1987) sample of 87 U.S. Air Force fathers was 76% white. Greif's (1990) sample of 1,132 (see also Greif & DeMaris, 1989; 1990), gained in the late 1980s from the membership of Parents Without Partners and court records in three east coast cities, had a mean income slightly above the national average, but one-quarter held no more than a high school education and were clearly not middle-class. One review of three different data sources places single custodial fathers' income between that of single mothers and married fathers (Meyer & Garasky, 1993). Income though has not been found to have a significant impact on parent-child relationships (Hanson, 1981) or on a variety of parenting experiences (Greif, 1985b). What was significant was a *change* in a father's income; that is, fathers whose incomes declined because of being a single father were believed to have more difficulties (Greif, 1990).

Fathers tended to be in their late 30s and to be raising between one and two children with an average age above five years. There was a slightly greater likelihood for the child in the home to be male than female (Chang &

Deinard, 1982; Greif, 1985b; Greif, 1990) but variations ranged even to the point of a majority of the children raised in one study being girls (Mendes, 1976b).

One question that remains is whether the demographic profile is changing. As it becomes increasingly common for fathers to gain custody, it can be hypothesized that their profile will more typically represent fathers in general, rather than the somewhat more affluent well-educated fathers who comprised the early pioneers of custody-seeking males.

INTERNAL FUNCTIONING OF THE SINGLE FATHER-HEADED FAMILY

The first content area to be considered centers on the *internal* functioning of the single father-headed family; that is, how the father feels about his parenting situation and how he handles home-related tasks. An important or relevant question is: Is there a relationship between the fathers' early experiences as a child, their initial experiences in the marriage and their later experiences when they have custody? In general, the answer is no. Gersick (1979) found no difference between 20 fathers with custody and 20 fathers without custody in whether they came from a single parent home or in their participation in childrearing in the intact marriage. He did discover, though, that fathers with custody seemed to be closer with their own mothers than those without custody. Greif's (1990) survey of 1,132 fathers, which included in-depth interviews with a subsample, also found no connection between being a custodial father and being raised in a single parent family. In addition, the majority said they had not given much consideration to childrearing when they were young. During the early stages of their marriages, they did not describe themselves as overly involved in childrearing though many had been present at the birth of the child. Hanson's (1981) study of 37 father-child pairs did not find any significant link between quality of the current father-child relations and the relationship the fathers had experienced with their own fathers in their original family of origin. As might be expected, fathers who choose to become custodians, a group Mendes (1976b) refers to as seekers, seem to have an easier time adjusting to a variety of parenting tasks than those who assent to the role (see also Hanson, 1981; Greif, 1985b). With occasional exceptions, the fathers seem to have few problems handling housekeeping even though the question of who they hire or solicit to help them is often asked. Contrary to popular belief, housekeepers are rarely hired (Risman, 1986; Bartz & Witcher, 1978) with the highest utilization of outside help totalling no more than one in three in any given sample (Gasser & Taylor, 1976). Greif (1985b) reports that men adjust to the housework following an initial period of confusion and that some share their housework with their children (see also Smith & Smith, 1981) while others feel the necessity to run things on their own as a way of proving their competence. One study of the division of chores within the single father home found that children helped out more as they aged and that daughters assisted more than sons (Greif, 1985c).

Unlike housekeeping, arranging child care is a concern, as it is for most working parents. If the father provides it himself it often means a redefinition of what it means to be a father and a man (Keshet & Rosenthal, 1978). As the vast majority of fathers in the studies were working, paid day care and sitters were used extensively, with relatives used less often. The problems posed by children vary by age. Child care is the most stressful for fathers with children in the 5 to 11 year old range because of the temptation to leave them on their own when they are not yet ready. Younger children clearly need child care and older ones can be left on their own (Greif, 1985b). Finding child care was ranked fifth in difficulty out of 11 categories by fathers in Chang and Deinard's (1982) study and as a major concern in Bartz and Witcher's (1978). Day care and out of home sitters proved more satisfactory than in-home situations in some families as there was more consistency in the adult caregivers (Mendes, 1976a). Time management, i.e., having enough time for the children, was also a frequently mentioned problem for the fathers (Chang & Deinard, 1982).

Another "internal" area explored is the feelings the fathers have about their role as father. Rosenthal and Keshet (1981) describe how fathers, when they first gained custody, sought reassurance from their children to an unhealthy degree. Some fathers became frustrated and upset with being unable to understand their children's feelings when the children cried or were unmanageable. Almost half received help with their children's feelings from friends, family members, or professionals (Keshet & Rosenthal, 1976). Only with time did most of the fathers move past the need to rely on their children for validation.

Mendes (1976a) points out how children raise different issues for the fathers depending on the child's age and gender. Love and affection were shared more openly with younger than older children and fathers raising daughters expressed concerns about their daughters' sexuality. Bartz and Witcher (1978) and to a lesser extent Orthner et al. (1978) also described fathers who were uncomfortable raising daughters and may have hesitated to actively seek custody of them because of their gender.

Greif (1985b) states that, while fathers had more questions about raising daughters, they were not necessarily having more trouble with them. DeMaris and Greif (1992), using Hudson's Index of Parental Attitudes Scale and examining fathers raising children in three age groups and comparing them also by gender, concluded that fathers felt the best toward their pre-adolescent daughters.

The other question about the father's feelings concerns itself with his level of comfort. Greif and DeMaris (1990) found 28% of the sample to be "mixed" or uncomfortable in the role of single father, a level similar to that found by Smith and Smith (1981). A logistic regression analysis revealed seven variables that were related to a diminution in discomfort: the number of years of sole custody, satisfaction with a social life; not having a religious affiliation; an increasing income; having a higher rating of himself as parent; a good relationship with the children; and if visitation is handled amicably or if there is no visitation (as opposed to visitation occurring under "somewhat" amicable conditions.) Facchino and Aron (1990) came to similar conclusions, with older and better educated fathers having an easier adjustment. Loneliness has also been noted to be a barrier to happiness (Smith & Smith, 1981).

Other studies have used standardized measures to further analyze issues of competence and comfort. Nieto (1990) administered the California Psychological Inventory to the 213 fathers in his survey and found reasonably high degrees of self-worth. Consistent with other findings, only one-fifth felt that others regarded them negatively as a single parent and about one-quarter believed that a single father-headed family was a pathological family structure.

Stewart et al. (1986), using the Beck Depression Inventory and other measures, learned that custodial fathers exhibited less anxiety and depression than noncustodial fathers and had similar levels of adjustment as fathers who were married. The presence of children in the father's life was hypothesized to explain some of the difference between groups. (For additional research on children being raised by single fathers, see Ambert, 1982; Downey & Powell, 1993; Santrock & Warshak, 1979; Schnayer & Orr, 1989).

EXTERNAL FUNCTIONING OF THE FATHER-HEADED FAMILY

Slightly less attention has been paid in the research to the relationship of the father with the external systems with which he comes in contact. Not only must a father maintain the status quo within his home, he also must cope with such issues as balancing work and childrearing, dating, establishing a relationship with his ex-wife, and navigating the court system.

Perhaps one of the most difficult areas to balance is that of work and childcare. Many men in today's society feel judged by their success at work. When they cannot pursue a career to the extent they wish because of their single parenting responsibilities, their self-esteem may suffer as well as their financial stability. Gasser and Taylor (1976) reported that almost half of their sample found the pursuance of job possibilities problematic and over half had difficulty arranging business trips. Lack of employment flexibility was one of the top concerns of fathers in Chang and Deinard's (1982) research. Greif (1985b) learned that the most frequently reported work-related changes were having to arrive late or leave early, having to miss work, and having to reduce work-related travel. Occasionally fathers were fired or had to quit. The more children the father raised, the more difficult his work situation was. Only one-quarter reported no work related changes because of assuming sole custody.

Dating also poses problems for many of the fathers, even though their social lives are active. In one study, 95% of the fathers reported recent dating activity, with most "playing the field" rather than seeing one person (Orthner et al., 1976). Another noted that 80% of the fathers were dating with almost the same percentage bringing dates home to meet their children (DeFrain & Eirick, 1982). Two other studies found dating posed a problem for between 40% (Chang & Deinard, 1982) and over half of those interviewed (Gasser & Taylor, 1976). Some, feeling vulnerable and hurt following the breakup of the marriage, found it difficult to date. Others feel constrained by the demands of childrearing or the vocal objections of their children who are lobbying for their parents to reconcile. In many cases, socializing does not begin until a few months after the breakup (Greif, 1985b) and does not become serious until three years post-separation (Greif, 1990). Satisfaction with dating is not always correlated with frequency though social satisfaction is more likely if the father is having sexual relations (Greif, 1990).

A third area to examine in the fathers' external involvements is the co-parental relationship with the ex-wife. This, when functioning well, can be a cornerstone of the family's adaptation. When relations are smooth, the ground is set for an easier transition to the single parent family. Yet it often mirrors the contentiousness and ambivalence of the breakup. As with all post-marital relationships, there is great variation. Distrust between the father and his ex-wife is often high (Greif, 1985b). Some wish their ex-wives were more involved with the children while others believe they are too involved. At times the fathers took steps to reduce her involvement.

DeFrain and Eirick (1981) report that one-third of the fathers they interviewed tried to coax the children into siding with them against the mother.

Research on non-custodial mothers shows a similar pattern. They tend to have a favorable view of the father's ability to parent, with only one in five rating the father as a poor parent. Half, though, said they were never consulted about the children, confirming the impression given above that some fathers may try to actively impede contact (Greif & Pabst, 1988).

The final external area explored is the interaction between the father and the legal system. Despite many fathers having custody, and most gaining it without a court battle, the situation surrounding court contact is clearly stressful both emotionally and financially for all family members. Fathers often perceive bias against them because of maternal presumption even though most state laws by the mid 1980s were supposed to protect them against such a presumption. They tended to go to court only when they believed they had a good chance of winning (Rosenthal & Keshet, 1981). Greif and DeMaris (1989) explored the differences between fathers who fought for custody in court (20% of their sample) and those who were awarded it without a battle. Those who battled reported more conflict at the time of the breakup and had a tendency to be seeking custody of girls. Income, the age of the children, and the father's involvement with the children before the breakup were not significantly related to having fought for custody. Returning to court after an agreement is noted to be rare (Greif, 1990).

What happens to these fathers over time? In a followup study of 28 fathers who remained single three years after participating in a survey (Greif, 1987), the ex-wives' involvement was reported to have increased (see also Greif & Emad, 1989) and the fathers gave themselves a slightly higher rating as a parent. No other significant changes were noted in such areas as satisfaction with social life, comfort being single, satisfaction with child care or in the relationship with the children, or in the rating the father gave the mother.

In general, single parent or single fathers report a fairly high level of comfort with their situation. Over time, while they show some improvement in a few areas, other problems loom. For example, even though housework and child care get easier to manage as children become more responsible and independent, raising older children poses new challenges. Adolescent sexuality and peer pressures challenge many parent-child relationships in ways that they have not been challenged before. Also, over time, loneliness may increase as the hope of a new marriage (if desired) diminishes. One potential bright spot is that, in many cases, the co-parental relationship with the ex-wife grows more satisfactory.

POLICY IMPLICATIONS

With the democrats reclaiming the White House in 1993, renewed interest is being devoted to children in the context of their families. Whereas issues such as family leave and greater access to child care have applicability to both fathers and mothers, two areas of particular note to fathers are custody decisions and child support. These need to be considered in relation to the status of men in broader society. It is well-established that, in the past, some fathers never pursued custody because they believed the courts were biased toward the mother (McCant, 1987). If men have not been valued in the home as the caretaker, how can they assume they would win custody? More recently, and with changing legislation, debate has focused on whether one parent has the advantage over the other in a custody dispute. Both fathers' and mothers' rights activists argue that the other has the upper hand. Atkinson (1984) contends that men win about half the time when they contest. Others think men win more often as financial stability is increasingly used as a yardstick. Despite custody laws being written in gender neutral language, the *perception* among many fathers is that the courts, even in the 1990s, remain biased. Thus as they consider sole or even joint custody they worry that they will not be able to win. Others fret that once they win custody, they will not be able to retain it. This last point is noteworthy as the research suggests that fathers do not tend to lose custody in court after they have won it. Yet it is also a fact that children of divorce frequently go back and forth voluntarily between their parents.

From a policy perspective the integrity of the custody process must be preserved. Fathers, as well as mothers must be convinced that decisions are made on the basis of the best interests of the child and not gender. Until fathers can feel validated by court personnel and lawyers in their quest for custody, and until they feel that their attempts for custody are being measured on their own merits, the process will be more stressful and less successful than it need be. Such stress can clearly have a negative impact on the children if they are swept along into a traumatic decision-making process which even defies mediation (e.g., Johnston & Campbell, 1988). With these warnings, every indication is that the courts have become much more responsive to the needs of fathers and their children.

Closely connected to this is the issue of child support which is linked to economic equity between men and women. In one study of data from Wisconsin, fathers were much less likely to be awarded child support than mothers (Meyer & Garasky, 1993). Social policy is written primarily for the intention of gaining support payments from non-paying fathers for mothers. Yet how it is written also affects the support of custodial fathers.

Both women and men have a poor history of child support payments when they have been court-ordered to pay.

The policy issue revolves around models of child support payments that are gender neutral and fair. Most cases are not easily resolved by simple formulae (Takas, 1992) and thus whatever criteria are used must be flexible enough to meet the complicated demands of situations that account for, among other things, changing incomes, changing marital statuses, and changing age of children. The payment of child support and visitation often become intertwined (Czapanskiy, 1989) such that if payments are not being made, visitation is hampered. They need to be considered separately so that contact with the noncustodial parent will not be unfairly affected if he or she is in arrears.

Some research on child support shows a relationship between consistent payment by the father and visitation (Seltzer, Schaeffer, & Charng, 1989; Teachman & Polonko, 1990). In the single father research it has been found that fathers rarely receive child support (14.3% of mothers without custody in one study claimed they paid (Greif, 1986a) and 23% of fathers with custody in another claimed they were court ordered to receive it (Greif & DeMaris, 1991)). Mothers who do pay support visited more and had higher incomes than those who did not visit (Greif, 1986a). Fathers report that when the ex-wife's income is known and it is higher than his, the chances of being awarded support increase (Greif & DeMaris, 1991).

This last point bodes well for the fair treatment of fathers in these matters. Yet again, the perception is that getting custody in court in a "biased" system is enough of a success. Being awarded child support in addition is rarely expected. Fathers behave accordingly and are loathe to seek both custody and child support, even though it is clearly within their rights.

PRACTICE AND EDUCATIONAL IMPLICATIONS

Mental health practitioners need to work on a number of fronts to help single fathers, particularly those, as Hanson (1985) suggests, having the most trouble coping. The first task is to educate others in the community, e.g., churches, schools, child care centers, employers, etc., about the viability of these families (Schnayer & Orr, 1989; Risman, 1986). Second, is to inform them of the potential service and psychological needs of these families (Orthner et al., 1976; Bartz & Witcher, 1978). Third, practitioners need to be aware of the clinical issues. These families, while homogenous in many ways, present a diverse picture to the practitioner (Risman, 1986). A sound assessment of the issues facing the father-headed family must be undertaken to avoid stereotyping and insensitive treatment approaches.

Specifics to consider in clinical work are judging the appropriateness of individual, or group, or family work. If family therapy is needed, the structural approach (Greif, 1986b) has been noted as an effective model. Support groups for single parents have also been helpful. Those seeking treatment will most likely be experiencing some of the common difficulties of single parenthood–loneliness, difficulty adjusting to being single, problems balancing work and child care, and problematic relations with their children or a lack of knowledge about how to raise them (Greif, 1985d). These issues require empathy and concrete assistance as well as a keen awareness of the isolation that these parents experience. Family of origin issues may need exploration (Greif & DeMaris, 1990). Many men were raised in a time when parenting was the purview of the mother. Their fulfilling this role has implications for how they see their own masculinity and for how they attempt to meet the competing demands they face.

The availability of resources for assisting fathers varies by community. Parents Without Partners, which primarily focuses on socializing but also provides education, has chapters in many cities. Its national chapter is in Silver Spring, Maryland where it also publishes a magazine, *The Single Parent*, containing a variety of helpful articles. For the more litigious minded single father, some cities have chapters of Fathers United for Equal Rights, (or other similar groups), that fight locally for a fairer hearing for men in court. In extreme cases, if a father has been denied custody due to an abduction, the father can contact the National Center for Missing and Exploited Children, in Arlington, Virginia. *Full-time Dads*, (P.O. Box 577, Cumberland, ME 04021) a quarterly publication for fathers, may also be a beneficial resource as will be the literature cited in this article. Fathers fighting for custody may be further interested in issues of *Family Advocate*, (see Winter 1993) a journal published by the Family Law Section of the American Bar Association.

Educators must guard against teaching students to assume that single parent families are automatically headed by mothers. The anecdotal literature is replete with examples of teachers who tell children to share school-related issues with their mothers rather than with their parents. University-level educators, whether teaching practitioners, other educators, or social policy theoreticians, should insure that content in their courses is relevant to the changing domestic scene and the greater involvement of fathers in the intact family.

RESEARCH IMPLICATIONS

Gaps in the literature remain. Representative samples are difficult to obtain. The fathers who participated in these studies were volunteers who either responded to a direct personal, mail, or media-generated request, or saw a questionnaire in a magazine. It is unclear what the potential biases are in the samples. Who were the fathers who were not contacted or elected not to participate when they were asked? Did the fathers who responded participate because they were proud of their parenting experience or because they were in need of assistance?

Most striking is the lack of variation in the research findings. Is this really as unproblematic a parenting arrangement as reported? The following explanations are possible: (1) men underreport their concerns; (2) men have been socialized to not experience concerns in the same way that women do and thus have fewer complaints to discuss; and/or (3) are the samples skewed? These are all volunteer respondents. Would, for example, a random telephone survey draw a markedly different and more troubled sample?

Most likely, before significant advances can be made in understanding these fathers, major funding will be needed. Research on other key social phenomena, like child abuse, is being sufficiently funded to design more elegant research and, at times, to offer participants money. For example, funding to interview and test all fathers who come through the court system would potentially produce a larger range of fathers. Methods would still have to be devised to attract fathers who gain custody without court-related involvement.

In gaining a wider sample, racial minorities, a group that has been difficult to reach, could be included. The number of children being raised by black single fathers has doubled from 1980 to 1991 to 358,000, a much greater percentage increase than the numbers of children being raised by black single mothers (U.S. Department of Commerce, 1992). Obtaining a more ethnically diverse population would aid understanding of a much broader range of fathers and would inform theory building and practice.

More longitudinal research is also needed. No detailed understanding exists as to what changes these fathers undergo over time. An important question to explore would be: Do they adjust or do they instead experience little improvement and even a diminution in satisfaction as what some believe to be a temporary situation takes on the specter of being a more permanent one?

CONCLUSIONS

While many fathers claim to feel comfortable as the sole custodian, there are those who clearly suffer. As it becomes easier for fathers to gain sole custody, the outlook for these men as a group is unclear. It may be that more will experience difficulty with this role than their predecessors. Previous generations of single fathers may have been more capable parents than the current ones as it was more difficult to obtain custody in the past. At the same time there is greater acceptance of and more services geared towards single parents than before. Despite these questions, the research clearly indicates that single father-headed families are viable. Particular areas of stress tend to center on balancing the demands of work and child care, socializing, and negotiating with the court system.

There is every indication that the population of single father-headed families will continue to grow. We have to be prepared to understand them and to meet their needs. Without including them in practice, education, and social policy we are dooming them and their children to a nether world where mothers will continue to be seen as the only logical course when it comes to child rearing. As one single father once wrote across a questionnaire he returned for a survey, "Send me the results (of the survey) quickly. How many other freaks are there out there like me?" (Greif, 1985b, p. 151). Let us not sentence the next generation of single fathers to the same feeling.

REFERENCES

Ambert, A.-M. (1982). Differences in children's behavior towards custodial mothers and custodial fathers. *Journal of Marriage and the Family, 44*, 73-86.

Atkinson, J. (1984). Criteria for deciding child custody in the trial and appellate courts. *Family Law Quarterly, 28*, 1-42.

Bartz, K.W. & Witcher, W.C. (1978). When father gets custody. *Children Today*, 7(5): 2-6, 35.

Bowen, G.L. (1987). Single fathers in the Air Force. *Social Casework, 68*, 339-344.

Brown, V. & Ralph, T. (1988). Sole-supporting fathers: A study, Primary Health Care Unit–Community Research Project, Tasmanian State Institute of Technology, November.

Chang, P. & Deinard, A.S. (1982). Single-father caretakers: Demographic characteristics and adjustment processes. *American Journal of Orthopsychiatry, 52*, 236-242.

Czapanskiy, K. (1989). Child support and visitation: Rethinking the connections. *Rutgers Law Journal, 20*, 619-665.

DeFrain, J. & Eirick, R. (1981). Coping as divorced single parents: A comparative study of fathers and mothers. *Family Relations, 30*, 265-273.

DeMaris, A. & Greif, G.L. (1992). The relationship between family structure and parent-Child relationship problems in single father households. *Journal of Divorce & Remarriage, 18*, 55-77.

Downey, D.B. & Powell, B. (1993). Do children in single-parent households fare better living with same-sex parent? *Journal of Marriage and the Family, 55*, 55-71.

Facchino, D. & Aron, A. (1990). Divorced fathers with custody: Method of obtaining custody and divorce adjustment. *Journal of Divorce, 13*, 45-56.

Ferri, E. (1973). Characteristics of motherless families. *British Journal of Social Work, 3*, 91-100.

Ferri, E. & Robinson, H. (1976). *Coping Alone*. England: NFER Publishing.

Gasser, R.D. & Taylor, C.M. (1976). Role adjustment of single parent fathers with dependent children. *The Family Coordinator, 25*, 397-401.

George, V. & Wilding, P. (1972). *Motherless families*. London: Routledge and Kegan Paul.

Gersick, K. (1979). Fathers by choice: Divorced men who receive custody of their children. In G. Levinger & O.C. Moles (eds.) *Divorce and separation*. New York: Basic Books, pp. 307-323.

Giles-Sims, J. & Urwin, C. (1989). Paternal custody and remarriage. *Journal of Divorce, 13*, 65-79.

Greif, G.L. (1985a). Single fathers rearing children. *Journal of Marriage and the Family, 47*, 185-191.

Greif (1985b). *Single fathers*. New York: MacMillan/Lexington Books.

Greif (1985c). Children and housework in the single father family. *Family Relations, 34*, 353-357.

Greif, G.L. (1985d). Practice with single fathers. *Social Work in Education, 7*, 231-243.

Greif, G.L. (1986a). Mothers without custody and child support. *Family Relations, 35*, 87-93.

Greif, G.L. (1986b). Clinical practice with the single father: A structural approach. *International Journal of Family Psychiatry, 7*, 261-275.

Greif, G.L. (1987). A longitudinal examination of single custodial fathers: Implications for treatment. *American Journal of Family Therapy, 15*, 253-260.

Greif, G.L. (1990). *The daddy track and the single father*. New York: MacMillan/Lexington Books.

Greif, G.L. & DeMaris, A. (1989). Single custodial fathers in contested custody suits. *The Journal of Psychiatry & the Law, 17*, 223-238.

Greif, G.L. & DeMaris, A. (1990). Single fathers with custody. *Families in Society, 71*, 259-266.

Greif, G.L. & DeMaris, A. (1991). Single fathers who receive child support. *American Journal of Family Therapy, 19*, 167-176.

Greif, G.L. & Emad, F. (1989). A longitudinal examination of mothers without custody: Implications for treatment. *American Journal of Family Therapy, 17*, 155-163.

Greif, G.L. & Pabst, M.S. (1988). *Mothers without custody*. New York: MacMillan/Lexington Books.

Greif, G.L. & Zuravin, S. (1989). Natural fathers: A placement resource for abused and neglected children? *Child Welfare, 68*, 479-495.

Hanson, S.M.H. (1981). Single custodial fathers and the parent-child relationship. *Nursing Research, 30*, 202-204.

Hanson, S.M.H. (1985). Single custodial fathers. In S.M.H. Hanson & F.W. Bozett (Eds.), *Dimensions of fatherhood* (pp. 369-392). Beverly Hills, CA: Sage Publications.

Hanson, S.M.H. (1988). Divorced fathers with custody. In P. Bronstein & C.P. Cowan (Eds.). *Fatherhood today: Men's changing role in the family*, pp. 166-194. NY: John Wiley.

Johnston, J.R. & Campbell, L.E. (1988). *Impasses of divorce: The dynamics and resolution of family conflict*. New York: The Free Press.

Katz, A.J. (1979). Lone fathers: Perspectives and implications for family policy. *The Family Coordinator, 28*, 521-528.

Keshet, H.F. & Rosenthal, K.M. (1976). Single parent families: A new study. *Children Today, 7*(3), 13-17.

McCant, J.W. (1987). The cultural contradiction of fathers as nonparents. *Family Law Quarterly, 21*, 127-143.

Mendes, H.A. (1976a). Single fathers. *The Family Coordinator, 25*, 439-444.

Mendes, H.A. (1976b). Single fatherhood. *Social Work, 21*, 308-312.

Meyer, D.R. & Garasky, S. Custodial fathers: Myths, realities, and child support policy. *Journal of Marriage and the Family, 55*, 73-89.

Mitchard, J. (1992). TV's pop culture: A short, illustrated history of single dads. *Reader's Digest*, June 13, 9-12.

Murch, M. (1973). Motherless families project. *British Journal of Social Work, 3*, 365-376.

Nieto, D.S. (1990). The custodial single father: Who does he think he is? *Journal of Divorce, 13*, 27-43.

Orthner, D.K., Brown, T., and Ferguson, D. (1976). Single-parent fatherhood: An emerging family life style. *The Family Coordinator, 25*, 429-437.

Risman, B.J. (1986). Can men "mother"? Life as a single father. *Family Relations, 35*, 95-102.

Rosenthal, K.M. & Keshet, H.F. (1981). *Fathers without partners*. Totowa, NJ: Rowman and Littlefield.

Santrock, J.W. & Warshak, R.A. (1979). Father custody and social development in boys and girls. *Journal of Social Issues, 35*, 112-125.

Saunders, E.B. & Melville, C. (1987). Custodial fathers, custodial mothers and their former spouses in protracted custody disputes: Clinical opinions and data. *The Journal of Psychiatry & Law, 15*(Winter), 555-570.

Schlesinger, B. & Todres, R. (1976). Motherless families: An increasing societal pattern. *Child Welfare*, *55*, 553-558.

Schnayer, R. & Orr, R.R. (1989). A comparison of children living in single-mother and single-father families. *Journal of Divorce*, *12*, 171-184.

Seltzer, J.A., Schaeffer, N.C., & Charng, H.-W. (1989). Family ties after divorce: The relationship between visiting and paying child support. *Journal of Marriage and the Family*, *51*, 1013-1031.

Shu, R. L.-H. (1989). A model to analyze single parent families in Taiwan. *Journal of Social Sciences and Philosophy*, (78/11), 101-153.

Smith, R.M. & Smith, C.W. (1981). Child-rearing and single parent fathers. *Family Relations*, *30*, 411-417.

Stewart, J.R., Schwebel, A.I., & Fine, M.A. (1986). The impact of custodial arrangement on the adjustment of recently divorced fathers. *Journal of Divorce*, *9*, 55-65.

Takas, M. (1992). Improving child support guidelines: Can simple formulas address complex families. Paper published by the American Bar Association Center on Children and the Law.

Teachman, J.D. & Polonko, K. (1990). Negotiating divorce outcomes: Can we identify patterns in divorce settlements? *Journal of Marriage and the Family*, *52*, 129-139.

Todres, R. (1978). Runaway wives: An increasing North-American phenomenon. *The Family Coordinator*, *27*, 17-21.

Turner, J.R. (1984). Divorced fathers who win contested custody of their children: An exploratory study. *American Journal of Orthopsychiatry*, *54*, 498-501.

U.S. Department of Commerce, Bureau of the Census. (1989). Studies in marriage and the family. Series P-23, No. 162, Washington, DC: U.S. Government Printing Office.

U.S. Department of Commerce, Bureau of the Census. (1990). Household and family characteristics; March 1990 and 1989. Series P-20, No. 447, Washington, DC: U.S. Government Printing Office.

U.S. Department of Commerce, Bureau of the Census. (1991). Marital status and living arrangements: March 1990. Series P-20, No. 450, Washington, DC: U.S. Government Printing Office.

U.S. Department of Commerce, Bureau of the Census. (1992). Marital status and living arrangements: March 1991. Series P-20, No. 461, Washington, DC: U.S. Government Printing Office.

Wilson, J. (1988). Working with single fathers: Suggestions for effective practice. *Australian Child and Family Welfare*, *13*, 12-15.

Wilson, J. (1989). Single fathers: Their experiences in court. *Law Institute Journal*, *63*, 258-261.

Chapter 11

Noncustodial Mothers Following Divorce

Catalina Herrerías

SUMMARY. Historically women have been responsible for providing the primary care of their children. This notion of responsibility for the care and well-being of children is central to the definition of motherhood. When mothers relinquish custody of their children prior to their 18th birthday, they elicit suspicions of deviance and nonnormality. There are an estimated 500,000 to 1,200,000 noncustodial mothers in the United States, with approximately 75% being voluntary relinquishers. This chapter identifies, through a review of the social science literature on maternal noncustody and examination of a specific study, the broad range of reasons for becoming a noncustodial mother, as well as provides a clearer picture of the noncustodial mother-child relationship pursuant to relinquishment. An overall theme from the literature was a general societal disapproval regarding maternal custody relinquishment, which in the study described, negatively affected respondents self-perceptions.

This study describes the social situation of women who voluntarily gave up custody of one or more biological children. Retrospective data identifying the factors influencing custody relinquishment and the events leading up to giving up custody are examined. Rela-

---

Catalina Herrerías is Regional Director for the Lutheran Children and Family Service, 101 E. Olney Avenue, Box C-12, Philadelphia, PA 19120.

[Haworth co-indexing entry note]: "Noncustodial Mothers Following Divorce." Herrerías, Catalina. Co-published simultaneously in *Marriage & Family Review* (The Haworth Press, Inc.) Vol. 20, No. 1/2, 1995, pp. 233-255; and: *Single Parent Families: Diversity, Myths and Realities* (ed: Shirley M. H. Hanson et al.) The Haworth Press, Inc., 1995, pp. 233-255. Multiple copies of this article/chapter may be purchased from The Haworth Document Delivery Center [1-800-3-HAWORTH; 9:00 a.m. - 5:00 p.m. (EST)].

tionships between noncustodial mothers and their children are explored pursuant to relinquishment, as well as the extent to which mothers regretted giving up their children.

A sample of 130 noncustodial mothers responded to a 137-item life history questionnaire and three clinical assessment scales. One-hundred-and-two of the participants engaged in two- to five-hour interviews. Findings revealed that approximately 86% of the respondents cited multiple reasons for custody relinquishment. Financial considerations, emotional problems, threats of legal custody fights, and being in a destructive relationship with mate emerged as the most frequently reported reasons for giving up one's children. The reasons for relinquishment as well as how the decision was handled with children had the greatest impact on the mother-child relationship. Almost 97% of the mothers actively maintained relationships with children following relinquishment. Seventy percent of those sampled were satisfied with their decision to relinquish in retrospect.

Finally, recommendations for policy and practice were discussed. Agency and legal policies and procedures should reflect a sensitivity to conditions under which most mothers relinquish their minor children, especially a supportive national family policy. The provision of a child or family allowance, compulsory court-based mediation, and a more uniform state-to-state support enforcement are recommended. Practitioners need to employ contextually-specific interactions for noncustodial mothers and their families, as high anxiety may characterize the emotions of this variable type of single parent. Professionals interacting with potential noncustodial mothers should provide for them to make a more informed and less pressured decision regarding relinquishment.

KEYWORDS. Mothers, Noncustodial mothers, Child custody, Divorce

INTRODUCTION

Historically women have been responsible for providing the primary care of their children. This notion of responsibility for the care and well-being of children is central to the definition of motherhood (Tip, 1986; Taws, 1978; Dally, 1982; Miller, 1991). Up to now, women have been first and foremost societally defined as mothers and any significant variation from this norm elicits suspicions of unfitness and deviance (Chesler, 1986), mental illness (Al-Issa, 1980), and engenders guilt and social disapproval (Miller, 1991). At the most basic level, mothers are held accountable when children's needs are not met (Hutchison, 1992). While the child caretaking role can equally be performed equally by males or females, in this country the role responsibility for taking care of children is almost exclusively relegated to women (Schaefer, 1990).

According to Meyer and Garasky (1993), males are receiving child custody at increasing rates over single mother families. They report that the number of father only families has multiplied by 300% over the last three decades. There is also a concomitant increase in the numbers of mothers voluntarily relinquishing custody of their offspring. Questions that arise from this trend are for instance: What factors lead a mother to relinquish custody of her children? Are the children's preferences for where they want to live taken into consideration or are they merely informed of the decision that they will be living with their father or other caretaker? What kind of a relationship do mothers and children have following custody relinquishment? Do mothers regret their decisions to have given up their offspring?

There are an estimated 500,000 to 1,200,000 noncustodial mothers in the United States, with approximately 75% of that number being voluntary relinquishers (Doudna, 1982; Grief, 1987; Grief & Pabst, 1988; Paskowicz, 1982). A noncustodial mother is defined as a woman who either currently lives apart from or has at some time lived separately from one or more biological children under the age of 18 (Herrerías, 1984). A *voluntary* noncustodial mother refers to either a formalized legal or informal agreement willingly entered into by the mother whereby one or more children will reside with another caretaker, in most cases the children's biological father. An *involuntary* noncustodial mother indicates some form of protective services intervention, criminal confinement, long-term mental or physical health convalescence, child kidnapping, or court custody finding on behalf of another caretaker for the mother's minor children. Noncustodial status excludes children given up at birth for adoption.

The study on which this chapter is based represents one of the most in-depth investigations into the social situation of noncustodial mothers available (Herrerías, 1984). The study used a symbolic interactionist theoretical framework to explore the self-concept of noncustodial mothers; assess problems with self-esteem, nonpsychotic depression, and relationships with their children; examine noncustodial mothers' life histories from birth to the present, probe details of marriages and divorces; identify the factors that influenced custody relinquishment; compare noncustodial mothers' interactions with significant and not-so-significant others with their self-feelings around the social act of custody relinquishment; and analyze respondents' decisions to relinquish in retrospect.

This chapter extrapolates some of the findings from the larger study to accomplish several objectives. First, it identifies the factors that influenced women's decisions to give up custody of their children. Second, it examines the process that led up to the relinquishment, including the role children had in the actual decision. Third, it sheds light on the mother-child relationship following relinquishment and discusses women's decisions in retrospect. A limited number of excerpts from recorded interviews are used to further enhance findings by giving voice to noncustodial mothers' experiences. Finally, this chapter discusses implications for policy and practice.

REVIEW OF LITERATURE

In recent years, mothers without custody of their children have garnered a significant measure of national attention vis-à-vis the print media (Campbell, 1981; Evans, 1980; Feldman, 1983; Foreman, 1981; Forman, 1982; Goldstein, 1980; Greenberg, 1980; Hannah, 1983; Hoover, 1982; Mall, 1981; Markey, 1982; *Ms.*, 1983; *Psychology Today*, 1983; Scott, 1983). This unique group of women have also been the focus of trade books (Brenton, 1978; Chesler, 1986; Edwards, 1989; Fielding, 1981; Meyers & Lakin, 1983; Paskowicz, 1982; Sklar, 1976; Trudeau & Morehead, 1979; Weitzman, 1985) and television talk shows, such as Phil Donahue, Sally Jessy Rafael and Oprah Winfrey. Up to now, however, there has been a paucity of information concerning this group in the professional helping literature (Corcoran & Herrerías, 1985; Fischer & Cardea, 1981; Fischer, 1983; Greif, 1987; Greif & Pabst, 1988; Lupenitz, 1982).

A review of the social science literature found several studies dealing with the subject of maternal noncustody. Keller (1975, 1981) represented a pioneer attempt to empirically investigate 15 women who identified they had made a "highly deviant" life choice generally perceived as unacceptable. These females were reportedly strongly dissatisfied with the mothering role and felt burdened with tremendous emotional and financial pressures. Sklar (1976) discussed more than 50 women (the exact number was not disclosed) who left their homes. Some of the women left one or more children behind due to emotional difficulties in coping with offspring or personal fears of being unable to financially provide for children. Polson (1977) compared three groups of 30 women who had retained custody, relinquished custody, or were married with adolescent children. No discernible differences in upbringing across the three groups were noted. Findings did reflect, however, a higher degree of self-actualization among noncustodial mothers than divorced women with custody or married women with adolescents.

Todres (1978) studied 38 "runaway" wives in Canada who reported the primary reasons for leaving were prompted by desires for the financial security and emotional welfare of their children. Brenton (1978) focused on different groups of runaways, including children, husband, wives, and parents. He reported that 50% of the runaways in 1975 were women, representing the path of least resistance rather than contending with confrontations, contested divorces and/or child custody battles.

Berke, Black, Byrne, Fields, Gallaher, & Paley (1979) conducted an exploratory study (N = 99) wherein 79% reported that relinquishing the parental role was in the best interests of the children. Isenhart (1979, 1983) compared two groups of divorced women who had retained (N = 17) or relinquished (N = 18) custody of their children. No measurable differences between the groups were found on social conformity, value orientations or personal resources.

Fischer and Cardea (1981) studied two groups of women with (N = 14) and without (N = 17) custody. Twenty-nine percent of the noncustodial group believed it was in the best interests of the children to have relinquished custody. Paskowicz (1982) surveyed 100 women across Canada, Europe and the United States. Of that number, she determined that overall about 60% were psychologically troubled. While approximately 61% were *involuntary* noncustodial mothers, Paskowicz made no distinction between this group and *voluntary* relinquishers regarding the extent of any existing emotional problems.

Rosenblum (1982) investigated ten women who were either in the process of relinquishing custody or who had already relinquished custody. Women gave up custody due to: (1) factors external to the relationship with children, (2) idiosyncracies of a particular mother-child relationship, and (3) mothers' personality factors that impeded their being "good mothers." Meyers and Lakin (1983) interviewed 70 women whose decisions to live apart from their children were induced by financial difficulties, the desire for children's stability, the pursuit of new or disrupted careers, to establish a better sense of identity, and to comply with children's preference to live with the other parent.

Probst (1983) sampled 53 mothers without custody and found that 68% indicated that relinquishing custody was in the best interests of their children. Greif (1987) sampled 517 noncustodial mothers who reported their primary reasons for custody relinquishment resulted from fiscal considerations (e.g., mothers' disbelief they could financially provide for their children, children preferred to live with their fathers due to perceptions of material gain, and fathers could better afford to hire an attorney).

More recently, Edwards (1989) studied 100 women from 41 states who ranged from being in the process of relinquishing custody to having given up custody forty years prior. More than 90% of those responding expressed satisfaction with their decision to have relinquished custody of their children.

Empirical investigations identify the principal factors contributing to maternal noncustody to be financial considerations, and avoiding a court custody battle. Avoidance of a court custody battle was the most commonly reported reason for relinquishment (Fischer & Cardea, 1981; Paskowicz, 1982; Probst, 1983). Other commonly cited reasons for custody relinquishment include the desire to attend college, a perception that the father was the "more natural" parent, and children's stated preference to live with the other parent.

Although many of the studies identified additional reasons for maternal custody relinquishment, such as a desire for self-actualization (Greif, 1987; Paskowicz, 1982; Probst, 1983), being tired of motherhood (Berke et al., 1979; Isenhart, 1979, 1983; Probst, 1983), or the existence of relational problems between mothers and children (Fischer & Cardea, 1981; Rosenblum, 1982), women citing these reasons were few. A final theme found throughout the studies was a general societal disapproval regarding maternal custody relinquishment which negatively affected respondents' self-perceptions.

This chapter seeks to identify a broader range of reasons for becoming a noncustodial mother, as well as to provide a clearer picture of the noncustodial mother-child relationship pursuant to relinquishment through examination of a particular study (Herrerías, in press). A summary of the study's methodology is provided for contextual purposes and to enhance the reader's appreciation of the comprehensiveness of the data collected.

SUMMARY OF THE METHODS

A descriptive-exploratory study which combined elements of both quantitative and qualitative research methodologies was designed to: (1) examine noncustodial mothers' self-concepts; (2) examine the existence of problems with self-esteem, depression, and mother-child relationships; (3) explore the process leading up to custody relinquishment; (4) identify the factors influencing custody relinquishment; (5) explore the respondents' social interactions with others relevant to custody relinquishment; (6) explore respondents' relationships with their living apart children; and (7) assess the respondents' retrospective evaluations of their custody decisions (Herrerías, 1984).

A sample of 130 noncustodial mothers was generated through the use of the print media when conventional sampling strategies failed to yield sufficient numbers of study participants (Herrerías, in press). In order to participate in the study, respondents must have: (1) given birth to one or more children; (2) provided the primary parenting for one or more biological children, (3) voluntarily relinquished custody of at least one child; and (4) relinquished custody for the period of at least one year prior to participating in the research.

Data were primarily collected throughout Southwest. Notably, about 60% of the respondents were born and reared in 28 states, representing diverse personal value and regional orientations. Noncustodial mothers were administered the Twenty Statements Test (TST), a relatively unstructured measure of self-concept, and three clinical scales to measure the extent of clinically significant problems with self-esteem, nonpsychotic depression and parental attitude (Hudson, 1982). The respondents also completed a 137-item life history questionnaire that asked questions regarding childhood, family of origin, [multiple] marriages and divorces, parenting and custody relinquishment, current mother-child relationships, and retrospective evaluations of the custody decision.

Of the 130 noncustodial mothers sampled, in-depth interviews lasting from two to five hours were audiorecorded with 102 study participants. The remaining 28 respondents who resided outside of a 400-mile radius of the author's former residence responded by mail to the life history questionnaire, as well as to an additional eight-page series of open-ended questions regarding their initial expectations for marriage and motherhood, the process leading up to the decision to relinquish their children, their parenting relationship following relinquishment, and current feelings about their decision to give up custody. Primary limitations of the study included respondent self-selection, lack of generalizability, and homogeneity of the sample (Herrerías, 1984).

PROFILE OF NONCUSTODIAL MOTHERS AND THEIR CHILDREN

Noncustodial Mothers

The noncustodial mothers reported a mean age of 35.7 years, and ranged from 22 to 49 years old. Respondents married at an average age of

19 years, gave birth to their first child by 20 years, and divorced at the age of 28 years. Thirty percent of the respondents were pregnant at the time of their marriage. Almost 53% of the respondents were currently divorced or separated. Of the 45.3% either married or cohabiting, 32% were in a third or subsequent marriage. Most of the respondents were white, Protestant and had earned baccalaureate degrees. Median income of respondents ranged from $15,000 to $20,000. Women were employed across a broad range of occupations, with 15 respondents enrolled as full-time college students. At the time of custody relinquishment, only 37% of the respondents had any experience with full-time gainful employment. Table 1 summarizes sociodemographics of the sample.

The majority of noncustodial mothers (98.5%) reported having grown up with their biological mothers, whereas only two respondents reported being children of noncustodial mothers themselves. Forty percent of respondents' mothers had been full-time homemakers, and 28% worked either part-time or intermittently, indicating a maternal presence in the home throughout respondents' formative years.

Overall, nearly 70% of the respondents cited the existence of social problems in their homes of origin. One-half of the noncustodial mothers reported growing up in households where parental alcoholism or drug abuse were common. Fifty-five percent said they had experience with either being a child victim of physical or sexual abuse or having witnessed their mother being battered by either a father or stepfather. An estimated 43% experienced both chemical abuse and domestic violence during their childhood and adolescence in one form or another.

Seventy-four percent of respondents were reared in predominantly intact households with both biological parents. Even so, the data reflect a history of family social problems with potentially serious personal consequences and with far-reaching implications concerning trust issues, difficulty with communication, future selection of and interaction with intimate partners and managing other significant relationships.

Children of Noncustodial Mothers

Respondents had a total of 288 children, averaging 2.2 children each. Mothers with two children comprised the largest family group (38.2%). Only three of the respondents had between 6 to 12 children. Custody was given up on 249 children, with 39 of them retained by mothers in a limited number of split custody situations. Seventeen women kept at least one child and relinquished from one to five. Women were as likely to relinquish male children (87.1%) as female children (85.6%).

Children averaged 8 years of age at relinquishment, ranging from 6

TABLE 1. Sociodemographic Characteristics of Noncustodial Mothers

(N = 130)

	No.	Percent
Marital Status		
Married	41	31.5
Not married/cohabiting	18	13.8
Divorced	60	46.2
Separated	8	6.2
Never married	3	2.3
Ethnic/Racial Background		
White	114	87.7
American Indian	5	3.8
Asian American	1	.8
Black	2	1.5
Hispanic	8	6.2
Educational Level of Respondents		
Less than high school	2	1.5
High school	17	13.0
Some college	54	41.5
Baccalaureate degree	32	24.6
Masters degree	21	16.2
Doctoral degree	4	3.0
Religious Affiliation		
Protestant	62	47.7
Catholic	22	16.9
Jewish	3	2.3
Nondenominational	11	8.5
Other	4	3.1
None	28	21.5
Occupational Status		
Professional, technical	32	24.6
Managers, administrators	20	15.3
Salesworkers	11	8.5
Clerical	42	32.3
Others	10	7.8
Full-Time student	15	11.5
Income		
Less than $5,000	6	4.6
$5,001-$10,000	17	13.1
$10,001-$15,000	24	18.5
$15,001-$20,000	30	23.1
$20,001-$25,000	20	15.4
$25,001-$30,000	12	9.2
Over $30,000	14	10.8
Various benefit programs	7	5.4

months (N = 1) to 18 years old (N = 17). The largest percentage of relinquished children was between 5-11 years (50.2%), followed by children under 5 (27.4%). Overall, the average number of children relinquished by respondents was 1.9. At the time of the study, children's mean age was 13 years, and the average length of relinquishment was 5 years. Almost 7% of the children were 18 years or over at relinquishment, representing older siblings in families where younger siblings were being relinquished as well.

Mean geographic distance between respondents and their living apart children is 577 miles and some of the respondents have children residing in more than one state. At the time of custody relinquishment, more than 95% of all relinquished children went to live with their biological father. Of the 16 respondents of color, almost half were relinquished to a relative other than the father. Extended kinship systems are more readily used as important sources of support by many ethnic and racial minority groups (Attneave, 1982; Garcia-Preto, 1982; Hines & Boyd-Franklin, 1982; Logan et al., 1990; Stack, 1974).

Unpublished follow-up data obtained later than the original collection, found that in approximately 20% of the cases children whose custody had been relinquished returned to live with their mothers. Notably, every one of the Hispanic respondents' children with one exception returned to their biological mother within two years of relinquishment. Since children represent such an integral part of the Hispanic family, it may be that the strength of these cultural norms influence mother-child reunification in unique ways (Falicov, 1982; Garcia-Preto, 1982).

FACTORS INFLUENCING CUSTODY RELINQUISHMENT

Approximately 86% of the respondents declared more than one reason for relinquishing custody, with an average of 3.3 reasons cited for giving up children. Financial considerations, emotional problems, threats of legal custody fights, and being in a destructive relationship with mate emerged the most frequently cited reasons for giving up one's children. Custody relinquishment for financial reasons included two groups of respondents, those giving up custody at the time of divorce (N = 28) and those giving up custody one or more years pursuant to divorce (N = 37). Examples of relinquishment for economic reasons follow:

> Mary gave up two daughters ages 5 and 7 at the time of divorce: *For some reason I felt I couldn't make it on my own economically–I never considered he would have to help. I felt that I would have to do it all on my own. I was in a state of emergency.*

> Sandra gave up a 5-year-old son and 6-year-old daughter one year after her divorce: *I was broke, and it was having a very adverse affect on my children. He refused to pay child support. I had to sell my home and moved to the ghetto. I was broke. Hell, I was at rock bottom. . . .*

Respondents gave compelling reasons for relinquishment when being threatened with a custody fight and for emotional troubles as well:

> Susan gave up a 2-year-old boy and 4-year-old girl, retaining an 8-year-old son from her first marriage when threatened with a custody battle: *My husband let me know early on that if I ever intended to leave him it would have to be some sort of midnight escape because he would never let me take the children. I had no money, no family. . . . So [CRYING] finally I said, 'I give up, I surrender, you take the kids.' I didn't know what else to do.*

> Candy gave up her 3-year-old son for emotional reasons: *I didn't even think about it. The situation inside myself was so tumultuous that all I thought of was 'I'm falling apart,' and all that held me together was bits of energy. It was completely spontaneous. The question was survival at that point–mental survival.*

An overwhelming number of respondents cried through parts of the interviews regardless of the number of years that had passed from the time children were relinquished. Sometimes both the noncustodial mother and author cried together–the reasons for relinquishment were as different as they were similar. For most, the pain involved in making the decision had been and was still vividly experienced.

Some of the other influential factors for relinquishment included the perception that respondent and mate were involved in a destructive relationship, the belief that the children's father could provide more security or was the more "natural" parent, and the desire to attend college. Table 2 provides the list of factors influencing custody relinquishment.

The decision to relinquish custody of one's children is a difficult, painful act often complicated by a series of uncontrollable events. Clearly, custody relinquishment was not something that had been planned over a long period of time. Usually, the alternative of relinquishment emerged out of bare necessity, was briefly discussed, decided and acted upon all within a relatively short time. Ultimately, 84% of the decisions were legally formalized.

By definition, the respondents are all voluntary relinquishers, however, the compelling nature of the majority of the factors identified as in-

TABLE 2. Factors Influencing the Decision to Relinquish Custody

Influencing Factors	N*	%
Financial considerations	65	50
Emotional difficulties	64	49.2
Threat of legal custody fight	53	40.8
Destructive relationship with mate	52	40
Tired of the mothering role	32	24.6
Desire to attend college	30	23.1
Father could provide more security	26	20
Father was the more "natural" parent	25	19.2
Desire to self-actualize	23	17.7
Involvement in intimate relationship	17	13
Children's preference to live apart	15	11.5
Discovered or chose lesbian lifestyle	4	3.1
Other reasons	22	16.9

*Noncustodial mothers averaged 3.3 reasons each for relinquishment.

fluencing relinquishment question the true voluntariness of this decision. One respondent summed it all up with: *When I consider the fact that at the time I had no money or marketable skills, little confidence in my ability to make it or in my husband to follow through with child support, what other choice did I have but to let the kids live with their father who had the house, a stable income, and could continue to provide for them?* The factors influencing relinquishment in and of themselves do not adequately convey the complexity of the actual process involved in the socio-legal act of maternal custody relinquishment.

THE PROCESS LEADING TO CUSTODY RELINQUISHMENT

A series of questions related to the process involved in reaching the decision to relinquish custody arrangements, child support, and frequency of contact with children yielded an array of issues with which to contend. Noncustodial mothers elected to first discuss the alternative of custody relinquishment with their children's father in 30.8% of the cases, particularly since 95% of those relinquished went to live with their fathers. On the other hand, fathers broached the subject with respondents in 45.4% of the instances. Only 23% of the children actively participated in the decision-making process involving custodial arrangements in any way.

Children were informed about the impending custody reversals by one or both parents. Thirty-three percent of the children were told by their mothers, 18% by their fathers, and 26.2% were conjointly informed by their parents. The remaining children were told nothing because parents felt they were too young to understand the situation.

Initially, the reasons given for relinquishing custody as well as how the decision was eventually handled had the greatest impact on the mother-child relationship. Despite obvious spousal conflict in the home, children still residing with both parents were reportedly shocked by the news of an imminent divorce and custodial change. Respondents involved in destructive relationships with mates were more apt to leave unannounced out of fear for their own safety. Understandably, these mothers believed their children felt abandoned or unloved to a greater extent than those respondents who explained their decisions to offspring. Yet others who clearly gave up custody due to emotional reasons, a belief that the father was the more natural parent, or children's preference to live with their father felt that if children, especially younger ones, did not readily understand the rationale for relinquishment. Findings revealed that they would, with time, understand, given the extenuating circumstances surrounding their decision.

When asked how respondents perceived their children's original reaction to the custody decision and how, in turn, they felt about those reactions, responses fit into four categories. Mothers felt children disapproved of the relinquishment in 21.6% of the cases, while another 26.9% of the respondents believed their children supported the decision. No discernible reaction was reported for 29.2% of the children, and the remainder were perceived as too young to know the difference.

At the same time, 38.5% of the respondents indicated feeling somewhat negative, guilty or like a failure, with 16.9% saying that despite offspring's positive responses or the extent of support they received from others, they continued to experience negative self-feelings. Another 25.2% of the non-custodial mothers said they felt at least somewhat positive about their children's reactions. Irrespective of the handling of the custody decision, almost 80% believed that children felt confused, abandoned, unloved or hurt at actually being given up by mothers. These mothers may have even projected some of their own feelings of separation anxiety onto their offspring.

The data shows that prior to custody relinquishment, respondents were fully engaged in the more traditional tasks of motherhood. They reported assuming greater responsibility than fathers for attending to children's health care (87.7%), staying at home with sick children (94.5%) and visiting children's schools (89.3%). Since respondents felt they had borne the "lion's share" of the primary parenting for their children, this perception exacerbated issues of low self-esteem, depression, and necessary role transitioning.

There was anywhere from one week to three months from the time the custody decision was made until the maternal separation took place. One-third of all relinquishments occurred within 30 days, with the remainder being accomplished in three months. For the most part, respondents continued with daily routines in an attempt to normalize the situation surrounding the impending custodial change as much as possible. Half of the noncustodial mothers noted their satisfaction with the manner in which they handled the final days with their children. Thirty-six percent were not satisfied at all, and 14% did not recall events during that time period.

Nevertheless, emotions between mothers and children were reportedly intense the final week before parting. Twenty-one percent of the respondents described feelings of contentment, satisfaction with having spent quality time with their children, and with having reassured offspring that everything would be all right following their separation. Conversely, 66.7% of the women recalled deep sadness, negative feelings (e.g., anger with children who stated a preference to live with their father), or a sense of numbness in order to avoid further psychic pain. Another 12.3% said they were not consciously aware of the final days with their children prior to the separation.

In asking women what they would have done differently, 45% said "Nothing," 14% would not have given up their children, and 12% would have done more talking with their children about the change in custody. Other things mothers would have done differently the final days they lived with their children were (1) not to have gotten angry with older children who opted to live with their father, (2) taken a special trip with 6- to 11-year-olds, or (3) simply held the younger children physically close for a longer period of time.

Immediately following the change of custody, mothers either cried for days to weeks at a time (reported by 80%) or else engaged in other activities as a way of not focusing on their children, their own feelings, or what others might be thinking about their act of relinquishment. Fifty-five percent of the children remained in the family home, while mothers and fathers physically changed residential locations.

One respondent voiced the feelings of many when she shared: *I felt guilty all the time but I didn't feel I made the wrong decision. But I still felt somewhere I must have failed. Under the circumstances, I would have made it again. But somewhere I must have failed. [CRYING] Because it hurt so much. I hurt them and I hurt me. Somewhere I screwed up. I didn't really blame myself. I felt guilty and somehow felt inadequate because I didn't have enough strength or money to change the circumstances.*

As mentioned earlier, fathers assumed primary custodial responsibility in 95% of the cases. Custody arrangements were almost evenly divided between mothers having access to children as often as was mutually convenient and visitation on alternate weekends and holidays. Almost three-quarters of respondents expressed satisfaction with the custody arrangements. Dissatisfied noncustodial mothers argued that the "as often as was mutually convenient" clause in many legal documents was ambiguous and subject to being grossly manipulated by custodial fathers' on their own behalf.

VISITATION AND SUPPORT BY NONCUSTODIAL MOTHERS

Most of the respondents exercised their prerogative to see their children regularly. Slightly more than 26% of the women reported spending time with their children on a weekly basis. Additionally, 24.6% of the respondents saw their children on a monthly basis, which means that one-half of the mothers interact with their children fairly frequently. Another 36.2% asserted visiting their children on a quarterly basis. While annual visits were the rule for 7.7% of the respondents and their children, these more often than not represented two- to three-month summer visits. These findings suggest that the frequency of contact between noncustodial mothers and their children exceeds that of most noncustodial fathers with their children (Furstenberg et al., 1983; Luepnitz, 1982).

A small percentage of noncustodial mothers (3.4%) were no longer in contact with their children. These women were either still terrified of their former spouses knowing their whereabouts or believed it was in their child's best interest to withdraw entirely from his/her life.

In terms of child support, 24.6% of the noncustodial mothers were court ordered to pay support and of those, 84% (N = 27) paid the amount stipulated. Respondents made average annual child support payments of $2,100, which was equal to $1,105 per child (1984 dollars) and a mean of

1.9 children. The amount of child support paid is comparable with that cited by Greif (1987), and Greif and Pabst (1988).

Overall, 16% of noncustodial mothers retained at least one child, and of those, 70% received no child support whatsoever. Garfinkel and McLanahan (1986) state that only about half of the eligible children who are awarded child support receive the full amount stipulated, and that almost 30% receive nothing at all. Comparable data on noncustodial mothers and child support payments do not exist, thus any interpretations between noncustodial mothers and fathers are speculative at best.

Noncustodial mothers echo the stark reality faced by divorced and single mothers with children throughout this country who receive partial or no child support. These voices, if you will, provide a glimpse into the uncertainty experienced by some of the respondents as they considered custody relinquishment out of fear that child support would not be forthcoming. Given that at the time this particular research was completed child support enforcement was barely in its infancy and states were working out complexities in their tracking and reporting systems, there was little assurance that child support would be paid or received on any consistent basis (Garfinkel & McLanahan, 1986).

MOTHER-CHILD RELATIONSHIPS FOLLOWING RELINQUISHMENT

Although mothers had lived apart from their children for an average of five years, almost 97% continued to maintain ongoing relationships with their offspring. Of those respondents, almost 71% were reportedly satisfied with their mother-child relationships since relinquishment. Twenty-nine percent of the mothers expressed dissatisfaction with what they perceived to be a lack of rapport or emotional intimacy with their children.

Nearly 77% of respondents described close and caring relationships with their children. A comparatively small number (11.6%) admitted that their relationships with children were somewhat strained. Nine percent stated they were experiencing relational problems with one of their children but not the others. This was corroborated by the results on the Index of Parental Attitudes measuring clinically significant problems with respondents' attitudes toward their children.

It is entirely possible that respondents currently have few relational problems with offspring, but that at the time of or following relinquishment problems may have been significantly greater. It is also conceivable that currently respondents are either more accepting or tolerant of their children, particularly given that children are older and more self-sufficient.

Mothers may also be sensitive to having given up custody and are predisposed to giving socially desirable responses.

Notwithstanding, 38% of the noncustodial mothers expressed a desire for more frequency of contact with their children. Respondents gave two major complaints concerning their inability to see children more frequently. First, the full financial responsibility for children's travel in conjunction with visitation is borne by the respondents. And, as one-half of the respondents lived in different states than their children, and the inability to pay for travel expenses substantially curtailed mother-child visitation. Another complaint from respondents was the lack of available money to spend on children during visitation, which was a similar sentiment expressed by noncustodial fathers in Arditti (1995). The second major complaint involved changes in the visitation schedule by former mates.

Complaints were also levelled against children's stepmothers. If the former mate remarried, which occurred within a year or two of assuming custody in almost two-thirds of the cases, conflicts often arose between noncustodial and stepmothers. Even though 28% of the noncustodial mothers maintained close relationships with their former mates, close to 43% stated that relations were quite tenuous and could definitely be better. Respondents felt that their children were frequently triangulated in the communication process between themselves and the custodial parent.

Despite many obstacles, mothers felt their relationship with children was relatively positive. As one respondent commented: *I talk to the kids a lot and they visit quite a while. They live 300 miles away. I see them about four times a year: Thanksgiving, Christmas, Spring Break, and I have them all summer. We talk on the phone weekly and write back and forth.* At least half of the respondents did not feel that the relationship they shared with former mates affected the mother-child relationship in any long-lasting, meaningful way.

CUSTODY DECISIONS IN RETROSPECT

Seventy percent of the noncustodial mothers maintained that giving up custody was the right decision. Only 2.3% said it was not the right decision for all children concerned. Twenty-nine of the respondents (22.3%) believed that giving up custody had been the wrong decision. Women who regretted their custody decision were found to have problems with self-esteem and nonpsychotic depression at statistically significant levels of $p = .0015$ and $p = .003$, respectively. There is no way to discern whether respondents were suffering from low self-esteem and depression at the time the relinquishment decision was made and their state of mind influenced the particular course of action taken, or if giving up custody of their children led to feelings of low self-esteem and depression. Another explanation might be that something entirely separate from the custody relinquishment issue was principally responsible for the clinical problems uncovered. Respondents demonstrating clinically significant problems as measured by any of the assessment instruments were immediately informed of the results and referred to counseling. Approximately one-quarter of the respondents were referred for counseling as an outcome of their research participation.

Clearly, noncustodial mothers have many issues with which they have had to contend. Be that as it may, many of these respondents probably would not have decided to relinquish custody had critically needed social, psychological, or material supports been available. Most of the respondents believe they did the best they could given scarce resources. The politics of custody relinquishment are certainly not in favor of women with children.

IMPLICATIONS AND RECOMMENDATIONS FOR POLICY AND PRACTICE

Several issues emerged from this research with clear implications for policy and practice and are discussed below.

Implications for Policy

Giving up custody of one's children due to the fear of not being able to provide the family with life's necessities makes an incredibly powerful statement about the lack of a national family policy and guaranteed income that would establish an essential safety net for women and children. Provision of a child or family allowance, improvement in the child support collection system, expanded earned income tax credits, and increased medical care coverage can help ameliorate the widespread poverty faced by children in mother-only families (Garfinkel & McLanahan, 1986; Plotnick, 1989).

Additional recommendations include court-based mediation in divorce actions where minor children are involved and nationwide reciprocal laws that would uphold the integrity of child custody orders from one state to the next at comparable levels. Expecting parents to make an objective, rational decision regarding the best interests of their children amidst the chaos evident in most marital disruptions is unrealistic. Compulsory mediation in cases of divorcing couples with minor children or legal petitions to change already established custodial arrangements could help guide estranged couples involved to a more informed and workable decision while minimizing the trauma to all concerned. Low- or no-cost legal representation in divorce and custody cases is also critical, particularly as described by mothers threatened with court custody fights they could ill afford.

The absence of more uniform state-to-state reciprocal child support enforcement policies often set up unrealistic expectations, undue delays in the collection of support which is usually desperately needed, extreme financial hardships, and intense frustration. It is the lack of adequate child support payments that has heavily contributed to the impoverished economic condition of women and their children (Garfinkel & McLanahan, 1986). Increased standardization and equity regarding the formulas used for computing size of child support cash awards are needed (Hagen, 1992). Further, a more responsive system is essential in order to more effectively and efficiently collect and transmit child support to appropriate families, the majority of whom are single female-headed households.

Implications for Practice

The high number of noncustodial mothers giving up custody for emotional difficulties requires the existence of low- or no-cost, reasonably accessible community-based mental health services. Unbiased, genuinely supportive helping professionals who are knowledgeable about the unique challenges confronting noncustodial mothers and their families are a key resource. Regardless of the specific reasons *why* a mother is considering giving up or has given up custody, total acceptance is a critical element in establishing an effective therapeutic relationship. Some of the problems faced by these women include low self-esteem and depression; feelings of guilt, anxiety, isolation, and loss of control over children's daily lives. If not initially experienced, feelings of guilt are usually engendered in the course of interactions with others. A supportive listener, as well as help with role playing responses to insensitive and hurtful comments are initial steps toward empowerment of noncustodial mothers.

Maternal noncustody oftentimes elicits feelings of anxiety partially due to the belief that their children would someday hate or resent them for being relinquished. These feelings are exacerbated when the relationship between noncustodial mother and custodial father are conflictual. Loss of control over the daily lives of their children also poses a problem for mothers, particularly the perceived loss of relational intimacy. Instead, noncustodial mothers can be guided toward redefining their relationships with children in new, healthy ways that will help to build a new foundation for the future. Moreover, noncustodial mothers should be encouraged to "try on" new and different social roles as they explore greater freedom to pursue education, career or social avenues. Finally, establishment of support groups comprising other noncustodial mothers can serve to enhance self-esteem and decrease the sense of social isolation reported by so many noncustodial parents (Arditti, in this volume; Greif & Kristall, 1993; Herrerías, 1984).

Up to now, there is only one national support group which focuses exclusively on women who relinquish child custody. For more information, the following group can be contacted via written correspondence: Mothers Without Custody, P.O. Box 27418, Houston, TX 77227-7418 and their telephone number is 1-800-457-6962.

CONCLUSIONS

This chapter examined the harsh realities of women who voluntarily and painfully relinquished custody of at least one biological child. The reasons given for relinquishment principally pointed to economic difficulties, women's emotional problems, fears engendered by threats of protracted court custody battles women could ill afford, and being in a physically or emotionally destructive spousal relationship. Under these circumstances, a serious question emerges about the true voluntariness of child relinquishment. Faced with the potential loss of food, clothing, housing, and income, child relinquishment is interpreted more as an unfortunate outcome of unexpected events than a viable custodial alternative.

Most mothers will likely continue to provide the primary parenting for their children. However, women electing to do otherwise for whatever reason should have the freedom to base their decision on personal preference and not as a consequence of coercion or the lack of essential resources.

REFERENCES

Al-Issa, I. (1980). *The psychopathology of women.* Englewood Cliffs, NJ: Prentice-Hall.

Arendell, T. (1986). *Mothers and divorce: Legal, economic, and social dilemmas.* Berkeley, CA: University of California Press.

Arditti, J. A. (1995). Noncustodial Parents: Emergent Issues of Diversity and Process. In S. Hanson, M. Heims, D. Julian, and M. Sussman (Eds.), *Marriage & Family Review, 20*(1/2), pp. 283-304.

Attneave, C. (1982). American Indians and Alaska Native Families (pp. 55-83). In M. McGoldrick, J. K. Pearce, & J. Giordano (Eds.), *Ethnicity and Family Therapy*. New York: Guilford.

Berke, P., Black, M., Byrne, M., Fields, F., Gallagher, B., & Paley, N. (1979). *A study of natural mothers who terminated the primary parental role*. Unpublished Master's thesis, University of Southern California, Los Angeles.

Brenton, M. (1978). *The runaways*. Boston: Little, Brown, and Co., 120-137.

Campbell, B. M. (1981, October). Mothering long-distance. *Essence*, pp. 92, 142-144, 147, 149.

Chesler, P. (1986). *Mothers on trial: The battle for children and custody*. Seattle, WA: Seal Press.

Chodorow, N. (1978). *The reproduction of mothering*. Berkeley, CA: University of California Press.

Corcoran, K. & Herrerías, C. (1985). Measuring nonpsychotic depression and self-esteem: Additional reliability and validity data. *Social Work Research & Abstracts*, *21*, 30-31.

Dally, A. (1983). *Inventing motherhood: The consequences of an ideal*. New York: Schocken Books.

Doudna, C. (1982, October 3). The weekend mother. *The New York Times Magazine*, pp. 72-75, 84-88.

Edwards, H. (1989). *How could you? Mothers without custody of their children*. Freedom, CA: The Crossing Press.

Evans, I. L. (1980, May 28). Even without children's custody, they're still mothers. *Denver Post*, p. D1.

Falicov, C. J. (1982). Mexican families. In M. McGoldrick, J. K. Pearce, & J. Giordano (Eds.), *Ethnicity and Family Therapy* (pp. 134-163). New York: Guilford Press.

Feldman, C. (1983, May 15). When moms don't have custody . . . *Houston Chronicle*, Section 6, pp. 1, 6, 7.

Fielding, J. (1981). *Kiss mommy goodbye*. Garden City, NY: Doubleday & Co.

Fischer, J. L. (1983, July). Mothers living apart from their children. *Family Relations*, *32*, 351-357.

Fischer, J. L. & Cardea, J. M. (1981, May). Mothers living apart from their children: A study in stress and coping. *Alternative Lifestyles*, *4*, 218-227.

Foreman, J. (1981, May 10). Motherhood begins a new chapter. *The Boston Globe*, pp. A1, A4.

Forman, D. (1982, April). Losing Sara. *Boston Magazine*, pp. 110-113, 166-168.

Furstenberg, F. F., Nord, C. W., Peterson, J. L., & Zill, N. (1983, October). The life course of children of divorce: Marital disruption and parental contacts. *American Sociological Review*, *48*, 656-668.

Garcia-Preto, N. (1982). Puerto Rican families (pp. 164-186). In M. McGoldrick, J. K. Pearce, & J. Giordano (Eds.), *Ethnicity and Family Therapy*. New York: Guilford.

Garfinkel, I., & McLanahan, S. S. (1986). *Single mothers and their children: A new American dilemma*. Washington, DC: Urban Institute.

Goldstein, M. (1980, November). What's it like to leave the family behind and become a weekend mom? *Glamour*, pp. 89-91.

Greenberg, D. (1983, May 1). When mothers give up custody. *The New York Times*.

Greif, G. L. (1987). Mothers without custody. *Social Work, 32*, 11-16.

Greif, G. L. & Kristall, J. (1993). Common themes in a group for noncustodial parents. *Families in Society, 74*(4), 240-245.

Greif, G. L. & Pabst, M. S. (1988). *Mothers without custody*. Lexington, MA: DC Heath.

Hagen, J. L. (1992). Women, work, and welfare: Is there a role for social work? *Social Work, 37*(Jan.), 9-14.

Hannah, M. (1983, March 20). Giving up kids lays guilt on mother: Custody reversal hard choice even when best for children. *Austin American Statesman*, pp. E1, E15.

Herrerías, C. (in press). Use of the print media to attract "hard-to-reach" research participants. *Journal of Social Service Research*.

Herrerías, C. (1984). Noncustodial mothers: A study of self-concept and social interactions. University of Texas at Austin. Unpublished Doctoral dissertation.

Hines, P. M., & Boyd-Franklin, N. (1982). Black families (pp. 84-100), In M. McGoldrick, J. K. Pearce, & J. Giordano (Eds.), *Ethnicity and Family Therapy*. New York: Guilford.

Hoover, B. (1982, April 21). When mothers give up custody. *The Detroit News*, p. 1.

Hudson, W. W. (1982). *The clinical measurement package*. Homewood, IL: Dorsey Press.

Hutchison, E. D. (1992). Child welfare as a women's issue. *Families in Society, 73*(2), 67-77.

Isenhart, M. A. (1983). Divorced women: A comparison of two groups who have retained or relinquished custody of their children. (Doctoral dissertation, California School of Professional Psychology, San Diego, 1979) *Dissertation Abstracts International, 40*, 5628-A.

Keller, F. O. (1981). The childless mother: An evaluation of deviancy as a concept in contemporary culture. (Doctoral dissertation, California School of Professional Psychology, San Francisco, 1975). *Dissertation Abstracts International, 36*, 4164-B.

Logan, S. M. L., Freeman, E. M. & McRoy, R. G. (1990). *Social work practice with Black families*. New York: Longman.

Luepnitz, D. A. (1982). *Child custody: A study of families after divorce*. Lexington, MA: DC Heath Books.

Mall, J. (1981, September 20). Support for women without custody. *Los Angeles Times*.

Markey, J. (1982, May 19). Exit mom, sans kids. *The Floridian*.

Meyer, D. R. & Garasky, S. (1993). Custodial fathers: Myths, realities, and child support policy. *Journal of Marriage and the Family, 55*, 73-89.

Meyers, S. & Lakin, J. (1983). *Who will take the children?* New York: Bobbs-Merrill.

Miller, D. C. (1991). *Women and social welfare: A feminist analysis*. New York: Praeger Books.

Ms. (1983, April). Mothers without custody, pp. 78-79.

Paskowicz, P. (1982). *Absentee mothers*. New York: Universe Press.

Plotnick, R. D. (1989). Directions for reducing child poverty. *Social Work*, *34*(6), 523-530.

Polson, D. (1977). Runaway wives: A comparison study of marital status, feminism and self-actualization. Unpublished Master's thesis, U. S. International University, San Diego.

Probst, P. S. (1983). Mothers without custody of their children. Unpublished Master's thesis, University of Missouri-Columbia.

Psychology Today. (1983, February). Pariah Mothers.

Rosenblum, K. E. (1982, March). The route to voluntary non-custody: How mothers decide to relinquish child custody. Revised version of a paper presented at the Annual Meeting of the American Orthopsychiatric Association, San Francisco.

Schaefer, R. T. (1990). *Racial and ethnic groups*. (4th Ed.). Glenview, IL: Scott, Foresman/Little, Brown.

Scott, N. (1983, November 10). Divorced mothers giving up custody are judged unfairly. *Houston Chronicle*, p. 8.

Shon, S. P., & Ja, D. Y. (1982). Asian families (pp. 208-228). In M. McGoldrick, J. K. Pearce, & J. Giordano (Eds.), *Ethnicity in Family Therapy*, New York: Guilford.

Sklar, A. (1976). *Runaway wives*. New York: Coward, McCann & Geoghegan, Inc.

Stack, C. (1974). *All our kin: Strategies for survival in a black community*. New York: Harper & Row.

Todres, R. (1978). Runaway wives: An increasing North-America phenomenon. *The Family Coordinator*, *27* (Jan.), 17-22.

Trudeau, M. & Moorehead, C. (1979). *Beyond reason*. New York: Pocket Books.

Weitzman, L. J. (1985). *The divorce revolution: The unexpected social and economic consequences for women and children in America*. New York: The Free Press.

Chapter 12

Noncustodial Fathers Following Divorce

Greer Litton Fox
Priscilla White Blanton

SUMMARY. Noncustodial fathers are men whose parental rights and obligations have been altered through judicial action, usually accompanying marital separation and divorce. In the majority of divorces, physical and legal custody of children is taken from fathers and reassigned to mothers only. Despite the curtailment of their decision-making authority and despite the limitations imposed on their day-to-day presence in their children's lives, in the majority of divorces fathers retain the duty to provide economic support for their minor children. The bulk of quantitative research on the post-divorce involvement of men as noncustodial fathers is structured by exploration of the interrelationships among these parameters: child custody awards, visitation privileges and performance, child support awards and compliance, and child well-being. The documentation of important linkages between child support compliance and child outcome have focused both social science and legislative attention on means to foster greater paternal acceptance of responsibility for children. Research using open-ended interviews and smaller surveys of limited samples have been of great importance in providing a richer understanding of the noncustodial father-child relationship. To retain

Greer Litton Fox and Priscilla White Blanton are affiliated with the University of Tennessee, Knoxville.

[Haworth co-indexing entry note]: "Noncustodial Fathers Following Divorce." Fox, Greer Litton, and Priscilla White Blanton. Co-published simultaneously in *Marriage & Family Review* (The Haworth Press, Inc.) Vol. 20, No. 1/2, 1995, pp. 257-282; and: *Single Parent Families: Diversity, Myths and Realities* (ed: Shirley M. H. Hanson et al.) The Haworth Press, Inc., 1995, pp. 257-282. Multiple copies of this article/chapter may be purchased from The Haworth Document Delivery Center [1-800-3-HAWORTH; 9:00 a.m. - 5:00 p.m. (EST)].

(or for some, to build for the first time) a meaningful paternal relationship, men are challenged to find new ways to confront issues of autonomy, connectedness and power. However, societal supports for moving beyond the traditional polarization of genders and roles through which families have been organized are sorely lacking. The ways in which men respond to the changes precipitated by divorce are influenced by a number of factors related to their own self-definition as well as to the broader social context in which they operate. In order to design psychoeducational or therapeutic interventions that allow noncustodial fathers to adapt in ways that are beneficial to themselves and ultimately to their children, an awareness of these factors is imperative.

KEYWORDS. Fathers, Fatherhood, Noncustodial fathers, Divorce, Child custody

NONCUSTODIAL FATHERS FOLLOWING DIVORCE

This chapter reviews recent research on divorced or separated noncustodial fathers. The contours of noncustodial fathering is explored, as shaped by changing demographic patterns and shifts in legal frameworks defining parenting rights and obligations. Research is examined on the nature of fathering outside the customary social setting of the father role–the maritally intact, coresidential family. Incorporated throughout the chapter are suggestions for research, directions for divorce-related social policy and strategies for psychoeducational and therapeutic interventions for men–and their families–who are confronted with the extraordinary challenges of renegotiating their relationships following divorce.

The term "noncustodial father" refers to men whose rights and obligations as fathers are curtailed and reassigned through judicial action, usually accompanying marital separation or divorce. For noncustodial fathers the parent role has been legally altered so as to vest only in the mother the father's usual "powers, rights, and duties" with respect to his children (Krause, 1977). However, the term can also be extended to fathers whose children are born outside of marriage. "Noncustodial father," then, refers to men who live apart from their children either because of marital disruption through separation and divorce or because of nonmarriage with the child's mother.

HISTORIC TRENDS, CURRENT STATISTICS, AND DATA LIMITATIONS

Two patterns in American family life have converged to make noncustodial fatherhood increasingly common in contemporary American society: marital dissolution through separation and divorce and nonmarital childbearing in the absence of parental coresidence. The current high rates of marital dissolution and nonmarital childbearing are not new demographic developments, but rather are continuations of long-term trends affecting the character of contemporary family life in America (Bumpass, 1990). Recent estimates suggest that when current divorce rates are projected forward, three-fifths to two-thirds of first marriages contracted during the 1980s will end in divorce (Bumpass, 1990; Castro Martin and Bumpass, 1989), and that roughly one of every two children can expect to live for a time in a single-parent household (see Bianchi, in this volume). This implies that young couples who are considering marriage and family-building today must wrestle with an uncertain marital future including the high probability that at some point their relationship will be that of co-parental former spouses. If current custody patterns continue, large segments of young married women face the strong likelihood that a portion of their lives will be lived as single mothers with custody of their children; and in their turn, young fathers must contemplate the risk of becoming noncustodial fathers living apart from their children.

Also having significance for the numbers of men who are noncustodial fathers are trends in childbearing outside of marriage. Using life table procedures with current rates of nonmarital childbearing, Bumpass (1990) estimates that as many as 1 in 6 white women and 7 in 10 black women will have children outside of marriage if current trends continue. Currently, most research, policy and media attention is given to the large numbers of nonmarital births to teens, but a substantial portion occur to older women as well. Clearly major changes have occurred and are occurring in the meanings of and linkages among fathering, mothering, and marriage. Very little is known about the claims to fatherhood that nonmarital fathers make for their children born outside of marriage, although the limited research is illuminating (see Marsiglio, in this volume; Mott, 1990).

Neither the absolute numbers of noncustodial fathers in the population nor the prevalence and incidence of noncustodial fathering have been discussed. In an earlier review, Fox (1985) outlined the limitations of existing data for developing counts and descriptions of the noncustodial father population. The limitations still apply (see also Garfinkel and Oellerich, 1989; see Bianchi, in this volume). What is needed is a childbearing history for men, data that are rarely collected because of problems of validity, reliability, accuracy and coverage of events. In the absence of the necessary data, analytic improvisation is necessary. A very crude estimate of the numbers of noncustodial fathers in 1989 is 8.25 million, estimated by inflating by 60% the Current Population Survey (CPS) count of 4.95 million women with children under 21 who were due child support (Lester, 1991). The inflation factor reflects that generally only 60% of women with dependent children are awarded child support.

Long overdue are the methodological improvements necessary to obtain adequate data from men themselves on their procreative behaviors and subsequent contacts and relationships with any children resulting from such unions. Shifts are also needed in social expectations for men's reporting accurately their fathering behavior–whether they have begat children; the number, ages, locations and identities of any such children; and whether and what kinds of contact fathers have had with those children during the child's lifetime.

THE LEGAL FRAMEWORK: CUSTODY DISPOSITIONS, VISITATION, AND CHILD SUPPORT

The legal parameters of noncustodial fatherhood are set by state law, judicial discretion, case precedent, and increasingly, federal statute. That is, what it means to be a noncustodial father is negotiated not solely by the players in the former familial triangle of father-mother-child/ren. But in addition, through the mechanisms of custody dispositions, visitation privileges and child support awards, the society at large becomes an important player in constructing the post-divorce family. Normative expectations and values about appropriate family relations are expressed through custody, visitation, and child support; so it is important to consider each of these three areas as guidelines for and constraints upon parenting in the post-divorce context.

Custody

Currently an array of custody options is seen following divorce, including *sole* custody, that is, physical (residential) and legal (decision-making) custody award of children to one parent; *joint* custody with shared legal custody and either joint or sole physical custody awarded to one parent; *split* custody in which children are divided between the parents; and other combinations of residential and legal custody dispositions.

In most divorces today legal and physical custody of children is awarded solely to the mother; Seltzer (1990) reports 73% and Weitzman (1985) reports 90%. This pattern notwithstanding, at least 35 states mandate a preference for joint custody, that is, parentally shared legal custody (Freed and Walker, 1987; Kitson and Morgan, 1990; Seltzer, 1990). This shift in custody law reflects several societal trends in parenting ideology, including the recognition of the contributions of both parents to children's socioemotional development, wholly apart from their economic contributions to child well-being.

Empirical research on determinants of custody decisions is sparse. Researchers have difficulty gaining access to and capturing the intensity of on-going negotiations about future co-parenting between divorcing parties. Maccoby and Mnookin (1992) circumvent these difficulties to an extent in their research on the negotiation of divorce outcomes in a panel study of 1,100 families in California. Among the wealth of findings from this study are that parents in 80% of the cases did not make conflicting requests for child custody; mothers were more likely than fathers to ask for custody and to obtain a positive ruling on their requests. The most common conflict arose when mothers requested sole physical custody and fathers requested joint custody; in 67% of these cases, the mother was granted her request. Legal representation of either party led to joint legal custody. When the mother only was represented, her chances of receiving sole physical custody were only slightly higher than when neither party had representation; by contrast, legal representation of the father increased his chances of receiving joint physical or sole physical custody. Seltzer (1990) investigated custody adjudication in a sample of Wisconsin divorce cases filed during 1980-1985. Using multinomial logit analysis, Seltzer reported that in contrast to sole custody awards to mother, joint custody was more likely if the father's income was higher and the divorce action was more recent. Physical custody awards to mothers were more likely when the children were younger, reflective of the "tender years" doctrine that has predominated in custody decision-making during most of this century.

Working with a divorced female subsample of the National Longitudinal Survey of the Class of 1972 (NLS-72), Teachman and Polonko (1990) used latent-class analysis and logistic regression to understand factors important in predicting whether divorces resulted in the "standard divorce" (mother with custody, father with visitation, and a child support award). The standard divorce was more likely the lengthier the marriage, the higher the husband's income at the time of divorce, and when at least one child under six years old was present. The mother's not having a lawyer decreased the likelihood of reaching the standard divorce outcome. Fox and Kelly (1993) investigated custody awards in 879 Michigan divorce cases filed in 1982-83. Factors identified in logit regression models that increased the likelihood of physical custody awards to fathers included having a son as the eldest/only child, having "older" youngsters, the father's role as plaintiff and the inclusion of Friend of the Court investigations in the divorce record. Factors that decreased the likelihood of physical custody awards to fathers included his unemployment, higher income, and being in arrears for one or more periods of child support. It is notable that all four studies find legal process, socioeconomic, and family composition variables to affect custody outcomes. More research is needed that will allow further specification of the conditions under which fathers (and mothers) are likely to receive custody awards of different types, including studies focused directly on negotiation processes and on the question of trade-offs among custody, child support, alimony, and visitation (see Seltzer and Garfinkel, 1990).

Visitation

The significance of visitation to noncustodial parents cannot be overstated. It is through visitation that the noncustodial parent is able to maintain some semblance of a paternal relationship with his child or children. Parenting by noncustodial fathers is circumscribed by the visitation arrangements set forth in the final divorce settlement. Therefore, the nature and protection of visitation privileges are of paramount importance to the maintenance of the parent-child bond (Fox, 1985; Novinson, 1983). Visitation arrangements are customarily stipulated in the final divorce settlement and vary widely both in the amount of contact time awarded and in the degree of specificity of arrangements. A blanket "right of reasonable visitation" is often granted, leaving the determination and implementation of that right in the hands of the divorcing parents.

Missing from the research literature is the relationship between de facto and de jure (factual versus legal) visitation arrangements. Certainly lawyers and counselors can draw on much anecdotal evidence of informal visitation arrangements engineered by co-parents after divorce that vary widely from those stipulated in divorce settlements. Because visitation is second only to support complaints in bringing parties back into litigation, it would be worthwhile to learn how divorced parents successfully work out satisfactory visitation arrangements and whether the degree of satisfaction varies with such factors as specificity, amount and patterning of contact time, that can be regulated by the courts at the time of the decree. Such information could be useful in making initially more satisfactory visitation settlements, potentially avoiding costly post-divorce litigation over visitation disputes.

For most fathers, contact with children tapers off sharply following marital separation. Using data from the National Survey of Children, Furstenberg (Furstenberg and Nord, 1985; Furstenberg, Morgan, and Allison, 1987; Furstenberg, Nord, Peterson, and Zill, 1983) documents decreasing levels of father involvement over time, such that most children reported rare or no contact with their fathers in the preceding year. Only 16% reported visits at least weekly with the noncustodial father. Seltzer (1991b) reports somewhat higher rates of father-child visiting after divorce with NSFH data: close to 25 percent of children of divorce saw their noncustodial fathers at least weekly. One-third of formerly married fathers and one-half of never-married fathers were reported to have visited their children once a year or less in the year preceding the survey (Seltzer, 1991b). Even more important than delineation of overall patterns of father-child contact is to understand the conditions that foster or impede post-separation continuation of the father-child relationship. Several recent research efforts have identified factors associated with maintenance of father-child contact following divorce, including *time since separation/divorce*, such that the more recent the separation, the more frequent are father-child visits (Furstenberg et al., 1983; Seltzer, 1991b; Seltzer, Schaeffer, and Charng, 1989); *payment of child support* increases the likelihood of visitation (Furstenberg et al., 1983; Seltzer, 1991b), *remarriage of the mother and/or of the father* decreases the likelihood of visitation (Furstenberg et al., 1983; Seltzer, 1991b; Seltzer et al., 1989); *educational level of mother and/or father* increases the likelihood of visitation (Furstenberg et al., 1983; Seltzer, 1991b; Seltzer et al., 1989); and *proximity of residence* facilitates parent-child contact (Furstenberg et al., 1983; Seltzer, 1991b; Seltzer et al., 1989).

The findings from national surveys on maintenance of the father role through visitation might be construed as evidence of the lack of salience or meaningfulness of the father role to many men. Such an interpretation contrasts very sharply with research that allows noncustodial fathers to speak for themselves. Grief reactions, feelings of displacement and of having lost their children, and unremitting anger have been reported (Arditti, 1992; Arendell, 1992; Guttman, 1989; Hetherington, Cox, and Cox, 1978; Myers, 1986; Tschann, Johnston, and Wallerstein, 1989; Wallerstein and Kelly, 1980; Weiss, 1975). Some have suggested that the inconsistency between men's expressions of intense longings for their children and the lack of regular or frequent contact with children can be more readily understood if one takes into account post-separation or post-divorce familial conflict, degree of attachment (positive and negative) between ex-spouses, and alternative sources of social contact or social support available to the former spouses (Arditti, 1992; Guttman, 1989; Tschann et al., 1989). When contacts with the former spouse are aversive, noncustodial fathers become dissuaded from their attempts to maintain a relationship with their former families, with the resulting rapid attenuation of ties with their children. The pain of the visits themselves–their brevity, their intensity, their insufficiency–and the father's sense of guilt and anger over the divorce also inhibit consistent and frequent visitation (Arditti, 1992; Arendell, 1992; Wallerstein and Kelly, 1980). In the final section of this chapter, an assessment is offered of the contribution of traditional sex role socialization and communication patterns and gendered parent roles in undermining the father-child relationship in nonfamilial settings, such as visitation.

In response to problems with visitation, most noncustodial fathers apparently manage to work out sets of arrangements with their former spouses that accommodate their level of conflict and continuing post-divorce attachments (Isaacs, 1988; Maccoby, Depner, and Mnookin, 1990). A minority of fathers respond to visitation problems (among other divorce-related grievances) with public political mobilization in advocacy efforts for parental rights for noncustodial fathers. Others channel their efforts into private acts of aggression, including continued post-divorce litigation (Arendell, 1992) and abduction of their children in defiance of custody and visitation orders (Finkelhor, Hotaling, and Sedlak, 1991). Finkelhor and his colleagues (1991) report more than 350,000 child abductions associated with violations of custody agreements, using data from the 1988 National Incidence Survey of Missing, Abducted, Runaway, and Thrownaway Children.

State legislatures and courts have moved in recent years to clarify the nature of visitation, to specify visitation privileges for affinal kin and other relatives of the child, and to strengthen the enforcement of visitation orders. Additionally, some states are wrestling with the issues of relocation rights of custodial and noncustodial parents; that is, whether co-parents have a right to relocate at a distance that prohibits the exercise of the other parent's "reasonable rights of visitation" and full exercise of adjudicated custody privileges. The potential impact of new legislation on visitation difficulties is unclear. What is certain, however, is that the numbers of families facing such issues is large and growing. Not only is more empirical research needed on legal and social factors associated with noncustodial parent visitation, but work is also needed in counseling and clinical areas on means of reducing the high levels of conflict and pain associated with marital separation and post-divorce contact.

Child Support

The obligation to support one's child is central to our understanding of the rights and duties of parenthood, but recent changes in context and texture of marriage, divorce and parenting have raised significant questions about the universal applicability of this obligation (Krause, 1990). Indeed, Krause argues that noncustodial fathers with support awards in some jurisdictions have become obligated to provide levels of support in excess of those required of custodial residential fathers.

Moved largely by embarrassment and dismay at the steadily increasing proportions of American children living in single-parent homes in poverty or near poverty, along with indisputable evidence that despite the financial capacity to do so, the majority of noncustodial fathers responsible for child support payments failed to comply regularly or fully with child support payment schedules, the U.S. Congress enacted legislation during the 1980s to address the issue of parental and societal support obligations for children, while acknowledging at the same time the enormous demographic and normative shifts in marriage, family, and work patterns among U.S. adults (Calistri, 1990; Krause, 1990). These efforts culminated in the Family Support Act of 1988. The child support provisions of this act are designed to increase the likelihood that eligible children will receive awards, primarily by improving state efforts to establish paternity, to shift states toward uniformity via mandatory guidelines for size of awards based on numbers and ages of children, and to increase the effectiveness of collection efforts by moving states away from punitive actions such as incarceration, and toward bureaucratic mechanisms for enforcement (including mandatory wage-withholding, periodic review, and strengthened interstate cooperation) (Garfinkel and McLanahan, 1990; Krause, 1990). Both state and national assessments of the impact of these provisions are currently underway (Moore, 1992; Thoennes, Tjaden, and Pearson, 1991).

Support Awards and Compliance. Not all divorces obligate the noncustodial parent to contribute to continued support of children, and not all parents ordered to pay support do so regularly or fully. Indeed, Lester (1991) estimates that just over half (51%) of the close to five million women with children under 21 who were due child support payments actually received the payments in full; another 24% received partial payment, and the remainder received nothing of what was due. These data, however, include both never married and ever married women. Compliance figures are higher when only ever married mothers are considered;

roughly 80% are awarded child support and compliance with support awards reaches 60% (Beller and Graham, 1986; Teachman, 1991). Ellis and Lino (1992) provide information on child support from the perspective of those making payments. Using data from the 1988-89 Consumer Expenditure Survey, they report that 2.91 million householders made child support payments in the survey year, averaging $3,339 and comprising 9% of household before-tax income (see also Bianchi, this volume).

Child well-being is expected to be affected by income transfers from noncustodial parents in the form of child support, both directly through improvements in the child's standard of living, and indirectly through the positive association found between regular payment of support awards and other forms of parental contact (Seltzer et al., 1989). Thus, the separate questions of who is granted a support award at divorce and given an award, and who pays are important. As the child support provisions of the Family Support Act of 1988 are implemented more fully across the U.S., the awarding of child support at the time of divorce can be expected to reflect "need factors," such as number and ages of children and custodial parent's employment status and income, along with "ability-to-pay factors" such as the noncustodial parent's income. Factors that index the former spouses' relative bargaining power or negotiating ability–each one's education, use of attorneys, judicial discretion–can be expected to become less significant in accounting for who is awarded support. Further, as enforcement becomes more effective and uniform across the states, models of payment (who pays how much?) should reflect size of award and ability to pay rather than motivational variables assessing the noncustodial parent's willingness to pay, post-divorce negative attachments and the like.

Patterns of child support compliance identified by current research necessarily reflect the experiences of men and women whose divorces and subsequent post-divorce custody and child support arrangements have taken place in the midst of the present period of statutory and regulatory transition, ideological change in parenting norms and stagnation in gender roles. Teachman (1990) explored conditions associated with child support awards at divorce among a subsample of ever-divorced mothers from the NLS-72 (National Longitudinal Class of 1972) and found the likelihood of being awarded child support was positively associated with the mother's income, her having at least some college education at the time of divorce, the presence of children aged 6 or younger, and the length of the marriage. When amount of award was examined, Teachman found that awards were larger when the mother had at least some college education, the higher the father's earnings at divorce, the larger the number of children, and the longer the marriage. The size of the child support award was not affected by legal factors (mother's having an attorney, state divorce statutes), the mother's income at divorce or race. Teachman concludes that in this sample, support award outcomes reflect both the relative negotiating strengths of the former spouses and, at least in the voluntary arrangements, the motivation of the husband to continue to support his former family. It is also evident that need factors, such as number and age of children, affect the likelihood and amount of award.

Considerably more attention has been directed to the question of who complies with child support orders, or alternatively, under what circumstances is compliance enhanced? Teachman (1991) focused on receipt of child support payments among a subsample of ever-divorced mothers taken from the larger NLS-72 national survey. He concluded that receipt of child support does not depend on such need factors as mother's income or child characteristics (age, gender, number) but rather on characteristics and circumstances of the father, which reflect both his ability and his motivation to pay. Receipt of child support was positively predicted by father's income at the time of divorce, his having remarried, geographic proximity, father visitation, voluntariness of the child support award, and size of the award. Neither indicator of legal factors (mother's having an attorney; divorce in a no-fault state) was associated with payment of support. These results–the greater importance of the father's than of the mother's circumstances in determining child support compliance–echo the conclusions of Peterson and Nord (1990) with the national Survey of Income and Program Participation and those earlier of Beller and Graham (1986) using 1979 CPS data.

Seltzer has also explored child support compliance in a series of research efforts (Seltzer et al., 1989; Seltzer, 1991a; and Seltzer, 1991b), examining the complex covariation of custody awards, visitation, child support compliance, paternal participation in parenting, and child well-being. Among her conclusions are that much of the covariation of visitation and child support compliance can be accounted for by their common demographic antecedents, such as parental income, education, proximity, and the like. However, she also concludes that visiting and child support payment are complementary activities; and as such, ". . . legal reforms to the child support system will increase the amount of time that noncustodial parents and children spend together" (1989: 1027).

The impact of custody arrangements on child support compliance was investigated in a separate study (Seltzer, 1991a). Seltzer found that the size of support awarded was higher in divorces with joint legal custody dispositions, but the association is explained by a selectivity factor; that is, fathers with higher incomes are more likely to receive joint legal custody and to have higher payments ordered. When only those with joint legal custody are considered, the income of the father was closely associated with the payments actually made, regardless of the size of the support order awarded by the court. Seltzer concludes that ". . . joint legal custody may encourage fathers to make child-support contributions contingent on their own personal circumstances" (1991a: 923).

One might derive from Seltzer's work support for current policy manipulations of two of the external parameters or constraints on the noncustodial father-child relationship, changes that are designed in part to buttress that fragile relationship. Specifically, joint custody is to be preferred over other forms of custody, since it appears to bolster child support compliance. Moreover, improvements in state mechanisms for child support enforcement are to be applauded, because regular payment of child support enhances father-child contact through more frequent and enduring visitation patterns.

Arendell (1992) sounds a cautionary note, however, against overly sanguine interpretations of child support compliance by noncustodial fathers. In an ethnographic study of 75 divorced fathers, she finds considerable support for viewing payment of child support as motivated as much by a desire to maintain control over the post-divorce existence of the ex-wife as by a desire to contribute to the well-being of their mutual children. Maccoby et al. (1990: 154) express similar reservations about joint custody. Research using intensive interviews underscores the need to take into account the post-divorce relationships between ex-spouses (e.g., conflict, cooperation) in shaping the underlying meanings of overt behaviors measured with quantitative assessments. It is also valuable in suggesting potentially healthful directions of psychoeducational interventions with men and women after divorce, as outlined in the final section of this chapter.

FATHERING BY NONCUSTODIAL FATHERS

Despite the assumption that continuing contact with the noncustodial father is important to a child's well-being following divorce, the empirical evidence to support this assumption is surprisingly thin (Furstenberg and Nord, 1985; Hawkins and Eggebeen, 1991). The positive outcomes of noncustodial father contact were noted in early studies that involved small, nonrepresentative samples of divorcing couples characterized by higher socioeconomic backgrounds (Wallerstein and Kelly, 1980). The early results have been difficult to replicate consistently in subsequent studies that rely upon survey data from larger, representative samples (Furstenberg, Morgan and Allison, 1987; Hawkins and Eggebeen, 1991; King, 1994; Thomson, McLanahan, and Curtin, 1992).

It is not difficult to demonstrate differentials in child well-being by family structure or marital disruption (Baydar, 1988; Dawson, 1991; McLanahan and Booth, 1989). The problem is tying down exactly what it is about noncustodial fathers that affects their children–their limited presence? their behaviors? their effects on others? This problem in research with noncustodial fathers is exacerbated by the absence of comparable research with custodial fathers. In truth, the recognition among family scientists that parenting by men might reasonably be operationalized as a set of behaviors, in active terms as the ungendered "parent," rather than as a status, "father," is quite recent. Consequently, few common understandings about what to measure and even fewer standardized instruments exist for measuring parenting behaviors among men (see the recent efforts of Harris and Morgan, 1991; Ihinger-Tallman, Pasley, and Buehler, 1993; Marsiglio, 1991; and Thompson et al., 1992). Seltzer (1991b) using NSFH data operationalized fathering following separation as (mother's reports of) contact with the child, economic support, and involvement with the coparent in decision-making about the child. The three behaviors covaried, such that an increase in one was accompared by involvement in the other two indicators of parenting. Importantly, Seltzer demonstrated stability over time in the linkage among the behaviors, such that once patterns were established, they "held together" in a parenting bundle regardless of time since separation. Furstenberg and Nord (1985) draw on children's reports in the NSC to describe parallel parenting among noncustodial fathers, in which the father's parenting is independent of the custodial mother.

Studies based on interviews with noncustodial fathers themselves report several common difficulties, including relative inexperience in the full complement of caregiving activities involved in the parent role; situational problems in providing a home or home-like environment in which to enact family behaviors during visits, the challenge of meeting the needs of each child during visits with more than one child; communication problems with children at different stages of development; and resistance from children to the father's new social involvements (see Fox, 1985 and Guttman, 1989 for reviews of this work).

The one factor identified consistently across studies as most salient in constraining the relationship with their children, however, is the nature of the relationship with the former wife. The relative balance of conflict and cooperation colors many aspects of men's contacts with their children

(Ahrons, 1983; Arendell, 1992; Bowman and Ahrons, 1985; Coysh, Johnston, Tschann, Wallerstein, and Kline, 1989; Isaacs, 1988; Koch and Lowery, 1984; Kurdek, 1986; Tschann, Johnston, and Wallerstein, 1989; Wright and Price, 1986.) Maccoby and her colleagues, (Maccoby et al., 1990; Maccoby and Mnookin, 1992) are investigating the interaction of conflict between coparental former spouses with different custody arrangements and the nature of coparenting relationships. At the 18-month followup, they found that noncustodial parents were less satisfied with custody arrangements than parents who shared residential custody of their children; further, they found continuity in levels of conflict across the divorce process, such that predivorce conflict predicted post-divorce conflict levels. Sharing residential custody neither exacerbated nor lessened levels of coparental conflict, and noncustodial parents were more satisfied with their custody situation when the coparents either were cooperative or had completely severed their ties with each other. Clearly, any understanding of noncustodial fathers must start with the nature of the continuing relationship with his former spouse.

INTERVENTIONS WITH NONCUSTODIAL FATHERS

A description of the ways in which noncustodial fathers behave and the situations they typically experience provides a basis for understanding how they, as well as their former wives and children, adapt following divorce. In order to facilitate more positive adaptations through psychoeducational or therapeutic interventions, a basic understanding of the impact of divorce on family systems needs to be conceptualized. Ahrons (1980), most notably, and others have postulated stages in the process of adjustment for families in response to divorce. Her description entails an emphasis on cognitive, affective, and boundary issues in families and is helpful in emphasizing important role transitions and tasks facing families. There are, however, some more basic lenses or perspectives through which the impact of divorce can be described when viewed in a broader sociocultural perspective.

Recent work from the feminist perspective on family therapy provides a basis for such a conceptualization of the impact of divorce on family systems. The field of family therapy typically has not viewed family systems through the important lens of gender when attempting to describe how family systems function. Neither have attempts to devise systemic interventions taken gender into account (McGoldrick, Anderson, and Walsh, 1989; Walters, Carter, Papp and Silverstein, 1988). A gender-sensitive view of family systems as described by Goldner (1988) ". . . means conceptualizing gender as an irreducible category of clinical observation and theorizing, as fundamental to the family therapy paradigm as the concept of generation . . . gender and generation are best understood as the two fundamental, organizing principles of family life" (p. 44).

Two important aspects of these organizing principles for families are the impact of autonomy and connectedness as well as power in families. Walters et al. (1988) pointed out that in systemic views of male-female and intergenerational relationships, the ideal is seen as interdependence with maturity being defined as autonomy-with-connectedness. This is not the reality, however, in our patriarchal society; the tie between autonomy and connectedness is severed, and "autonomy" (distorted to separateness) is assigned to men and "connectedness" (distorted to dependency) to women. The gendered assignment and distortion of these processes has resulted in adverse effects for both men and women in families.

In line with the lack of attention given to gender in understanding family systems, the concept of power has not been adequately utilized in explaining how families function. Although some theories have taken into account the concept of power, it has been viewed in a generational rather than a gender context (Walsh and Scheinkmen, 1989). In families, as is true of the broader social context, men and women have had unequal access to differential types of power. Hansen (1965) differentiated two kinds of power in groups. The first involves the influence members have on another because of their personal relationship and is termed personal power; the second involves the influence they have on another because of their position in the group structure and is termed positional power. Certainly these concepts of power apply to our social order as well as individual family systems. Men have had much greater access to positional power based on status and economic control. Women have had much greater access to personal power or as Walters et al. (1988) described it ". . . exerting authority more through relationship . . ." (p. 24).

How does such a perspective on family systems help us better understand the experiences of noncustodial fathers? Fundamentally, divorce creates significant changes in the organization of a family system in terms of both gender and generation. Processes of autonomy, connectedness, and power must be realigned in families but within a broader sociocultural context in which a patriarchal family structure is still most likely to be valued and supported. Essentially, divorce creates, and to some extent necessitates, opportunities for men and women to deal in new ways with the issues of autonomy, connectedness, and power. However, societal supports for moving beyond the traditional polarization of genders and roles through which families have been organized and masculinity and femininity have been defined are sorely lacking.

Following divorce, noncustodial fathers lose much of the basis for the positional power that undergirded their authority with wives and children. They must also deal with issues of autonomy or connectedness in very different ways; no longer can they count on a relationship with wives, as is often the case, for the only context in which they allow themselves to experience intimacy. Neither can they depend on wives to facilitate and mediate their relationships with children and to provide physical care-giving. Men are thus thrust into a situation in which they are faced with issues and tasks that often leave them feeling bewildered, lonely, powerless, and detached. Unfortunately, some noncustodial fathers continue to use the control of money and/or regular contact with children as last ditch measures to maintain and exert positional power (Berkman, 1986).

The ways in which men respond to the changes precipitated by divorce are influenced by a number of factors related to who they are as a person as well as the broader social context in which they operate. In order to design psychoeducational or therapeutic interventions that allow noncustodial fathers to adapt in ways that are beneficial to themselves and ultimately to their children, an awareness of these factors is imperative. The ultimate objectives of such interventions are: to empower men so they can recognize, value, and exert the influence open to them through a greater utilization of personal power rather than primarily positional power; and to assist men to find ways of maintaining emotional connection to their children in ways that allow them to be truly autonomous rather than detached or cut-off from them.

In general, these are goals that have been achieved by only a minority of noncustodial fathers. In order to work toward such outcomes entails reformulations of how men have been socialized to view both their masculinity as well as their role as fathers. McKenry and Price (1990) offered a cogent review of the literature on the impact of divorce on men by attempting to answer the question of the extent to which men are at risk for negative consequences of divorce. They concluded that:

> Although research is limited, increasing evidence suggests that men, because of their traditional sex role socialization, are particularly vulnerable to many negative consequences of divorce. Also, because of this socialization, men involved in divorce are neither able to acknowledge their symptomatology nor to seek help. (p. 112)

In recognition of the growing numbers of men who want to move in this direction, interventions are needed that provide them with support and assistance in dealing with opportunities, issues, and tasks that they are facing rather than ignoring or denying them. Some guidelines for such interventions are offered.

Noncustodial fathers need to be helped to recognize the important role that they can play in the on-going development and well-being of their children. Wallerstein and Kelly (1980) concluded that the more cooperative divorced parents could be in the process of coparenting their children, the better children fared developmentally and emotionally following parental divorce. They also found that the great majority of children in their sample felt that they did not get to see the noncustodial father often enough (the most typical visitation arrangement was every other weekend). Regularity and accessibility of contact between fathers and their children following divorce is beneficial not only to the post-divorce adjustment of children, but also of fathers (Ambrose, Harper, & Pemberton, 1983; Clarke-Stewart & Bailey, 1990; Stewart, Schevebel, & Tine, 1986). Helping noncustodial fathers become aware of the positive influence they can have on children's development following divorce can introduce them to and help them appreciate the importance of the personal power they continue to have or are able to foster with their children following divorce.

With increasing frequency, the issues that bring noncustodial fathers to therapy are issues about their relationships with their children; frequently they feel powerless to effect change or fear losing their children (Brown, 1989; Feldman, 1990). Although the extent to which fathers were involved in the process of parenting prior to divorce varies, in almost all cases mothers have had primary responsibility for both the physical and emotional care of children. Following divorce, fathers find themselves in a situation where, ". . . presence can no longer serve as a cover for inaction. In a two-parent home the father is assured of the availability of his children. But once he leaves, his fatherhood must be earned" (Guttmann, 1989, p. 252). Interventions must be devised so that fathers feel encouraged, informed, and supported in their attempts to "earn their fatherhood" through exerting their authority through their personal relationship with their children. Information and help in interpreting the responses and reactions of children following divorce is, thus, very useful to most fathers. The age, gender, and birth order of children will impact both on the ways in which they deal with parental divorce as well as how they respond and relate to the noncustodial father (Brody & Forehand, 1990; Healy, Malley, & Stewart, 1990; Wallerstein & Blakeslee, 1989; Wallerstein & Kelly, 1980). Brown (1989) pointed out that frequently men are eager to learn more about children and parenting ". . . and a divorce may present the first opportunity to learn how to keep relationships alive and well" (p. 393).

The other broad goal to be addressed in devising interventions for working effectively with noncustodial fathers is helping them find alternatives that allow them to redefine relationship with children and former spouses so that genuine autonomy can be experienced in the context of genuine connection. As was mentioned earlier, our patriarchal society has distorted these concepts so that often autonomy is seen as separateness and connection is seen as dependency. Further, traditional gender-role socialization has emphasized separateness as the primary feature of men's relationships and dependency as the primary characteristic of women's relationships. Rubin (1983) has pointed out that these broader sociocultural norms have created a situation in which typically only mother-child relationships have been the context in which children experience connection. As a result, in adult life issues of autonomy are more difficult and threatening for women and issues of connection are more difficult and threatening for men. This reality is reflected in the ways in which men and women experience not only marriage, but also divorce. McKenry & Price (1990) summarized their review of research on separation-related stress and the emotional impact of divorce on men by noting that there is growing evidence that men experience greater distress than do women following separation and divorce. "These gender differences have been attributed to men's tendency to deny their dependency needs and their feelings about the loss of their children, friends, home, possessions, and sometimes status" (p. 97).

One important aspect of working therapeutically with noncustodial fathers is helping them become aware of the emotional impact of their divorce and then helping them reframe their reactions in a way that makes them more understandable and acceptable to them. Weiss (1975) articulated a perspective for understanding the emotional impact of divorce in terms of the concepts of attachment and separation distress. Helping noncustodial fathers reframe their emotional responses from such a perspective often makes their reactions far less threatening, and easier to acknowledge and accept.

The post-divorce relationships of former spouses are frequently characterized by conflict, anger, and ambivalence (Levant, 1990; Weiss, 1975). Noncustodial fathers must be helped to find constructive ways of handling their feelings of often intense emotional reactivity with former spouses. Helping men find effective ways for handling their anger in relationships with former spouses is crucial. Although Lerner (1985) focused on helping women learn to deal with anger, many of her strategies are equally applicable to men and can help them find ways of dealing with anger other than to cut themselves off from their former spouse and children. Such cut-off is adverse for noncustodial fathers as well as their children and former spouses. But all too often this is the route men take in a distorted attempt to protect themselves from pain and conflict (Guttman, 1989). Levant (1990) provided an interesting analysis of the post-divorce family and what he termed the "new father role."

> Noncustodial fathers are at a particular disadvantage for dealing with post-divorce conflict because of the shift in the balance of power in favor of their wives. As mentioned above, men of this generation have not, in general, been prepared to be good listeners or flexible negotiators; in fact, as boys they were trained to resolve conflicts through the exercise of power, in the form of physical strength, verbal facility, or a superior strategy. I would advance the hypothesis that many men call it quits with visitation because they cannot tolerate feeling so powerless in the face of unremitting conflict. (p. 87)

Certainly an important part of formulating effective interventions with noncustodial fathers is help them become aware of and sensitive to gender differences in styles of communication and ways of approaching conflict. Tannen's (1990) descriptions of the differing communication styles of men and women is a very useful resource for helping noncustodial fathers learn more effective ways to interact with former spouses so that their messages have a greater likelihood of being understood and accepted. A realistic perspective is that noncustodial fathers may learn more effective ways to *manage* conflict with former spouses, rather than to resolve conflicts. In situations where former spouses are bitterly angry and uncooperative the process of managing conflicts will be especially problematic. Unfortunately, in some instances, these conflicts impinge on the noncustodial father's relationships with children when mothers overtly or covertly interfere with the father's attempts to be involved with their children (Hodges, 1986). Even in these situations, however, the disruptive effects can perhaps be minimized if noncustodial fathers can learn new and more effective strategies for dealing with anger and conflict. For both former spouses the intensity and frequency of conflicts usually does diminish over time (Hetherington, Cox, & Cox, 1978) and recognition of this reality can be helpful. Hope is an important part of coping with stress in a variety of situations.

According to Kegan (1982), autonomy involves a sense of one's self as an individual beyond a relational context. It also involves being clear about the things you are responsible for as well as the things for which you are not responsible. Noncustodial fathers should be helped to claim their responsibility for the emotional and financial well-being of their children. Neither over-responsibility (feeling they should attempt to solve all of the problems experienced by former spouses and children) or under-responsibility (becoming separated and detached) are healthy and effective responses. Achieving autonomy in the context of connectedness is truly a complex and ever-changing balance to maintain. It is indeed unfortunate that for many men the only context in which they come to terms with these issues squarely is in the milieu of divorce. It is also unfortunate that a minority of men are able to confront and deal with these issues even when faced with the disruption of attachment relationships and distress that divorce creates for them.

CONCLUSION

An attempt has been made to understand the post-divorce responses and reactions of noncustodial fathers using gender and power as crucial concepts in both familial and broader sociocultural contexts. Obviously, this perspective can be broadened to include the post-divorce reactions and responses of custodial mothers although that task was beyond the scope of the present review. A more complete understanding of how family systems are affected by divorce would necessitate such an extension of this perspective. The "best of all possible worlds" for mothers, fathers, and children following divorce would be when *both* mothers and fathers develop ways to utilize personal and positional power and to be autonomous in the context of connectedness to their children.

Yet families exist in a broader sociocultural context which works against men and women dealing effectively with such processes. Our patriarchal social order assigns processes to familial roles on the basis of gender. Men and women learn different ways of understanding the world and their experience (Belenky, Clinchy, Goldberger, & Tarule, 1986). The unequal access of women to occupational and economic resources is clearest in the context of the post-divorce family and has resulted in what Rix (1980) aptly termed the "feminization of poverty." The well-being of families, whether intact or divorced, ultimately rests on changes in the broader social order that support greater equality in the access to bases of power and sensitivity to the demands faced by parents. Only then will women have greater economic viability and will men be more engaged in familial relationships.

It is a sad commentary indeed that for some women and more men moving away from gender-stratified roles and behaviors occurs most fully following divorce. Both men and women reported that the decision for marital separation (not just divorce) was more frequently initiated by women (Zeiss, Zeiss, & Johnson, 1981). The conditions of a patriarchal organization of the family are becoming somewhat less tolerable for women as they are shouldering the sharing of the provider role without concomitant changes on the part of husbands and fathers in sharing in the physical care and emotional processes of families that have traditionally been assigned or relegated to wives and mothers. "What distinguishes our time and place from others is that women's subordination to men has become morally unacceptable. Nonetheless, it persists" (Goldner, 1989, p. 49). If men and women were able to move away from a family organization based on roles polarized by gender and were able to utilize both personal and positional power in families with a focus on tasks rather than roles, perhaps rates of divorce would decrease as marriages became more equitable for women. Men would reap the rewards of greater involvement and connectedness with both their wives and children if such changes occurred prior to divorce.

As social scientists and helping professionals we must guard against "father bashing" in our descriptions of noncustodial fathers. Certainly the behavior of many noncustodial fathers is not to be admired in terms of the limited on-going responsibility they assume for the financial and emotional well-being of their children. But such fathers are not necessarily hard-hearted and narcissistic individuals. They are men faced with issues and tasks that are most difficult for them to handle effectively because of the gender-typed socialization occurring in our culture. Often the support needed from their social milieu for changes that move them away from traditionally "masculine" roles and behaviors are lacking. As a culture, the more traditionally "feminine" roles and behaviors they may be attempting to assume are devalued. If the dilemmas of noncustodial fathers are to be fully understood, they must be cast in the context of our broader social order.

REFERENCES

Ahrons, C. R. (1980). Divorce: A crisis of family transition and change. *Family Relations*, *29*, 533-540.

Ahrons, C. R. (1983). Predictors of paternal involvement postdivorce: Mothers' and fathers' perceptions. *Journal of Divorce*, *6*, 55-69.

Ambrose, P., Harper, J., & Pemberton, R. (1983). *Surviving divorce: Men beyond marriage*. Rowman & Allanheld.

Arditti, J. A. (1992). Factors related to custody, visitation, and child support for divorced fathers: An exploratory analysis. *Journal of Divorce & Remarriage*, *17*, 23-42.

Arendell, T. (1992). After divorce: Investigations into father absence. *Gender and Society*, *6*, 562-586.

Baydar, N. (1988). Effects of parental separation and reentry into union on the emotional well-being of children. *Journal of Marriage and the Family*, *50*, 967-982.

Belenky, M. F., Clinchy, B. M., Goldberger, N. R., & Tarule, J. M. (1986). *Women's ways of knowing: The development of self, voice, and mind.* New York: Basic Books.

Beller, A. H., & Graham, J. W. (1986). Child support awards: Differentials and trends by race and marital status. *Demography, 23*, 231-246.

Berkman, B. G. (1986). Father involvement and regularity of child support in post-divorce families. *Journal of Divorce, 9*, 67-74.

Bowman, M. E., & Ahrons, C. R. (1985). Impact of legal custody status on fathers' parenting postdivorce. *Journal of Marriage and the Family, 47*, 481-488.

Brody, G., & Forehand, R. (1990). Interparental conflict, relationship with the noncustodial father and adolescent post-divorce adjustment. *Journal of Applied Developmental Psychology, 11*, 139-147.

Brown, F. H. (1988). The postdivorce family. In M. McGoldrick & B. Carter (Eds.), *The changing family life cycle: A framework for family therapy.* New York: Gardner Press.

Bumpass, L. L. (1990). What's happening to the family? Interactions between demographic and institutional change. *Demography, 27*, 483-498.

Calistri, B. L. (1990). Child support and welfare reform: The child support enforcement provisions of the Family Support Act of 1988. *Journal of Legislation, 16*, 191-201.

Castro Martin, T., & Bumpass, L. L. (1989). Recent trends in marital disruption. *Demography, 26*, 37-51.

Clarke-Stewart, K. A., & Bailey, B. (1989). Adjusting to divorce: Why do men have it easier? *Journal of Divorce, 13*, 75-94.

Coysh, W. S., Johnston, J. R., Tschann, J. M., Wallerstein, J. S., & Kline, M. (1989). Parental postdivorce adjustment in joint and sole physical custody families. *Journal of Family Issues, 10*, 52-71.

Dawson, D. A. (1991). Family structure and children's health and well-being: Data from the 1988 National Health Interview Survey on Child Health. *Journal of Marriage and the Family, 53*, 573-584.

Ellis, W., & Lino, M. (1992). Payments of child support and alimony. *Family Economics Review, 5(2)*, 12-18.

Feldman, L. B. (1990). Fathers and fathering. In R. L. Meth & R. S. Pasick (Eds.), *Men in therapy: The challenge of change.* New York: Guilford Press.

Finkelhor, D., Hotaling, G., & Sedlak, A. (1991). Children abducted by family members: A national household survey of incidence and episode characteristics. *Journal of Marriage and the Family, 53*, 805-818.

Fox, G. L. (1985). Noncustodial fathers. In S. H. H. Hanson & F. N. Bozett (Eds.), *Dimensions of fatherhood* (pp. 393-415). Beverly Hills, CA: Sage.

Fox, G. L. and Kelly, R. F. (1993). Socioeconomic and legal determinants of maternal and paternal physical custody arrangements at divorce. Paper presented at the North American Conference of the International Society of Family Law. Jackson Hole, Wyoming.

Freed, D. J., & Walker, T. B. (1988). Family law in the fifty states: An overview. *Family Law Quarterly, 21*, 417-573.

Furstenberg, F. F., Jr., Morgan, S. P., & Allison, P. D. (1987). Paternal participation and children's well-being after marital dissolution. *American Sociological Review, 52*, 695-701.

Furstenberg, F. F., Jr., & Nord, C. W. (1985). Parenting apart: Patterns of childrearing after marital disruption. *Journal of Marriage and the Family, 47*, 893-904.

Furstenberg, F. F., Jr., Nord, C. W., Peterson, J. L., & Zill, N. (1983). The life course of children of divorce. *American Sociological Review, 48*, 656-667.

Garfinkel, I., & McLanahan, S. (1990). The effects of the child support provisions of the Family Support Act of 1988 on child well-being. *Population Research and Policy Review, 9*, 205-234.

Garfinkel, I., & Oellerich, D. (1989). Noncustodial fathers' ability to pay child support. *Demography, 26*, 219-233.

Goldner, V. (1989). Gender and generation: Normative and covert hierarchies. In M. McGoldrick, C. Anderson, & F. Walsh (Eds.), *Women in families: A framework for family therapy*. New York: W. W. Norton.

Guttmann, J. (1989). The divorced father: A review of the issues and the research. *Journal of Comparative Family Studies, 20*, 247-261.

Hansen, D. A. (1965). Personal and positional influence in formal groups: Propositions and theory for research on family vulnerability to stress. *Social Forces, 44*, 202-210.

Harris, K. M., & Morgan, S. P. (1991). Fathers, sons, and daughters: Differential paternal involvement in parenting. *Journal of Marriage and the Family, 53*, 531-544.

Hawkins, A. J., & Eggebeen, D. J. (1991). Are fathers fungible? Patterns of coresident adult men in maritally disrupted families and young children's well-being. *Journal of Marriage and the Family, 53*, 958-972.

Healy, J. M., Malley, J. E., & Stewart, A. J. (1990). Children and their fathers after parental separation. *American Journal of Orthopsychiatry, 60*, 531-543.

Hess, R. D., & Camara, K. A. (1979). Post-divorce family relations as mediating factors in the consequences of divorce for children. *The Journal of Social Issues, 35(4)*, 79-96.

Hetherington, E. M., Cox, M., & Cox, R. (1978). The aftermath of divorce. In J. H. Stevens, Jr. & M. Matthews (Eds.), *Mother/child, father/child relationships*. Washington, DC: National Association for the Education of Young Children.

Hodges, W. F. (1986). *Interventions for children of divorce: Custody, access, and psychotherapy*. New York: Wiley.

Ihinger-Tallman, M., Pasley, K., & Buehler, C. (1993). Developing a middle-range theory of father involvement postdivorce. *Journal of Family Issues*, 15: in press.

Isaacs, M. B. (1988). The visitation schedule and child adjustment: A three-year study. *Family Process, 27*, 251-256.

Kegan, R. (1982). *The evolving self*. Cambridge, MA: Harvard University Press.

King, V. (1994). Nonresidential father involvement and child well-being: Can dads make a difference? *Journal of Family Issues*, 15: in press.

Kitson, G. C., & Morgan, L. A. (1990). The multiple consequences of divorce: A decade review. *Journal of Marriage and the Family, 52*, 913-924.

Koch, M. A. P., & Lowery, C. R. (1984). Visitation and the noncustodial father. *Journal of Divorce, 8(2)*, 47-65.

Krause, H. D. (1990). Child support reassessed: Limits of private responsibility and the public interest. *Family Law Quarterly, 24*, 1-34.

Kurdek, L. A. (1986). Custodial mothers' perceptions of visitation and payment of child support by noncustodial fathers in families with low and high levels of preseparation interparent conflict. *Journal of Applied Developmental Psychology, 7*, 307-323.

Lester, G. H. (1991). *Child support and alimony: 1989* (Current Population Reports, Consumer Income, Series P-60, No. 173). Washington, DC: U. S. Department of Commerce, Bureau of the Census.

Levant, R. F. (1990). Coping with the new father role. In D. Moore & F. Leafgren (Eds.), *Problem solving strategies and interventions for men in conflict*. Alexandria, VA: American Association for Counseling and Development.

Maccoby, E., and Mnookin, H. (1992). *Dividing the Child: Social and Legal Dilemmas of Custody*. Cambridge, MA: Harvard University Press.

Maccoby, E. E., Depner, C. E., & Mnookin, R. H. (1990). Coparenting in the second year after divorce. *Journal of Marriage and the Family, 52*, 141-155.

Marsiglio, W. (1991). Paternal engagement activities with minor children. *Journal of Marriage and the Family, 53*, 973-986.

McGoldrick, M., Anderson, C., & Walsh, F. (1989). Women in families and family therapy. In M. McGoldrick, C. Anderson, & F. Walsh (Eds.), *The changing family life cycle: A framework for family therapy*. New York: W. W. Norton.

McKenry, P., & Price, S. J. (1990). Divorce: Are men at risk? In D. Moore, & F. Leafgren (Eds.), *Problem solving strategies and interventions for men in conflict*. Alexandria, VA: American Association for Counseling and Development.

McLanahan, S., & Booth, K. (1989). Mother-only families: Problems, prospects, and politics. *Journal of Marriage and the Family, 51*, 557-580.

Moore, K. (1992). Personal communication, January 26.

Mott, F. L. (1990). When is a father really gone? Paternal-child contact in father-absent homes. *Demography, 27*, 499-518.

Myers, M. F. (1986). Angry, abandoned husbands: Assessment and treatment. *Marriage and Family Review, 9:3/4*, 31-42.

Novinson, S. L. (1983). Post-divorce visitation: Untying the triangular knot. *University of Illinois Law Review, 1*, 119-200.

Peterson, J. L., & Nord, C. W. (1990). The regular receipt of child support: A multistep process. *Journal of Marriage and the Family, 52*, 539-551.

Rix, E. (1988). *The American woman, 1987-88: A report in depth*. New York: W. W. Norton.

Rubin, L. (1983). *Intimate strangers: Men and women together.* New York: Harper & Row.

Seltzer, J. A. (1990). Legal and physical custody arrangements in recent divorces. *Social Science Quarterly, 71*, 250-266.

Seltzer, J. A., & Garfinkel, I. (1990). Inequality in divorce settlements: An investigation of property settlements and child support awards. *Social Science Research, 19*, 82-111.

Seltzer, J. A. (1991a). Legal custody arrangements and children's economic welfare. *American Journal of Sociology, 96*, 895-929.

Seltzer, J. A. (1991b). Relationships between fathers and children who live apart: The father's role after separation. *Journal of Marriage and the Family, 53*, 79-101.

Seltzer, J. A., Schaeffer, N. C., & Charng, H. (1989). Family ties after divorce: The relationship between visiting and paying child support. *Journal of Marriage and the Family, 51*, 1013-1032.

Stewart, J. R., Schwebel, A. I., & Fine, M. (1986). The impact of custodial arrangement on the adjustment of recently divorced fathers. *Journal of Divorce, 9*, 55-65.

Tannen, D. (1990). *You just don't understand: Women and men in conversation.* New York: Ballantine Books.

Teachman, J. D. (1990). Socioeconomic resources of parents and award of child support in the United States: Some exploratory models. *Journal of Marriage and the Family, 52*, 689-699.

Teachman, J. D. (1991). Who pays? Receipt of child support in the United States. *Journal of Marriage and the Family, 53*, 759-772.

Teachman, J. D., & Polonko, K. (1990). Negotiating divorce outcomes: Can we identify patterns in divorce settlements? *Journal of Marriage and the Family, 52*, 129-139.

Thoennes, N., Tjaden, P., & Pearson, J. (1991). The impact of child support guidelines on award adequacy, award variability, and case processing efficiency. *Family Law Quarterly, 25*, 325-345.

Thomson, E., McLanahan, S. S., & Curtin, R. B. (1992). Family structure, gender, and parental socialization. *Journal of Marriage and the Family, 54*, 368-378.

Tschann, J. M., Johnston, J. R., & Wallerstein, J. S. (1989). Resources, stressors, and attachment as predictors of adult adjustment after divorce: A longitudinal study. *Journal of Marriage and the Family, 51*, 1033-1046.

Wallerstein, J. S., & Blakeslee, S. (1989). *Second chances: Men, women, and children a decade after divorce.* New York: Ticknor & Fields.

Wallerstein, J. S., & Kelly, J. B. (1980). *Surviving the breakup: How children and parents cope with divorce.* New York: Basic Books.

Walsh, F., & Scheinkmen (1989). (Fe)male: The hidden gender dimension in models of family therapy. In M. McGoldrick, C. Anderson, & F. Walsh (Eds.), *Women in families: A framework for family therapy.* New York: W. W. Norton.

Walters, M., Carter, B., Papp, P., & Silverstein, O. (1988). Toward a feminist perspective in family therapy. In M. Walters, B. Carter, P. Papp, & O. Silverstein (Eds.), *The invisible web: Gender patterns in family relationships*. New York: Guilford Press.

Weiss, R. S. (1975). *Marital separation: Coping with the end of a marriage and the transition to being single again*. New York: Basic Books.

Weitzman, L. (1985). *The divorce revolution*. New York: The Free Press.

Wright, D. W., & Price, S. J. (1986). Court-ordered child support payment: The effect of the former-spouse relationship on compliance. *Journal of Marriage and the Family, 48*, 869-874.

Zeiss, A. M., Zeiss, R. A., & Johnson, S. M. (1980). Sex differences in initiation of and adjustment to divorce. *Journal of Divorce, 4*, 21-34.

Chapter 13

Noncustodial Parents: Emergent Issues of Diversity and Process

Joyce A. Arditti

SUMMARY. Beyond documentation of noncustodial fathers' failure to pay child support or visit, little is known about the dynamics of noncustodial parenting. Even less is known about the experience of noncustodial mothers. Both of these noncustodial relationships need to be studied, as the data can inform us concerning the role of residential status in relation to the quality of the parent-child relationships. This paper seeks to move beyond status-laden conceptualizations of parenthood which emphasize deficiencies associated with noncustodial parenting situations, and examine specific constraints and opportunities inherent in such arrangements. After divorce, noncustodial parents experience diversity and variation in the quality of relationships with their child(ren) and former spouses. This diversity and variation also emerges in relation to economic circumstances for noncustodial parents. More progressive conceptualizations of parenthood are explored which focus on the *quality* of nonresidential parent-child relationships as well as how parents implement parenting arrangements postdivorce. Recommendations for methodologies which are sensitive to issues related to diversity and process, as well as policy implications are offered.

Joyce A. Arditti is affiliated with the Department of Family and Child Development, Virginia Polytechnic Institute and State University, Blacksburg, VA 24061-0416.

[Haworth co-indexing entry note]: "Noncustodial Parents: Emergent Issues of Diversity and Process." Arditti, Joyce A. Co-published simultaneously in *Marriage & Family Review* (The Haworth Press, Inc.) Vol. 20, No. 1/2, 1995, pp. 283-304; and: *Single Parent Families: Diversity, Myths and Realities* (ed: Shirley M. H. Hanson et al.) The Haworth Press, Inc., 1995, pp. 283-304. Multiple copies of this article/chapter may be purchased from The Haworth Document Delivery Center [1-800-3-HAWORTH; 9:00 a.m. - 5:00 p.m. (EST)].

KEYWORDS. Noncustodial, Divorce, Child support, Visitation, Custody

INTRODUCTION

Stereotypical monolithic portrayals, most commonly the "deadbeat dad," obscure tremendous differences in terms of the parenting process postdivorce as well as differences between parents and different children within the same family. The idea of noncustodial "parenting" is paradoxical in and of itself. Biological in-residence parenting is the standard against which all other parenting arrangements are measured. Hence, other types of parenting arrangements, such as stepparenting and noncustodial parenting, lack social guidelines and legitimacy, forcing individuals to construct their own sense of how they should parent and what they are responsible for with respect to the children involved. Cherlin's (1978) explanation of the causes of instability in remarriages following divorce, most notably the absence of commonly understood guidelines for family interaction, applies to problems associated with noncustodial parenting as well. He states: "problems are created by a complex family structure which cannot occur in first marriages. Because of the lack of social regulation, each family must devise its own solutions to these problems . . ." (p. 640). Wallerstein and Kelly (1980) observed over a decade ago that the visiting relationship between noncustodial father and child is the singular relationship that has no counterpart in the intact marriage. Subsequently, parents find themselves unprepared for or unable to deal with the realities of renegotiating their relationships with their children after divorce.

Certain structural constraints are inherent in nonresidential parenting arrangements and raise questions pertaining to noncustodial parents rights and responsibilities. These constraints are often ignored or minimized in studies examining parent-child relationships postdivorce. For example, the problem of mobility after divorce is rarely fully acknowledged despite the fact that we already know that distance between noncustodial parent's residence and children's residence is one of the most important predictors of contact postdivorce (Arditti, 1992; Furstenburg, 1988). Given the likely possibility that one or both parents typically move during or after a divorce the important question which arises is: how do we reconcile the different needs between each parent and the children? Mandates which require joint custodians to obtain permission from a judge to move is one way in which the legal system has attempted to keep both parents in close proximity to their children. However, even these policies do not necessarily insure that this will happen and fail to address the broader issue of supporting the integrity of parent-child relationships postdivorce regardless of residence.

The review in this paper integrates the research available on noncustodial parents by highlighting aspects which to a large extent, determine outcomes for parent-child relations postdivorce as well as methodological problems in the research. The review is not all inclusive but will emphasize the most important areas of study and significant research. In closing the discussion, a theoretical framework from which to conceptualize noncustodial parenting will be explored. Such a framework encompasses all styles of parenting, with residence being an important contextual feature of any parenting situation. Thus parenting would be defined as a "dynamic process that is in continual development over the life course, subject to change as parents circumstances, preferences, and children's developmental needs change." Within such a framework, custodial status is a divorce related outcome with important implications for parenting–divorce being a likely transition in the life course of many parents. Suggestions for future research, policy and practice directions will also be offered.

NONCUSTODIAL FATHERS

In the following discussion, several issues are considered that are central to understanding existing research as well as pointing to gaps in the literature. Visitation and child support, traditional indicators of paternal involvement postdivorce, are examined as well as the quality of father-child relations. The role coparental relations may have in determining the nature of fathers relations with their children following divorce is then explored. Finally, factors contributing to diverse circumstances for noncustodial fathers and their children are identified and discussed.

Visiting and Paying

Much of our knowledge regarding noncustodial fathers' experiences and parenting postdivorce comes from custodial mothers. While some researchers believe the mothers' reports regarding fathers' activities are relatively accurate (Cherlin, Griffith, and McCarthy, 1983; Teachman, 1991), other studies have shown that mothers tend to underestimate fathers' involvement and child support payment (Ahrons, 1983; Goldsmith, 1982; Seltzer, 1991; Wright & Price, 1986). Also problematic is the narrow view often taken of the fathers' role after divorce. Fathers' parenting postdivorce tends to be operationalized as visitation frequency or child support payment and/or compliance. Clearly the focus is not necessarily how noncustodial fathers negotiate the challenges of parenting children in another household, or qualitative aspects of the nature of parenting postdivorce, but on limited indicators of father child contact and formal financial support. Granted, these outcomes *are* important–especially to children and mothers, and a certain pattern has emerged regarding noncustodial fathers' parenting based on these indicators.

It has been rather well documented that fathers tend to decrease the frequency and duration of their visits over time (Furstenburg, Peterson, Nord, & Zill, 1983; Hetherington et al., 1976; Wallerstein & Kelly, 1980). However, not all studies are in agreement regarding how much noncustodial fathers actually see their children. Much of the variance in findings is probably due to differences in sample composition, sample selectivity, and biases inherent in self-report. For example, Furstenburg et al. (1983) reported that 35% of the fathers in their study had not seen their children for 5 or more years. Weitzman (1985) also reported dismal results–23% of the fathers in her California sample saw their children less than yearly. Haskins, Richey, and Wicker (1987) and Arditti (1992) reported more positive results based on fathers' self reports. Only about 10% in the Haskins study and 13% in Arditti's study reported seeing their children less than once a month.

Figures also vary with regard to how many children receive child support and what the financial situation of their custodial mothers and noncustodial fathers may be. Weitzman's (1985) study of the effects of no-fault divorce on women and children has probably provided the most visible data on this issue. She reported that 73% of custodial mothers experience a downward financial spiral after divorce while 43% of divorced fathers experience an improved financial situation. Recently, there have been questions regarding the accuracy of these findings. While the downward financial trend for women and slight increase in men's financial situation has been corroborated by other studies, the extent of their plunge and men's upward mobility postdivorce as reported by Weitzman has not been replicated and has been the subject of controversy (Faludi, 1991). Furthermore, it is important to keep in mind that findings regarding men's upward mobility after divorce are usually based on middle-class or upper middle-class samples. Men in lower SES brackets generally report economic distress postdivorce and difficulties in financially covering the most basic necessities. For example, a surprising number of the men in Haskins' (1988) study reported that they were unable to afford rent or mortgage payments and were forced to move in with family members in order to meet their financial obligations.

Several studies have explored the relationship between father-child contact and child support payment. Seltzer, Schaeffer, and Charng (1989) summarize three of the most common premises that have been utilized in examining the potential relationship between visiting and paying: (1) that visiting and paying are a result of the same demographic and family characteristics; (2) that visiting and paying support are determined by some unobserved social-psychological construct; and (3) that visits and payments are causally related to each other. The actual evidence is inconclusive regarding the relationship between visiting and paying. Certain studies have found a positive relationship between visiting and paying (Furstenburg, Pearson, Nord, & Zill, 1983; Seltzer, Schaeffer, & Charng, 1989; Teachman, 1991). Other studies, however, have either failed to substantiate a relationship between father-child contact and child support payment (Arditti, 1992a; Berkman, 1986; Pearson & Thoennes, 1988) or report a relationship in the opposite direction, i.e., frequent visitation was associated with lower child support amounts (Arditti & Keith, in press).

Hence, a rather pessimistic picture has emerged from the literature of devitalized father-child relations postdivorce (see for example Furstenburg & Cherlin's portrayal of "fading fathers," 1991). But what the literature fails to tell us is exactly what noncustodial parenting is all about. We do not get a real sense of the quality of relations between fathers and children. Five years ago Furstenburg, Morgan, and Allison (1987) pointed out that the quantity of paternal participation is only loosely indicative of the quality of relations between fathers and children and yet this is still the most commonly used indicator. One is left wondering, exactly what should these fathers be doing beyond visiting and paying? What kinds of qualitative changes occur in the father-child relationship as a result of moving to a separate residence?

Fathering Postdivorce and Coparental Relations

From a theoretical standpoint, the coparental relationship between husband and wife is an important influence on father's involvement postdivorce. Family systems theory suggests that ex-spouses continue to exert an influence on each other after divorce (Ahrons, 1981; Bowen, 1978; Kerr & Bowen, 1988). Based on this framework, the level of interparental conflict postdivorce is seen as having an important role in determining visitation patterns and fathers' feelings of warmth for their children (Koch & Lowery, 1984). Indeed, several studies have shown that hostile relations between ex-spouses and little discussion regarding child rearing are negatively associated with father involvement and contact with children (Ahrons, 1983; Hetherington et al., 1976; Lund, 1987).

From a legal standpoint, mothers' role is also significant in terms of whether she is supportive of fathers' visitation or opposed to his involvement. Novinson (1983) considers the legal implications of mothers' denying fathers' access to children. He argues that visitation is the essence of parental rights for noncustodial parents and that to deny visitation is the equivalent of terminating parental rights and is therefore unconstitutional. Fox (1985) and Fox and Blanton (this volume) also points out that visitation arrangements as specified by the court vary widely in terms of the amount of visitation awarded and in their degree of specificity. She notes that the literature fails to address the relationship between "de jure" (i.e., court ordered) and "de facto" (actually existing) visitation arrangements. Fox argues that because disagreements over visitation are only second to complaints over child support in bringing divorced parties into litigation, it is important to understand how parents actually negotiate and implement visitation arrangements (see Fox & Blanton in this volume). For example, it would be worthwhile to examine whether satisfactory arrangements postdivorce differ in terms of specificity and amount of access from visitation that was originally ordered by the courts at the time of divorce.

Thus from a theoretical as well as a legal standpoint, custodial mothers' role in determining the nature and extent of noncustodial fathers' visitation should not be ignored. Mothers' often act as the "gatekeeper" of fathers' involvement; that is, fathers generally must go through mothers to see their children. The younger the children, the more central mothers' role is in overseeing visitation. This is reflected not only by the fact that many fathers are awarded visitation rights that are only loosely stated (that is reasonable times at reasonable places given reasonable notice) and must go through the mother to determine what is indeed reasonable, but also by the fact that mothers' denial of visitation is only rarely admonished. Whether truth or fantasy, fathers seem to perceive mothers as having a tremendous amount of power in determining their relationships with children after divorce (Arditti & Allen, in press) and view this power differential as inequitable. Furthermore, mothers interference with visitation is seen as a problem by many noncustodial fathers (Dudley, 1991; Haskins, 1987; Arditti, 1992).

The Quality of Father-Child Relations

Qualitative aspects of the relationship between fathers and children postdivorce have not received a lot of attention in the literature. As mentioned previously, research looking at the role of noncustodial fathers has relied primarily on structural measures such as child support payment or visitation frequency, but some has looked at father/child relationships (Hanson, 1988). Another recent investigation by Munsch, Woodward, and

Darling (1992) is one of the few studies to examine the qualitative aspects of the relationship between children and nonresidential fathers by comparing the perceptions of two groups of adolescents (one which lives with their father, n = 218, and one which lives apart, n = 78) regarding the quality of their relationship with their fathers. This study is particularly interesting in that it specifically considers the functional roles filled by fathers and the adolescents' use of their father as a source of support in a time of stress. Residential status of the father affected only the likelihood that a father would be called upon to provide support in a time of stress, with co-residing fathers being more likely to be mobilized. However, co-residing fathers did not differ significantly from nonresidential fathers on measures of social support functions and general relationship qualities (i.e., helpfulness, advice, sharing of feelings, understanding, and acceptance). Most interesting was the finding that nonresidential fathers were perceived as providing a greater amount of emotional support than co-residing fathers. The authors conclude that custodial and noncustodial fathers are seen by their adolescent children as functioning in similar ways and as having qualitatively similar relationships.

Stereotypes of the "Disneyland Dad" portray noncustodial fathers as the fun parent. Discipline is lax or nonexistent and expectations for mature, age appropriate behavior are low (Furstenburg & Nord, 1985). Weekend visits have been described as opportunities to bestow presents on children and take them on special activities (Hetherington, Cox & Cox, 1976). Custodial mothers are left with the day to day work of parenting; e.g., discipline, homework, chores and keeping the children's ears clean. Furstenburg and Nord (1985) attempted to look at qualitative differences in parenting across family structures. As expected, they found that noncustodial fathers' contacts were more social and recreational in nature than either custodial fathers' or noncustodial mothers'. While this finding may represent an important superficial difference, we are still left to disentangle the implications of this finding for ourselves. To what extent are qualitative aspects of parenting due to gender and individual differences as well as social constructions of parental identity?

The "Disneyland Dad" should really come as no surprise–typical patterns of parenting in two parent families mimic the pattern Furstenburg and Nord (1985) uncovered. Furstenburg and Cherlin (1991) observe that child-care arrangements after marriage in terms of which parent has responsibility for basic caregiving generally resemble those before the marriage ended–i.e., women perform most of the child care responsibilities. Subsequently, it seems probable that fathers tend to be the fun parent regardless of family structure. Specifically, the majority of fathers are relegated to the role of "secondary caregiver" and as a result of this secondary caregiver role, fathers' style of interaction appears distinct from that of mothers'–especially in the area of play (Belsky, Lerner, & Spanier, 1984). In general, fathers engage in more novel, arousing play with their children than mothers and are less involved with the day to day responsibilities of caretaking (Belsky, Lerner, & Spanier, 1984; Hill, 1985).

It appears then that there probably are qualitative differences between fathers' and mothers' relationships with children given gender differentiated parenting styles; however, it is far less clear regarding the role of residential status on qualitative aspects of parenting. Currently, there is not enough available research to definitively state whether residential status in and of itself makes a difference–especially in terms of children's perceptions. While Furstenburg and Nord (1985) find modest differences between residential and nonresidential fathers, they find no such differences for mothers. Moreover, Munsch et al. (1992) find very few qualitative differences between custodial and noncustodial fathers, at least from their children's reports. Future research in this area needs to disentangle the effects of residence, and gender, on the quality of parent-child relationships.

Diversity for Fathers and Children

In spite of the fact that fathers' participation in childcare has increased only slightly (Pleck, 1985), changing societal attitudes promoting involved, responsible fathering have raised our expectations regarding what a noncustodial father should and shouldn't be. Society thinks he should be involved and he should visit. He should pay his child support in a timely manner and it should cover a reasonable proportion of his children's expenses. He should cooperate with his ex-wife. But what is virtually ignored is the diversity of circumstances noncustodial fathers find themselves in postdivorce and the influence of important social stratifiers such as race and socioeconomic status (SES) on the nature and extent of paternal participation.

Results are mixed regarding the role SES plays with respect to child support payment with some studies finding a positive association (Arditti, 1992; Arditti & Keith, in press) and others finding men's ability to pay has no bearing on mother's receipt of support (Weitzman, 1985). In one of the few studies that specifically studied low SES men, Haskins (1987) documented not only fathers' attempts to provide support despite their financial inadequacy, but also high levels of involvement between these men and their children. These findings dispute stereotypical portrayals of "deadbeat dads" who are financially better off postdivorce and relatively uninvolved. Moreover, the few studies that examined the effects of race on paternal involvement postdivorce turned up mixed results. While Seltzer (1991) found that black fathers were more likely to maintain ties to children than nonblacks postdivorce, Isaacs and Leon (1987) as well as Seltzer and Bianchi (1988) found no differences between blacks and whites in visiting patterns.

Also generally ignored in research on noncustodial fathers is the impact child characteristics and temperament may have on parenting. Different children elicit different responses from parents, different styles of parenting, and different levels of parental involvement (Belsky, Lerner, & Spanier, 1984). Little is known regarding how various child characteristics influence postdivorce outcomes like visitation. Dudley (1991) found that children's increasing age, and changing developmental needs, was negatively associated with father-child contact for some fathers. In these cases, fathers believed that their children preferred to be with their friends, or had jobs, and did not have as much time to spend with them as when they were younger. Other studies have examined whether the gender of the child influences visitation patterns. Results tend to be mixed, but when significant effects are found, noncustodial fathers tend to visit sons more than daughters (Hess & Camara, 1979; Hetherington, Cox, & Cox, 1982). But beyond considering superficial characteristics like the gender or age of the child, comprehensive assessments of how other factors, i.e., children's temperament, personality, or activity level, may influence father involvement postdivorce are scarce or nonexistent.

In summary, we must ask ourselves whether fading fatherhood and "deadbeat dadding" is simply a response to the dynamics of nonresidential parenting. Perhaps in the initial frenzy to study noncustodial fathers, researchers lost sight of what is truly realistic and necessary, and therefore overstated the importance of noncustodial fathers. Men were held against an ideal, which most of them failed to live up to; hence, the familiar story of the "deadbeat." Furstenburg and Cherlin (1991) are perhaps painfully realistic when they contend that noncustodial fathers may not be as influential to their children's development as previously believed.

NONCUSTODIAL MOTHERS

Although in recent years, mothers without custody have received some attention in the print media (see Herrerías, this volume), noncustodial mothers tend to be understudied in the social science literature for a variety of reasons. Some of these reasons include: difficulty in locating them, prevailing negative stereotypes, and the relatively small number of noncustodial mothers in the past (Fischer & Cardea, 1981). Understanding the experience of noncustodial mothers is important as this possibility is becoming more and more likely given trends in child custody placement (Smart, 1989), recent challenges to the "tender years doctrine" (Salt, 1985-86), and greater involvement on the part of fathers predivorce (Thompson, 1983).

Some experiences of noncustodial mothers are related to their noncustodial status, hence they are comparable to the experience of noncustodial fathers. For example, both mothers and fathers may experience guilt over not living with their children and feelings of helplessness regarding the process of assigning custody (Arditti & Allen, in press; Arditti & Madden-Derdich, in press; Wilbur & Wilbur, 1988). They also have to deal with the constraints not living with their children puts on their relationship with them (such as mourning the loss of the day to day activities of parenting, missing their children, etc.). Mothers reported a drop in involvement in their children's activities and a decline in closeness postdivorce (Arditti & Madden-Derdich, in press)–a well documented pattern for noncustodial fathers. Mothers also had similar complaints as fathers regarding visitation. Arditti and Madden-Derdich (in press) found that mothers' top three visitation complaints were: (1) not having enough money to do things with their children, (2) visits were too short and infrequent, and (3) other parent interfered with visits. The problems were the same ones reported by a larger sample of noncustodial fathers (Arditti, 1992). The following discussion will consider similarities and differences between noncustodial mothers and fathers, as well as exploring the implications women's financial vulnerability may have with respect to noncustodial parenting situations.

Comparability to Noncustodial Fathers

Despite the similarities, there are important differences in the experiences of noncustodial mothers and fathers. Social attitudes toward noncustodial mothers tend to be much more negative than attitudes toward noncustodial fathers putting these mothers at greater risk for social isolation and depression (Chesler, 1986; Fischer, 1983; Paskowicz, 1982). A central component of mothers' experience with noncustodial parenting appears to be a perceived lack of support for their decision to relinquish custody and intensive discomfort with their noncustodial status (Arditti & Madden-Derdich, in press). The nature of their discomfort is unique to their gender given the appearance or the belief on the part of others that they have rejected their parenting role.

Chesler (1986) has documented that noncustodial mothers express more guilt than noncustodial fathers. She explains that mothers' greater guilt is rooted in different conceptions of parental responsibility. Chesler suggests that fathers may have internalized a concept of fatherhood which has a limited responsibility while mothers internalized a concept of motherhood which has an unlimited responsibility. For mothers then, noncustodial parenting may be very incongruent with their internalizations of unlimited responsibility. In a similar argument, Greif (1987) states that mothers have historically been seen as the primary parent following divorce. Mothers without custody are seen as extraordinary and nonnormative. The findings revealed opinions that it is different for a mother to give up her primary role as caregiver to her children than for a father to give up the caregiver role, which may not have been his primary role (Greif, 1987).

In 1983, Furstenburg et al. noted some important differences between noncustodial mothers and fathers. First, their overall impression was that contact with children did not drop off as sharply over time for mothers as it did for fathers, although their sample of mothers was small (n = 28) compared to the number of noncustodial fathers in the study (n = 395). Specifically, noncustodial mothers were more likely to visit their children regularly, have overnight visits, and maintain indirect contact through phone calls and letters than noncustodial fathers. Children were more likely to report that they had places to store things at their mothers house and that it felt like home. In addition, a strong similarity existed in children's feelings about their mothers regardless of their residential situation whereas residential status appeared influential regarding children's feelings about their fathers. Children tended to express more discontent about their relationships with noncustodial fathers than residential fathers. Furstenburg et al. (1983) offer several explanations for these differences between nonresidential mothers and fathers speculating that they could be attributed to differences in levels of contact rather than gender. Children's higher assessment of their relationships with their mother could be due to higher levels of contact. However, it appeared that even when level of contact was taken into consideration, children still evaluated their relationships with noncustodial mothers more positively.

These differences between mothers and fathers are important for several reasons. First, they tell us something about what kinds of expectations are brought to parenting, regardless of residence. Apparently, children expect to be closer to their mothers and report this–mothers also expect to be primary to their children and appear to make efforts to do this, even when they are not living in the same household. Also, one can speculate that the predivorce nature of the parent-child relationship has implications for parenting postdivorce. If mothers typically are primary caregivers predivorce, it is logical that they would stay as involved as possible postdivorce. The transition from custodial and noncustodial parenting, although perhaps more difficult for mothers, may make less of a difference with regard to qualitative aspects of the relationship. It seems less likely that she will become a "Disneyland Mom" given typical parenting patterns predivorce. However, to date, there are no studies that examine in sufficient depth the nature and extent of mothers' parenting before they relinquish custody, and whether dominant parenting arrangements with the mother as the primary caregiver are typical.

Women and Financial Vulnerability

Without overstating the importance of gender given that certain aspects of noncustodial parenting do seem comparable, it is important not to overlook structural inequities between men and women in the macrosystem. Women in general are more vulnerable financially regardless of their custodial status. It is highly unlikely that noncustodial mothers would report tremendous financial gains postdivorce to the same extent that noncustodial fathers might. This is largely still speculation since researchers have been unable to study large enough samples of noncustodial mothers to adequately generalize and draw firm conclusions. Preliminary evidence does exist that noncustodial mothers, like their custodial sisters, are ill-prepared to adequately support themselves, or their children, postdivorce. In fact, mothers felt their lack of financial resources contributed to their decision to relinquish custody or their inability to fight for custody (Arditti & Madden-Derdich, in press; Herrerías, this volume).

A recent study by Christensen, Dahl, and Rettig (1990) which examined the differences in treatment of noncustodial mothers and noncustodial fathers by the courts also turned up some interesting findings with respect to women's financial vulnerability and custody status. Although they found that noncustodial mothers pay proportionately less child support than noncustodial fathers (20% of their net income compared to 25% for men), a closer inspection of mothers' financial situations revealed why this apparent inequity in treatment may have been warranted. Not surprisingly, noncustodial mothers had a net median yearly income of only 62.8% of that of noncustodial fathers. Furthermore, the noncustodial mothers in their sample had a dramatically lower net median income when compared with custodial fathers than did noncustodial fathers when compared with mothers. Noncustodial mothers were likely to be employed in jobs with few fringe benefits and were also less likely to have rights to a pension than noncustodial fathers. The authors concluded that noncustodial mothers experienced incomes closer to the poverty level than custodial father families, even before the transfer of child support.

It appears then, that gender is an important stratifier, like race and class, which has bearing on the construction and meaning of parenting arrangements. Stratification systems serve as lens through which people are "viewed and arranged" (Glenn, 1987, p. 245) and reflect differences in privilege and power. Central to gender stratification systems and most relevant to examining beliefs about parenting, is the social mythology surrounding women's work and the natural superiority of women to nurture and care for children. Alternative caregiving arrangements which place mothers outside of their children's primary residence subsequently are seen as "unnatural" and deficient, thus making the transition to noncustodial parent one of the most difficult and painful experiences a woman could undergo (Edwards, 1989).

DIVERSITY AND PROCESS: AN INTEGRATIVE FRAMEWORK FOR RESEARCH

Two themes emerged from this review that hold promise in terms of integrating existing research and providing researchers with new directions. First and foremost is the issue of diversity. Clearly, there are wide variations in the nature and extent of noncustodial parents' involvement with their children. What little research we have available to us that even addresses the issue of diversity indicates there may be differences between noncustodial fathers and mothers (Furstenburg et al., 1985), as well as differences within groups. What remains to be fully explored however, is considering how racial, ethnic, and economic diversity may influence noncustodial parenting postdivorce. For example, SES is almost always included in analyses of parent-child relationships postdivorce, however, we really do not get a good sense of why SES may be important and how SES may impact noncustodial parenting arrangements.

Race and ethnicity have been all but ignored in the literature and must be included in research on parenting postdivorce. Given what we know about diversity in racial and cultural attitudes about parenting, children, and close relationships (see Billingsley, 1968; Burton, 1990; Peters & McAdoo, 1983; and Stack, 1974), such an omission probably means that existing research obscures or misrepresents the experiences of minorities. Harsh economic realties that typify a large proportion of minority families as well as cultural prescriptions defining acceptable parental behavior have important implications for parenting postdivorce. A challenge for future researchers would involve greater attention and more rigorous investigation of the effects of race and ethnicity on noncustodial parenting. Furthermore, research that is sensitive to diversity also encompasses not only race, ethnic background, and SES, but also acknowledges the implications of parents' gender. The issue of gender has been discussed elsewhere in this article; however, a reiteration of its importance in understanding the experience of noncustodial mothers is useful. Noncustodial mothers represent a growing minority of parents with unique difficulties as well as strengths.

A second theme which holds promise in terms of integrating existing research and providing a progressive research direction is that of process. Central to process theory is the phenomena of interdependence, i.e., two or more persons mutually influencing each other. Scanzoni, Teachman, Polonko, and Thompson (1989) discuss how the notion of shared interdependence cuts across all varieties of living arrangements, household patterns, and legal/residential structures as well as emphasizing the ongoing decision-making processes that occur within these arrangements. Thus a process approach focuses attention on *how* the transition to noncustodial parenting is negotiated as well as the way in which parents implement parenting relationships postdivorce. Primary to this approach is a focus on shared interdependencies between former spouses and between parents and children pre- and postdivorce. As already discussed, existing research has indicated that coparental relations have an important influence on noncustodial parents postdivorce in terms of the nature and extent of their involvement with children. We know much less about the role children may play in eliciting involvement from noncustodial parents. Such information is essential in understanding the dynamics of parent-child relationships postdivorce.

A focus on process deemphasizes structural aspects of parenting and emphasizes the quality of relationships. An emphasis on structure typically idealizes residential, biological parenting, and obscures the wide variations in the quality of parent-child relationships that exist irrespective of domicile. A structural approach also treats parenthood as a *status*, which by definition, precludes a variety of parenting arrangements, for statuses are immovable and unyielding to circumstance and individual preference (Rothman, 1989). A process approach acknowledges the complexity of family arrangements: parents often have multiple statuses, i.e., noncustodial father, stepfather, and father, which may translate into different parenting styles, responsibilities, and levels of involvement. Scanzoni et al. (1989) point out that with respect to close relationships between adults and adults and children, it is widely presumed that love and caring is connected with coresidence. They suggest instead of using residence to define relationships, a continuum of physical togetherness, irrespective of residence or legal status (i.e., custody status), more adequately describes the character of relationships (pp. 86-87).

Along with the issue of residence vs. physical togetherness having implications for noncustodial parent-child relationships is the issue of quality vs. quantity of contact. Most studies fail to consider the quality of visitation focusing instead on measures of frequency or duration of contact as indicators of involvement. For example, while Seltzer et al. (1989) acknowledge that visiting is a multidimensional phenomena and can be measured by the frequency of visits, the total time that noncustodial parents and children spend together, and the types of activities that parents and children pursue during visits, they assume that these components are *probably* highly correlated and choose only to consider visitation frequency in their analysis.

It is important to recognize that frequent or regular visitation may or may not reflect quality and a loving or concerned parent. In their study of noncustodial fathers, Furstenburg et al. (1987) speculate that the quantity of paternal participation is only loosely indicative of the quality of relations between fathers and children. They explain: "Children may closely identify with their fathers even though they see them infrequently or, . . . those who have frequent contact may experience greater conflict with their father . . ." (p. 698). Arditti and Keith (in press) also discuss the importance of conceptually distinguishing between visitation frequency and visitation quality; especially with respect to the relationship between visiting and paying. They found that while visitation frequency was related to both quality and child support, visitation quality and support appeared unrelated. And even if quality and frequency are highly related, they apparently are tapping into two very separate domains given their differential association with child support payment.

Theorizing about the meaning of time holds promise in terms of discerning the difference between quality and quantity. Daly (1992) discusses the emergence of a quantity/quality distinction as a way of understanding and justifying competing expectations in parents' lives, for example: work and family demands. In his study of how residential fathers make and use time, Daly found that *how* men create social constructions of time played a powerful role in the way that men perceived their family lives. Men's discourse about what it meant to be a father suggested that time was a highly valued commodity. Fathers struggled to "spend time, make time, give time and put in time with their children" (p. 4). Daly concluded that work structures dominated the way men organize their lives in terms of taking the biggest bite out of men's life and was the primary constraint in terms of their experience as fathers. As a result of this time scarcity, spending time with children became the primary goal, often with scant attentiveness given to how the time will actually be spent. Daly states: "the production of time for children becomes the obsessive focus that supersedes the construction of the experience with children" (p. 4).

Daly's findings are directly relevant to research on noncustodial parents. Researchers are far more focused on the frequency of contact than how the time is spent and what the time spent together means to parents and children. Clearly, nonresidence is an important constraint on parents' available time with children. Exploration of noncustodial parents' construction of the meaning of time would provide important insights in terms of how they see themselves as parents and probably shapes to a certain extent their experience with their children.

Methodological Considerations

An emphasis on diversity and process pose certain methodological challenges for researchers. Sampling has generally been problematic in studies of noncustodial parents–the most notable difficulty being self-selection and the subsequent possibility of bias. Gathering data on noncustodial mothers is even more difficult than sampling fathers given their lesser numbers and greater invisibility. While it is impossible to completely overcome the problem of self-selection, greater utilization of national data sets that include minorities and are also geographically diverse provide one avenue to address the problem of bias. Greater efforts on the part of researchers to include racial, SES, and ethnic diversity should be made whenever funding and geographic location permits.

Another source of data that may be underused is public civil court records. Court records generally document the divorce proceedings and various postdivorce outcomes such as custody, visitation, property settlement and child support. In examining how parents negotiate and implement visitation, court records are an important starting point of that process. Many families develop "informal" arrangements that can differ considerably from those that are formally ordered in the divorce settlement. The extent to which parents negotiate and maintain informal arrangements, or adhere to formal prescriptions is of interest in terms of understanding family process postdivorce and how individuals weather the transition from residential to nonresidential parent.

Methodologies which deal with time and change over time are also necessary to adequately address the notion of process. Time-series, and multiple time-series or panel data are two potential plans for obtaining data that allows one to look at change over time. While these data plans are not without technical problems (such as sample attrition, testing and selection bias) they are advantageous in allowing researchers to answer questions about process and continuous outcomes. Since cost is typically a problem associated with panel designs, alternative procedures may be incorporated to collect the required data. For example, court records could be used as information for the "first wave" of a study or respondents could be interviewed for one wave of a study and then one could access their matched court records to represent an earlier wave. Cross-sectional data could be used to locate respondents for follow-up as well. Finally, various statistical techniques have emerged over the past decade which allow researchers to test-time lagged designs. LISREL (Joreskog, K.G., & Sorbom, D., 1989) is one of the better known statistical packages available which utilizes latent variable structural equations analysis. Whether structural equations modeling can be used to test models based on cross-sectional data is generally a source of controversy (Biddle & Marlin, 1987). Some methodologists believe these techniques are acceptable if conservatively applied and if the model tested is logically and theoretically grounded.

Qualitative methodologies are also useful in providing researchers with the necessary tools to fully consider issues pertaining to diversity and process. Qualitative methods have the advantage of enabling researchers to obtain information right from the source and allow people to speak in their own voices (Gilgun, Daly, & Handel, 1992). Qualitative data provide in-depth analyses of people's experience and lives that are essential if we are to truly understand the point of view and experience of noncustodial parents. Related to qualitative methodologies are feminist methodologies which although largely used to document the experience of women, have relevance for all marginalized groups (Allen & Baber, 1992; Collins, 1990). One could argue that noncustodial parents, given their role ambiguity and "outsider" status, are in essence marginalized. A feminist framework is particularly useful in guiding research on noncustodial parents which includes minorities and/or women (i.e., hard to obtain "random" sample). Small sample size is not necessarily a limitation from a feminist perspective vs. a mainstream approach. Rather, this approach values people's experience as a valid source of knowledge and considers the individual(s) studied as authorities on their own lives (Thompson, 1992). Hence, the concern is not necessarily generalizing findings but rather understanding how people construct meaning given a certain set of constraints and/or inequities.

CONCLUSIONS

Families where parents do not live together encompass a wide range of situations with a variety of socio-emotional, developmental, and financial needs. Furthermore, each family member's needs may or may not be in the best interests of other family members. For example, it is plausible that certain strategies (such as mediation) and outcomes (joint custody) may be beneficial for noncustodial parents, but not in the best interests of custodial parents and/or children. In the case of competing interests, which is commonly problematic in divorce, a prioritization of needs is essential. Children's needs typically have been seen as paramount. Furstenburg and Cherlin (1991) suggest that policies which support mothers' parenting, since they are typically the primary caregivers of children pre- and postdivorce, should be paramount as well. They support a new "primary-caregiver standard" to replace the "best interest standard" which they believe is vague and currently gives judges too much discretion potentially increasing the possibility of conflict for those couples who cannot agree on custody. Such legislation would instruct judges to award custody of children to the parent "who has performed a substantial majority of the caregiving tasks for the child . . ." (Furstenburg & Cherlin, 1991, p. 115).

Policies which promote noncustodial parents involvement must be carefully considered on a case to case basis prior to implementation. In general, it is recommended that nonresidential parents should be allowed shared legal responsibility and frequent visitation unless there are compelling contraindications (Furstenburg & Cherlin, 1991). Until the family reorganization that Fox and Blanton (see this volume) envision becomes a reality whereby parents are equally involved in the caregiving of their children, it is important to consider the context of parenting patterns prior to separation in negotiating postdivorce parenting arrangements. Such arrangements may evolve as parents decisions about the extent of their own involvement changes and children's developmental needs change. For example, it is possible that a father, who may not have been particularly active with his children while married, desires greater involvement with his children postdivorce.

Finally, it is vital that the interdependence between divorce related outcomes be acknowledged. While implementing one strategy may potentially benefit one set of outcomes, unanticipated outcomes may crop up somewhere else. A recent study by Arditti and Keith (in press) highlights the potential for complications on the policy front quite well. They found that while frequent visitation was associated with better quality visits between fathers and children (hence the clear policy initiative to support frequent visits), frequent visitation was associated with *lower* child support payments!

In conclusion, new directions theoretically as well as methodologically for research on noncustodial parents is important in order to fully understand the experience of families where parents divorce and move us beyond stereotypes of "the deadbeat." Such research is essential in order to develop effective mental health interventions, educational programs, and public policy initiatives and to demonstrate the changing definitions and views. More progressive conceptualizations of parenthood that acknowledge the diversity and tenacity of parenting arrangements are essential in guiding research in this area.

REFERENCES

Ahrons, C. (1981). The continuing coparental relationship between divorced spouses. *American Journal of Orthopsychiatry, 51*, 415-428.

Ahrons, C. (1983). Predictors of paternal involvement postdivorce: Mothers' and fathers' perceptions. *Journal of Divorce, 6*, 55-69.

Allen, K. R., & Baber, K. N. (1992). Ethical and epistimological tensions in applying a postmodern perspective to feminist research. *Psychology of Women Quarterly, 16*, 1-15.

Arditti, J. A. (1992). Factors related to custody, visitation, and child support for divorced fathers: An exploratory analysis. *Journal of Divorce & Remarriage, 17*, 23-41.

Arditti, J. A., & Allen, K. R. (in press). Distressed fathers perceptions of legal and relational inequities. *Family & Conciliation Courts Review.*

Arditti, J. A., & Keith, T. Z. (in press). Visiting, paying, and the father-child relationship postdivorce. *Journal of Marriage and the Family.*

Arditti, J. A., & Madden-Derdich, D. (in press). Noncustodial mothers: Developing strategies of support. *Family Relations.*

Belsky, J., Lerner, R., & Spanier, G. (1984). *The child in the family.* Reading, MA: Addison-Wesley.

Berkman, B. G. (1986). Father involvement and regularity of child support in post-divorce families. *Journal of Divorce, 9*, 67-74.

Biddle, B. J., & Marlin, M. M. (1987). Causality, confirmation, and structural equation modeling. *Child Development, 58*, 4-17.

Billingsley, A. (1968). *Black families in white America.* Englewood Cliffs, NJ: Prentice-Hall.

Bowen, M. (1978). *Family therapy in clinical practice.* N.Y.: Jason Aronson.

Burton, L. M. (1990). Teenage childbearing as an alternative life-course strategy in multigeneration black families. *Human Nature, 1*, 123-143.

Cherlin, A. (1978). Remarriage as an incomplete institution. *American Journal of Sociology, 84*, 634-650.

Cherlin, A., Griffith, J., and McCarthy, J. (1983). A note on maritally disrupted men's reports of child support in the June 1980 current population survey. *Demography, 20*, 385-390.

Chesler, P. (1986). *Mothers on trial.* Seattle: The Seal Press.

Christensen, D. H., Dahl, C. M., & Rettig, K. D. (1990). Noncustodial mothers and child support: Examining the larger context. *Family Relations, 39*, 388-394.

Collins, P. H. (1990). *Black feminist thought.* Boston: Unwin Hyman.

Daly, K. J. (1992). Family time as a commodity: How fathers make, give, and spend time. Summary report to accompany a poster session presented at the National Council on Family Relations, Orlando, Florida, Nov., 1992.

Dudley, J. (1991). Increasing our understanding of divorced fathers with infrequent contact with their children. *Family Relations, 40*, 279-285.

Edwards, H. (1989). *How could you: Mothers without custody of their children.* Freedom, CA: The Crossing Press.

Faludi, S. (1991). *Backlash: The undeclared war against American women.* New York: Crown.

Fischer, J. (1983). Mothers living apart from their children. *Family Relations, 32*, 351-357.

Fischer, J., & Cardea, J. M. (1981). Mothers living apart from their children: A study in stress and coping. *Alternative Lifestyles, 4*, 218-227.

Fox, G. L. (1985). Noncustodial fathers. From S. Hanson & F. Bozett (Eds.), *Dimensions of Fatherhood* (pp. 393-415). Beverly Hills: Sage.

Furstenburg, F. (1988). Marital disruptions, child custody, and visitation. In S. Kamerman & A. Kahn (Eds.), *Child support: From debt collection to social policy* (pp. 277-305). Beverly Hills: Sage.

Furstenburg, F., & Cherlin, A. (1991). *Divided families: What happens to children when parents part.* Cambridge, MA: Harvard University Press.

Furstenburg, F., Morgan, P., & Allison, P. (1987). Paternal participation and children's well-being after marital dissolution. *American Sociological Review, 52*, 695-701.

Furstenburg, F., & Nord, C. W. (1985). Parenting Apart: Patterns of childrearing after marital disruption. *Journal of Marriage and the Family, 47*, 893-904.

Furstenburg, F., Peterson, J. L., Nord, C. W., & Zill, N. (1983). The life course of children of divorce: Marital disruption and parental contact. *American Sociological Review, 48*, 656-678.

Gilgun, J. F., Daly, K., & Handel, G. (1992). *Qualitative methods in family research.* Newbury Park: Sage.

Glenn, E. N. (1987). Gender and the family. In B. Hess and M. Ferree (Eds.), *Analyzing gender: A Handbook of social science research.* Newbury Park: Sage.

Goldsmith, J. (1981). Relationships between former spouses: Descriptive findings. *Journal of Divorce, 4*, 1-20.

Greif, G. (1987). Mothers without custody. *Social Work, 32*, 11-16.

Hanson, S. M. H. (1988). Divorced fathers with custody. In P. Bronstein & C. P. Cowan

(Eds.), *Fatherhood today: Mens changing role in the family* (pp. 166-194). New York: John Wiley.

Haskins, R. (1988). Child support: A father's view. In S. Kamerman & A. Kahn (Eds.), *Child support: From debt collection to social policy* (pp. 306-327).

Haskins, R., Richey, T., & Wicker, F. (1987). Paying and visiting: Child support enforcement and fathering from afar. Unpublished manuscript.

Herrerías, C. (1995). Noncustodial mothers following divorce. *Marriage & Family Review, 20*, 233-255.

Hess, R. D., & Camara, K. A. (1979). Postdivorce family relationships as mediating factors in the consequences of divorce for children. *Journal of Social Issues, 35*, 79-96.

Hetherington, E. M., Cox, M., & Cox, R. (1982). Effects of divorce on parents and children. In M. Lamb (Ed.), *Nontraditional families: Parenting and child development* (pp. 233-288). Hillsdale, NJ: Erlbaum.

Hetherington, E. M., Cox, M., & Cox, R. (1976). Divorced fathers. *The Family Coordinator, 25*, 417-428.

Hill, M. S. (1985). Patterns of time use: In F. Justen & F. Stafford (Eds.), *Time, goods, & well being*. Ann Arbor, MI: University of Michigan.

Isaacs, M. B., & Leon, G. H. (1987). Race, marital dissolution, and visitation: An examination of adaptive family strategies. *Journal of Divorce, 11*, 17-31.

Joreskog, K. G., & Sorbom, D. (1989). *LISREL 7: A guide to the program and applications*. Chicago: SPSS Inc.

Kerr, M., & Bowen, M. (1988). *Family Evaluation*. N.Y.: W. W. Norton.

Koch, M. A., & Lowery, C. (1984). Visitation and the noncustodial father. *Journal of Divorce, 8*, 47-65.

Lund, M. E. (1987). The noncustodial father: Common challenges in parenting after divorce. In C. Lewis & M. O'Brian (Eds.), *Reassessing fatherhood* (pp. 212-224). Beverly Hills: Sage.

Munsch, J., Woodward, J., & Darling, N. (1992). Fathers as providers of support: A comparison of custodial and non-custodial fathers. Poster presented at the annual meeting of the National Council on Family Relations, Orlando, FL, Nov. 1992.

Novinson, S. L. (1983). Post-divorce visitation: Untying the triangular knot. *University of Illinois Law Review, 1*, 119-200.

Pasowicz, P. (1982). *Absentee mothers*. New York: Universe.

Pearson, J., & Thoennes, N. (1988). Supporting children after divorce: The influence of custody on child support levels and payments. *Family Law Quarterly, 22*, 319-339.

Peters, M. F., and McAdoo, H. P. (1983). The present and future of alternative lifestyles in ethnic American cultures. In E. D. Macklin and R. H. Rubin (Eds.), *Contemporary families and alternative life-styles* (pp. 288-307). Beverly Hills, CA: Sage.

Pleck, J. (1985). *Working wives/working husbands*. Beverly Hills: Sage.

Rothman, B. K. (1989). *Recreating motherhood: Ideology and technology in a patriarchal society*. New York: W. W. Norton & Co.

Salt, R. (1985-1986). The legal rights of fathers in the U.S. *Marriage and Family Review, 9*, 101-115.

Scanzoni, J., Polonko, K., Teachman, J., & Thompson, L. (1989). *The sexual bond: Rethinking families and close relationships*. Beverly Hills: Sage.

Seltzer, J. (1991). Relationships between fathers and children who live apart: The father's role after separation. *Journal of Marriage and the Family, 53*, 79-101.

Seltzer, J., & Bianchi, S. (1988). Children's contact with absent parents. *Journal of Marriage and the Family, 50*, 663-677.

Seltzer, J., Schaeffer, N., & Charng, H. (1989). Family ties after divorce: The relationship between visiting and paying child support. *Journal of Marriage and the Family, 51*, 1013-1032.

Smart, C. (1989). Power and the politics of child custody. In C. Smart & S. Selma Sevenhuijsen (Eds.), *Child custody and the politics of gender.* New York: Routledge.

Stack, C. (1974). *All our kin: Strategies for survival in a black community.* New York: Harper & Row.

Teachman, J. (1991). Who Pays? Receipt of child support in the U.S. *Journal of Marriage and the Family, 53*, 759-772.

Thompson, L. (1992). Feminist methodology for family studies. *Journal of Marriage and the Family, 54*, 3-18.

Thompson, R. A. (1983). The father's case in child custody disputes: The contributions of psychological research. In M. Lamb & A. Sagi (Eds.), *Fatherhood and family policy* (pp. 53-1000). Hillsdale, New Jersey: Lawrence Erlbaum Assoc.

Wallerstein, J., & Kelly, J. (1980). *Surviving the breakup: How children and parents cope with divorce.* New York: Basic Books.

Weitzman, L. (1985). *The divorce revolution: The unexpected social and economic consequences for women and children in America.* New York: The Free Press.

Wilbur, J., & Wilbur, M. (1988). The noncustodial parent: Dilemmas and interventions. *Journal of Counseling and Development, 66*, 434-437.

Wright, D., & Price, S. (1986). Court-ordered child support payment: The effect of the former spouse relationship on compliance. *Journal of Marriage and the Family, 48*, 869-874.

Chapter 14

Never Married/Biological Teen Mother Headed Household

Loretta Pinkard Prater

SUMMARY. This chapter is a review and analysis of literature examining the dynamics of never married female parents who are teenage heads of households. In reporting the findings, three theoretical models are utilized: deficit, decision-making, and subjective utilities models. The synthesis of the research includes intra- and interrelationships among the models, demographic patterns, and public policy and research implications.

The transition from being childless to becoming a mother is a challenge for females of any age. However, the reality of parenthood, with its many responsibilities, can be a culturally shocking experience for a teenager. Adolescence is a period when many changes are occurring. When these two are coupled, adolescence and parenthood, a very demanding situation is created. When adding a third and fourth variable, that of becoming a household manager and remaining unmarried, a life long struggle for survival may become reality.

Extended family, service providers and policymakers must help these young women reach self-sufficiency. This can only be realized through strategies resulting in long term benefits for single adolescent mothers and their children. Failure to do so will likely perpetuate a continuous intergenerational cycle of poverty. These techniques must be proactive, innovative, and strategically focused.

Loretta Pinkard Prater is affiliated with the Department of Human Ecology, University of Tennessee at Chattanooga, Chattanooga, TN 37403.

[Haworth co-indexing entry note]: "Never Married/Biological Teen Mother Headed Household." Prater, Loretta Pinkard. Co-published simultaneously in *Marriage & Family Review* (The Haworth Press, Inc.) Vol. 20, No. 3/4, 1995, pp. 305-324; and: *Single Parent Families: Diversity, Myths and Realities* (ed: Shirley M. H. Hanson et al.) The Haworth Press, Inc., 1995, pp. 305-324. Multiple copies of this article/chapter may be purchased from The Haworth Document Delivery Center [1-800-3-HAWORTH; 9:00 a.m. - 5:00 p.m. (EST)].

KEYWORDS. Adolescent mothers, Adolescent parents, Teenage mothers, Teenage parents, School-age parents

INTRODUCTION

Adolescence is a dynamic period in the life cycle. During the years between childhood and adulthood, major transitions occur. It is significant to consider that the period of adolescence has been, at best, described as potentially stressful (McCubbin & Patterson, 1986). Because of the complexity of changes, family scientists may not always agree about the time span for the beginning and ending of adolescence. For the purpose of this discussion, adolescence will be used synonymously with teenager, representing ages 13 through 19.

Adolescents pass through various developmental stages which may precipitate confusion. The teenager is in an ambiguous state. This brings about the commonly used phrase "identity crisis." They are beginning to establish an identity separate from the family of origin (Erickson, 1963). Also, the concept of "Push versus Pull" is initiated, when the family is pushing the adolescent at the same time that the peer group is pulling (Smith, 1976). This period is especially ambiguous for adolescent parents. More than marriage, parenthood signifies adulthood–the final irreversible end of youthful roles (Strong & Devault, 1992). However, when parenthood occurs chronologically with childhood, various immediate accommodations are necessary. This is an abrupt transition for which the teenager is ill prepared.

Heads of household assume many responsibilities. Generally, household heads are expected to be in charge of the physical needs of family members, that of providing food, clothing, shelter, and health care. Attending to social and psychological needs are also added to the list of responsibilities, including providing an acceptable socialization process for children. Additionally, money management and interacting with the community are part of what seems to be an endless list of things to do. This role as head of household is overwhelming for many adults. Traditionally, married men assumed this responsibility as head of household, which was primarily that of wage earner. Wives took on a more subservient role, that of remaining at home to care for the family's daily physical needs and childrearing (Mintz & Kellogg, 1988). The emphasis on childrearing and housework as the proper duties for women continued unchallenged until the 1940s. After World War II, the traditional role of women began to change (Lasswell & Lasswell, 1991).

The almost exclusive scenario of father headed households has changed today, as an increasing number of single mothers head households. In fact, single parent families are the fastest growing family form in the United States. In 1950, there were 1,531,000 one parent families (U.S. Bureau of the Census, 1955). However, in 1990, there were 7,383,000 families identified as one parent (U.S. Bureau of the Census, 1993). These single parent families tend to be created by marital separation, divorce, or births to unmarried women, rather than by widowhood. An exceptionally large number of these new single parents are teenagers. For example, Hayes (1987) reported that of 261,000 teenagers who gave birth without marriage, 249,000 became single parents. Moreover, adolescent pregnancy and childbearing account for a significant proportion of the growth of female headed households over the past two decades (Franklin, 1988). Also see Bianchi, (1995) this volume, for recent statistics.

An unmarried adolescent female taking on the dual roles as head of household and parent is thrust into a potentially stressful situation. However, heading a household is not the responsibility of all teenage parents. For instance, in one study of 87 parenting teenage mothers, it was determined that 75% continued to live in their parents' homes and were primarily dependent on them (Unger & Wandersman, 1988). The fact that the majority of adolescent parents may remain at home doesn't lessen the burden for those who leave their parents to establish separate households. According to Taeuber (1991), approximately 128,000 fifteen to 17 year olds and 190,000 eighteen to 19 year olds reportedly function as teenage female heads of household.

If the traditional two-parent model of family structure were followed, hypothetically, there would be no single parents fitting the description of adolescent female head of household. Adolescents are theoretically expected to move through a traditional developmental period where the biggest decisions are what to wear or what events to attend. After reaching adulthood, marriage and childbearing would follow. Many young women prematurely have obligations traditionally reserved for adults, partly resulting from a trend for males and females to participate in sexual activity before marriage (Fox, 1986).

For approximately 400,000 adolescents yearly, the responsibilities of parenthood are added to the dynamics of adolescence (Turner, Grindstaff, & Phillips, 1990). Half of these teen mothers are less than 18 years of age (Cooley & Unger, 1991). This is a big concern in society, considering that these young women are still developing and considered to be children themselves (Wallis, 1985). Actually, many may not choose parenthood, but become parents by neglecting to use measures to prevent pregnancy (Prater, 1990). One speculation for this occurrence may be rooted within immature cognitive functioning (Piaget, 1952). For instance, junior high school students are deficient in their ability to make valid generalizations, use symbols, process information with objectivity and engage in formal reasoning (Hamburg, 1986; Peterson & Crockett, 1986). Therefore, they may not internalize and synthesize information regarding pregnancy prevention.

The United States has the highest rates of pregnancy and childbearing in the industrialized world. Within the United States, the highest rates are found among low-income black adolescents (Franklin, 1988a). Black teenagers are at greater risk of nonmarital pregnancy than whites because, proportionately, more black adolescents are sexually active and fewer are married (Hayes, 1987). Also, unmarried white females are more likely to get an abortion than blacks (Trussell, 1988). Therefore, unmarried black females are more likely to carry the baby to term.

Parenthood is a challenge in any female's life, regardless of age, race, or marital status. However, for an unmarried adolescent, the situation is greatly intensified. It adds another level of complexity to an already complex period of physical and emotional change (Atkins, Protinsky, & Sporakowski, 1982; Turner, Grindstaff, & Phillips, 1990). According to Porter (1990), teen mothers are at risk for childrearing failure, considering the enormous responsibility involved in satisfying the needs of children. Of further significance is the fact that many of these young mothers have more than one child. In fact, there is a 26% likelihood that unmarried women who first gave birth at ages 16 or younger will bear a second child within the next two years (Mott, 1986).

The purpose of this discussion is to alert the public (e.g., family members, service providers, and policymakers) of the potentially negative consequences for these mothers and their children in current U.S. society. Effective intervention may cushion some of the negative impact of early single parenting. The goal of the author is to produce a practical, applied document to stimulate activity in the development and implementation of support services available to these young families.

CONCEPTUAL FRAMEWORK

In reviewing teenage pregnancy literature, it is apparent that a system of interrelated factors are involved in one becoming an adolescent female head of household. Through Bronfenbrenner's ecosystem (1977), it is acknowledged that such entities as the home, school, work, community, government and societal traditions/attitudes form an interactional environment. Therefore, no element in the system acts independently. Within this dynamic framework, any change in one element causes a change in other components of the total environment. For the purpose of this discussion, the basic element within the system is the unmarried adolescent mother who is head of household.

There are numerous articles which report research on adolescent pregnancy and parenting. As anticipated, most investigate isolated factors rather than all of the variables within the system. For instance, some studies report on contraceptive behavior, others investigate relationships with other people, and numerous others report various disadvantages of early parenting. After reviewing the literature, this author identified common themes of research topics which tended to be clustered within the frameworks of decision-making, deficit, and subjective utilities models. These models are quite applicable in reporting the dynamics present after pregnancy and delivery. First, the decision-making model examines the process through which people choose among alternatives to reach a certain decision. Second, the deficit model proposes that specific circumstances were detrimental to the well-being of persons involved. In other words, the assumption is that unmarried teenage pregnancy presents "problems." Third, the subjective utilities model proposes that significant individuals and relationships within the individual's environment directly influence behavior and well-being.

Decision-Making Model

This model examines the process of selecting a course of action from among alternatives. For example, for a young woman to be head of a household, as an unmarried teenage mother, a series of decisions were made. There was a decision to engage in unprotected premarital sexual relations, carry the baby to term, keep the baby, and remain unmarried. Of the teenagers who carry their babies to term, many will decide to keep the babies (Hayes, 1987). More precisely, nine out of ten black children and four out of ten white children born to unmarried mothers are kept by the mother (Spanier, 1989). Unmarried adolescent mothers choosing to place their children for adoption were more likely to be of higher socioeconomic status, have higher educational aspirations, and reside in suburban communities (Resnick, Blum, Bose, Smith, & Toogood, 1990). This fact suggests that those less able to economically support a child are more likely to select single parenting from among other perceived alternatives.

Decision to remain single. Marriages of adolescents to legitimize births has declined dramatically in the United States in recent years (Farber, 1990; Gispert, Brinich, Wheeler, & Krieger, 1984). Reasons for this decision include social acceptability of unwed status, the boyfriend's unwillingness to marry, the girl's own beliefs, and her family's belief that she was too young for marriage (Prater, 1990). Although this may not necessarily influence most adolescents, Farber (1990) explained that increased employment opportunities for American women may contribute to the rising rates of single-mother families. Increasingly women do not look to men and marriage to support them and their children. The absence of this expectation is reinforced by the fact that many teens are involved with young men who are unable to support them. Also, even if they had decided to marry, they probably would become single parents by divorce. Statistics indicate a low probability of marital success for these couples (Norton & Moorman, 1987).

Decision to head household. Most unmarried teenage parents do not consciously plan to become head of household. Young mothers have ideal visions that are congruent with traditional values about family formation. They probably had planned to live with their family of origin until adulthood. Ideally, they thought they would marry before having children (Farber, 1990). In more recent years, there seems to be more of a thrust to accept differences and alternative lifestyles. Therefore, there is less pressure to conform to the ideal family than in previous years.

The decision to set up a household, independent of parents, may represent a lack of alternatives rather than an actual choice. Because of familial conflicts, some young women are asked to move out, whereas, others leave voluntarily. Those wanting to maintain their own households seek to establish their identity as an adult and parent (Prater, 1990). Their youth and inexperience serve as a barrier to their ability to envision the ripple effect of such a decision. As cited earlier, in the United States there are approximately 128,000 fifteen to 17 year olds and 190,000 eighteen to 19 year olds who are classified as female, single-parent heads of household (Taeuber, 1991).

Deficit Model

The deficit model proposes that teenage pregnancy presents problems for the mothers and their children, as well as concerns in communities, social agencies, and various levels of government. Much of the community's concern is stimulated by the numbers of youth involved in early parenting. There are approximately 1,000,000 teenagers who become pregnant yearly (vonWindeguth & Urbano, 1989). Although 40% of these pregnancies are terminated voluntarily and 100,000 end in miscarriage, the remainder are carried to term (Hayes, 1987). Those who terminate pregnancies are more likely to come from intact families, have fewer siblings, have a higher socioeconomic status, and more education than term clients (Olson, 1980). Those who carry their babies to term are faced with consequences identified by society as adverse, both for teenage mothers and for their children (Furstenberg, 1987; Turner, Grindstaff, & Phillips, 1990). Areas of concern which have long term effects include poverty, education, health, and parenting skills.

Poverty. Having inadequate financial resources to manage a household is a deficit. Young unmarried mothers and their offspring are at high risk of experiencing long-term poverty and associated disadvantages (Cooley & Unger, 1991; Farber, 1990; Furstenberg, Brooks-Gunn & Morgan, 1987). A job is the socially acceptable method of earning a living to support a family. Teenage parents have little success in locating jobs which provide an adequate and secure income. Therefore, they have diminished employment success, both in salary and job satisfaction, which can lead to poverty (Turner, Grindstaff, & Phillips, 1990). According to Garfinkel and McLanahan (1986), this poverty and economic insecurity are a consequence of three factors: (1) the low earnings capacity of single mothers, (2) the lack of child support from fathers, and (3) the meager benefits provided by public assistance programs.

For those who cannot get economic support from a job, their families, or the father of the baby, Aid to Families with Dependent Children (AFDC or Welfare) is their major source of income. Many will come to rely on welfare, because fathers of children born outside of marriage generally have a minimal role in providing economic support (Presser, 1980). The level of income from public assistance qualifies them and their children as persons living in poverty. Therefore, receiving such payments is not a conscious incentive for adolescents to parent outside marriage (Finkel & Finkel, 1983; Moore, 1985). As an example, Prater (1990) found that an 18 year old mother with 3 children was receiving an allotment of $238.00 monthly plus food stamps. Selection of the daily meals to prepare is often determined by the amount of food stamps available in the house (Platt-Koch, 1984). Unfortunately, this life of poverty often becomes a lifestyle. This economic situation is especially dismal for black single mothers, who are financially less well off than their white counterparts (Besharov, 1992). Although many teenagers feel that they will eventually marry (Scott, 1983), the welfare rolls are filled with single adult women who first gave birth as teenagers. However, adolescent mothers comprise a small number of welfare recipients compared to the total welfare population (Boxill, 1987).

Education. Teenage heads of household have educational deficits which translate into lack of adequate job preparation. Reports are consistent that education of an adolescent is hindered by pregnancy (Furstenberg, 1976; Hayes, 1987; Mott & Marsiglio, 1985; Prater, 1990; Prater, 1991; Prater, 1992; Turner et al., 1990). More directly, this curtailment of education is viewed as the most far-reaching consequence of teen pregnancy (Finkel & Finkel, 1983). Lack of education makes it more likely that they will live a life of poverty, as cited earlier. Also, this low level of educational attainment puts these mothers at a disadvantage when trying to assist their children with learning.

Children of teenage parents experience educational deficits, including scoring lower on IQ tests and demonstrating below-average academic achievement (Hayes, 1987; Hofferth, 1987; vonWindeguth & Urbano, 1989). However, factors other than merely the age of mother must be considered when examining the cognitive development of these children (Ketterlinus, Henderson, & Lamb, 1991). Furstenberg and colleagues (1987) reported that children of mothers who had three children, who had remained unmarried, who received welfare and had not gone back to school after the first child's birth, were educationally disadvantaged. In fact, they scored 30 points lower on the Caldwell Preschool Inventory scale than a child whose mother was married, had no other children, was not receiving public assistance and had returned to school for at least two years. This report gives a clear indication of the far-reaching educational deficits.

Physical health. Another deficit which is linked to early pregnancy and parenting is adverse health and psychosocial outcomes for young mothers and their children (McCormick & Moore, 1985; Shapiro & Starfield, 1984; Wallis, 1985; Wasserman, Rauh, Brunelli, Garcia-Castro, & Necos, 1990). It is reported that adolescents experience problems with pregnancy ranging from excessive weight gain to maternal mortality, and include anemia, nutritional deficiencies, toxemia, prolonged or abrupt labor, and caesarean sections (Hamburg, 1986). Also, babies born to these young mothers are more likely to be physically disadvantaged than babies born to non-teens (Turner et al., 1990; Wasserman et al., 1990). In fact, babies born to teenagers are more likely to die in their first year than babies born to women in their twenties and there is a high percentage of low birth rate babies born to teenage mothers (Garn, Pesick, & Petzoid, 1986). Other negative outcomes evidenced by these infants include prematurity, congenital malformations, neurological defects, perinatal mortality and childhood growth failure (Hamburg, 1986). Although many deficits are reported regarding the health of young mothers and their infants, some research indicate that adolescence may be a healthier time for low income black women to have a baby rather than waiting later (Geronimus, 1987).

As expected, this view tends to create controversial dialogue between scholars and service providers. Further research is warranted.

In a study conducted by the Child Welfare League of America (cited by Miller, 1984), 16% of the infants born to young adolescents could not go home from the hospital with their mothers. This early separation rate was much higher than the 7% rate for the general population of married women. Many of these babies have physical and mental health problems that may be continuous. As summarized by Cooley and Unger (1991):

> Perhaps the most serious outcomes resulting from teen pregnancy are the negative consequences for the growth and development of the children in these families. Immediate effects on children include less prenatal care, lower birth weight, increased prematurity, a higher incidence of illness and developmental disabilities, and poorer developmental outcomes than for children born to older mothers. (p. 218)

This is especially unfortunate considering the fact that teenage mothers, especially those heading households, lack the financial, emotional, and educational resources necessary to effectively care for disabled and/or exceptional children. Unfortunately, some of these children also become victims of child abuse (vonWindeguth & Urbano, 1989). Parenting by adolescents is explored further in the next section.

Mental health. Health deficits regarding psychological well-being should also be addressed. Adolescents parenting independently of their own parents are at a higher risk of depression (Turner et al., 1990). Therefore, the mental health status of these single young mothers is of special concern. A healthy mental state is beneficial in any situation, but especially for parents of young children. Maternal mental health is important for effective parenting (Wasserman et al., 1990). However, the task imposed by motherhood increases turmoil and emotional strain for these adolescents (Atkins, Protinsky, & Sporakowski, 1982; Barnes, 1987). The mental state of these young unmarried mothers, residing independent of family members, is reflected in their perceptions and behavior in the role of sole caregiver.

Parenting skills. When a young woman becomes a parent during the transition period from childhood to adulthood, one would anticipate that parenting skills would be poorly developed. After all, prior educational preparation had been concentrated within the cognitive areas, that of acquiring skills in reading, writing, and computations. These parenting deficits are compounded by the fact that family composition in teen pregnancy reflects higher numbers of births, shorter spacing between births, and more than one non-marital birth (Cooley & Unger, 1991; Ford, 1983;

Moore & Hofferth, 1978; Phipps-Yonas, 1980). Older girls, in comparison to younger ones, are more likely to have sufficient cognitive and psychosocial maturity, as well as appropriate knowledge and experience to function as an adequate parent (Peterson & Crockett, 1986; Porter, 1990; vonWindeguth & Urbano, 1989). Of course, one might wonder exactly what may be classified as adequate. Also, there is little comfort in the well-being of children of older adolescents, considering the reality that many adolescents become parents in their early teens. Additionally, younger adolescents are at a higher risk of a repeat pregnancy, a situation which puts them at an increased risk for depression (Turner et al., 1990). Hence, this increased risk for psychological problems place their children at a higher risk due to inadequate or inappropriate parenting. Cooley and Unger (1991) reported that seeking help from extended family members can help adolescent mothers acquire the skills needed in successful parenting.

Focusing on the parenting skills of adolescent parents is of great importance, considering that teenagers now bear and rear about one out of every six children in the United States (Porter, 1990). Porter further reported that teen mothers from urban, lower socioeconomic status tended to prefer physical punishment as discipline for their children, displayed minimal infant verbal stimulation, and had meager ideas about age-appropriate stimulation. Interestingly, young mothers on welfare were significantly more likely to rate their child as being uncooperative, rude and disobedient (Furstenberg et al., 1987). According to Porter, the most consistent findings have been that teen mothers (a) lack awareness of their infants' needs; (b) are verbally and emotionally unresponsive; and (c) possess inadequate knowledge of growth and development. Whereas, adolescent mothers may be lacking in parenting skills, they were not lacking in perceived love for their child (Prater, 1990).

Subjective Utilities Model

Although an unmarried adolescent parent may be head of household, this is not to suggest that she is insulated from the influences of others. There are various persons who are significant in the lives of these young mothers who influence their emotional, psychological and physiological well-being and that of their children. These persons usually include relatives and friends. Unfortunately, teenage mothers are likely to receive little in the form of direct caregiving from the baby's father (Cooley & Unger, 1991). Some adolescent mothers react to this lack of support from the father by responding to the child in a punitive and rejecting manner (Furstenberg, Brooks-Gunn, & Morgan, 1987).

Social support networks. In addition to family and friends, institutions, such as schools, community agencies and government services can serve as a source of support through providing resources. Single mothers who participate in activities outside the home reported higher self-esteem (Burns, Doremus, & Potter, 1990). This is significant, because parents with high self-esteem are said to be able to provide an atmosphere that nurtures positive parent-child relationships (Porter & Sobong, 1990). Therefore, access and use of these support networks can make the difference between progress or disaster, and tend to buffer the stress of managing alone. An adolescent head of household is not alone if these resources are used effectively. Support networks can fulfill many of the expectations of a marital partner. These extended associations in the form of networks can serve as surrogate parents through assuming responsibilities theoretically attributed to parents. Therefore, the subjective utilities model recognizes the significance of these external relationships. Also, see Marciano, this volume.

Turner, Grindstaff, and Phillips (1990) reported that social support involved the presence and products of stable human relationships. Three types were important: (1) Social embeddedness which is the connection of individuals to significant others in their social environment; (2) Perceived social support, which is the belief that there is help available; and (3) Enacted support which are actions that others perform in rendering assistance.

Impact of support. An adolescent mother who receives support is more likely to be less distressed, more responsive and attentive to her children, have time to spend with them, and have more interest in child development and educational activities (Cooley & Unger, 1991). Furthermore, Cooley and Unger found that support in the form of advice, emotional support, and financial assistance led to decreased aggressive behaviors, rejection, scolding, neglectful interactions and depression in teen mothers. Social support provided a variety of functions, such as guidance, social reinforcement, practical assistance with tasks of daily living, and social stimulation. This would seem especially important in a home headed by an unmarried adolescent mother.

Most unmarried teenagers, who become parents, do not establish their own households. The majority will remain with their families of origin after the birth of their babies (Wasserman et al., 1990). Also, the younger the mother at the birth of the child, the more likely she is to remain in her mother's home through the baby's childhood (Cooley & Unger, 1990). This living arrangement tends to be beneficial, according to Cooley and Unger, who reported that teens who lived with their parents or relatives were more likely to have returned to school and to have graduated, to be employed, and to be non-welfare recipients.

PROFILE OF BIOLOGICAL TEEN MOTHER HEAD OF HOUSEHOLD

Although each person brings individuality into every situation, there are some common experiences shared by these young women. In her study, Platt-Koch (1984) described adolescent unmarried mothers, who were heads of households, as being welfare dependent, inner-city residents, persons with no job skills, and whose daily life with their children had an unvarying routine. She also noted that television represented their connection to the outside world, especially soap operas. Platt-Koch reported an interesting analysis by A. F. Kilguss in describing the impact of television on these young mothers. She stated:

> Many of the soap opera themes reinforce the adolescent's misconceptions about the world. Pregnancy and motherhood are portrayed as entirely blissful states. The demands of a real-life baby are not shown. Birth control is rarely used; affairs are punished with unwanted pregnancy. "Traditional" women almost invariably are rewarded with happiness and career women with misery; this tends to reinforce the view that a woman's place is always in the home. Women are often victims, as if it were their natural lot to bear pain. (p. 1246)

The profile can also include an intergenerational cycle of teenage parenting. Many of these young mothers have mothers and sisters who were teenage parents. Because many of them grew up in single parent households, the family structure they have formed was the one modeled for them during their childhood years. Also, most of their childhood friends became teenage parents (Gispert & Falk, 1976; White, 1981).

As noted earlier, these young mothers were likely to experience maternal depression. As reported by Greywolf, Reese, and Belle (cited in Burns et al., 1990), variables associated with these mothers included low-income, single-parent status, at least one child under the age of six, three or more children, unsafe living environment, second or third generational poverty, lack of support with child care, and lack of a supportive confidant.

PUBLIC POLICY IMPLICATIONS

Local community and government agencies are a resource for teen mothers. Available agencies can serve as surrogate parents by assisting these young women to carry the responsibilities of parenting and household management. However, in order for these mothers to become self-sufficient, the public must be more responsive. It is realized that some citizens may be reluctant to offer assistance, because they view the plight of these young women as being punishment for deviating from society's norms and values. However, in terms of economics, it is more cost-effective to help these young women to elevate themselves above their present condition. Not only will the mothers benefit, but the quality of life for future generations will be enhanced through providing a more nurturing environment for the children. In other words, the goal of social support should be that of empowerment, providing people the opportunity to help themselves.

Providing public assistance may not necessarily mandate increased funding. It may merely mean using the available money differently, focusing the responsibilities of existing staff, using under-utilized school buildings in their neighborhoods, or combining services and resources. Innovation is the operational concept for addressing these concerns. An example of such an effort was the Early Childbearing Program at the Dorchester House Multi-Service Center in Boston, MA. In this program, clinicians visited young mothers in their own homes to offer emotional support and education about parenting. It was surmised that this natural setting provided a more accurate assessment of the mother-child relationship (Platt-Koch, 1984). Also, by going to the parents' home, two problems were eliminated–that of finding baby sitters and transportation.

Programs must be created within a comprehensive structure. It can be very frustrating for young teens to go "agency hopping." Young mothers do not possess the sophistication and knowledge to access numerous agencies and complete massive paperwork (Prater, 1990). An umbrella concept, that of clustering services at only one location, must be enhanced and supported. Also, other barriers for use should be removed. For instance, there may be a job training program in the community for which teens are eligible, but constrained by lack of baby sitters or transportation. Including teenage mothers in the planning process of support programs and employing them as workers in these efforts would be a proactive step. Possibly, agencies could avoid the wasting of resources on programs in which adolescent parents will not participate.

Attitudes of employees of agencies must be assessed and adjusted. Services must be acceptable to clients and "user friendly." Single adolescent mothers, especially those living in public housing, can be stereotyped unfavorably. For instance, some taxpayers believe the "brood sow" theory which proposes that adolescents have babies in order to qualify for welfare and continue to have children to increase welfare allotments (Dunston, Hall, & Thorne-Henderson, 1987). Research findings do not support this theory. What has probably happened is that these adolescent heads of household experienced the "domino effect." Early parenting triggered the fall of the first domino which knocked down everything in its path, including high educational attainment, well paying jobs, financial security, time for personal growth and development, and all other advantages associated with delayed parenting.

As cited earlier, helping these young women to become self-sufficient is very cost effective and can have far-reaching implications for the future. For instance, providing school based day care, coupled with child development classes, could assist teenage mothers to complete their high school education while developing parenting skills. Without such assistance, approximately 80% of teenage mothers will not finish high school; and it is their children who are likely to become teenage parents themselves in another 14 or 15 years (Schmidt, 1985).

For those adolescents who manage to complete high school and job training, public policy must not punish them for working. It is rare that a teenager, regardless of the level of skill and intelligence, will be employed in a job with enough income to be self-sufficient as a head of household. However, the salary from jobs that they may acquire could cause curtailment of all public assistance. Therefore, many desire to work, but cannot afford to work. Policy adjustments are definitely warranted.

RESEARCH IMPLICATIONS

Given that we have families structured with unmarried adolescent heads of household, more attention should be focused to this population. Numerous studies have been done on teenage pregnancy. Future investigations should examine in greater depth the teen mother who has no legal spouse or partner. Parenting, with all of its many ramifications of responsibility, can become a crisis situation. Possibly, if additional research were completed in this area, there would be increased guidance for creating programs with long-term positive results, especially if some of these were empirical investigations. Also, additional professional collaborations between practitioners and scholars should occur. This collaboration should include longitudinal studies.

In future research, the selection of methodology should be more carefully structured. According to Porter (1990), research on this subject has frequently lacked rigorous methodology, used weak measurement techniques, and was not usually developed using a sound theoretical basis. Specific limitations cited by Porter included the use of small samples, questionable instrumentation, unstructured observations, and the treatment of subjects with diverse demographic characteristics as homogeneous groups.

CONCLUSION

As another century draws near, there is an increasing recognition of diversity of family forms. The traditional family, legally married adult male and female parents, is not the model used by all who identify themselves as families. Also, as the demographic patterns shift, it becomes more difficult to stratify behaviors according to age. The common belief is that parenthood is for adults. However, when does adulthood begin and childhood end? Is adulthood when one gets a job and takes care of him/herself? Is adulthood when one can buy alcoholic beverages, go off to war or get married? Or is adulthood when one can give birth to a baby? Is a 13 year old who becomes a mother an adult or a child?

If America is truly a child-centered culture, then there is a responsibility to care for all children, particularly if they become parents. These teen mothers, who are trying to head households, have taken on an almost impossible task. Successfully coupling parenthood with household management as an adolescent can only be accomplished with a strong support network of family, friends, and social service agencies. Collectively, individuals and institutions must form a community to help rear the children, mothers and their offspring. In black families, especially, the extended family served as an integrated support network to rear the children. Today, this attitude of support must extend beyond biological relatives.

The best strategy is to establish programs aimed at supporting personal self-esteem and social acceptance. The worst way to use time and energy is to blame and criticize, and discuss how they have ruined their lives. These young women, in many ways, are still children. Regardless of the behavior which led to their circumstance, society has a responsibility to continue to nurture them and assist with the transition to adulthood. Without societal support, fairly accurate predictions may be made about the outcomes for teen mothers and their children. Living in poverty is one of the predictions. If, indeed, there is a culture of poverty, other predictions may be made. Children from this culture will more likely be undereducated. They will live in communities with a high crime rate. The mothers will likely have other children who will have the same disadvantages as the firstborn. Therefore, if predictions can be made about what will happen in these families, proactive solutions can be developed.

REFERENCES

Atkins, P., Protinsky, H., & Sporakowski, M. (1982). Identify formation: Pregnant and non-pregnant adolescents. *Adolescence, 225*(65), 73-79.

Barnes, A.L. (1987). *Single parents in Black America: A study in culture and legitimacy*, IN.: Wyndham Hall Press.

Besharov, D.J. (1992). Not all single mothers are created equal. *American Enterprise*. 13-17.

Beyer, M. (1983, Spring). The problems of teenage parenthood: Put my future on hold. *Teen Times*, pp. 12-13.

Bianchi, S.M. (1995). The changing demographic and socioeconomic characteristics of single parent families. In S. Hanson, M. Heims, D. Julian, & M. Sussman (Eds.), *Marriage & Family Review, 20*(1/2) (pp. 71-97).

Boxill, N.A. (1987). "How would you feel . . . ?": Clinical interviews with black adolescent mothers. In S.F. Battle (Ed.), *Child and Youth Services: The Black Adolescent Parent, 9*(1), 41-51.

Bronfenbrenner, U. (1977). Toward an experimental ecology of human development. *American Psychologist, 32*, 513-531.

Burns, E.I., Doremus, P.C., & Potter, M.B. (1990). Value of health, incidence of depression, and level of self-esteem in low-income mothers of pre-school children. *Issues in Comprehensive Pediatric Nursing, 13*, 141-153.

Card, J.J., & Wise, L.L. (1978). Teenage mothers and teenage fathers: The impact of early childbearing on the parents' personal and professional lives. *Family Planning Perspectives, 10*, 199-205.

Cooley, M.L., & Unger, D.G. (1991). The role of family support in determining developmental outcomes in children of teen mothers. *Child Psychiatry and Human Development, 21*(3), 217-234.

Donati, T. (1995). Single parents and wider families in the new context of legitimacy. In S. Hanson, M. Heims, D. Julian, & M. Sussman (Eds.), *Marriage & Family Review, 20*(1/2) (pp. 27-42).

Dunston, P.J., Hall, G.W., & Thorne-Henderson, C. (1987). Black adolescent mothers and their families: Extending services. In S.F. Battle (Ed.), *Child and Youth Services: The Black Adolescent Parent, 9*(1), 95-110.

Erikson, E. (1963). Childhood and Society, New York: Norton.

Farber, N. (1990). The significance of race and class in marital decisions among unmarried adolescent mothers. *Social Problems, 37*(1), 51-63.

Finkel, M.L., & Finkel, D.J. (1983). Public policy and adolescent sexual behavior in the United States. *Social Biology, 30*(2), 140-149.

Ford, K. (1983). Second pregnancies among teenage mothers. *Family Planning Perspectives, 15*, 268-272.

Fox, G.L. (1986). The family context of adolescent sexuality and sex roles. In G. Leigh & G. Peterson (Eds.), *Adolescents in families* (pp. 179-204). Cincinnati: South-Western.

Franklin, D.L. (1988a). Race, class, and adolescent pregnancy: An ecological analysis. *American Journal of Orthopsychiatry, 58*(3), 339-354.

Franklin, D.L. (1988b). The impact of early childbearing on developmental outcome: The case of black adolescent parenting. *Family Relations, 37*, 268-274.

Furstenberg, F.F. (1976). The social consequences of teenage parenthood. *Family Planning Perspectives, 8*, 148-164.

Furstenberg, F.F., Brooks-Gunn, J., & Morgan, S.P. (1987). Adolescent mothers and their children in later life. *Family Planning Perspectives, 19*, 142-151.

Garfinkel, I., & McLanahan, S.S. (1986). *Single mothers and their children: A new American dilemma.* Washington D.C.: The Urban Institute.

Garn, S.M., Pesick, S.D., & Petzoid, A.S. (1986). The biology of teenage pregnancy: The mother and the child. In J.B. Lancaster & B.A. Hamburg (Eds.), *School age pregnancy and parenthood*, (pp. 77-93). New York: Aldine De Gruyter.

Geronimus, A.T. (1987). On teenage childbearing and neonatal mortality in the United States. *Population and Development Review, 13*,(2), 245-273.

Gispert, M., & Falk, F. (1976). Sexual experimentation and pregnancy in young black adolescents. *American Journal of Obstetrics and Gynecology, 126*, 459-466.

Hamburg, B.A. (1986). Subsets of adolescent mothers: Developmental, bio-medical, and psycho-social issues. In J.B. Lancaster & B.A. Hamburg (Eds.), *School age pregnancy and parenthood* (pp. 115-146). New York: Aldine De Gruyter.

Hayes, C.D. (Ed.) (1987). *Risking the future: Adolescent sexuality, pregnancy, and childbearing (Vol. 1)*. Washington, D.C.: National Academy Press.

Hofferth, S.L. (1987). The children of teen childbearers. In S.L. Hofferth & C.D. Hayes (Eds.), *Risking the future: Adolescent sexuality, pregnancy, and childbearing (Vol. II)* (pp. 174-206). Washington, D.C.: National Academy Press.

Jones, E.F., Forrest, J.D., Goldman, N., Henshaw, S.K., Lincoln, R., Rosoff, J.I., Westoff, C.F., & Wulf, D. (1985). Teenage pregnancy in developed countries: Determinants and policy implications. *Family Planning Perspectives, 17*, 53-63.

Kitterlinus, R.D., Henderson, S., & Lamb, M.E. (1991). The effects of maternal age-at-birth on children's cognitive development. *Journal of Research on Adolescence, 1*(2), 173-188.

Lasswell, M., & Lasswell, T. (1991). *Marriage and the family.* (3rd ed.) Belmont: Wadsworth Publishing.

McCormick, M.C., Shapiro, S., & Starfield, B. (1984). High-risk young mothers: Infant mortality and morbidity in four areas in the United States, 1973-1978. *American Journal of Health, 74*(1), 18-23.

McCubbin, H.J., & Patterson, J.M. (1986). Adolescent stress, coping, and adaptation: A normative family perspective. In G.K. Leigh & G.W. Peterson (Eds.), *Adolescents in families* (pp. 256-276). Cincinnati: South-Western Publishing.

Miller, S.H. (1984). Childbearing and childrearing among the very young. *Children Today, 13*, 26-29.

Mintz, S., & Kellogg, S. (1988). *Domestic revolutions: A Social history of American family life*. New York: The Free Press.

Moore, K.A. (1985). Teenage pregnancy: The dimensions of the problem. *New Perspectives*, (Summer), 11-15.

Moore, K., & Hofferth, S. (1978). *The consequences of age of first birth.* Washington D. C.: Urban Institute.

Mott, F.L. (1986). The pace of repeated childbearing among young American mothers. *Family Planning Perspectives*, *18*, 5-12.

Mott, F.L., & Marsiglio, W. (1985). Early childbearing and completion of high school. *Family Planning Perspectives*, *17*, 234-237.

Norton, A.J., & Moorman, J. (1987). Current trends in marriage and divorce among American women. *Journal of Marriage and the Family*, *49*, 3-14.

Peterson, A.C., & Crockett, L. (1986). Pubertal development and its relationship to cognitive and psycho-social development in adolescent girls: Implications for parenting. In J.B. Lancaster & B.A. Hamburg (Eds.), *School age pregnancy and parenthood* (pp. 147-176). New York: Aldine De Gruyter.

Piaget, J. (1952). *The origins of intelligence in children.* New York: International University Press.

Platt-Koch, L.M. (1984). Soap opera: Catalyst to communication. *American Journal of Nursing*, *84*(2), 1244-1246.

Porter, C.P. (1990). Clinical and research issues related to teen mothers' child-rearing practices. *Issues in Comprehensive Pediatric Nursing*, *13*, 41-58.

Porter, L.Z., & Sobong, L.C. (1990). Differences in maternal perception of the newborn among adolescents. *Pediatric Nursing*, *16*(1), 101-104.

Prater, L.P. (1990). *Rationale for repeat term pregnancy among Black adolescents.* Unpublished Doctoral dissertation, University of Tennessee, Knoxville.

Prater, L.P. (1991, June). *Adolescent African-American single parents: Barriers to self-sufficiency*. Paper presented at the New Perspectives: Single Parents and Self-Sufficiency Annual Conference, Lexington, KY.

Prater, L.P. (1992). Early pregnancy and academic achievement of African-American youth. *Exceptional Children*, *59*(2), 141-149.

Presser, H.B. (1980). Sally's corner: Coping with unmarried motherhood. *Journal of Social Issues*, *36*(1), 107-129.

Resnick, M.D., Blum, W., Bose, J., Smith, M., & Toogood, R. (1990). Characteristics of unmarried adolescent mothers: Determinants of child rearing versus adoption. *American Journal of Orthopsychiatry*, *60*(4), 577-584.

Schmidt, A.V. (1985). Teenage mothers: School-based child care puts diploma in reach. *Children Today*, *14*, 16-18.

Smith, T.E. (1976). Push versus pull: Intra-family versus peer-group variables as possible determinants of adolescent orientations toward parents. *Youth and Society*, *8*, 5-26.

Spanier, G. (1989). Bequeathing family continuity. *Journal of Marriage and the Family*, *51*, 3-13.

Strong, B., & Devault, C. (1992). *The marriage and family experience* (5th ed.). St. Paul, MN: West.

Taeuber, C. (Ed.) (1991). *Statistical handbook on women in America.* Phoenix, AZ: Oryx Press.

Turner, R.J., Grindstaff, C.F., & Phillips, N. (1990). Social support and outcome in teenage pregnancy. *Journal of Health and Social Behavior, 43*, 43-57.

Unger, D.H., & Wandersman, L.P. (1988). The relation of family and partner support to the adjustment of adolescent mothers. *Child Development, 59*, 1056-1060.

U.S. Bureau of the Census. (1955). *Census of Population: 1950*, Vol. IV, Part 2, Chapter A. *General Characteristics of Families.*

U.S. Bureau of the Census. (1993). *Census of Population: 1990*, Vol. 1, *General Population Characteristics, U.S. Summary.*

vonWindeguth, B.J., & Urbano, R.C. (1989). Teenagers and the mothering experience. *Pediatric Nursing, 15*(5), 517-520.

Wallis, C. (1985, December 9). Children having children. *Time*, pp. 78-82.

Wasserman, G.A., Rauh, V.A., Brunelli, S.A., Garcia-Castro, M., & Necos, B. (1990). Psychosocial attributes and life experiences of disadvantaged minority mothers: Age and ethnic variations. *Child Development, 61*, 566-580.

White, M.S. (1981). Adolescent pregnancy status convergence for the well-socialized adolescent female. *Youth and Society, 12*(4), 443-464.

APPENDIX

Glossary

Noncustodial mother	A woman who currently does not or at some previous time did not physically share the same abode as one or more biological children under the age of 18 for whatever reason.
Voluntary noncustodial	A woman who does not physically share the same abode as mother of one or more biological children under the age of 18 as a result of a personal choice, whether legally formalized or not.
Involuntary noncustodial	A woman who does not physically share the same abode as mother of one or more biological children under the age of 18 as a result of some form of protective services intervention, criminal confinement, long-term mental or physical health convalescence, court custody determination, or child kidnapping.

Following divorce, noncustodial fathers lose much of the basis for the positional power that undergirded their authority with wives and children. They must also deal with issues of autonomy or connectedness in very different ways; no longer can they count on a relationship with wives, as is often the case, for the only context in which they allow themselves to experience intimacy. Neither can they depend on wives to facilitate and mediate their relationships with children and to provide physical care-giving. Men are thus thrust into a situation in which they are faced with issues and tasks that often leave them feeling bewildered, lonely, power-less, and detached. Unfortunately, some noncustodial fathers continue to use the control of money and/or regular contact with children as last ditch measures to maintain and exert positional power (Berkman, 1986).

The ways in which men respond to the changes precipitated by divorce are influenced by a number of factors related to who they are as a person as well as the broader social context in which they operate. In order to design psychoeducational or therapeutic interventions that allow noncus-todial fathers to adapt in ways that are beneficial to themselves and ulti-mately to their children, an awareness of these factors is imperative. The ultimate objectives of such interventions are: to empower men so they can recognize, value, and exert the influence open to them through a greater utilization of personal power rather than primarily positional power; and to assist men to find ways of maintaining emotional connection to their children in ways that allow them to be truly autonomous rather than detached or cut-off from them.

In general, these are goals that have been achieved by only a minority of noncustodial fathers. In order to work toward such outcomes entails reformulations of how men have been socialized to view both their mascu-linity as well as their role as fathers. McKenry and Price (1990) offered a cogent review of the literature on the impact of divorce on men by at-tempting to answer the question of the extent to which men are at risk for negative consequences of divorce. They concluded that:

> Although research is limited, increasing evidence suggests that men, because of their traditional sex role socialization, are particularly vulnerable to many negative consequences of divorce. Also, because of this socialization, men involved in divorce are neither able to acknowledge their symptomatology nor to seek help. (p. 112)

In recognition of the growing numbers of men who want to move in this direction, interventions are needed that provide them with support and assistance in dealing with opportunities, issues, and tasks that they are

(Ahrons, 1983; Arendell, 1992; Bowman and Ahrons, 1985; Coysh, Johnston, Tschann, Wallerstein, and Kline, 1989; Isaacs, 1988; Koch and Lowery, 1984; Kurdek, 1986; Tschann, Johnston, and Wallerstein, 1989; Wright and Price, 1986.) Maccoby and her colleagues, (Maccoby et al., 1990; Maccoby and Mnookin, 1992) are investigating the interaction of conflict between coparental former spouses with different custody arrangements and the nature of coparenting relationships. At the 18-month followup, they found that noncustodial parents were less satisfied with custody arrangements than parents who shared residential custody of their children; further, they found continuity in levels of conflict across the divorce process, such that predivorce conflict predicted post-divorce conflict levels. Sharing residential custody neither exacerbated nor lessened levels of coparental conflict, and noncustodial parents were more satisfied with their custody situation when the coparents either were cooperative or had completely severed their ties with each other. Clearly, any understanding of noncustodial fathers must start with the nature of the continuing relationship with his former spouse.

INTERVENTIONS WITH NONCUSTODIAL FATHERS

A description of the ways in which noncustodial fathers behave and the situations they typically experience provides a basis for understanding how they, as well as their former wives and children, adapt following divorce. In order to facilitate more positive adaptations through psychoeducational or therapeutic interventions, a basic understanding of the impact of divorce on family systems needs to be conceptualized. Ahrons (1980), most notably, and others have postulated stages in the process of adjustment for families in response to divorce. Her description entails an emphasis on cognitive, affective, and boundary issues in families and is helpful in emphasizing important role transitions and tasks facing families. There are, however, some more basic lenses or perspectives through which the impact of divorce can be described when viewed in a broader sociocultural perspective.

Recent work from the feminist perspective on family therapy provides a basis for such a conceptualization of the impact of divorce on family systems. The field of family therapy typically has not viewed family systems through the important lens of gender when attempting to describe how family systems function. Neither have attempts to devise systemic interventions taken gender into account (McGoldrick, Anderson, and Walsh, 1989; Walters, Carter, Papp and Silverstein, 1988). A gender-sensitive view of family systems as described by Goldner (1988) ". . . means conceptualizing gender as an irreducible category of clinical observation

fathers with higher incomes are more likely to receive joint legal custody and to have higher payments ordered. When only those with joint legal custody are considered, the income of the father was closely associated with the payments actually made, regardless of the size of the support order awarded by the court. Seltzer concludes that "... joint legal custody may encourage fathers to make child-support contributions contingent on their own personal circumstances" (1991a: 923).

One might derive from Seltzer's work support for current policy manipulations of two of the external parameters or constraints on the noncustodial father-child relationship, changes that are designed in part to buttress that fragile relationship. Specifically, joint custody is to be preferred over other forms of custody, since it appears to bolster child support compliance. Moreover, improvements in state mechanisms for child support enforcement are to be applauded, because regular payment of child support enhances father-child contact through more frequent and enduring visitation patterns.

Arendell (1992) sounds a cautionary note, however, against overly sanguine interpretations of child support compliance by noncustodial fathers. In an ethnographic study of 75 divorced fathers, she finds considerable support for viewing payment of child support as motivated as much by a desire to maintain control over the post-divorce existence of the ex-wife as by a desire to contribute to the well-being of their mutual children. Maccoby et al. (1990: 154) express similar reservations about joint custody. Research using intensive interviews underscores the need to take into account the post-divorce relationships between ex-spouses (e.g., conflict, cooperation) in shaping the underlying meanings of overt behaviors measured with quantitative assessments. It is also valuable in suggesting potentially healthful directions of psychoeducational interventions with men and women after divorce, as outlined in the final section of this chapter.

FATHERING BY NONCUSTODIAL FATHERS

Despite the assumption that continuing contact with the noncustodial father is important to a child's well-being following divorce, the empirical evidence to support this assumption is surprisingly thin (Furstenberg and Nord, 1985; Hawkins and Eggebeen, 1991). The positive outcomes of noncustodial father contact were noted in early studies that involved small, nonrepresentative samples of divorcing couples characterized by higher socioeconomic backgrounds (Wallerstein and Kelly, 1980). The early results have been difficult to replicate consistently in subsequent studies that

Chapter 15

Young Nonresident Biological Fathers

William Marsiglio

SUMMARY. This paper summarizes research, policies, and programs related to nonresident, adolescent and young adult biological fathers and outlines avenues for future initiatives in these areas. The discussion is informed by a conceptual model that illustrates how a set of interrelated macro and micro factors affect the way young fathers respond to their paternity and father roles.

Research on nonresident young fathers is limited because it is largely based on data from small convenience samples. While several studies use national survey data to address issues relevant to young fathers, they are restricted because the samples are not representative of those who have fathered a child, many young men are unwilling or unable to provide an accurate report of their paternity history, surveys either omit or include only cursory measures of key concepts that address fatherhood issues, data are not collected as part of a larger conceptual framework, and data are based on older cohorts of youth. Survey data do indicate that young unwed fathers are generally less well educated, have lower academic abilities, commit more crimes, and are more likely to have been raised in a family that was economically disadvantaged compared to other young men, with these differences being much larger among white than black unwed fathers.

The discussion focuses on how social agents have expanded their efforts to establish paternity for births to unmarried parents and have

---

William Marsiglio is affiliated with the Sociology Department, Turlington Hall, University of Florida, Gainesville, FL 32611.

[Haworth co-indexing entry note]: "Young Nonresident Biological Fathers." Marsiglio, William. Co-published simultaneously in *Marriage & Family Review* (The Haworth Press, Inc.) Vol. 20, No. 3/4, 1995, pp. 325-348; and: *Single Parent Families: Diversity, Myths and Realities* (ed: Shirley M. H. Hanson et al.) The Haworth Press, Inc., 1995, pp. 325-348. Multiple copies of this article/chapter may be purchased from The Haworth Document Delivery Center [1-800-3-HAWORTH; 9:00 a.m. - 5:00 p.m. (EST)].

also begun to apply a long term perspective to the child support issue. To date, paternity establishment efforts have achieved limited success. However, a number of innovative strategies have been proposed that would enable most young fathers to develop a pattern of support from the outset irrespective of their educational and financial resources. The discussion also speculates on how these strategies could be enhanced if insights are gleaned from social psychological scholarship on identity processes and the commitment concept.

KEYWORDS. Fathers, Fatherhood, Adolescent fathers, Teenage fathers, Nonresident fathers

INTRODUCTION

During the past decade, researchers, social service providers, and policy makers have begun to reconceptualize adolescent childbearing issues in a manner that incorporates young fathers. Adolescent and young adult men who have made a serious commitment to their partner (and child) by cohabitating with or marrying her before or shortly after their child is born represent one group of fathers that has received this attention. The large percentage of young fathers who either never experienced a serious commitment with the mother of their child or separated/divorced after a short period of time together have also been of interest to persons dealing with early childbearing issues.

Despite the rapid increase in the rate of single-father families in recent decades, data from the 1990 Current Population Survey indicates that this family form represents only about 14% of all single parent families where a stepparent is not present (Meyer & Garasky, 1993; see also Bianchi, this volume). Single-father families are particularly rare among young parents. Only about 5.5% of all single parent families in which the resident parent is under age 21 are single-father families. Because this volume focuses on single parents[1] and researchers have not studied young resident single-father families as a unique group, this review primarily addresses issues relevant to nonresident adolescent/young adult fathers. (For additional and broader reviews of related issues see Adams & Pittman, 1988; Family Impact Seminar, 1990; Fox & Blanton, this volume; Parke & Neville, 1987; Smollar & Ooms, 1987).

It is well known that researchers interested in adolescent childbearing issues define their sample populations in diverse ways. Some studies of

fathers (Lerman, 1986) include and others (Marsiglio, 1987) exclude fathers who are in their early twenties without taking into account the mother's age at birth. Meanwhile, there are those researchers (Furstenberg & Harris, in press; Hardy, Duggan, Masnyk, & Pearson, 1989) who define their sample in terms of the mother's age irrespective of the fathers' age as well as those who restrict their research to adolescent pregnancy/childbearing issues specifically relevant to teenage parents or hypothetical teen parents (Marsiglio, 1988; 1989; Marsiglio & Menaghan, 1990). The fact that young men are often a few (or more) years older than their female partners complicates efforts to simplify sample definitions (Adams & Pittman, 1988; Hardy et al., 1989; Lamb, Elster, Peters, Kahn & Tavare, 1986). This review, for the most part, focuses on adolescent fathers and young adult males who have fathered a child with an adolescent mother.[2] This approach assumes that young fathers in their early twenties may in some instances encounter problems similar to those of their younger counterparts. Likewise, the problems adolescent mothers and their children experience may often be comparable whether the fathers are teenagers or young adults in their twenties.

Fathering a child as an adolescent, or in some cases as a young adult, can have both personal and social implications. Unlike young mothers who tend to keep and live with their child, many fathers do not live with or even financially assist in the support of their child. Thus, the extent to which paternity affects young men will depend on the extent to which they commit themselves to the social and financial aspects of fatherhood. This commitment, especially among whites, still frequently involves the decision to marry or cohabitate with the child's mother (Marsiglio, 1987). However, rates of out-of-wedlock childbearing among young whites have increased significantly in recent years (NCHS, 1993) and fathers can be committed to the social role of father without living with their child (Danzinger & Radin, 1990). Meanwhile, the child's well-being can be affected by the father's actions whether or not the father is committed to his father roles. One of the obvious ways a child may suffer is economically when nonresident fathers pay little or no child support.

This review of previous research and policies/programs relevant to nonresident, biological young fathers is organized around the conceptual model illustrated in Figure 1 (slightly modified versions of this model are found in Marsiglio, 1991a; Marsiglio & Scanzoni, 1990). This model, which is drawn upon selectively here (focusing only on males and relevant variables), depicts how young parents' attitudes, life style adaptations, and well-being are interrelated and affected by the larger social context that includes elements of social structure, cultural and subcultural values and

FIGURE 1. Conceptual Model for Pregnant/Parenting Teens and Their Male Partners: Pregnancy Resolution Decisions, Life-Style Adaptations, and Well-Being

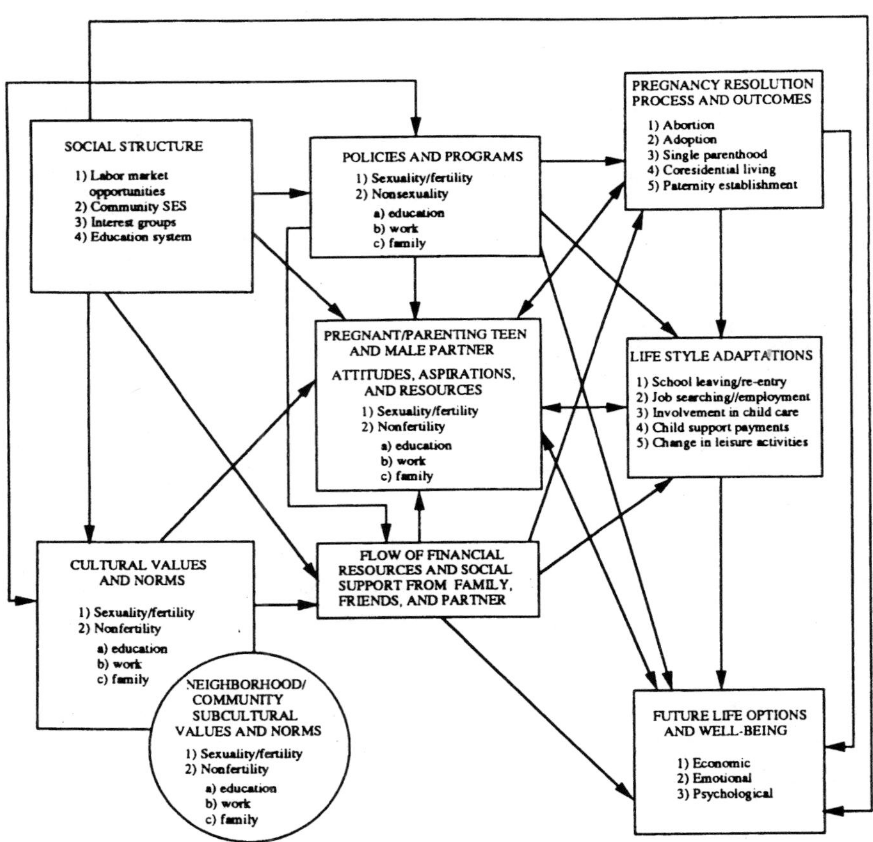

norms, social policies and programs, and the availability of financial resources and social support at the micro level. In addition to reviewing the literature in this area this model is used to develop an agenda for research, theory, policies, and programs that reflects the ongoing struggle to improve the lives of adolescent parents and their children.

RESEARCH AND POLICY ISSUES

Data Sources and Descriptive Overview

Much of the empirical research on adolescent and young adult fathers has been conducted since the mid 1980s and continues to be limited by a number of methodological shortcomings. As Parke and Neville (1987) noted, one of the major limitations of this body of research is that it is largely based on data from small convenience samples. Several studies use national survey data to address issues relevant to adolescent/young adult fatherhood (Card & Wise, 1978; Hanson, Morrison, & Ginsburg, 1989; Lerman, 1986; Lerman, in press-a, in press-b; Marsiglio, 1987). However, they are restricted because the data either omit or include only cursory measures of key concepts that address paternity issues, they were not collected as part of a larger conceptual framework, and the data are based on older cohorts of youth.[3] One of the major problems with these data is that since relevant attitudinal measures are not available, it is impossible to assess directly the underlying processes that shape young fathers' experiences. Furthermore, high quality national demographic data on young fathers is not available because at least 32% of unwed mothers (many of whom are adolescents) do not report the age of the father on the birth certificate (NCHS, 1983), and a significant number of men are unable or unwilling to provide an accurate report of their paternity history (Mott, 1983).

Notwithstanding these limitations, national survey data do provide some basic demographic information on young fathers and more specifically on those young fathers who do or do not live with their child shortly after the child's birth. Data based on male respondents interviewed in 1979 and 1984 from the youth cohort (20-27 years of age in 1984) of the National Longitudinal Survey of Labor Market Experience (NLSY) indicated that 6.8% reported fathering a child while they were a teenager and 5.5% were responsible for a *nonmaritally conceived* first birth (Marsiglio, 1987). Of those who were responsible for a nonmaritally conceived first birth, 1.7% were between 11-17 years of age while 3.8% were either 18 or 19 years old when they became a father for the first time. This study also documented the living arrangement patterns of fathers of nonmaritally conceived first born children. About 23% of nondisadvantaged whites, 42% of disadvantaged whites, 52% of Hispanics, and 85% of black teenagers were *not* living with their first born child at the initial observation date after the child's birth. Lerman's (1986) analysis of NLSY data focused on fathers who were 18-25 years of age in 1983 and had fathered at least one child at some point in their life who was not living with them for reasons other than death and schooling (the mother was not always a teenage mother). He found that about one third of all fathers 18-25 lived away from at least one of their children irrespective of whether they were conceived within or outside of marriage. In addition, 5% of 18-21 year old and about 20% of 22-25 year old "absent" fathers, lived with some, but not all of their children, a pattern that was most pronounced among Hispanic men.

A Conceptual Model and Literature Review

One approach to reviewing the literature that focuses on nonresident young fathers is to examine the relevant issues within a larger conceptual framework. Figure 1 displays such a framework. It indicates that social structural factors and cultural values/norms are interrelated and play an important role in shaping the macro and micro context within which young men experience aspects of their paternity and alter their lifestyle in response to becoming a father. For example, the availability of jobs within the local community for young persons, many of whom have little work experience and limited skills, in combination with cultural norms regarding fathers' provider role responsibilities, can have profound implications for young fathers, their partners, and children. These factors can directly affect young fathers' attitudes, aspirations, and resources. They also may be important indirectly through their association with particular social policies/programs and the flow of financial and social support from significant others to young fathers and their children. Qualitative studies have indicated that since many disadvantaged fathers feel inadequate about their ability to fulfill the breadwinner role they often dissociate themselves from it in order to minimize their sense of inadequacy (Anderson, 1989; Furstenberg, 1991; Sullivan, 1985). Recent policy and programmatic initiatives address this dilemma by providing fathers opportunities, especially during their child's first few years of life, to demonstrate their commitment to their child in ways other than through direct financial support (Johnson & Sum, 1987; Savage, 1987).

This model indicates that these interrelated macro and micro phenomena can affect the way young fathers respond to a pregnancy and birth. In addition, it shows how the larger social and political context is likely to affect young fathers' future life options and well-being. In other words, young men's decisions about matters involving marriage, cohabitation, participation in school or work programs, and child care are affected by various legislative measures and the availability of specific educational and work initiatives. Likewise, the level and type of support young men receive from family members and friends may enable them to make certain choices about their education, work, and social life. These choices will have implications not only for the way they express themselves as fathers, but their partner's and children's life experiences as well. For instance, when grandparents of a young father's child provide financial and child care support, a young father (and his partner) may have the chance to further his education prior to seeking full-time employment without compromising his child's well-being. Consequently, his long-term potential to provide for his child may be enhanced.

Given space limitations and the scope of this model, the following discussion focuses on selective aspects of it. Young men's paternity experiences are discussed in relation to social structure (socioeconomic factors in particular), cultural values and norms, policies and programs, and financial and social support.

Social Structure. The first two columns of Figure 1 illustrate, among other things, the notion that young men's economic opportunities and socioeconomic background may be related to the types of policies and programs targeted at them, the resources they possess, as well as their values and life aspirations regarding education, work, and family. A common observation in this area has been that young fathers are often disadvantaged economically and have completed fewer years of schooling than their childless peers (Lerman, 1986, in press-a; Marsiglio, 1987). In his analysis of data from the NLSY (cohort of young men 23-27 in 1987), Lerman (in press-a) found that young men who were unwed fathers as of 1984 (not controlling for the age of the mother) worked fewer hours and earned considerably less than their peers in 1983. This disparity continued to increase by 1987 at which time unwed fathers were working 400-500 fewer hours and earning between $5,000-9,000 less per year compared to their counterparts who were single without a child, married without a child, or married fathers. Lerman (in press-b) has also shown that while unwed fathers are generally less well educated, have lower academic abilities, and engage in more crime than other young men, these differences are much larger among white than black unwed fathers.

Young fathers' ability to make a financial contribution to their child and partner will tend to be influenced by their family of origin's socioeconomic status. Lerman (1986) found that young men 18-25 years of age who became a nonresident father by 1983 were more likely to have been raised in a family that was economically disadvantaged; 27% of nonresident fathers lived in a family who received welfare in 1978 whereas only about 9% of other young men (resident fathers and childless peers) in 1983 had lived in an impoverished family in 1978. He also reported that family income levels in 1978 for those young men who were living with their parents and had not fathered a child as of 1979, but who would eventually become nonresidential fathers, were considerably lower than the family incomes of those who remained childless through 1983. Family income levels were 48% lower for whites, 35% lower for Hispanics, and 20% lower for blacks.

Although data are not available to document the extent to which young fathers' parents financially support their grandchildren, it is assumed that more advantaged grandparents, on average, will provide more assistance to their grandchildren than grandparents who are less advantaged financially.[4] Furthermore, young fathers who work–especially full time, compared to their school attending peers who do not work, may in some instances be in a better position to support their children financially in the short term when their children are very young. But, young fathers who are not working may be in a better position to provide financial assistance later on in life if they promptly complete their high school and perhaps college education.

Young fathers' attitudes about and their responses to their paternity may be related to another parental resource, education. Marsiglio's (1987) study using NSLY data indicated that among males who fathered a child as a teenager, 42% reported having a father and 45% reported having a mother who had not completed high school, whereas the comparable figures for young men who had not fathered a child as a teenager were 28.5% and 27% respectively. This pattern was most pronounced when young fathers whose first child was maritally conceived were compared to those who had not fathered a child as a teenager. This study also revealed that while parental education (especially father's) was related to teenage paternity status in a bivariate context, parental education was not related to the probability that an adolescent father was living with his non-maritally conceived child at the time of the subsequent interview. Parental education also was not related to the probability of getting married within 12 months of conception in a multivariate context. These findings, in conjunction with the data presented above on family socioeconomic status, suggest that adolescent fathers are less apt than their childless peers to have access to the types of familial resources that would enhance their chances of providing for their child financially.

Cultural Values/Norms. Young fathers' attitudes, aspirations, and resources will also be shaped by their exposure to cultural/subcultural values and normative expectations associated with particular statuses such as student, worker, and father, as well as their perceptions (and others) about their ability to fulfill them (Teti & Lamb, 1986). Sometimes young men may interpret and respond to these messages in contradictory ways. For example, some but not all young men will be exposed to cultural images that stress the financial role related to fatherhood. Lerman (in press-a) recently found indirect evidence of this pattern and concluded, after analyzing young fathers' 1986 earnings, that the "requirement and/or the desire to pay child support helped stimulate increased earnings."

It is also possible that young men may view paternity as a means to earn respect from their peers when they perform poorly in school and perceive (correctly or incorrectly) that few decent economic opportunities are available for them as unskilled workers. In a 1988 national survey of never married 15-19 year old males (Marsiglio, 1993), youth from more disadvantaged backgrounds were significantly more likely to report that fathering a child now would make them feel like a "real man" and that they would be less upset (or even pleased) if this were to happen. However, some young men may feel inadequate once their child is born because they are unable to find the kind of employment that would enable them to provide financially for their child and partner. This pattern is exacerbated by the fact that employment opportunities for young men, minority youth in particular, are generally poor (Betsy, Holister & Papageogious, 1985; Freeman & Holzer, 1985; Johnson & Sum, 1987). Not surprisingly, if young men believe there is little chance for them to play a specific role successfully, they will probably abdicate it and pursue a life style that provides them with a greater chance to succeed and increase their self-esteem.

One of the more important discussions about cultural values and norms in the adolescent childbearing literature has focused on apparent race differences in the rate of births to unmarried parents among blacks and whites (Marsiglio & Scanzoni, 1990; NCHS, 1993; O'Connell & Rogers, 1984). Scholars and policy makers have debated extensively how differences in self-reported sexuality/fertility values and norms among blacks and whites affect family formation patterns involving unplanned pregnancies. Controlling for social class, survey results published in the 1980s indicated that blacks were more likely than whites to report a desired age for childbearing that was younger than their desired age for marriage (Cherlin, 1981; Clark, Zabin & Hardy, 1984; Heiss, 1981; see also Moore, Simms, & Betsey, 1986; St. John & Rowe, 1990). Clark et al. (1984) found that black male students in grades 7-12 reported the ideal age for fathering a child to be 22.5 while their ideal age for getting married was 24.5. Thus, some observers have assumed that blacks have been less likely than whites to marry or cohabitate in response to an unplanned birth (Hayes, 1987), *in part*, because they have not felt the same type of pressure from either their same-race partner, parental figures, or significant others to "legitimate" their child's birth through marriage or at least cohabitation (see Marsiglio, 1988, 1989; Marsiglio & Menaghan, 1990). Nevertheless, ethnographic evidence based on small inner-city samples suggests that black male youth usually acknowledge their paternity, although the process of establishing paternity is sometimes complicated and protracted (Anderson, 1989; Sullivan, 1985). These researchers also note that the black community frequently supports young fathers' participation in informal child support/care arrangements. In recent years, the black middle class has supplemented these informal efforts by attempting to marshal community support for its campaign to encourage young black men, especially those living in central city areas, to interact with their partners and children in a more responsible manner (National Urban League, 1987).

Policies, Programs, Financial and Social Support. One of the key social policy developments of recent years related to family issues has been the growing commitment to encourage, and demand if necessary, that fathers (adolescent and older ones) act more responsibly, particularly in terms of child support. An important impetus for this policy shift has been the growing concern with the poverty status of children born to unwed parents and welfare dependency (Family Impact Seminar, 1990; Garfinkel & McLanahan, 1986). This concern is central to the issues reviewed here since many of the fathers of these children are economically disadvantaged adolescents or young adults. The basic policy objective, exemplified by the Family Support Act of 1988, is thus buttressed by the general fatherhood ideology that emphasizes the breadwinner role and is reinforced by liberal feminists' concerns with the feminization of poverty. Profeminist values have also influenced specific social programs and media campaigns designed to promote greater paternal involvement in the emotional and psychological aspects of fathering. While it is beyond the scope of this review to critique at length the various interventions that attempt to enhance paternal involvement among young fathers, there is a burgeoning literature that assesses the critical policy issues, social supports, and programs in this area (see Adams & Pittman, 1988; Barth, Claycomb, & Loomis, 1988; Cervera, 1991; Danzinger, Kastner, & Nickel, in press; Howe, in press; Family Impact Seminar, 1990; Freeman, 1989; Hendricks & Solomon, 1987; Johnson & Sum, 1987; Joshi & Battle, 1990; Mellgren, in press; Smollar & Ooms, 1987; Sullivan, 1990; Pirod-Good, in press; Pittman & Adams, 1988; Public/Private Ventures, 1990; Smith, 1989; Watson & Kelly, 1989; Wattenberg, in press; Westney, Jackson, & Munford, 1989; Zayas & Schinke, 1987).

There appears to be widespread public support for the idea that young fathers should act responsibly, but there is far less agreement about what constitutes responsible behavior (Adams & Pittman, 1988; Family Impact Seminar, 1990; Marsiglio, 1991b). At minimum, most observers seem to agree that fathers should demonstrate some interest in their child's emotional, psychological, and financial well-being. Fathers' initial step in this direction would be to acknowledge their paternity (Nichols-Casebolt & Garfinkel, 1991; Rozie-Battle, 1989). This behavior can be considered within the context of the pregnancy resolution process or an outcome of it, as is depicted in Figure 1.

Beginning in the mid 1980s, various social agents accelerated their efforts to secure the formal establishment of paternity in instances of out-of-wedlock births. A number of states have developed strategies beyond those mandated by federal law to improve rates of paternity establishment (Danzinger et al., in press). While some of these efforts have proven to be somewhat successful in increasing the rate for establishing paternity (Aron, Barnow & McNaught, 1989; Family Impact Seminar, 1990), the overall percent of paternity adjudications for U.S. out-of-wedlock births (based on crude estimates) increased only slightly from 28.2 in 1983 to 31.0 in 1989 (Wattenberg, in press; see also Wattenberg, Brewer, & Resnick, 1991). As Wattenberg's (1988) organizational analysis revealed, paternity cases are often mishandled and involve individuals as well as agencies with conflicting interests.

The Paternity Affidavit Project initiated in 1988 in the state of Washington may be the most successful program in this regard (Child Support Report, 1990). In cases of births to unwed parents, a new law requires that a "physician, midwife or their agent must provide an opportunity for parents to sign the paternity affidavit." The new parents' participation is completely voluntary and a father who signs this form can request a blood/genetic test at a later date if he changes his mind about paternity.

In addition to the symbolic significance of establishing paternity, it is the requisite first step to securing a father's formal child support commitment. Although it is well documented that a large percentage of nonresident fathers provide only partial or no child support (Meyer & Garasky, 1993; Savage, 1987; Seltzer, 1991; U.S. Bureau of Census, 1991), precise estimates of young nonresident fathers' child support expenditures are not readily available (Rievera-Casale, Klerman, & Manela, 1984). Young fathers typically provide less financial child support than their older counterparts. Many not only lack resources, but unmarried mothers are three times less likely (24% to 72%) to be awarded child support awards than other mothers, and young mothers are more likely to have children outside of marriage (NCHS, 1993).

A number of small scale studies, most focusing on minority youth in central city areas, have indicated that many young unwed fathers make some type of informal contribution to their child's care, or would be willing to do so if given the opportunity (Anderson, 1989; Christmon, 1990; Sander & Rosen, 1987; Sullivan, 1985; see also Marsiglio, 1993). These efforts tend to be rather modest and decline over time though, and Hardy et al. (1989) found that a large percentage of young mothers report being dissatisfied with the father's contribution.

As noted earlier, many young fathers are unable to fulfill typical child support obligations during the first several years of their child's life because they are unemployed or underemployed. However, many policy advocates have begun to apply a long term perspective to the child support issue by proposing a number of innovative strategies that would enable most young fathers to develop a pattern of support from the outset (see, Adams & Pittman, 1988; Danzinger et al., in press; Smollar & Ooms, 1987). In some instances young fathers may be required to pay only a token $1-2 award per week and they may in some instances receive child support credit for attending school, taking GED preparation classes, or being involved in a jobs training program.

The Teen Father Collaboration project, launched in 1983 in eight U.S. communities, is perhaps the most ambitious and successful programmatic effort to assist young fathers. It was designed to provide a comprehensive set of social services and training that would meet fathers' needs and enable them to assume a responsible role in their children's lives (Klinman, Sander, Rosen, Longo, & Martinez, 1985). One of the major objectives of this multifaceted outreach approach was to develop young fathers' employment, education, and parenting skills. This project represents an invaluable source of information for various types of service providers interested in dealing with young fathers.

RESEARCH AND POLICY: AN AGENDA FOR THE FUTURE

Aspects of the model presented above, in addition to those not explicitly discussed, can inform the development of a research and policy agenda that targets adolescent and young adult fathers. The significance of doing research in this area has been well established among researchers, social service providers, and policy advocates during recent years. The time has come though to initiate a more ambitious, theoretically guided research agenda based on national survey data, smaller scale intensive interviews, evaluation studies, and longitudinal designs. This agenda should address a variety of theoretical and policy issues relevant to young fathers as well as their partners and children. The conceptual model discussed here suggests that understanding the theoretical linkages between social structure, culture, financial and social resources, and social psychological processes involving young fathers will lead to more meaningful intervention strategies that include these fathers and enhance the quality of life for young parents and their children.

One area of research that warrants further study involves young fathers' attitudes, aspirations, and resources in areas such as education, work, and family life. It is important to develop a better understanding of how both structural and cultural factors affect young fathers in this regard. Researchers also need to examine more closely how young fathers adapt to an unplanned pregnancy. In this regard, it is critical that scholars examine why some young men are more willing than others to act responsibly toward their children, especially in terms of their financial assistance. Young fathers' willingness as well as their ability to fulfill this type of responsibility should be considered. Researchers and social service providers must also recognize that fatherhood can include an emotional and psychological component as well as a financial one. This greater awareness of the multifaceted nature of fatherhood should be accompanied by a heightened sensitivity to the developmental aspects of young fathers' (especially adolescents) personality. As Parke and Neville (1987) suggest, it would be instructive to move beyond the "age" variable and to assess young fathers' cognitive, emotional, and social status.

One approach that relates theory to policy issues for young fathers draws upon identity theory and the *commitment* concept. While it is beyond the scope of this review to elaborate fully on the potential policy implications of applying identity theory to the study of young fathers, a brief discussion of the key features of this theory is warranted.

Identity theory has been articulated by structural symbolic interactionists in various ways (see Burke & Reitzes, 1981, 1991; McCall & Simmons, 1966; Stryker, 1980, 1987; Stryker & Serpe, 1982). Theorists basically agree though that an individual's self is comprised of a variety of identities or "role identities" that are ordered according to their salience or centrality to the person's self. Some scholars have not always explicitly differentiated the term "role identity" from "status" (e.g., Stryker, 1980). It is instructive to note then that the various roles (e.g., breadwinner, nurturer, moral teacher) associated with a particular status (e.g., father) may themselves be ranked and ordered in a manner similar to how statuses or "role identities" are ranked relative to one another (Ihinger-Tallman, Pasley, & Buehler, in press). Burke and Reitzes' (1991) recent definition of identity as the "shared social meanings that persons attribute to themselves in a role" seems consistent with this observation (p. 242). They also observe that identities are: (a) social products because the self is situated in social categories (statuses and roles) and is experienced through an interaction process with others that is guided by individuals' perceptions about meanings and behaviors associated with these categories, (b) self-meanings that emerge through specific situations of role behavior, (c) symbolic and reflexive in that the meanings can produce similar responses among individuals while also serving as a standard for individuals to evaluate their behaviors, and (d) a stimulus for action (p. 242).

Formulations of identity theory have varied to a large extent because theorists have conceptualized the commitment concept differently. This review briefly highlights two conceptualizations relevant to a discussion of young fathers; more extensive summaries of these formulations appear elsewhere (Burke & Reitzes 1991; Ihinger-Tallman et al., 1993).

One conceptualization posits that commitment links persons to specified role partners (Stryker, 1968, 1980; Stryker & Serpe, 1982). Commitment is thought to be a function of: (a) the extent to which persons must be a particular type of person in order to maintain specific relationships, (b) the number of relationships persons have based on a specific role identity, and (c) the extent to which persons feel it is important for them to maintain these relationships. Accordingly, commitment is measured by assessing the perceived costs associated with the dissolution of specific relationships.

Meanwhile, Burke and Reitzes (1991) draw upon identity theory and affect control theory (Heiss, 1979, 1988; Smith-Lovin & Heiss, 1988) to advance Foote's (1951) work on the commitment concept. They view commitment as "linking a person to a stable set of self-meanings (identity). That connection, in turn, produces apparent ties to actions, organizations, and persons" (p. 240). They add that commitment refers to the "sum of the forces, pressures, or drives that influence people to maintain congruity between their identity setting and the input of reflected appraisals from the social setting" (p. 243). A person's identity provides him or her with the opportunity to assess the match between the "reflected appraisals" (specific feedback from others) toward him or her and his or her identity which serves as a basis for comparison. This process encourages individuals to act in any number of ways so as to make the meanings of the inputs consistent with those of their identity. There are both cognitive (e.g., rewards and avoided costs) and socioemotional (e.g., sense of "we-ness," warmth, belonging) bases for commitment. The strength of these forces will vary among individuals and the level of commitment will affect the manner and extent to which individuals attempt to maintain congruity between their reflected appraisals and identity standard. In conceptualizing commitment as part of the larger identity process, Burke and Reitzes treat the self as an active agent that links the individual to social structure. However, they do not explicitly consider the ways in which standards about role behavior are established, disseminated, or processed.

This summary of the key aspects of identity theory and the commitment concept, though brief, highlights the theoretical and policy significance of conducting research on young fathers' perceptions about their father role identities, their reflected appraisals, and the actual perceptions others have of them as fathers. Future research needs to clarify more fully, building upon previous qualitative interviews with fathers, the nature of the primary dimensions of meaning young fathers and others associate with the father status and its associated roles. Consistent with this theme, it would be useful to extend Burke and Reitzes' (1991) theoretical approach by considering the cultural sources and interpersonal processes that shape individuals' perceptions about fatherhood and the way young fathers in particular experience the emotional and psychological aspects of fatherhood (Marsiglio, 1993). Individuals' perceptions about father roles are probably shaped to some extent by the cultural images of fatherhood they encounter in movies, television, and advertising. Interpersonal experiences among family, friends, and coworkers will also serve to either reinforce these media images or challenge them. Peer groups can also be quite powerful in creating and reinforcing subcultural views about fatherhood that evolve independent of media images (Anderson, 1989; Sullivan, 1985). Thus, the processes by which young men incorporate or reject these images as part of their own identity standard need to be examined. In a related context, researchers should examine how young fathers model their own fathering style after specific individuals or a fragmented set of behaviors displayed by different individuals (see Daly, in press). It would be useful to assess, from a social learning perspective (Bandura, 1977), whether the mechanisms underlying this role modeling process vary by young men's social class and racial background.

The version of identity theory that links individuals' commitment level to their relationship with specific role partners may be useful for studying another aspect of young fathers' interpersonal experiences as well. It has become increasingly apparent in recent decades that many fathers' commitment to their children is contingent upon the quality of their relationship with their partner (Furstenberg, 1988; Marsiglio, 1991b, 1993). Research guided by this theoretical formulation could focus on the underlying factors and processes that entangle men's romantic partner and father role identities; and, in turn, inform policy or programmatic efforts designed to strengthen fathers' interest in their children independent of their relationship with their partner.

The research topics described above are consistent with the emerging philosophy that it is often desirable to secure and nurture young fathers' involvement with their children when they are newborns even if fathers are unable to make a significant financial contribution to them. It seems wise then to experiment with multifaceted and nonpunitive policies, media campaigns, educational curricula, and social programs that will foster young fathers' genuine, and therefore voluntary interest, in being more conscientious about their sexual/contraceptive behavior and willingness to be involved in their children's lives from the outset–if they do beget children (see Fox & Blanton, in press). These institutional efforts are likely to be most effective if they can promote meaningful peer support for values and norms associated with being a responsible father.

Young males' orientation toward the reproductive realm will need to be altered in a fundamental way for nonpunitive interventions to be successful. A combination of "carrot" and "stick" approaches, such as, the provision of flexible options to disadvantaged and school age fathers for fulfilling child support responsibilities and more aggressive paternity establishment and child support collection efforts, are probably necessary. Some scholars are quite skeptical though about the viability of any efforts to increase paternal involvement in a society such as the U.S. (Ehrenreich, 1983; see also Furstenberg, 1988 for a critique of specific "carrot" and "stick" strategies).

Those who develop social programs to increase paternal involvement should draw upon the experience of others who have already attempted to provide outreach programs for young fathers (Hendricks & Soloman, 1987; Sander & Rosen, 1987). Ideally, these initiatives should include a well-designed evaluation component to assess their short and long term consequences for young fathers, partners, and children (Mellgren, in press; Pirog-Good, in press). The outcome measures should include assessments of financial and informal child support as well as diverse well-being measures that apply to those immediately affected by the unplanned birth.

CONCLUSION

This review indicated how a number of interrelated macro and micro factors shape young nonresident fathers' responses to their early fatherhood experiences. The discussion explored some potential links between theory, research, and policy in this area by drawing upon identity theory. Significant advances in understanding young nonresident fathers will require that large scale studies employ innovative sampling strategies and more thorough measures of fathers' attitudes and experiences. While research on young nonresident fathers is limited in various ways, one of the consistent findings is that this group of fathers is more likely to be economically disadvantaged than their counterparts who either live with their child or have not fathered a child.

Future policies and programs intended to increase nonresident fathers' involvement with their children will continue to be fraught with political and legal controversy (Howe, in press; Walters & Abshire, this volume). The major policy challenge of the future will be to intensify efforts to increase nonresident fathers' commitment to their children while being sensitive to young mothers' parental rights. These initiatives will occur within a sociopolitical climate in which the larger ideology of fatherhood, including expectations about fathers' rights, obligations, and ideal behaviors, will continue to evolve in response to the ongoing public discourse about father roles. Hence, perceptions about fathers as a general category of parents will influence strategies designed to deal specifically with adolescent and young adult fathers.

NOTES

1. The term "single parent" is typically used to refer to a single parent household where one parent lives with his/her child(ren) and has sole or primary custody of the child. In general, this term lacks precision because the noncustodial or nonresident parent may assume a great deal of parental responsibility (or a cohabitating partner with no biological connection to the resident child may assume a similar role). Given the focus of my paper, I will use the terms "nonresident" and "absent" father interchangeably.

2. Some of the data I refer to discusses young fathers of a particular age range (e.g., 18-25) without specific reference to the age of the mother. I use these data because national data that specifically address young fathers whose partner is an adolescent mother are scarce.

3. The National Survey of Adolescent Males includes a more extensive series of attitudinal questions dealing with fatherhood issues; however, only 218 young men reported being a father as of their 1991 interview (Pleck, 1993).

4. In 1985, Wisconsin enacted the first law that made grandparents financially liable for the offspring of their children under 18 years of age (see Savage, 1987). The practical value of this law was limited because there were no provisions for bringing legal action against grandparents. Consequently, the law's application was restricted essentially to AFDC recipients. Although this law was not evaluated favorably by social service staff, district attorneys, or child support direc-

tors, future legislation in other states might also incorporate stricter enforcement provisions and build upon the premise that grandparents should be held accountable for their minor children's actions. However, if grandparents only have a financial responsibility for their grandchildren while their son is a minor, the overall benefit of this type of legislation will be limited.

REFERENCES

Adams, G. & Pittman, K. (1988). *Adolescent and young adult fathers: Problems and solutions*. Washington, D.C.: Children's Defense Fund, Adolescent Pregnancy Prevention Clearinghouse Report.

Anderson, E. (1989). Sex codes and family life among poor inner-city youth. *Annals of the American Academy of Political and Social Science, 501*, 59-78.

Aron, L. Y., Barnow, B. S., & McNaught, W. (1988). *Paternity establishment among never-married mothers: Estimates from the 1986 Current Population Survey Alimony and Child Support Supplement.* Report prepared by Lewin/ICF for Office of Income and Security Policy, ASPE/DHHS. November.

Bandura, A. (1977). *Social learning theory.* Englewood Cliffs, CA: Prentice-Hall.

Barth, R. P., Claycomb, M. & Loomis, A. (1988). Services to adolescent fathers. *Health and Social Work, 13*, 277-287.

Betsy, C. L., Holister, R. G., & Papageogious, M. R. (1985). *Youth employment training programs: The YEDPA years*. Committee on Youth Employment Programs, National Research Council. Washington, D.C.: National Academy Press.

Bianchi, S. M. (1995). The changing demographic and socioeconomic characteristics of single parent families. In S. Hanson, M. Heims, D. Julian, & M. Sussman (Eds.), *Marriage & Family Review, 20*(1/2) (pp. 71-97).

Burke, P. J. & Reitzes, D. C. (1981). The link between identity and role performance. *Social Psychology Quarterly, 44*, 83-92.

Burke, P. J. & Reitzes, D. C. (1991). An identity theory approach to commitment. *Social Psychology Quarterly, 54*, 239-251.

Card, J. J. & Wise, L. L. (1978). Teenage mothers and teenage fathers: The impact of early childbearing on the parents' personal and professional lives. *Family Planning Perspectives, 10*, 199-205.

Cervera, N. (1991). Unwed teenage pregnancy: Family relationships with the father of the baby. *Families in Society: The Journal of Contemporary Human Services, 72*, 29-37.

Cherlin, A. (1981). *Marriage, divorce, remarriage: Social trends in the United States*. Cambridge, MA: Harvard University Press.

Child Support Report (1990). Involved from the start: In-hospital paternity establishment." *Child Support XII (7)*, Publication of the National Child Support Enforcement Reference Center MS OCSE/RC, 370 L'Enfant Promenade, S.W., Washington, D.C.

Christmon, K. (1990). Parental responsibility of African-American unwed adolescent fathers. *Adolescence, XXV*, 645-653.

Clark, S. D., Jr., Zabin, L. S., & Hardy, J. G. (1984). Sex, contraception and parenthood: Experience and attitudes among urban black young men. *Family Planning Perspectives, 16*, 77-82.

Daly, K. (in press). Reshaping fatherhood: Finding the models. *Journal of Family Issues*.

Danzinger, S. & Radin, N. (1990). Absent does not equal uninvolved: Predictors of fathering in teen mother families. *Journal of Marriage and the Family, 52*, 636-642.

Danzinger, S. K., Kastner, C. K., & Nickel, T. (1993). The problems of child support policies. In T. Ooms & R. Lerman (Eds.), *Young unwed fathers: Changing roles and emergent policies*. Philadelphia, PA: Temple University Press (pp. 235-250).

Ehrenreich, B. (1983). *The hearts of men: American dreams and the flight from commitment*. New York: Anchor Press.

Family Impact Seminar (1990). Encouraging fathers to be responsible: Paternity establishment, child support and JOBS strategies. Background Briefing Report, The AAMFT Research and Education Foundation, Washington, D.C.

Foote, N. N. (1951). Identification as the basis for a theory of motivation. *American Sociological Review, 26*, 14-21.

Fox, G. L. & Blanton, P. W. (1995). Noncustodial fathers following divorce. In S. Hanson, M. Heims, D. Julian, & M. Sussman (Eds.), *Marriage & Family Review, 20*(1/2) (pp. 257-282).

Freeman, E. (1989). Adolescent fathers in urban communities: Exploring their needs and role in preventing pregnancy. *Journal of Social Work and Human Sexuality, 8*, 113-131.

Freeman, R. B. & Holzer, H. J. (1985). Young blacks and jobs–What we now know. *Public Interest, 768*, 18-31.

Furstenberg, F. F., Jr. (1988). Good dads–bad dads: Two faces of fatherhood. In A. Cherlin (Ed.), *The changing American family and public policy* (pp. 193-218). Washington, DC: Urban Institute.

Furstenberg, F. F., Jr. (1991). Daddies and fathers: Men who do for their children and men who don't. Paper prepared for the Manpower Demonstration Research Corporation.

Furstenberg, F. F., Jr. & Harris, K. M. (1993). When and why fathers matter: Impacts of father involvement on the children of adolescent mothers. In R. Lerman & T. Ooms (Eds.), *Young unwed fathers: Changing roles and emerging policies*. Philadelphia, PA: Temple University Press (pp. 117-138).

Garfinkel, I. & McLanahan, S. S. (1986). *Single mothers and their children: A new American dilemma*. Washington, DC: Urban Institute.

Hanson, S. L., Morrison, D. R., & Ginsburg, A. L. (1989). The antecedents of teenage fatherhood. *Demography, 26*, 579-596.

Hardy, J. B., Duggan, A. K., Masnyk, K. & Pearson, C. (1989). Fathers of children born to young urban mothers. *Family Planning Perspectives, 21*, 159-163, 187.

Hayes, C. (1987). *Risking the Future: Adolescent sexuality, pregnancy, and child-bearing*. Washington, DC: National Academy Press.

Heiss, D. R. (1979). *Understanding events: Affect and the construction of social action*. Cambridge: Cambridge University Press.

Heiss, D. R. (1988). Affect control theory: Concepts and model. In L. Smith-Lovin & D. R. Heiss (Eds.), *Analyzing social interaction: Advances in affect control theory* (pp. 1-34). New York: Gordon and Breach.

Heiss, J. (1981). Women's values regarding marriage and the family. In H. McAdoo (Ed.), *Black families* (pp. 186-197). Beverly Hills, CA: Sage.

Hendricks, L. E. & Solomon, A. M. (1987). Reaching black male adolescent parents through nontraditional techniques. *Child & Youth Services, 9*, 111-124.

Howe, R. (1993). Legal rights and obligations: An uneven evolution." In R. Lerman and T. Ooms (Eds.), *Young unwed fathers: Changing roles and emergent policies*. Philadelphia, PA: Temple University Press (pp. 141-169).

Ihinger-Tallman, M., Pasley, K., & Buehler, C. (in press). Developing a middle-range theory of father involvement postdivorce. *Journal of Family Issues*.

Johnson, C. & Sum, A. (1987). *Declining earnings of young men: Their relation to poverty, teen pregnancy, and family formation*. Washington, D.C.: Children's Defense Fund, Adolescent Pregnancy Prevention Clearinghouse Report.

Joshi, N. P. & Battle, S. F. (1990). Adolescent fathers: An approach for intervention. *Journal of Health & Social Policy, 1*, 17-33.

Klinman, D. G., Sander, J. H., Longo, K. R., & Martinez, L. P. (1985). *Reaching and serving the teenage father*. The Teen Parent Collaboration. N.Y., Bank Street College of Education.

Lamb, M. E., Elster, A. B., Peters, L. J., Kahn, J. S., & Tavare, J. (1986). Characteristics of married and unmarried adolescent mothers and their partners. *Journal of Youth and Adolescence, 15*, 487-496.

Lerman, R. I. (1986). Who are the young absent fathers? *Youth & Society, 18*, 3-27.

Lerman, R. I. (1993). Employment patterns of unwed fathers and public policy. In R. Lerman and T. Ooms (Eds.), *Young unwed fathers: Changing roles and emerging policies*. Philadelphia, PA: Temple University Press (pp. 27-61).

Lerman, R. I. (1993). A national profile of young unwed fathers. In R. Lerman and T. Ooms (Eds.), *Young unwed fathers: Changing roles and emergent policies*. Philadelphia, PA: Temple University Press (pp. 27-61).

Marsiglio, W. (1987). Adolescent fathers in the United States: Their initial living arrangements, marital experience and educational outcomes. *Family Planning Perspectives, 19*, 240-251.

Marsiglio, W. (1988). Commitment to social fatherhood: Predicting adolescent males' intentions to live with their child and partner. *Journal of Marriage and the Family, 50*, 427-441.

Marsiglio, W. (1989). Adolescent males' pregnancy resolution preferences and family formation intentions: Does family background make a difference for blacks and whites. *Journal of Adolescent Research, 4*, 214-237.

Marsiglio, W. (1991a). Pregnant teens and pregnancy resolution decisions: The role of male partners. *TEC Networks*, Newsletter of the Too-Early-Childbearing Networks of Programs funded by the Charles Stewart Mott Foundation, June.

Marsiglio, W. (1991b). Male procreative consciousness and responsibility: A conceptual analysis and research agenda. *Journal of Family Issues, 12*, 268-290.

Marsiglio, W. (1993). Adolescent males' orientation toward paternity and contraception. *Family Planning Perspectives, 25*, 22-31.

Marsiglio, W. (in press). Contemporary scholarship on fatherhood: Culture, identity, and conduct. *Journal of Family Issues.*

Marsiglio, W. & Menaghan, E. G. (1990). Pregnancy resolution and family formation: Understanding gender differences in adolescents' preferences and beliefs. *Journal of Family Issues, 11*, 313-333.

Marsiglio, W. & Scanzoni, J. H. (1990). Pregnant and parenting black adolescents: Theoretical and policy perspectives. In A. R. Stiffman & L. Davis (Eds.), *Advances in adolescent mental health: Ethnic issues* (pp. 220-244). Newbury Park, CA: Sage.

McCall, G. & Simmons, J. L. (1966). *Identities and Interactions*. New York: The Free Press.

Mellgren, L. (1993). Creating federal leadership in research and policy development. In R. Lerman and T. Ooms (Eds.), *Young unwed fathers: Changing roles and emergent policies*. Philadelphia, PA: Temple University Press (pp. 193-212).

Meyer, D. R. & Garasky, S. (1993). Custodial fathers: Myths, realities, and child support policy. *Journal of Marriage and the Family, 55*, 73-89.

Moore, K. A., Simms, M. C., & Betsey, C. L. (1986). *Choice and circumstance: Racial difference in adolescent sexuality and fertility*. New Brunswick, NJ: Transaction Books.

Mott, F. L. (1983). *Fertility-related data in the 1982 National Longitudinal Surveys of Work Experience of Youth: An evaluation of data quality and some preliminary analytical results*. Columbus, Ohio: Ohio State University, Center for Human Resource Research.

National Center for Health Statistics (1983). Advance report of final natality statistics, 1981. *Monthly Vital Statistics Report, 32(9).*

National Center for Health Statistics (1993). Advance report of final natality statistics, 1990. *Monthly Vital Statistics Report, 41(9).*

National Urban League (1987). *Adolescent male responsibility pregnancy prevention & parenting program: A program development guide*. New York: Author.

Nichols-Casebolt, A. & Garfinkel, I. (1991). Trends in paternity adjudications and child support awards. *Social Science Quarterly, 72*, 83-97.

O'Connell, M. & Rogers, C. C. (1984). Out-of-wedlock births, premarital pregnancies and their effect on family formation and dissolution. *Family Planning Perspectives, 16*, 157-162.

Parke, R. D. & Neville, B. (1987). Teenage fatherhood. In S. Hofferth & C. Hayes (Eds.), *Risking the future: Adolescent sexuality, pregnancy and childbearing (Vol. 2)* (pp. 145-173). Washington, D.C.: National Academy Press.

Pirog-Good, M. A. (1993). In-kind contributions as child support: The teen alternative parenting program. In R. Lerman and T. Ooms (Eds.), *Young unwed fathers: Changing roles and emergent policies*. Philadelphia, PA: Temple University Press (pp. 251-266).

Pittman, K. & Adams, G. (1988). *What about the boys? Teenage pregnancy prevention strategies*. Washington, D.C.: Children's Defense Fund, Adolescent Pregnancy Prevention Clearinghouse Report.

Pleck, J. H. (1993). Personal communication, January.

Public/Private Ventures (1990). *The young unwed fathers demonstration project: A status report*. Philadelphia, PA: Public/Private Ventures, 399 Market Street, 19106.

Rivera-Casale, C., Klerman, L. V., & Manela, R. (1984). The relevance of child-support enforcement to school-age parents. *Child Welfare, LXII*, 521-532.

Rozie-Battle, J. L. (1989). Adolescent fathers: The question of paternity. *National Urban League Review, 12*, 129-137.

St. John, C. & Rowe, D. (1990). Adolescent background and fertility norms: Implications for racial differences in early childbearing. *Social Science Quarterly, 17*, 152-162.

Sander, J. & Rosen, J. (1987). Teenage fathers: Working with the neglected partner in adolescent childbearing. *Family Planning Perspectives, 19*, 107-110.

Savage, B. D. (1987). *Child support and teen parents*. Washington, DC: Children's Defense Fund, Adolescent Pregnancy Prevention Clearinghouse.

Seltzer, J. A. (1991). Relationships between fathers and children who live apart: The father's role after separation. *Journal of Marriage and the Family, 53*, 79-101.

Smith, A. (1989). Responsibility of the African-American church as a source of support for adolescent fathers. *The Urban League Review, 12*, 83-90.

Smith-Lovin, L. & Heise, D. R. (1988). *Analyzing social interaction: Advances in affect control theory*. New York: Gordon and Breach.

Smollar, J. & Ooms, T. (1987). *Young unwed fathers: Research review, policy dilemmas and options*. Summary Report to U.S. Department of Health and Human Services. Family Impact Seminar, Catholic University of America.

Stryker, S. (1968). Identity salience and role performance. *Journal of Marriage and the Family, 4*, 558-564.

Stryker, S. (1980). *Symbolic interactionism: A social structural version*. Menlo Park: Benjamin Cummings.

Stryker, S. (1987). The vitalization of symbolic interactionism. *Social Psychology Quarterly, 50*, 83-94.

Sullivan, M. L. (1985). *Teen fathers in the inner city: An exploratory ethnographic study*. New York: Vera Institute of Justice.

Sullivan, M. L. (1990). *The male role in teenage pregnancy and parenting: New directions public policy*. New York: Vera Institute of Justice.

Teti, D. M. & Lamb, M. (1986). Sex-role learning and adolescent fatherhood. In

A. B. Elster & M. E. Lamb (Eds.), *Adolescent Fatherhood* (pp. 19-30). Hillsdale, NJ: Lawrence Erlbaum Associates.

U.S. Bureau of the Census. (1991). Child support and alimony: 1989. *Current Population Reports*, Series P-60, No. 173. Washington, D.C.: U.S. Government Printing Office.

Walters, L. H. & Abshire, C. R. (1995). Single parenthood and the law. In S. Hanson, M. Heims, D. Julian, & M. Sussman (Eds.), *Marriage & Family Review, 20*(1/2) (pp. 161-188).

Watson, F. I. & Kelly, M. J. (1989). Targeting the at-risk male: A strategy for adolescent pregnancy prevention. *Journal of the National Medical Association, 81*, 453-456.

Wattenberg, E. (1988). Establishing paternity for nonmarital children. *Public Welfare, Summer*, 9-48.

Wattenberg, E. (1993). Paternity actions and young fathers. In R. Lerman and T. Ooms (Eds.), *Young unwed fathers: Changing roles and emergent policies*. Philadelphia, PA: Temple University Press (pp. 213-234).

Wattenberg, E., Brewer, R., & Resnick, M. (1991). A study of paternity decisions of young unmarried parents. Final report to the Ford Foundation, February 12.

Westney, O. E., Cole, J., & Munford, T. L. (1988). The effects of prenatal education intervention on unwed prospective adolescent fathers. *Journal of Adolescent Health Care, 9*, 214-218.

Zayas, L. H. & Schinke, S. P. (1987). Hispanic adolescent fathers: At risk and underresearched. *Children and Youth Services Review, 9*, 235-248.

APPENDIX

Resources on Social Policy Issues and Intervention Strategies

Write to: Publications, Children's Defense Fund, 122 C Street, N. W., Washington, D.C., 20001, (202) 628-8787 for the following publications:

a. Adams, Gina & Pittman, Karen (1988). *Adolescent and young adult fathers: Problems and solutions.* Adolescent Pregnancy Prevention Clearinghouse Report.
b. Pittman, Karen & Adams, Gina (1988). *What about the boys? Teenage pregnancy prevention strategies.* Adolescent Pregnancy Prevention Clearinghouse Report.
c. Savage, Barbara (1987). *Child support and teen parents.* Adolescent Pregnancy Prevention Clearinghouse Report.

Write to: Family Support Administration, Office of the Administrator, Suite 600, 370 L'Enfant Promenade, S. W., Washington, D.C., 20447 for: Smollar, Jacqueline & Ooms, Theodora (1987). *Young unwed fathers: Research review, policy dilemmas and options.* Summary Report to U.S. Department of Health and Human Services.

Write to: Family Impact Seminar, American Association for Marriage and Family Therapy, Research and Education Foundation, 1100 Seventeenth Street, N.W., The Tenth Floor, Washington, D. C., 20036 or phone (202)-467-5114 for: Family Impact Seminar (1990). Encouraging fathers to be responsible: Paternity establishment, child support and JOBS strategies. Background Briefing Report, The AAMFT Research and Education Foundation, Washington, D.C.

Chapter 16

Context and Surrogate Parenting Among Contemporary Grandparents

Linda M. Burton
Peggye Dilworth-Anderson
Cynthia Merriwether-deVries

SUMMARY. This paper provides a conceptual discussion of the relationship between the surrogate parenting role of contemporary American grandparents and temporal, developmental, and ethnic/racial contexts of the life course. Grandparents who are surrogate parents, either operate as co-parents by assisting their adult children in the rearing of their offspring, or they assume total responsibility for providing the necessary care and socialization their grandchildren require when their parents cannot. The surrogate parenting responsibilities of grandparents are hypothesized to be affected by: (1) temporal context, which concerns the sequencing and synchronization of the assumption of surrogate parenting responsibilities by grandparents relative to their age, peer relationships, and other social role respon-

Linda M. Burton is Professor in the Department of Human Development and Sociology, The Pennsylvania State University, University Park, PA 16802. Peggye Dilworth-Anderson is Professor of Child Development and Family Relations, University of North Carolina, Greensboro, NC 27412. Cynthia Merriwether-deVries is a Doctoral Candidate in the Department of Human Development and Family Studies, The Pennsylvania State University, University Park, PA 16802.

[Haworth co-indexing entry note]: "Context and Surrogate Parenting Among Contemporary Grandparents." Burton, Linda M., Peggye Dilworth-Anderson, and Cynthia Merriwether-deVries. Co-published simultaneously in *Marriage & Family Review* (The Haworth Press, Inc.) Vol. 20, No. 3/4, 1995, pp. 349-366; and: *Single Parent Families: Diversity, Myths and Realities* (ed: Shirley M. H. Hanson et al.) The Haworth Press, Inc., 1995, pp. 349-366. Multiple copies of this article/chapter may be purchased from The Haworth Document Delivery Center [1-800-3-HAWORTH; 9:00 a.m. - 5:00 p.m. (EST)].

sibilities; (2) developmental context, which focuses on how grandparents' personal development is hindered or facilitated by the assumption of the surrogate parenting role; and (3) ethnic/racial context, which refers to the cultural influences grandparents bring to the surrogate parenting role. The implications of these contexts for the surrogate parenting role of grandparents relative to research, policy, programs, and education are discussed.

KEYWORDS. Grandparents/grandparenting, Surrogate parents, Parenting, Single parenting, Primary parenting

INTRODUCTION

After prolonged neglect, grandparenthood is now receiving considerable attention in the literature on adulthood, family development, and intergenerational relations (for a current review see Tinsley & Parke, 1982; Barranti, 1985; Bengtson & Robertson, 1985; Troll, 1985; Hagestad & Lang, 1986; Roberto, 1990; Kivett, 1991; McGreal, in press). The growth of conceptual discussions and empirical research on grandparenthood is owing, in part, to the dramatic decline in mortality during the last century (Watkins, Menken, & Bongaarts, 1987; Bengston, Rosenthal, & Burton, 1990; Himes, 1992). Life expectancy has increased, on average, 27 years since 1900 (Uhlenberg, 1980; Gee, 1987). The number of people, 65 and older, has more than doubled in the last century. In the U.S., 12.2 million (8.1%) (1950) fit this category; in 1988, greater than 30.4 million people (12.4%) did (National Center for Health Statistics, 1991). This extension of the life course has direct implications for the duration of the grandparent role (Ruggles & Goeken, 1992; Burton & Dilworth-Anderson, 1991). For example, in the early nineteenth century, given higher rates of mortality at younger ages, grandparents and grandchildren may have only shared a decade of life together (Juster & Vinovskis, 1987). By comparison, today's grandparents are likely to witness their grandchild's transition to adulthood as well as the early years of life of their great-grandchildren–a period of time which could extend well beyond 30 years (Hagestad & Burton, 1985; Hagestad, 1988).

While the lengthening of the grandparental life course has generated much of the current discourse on grandparenthood in the social science literature, several additional demographic trends as well as challenging family circumstances have resulted in a plethora of popular media and social service agency attention to the role (SysteMetrics/McGraw-Hill, 1989). The demographic trends include increases in parental joblessness

(Wilson, 1987; Pearson, Hunter, Ensminger, & Kellam, 1990), teenage "out-of-wedlock" childbearing (Smith, 1975; Flaherty, 1988; Burton, 1990; Furstenberg, Brooks-Gunn, & Chase-Lansdale, 1989; Apfel & Seitz, 1991), divorce (Ahron, & Bowman, 1982; Matthews & Sprey, 1984; Cherlin & Furstenberg, 1986; Johnson, 1993), single-parent households (Wilson, 1986; Garfinkel & McLanahan, 1986; Hogan, Hao, & Parish, 1990), and poverty (Bianchi, 1990; Chase-Lansdale & Brooks-Gunn, in press). The family circumstances comprise chronic illnesses of grandchildren (Dilworth-Anderson, in press), the illicit drug addiction of young-adult parents (Burton, 1992; Minkler & Roe, 1992), and the incarceration of young mothers and fathers (Gibbs, 1988). These demographic trends and family circumstances are often cited as factors that affect the assumption of a specific type of grandparent role–surrogate parenting.

Grandparents who are surrogate parents either operate as co-parents by assisting their adult children in the rearing of their offspring, or they assume total responsibility for providing the necessary care and socialization their grandchildren require when the children's parents cannot (Burton & Merriwether-deVries, 1993; Chescheir, 1981; Tomlin & Passman, 1989). The duration of the surrogate parent role is often variable. In some situations grandparents may only assume short-term responsibility for parenting their grandchildren. In others, grandparents assume permanent responsibility for their grandchildren, often raising them from infancy to adulthood. Grandparents also can be single persons and thus operate as single parents in their surrogate role.

The popular media and social service agency accounts of grandparents who are surrogate parents suggest that there is an urgent need to explore the parameters of this role (Burton, 1992). Despite this popular attention, however, there has been relatively little systematic study of the scope and nature of grandmothers and grandfathers who parent their grandchildren. What little is known about the role appears in the ethnographic and historical literature on extended kin relationships among ethnic minority families (Burton & Sorenson, 1990; Jarrett, 1990). This literature suggests that how grandparents negotiate the surrogate parent role is largely dependent on contextual factors. For example, ethnographic research on African-American families report that cultural context has historically influenced the frequent assumption of parenting responsibilities by African-American grandparents (Frazier, 1939; Aschenbrenner, 1975; Huling, 1978; Lesnoff-Caravaglia, 1982; Scott, 1991; Stack & Burton, 1993).

This paper provides a conceptual discussion of three contextual factors that may influence the surrogate parenting role of grandparents in contemporary American society: temporal, developmental, and ethnicity/race.

Using a life course perspective, *temporal context*, as it is discussed here, focuses on the timing of entry to the role–that is the sequencing and synchronization of the assumption of surrogate parenting responsibilities by grandparents relative to their age, peer relationships, and other social role responsibilities (Elder, 1987; Hagestad, 1990). *Developmental context* concerns (1) how the assumption of parenting responsibilities either hinders or facilitates the individual development of grandparents, and (2) the compatibility of developmental stages between the parenting grandparents and the grandchildren they are rearing (Burton & Sorenson, 1993). The *ethnic/racial context* refers to the cultural influences Hispanic, African-, Asian-, European-, and Native Americans bring to the surrogate parenting role (Dilworth-Anderson, Burton, & Boulin-Johnson, 1993; Dilworth-Anderson, Burton, & Turner, 1993). Each of these three contexts will be elaborated in the following discussion.

TEMPORAL CONTEXT

Since the 1960s, the impact of time on social roles and interactions has received considerable attention from social scientists, particularly those interested in the life course perspective (Bengeston & Allen, 1993; Clausen, 1986; Elder, 1985; Hagestad & Neugarten, 1985; Hogan, 1987; Kertzer, 1983; Plath, 1980; Rossi, 1980). Studies of the life course "trace individuals as social personas and their pathways along an age-differentiated, socially marked sequence of transitions" (Hagestad, 1990, p. 151).

In understanding temporal context and the life course, the issue of timing, that is, the sequencing and synchronization of major life role transitions such as marriage, parenthood, and grandparenthood, is central. The timing of these role transitions, in some societies, is gauged by social timetables. Social timetables are shared ideas of when key life changes ought to happen. They serve as guides to individuals about what the appropriate or inappropriate times are to enter and exit specific roles over the course of life (Hogan, 1978; Neugarten, Moore, & Lowe, 1965; Wood, 1971).

Current research suggests that an inappropriate or "off-time entry" to certain roles may be associated with negative consequences for the individual and subsequently the family (Burton & Bengston, 1985; Giorsca, 1972; Seltzer, 1976; Brim & Ryff, 1980; Nydegger, 1973; Elder & Rockwell, 1976). Neugarten (1970:86) comments:

> It is the unanticipated, not the anticipated, which is likely to represent the traumatic event. Major stresses are caused by events that

> upset the sequence and rhythm of the expected life cycle, as when the death of a parent comes in adolescence rather than in middle age; when the birth of a child is too early or too late; when occupational achievement is delayed; when the empty nest, grandparenthood, retirement, major illness, or widowhood occur off-time.

The few empirical studies that do exist on the surrogate parenting role of grandparents in contemporary American society suggest that this role is invariably assumed "off-time" or as the product of unanticipated non-normative life events. With respect to the "off-time" nature of the role, Burton's (1985) study of young great-grandmothers who assume the primary care for the offspring of their adolescent grandchildren, reports that her respondents experienced considerable stress given the overload of role demands associated with their "later life" childrearing responsibilities. Burton and Merriwether-deVries (1992), in an analysis of the challenges and rewards of surrogate parenting among 101 African-American grandparents and great-grandparents, identified four sources of stress related to the off-time assumption of their role. Grandparents who assumed the role either off-time or as a function of non-normative life events in the family often experienced (1) a pile-up of family responsibilities, (2) difficulty in keeping up with the school, social, and physical activities of their grandchildren, (3) financial hardships, and (4) not enough time to meet their own personal needs. Despite these challenges, however, these grandparents and great-grandparents indicated that their surrogate parenting roles also had rewards. The rewards included the grandparents' opportunity to (1) have yet another chance to raise a child right, (2) nurture family legacies through the lives of their grandchildren and, (3) receive the love and companionship of a child.

In terms of unanticipated, non-normative life events, Minkler (1992) and Burton (1992), in studies of the impact of illicit drug addiction among young adult parents on the surrogate parenting role of grandparents, have identified high levels of stress among their respondents. Dilworth-Anderson (in press), in a study of the role grandparents assume in the care of their grandchildren with sickle cell anemia, did not directly address the issue of stress, but reported that grandparents were heavily involved for long durations of time in co-parenting these chronically ill children. Dilworth-Anderson suggests that grandparents who perform this role may, in the long run, need social service interventions to assist them in continuing to play this high profile, demanding role in the lives of their grandchildren.

An additional aspect of temporal context that is important for understanding the role of grandparents who are surrogate parents concerns what Burton and Sorensen (1993) identify as peer time. Peer time is the temporal spacing of role acquisitions among age-mates, friends, or colleagues.

The relationship between peer time and the surrogate parent role is hypothesized as follows: When a group of age-mates, friends or colleagues assume primary responsibility for the care of their grandchildren at about the same age and time, they are more likely to view their roles more positively than those individuals who do not have peers that are also surrogate grandparents. Peers who are surrogate parents are more likely to foster feelings of group solidarity and be supportive to one another because of their common life experience.

Burton and Sorensen (1993), reporting findings from their ethnographic study of the caregiving responsibilities of African-American grandparents, indicate that those respondents who did not have peers that were also surrogate parents felt isolated and "out of synch" with respect to the roles their age-mates engaged in. In contrast, those grandparents who did have peers that were also surrogate parents felt a stronger sense of social support because as one of their respondents commented that "her friends were dealing with the same frustrations and joys in raising her grandchildren as she was."

DEVELOPMENTAL CONTEXT

The second contextual factor influencing the surrogate parenting role of grandparents is developmental. Developmental context concerns (1) how the assumption of parenting responsibilities either hinders or facilitates the individual development of grandparents, and (2) the compatibility of developmental stages between the parenting grandparents and the grandchildren they are rearing (Burton & Sorenson, 1993). To explore this dimension of context, themes from developmental psychology and the life course perspective are used.

Authors from both developmental psychology and the life course perspective discuss notions of "the normal expectable life"–a set of seasons with characteristic preoccupations, changes, challenges, and rewards (Levinson, 1978). In psychodynamic approaches to individual life time, the emphasis is on how developmental changes and the social context in combination present individuals with a series of developmental tasks (Erickson, 1982; Havighurst, 1972). Erickson (1963, 1980) for example, described late adolescence and young adulthood as a period in which personal identity and intimacy must be achieved, whereas the central theme in middle age is attaining a sense of generativity. Havighurst (1972) described the developmental tasks of young adulthood as involving the differentiation from one's family of origin and the establishment of a new family on one's own. In contrast, the developmental tasks for late life involve attaining integrity (Erickson, 1980), adjusting to the limitations created by diminished physical strength, shrinking social networks, and reduced income (Havighurst, 1972). Inherent in each of these developmental tasks is the process of negotiating and resolving psychosocial tensions at each stage of life.

Within the life course perspective, the emphasis in examining developmental stages is on role transitions. As discussed earlier, role transitions often follow timetables and established sequences. Individuals build expectations about what life will bring, and crises are often presented by events that represent breaches of such expectations. Thus, the timing of taking on the surrogate parent role has implications for the psychosocial development of the grandparents and grandchildren. For example, the timing of assuming primary responsibility for the care of a grandchild may in some cases, interfere with, and in others facilitate the immediate developmental tasks individuals face in different periods of their lives.

The process of negotiating developmental tasks is also affected by the individual's involvement with other people, with institutions, and with the society at large (Kivnick, 1985). The assumption of "off time" parenting responsibilities by grandparents can conflict with some of these involvements and thereby hinder the achievement of developmental tasks. For example, the main tasks of young adulthood involve establishing an identity, differentiating from the family, and achieving intimacy. Burton (1992), in a study of "early" grandparents age 27-36 who assumed the role of principal care provider for their grandchildren, reports that the majority of her respondents felt that they had not had enough time in their lives without the responsibilities of childrearing "to grow up, do what other people their ages were doing, truly learn about who they were as individuals, and make decisions about what they wanted in life."

The second aspect of developmental context to explore is the compatibility of developmental stages between the grandparent and their grandchildren. Kivnick (1985) argues that grandparenting represents an "age-appropriate involvement through which the grandparent may reface issues directly related to parenting (Generativity versus Stagnation), and perhaps less directly related to such other tensions as Identity versus Identity Confusion; Industry versus Inferiority; Autonomy versus Shame and Doubt" (p. 157). Thus grandparenthood may give individuals the opportunity to renew earlier psychosocial balances. Reciprocally, grandchildren, as they move through developmental stages, may have the opportunity to "pre-face" the tensions they will experience later in life through interacting with their grandparents.

Current research suggests that from a developmental perspective, the connectedness between grandparents and their grandchildren are particularly beneficial for teenagers (Dellmann-Jenkins, Papalia & Lopez, 1987; Matthew and Sprey, 1985). Baranowski (1982) suggests that close relationships between teens and their grandparents may be beneficial to the successful resolution of adolescent's identity issues. Elkind (1990) comments:

> For teenagers, grandparents can be a sensitive sounding board for life plans, a nonjudgmental listener to their fears of personal inadequacy or failure, and a wonderfully appreciative audience for their performances and achievements. (p. 169)

The research cited concerning the benefits of the synchrony between the developmental stages of grandparents and grandchildren principally explores the relationship among white middle class families where grandparents do not necessarily assume the surrogate or co-parent role. Consequently, a number of questions emerge with respect to developmental synchrony in the situation of surrogate parents. This lack of specific data raises several important questions: Under what surrogate parenting conditions does developmental compatibility occur for grandparents and grandchildren? Is the developmental life course similar for children who are raised by their grandparents as compared to those who were raised by their parents? What are the developmental rewards and liabilities for grandparents and grandchildren in surrogate parent relationships? Are there ethnic/racial similarities and differences in developmental synchrony between grandchildren and their surrogate parents?

ETHNIC/RACIAL CONTEXT

The third contextual factor influencing grandparenting is ethnic/racial. While the past decade has led to an increased awareness of the importance of considering ethnicity and race in discussions of grandparenting, conceptual and empirical literature in this area remains relatively sparse (Burton, Dilworth-Anderson, & Bengston, 1992). The existing literature discusses the issue of the surrogate parenting role of grandparents in the context of cultural family norms. For example, among the Navajo and Apache (tribes) kinship patterns proscribe specific circumstances in which grandparents must serve as parent. Within their matrilocal family structure the grandmother is the core of the family and performs the roles that modern Americans associate with the mother (Ryan, 1981).

The Mescalro Apache nation assigns a similar role to the elderly male. In this society the tasks of parenting and child care are prized and revered.

This pattern has been observed for several decades of reservation resident Native-Americans. While little research has been done to explore urban resident Native-American family configurations, speculation is that these patterns are still valued even if not actively practiced. It is clear from the research and empirical evidence that grandparents, and especially grandmothers, are central figures among many nations and that parenting as grandparents is considered normative (John, 1988).

Ethnographic research within urban northeastern Puerto Rican communities also illustrates this point. Foster and surrogate parenting is culturally proscribed even though intergenerational co-residence is not as common as it is for other Hispanic family groups. The role is legitimized by the linguistic recognition of "hijos de crianza" or informal adoption (Sanchez-Ayendez, 1988) and the relationship "padres de crianza" or parents of rearing (Jarrett, 1990). These phrases are often used to refer to, though not exclusively reserved for, the grandparents. Family interdependence and reciprocity are aspects of the Puerto Rican-American family that some earlier studies indicated may be declining (Sanchez-Ayendez, 1988). More recent work indicates that strong kinship bonds are clearly articulated as normative values and practices (Jarrett, 1990).

Cultural components of the Mexican-American family system contribute to increased access to grandparents. Among Mexican-American families, the primacy of the maternal role enhances the tendencies toward expressions of familialism that include surrogate parenting for grandchildren (Jarrett, 1990). High levels of intergenerational co-residence and socio-emotional exchanges also contribute by providing increased access to grandparents (Rogler & Cooney, 1989).

Asian-American families of Korean and Vietnamese origin also prize family cohesion but they are often manifested in forms that differ from the groups previously discussed. Specific cultural components such as the reluctance of the Vietnamese elderly to learn English and abandon the traditional practices (Van Tran, 1988) may reduce their effectiveness in the role of parenting grandparents. Vietnamese-American elderly are less likely to hold the position of reverence in the family that would be bestowed in Vietnam. Co-residence of Vietnamese families does not provide the same level of interaction among family members for three primary reasons. First, the tendency of Vietnamese young people is to not learn the language of their elders; therefore grandparents and grandchildren who do not speak the same language are not prime candidates for a caregiving relationship. Second, many Vietnamese are dual worker families who work for extended periods of time out of the home. Third, the elderly are considered to possess out-moded and obsolete knowledge in most aspects of life. Additionally, there are high levels of both physical and social isolation for the elderly in Vietnamese communities further reducing the ability to parent as grandparents (Van Tran, 1988).

Korean-Americans are also less likely to assume the role of parenting grandparent. In the case of this ethnic group the sanctions are more structural than cultural. Korean-Americans are more likely to be new immigrants, and less likely to reside in geographically segregated communities and have weaker ties to their native Korean cultural practices. Demographic profiles of Korean-Americans also indicate a higher number of young single person residences and nuclear families than extended or intergenerational families (Gap Min, 1988). These factors reduce the likelihood that grandparents are present to assume the parenting functions.

The socio/historical literature on the life course of extended black families suggests that many black grandparents have served as surrogate parents to their grandchildren (Burton & Sorensen, 1990; Frazier, 1939; Huling, 1978; Lesnoff-Caravaglia, 1982; Scott, 1991; White, 1985). The surrogate parent role was often enacted by grandparents in response to cultural precedence, historical events, and the needs of extended kin (Hill & Schackleford, 1977; Jackson, 1971; Wilson, 1985). For example, Jacqueline Jones (1985) notes that during the post-Civil War migration of blacks:

> Grandmothers cared for their children's children and all three benefitted, the elderly women gained companionship and, in some cases, a measure of economic support; their children were free to search for jobs elsewhere, and the grandchildren lived under the watchful eye of a relative who was often as strict . . . and as kind a person as she knew to be. (p. 228)

Similarly, Faustine Jones (1983) describes black grandmothers during the early 19th century to the mid-1960s as the lofty occupants of the extended kin surrogate parent role. She writes:

> As she [the black grandmother] grew older, she was even more respected and esteemed for her knowledge and for her contributions to people, for she willingly helped neighbors, as well as her own kin. In fact, it was not uncommon for the black grandmother to accept and rear, in addition to her own grandchildren, a niece, a nephew, a cousin, or even an orphan who has nowhere to turn for societal aid. (p. 20)

Although surrogate parenting by black grandparents has received the most attention from researchers, it should not be viewed as the normative grandparental role among older black Americans. Future studies of grandparenting among blacks must expand the current knowledge base by acknowledging heterogeneity in the role. Research must examine grandparenthood not only in highly dependent, at-risk intergenerational family networks, but also in families whose structure and composition offer alternative options for grandparental behavior.

Of all the ethnic groups studied, surrogate parenting among European-Americans has received virtually no attention. However, given that European-Americans are experiencing much of the same demographic changes (e.g., increase in divorce, and single parenthood) that other ethnic groups are, it seems plausible that such studies should soon be conducted.

IMPLICATIONS

Implications for Research

These data imply the need to explore the three contextual factors outlined in relation to grandparents rearing their grandchildren, taking account of both the grandparents as parents and the children they rear. Grandparents, both in their longevity and role expectations, are increasing in current society, therefore their influence on the quality of family life needs to be known. For example, a relevant question is: What are the health outcomes for chronically ill children who have both parents and grandparents caring for them? Another example of a relevant research issue to explore is the overall impact on the minor children of grandparents moving in and out of the parenting role with the biological parents. Overall, examination and testing of family theories and family practice models in relation to the intergenerational transitions and parenting activities involved in grandparents serving as surrogate parents could produce major changes in those theories, as well as in concepts and practice models.

Implications for Practice

Given the context of grandparents serving as both surrogate (replacement) parents and as co-parents to minor children, practitioners must carefully determine the role of grandparent in the child's life. That is, grandparents may serve in several different temporal, developmental or culturally sanctioned positions. Unverified assumptions about grandparent as parent are clearly inappropriate in interacting with grandparents in relation to assessment or intervention with families wherein the grandparent(s) is/are active participants in parenting. Professionals need to learn from grandparents to increase their understanding of socio-cultural variations.

Implications for Policy

Until the roles, practices and influences of the grandparent as surrogate parent are more well known, the impact of social policies regarding their parenting, the minor children in their care either temporarily or permanently cannot be surmised. What is known is that for most public and social policy, specific policies or laws regarding the grandparent as primary parent are minimal (see Henley Walters, this volume). Practitioners and researchers need to analyze situations specifically in order to determine policies in relation to grandparents as surrogate or primary parents. Furthermore, practitioners and policy-makers need to follow and analyze the organized efforts of grandparent-based groups as they seek economic, policy and legal support for their roles as primary parents for their adult children and their grandchildren.

Implications for Education

Students of family life and family health care must be informed about and competent to consider all the participants in the family. As grandparents and great-grandparents live longer and often undergo several developmental, temporal and contextual transitions in relation to their family members, their influence requires attention and consideration in order to gain a comprehensive view of the individual family's situation and address their specific issues. Educators have the responsibility of incorporating (integrating or including) grandparents into their formal coursework on the family, family developmental transitions, and any area or type of family practice.

CONCLUSION

The purpose of this chapter was to review the literature on grandparents as surrogate parents and examine the relationship between three dimensions of context (temporal, developmental, and ethnic-racial) and the surrogate parenting role of grandparents. Additionally the purpose was to present some beginning level implications for researchers, practice, social policy and education. Given the dramatic increase in popular attention to this role, conceptual as well as empirical discussions of this topic are in order. Unfortunately, to date, there has been little examination of this role by social scientists. Therefore the practice and social policy implications need particular attention.

The chapter suggests ways for social scientists to begin conceptualizing investigations of context and surrogate parenting for grandparents. Clearly there are additional contextual perspectives that can be assessed in examining this role (e.g., gender, political, socioeconomic, neighborhood). However, currently the underdeveloped nature of the literature in this area makes this a difficult task.

It is our hope that the ideas set forth in this paper raise more questions for research concerning the surrogate parent role of grandparents than answers. How many grandparents actually engage in this role? What are the parameters of the role? What are the implications of the role for grandparents, parents, and grandchildren? A rigorous research, practice, policy, and education agenda awaits us.

REFERENCES

Ahrons, C.R., & Bowman, M.E. (1982). "Changes in family relationships following divorce of adult child: Grandmother's perceptions." In E.O. Fisher (Ed.), *Impact of divorce on the extended family*, (pp. 49-68). New York: The Haworth Press, Inc.

Apfel, M.D., & Seitz, V. (1991). Four models of adolescent mother-grandmother relationships in black inner city families. *Family Relations*, *40*(4), 421-429.

Aschenbrenner, J. (1975). Extended families among black Americans. *Journal of Comparative Family Studies*, *4*, 257-268.

Barranti, C.C.R. (1985). "The grandparent/grandchild relationship: Family resource in an era of voluntary bonds." *Family Relations*, *34*, 343-352.

Baranowski, M.D. (1982). "Grandparent-adolescent relations: Beyond the nuclear family." *Adolescence*, *17*, 575-584.

Bengeston, V., & Allen, K.R. (1993). Life course perspectives applied to the family. In P.G. Boss, W. Dougherty, R. La Rossa, W. Schuman, & Steinmetz (Eds.), *Sourcebook of family theories and methods: A contextual approach.* New York: Plenum.

Bengston, V.L., Rosenthal, C., & Burton, L.M. (1990). "Families and aging." In R. Binstock and L. George (Eds.), *Handbook of Aging and the Social Sciences*, (pp. 263-287). New York: Academic Press.

Bengtson, V.L., & Robertson, J.F. (Eds.), (1985). *Grandparenthood*. Beverly Hills, CA: Sage Publications.

Brim, O.G., & Ryff, C.D. (1980). On the properties of life events. In P.B. Baltes & O.G. Brim (Eds.), *Lifespan development and behavior, Vol. 3*, (p. 386-388). New York: Academic Press.

Burton, L.M. (1985). Early and on-time grandparenthood in multi-generation black families. Unpublished dissertation for The University of Southern California Department of Sociology.

Burton, L.M. (1990). "Teenage childbearing as an alternative life-course strategy in multigeneration black families." *Human Nature*, *1*(2), 123-143.

Burton, L.M. (1992). "Black grandparents rearing children of drug-addicted parents: Stressors, outcomes, and social service needs." *The Gerontologist, 32*(6), 744-751.

Burton, L.M., & Bengston, V.L. (1985). "Black grandmothers: Issues of timing and meaning in roles." In V.L. Bengston and J. Robertson (Eds.), *Grandparenthood: Research and policy perspectives*, (pp. 61-77). Beverly Hills, CA: Sage Publications.

Burton, L.M., & deVries, M. (1992). "Challenges and rewards: African American grandparents as surrogate parents." *Generations, 17*, 51-54.

Burton, L.M., & Dilworth-Anderson, P. (1991). "The intergenerational family roles of aged black Americans." *Marriage & Family Review, 16*(3/4), 311-330.

Burton, L.M., Dilworth-Anderson, P., & Bengston, V.L. (1992). "Creating new ways of thinking about diversity and aging: Theoretical challenges for the twenty-first century." *Generations, 15*(4), 67-72.

Burton, L.M., & Sorensen, S. (1990). *Historical perspectives on black grandparents*. Presented at the annual meeting of the Social Science History Association, Minneapolis, MN.

Burton, L.M., & Sorensen, S. (1993). "Temporal dimensions of intergenerational caregiving in African-American multigeneration families." In S.H. Zarit, L.I. Pearlin, and K.W. Schaie (Eds.), *Caregiving systems: Informal and formal helpers*. New York: Erlbaum Associates.

Chase-Lansdale, L., Brooks-Gunn, J., & Zamisky, E.S. (In Press). Young African-American multigenerational families in poverty. *Child Development*.

Cherlin, A., & Furstenberg, F.F., Jr. (1986). *The new American grandparent: A place in the family, a life apart*. New York: Basic Books.

Cheshier, M.W. (1981). The use of elderly as surrogate parents: A clinical perspective. *Journal of Gerontological Social Work, 3*, 3-15.

Clausen, J.A. (1986). *The life course*. Englewood, NJ: Prentice-Hall.

Dellmann-Jenkins, M., Papalia, D., & Lopez, M. (1987). "Teenagers' reported interaction with grandparents: Exploring the extent of alienation." *Lifestyles: A Journal of Changing Patterns*, 3/4, 35-46.

Dilworth-Anderson, P. (In Press). "The importance of grandparents in extended kin caregiving to black children with sickle cell disease." *Journal of Health and Social Policy*.

Dilworth-Anderson, P., Burton, L.M., & Boulin-Johnson, L. (1993). "Reframing theories for understanding race, ethnicity, and family." In P. Boss, W. Doherty, R. Larossa, W. Schumm, and S. Steinmetz (Eds.), *Sourcebook of family theories and methods: A contextual approach*. New York: Plenum Press.

Dilworth-Anderson, P., Burton, L.M., & Turner, W. (1993). "The importance of values in the study of culturally diverse families." *Family Relations*.

Elder, G.H., Jr. (1985). Perspectives on the life course. In G.H. Elder, Jr. (Ed.), *Life course dynamics, trajectories and transitions, 1968-1980*, (pp. 22-49). Ithaca, NY: Cornell University Press.

Elder, G.H., Jr. (1987). Families and lives: Some developments in life-course studies. *Journal of Family History, 12*, 179-199.

Elder, G.H., Jr., & Rockwell, R. (1976). Marital timing and women's life patterns. *Journal of Family History, 4*, 34-53.

Elkind, D. (1990). *Grandparenting: Understanding today's children.* Glenview, IL: Scott, Foresman.

Erickson, E.H. (1963). *Childhood and society* (2nd Ed.). New York: Norton.

Erickson, E.H. (1980). On generational cycle: An address. *International Journal of Psychoanalysis, 61*, 213-233.

Erickson, E.H. (1982). *The life cycle completed.* New York: Norton.

Flaherty, M.J. (1988). "Seven caring functions of black grandmothers in adolescent mothering." *Maternal-Child Nursing Journal, 17*, 191-207.

Frazier, E.F. (1939). *The negro family in the United States.* Chicago: University of Chicago Press.

Garfinkle, I., & McClanahan, S. (1986). *Single mothers and their children: A new American dilemma.* Washington, DC: Urban Institute Press.

Gee, E.M. (1987). "Historical change in the family life course." In V. Marshall (Ed.), *Aging in Canada*, 2:120-132. Ontario: Fizhenry and White Side.

Gibbs, J.T. (1988). *Young, black and male in America: An endangered species.* Dover, MA: Auburn House.

Giorsca, V. (1972). On social time. In H. Yaker (Ed.), *The future of time* (pp. 10-37). Garden City, NY: Anchor Books.

Hagestad, G.O. (1988). Demographic change and the life course: Some emerging trends in the family research realm. *Family Relations, 37*, 405-414.

Hagestad, G.O. (1990). Social perspectives on the life course. In R. Binstock & L. George (Eds.), *Handbook of aging and social sciences*, (3rd Ed.), (pp. 35-61). New York: Van Nostrand & Reinhold.

Hagestad, G.O., & Burton, L.M. (1986). "Grandparenthood, life context, and family development." *American Behavioral Scientist, 29*, 471-484.

Hagestad, G.O., & Lang, M.E. (1986). "The transition to grandparenthood: Unexplored issues." *Journal of Family Issues, 7*, 115-130.

Hagestad, G.O., & Neugarten, B. (1985). Age and the life course. In R. Binstock & E. Shanans (Eds.), *Handbook of aging and the social sciences*, (2nd ed.), (pp. 35-61). New York: Van Nostrand & Reinhold.

Havighurst, R.J. (1972). *Developmental tasks and education*, (3rd ed.). New York: D. McKay.

Hill, R., & Schackelford, L. (1987). The black extended family revisited. *The Urban League Review, 1*, 18-24.

Himes, C.L. (1992). "Social demography of contemporary families and aging." *Generations, 17*, 13-16.

Hogan, D. (1987). The demography of life-span transitions: Temporal and gender comparisons. In A. Rossi (Ed.), *Gender and the life course*, (pp. 65-78). New York: Aldine.

Hogan, D.P. (1978). "The demography of life-span temporal and gender comparisons." In A. Rossi (Ed.), *Gender and the life course*, (pp. 65-78). New York: Aldine.

Hogan, D.P., Hao, L.X., & Parrish, W.L. (1990). Race, kin networks and assistance to mother-headed families. *Social Forces*, *68*, 797-812.

Huling, W.P. (1978). Evolving family roles for the black elderly. *Aging*, *287*, 21-27.

Jackson, J.J. (1971). Sex and social class variation in black aged parent-adult child relationships. *Aging and Human Development*, *2*, 96-107.

Jarrett, R.L. (1990). "A comparative examination of socialization patterns among low income African-Americans, Chicanos, Puerto Ricans, and whites: A review of the ethnographic literature." Report to the Social Science Research Council.

John, R. (1988). "The Native American family." In C.H. Mindel, R.W. Haberstein, and R. Wright, Jr. (Eds.), *Ethnic families in America: Patterns and variations*, (pp. 325-366). New York: Elsevier.

Jones, F.C. (1973). The lofty role of the black grandmother. *Crisis*, *89*.

Jones, J. (1985). *Labor of love, labor of sorrow: Black women, work and the family from slavery to the present*. New York: Basic.

Juster, S., & Vinovskiis, M. (1987). "Changing perspectives on the American family in the past." *Annual Review of Sociology*, *13*, 193-216.

Kertzer, D.I. (1983). Generation as a sociological problem. *Annual Review of Sociology*, *9*, 125-149.

Kitano, H.H.L. (1988). "The Japanese American family." In C.H. Mindel, R.W. Haberstein, and R. Wright, Jr. (Eds.), *Ethnic families in America: Patterns and variations*, (pp. 325-366). New York: Elsevier.

Kivett, V.R. (1991). The grandparent-grandchild connection. *Marriage & Family Review*, *16*(3/4), 267-290.

Kivnick, H.Q. (1985). *Grandparenthood and life cycle*. Paper presented at the annual meeting of the American Psychological Association, Toronto, Ontario.

Lensoff-Caravaglia, G. (1982). The Black granny and the Soviet babushka: Commonalities and contrasts. In R.C. Manuel (Ed.), *Minority aging: Social and psychological issues*. Westport, CT: Greenwood.

Levinson, D.J. (1978). *The seasons of a man's life*. New York: Ballantine Books.

Matthews, S.H., & Sprey, J. (1984). "The impact of divorce on grandparenthood: An exploratory study." *Gerontologist*, *24*, 41-47.

Matthews, S.H., & Sprey, J. (1985). "Adolescents' relationships with grandparents: An empirical contribution to conceptual clarification." *Journal of Gerontology*, *40*, 621-626.

McGreal, C.E. (In Press). "The family across generations: Grandparenthood." In L. L'Abate (Ed.), *Handbook of developmental family psychology and psychopathology*. New York: John Wiley and Sons.

Min, P.G. (1988). "The Korean American family." In C.H. Mindel, R.W. Haberstein, and R. Wright, Jr. (Eds.), *Ethnic families in America: Patterns and variations*, (pp. 325-366). New York: Elsevier.

Minkler, M. (1992). *Skipped generation parenting: When grandmother becomes mother*. Paper presented at the annual conference of the American Society on Aging, San Diego, CA.

Minkler, M. & Roe, K.M. (1992). The physical and emotional health of grandmothers raising grandchildren in the crack cocaine epidemic. *The Gerontologist, 32*, (6), 752-759.

National Center for Health Statistics. (1991). *Health, United States, 1990*. Washington, D.C.: Government Printing Office.

Neugarten, B. (1970). Dynamics of transition of middle to old age: Adaptation in the life cycle. *Journal of Geriatric Psychology, 4*, 71-87.

Neugarten, B.L., Moore, J.W., & Lowe, J.C. (1965). Age norms, age constraints, and adult socialization. *American Journal of Sociology, 70*, 710-717.

Nydegger, C. (1973). Timing of fatherhood: Role perception and socialization. Unpublished dissertation, Department of Individual & Family Studies, The Pennsylvania State University.

Pearson, J.L., Hunter, A.G., Ensminger, M., & Kellan, S.G. (1990). Black grandmothers in multigenerational households: Diversity in family structure and parenting involvement in the Woodlawn community. *Child Development, 61*(2), 434-442.

Plath, D. (1980). *Long engagements*. Stanford, CA: Stanford University Press.

Roberto, K.A. (1990). "Grandparent and grandchild relationships." In T.H. Brubaker (Ed.), *Family relationships in later life*. Newbury Park, CA: Sage Publications.

Rogler, & Clooney (1989). Puerto Rican families in New York City: Intergenerational processes. *Marriage & Family Review, 16*(3/4), 331-350.

Rossi, A. (1980). Life-span theories and women's lives. *Signs: Journal of Women in Culture and Society, 6*, 4-32.

Ruggles, S., & Goeken (1992). "Race and multigenerational family structure." In S.J. South & S.E. Tolnay (Eds.), *The changing American family*, (pp. 15-42). Boulder, CO: Westview Press.

Sanchez-Ayendez, M. (1988). The Puerto Rican American family. In C.H. Mindel, R.W. Haberstein and R. Wright, Jr. (Eds.), *Ethnic families in America: Patterns and variations* (pp. 173-198). New York: Elsevier.

Sanchez-Ayendez, M. In C.H. Mindel, R.W. Haberstein, and R. Wright, Jr. (Eds.), *Ethnic families in America: Patterns and variations.*

Scott, Y.K. (1991). *The habit of surviving*. New York: Ballantine Books.

Seltzer, M. (1976). Suggestions for the examination of time-disordered relationships. In J.F. Gubrium (Ed.), *Time, roles and self in old age*. New York: Human Sciences Press.

Smith, E.W. (1975). The role of the grandmother in adolescent pregnancy and parenting. *Journal of School Health, 45*, 278-283.

Stack, C.B., & Burton, L.M. (1993). "Kinscripts." *Journal of Comparative Family Studies, 24*(2), 157-170.

System Metrics/McGraw-Hill (1989). *Significant problems facing American children, youth, and families*. Lexington, MA: McGraw-Hill, Inc.

Tinsley, B.R., & Parke, R.D. (1982). "Grandparents as support and socialization agents." In M. Lewis (Ed.), *Beyond the dyad*, (pp. 161-194). New York, NY: Plenum.

Tomlin, A.M., & Passman, R.H. (1989). "Grandmothers' responsibility in raising two-year olds facilitates their grandchildren's adaptive behavior: A preliminary intrafamilial investigation of mothers' and maternal grandmothers' effects." *Psychology and Aging*, *4*, 119-121.

Troll, L. (1985). "The contingencies of grandparenthood." In V.L. Bengtson and J.F. Robertson (Eds.), *Grandparenthood.* Beverly Hills, CA: Sage Publications.

Uhlenberg, P. (1980). "Death and the family." *Journal of Family History, 5*(3), 313-320.

Van Tran, T. In C. H. Mindel, R. W. Haberstein and R. Wright, Jr. (Eds.), *Ethnic families in America: Patterns and variations.*

Watkins, S.C., Menken, J.A., & Bongaarts, J. (1987). "Demographic foundations of family change." *American Sociological Review, 52*, 346-358.

White, D.G. (1985). *Aren't I a woman? Female slaves in the plantation south.* New York: W.W. Norton & Co.

Wilson, J. (1987). *The inner city, the underclass and public policy.* Chicago: University of Chicago Press.

Wilson, M.N. (1986). The black extended family: An analytical consideration. *Developmental Psychology, 22*, 246-258.

Wood, V. (1971). Age-appropriate behavior for older persons. *The Gerontologist, 11*(3), 74-78.

GLOSSARY

Non-normative Parenting — Parenting when the person considers or perceives parenting not a normal, expectable event or role in relation to the social context and/or developmental events and tasks of life.

Normative Parenting — Parenting when the person considers or perceives parenting as a normal, expectable event or role in relation to the social context and/or the developmental events and tasks of life.

Grandparenting — One or both grandparents assume responsibility for primary caretaking and rearing of grandchildren.

Surrogate — One who acts in place of another, one that serves as a substitute.

Chapter 17

Adoptions by Single Parents

Joan F. Shireman

SUMMARY. Adoptions by single parents are thought by the public and by adoption professionals to be a plan for children needing adoption which is less advantageous for the child than a two parent adoption. For this reason, children who are difficult to find homes for are often placed with single parents; these are usually older children whose experiences have led to emotional and behavioral problems. Single persons who wish to parent an infant often adopt a child from another country. A review of the literature concerning single parent adoptions, and examination of the findings of a longitudinal study, indicate that the single persons who adopt are well able to carry out the responsibilities of parenting. They handle the special issues of adoption competently. Because children placed with single parents are frequently children with complex needs, and because single parents do not have a partner to share the responsibilities of parenting, continuing support from family and friends, the community, and from the adoption agency are important. Children adopted by single parents are as well adjusted as children adopted into two parent homes. There is some evidence that single parent homes may have unique strengths and be the placement of choice for some children.

KEYWORDS. Adoption of children, Single parent adoption

Joan F. Shireman is Professor with the Graduate School of Social Work, Portland State University, Portland, OR 97207.

[Haworth co-indexing entry note]: "Adoptions by Single Parents." Shireman, Joan F. Co-published simultaneously in *Marriage & Family Review* (The Haworth Press, Inc.) Vol. 20, No. 3/4, 1995, pp. 367-388; and: *Single Parent Families: Diversity, Myths and Realities* (ed: Shirley M. H. Hanson et al.) The Haworth Press, Inc., 1995, pp. 367-388. Multiple copies of this article/chapter may be purchased from The Haworth Document Delivery Center [1-800-3-HAWORTH; 9:00 a.m. - 5:00 p.m. (EST)].

INTRODUCTION

Adoption is considered a good way to plan for a permanent home for children whose birth parents have demonstrated inability to care for them. As a society, we have become convinced of the importance of family and of continuity in nurturing relationships during childhood. The adoptive home, buttressed by legal support, the approving sanction of society, and the love and caring of adoptive parents, seems to offer the best hope for children whose own parents are unable to care for them.

"It is difficult, but not impossible, for a single person to become a single parent," a recent handbook for single adoptive parents begins (Marindin, 1992, p. 1). The popular press raises concern about single parent families (Blankenhorn, 1992; Whitehead, 1993). Professionals working in adoption, many influenced by psychoanalytic theory, are also reluctant to expose children to the perceived adversity of a single parent home. Adoption agencies, and the community, thus tend to regard single parents as a "last resort" when children are so difficult to find adoptive homes for that continued foster care seems a probability. As a result, children placed with single parents are often "children with earlier experiences of deprivation, instability, and abuse (which) have led to substantially more emotional adjustment problems." (Fiegelman and Silverman, 1983, p. 185).

However, it is possible that these single parent homes have strengths comparable to those of two parent families. In this chapter, the research about single parent adoption is reviewed, and its interpretation enriched by reference to "first hand" accounts of single men and women who have adopted. The author's own research is often cited, for these are the single parents with whom she is best acquainted. In addition, the paucity of research in this area supports frequent references to this longitudinal study. The article examines the process of adoption for single parents, the characteristics of the single persons who adopt, and those of the children they adopt. Special issues of adoption are reviewed, and the manner in which they can be handled in single parent families examined. Finally, the outcome of single parent adoptions is explored. From this data a few conclusions can be drawn with a fair degree of certainty. Perhaps more interesting, there are some beginning indications of the factors which make these adoptions satisfactory for parent and child, and some indications of the particular strengths of single parent homes. These are the indicators which it will be interesting to follow in future research.

THE RESEARCH

There is remarkably little empirical literature on the adoption of children by single parents. There are five major research studies; single parents are included in the samples of studies of adoption which have focused on problems, and there are numerous first hand accounts of experiences with parenting.

Overview of Existing Research

Almost all of the studies of single parent adoption have focused on the experiences of parents who adopted children of their own race from agencies in the United States. Two approaches have been used. One was to recruit samples from adoptive parent support groups and use a mailed survey (Fiegelman and Silverman, 1983; Dougherty, 1978). The other approach was to follow agency placements with a longitudinal research design (Branham, 1970; Shireman and Johnson, 1976, 1985, 1986; Shireman, 1988). The former approach has produced larger numbers for study, the latter perhaps a more typical cross section of adoptions and more qualitative data. There is some data about how single parent adoptive families fare over time; Fiegelman and Silverman re-contacted adoptive parents six years after the original survey while the longitudinal study of Shireman and Johnson, described below, continued over fourteen years. Though older children with emotional difficulties are part of the sample of the Fiegelman and Silverman (1983) study, the first study to focus on single parent adoptions of special needs children appeared in 1991 with a large sample of agency placements (Groze and Rosenthal, 1991). There are some single parents represented in studies of special needs adoption (Nelson, 1985; Kagan and Reid, 1986; Partridge et al., 1986; Barth and Berry, 1988). Additionally, descriptive data has been collected by the Committee for Single Parent Adoptions since its founding in 1973; the data includes material on patterns of adoption, including adoption from foreign countries (Marindin, 1992).

The CCCS Study

In 1970, in Chicago, there were many black infants and toddlers awaiting placement in adoptive homes. Under pressure from the agency board to try single parent adoptions, the adoption workers at the Chicago Child Care Society (CCCS), a multi-service child welfare agency, rather reluctantly decided to begin making placements in single parent homes, on condition that they be followed and evaluated through the years. Thus began, under the direction of the author, a longitudinal study of single parent adoptions. A cohort of 118 black or mixed-race children placed in adoptive homes as infants or as toddlers have been followed from that date to the present. Case records were used to obtain pre-placement data, and every four years interviews with parents and children have taken place. The sample represented all of the placements made between June 1970 and June 1972 with single parents (31), half of those made with white couples (42) and a third of those made with black couples (45). Overall, 59% of the original sample was located in 1982-83 when the children were in early adolescence; among the single parents, 15 families were located.

THE ADOPTION PROCESS

The process of adopting a child can be confusing and complex for any family. The single parent finds it even more difficult. Community concern about single parents raising children is expressed in agency reluctance to place children for whom two parent homes could be found; thus agencies offer older, troubled children to single parents. International adoption, though which younger children are available, can become extraordinarily complex and uncertain. Independent adoptions present their own risks. The single parent who wishes to adopt must gather information and select the method most likely to lead to the desired outcome, and then proceed with patience and determination.

Agency Adoptions

The children available to single parents through adoption agencies have been those who were hard to place "special needs" children. In 1970, when the CCCS study began, special needs meant a child of color, beyond infancy, or an infant with a serious physical handicap. Two decades later, as the horizons of all adoptive families have expanded, these are older children, particularly children of color, children with serious physical or emotional handicaps, and siblings whom the agency wishes to keep together. Despite the argument that the single parent has fewer resources of family support, income, time, and energy to cope with a difficult child, these are the children placed in single parent homes.

Single persons who wish to adopt an infant or young child without serious problems have increasingly turned to adoption of a foreign-born child. These parents thus face the task of raising a child to be bi-cultural.

Most adoptions have been from Asian countries and the countries of Central America, countries in which there has been a civil or international war, where there is widespread poverty, and in which there are cooperative links between child welfare agencies and the governments. Not all countries accept applications from single women (Altstein and Simon, 1991); it is even more difficult for men to find a program which will accept them, because many cultures find the idea of men nurturing children to be alien (Stebbing and Edwards, in Marindin, 1992). There is no doubt that the process of adopting from a foreign country is more difficult, more expensive, and more fraught with risk than are domestic adoptions.

Independent Adoptions

Independent adoptions, adoptions without the services of a licensed child welfare agency, are legal in all but six states. Such adoptions may be arranged by a lawyer or doctor, or directly arranged by a birthparent who wants to choose the adoptive family for her child. Faced with the reluctance of agencies to place children with single parents, many single persons chose independent adoptions. Independent adoptions carry major risks for all parties; most importantly, a child may be placed in an inappropriate home. Birth mothers may not have sufficient counseling support and may make a decision about which they remain uncomfortable and guilt-ridden. Adopting parents may have worked with a specific pregnant woman and expect to receive a child, only to face loss when a birth mother changes her mind at the time of the child's birth, or they may face loss of a child later because legal matters were incompletely handled. Without the support of persons experienced in working with issues around the formation of the adoptive family (issues to be discussed later) there is also risk of the adoption disrupting the family unit. Major risks for the adopting parent can be minimized through selection of an agency to do a careful home study which will also provide follow-up services if necessary, and careful selection of a lawyer. Independent adoptions, domestic or foreign, not only carry more risk but are generally more expensive than adoptions arranged by agencies (Marindin, 1992).

Committee for Single Adoptive Parents

The Committee for Single Adoptive Parents, an organization formed to assist single adoptive parents, has available to its members information of use to those considering adoption. This includes a list of sources of domestic and foreign born children that have accepted single applicants, with additional information about the adoption process. The address is: Committee for Single Adoptive Parents, P.O. Box 15084, Chevy Chase, Maryland 20825.

Assessment of Parenting Skills

The law requires that there be a home study before a child is placed in a home for adoption. The home study evaluates the capacity of the applicants to care for a child, and certifies to the court that this is an appropriate home. The focus of a home study will vary with the circumstances of the applicant and with the philosophy of the investigating agency. Commonly, emphasis is placed on consideration of support systems available to help in a crisis and to provide role models to children, financial resources, "realism" in planning for child care while parents are at work, and enjoyment and knowledge of child rearing. Home studies which focus on the placement of older and disturbed children emphasize more the nature of the skills which will be required to parent children with particular difficulties. Focus is on the qualities which it is hypothesized will lead to success in parenting.

Placement of a Child

The final step in the adoption process is the matching of a child and parent, and the placement of the child in the adoptive home. The matching process is not well understood; appearance, intellectual potential, and temperament are all factors. However, it is difficult to identify the ingredients of the bond that forms between parent and child, sometimes instantly and sometimes over time (Shireman and Johnson, 1975).

The placement process itself is ideally a process of repeated visits as child and parent get to know each other and become comfortable with each other. If at all possible, the child needs the support of the person who has been its primary caregiver during the process, and at least one contact soon after the child has moved to the adoptive home.

CHARACTERISTICS OF SINGLE PARENT ADOPTERS AND THEIR CHILDREN

Most single parent adopters are women and most single parents adopt a child of the same sex (Shireman and Johnson, 1976; Fiegelman and Silverman, 1983; Groze and Rosenthal, 1991). About one in seven people who contact the National Committee for Single Adoptive Parents is a man, but probably a considerably smaller proportion of men succeed in adopting (Marindin, 1992). Children placed with single parents are complex in their needs.

Number of Single Parent Adoptions

It is difficult to estimate the number of single parent adoptions in the United States. Since 1975, adoption statistics have not been kept by the federal government, and state sources are difficult to synthesize. In 1975, 2.5% of the adoptions completed were with single parents (Meezan, 1980). Review of the literature, and conversations with those working in adoption, would indicate that this number has grown in subsequent years. In Oregon, probably a typical state, 5% of all placements made by Children Services Division in 1989 were with single parents; in 1991 they totaled 12% (Pierson, 1992, personal communication). In reviewing research on the adoption of special needs children, Groze found a range of single parent placements from 5% in a 1970 study to 34% in a 1984 study (Groze, 1991). The best current estimate available is that 25% of special needs children may be adopted by single men and women (National Adoption Center, reported in Harrison, 1991).

Parents

Information about the characteristics of single parent adopters comes mostly from data gathered from those who are members of single parent adoptive organizations. These data indicate that most single adoptive parents are in their mid to late thirties at the time of adoption, that a majority have graduate education, and that they hold stable jobs, usually in the helping professions (Dougherty, 1978; Fiegelman and Silverman, 1983; Marindin, 1992). The incomes of single parents tend to be lower than that of couples who adopt (Fiegelman and Silverman, 1983), although 40% of men adopters earn over $40,000 a year (Marindin, 1992).

Data gathered from studies of those who finalized an adoption of a special needs child during a given period paint a somewhat different picture of single parents who adopt in their mid to late forties. About a quarter of the women and 55% of the men have finished college, (Groze and Rosenthal, 1991). Incomes are markedly lower than those of couples who adopt (Groze and Rosenthal, 1991; Shireman and Johnson, 1985; Shireman, 1988). Single parents who adopt special needs children are more likely to be black, compared to couples who are more likely to be white (Groze and Rosenthal, 1991).

The single parents who formed the sample of the CCCS longitudinal study were mostly black women; there were 25 black women, 3 white women and 3 black men among the original 31. They ranged in age from 29 to 50 years, with a median age of 34. More than half of the women had been married; three had children. Twelve lived with extended family (parents, brothers, or sisters) and more than half planned to use extended family to meet child care needs. All were employed, about half in service professions. Incomes were low; the median income was $9000 (Shireman and Johnson, 1976).

Single parents seem to adopt for the same reasons that couples do: fulfillment of their own need to nurture and guide a child, and an enjoyment of children (Dougherty, 1978; Shireman and Johnson, 1976). In the CCCS study, a complex set of ratings concerning the extent to which the adopting parent's childhood needs were met, self-image, expectations of self, health, energy level, constructive use of defenses, capacity to nurture a child, and sensitivity to children were made. It was noted that most (80%) had their own childhood needs adequately met. Close relationships with extended families were common. The adopting parents thought they would be comfortable with talking about adoption to a child, and in explaining their "singleness" to a child. Obviously, since children were placed, all were considered to have capacity to raise children alone (Shireman and Johnson, 1976).

There is very little information on single adoptive fathers. The first formal adoption by a man took place in 1980 (Hanson, 1985). A 1985 unpublished survey, done by Timothy Gage, of 80 single men who had adopted or who wanted to adopt "convincingly demonstrated the value of these fathers as a resource for parenting special-needs children." (Marindin, 1992, p. 32). Most of the children adopted by the men in this survey were boys; 90% were school age, and 62% were identified by their fathers as having "special needs." Two respondents in the anonymous survey identified themselves as gay (Marindin, 1992). When single fathers are identified in the single parent adoption research, they have usually adopted boys, and usually older, troubled boys. Research on father-headed families indicates that fathers who seek custody of children (as adopting parents do) adjust most readily to their care (Hanson and Bozett, 1987). There is no evidence that the experiences of fathers differ from those of women who adopt, except that incomes are more adequate. Otherwise, they face the same stresses and cope with the same skill.

Some single parent adopters are gay or lesbian, probably many more than has been admitted by adoption agencies, though there is no data available. When a gay or lesbian adopter is in a committed relationship, the child is actually going to be raised as part of a two parent family; it is questionable whether such adoptions are really single parent adoptions. However, because of the reluctance of agencies and of courts to recognize such families, many such adoptions are completed by one parent as a single parent adoption. The tension created by the need to "select" a primary parent for legal purposes, when partners view themselves as co-equal, may be significant (Rohrbaugh, 1989). The suspicion that a man who wishes to adopt is gay, and that a homosexual may be sexually attracted to children, has made it very difficult for single men to adopt. In fact, child abuse statistics indicate that most child abuse is perpetrated by heterosexual men (Finkelhor, 1986).

Characteristics of Children

Children placed with single parents present challenges beyond those which adopting couples face. Dougherty (1978) found special needs children placed in two-thirds of the single parent adoptions studied. Groze and Rosenthal (1991) found single parents more likely than couples to adopt older, non-white, or mentally retarded children. Children adopted from other countries bring issues of racial differences, language differences (if they are beyond infancy) and the challenges of helping children know and value a culture and heritage different from that in which they are being raised. Single parents also accept the complexities of raising siblings. Some adopt sibling groups. There is little data, but such placements are described as "common" (Pierson, 1992). Other single parents adopt more than one child, building families as the years progress.

In the CCCS study, single adopting parents tended to receive children similar to those requested, i.e., toddlers, in good health and with good family histories and histories of good care in foster homes prior to adoption. Half of the 15 families remaining in the sample when the children were fourteen years old had adopted children over a year old at placement, and 30% had adopted children with developmental difficulties at placement. Approximately 25% of the single parents later adopted a second child.

SPECIAL ISSUES OF ADOPTION

There has been increasing recognition in recent years of the difficulties inherent in adoption. Working under the philosophy that every child who can benefit from family life should have the opportunity for adoption,

adoption agencies have placed children with increasingly serious physical and emotional difficulties, and have begun to recognize the need for continued support to the families that adopt them.

Loss and Identity

It has become apparent that even when a young infant is placed for adoption, the family is not identical to a family formed through birth, and that both parents and child will have lifelong issues related to adoption to resolve. Attempts to ignore the adoption, to treat the children "as if" they were birth children, are thought to lead to role confusion and difficulty (Kirk, 1983). Single parents have some advantage as adoptive parents, for there may be less tendency to pretend when the family structure is different.

Difficulties which are theoretically predicted for children adopted as infants are: (1) grief and loss due to separation from the birth mother; a loss which must be mourned before the child is free to make an attachment to the adoptive parent, and a loss of a sense of autonomy and control over what happens, (2) loss of continuity of care, due to placement with a new caretaker, (3) obvious physical and temperamental differences which impair the child's identification with the adoptive parent, (4) a core lack of self-worth, stemming from the perception that he or she was "given away" by the birth parents and (5) a need for information about biologic identity (Stein and Hoopes, 1985; Bourguignon and Watson 1987). The task of the adoptive parent is the recognition that he or she has "adopted" not only the child, but also his or her genetic heritage. If the bond between adoptive parent and child is exclusive, this may be difficult; if it is a relationship which can include others, the recognition of the biologic heritage and discussion of necessary issues is easier to accomplish.

Difficult Experiences

Children adopted when they are beyond infancy bring with them the memories of the experiences they have had. For older children, these experiences are often those of abuse and neglect before they were removed from parental homes, and experiences of moves from one caretaker to another. Recent research has demonstrated the long term impact of such experiences, with distorted expectations of family life and behavioral disturbances even when there is a move to a more benign environment (Kagan and Reid, 1987; Barth and Berry, 1988). The behavioral disturbance which is the aftermath of such experience creates continued stress in the adoptive family.

All too often these difficult experiences are followed by placement in more than one foster home prior to adoption. The negative impact of multiple placements has been extensively explored and is well documented. Though the impact of separation and loss differs with the developmental stage of the child, each successive placement makes the adoption more difficult, as each placement re-evokes the original loss and works to destroy the child's capacity to trust adults, and to risk a new attachment (Fahlberg, 1988). And each move further damages a child's self esteem. Clearly it is vital that supportive resources be in place, and that an adoptive family commit to permanency with this child.

The development of a value system is an issue when an older child is adopted. Often early experiences have not taught the child the values of the adoptive home, and mismatched expectations are perhaps most difficult to handle in this area (Tremitiere, 1992). The task of the adoptive family is to allow the child to bring his or her own values into the adoptive experience and, once accepted, be able gradually to build a value system modeled on that of the parent.

Being Different

Additionally, all adopted children must cope with the fact that they are different during a time of life when sameness is prized. The children of single adoptive parents will also experience the differentness of having only one parent for many years. One might speculate that it would be more difficult for children to handle the questions of a mysterious biologic identity when they are also seeking answers around the absence of a second parent in the home.

"At its very best, an adoptive family begins as a bitter-sweet mixture for both child and parent. Loss, love, hope, promise and peril are all mixed in. The recipe is enhanced by the faith of families and the courage of children" (Collins, Busch and Johnston, 1988, p. 1).

SINGLE PERSONS AS ADOPTIVE PARENTS

In addition to coping with the special issues of adoption discussed in the preceding section, single adoptive parents must handle issues of economic stress, social isolation, and role strain, just as all single parents do (Worell, 1988). These issues are discussed in the following paragraphs.

Economic Stress

Never-married single parent families typically have, by definition, one income; family income is thus markedly lower when comparisons are made with couples who adopt (Groze and Rosenthal, 1991; Fiegelman and Silverman, 1983). The income data is further skewed by the fact that most single parent adopters are women, whose incomes are lower than those of men. In the CCCS study, low income was a major problem for half of the sample, though as the children grew older and needed less expensive child care the problem became somewhat less acute (Shireman and Johnson, 1976, 1985; Shireman, 1988). However, the expenses of late adolescence and education after college were yet to be met for this sample.

Adoption subsidies are an attempt to remove the economic barrier to placement of special needs children. New York was the first state to enact legislation making public money available for adoption subsidies in 1965. Other states rapidly followed, but it was not until the passage of federal legislation, PL96-272, that there began to be much uniformity among state provisions for adoption subsidies. Now most state laws provide the following: (1) in order to be eligible for a subsidy, a child must be older, a member of a minority group, part of a sibling group, or handicapped in some way, and (2) the child must be eligible for the subsidy at the time of placement in the adoptive home. The amount of subsidy is determined by consideration of the needs of the child and the family's income. Subsidies can be used to meet the needs of a specific handicap, or they can be payments to supplement income for the daily care of the child. Subsidies thus help to remove one barrier to the adoption of children by single parents, and they can also be conceptualized as one of the supports to an adoptive placement.

Social Isolation

Data on the relationship of extended family is unclear. In the CCCS study, extended families tended to be close and supportive; one-third of our sample lived with relatives and more than half planned to use relatives for child care. In the research of Fiegelman and Silverman (1983), 55% of single adoptive parents saw extended family frequently; however, a higher proportion of adoptive couples (63%) had close family contact.

Generally, children did not have opportunity to interact with a single, important adult of the opposite sex over an extended period of time. Very few of the women in the CCCS sample made permanent alliances; male friends "disappeared," grandfathers and uncles died. Only one of the three men in this sample remained with the study; he lived with his parents during the child's pre-school years and after their deaths lived independently (Shireman and Johnson, 1985).

The community in which a child is raised can be important to the success of the adoption. Fiegelman and Silverman (1983) found that though families generally responded positively to single parent adoptions, friends of singles were not always as enthusiastic as were the friends of couples. The support of parents, neighbors, and friends was important in the adjustment to adoption.

Living patterns of single adopters may differ somewhat from those of couples who adopt. Single parents tend to remain in urban settings, rather than moving to suburbs (Fiegelman and Silverman, 1983; Shireman and Johnson, 1985). Lacking the suburban school systems, many single parents in the CCCS study invested in private schools for their children, despite their low incomes.

When the children in the CCCS study were four years old, interviewers were very concerned about the social isolation of seven of the families. These parents enjoyed their children and centered their lives around their homes, but did not have organizational or social contacts (Shireman and Johnson, 1976). However, the advent of the school years of the children changed this picture markedly, as mothers became involved in school-related organizations and made friends with other parents (Shireman and Johnson, 1985).

Role Strain

It would be expected that the energy of meeting all the demands of child care and employment without the support of a partner would engender greater role strain among single adopters than among couples. However, the research seems to indicate that being a single adoptive parent engenders no greater role strain than being part of an adoptive couple (Fiegelman and Silverman, 1983). Most of the detailed data on the nature of the role strain of being a single adoptive parent comes from the CCCS study with its interview data, and from the accounts of adopters of special needs children. In the CCCS study, it was clear that managing child care while maintaining employment was never a problem. Additionally, the single adopters showed capacity beyond that demonstrated by many parents in ability to cope with changes in family structure and with family crises, being able to recognize their own feelings, making necessary arrangements, and being sensitive to the feelings and needs of the children (Shireman and Johnson, 1985; Shireman, 1988).

Accounts by single parents of their experiences with special needs children are also revealing. Themes are the stress of dealing with difficult behavior without the support of a partner, and without the respite that a partner can provide. The need to care for oneself, and to use the respite provided by community resources such as schools, summer camp, and friends is stressed. The emotional support, and help in evaluating difficulties and decisions in parenting, that can be attained from parent support groups is repetitively noted. When an organized support group does not exist, single adoptive parents sometimes develop them for themselves (Ludden, 1992).

ACCOMPLISHING THE TASKS OF ADOPTION

All adoptive parents must work with their adoptive children through issues of grief and loss, and toward the formation of a new family. These issues were discussed in an earlier section of this paper. Indicators of success in accomplishing these tasks are found in the openness with which parents and children discuss adoption, the handling of issues of loss, and the building of trust and a shared value system.

Discussion of Adoption

There is little data on the degree to which single adoptive parents have been able to recognize the reality of adoption and discuss it openly. At each interview time during the CCCS longitudinal study, single parents have had more difficulty discussing adoption with their children, and have told them less and at a later age than have two parent adopters (Shireman, 1988). A partial explanation for this may lie in the very close parent-child attachment noted in pre-school years (Shireman and Johnson, 1976).

Handling Curiosity About Birth Parents

The questions of children concerning their birth parents seemed to be similar in one and two parent homes. It was notable that, with a very small sample of 3, eight year old boys adopted by single mothers were curious about their birth fathers, a dimension not evident among other adopted children, who asked questions only about birth mothers (Shireman and Johnson, 1985). This curiosity about birth fathers was not evident in early adolescence (Shireman, 1988).

In interviews, the young adolescents in the longitudinal study were asked about their concerns and worries. A theme of "loss" was evident among responses of adopted youngsters, and while non-adopted children tended to focus on personal adequacy, adopted children focused concerns on security and safety. There were no differences between single parent and two parent adoptive homes.

Building a Family

How do single adoptive parents deal with issues of the behaviors that follow from early abuse and neglect, of trust and attachment, and of building a value system? The children in the CCCS longitudinal study were all under two years of age when adopted, so our interview data offer limited insight into these questions. Issues of learning to trust new parents, after moves from foster care into adoption, were present for the children in our sample, and many single parents talked of early difficulties such as crying, reluctance to eat or sleep. These were handled through the continued attention and nurturing of the single parents, and an unusually close bond was observed between single parents and very young children (Shireman and Johnson, 1976). As the children grew, this seemed to mature into a relationship with which both parents and children were content (Shireman, 1988).

Follow up of single parent adoptions of special needs children, older children who are more likely to have been abused and/or neglected and to have had multiple moves, is the focus of work by Groze and Rosenthal (1991). Using standardized measures of behavior, completed by responding adoptive parents, they found that adopted children did, indeed, exhibit serious behavioral problems. At all ages, however, children adopted by single parents had the lowest percentage of scores in the problematic range (Groze and Rosenthal, 1991). This would indicate that single parents had been more successful than two-parent adoptive homes in integrating the children into their families.

THE ADJUSTMENT OF CHILDREN ADOPTED BY SINGLE PARENTS

The overall similarity of the responses, on various measures of outcome, among youngsters adopted by single parents, youngsters adopted by two parents, and youngsters with their birth families, in the research reviewed, makes it clear that single parent adoption is a good option for young children of the same race as the parent. Overall, outcomes for children who are older and emotionally troubled when placed for adoption seem to be as good, or perhaps better, when children are placed in single parent homes. There is, as yet, no research reported which examines the outcome of trans-racial, single parent adoption, though such adoptions are represented in most of the samples of adopted children which have been studied. Interestingly, the follow up studies which have been reviewed here, and other similar follow-up studies, also show that children adopted as infants are very similar to children raised in their birth homes with regard to self-concept and overall adjustment.

Identity Formation

Identity formation is an important concept in adoption, with all the possibilities for confusion which the adoptive situation engenders. In the CCCS study, measures of this concept capture the major dimensions of the overall adjustment of the children. Data from the CCCS study are consistent with other studies. When the children were in early adolescence, identity was carefully examined using the behavioral referents of (1) family relatedness, (2) peer relations, (3) gender identity, (4) school performance, and (5) self-esteem. Both parents and children were interviewed, together and separately, and a number of standardized paper-and-pencil assessment instruments were administered to the youngsters. In all of these measures, about two-thirds of the children adopted by single parents were without problems in the areas assessed. This was similar to the proportion among children adopted by same-race couples (Shireman, 1988).

Gender Identity

Gender identity was extensively investigated in the CCCS study. At age 4, children of single parents were clear in gender attribution (Shireman and Johnson, 1975). At age 8, the grade school age children's strong overt identification with children and activities of their own sex was evident (Shireman and Johnson, 1985). At age 14, gender identity was measured with a standardized scale; responses were similar to the distribution in same-race, two parent adoptive homes (Shireman, 1988).

Remediation of Emotional and Behavioral Problems

Whether these results can be generalized to the adoption of older, more troubled children has just begun to be investigated. Fiegelman and Silverman (1983) found a statistically significant relationship between single parenting and poorer emotional adjustment of children over six. In a follow up six years later, these differences remained, but were no longer statistically significant. They report, "When controlling for the age of the children adopted, both direct and indirect assessments of children's overall adjustments show fundamentally corresponding patterns among single parents and adoptive couples" (Fiegelman and Silverman, 1983, p. 191). If, indeed, more disturbed children are placed with single parents, the tendency of single parent adoptions to look like other adoptions over time would indicate strength in the single parent homes.

Groze and Rosenthal's (1991) follow up of special needs placements showed the same patterns. The children in their sample exhibited serious emotional problems. However, "comparisons of single parent and two parent adoptions showed that children in single parent families experienced fewer problems" (Groze and Rosenthal, 1991, p. 72). Additionally, the investigators found no significant differences between single parent and two parent families on school attendance, grades, or enjoyment of school (from the parent's perception) (Groze and Rosenthal, 1991).

The literature on adoptions which do not succeed, and disrupt when the adopted child is moved and placed into another home, provides additional evidence. In those studies in which data concerning single parents was reported, single and two parent families were equally represented among those adoptions in trouble (Barth and Berry, 1988; Kagan and Reid, 1986). A more indirect measure of handling serious behavior problems by single parents is found in the work on problematic adoptions, in which single parent homes are not identified as a risk factor (Groze, 1991).

SERVICES TO SUPPORT ADOPTIONS

As older and more difficult children have increasingly been placed in adoptive homes, it has become apparent that continuing support services are needed by many of these families. It might be expected that single parents, because they lack the support of a partner in parenting, would need and seek support services to an even greater degree than couples.

There is little research literature on this subject. Supportive extended family and supportive friends have been identified as helpful (Shireman and Johnson, 1985) and their presence is associated with fewer difficulties among the children (Fiegelman and Silverman, 1983). Groze and Rosenthal (1991) report that approximately one-third of the single parents in their sample and one-fourth of the two parent families were working with a family therapist. In addition, one-fourth of the families were in contact with other families who had adopted a special needs child. Contact with parent support groups was evaluated as being more helpful than contact with therapists (Groze and Rosenthal, 1991). Research on special needs adoptive families shows continued reliance on support systems, including family, informal networks, and the mental health services available in the community (Nelson, 1985); this need is presumed to be as great, or greater, for single parents.

One wonders if the relatively small percentage of single parent adopters in contact with parent support groups may be because of the relatively small numbers of single parent adoptions. The great help that such support groups can provide is attested to by many adoptive parents. The Committee on Single Adoptive Parents, referred to earlier, provides members with information about existing support groups and, on request, names of other single parent adopters in their states. One single adopting parent, in a rural area, talked of initially developing an informal support network of other single parents, and other parents whose children were having troubles, and finding it so helpful that over the years she had founded a support group of single adoptive parents (Ludden, 1992). Development of support groups is an activity which adoptive agencies might well incorporate into their adoption services.

IMPLICATIONS

Single parent adoptions have grown in number, until they now comprise between 12 and 15 percent of all non-relative adoptions. Applicants who are single are still considered "marginal" by adoption agencies, and almost always receive special needs or hard to place children. A good deal is known about black women who adopt young black children, and somewhat less about women and men who adopt older, special needs children. In general, adoption has been a good plan for children in these homes.

There is solid evidence that single parents are able to parent older, troubled children, children who are in great need of homes. Single parent homes may have particular strengths for children from deprived backgrounds, for there is a concentration on nurturing evident in these homes. The relative simplicity of relationship patterns may be easier for a child from a troubled succession of birth and foster homes to negotiate; certainly the capacity to manipulate and oppose one parent against the other, which troubles many placements, is aborted in the single parent home. We know that the main stress in single parent homes is economic, and that adoption subsidies are important in strengthening these placements. From the point of view of waiting children, the growing willingness of adoption agencies to make placements with single parents opens new opportunities for rich family life.

Implications for Further Research

There is a great deal that is not known about single parent adoptions. There has been no systematic research about the course of the adoption when single persons adopt young children from undeveloped countries;

almost all of this literature consists of the accounts of single persons seeking a child to adopt and recording their early days with the child. Single parent, transracial adoption has not been studied. Research does show that single parent adoptions do look, in the long run, a lot like two parent adoptions, and transracial adoptions look, in the long run, a lot like same race adoptions, so it is possible to be optimistic that these new single parent adoptions will work well.

Very little is known about men who adopt. They find it very difficult to adopt, but small numbers do adopt, usually boys who are older and troubled. It would be helpful to know what the particular strengths of these adoptions are, and which children these men are particularly gifted at raising. Until this research is completed, adoption workers must rely on the growing literature, represented in this volume, concerning men who are single parents.

Little is known about lesbian women and gay men who adopt. Again, this data is hidden in the studies of single parents, for surely many of them are lesbian or gay. Many of these adoptions are only nominally or legally single parent adoptions, for there is often a partner forming a two parent family. There is some literature indicating that there may be particular role strains when a gay or lesbian family takes on the raising of a child, but little detail about how such strains are resolved. Whether these households have special strengths in helping adopted children with particular problems is not known, nor is the impact of a lesbian or gay orientation on the capacity to seek adoption support groups or other help when there are difficulties known.

Implications for Policy and Practice

It is of concern that children who have special needs and make unusual demands are routinely placed with single parents. Single parents would appear to have fewer resources than couples in parenting these children. They lack the day-to-day support of a partner. Thus they face the responsibility of day-to-day decision making alone, and decisions about how to handle the behavior of children who have been abused and neglected, and who have difficulty establishing trusting relationships, can be difficult. They do not have a family member routinely available to provide respite from the demands of child care. Even infants from developing countries, who seem easy children at the time of placement, will eventually present complex challenges to their parents, as they grow and need to know their cultural heritage.

Adoption, however, is centered in the concept of providing for the best interests of the child, and there is reassuring evidence that these single parent homes are good and nurturing homes for children with special needs. Indeed, there is evidence that some children thrive better in these homes, perhaps because relationship patterns are less complex, perhaps because of the intensity of nurture and attention available. Thus, the interests of children are well served by single parent adoptions.

Nevertheless, it is clear that single adoptive parents need support systems in place as they undertake their difficult task. Agencies would do well to provide individualized counseling service to the new adoptive family for as long as is needed, as well as being available to help the family access such counseling at any point necessary during the child's development. This includes a responsibility to educate the mental health services of the community about the unique issues of the adoptive family, so that help will be appropriate. Adoption subsidies can aid in providing the income to support a child and the special services needed. There is also a need for support groups for single adoptive parents to be developed and nurtured by adoption agencies.

CONCLUSION

Single parents who adopt must combat the stereotypes of the young, unwed woman who has minimal or no employment. They must combat fears about homosexuality. The characteristics of single parents who adopt make clear that these are mature, hard-working, and well educated men and women. Gay, lesbian, or straight, they adopt for the same reasons that couples adopt. They face the same dilemmas as parents that couples do. They lack the support of a spouse, and the community support, that couples have to assist them in parenting. They deserve to have professional assistance in solving problems and in finding support groups as they undertake a difficult task.

Though there is much still to be learned about single parent adoption, it is evident that it is time for a change in thinking about single persons as adoptive parents. They are not applicants of less capacity than two parent families. Rather, these are families which have their unique strengths and can provide stable homes for children. In making adoptive placements, these are not homes in which to place children for whom two parent homes cannot be found. Rather, they are homes in which to place children whose background and experiences are such that they can best use the strengths of a home with one parent. Practitioners and those who develop and report research findings must work together in the years to come to identify more precisely the strengths of these single parent adoptive homes, and to identify the children who can best use these strengths.

REFERENCES

Altstein, H. & Simon, R. J. (1991). *Intercountry adoption*. New York: Praeger.

Barth, R. P. & Berry, M. (1988). *Adoption and disruption: Rates, risks, and response*. New York: Aldine De Gruyter.

Blankenhorn, D., Institute for American Values, New York: Reported in *The Oregonian*, November 14, 1992, p. A3.

Bourguignon, J. P. & Watson, K. (1987). *A manual for professionals working with adoptive families*. Springfield, IL: Illinois Department of Children and Family Services.

Branham, E. (1970). One parent adoptions. *Children, 17* (3), 103-107.

Collins, R. E., Busch, L. & Johnston, S. (1988). *The mental health challenge of special needs adoption*. Portland, OR: Oregon Health Sciences University.

Dougherty, S. A. (1978). Single adoptive mothers and their children. *Social Work, 32* (4), 311-314.

Fahlberg, V. (1988) A developmental approach to separation/loss. In Collins, R. E., Busch, L. & Johnston, S., *The mental health challenge of special needs adoption*. Portland, OR: Oregon Health Sciences University.

Fiegelman, W., & Silverman, A. R. (1983). *Chosen children: New patterns of adoptive relationships*. New York: Praeger.

Finkelhor, D. (1986). *A sourcebook on child sexual abuse*. Newbury Park: Sage Publications.

Groze, V. (1991). Adoption and single parents: A review. *Child Welfare, LXX* (3), 321-332.

Groze, V. K. & Rosenthal, J. A. (1991). Single parents and their adopted children: A Psychosocial Analysis. *Families in Society: The Journal of Contemporary Human Services, 9* (2), 67-77.

Hanson, S. M. H. (1985). Single fathers with custody: A synthesis of the literature. In Schlesinger, B., *The One Parent Family in the 1980's* (pp. 57-77). Toronto: University of Toronto Press.

Hanson, S. M. H. & Bozett, F. W. (1987). Fatherhood and changing family roles. *Family Community Health, 9* (4), 9-21.

Harrison, D. (1991). Single adoptive parents. *Growing Together*. Western Region, Children's Services Division.

Kagan, R. M. & Reid, W. J. (1986). Critical factors in the adoption of emotionally disturbed youths. *Child Welfare, 65*, 63-73.

Kirk, H. D. (1984). *Shared fate: A theory and method of adoptive relationships*. Port Angeles, WA: Ben Simon Publications.

Ludden, B. (1992). *Single parenting*. Presentation at Deschutes County Foster Parent Association Conference, October, 1992.

Marindin, H. (Ed.). (1992). *Handbook for single adoptive parents*. Chevy Chase, Maryland: Committee for Single Adoptive Parents.

Meezan, W. (1980). *Adoption services in the states*. (DHHS Publication No. OHDS 80-30288) Washington DC: U. S. Department of Health and Human Services.

Nelson, K. A. (1985). *On the frontier of adoption: A study of special-needs adoptive families.* New York: Child Welfare League.

Partridge, S., Hornby, H., & McDonald, T. (1986). *Legacies of less: Visions of gain: An inside look at adoption disruption.* Portland, Maine: University of Southern Maine.

Pierson, K., Manager, Permanent Planning and Adoption Services, Children's Services Division, State of Oregon. Personal communication, October, 1992.

Reid, W. J., Kagan, R. M., Kaminsky, A. & Helmer, K. (1987). Adoption of older institutionalized youth. *Social Casework, 68* (3) 140-149.

Rohrbaugh, J. T. (1989). Choosing children: Psychological issues in lesbian parenting. *Women & Therapy, 8* (1-2), 51-64.

Simon R. J. & Altstein, H. (1987). *Transracial adoptees and their families.* New York: Praeger.

Shireman, J. (1988). *Growing up adopted: An examination of some major issues.* Chicago: Chicago Child Care Society.

Shireman, J. & Johnson, P. (1976). Single persons as adoptive parents. *Social Service Review, 50* (1), 103-116.

Shireman, J. & Johnson, P. (1985). Single parent adoptions: A longitudinal study. *Children and Youth Services Review, 7* (4) 321-334.

Shireman, J. & Johnson, P. (1986). A longitudinal study of black adoptions: Single parent, transracial, and traditional. *Social Work, 31* (3) 172-176.

Stebbing, M. & Edwards, M. (1992). Adopting a child from abroad. In Marindin, H. (Ed.), *Handbook for single adoptive parents.* Chevy Chase, MD: Committee for Single Adoptive Parents.

Stein, L. M. & Hoopes, J. T. (1985). *Identity formation in the adopted adolescent.* New York: Child Welfare League of America.

Tremitiere, B. (1992). Coping, conscience, and the difficult child. Reprinted in H. Marindin (Ed.), *Handbook for single adoptive parents,* (pp. 46-49). Chevy Chase, MD: Committee for Single Adoptive Parents.

Whitehead, B. D. (1993, April). Dan Quayle was right. *The Atlantic Monthly,* pp. 47-84.

Worell, J. (1988). Single mothers: From problems to policies. *Women & Therapy, 7* (4) 3-13.

Chapter 18

Single Parenting in Families of Children with Disabilities

Glenna C. Boyce
Brent C. Miller
Karl R. White
Michael K. Godfrey

SUMMARY. Rearing a child with disabilities is a challenge, perhaps even more so for single parents who most often are women. Stress and negative psychological effects have been considered likely outcomes for parents of children with disabilities. With the increased family focus in the provision of services for children with disabilities, it becomes even more important to understand the sources of stress and the types of adaptations made in these families. The research literature was analyzed and similar results were found. Single mothers of children with disabilities often were younger, had less education, and lower incomes. Few studies included these socioeconomic factors. Findings indicate that gross differences between

Glenna C. Boyce is Research Associate at EIRI. Brent C. Miller is Professor of Family and Human Development at EIRI. Karl R. White is Professor of Psychology at EIRI. Michael K. Godfrey is a Doctoral Candidate in the Department of Family and Human Development, and Research Associate at EIRI.

Work reported in this manuscript was supported in part with funds from the U.S. Department of Education (Contract # HS90010001) to the Early Intervention Research Institute (EIRI) at Utah State University, Logan.

[Haworth co-indexing entry note]: "Single Parenting in Families of Children with Disabilities." Boyce, Glenna C. et al. Co-published simultaneously in *Marriage & Family Review* (The Haworth Press, Inc.) Vol. 20, No. 3/4, 1995, pp. 389-409; and: *Single Parent Families: Diversity, Myths and Realities* (ed: Shirley M. H. Hanson et al.) The Haworth Press, Inc., 1995, pp. 389-409. Multiple copies of this article/chapter may be purchased from The Haworth Document Delivery Center [1-800-3-HAWORTH; 9:00 a.m. - 5:00 p.m. (EST)].

single- and two-parent mothers tended to become nonsignificant when maternal education and income were taken into account. Stress levels and adaptation were not pervasively different for single mothers and mothers who were parenting with a partner, after SES variables were controlled. On a few dimensions–including family harmony, integration, and cohesion–some studies found mothers in single parent families to be at a slight disadvantage relative to two parent families. Research findings indicate that other factors need to be considered in research and in provision of services to understand the interplay between stress and adaptation and to facilitate the family's coping. Further study is needed on factors on two levels; task demands and emotional responses, the diversity among mothers, their life situations, and their task demands must be recognized, and socioeconomic conditions and participation by other adults in caregiving. Positive adaptation by single mothers of children who have disabilities is a reasonable expectation; services should build upon family strengths and competencies.

KEYWORDS. Children with disabilities, Stress, Single parents

Many single parents, most of whom are women,[1] face the challenge of rearing a child with disabilities. The actual number of children with disabilities who are being reared by a single mother is not available, but an approximation can be calculated. There are 80.5 million children aged 0-21 in the United States (National Center for Educational Statistics, 1992; Table 13). Slightly more than eleven percent are being served in some form of federally funded special education program (National Center for Educational Statistics, 1992; Table 50), resulting in over nine million children. Just under 12 per cent of children, ages 0 to 18, reside in single-mother-headed households (U.S. Bureau of the Census, 1991). Consequently, approximately 1.1 million children receiving special education (i.e., intervention services) are living in single parent families.

This figure may be a conservative estimate. Several researchers have acknowledged the possibility that children with disabilities are more likely to be from single parent families than their nondisabled counterparts. Some have pointed to a possible higher incidence of divorce among families of children with disabilities, and others have noted the possibility that never-married single mothers, often being younger, are more likely to have children with disabilities (Bristol, Schopler, & McConnaughey as cited in Jones, 1987; Cooke, Bradshaw, Lawton, & Brewer, 1986; Roesel & Lawlis, 1983). Other scholars reviewed the literature about marital status of parents of children with disabilities and arrived at similar conclusions (Bristol, Reichle, & Thomas, 1987; Foster & Berger, 1985; Longo & Bond, 1984). The research findings concerning the incidence of divorce in families of children with disabilities do not agree. In summarizing this literature, Wickler, Haack, and Intagliata (1984) concluded that when social class is held constant, the divorce rate between families with and without children with disabilities is nonsignificant. Despite the inconclusive nature of the results, a substantial number of single parents are rearing children with disabilities.

The purpose of this paper is to analyze the research literature about single parent families of children with disabilities in order to understand the dynamics of stress and adaptation in these families. First, an historical overview of the assumptions and directions of previous research concerned with families of children with disabilities as a basis for understanding the problems and concerns of single parent families is presented. Second, the conclusions and methodological concerns of a previous review about the stress of single parents who are rearing children with disabilities are presented. Third, the research studies are reviewed as to their sample characteristics and measures. Fourth, the research findings across studies are examined under the categories of stress, resources, and adaptation. Finally, implications for research, education policy, and practices are presented.

HISTORICAL OVERVIEW OF PREVIOUS RESEARCH

Researchers have actively studied children with disabilities and their families for over forty years. A clinical pathological model, focusing on the problems experienced by the families guided the early research (Byrne & Cunningham, 1985; Farber & Rowitz, 1986; Foster & Berger, 1985). Mothers of children with disabilities were expected to experience elevated stress and negative psychological outcomes from rearing children with disabilities. Early research corroborated this assumption of increased stress and psychological problems (e.g., Farber, 1959). However, subsequent research findings demonstrated that mothers of children with disabilities did not universally report high stress or psychological problems (e.g., Frey, Greenberg, & Fewell, 1989; Kazak, 1987), and more recent research suggests that mothers of children with disabilities are not necessarily more stressed than other mothers (Boyce, Behl, Mortensen, & Akers, 1991; Innocenti, Huh, & Boyce, 1992; Shonkoff, Hauser-Cram, Krauss, & Upshur, 1992).

These differences in findings need to be evaluated from an historical perspective. Since the mid-1970s, there has been a great increase in services including early intervention (i.e., prior to age 6) for children with disabilities, educational inclusion policies, and family support programs (Shonkoff et al.,

1992). During that time, variability in stress in families of children with disabilities has been noted (e.g., Gallagher, 1987; Shonkoff et al., 1992), and research has investigated a number of issues (e.g., family demographics, severity of disability, child age and sex, marital satisfaction) in a search for the factors that influence and mediate family stress and adaptation.

A likely stressor is family structure, i.e., having one or two parents in the home. Early research indicated that single motherhood in families of children with disabilities was related to increased stress (Beckman, 1983; Holroyd, 1974). Since then a limited number of studies investigated the effects of single parenting in families which included a child with disabilities. Outcome variables have varied, but the stress and/or coping of the mother have been the most common focus.

Financial difficulties of single mothers of children with disabilities have been noted (Gallagher, 1987). In the population as a whole, single parenthood is often associated with low income (see Bowen, this volume) and other stressors. Therefore, it is important to determine whether the stress reported in families of children with disabilities results from having a child with disabilities, being a single parent, or other factors often associated with single parenthood. Theoretical models of family adaptation (e.g., Double ABCX Model of Adjustment and Adaptation [McCubbin & Patterson, 1983]; Model of Stress, Coping, and Family Ecology [Crnic, Friedrich, & Greenberg, 1983]) encourage the examination of a number of variables, including stressors, available resources, the meaning of the event to the family, and interactions among the various contexts of the family.

CONCLUSIONS AND METHODOLOGICAL CONCERNS OF PREVIOUS REVIEW ABOUT STRESS

A number of reviews of literature concerned with family effects of having a child with disabilities in the home were analyzed (e.g., Byrne & Cunningham, 1985; Crnic et al., 1983; Foster & Berger, 1985); some discussed divorce findings of families of children with disabilities. One focused on the stress and adaptation of single mothers of children with disabilities. Bristol, Reichle, and Thomas (1987) concluded that:

> Results of these studies appear to indicate that single mothers of handicapped children experience more general stress and financial difficulties than married mothers . . . , although this is not consistent across all studies. (p. 59)

The authors then delineated several methodological issues for consideration in future research of single parent families of children with disabilities. First, differences in socioeconomic status between single- and two-parent mothers need to be controlled in the research design or the statistical analysis. Second, single mothers of children with disabilities are not necessarily a homogenous group. Findings may vary depending on whether single-parent status resulted from never-marrying, divorce, separation, or the death of the husband. Third, the amount of caretaking performed by the father varies, in both single and two parent families and might more properly be considered as a continuous, not a dichotomous, variable. Fourth, other persons may participate in the caretaking of the child. These concerns have been considered in this review.

REVIEW OF RESEARCH LITERATURE

In the present literature search, 15 studies[2] of mothers who are rearing children with disabilities were identified. Eight conducted single- vs. two-parent comparisons using analysis of variance designs (hereafter referred to as comparative studies). Seven studies examined the predictors (i.e., the family conditions) of stress (hereafter designated as correlational studies). The former group examined how mothers in single and two parent families differed on particular outcome measures, and the second group examined how a number of variables, including single parenthood, were related to parent stress, or other outcome measure. (Table 1 provides a listing of the studies reviewed, categorized by methodological design.) The studies spanned a 14-year period from 1978 to 1992. All measured some aspect of parent reaction or adaptation to caring for a child with, or at risk for developing, disabilities. Maternal stress and adaptation were measured in six of the comparison studies (Boyce, 1992; Burke, 1978; Gaudet & Powers, 1986; McCubbin, 1989; Salisbury, 1987; Schilling, Kirkham, Snow, & Schinke, 1986) and five of the correlational studies (Beavers, Hampson, Hulgus, & Beavers, 1986; Beckman, 1983; Boyce et al., 1991; Bradshaw & Lawton, 1978; Glidden, 1991). Perceptions of available resources and support, family adaptability and cohesion, and life satisfaction were measured in some of the studies.

Specific adaptations to caring for a child with, or at risk of developing, disabilities were investigated in four studies, including quality of stimulation (Allen, Affleck, McGrade, & McQueeney, 1984; Bristol et al., 1987), mothers' perceptions of infant temperament (Allen et al., 1984), future permanent planning (Kaufman, Adams, & Campbell, 1991), and out-of-home placement (Sherman, 1988).

The studies reviewed do not include Holroyd's paper (1974) which is frequently cited as evidence that, for families of children with disabilities,

TABLE 1. Studies Reviewed

Comparative Studies	Correlational Studies
Allen, Affleck, McGrade, & McQueeney (1984)	Beavers, Hampson, Hulgus, & Beavers (1986)
Boyce (1992)	Beckman (1983)
Bristol (1987) reported in Bristol et al. (1987)	Boyce, Behl, Mortensen, & Akers (1991)
Burke (1987)	Bradshaw & Lawton (1978)
Gaudet & Powers (1986)	Glidden (1991)
McCubbin (1989)	Kaufman, Adams, & Campbell (1991)
Salisbury (1987)	Sherman (1988)
Schilling, Kirkham, Snow, & Schinke (1986)	

single mothers of children with disabilities experience more stress than coupled mothers of children with disabilities. In her analysis of the single- vs. two-parent issue, families of children with and without disabilities were grouped together, introducing a possible confound.

Given the great variability among studies, information regarding sample characteristics and measures used are provided in the following order to help readers evaluate the findings. Samples are described, demographic characteristics measured are discussed, the measures used are outlined and, findings are discussed. Differences in findings are discussed in terms of statistical significance (p-value of .05 or less). The degree to which outcomes covary with other subject and study characteristics (e.g., severity of child's disability, family demographic characteristics, methodological quality of study) is also examined.

Study Characteristics

Samples. Finding adequate numbers of families of children with disabilities is problematic. Thus, samples are often limited in size and often include wide variations in maternal or child age, and types or severity of disability. Sample selection for studies investigating single parents of children with disabilities is further complicated by finding sufficient samples of single parents. All samples involved parents (almost always mothers) of children with disabilities. One study investigated only families who had adopted children with disabilities (Glidden, 1991).

The median number of families included in these studies was 60. All of the samples included less than 100 subjects, with the exception of four studies (Boyce, 1992; Boyce et al., 1991; Bradshaw & Lawton, 1978; Sherman, 1988). The two United States studies with large samples (Boyce, 1992; Boyce et al., 1991) used the Early Intervention Research Institute longitudinal studies extant data set (White, 1991) collected at 16 sites from different geographical regions of the U.S.

Two samples included an equal number of mothers in single and two parent families (Burke, 1978; McCubbin, 1989). In the other samples, there were fewer single-parent mothers than mothers in two parent families, with the proportion ranging from 14 to 51%. The number of single-parent mothers was particularly small in four studies (4 in Salisbury, 1987; 7 in Beavers et al., 1986; and 8 each in Beckman, 1983 and Gaudet & Powers, 1986). The families in some of the studies were young families, early in the family life cycle, with mothers in their 20s or 30s. Other studies investigated families more advanced in their family life cycle with mothers' ages ranging from the 40s through 60s.

Subgroupings (divorced, separated, never married, and widowed) were reported in some of the studies, but the subgroup divisions were not consistently defined across studies, and the proportions of subgroups varied across samples. The sample used by McCubbin (1989) is unique in that 45% of the single-parent mothers were widows. No study analyzed the data by single-parent subgroups, probably due to small numbers in each group.

Of those studies in which race of subjects was reported, samples were predominantly white with a smaller percent of African-Americans (e.g., Kaufman et al., 1991), Hispanics (e.g., Gaudet & Powers, 1986), and/or native Americans (McCubbin, 1989).

All samples were composed of families of persons at risk for, or with, identified disabilities (two studies also included single and two parent families of children without disabilities [Burke, 1978; Salisbury, 1987]). Multiple categories of disabilities were included in most of the studies (e.g., including Down syndrome, cerebral palsy, developmental delay), while four studies limited their samples to a particular diagnosis. These diagnostic groups included cerebral palsy (McCubbin, 1989), physical disabilities (Burke, 1978), medically fragile infants (Allen et al., 1984), and autism or communication impairment (Bristol, 1987). One study matched the samples on severity of disability (McCubbin, 1989). The ages of the persons with disabilities varied widely across studies. Most studies focused on infants, preschoolers, or school-age children; one (e.g., Kaufman et al., 1991) studied adults with disabilities.

Demographic comparisons. Five of the eight comparison studies reported comparisons of child and family characteristics between single and two parent families (Allen et al., 1984; Boyce, 1992; Bristol, 1987; Burke, 1978; Schilling et al., 1986). In these five studies, education and/or income was compared, with single-mother families generally reporting less education and/or income than the two-parent families. A younger mean age for the single mothers than the two-parent mothers was reported (Allen et al., 1984; Boyce, 1992). Two-parent families had more children than single-mother families (Boyce, 1992; Burke, 1978; Schilling et al., 1986). Single and two parent families did not differ on child age or severity of disability in the studies that completed these comparisons. Comparable distributions of race across single- and two-parent groups were reported in three studies (Allen et al., 1984; McCubbin, 1989; Schilling et al., 1986). One study, due to unequal distribution of racial groups across single- and two-parent groups, analyzed data by race (African-American and Euro-American) as well as by number of parents (Boyce, 1992).

Although demographic differences were found, only three studies controlled for these differences in their analyses (Allen et al., 1984; Boyce, 1992; Bristol, 1987). Matching of parents' age and gender and severity of child's disability was used to control differences in one study (McCubbin, 1989).

The correlational studies did not compare demographic characteristics of the mothers in the single- and two-parent groups due to the type of analyses used. However, across studies, the characteristics of income, socioeconomic status, and family size were generally found to be either associated with or a predictor of stress and adaptation. These are the same variables that often differentiated the mothers in the single and two parent families in the comparison studies discussed above.

Measures. The measures used to quantify the outcome variables were usually paper-and-pencil protocols that were completed by mothers in connection with an interview or part of a mailed survey. Measures generally included perceptions of family stress, family support and resources, and adaptation. Observational methodology was occasionally used (Allen et al., 1984; Beavers et al., 1986; Bristol et al., 1987).

Some of the measures were developed for use with families in the general population and have since been used with samples of families of children with disabilities (e.g., Social Adjustment Rating Scale [Holmes & Rahe, 1967]; Parenting Stress Index (PSI) [Abidin, 1983]). Others were developed specifically for use with families of children with disabilities (e.g., Questionnaire on Resources and Stress (QRS) [Holroyd, 1974]). Some have been used extensively by researchers, while others were specific to individual studies. The psychometric properties (e.g., reliability and validity) of these measures vary. Readers interested in greater detail should consult the specific references listed in Table 2.

FINDINGS RELATED TO STRESS, RESOURCES AND ADAPTATION

Several studies endeavored to understand the stress and adaptation experienced by families of children with disabilities. The comparison studies focused on the differences in stress and adaptation between mothers in single and two parent families, while the predictive studies attempted to describe those family conditions that related to stress and adaptation. Stress and adaptation are complex, interrelated phenomena that exist in the person-environment relationship and involve the environmental stressor, as well as the person's appraisal, beliefs, and resources (Friedrich, Greenberg, & Crnic, 1987; Lazarus, DeLongis, Folkman, & Gruen, 1985). These researchers have attempted to measure these phenomena in a variety of ways. Their findings are discussed here in relation to these three categories: stress, resources, and adaptation.

Stress. Eight studies (four comparison and four predictive) investigated maternal psychological stress and/or stressful life events. Across studies, no clear disadvantage for mothers in single parent families of children with disabilities was evidenced.

Four studies compared the stress of single- and two-parent mothers. Single mothers experienced greater stress than mothers in two parent families in two studies (Burke, 1978; Salisbury, 1987), while a third study found no difference in stress levels between mothers in single and two parent families (Schilling et al., 1986). The large multi-site study (Boyce, 1992) found single mothers more stressed only when the differences in age, education and income were not controlled in the analyses. Single mothers may be more stressed than mothers in two parent families, but resources, in terms of education and income, may mediate the stress.

Predictors of stress were examined in four studies (Beckman, 1983; Boyce et al., 1991; Bradshaw & Lawton, 1978; Glidden, 1991). The relationship between stress and the number of parents in the home varied from a moderate relationship to no relationship ($r = -.25$ to $.04$) (Beckman, 1983; Boyce et al., 1991; Glidden, 1991). In regression analyses, the number of parents in the home was not a significant predictor of stress (Boyce et al., 1991; Bradshaw & Lawton, 1978).

TABLE 2. Measures Used in Reviewed Studies

Outcome Measures	Studies Using the Measure
Beavers-Timberlawn Family Evaluation Scale (BT)*	Beavers et al. (1986)
Carolina Family Responsibilities Scale*	Bristol et al. (1987)
Centripetal/Centrifugal Family Style Scale (CP/CF)*	Beavers et al. (1986)
Coping-Health Inventory for Parents (CHIP) McCubbin, McCubbin, Nevin, & Cauble (1983)	Gaudet & Powers (1986) McCubbin (1989)
Family Adaptability and Cohesion Evaluation Scales (FACES I/III) Olson, Bell, & Porter (1978) Olson, Portner, & LaVee (1985)	McCubbin (1989) (FACES I) Boyce et al. (1991) (FACES III) Boyce (1992)(FACES III)
Family Inventory of Life Events and Changes (FILE) McCubbin, Patterson, & Wilson (1983)	McCubbin (1989) Boyce (1992) Boyce et al. (1991)
Family Inventory of Resources for Management (FIRM) McCubbin, Comeau, & Harkins (1981)	McCubbin (1989)
Family Resource Scale (FRS) Dunst & Leet (1985)	Boyce (1992) Boyce et al. (1991)
Family Support Scale (FSS) Dunst, Jenkins, & Trivette (1984)	Boyce (1992) Boyce et al. (1991)
Family System Strain Schedule (FSSS) Burke (1978)	Burke (1978)
Feetham Family Functioning Survey (FFFS) Roberts & Feetham (1982)	Schilling et al. (1986)
Home Observation for Measurement of the Environment (HOME) Caldwell & Bradley (1978)	Allen et al. (1984)

Home Quality Rating Scale Meyers, Mink, & Nihira (1981)	Bristol (1987)
Infant Characteristics Questionnaire Bates (1979)	Allen et al. (1984)
Malaise Inventory Rutter, Tizard, & Whitmore (1970)	Bradshaw & Lawton (1978)
Nelson Rating of Parental Satisfaction Nelson (1985)	Glidden (1991)
Parenting Stress Index (PSI) Abidin (1983)	Boyce (1992) Boyce et al. (1991)
Perception of Baby Temperament Pederson, Anderson, & Cain (1976)	Allen et al. (1984)
Placement Questionnaire*	Sherman (1988)
Quality of Life Survey (QLS) Olson et al. (1982)	Schilling et al. (1986)
Questionnaire on Resources and Stress (QRS) Holroyd (1974, 1985) Short Forms (QRS-F) Friedrich, Greenberg, & Crnic (1983) (QRS-SF) Salisbury (1987)	Beckman (1983) Salisbury (1987) (QRS-SFA) Glidden (1991) (QRS-F) Schilling et al. (1992) (QRS-F)
Social Adjustment Rating Scale (SARS) Holmes & Rahe (1967)	Beckman (1983)
Utah Stress Scale (USS) Sullivan et al. (1976)	Burke (1978)

* Author not identified

Four studies (Beckman, 1983; Boyce, 1992; Burke, 1978; McCubbin, 1989) examined life events/changes (e.g., death of husband, loss of job) to assess the number of stressors experienced by families during the previous year. No differences were found between mothers in single- and two-parent groups in the three comparison studies (Boyce, 1992; Burke, 1978; McCubbin, 1989). The study with a small sample reported that single parenthood correlated (r = –.43) with more life changes (Beckman, 1983).

In sum, the stress findings across studies are inconsistent. There is limited evidence that single mothers experience greater stress, but the stress may be more related to other aspects of their lives.

Resources. Findings from the two groups of studies (the comparison and correlational studies) appear to be in agreement concerning the socioeconomic characteristics. Single mothers as a group had less education and/or income, and consequently less socioeconomic resources, than mothers in two parent families (Allen et al., 1984; Boyce, 1992; Bristol, 1987; Burke, 1978). Income, and other measures of socioeconomic status, were associated with maternal stress (Boyce et al., 1991; Bradshaw & Lawton, 1978) and future planning or out-of-home placement (Kaufman et al., 1991; Sherman, 1988).

Perceptions of resources and social support were measured in four studies (Boyce, 1992; Boyce et al., 1991; McCubbin, 1989; Schilling et al., 1986). Mothers' perceptions of resources generally substantiated the socioeconomic findings. For example, mothers in single parent families reported greater concerns about their financial well-being than mothers in two parent families (McCubbin, 1989), indicating that the mothers realistically appraised their situation. Similarly, mothers' education and income was significantly associated with their perception of resources, and their perception of resources, in turn, was associated with their stress (Boyce et al., 1991).

Consequently, the findings across studies support the concern that socioeconomic differences between two parent and single parent families need to be included in the analyses and are necessary for interpreting the research findings (Bristol, 1987). Most of the studies did not perform multivariate analyses that would allow for the examination of the mediating effects of socioeconomic factors. One study reported results both with and without socioeconomic covariates (Boyce, 1992). Without these covariates single mothers reported more stress, more stressful life events, less cohesion, fewer resources, and less social support than mothers in two parent families. When mother's age, education, and income were entered into the analysis, most of the significant differences disappeared. Only differences in family cohesion remained (Boyce, 1992).

These findings lend support to the conjecture that social and economic problems common to many single parents are so overwhelming that they gravely complicate the effects of having a child with disabilities in the family (Schilling et al., 1986). The "feminization of poverty" is a very real problem for many single mothers in the general population (Hoffman & Duncan, 1988), with almost half (48.9%) of the families who were poor being headed by female householders with children under 18 years of age (U.S. Bureau of Census, 1991). The research reviewed herein indicates that it may well be so for many single mothers of children with disabilities.

Adaptation and coping. Family adaptation and coping were investigated in a variety of ways. Overall coping and adaptation were measured in two studies. Mothers in single and two parent families in the two studies reported similar coping and adaptation, except for the family integration subscale, on which single mothers reported more problems with family integration than mothers in two parent families (McCubbin, 1989).

Family adaptability (flexibility) and family cohesion, characteristics that should promote adaptation and coping, were measured in two studies. In the study where widows were numerous in the single-parent group, single mothers reported greater adaptability than mothers in two parent families (McCubbin, 1989). Conversely, in the sample that included a high proportion of never-married mothers in the single-parent group, single mothers reported less cohesion than mothers in two parent families (Boyce, 1992). The differences in samples may account for the differences in findings.

An observational study of 40 families investigated family functioning in the homes in terms of family flexibility, competence, and style (Beavers et al., 1986). The families were divided into two groups on the basis of observed family functioning (optimal/adequate families vs. midrange/borderline families). Only one of the seven single parent families was in the optimal/adequate group. This family included a mother and two young adult daughters who shared in the caretaking of the adolescent brother who had disabilities.

Specific family adaptations were also studied. Allen and associates (1984) examined environmental stimulation and perceptions of infant temperament of medically fragile infants at nine and 18 months of age. Single mothers provided less optimal home stimulation at both times, and perceived their infants' temperaments more negatively at the nine month assessment. Maternal age and education were controlled in the analyses. However, Bristol et al. (1987) found no differences in stimulation provided to children, ages 2 to 10, between single- and two-parent groups. Maternal education and age were controlled in the analyses. The age differences of the children in the studies may account for the differences in findings; however, the studies differed in the observational protocols used and the types of disabilities of the children.

The principle of minimal successive adaptations (Farber & Rowitz, 1985) suggests that families, while attempting to care for the child with disabilities, make as few changes in their lives as possible. Out-of-home placement is considered the final in a series of successive adaptations. One correlational study examined out-of-home placement (Sherman, 1988), and one examined future permanency planning for the person with disabilities (Kaufman et al., 1991). Single-parent status was found to relate to out-of-home placement, but not to permanency planning.

In sum, the evidence that single mothers experience significantly more stress or adapt less well than mothers in two parent families is limited. A lack of differences in findings across the single- and two-parent groups is common. However, certain findings (e.g., family disharmony [Glidden, 1991], family integration [McCubbin, 1989], family cohesion [Boyce, 1992]) suggest that single mothers face specific challenges in maintaining family closeness and integration that mothers in two parent families do not.

The finding across studies that single mothers, as a group, had less education and income, and in some studies were younger than their two-parent counterparts is compelling. These factors appeared to influence stress and adaptation (Boyce, 1992). Research with "typical" families (i.e., studies of families without disabilities) supports these findings (Simons, Beaman, Conger, & Chao, 1993).

In evaluating these findings it seems important to recognize the limitations of the studies reviewed. Thus far, the body of literature is small, samples are limited, and most of the research designs have not addressed the interactions among multiple variables. While a few studies addressed the mediating effect of socioeconomic variables, none have yet addressed the effects of other variables, such as single-parent subgroup (e.g., widowed, divorced, never-married), child age, or disability characteristics.

The lack of consistency in findings across studies, and the fact that findings disagree with the commonly held assumption that caring for a family alone results in more stress are troublesome. One wonders whether the measures used are able to tap differences that actually exist in stress and adaptation, or if the differences are limited or nonexistent. Some of the variation in findings are likely due to differences in measures used, sample characteristics, and research designs. Another problem may be that the present measures of family functioning are too global (Telleen, Herzog, & Kilbane, 1989). Additionally, stress and adaptation are difficult constructs to measure (Lazarus et al., 1985). Family and child characteristics explained little (i.e., 20% or less) in the perceptions of stress (Boyce et al.,

1991; Bradshaw & Lawton, 1978). Stress levels may be more strongly influenced by internal factors, such as beliefs and personality (Bradshaw & Lawton, 1978), or perceptions concerning the family's functioning (Boyce et al., 1991).

IMPLICATIONS FOR RESEARCH, EDUCATION, POLICY AND PRACTICE

The present findings are not conclusive, but they furnish issues for researchers, educators, policy makers and service providers to consider. The findings are relevant for family life educators and professionals who provide services for families of children without disabilities, as well as for service providers dealing with children who have disabilities. Families of children with disabilities are similar to other families, and, therefore, studies of these special families provide insights into the understanding of family functioning in general. Also, as families of children with disabilities are increasingly "mainstreamed" into society, professionals (e.g., therapists, social workers, and nurses) are more likely to interact with these families. For special educators, the findings provide relevant insights for formulating individual service plans and choosing appropriate services. Thus, professionals working with families or designing future research should consider the following.

First, the lack of definitive findings in stress and adaptation between single- and two-parent mothers should remind professionals not to automatically view single mothers of children with disabilities from a negative or pathological outlook. They are not necessarily more stressed. These families are probably more similar to, than different from, other families. Comparison studies of mothers in single parent families of children with and without disabilities would contribute to the understanding of the causes of stress in single parent families. Salisbury (1986) made this comparison and found no differences in stress scores, but the samples sizes were very small.

Second, there is great heterogeneity among single mothers of children with disabilities; each family has its own individuality. The reason for the single parent status (e.g., divorced/separated, widowed, never-married) may influence stress and adaptation. None of the studies reviewed compared stress and adaptation using the variables of single parent family. McCubbin's (1989) findings that more extended family support and adaptability were reported by single mothers than by mothers in two parent families is intriguing given that this is the only sample that included a high proportion of widows. Single mothers are also very diverse in age and stage of life cycle, education, race, and income, as well as in beliefs, attitudes, and expectations. Mother's life stage in some studies was limited, but no study has yet compared stress or adaptation of mothers in different stages, and only one study (Boyce, 1992) investigated racial effects. When the analyses were controlled for demographic differences there were no differences between African-American and Euro-American mothers on stress, adaptability, cohesion, or adequacy of resources or social support. However, African-American mothers reported fewer life changes. Consideration of diversity should influence future research and result in more individualized services.

Third, the influence of socioeconomic variables needs to be recognized in research designs and in provision of services. While education and job training are not usually part of family support services, connections to such programs could be provided. Professionals need to remember that provision of social support and coping techniques are no substitute for adequate economic and institutional supports (Schilling et al., 1986).

Fourth, the individual characteristics of the child with disabilities need to be considered. Some children have numerous medical complications which require frequent hospitalizations. Others are socially unresponsive or are difficult to control, while others require few adaptations.

Fifth, the degree to which help from additional adult caregivers (e.g., nonresident father, grandparent) alleviates maternal stress and improves family functioning needs to be further investigated. Although none of the studies investigated the relationship between assistance with child care and stress directly, the finding that one optimally functioning single parent family included two adult young women who helped their mother care for a younger brother with disabilities is intriguing (Beavers et al., 1986). Three maternal reports of experiences of being a single parent of a child with disabilities discuss the difficulty of finding suitable caregivers (Barnes, 1986; Lucas, 1992; McAnaney, 1989). One said, "The hardest part is not having someone to take over, . . . I can't hide in my room when I need a break (Lucas, 1992, p. E-3). Child care assistance and respite services should be considered, particularly if no other adult participates in caregiving."

Sixth, how families handle task demands needs to be evaluated. Early research indicated a relationship between child care demands and maternal stress in families of children with disabilities (Beckman, 1983). Other research indicates that mothers in single parent families make active manipulations in order to balance their child care demands with other activities. In one study, single mothers of children with disabilities often chose special education classes for their children over integrated classrooms because bus service and lunch were part of the special education program (Burke, 1975).

Other evidence of this juggling of demands comes from findings concerning the allocation of time across daily activities (i.e., time-use) (Barnett, 1987). Mothers of children with Down syndrome differed from mothers of children without disabilities in the time spent in child care, working for pay, and social activities (Boyce, Olson, & Saarelainen, 1992). Mothers of children with Down syndrome spent more time providing child care than mothers of children without Down syndrome, and consequently, spent less time in other activities, including working for pay and participating in social activities. Continuing analyses indicate that, within the sample of mothers whose children had Down syndrome, single mothers spent more time working and less time caring for their children than two-parent mothers, possibly adjusting their time because of work restraints.

Finally all of the findings speak to the need to be cognizant of the multiple and varied changes and stressors that families deal with daily. It is easy to define a family by the most visible problem (i.e., having a child with disabilities or being a single parent), but other sources of stress need to be recognized (Krauss, 1993). The strengths and coping strategies of a family must be identified in order to provide services that will complement their strengths. Although these families often face crises related to the child with disabilities, they also find joy. As one single mother of a boy with Down syndrome said, "He's brought more joy into my life than he's taken. . . . I'm never angry or bitter. I'm a better person for this" (Lucas, 1992).

NOTES

1. There are single fathers rearing children who have disabilities, however their numbers appear to be few. Although almost all of the papers reviewed studied mothers in single parent and two parent families, fathers were included in a few studies. McCubbin (1989)included one set of fathers, matched on age in the single- and two-parent groups. It appears Salisbury (1987) included father responses in the two-parent group, but not in the single-parent group. Two studies included father responses, but did not report whether they were in the single- or two-parent groups (Glidden, 1991; Kaufman, Adams, & Campbell, 1991).

2. Primary reference material included *PschInfo*, *ERIC*, *Psychological Abstracts*, and *Social Science Citation Index*. A number of recent journals were also reviewed. Active researchers in the area were telephoned to check for additional published and unpublished references.

REFERENCES

Abidin, R. R. (1983). *Manual for the Parenting Stress Index*. Charlottesville, VA: Pediatric Psychology Press.

Allen, D. A., Affleck, G., McGrade, B. J., & McQueeney, M. (1984). Effects of single-parent status on mothers and their high-risk infants. *Infant Behavior and Development*, *7*, 347-359.

Barnes, K. (1986). Surviving as a single parent. *The Exceptional Parent*, *16*(3), 47-49.

Barnett, S. W. (1987). *Time use in families of retarded children and adults*. Proposal funded by NICHD to the Early Intervention Research Institute, Utah State University, Logan.

Bates, J. (1979). *Infant characteristics questionnaire*. Unpublished document, Indiana University, Bloomington.

Beavers, J., Hampson, R. B., Hulgus, Y. F., & Beavers, W. R. (1986). Coping in families with a retarded child. *Family Process*, *25*, 365-378.

Beckman, P. J. (1983). Influence of selected child characteristics on stress in families of handicapped infants. *American Journal of Mental Deficiency*, *88*, 150-156.

Boyce, G. C. (1992, November). *Parenting a child with disabilities: A comparison of single- and two-parent families*. Poster presented at the Annual Conference of the National Council on Family Relations, Orlando, FL.

Boyce, G. C., Behl, D., Mortensen, L., & Akers, J. (1991). Child characteristics, family demographics, and family processes: Their effects on the stress experienced by families of children with disabilities. *Counselling Psychology Quarterly*, *4*, 273-288.

Boyce, G. C., Olson, S. T., & Saarelainen, S. B. (1992, December). *The division of parental time across daily activities in families of children with and without disabilities: Information for parents and services providers*. Paper presented at the Annual Conference for the Division of Early Childhood, Washington, DC.

Bradshaw, J., & Lawton, D. (1978). Tracing the causes of stress in families with handicapped children. *British Journal of Social Work*, *8*, 181-192.

Bristol, M. M. (1987). Methodological caveats in the assessment of single-parent families of handicapped children. *Journal of the Division for Early Childhood*, *11*, 135-142.

Bristol, M. M., Reichle, N. C., & Thomas, D. D. (1987). Changing demographics of the American family: Implications for single-parent families of young handicapped children. *Journal of the Division for Early Childhood*, *12*, 56-69.

Burke, S. O. (1978). *Familial strain and the development of normal and handicapped children in single and two parent families*. Unpublished Doctoral Dissertation. University of Toronto, Canada.

Byrne, E. A., & Cunningham, C. C. (1985). The effects of mentally handicapped children on families: A conceptual review. *Journal of Child Psychological Psychiatry*, *26*, 847-864.

Caldwell, B. M., & Bradley, R. H. (1978). *Home observation for measurement of the environment*. Little Rock: Center for Child Development and Education, University of Arkansas at Little Rock.

Cooke, K., Bradshaw, J., Lawton, D., & Brewer, R. (1986). Child disablement, family dissolution and reconstitution. *Developmental Medicine & Child Neurology, 28*, 610-616.

Crnic, K. A., Friedrich, W. N., & Greenberg, M. T. (1983). Adaptation of families with mentally retarded children: A model of stress, coping, and family ecology. *American Journal of Mental Deficiency, 88*, 125-138.

Dunst, C. J., & Leet, H. E. (1985). *Family Resource Scale.* Morgantown, NC: Western Carolina Center.

Dunst, C. J., Jenkins, V., & Trivette, C. M. (1984). Family support scale: Reliability and validity. *Journal of Individual, Family, and Community Wellness, 1*, 111-125.

Farber, B. (1959). Effects of a severely mentally retarded child on family integration. *Monographs of the Society for Research in Child Development*, No. 71.

Farber, B., & Rowitz, L. (1986). Families with a mentally retarded child. *International Review of Research in Mental Retardation*, 14, 201-224.

Foster, M., & Berger, M. (1985). Research with families with handicapped children: A multilevel systemic perspective. In L. L'Abate (Ed.), *The handbook of family psychology and therapy* (Vol. 2, pp. 741-780). Homewood, IL: The Dorsey Press.

Friedrich, W. N., Greenberg, M. T., & Crnic, K. A. (1987). The effects of developmental disabilities on children and families: Measurement issues and conceptual frameworks. In S. H. Landesman & P. M. Vietze (Eds.), *Living environments and mental retardation* (pp. 357-374). Washington, DC: American Association on Mental Retardation.

Friedrich, W. N., Greenberg, M. T., & Crnic, K. A. (1983). A short version of the questionnaire on resources and stress. *American Journal of Mental Deficiency, 88*, 41-48.

Frey, K., Greenberg, M., & Fewell, R. (1989). Stress and coping among parents of handicapped children: A multidimensional approach. *American Journal on Mental Retardation, 94*, 240-249.

Gallagher, J. J. (1987). *The Carolina institute for research on early education for the handicapped II final report* (Contract #300-82-0366). Chapel Hill: Frank Porter Graham Child Development Center, University of North Carolina at Chapel Hill.

Gaudet, L. M., & Powers, G. M. (1986). *Differences in coping patterns in parents of chronically ill children.* Unpublished Master's Thesis. (ERIC Document Reproduction No. ED 266 374).

Glidden, L. M. (1991). Adopted children with developmental disabilities: Post-placement family functioning. *Children and Youth Services Review, 13*, 363-377.

Hoffman, S., & Duncan, G. (1988). What are the economic consequences of divorce? *Demography, 25*, 641-645.

Holmes, T. H., & Rahe, R. H. (1967). The social readjustment rating scale. *Journal of Psychosomatic Research, 11*, 213-218.

Holroyd, J. (1974). The questionnaire on resources and stress: An instrument to measure family response to a handicapped member. *Journal of Community Psychology*, *2*, 92-94.

Holroyd, J. (1985). *Manual for the questionnaire on resources and stress.* Los Angeles: UCLA Neuropsychiatric Institute.

Innocenti, M. S., Huh, K., & Boyce, G. C. (1992). Families of children with disabilities: Normative data and other considerations on parenting stress. *Topics in Early Childhood Special Education*, *12*, 403-427.

Jones, C. W. (1987). Coping with the young handicapped child in the single-parent family: An ecosystemic perspective. *Family Therapy Collections*, *23*, 85-100.

Kaufman, A. V., Adams, J. P., & Campbell, V. A. (1991). Permanency planning by older parents who care for adult children with mental retardation. *Mental Retardation*, *29*, 293-300.

Kazak, A. E. (1987). Families with disabled children: Stress and social networks in three samples. *Journal of Abnormal Child Psychology*, *15*, 137-146.

Krauss, M. W. (1993, March). *Stability and change in the adaptation of families of children with disabilities.* Paper presented at the 1993 Annual Conference of the Society for Research in Child Development, New Orleans, LA.

Lazarus, R. S., DeLongis, A., Folkman, S., Gruen, R. (1985). Stress and adaptational outcomes: The problem of confounded measures. *American Psychologist*, *40*, 770-779.

Longo, D. C., & Bond, L. (1984). Families of the handicapped child: Research and practice. *Family Relations*, *33*, 57-65.

Lucas, L. (1992, January 19). For the love of Andrew. *The Press-Enterprise*, pp. E-1, E-3.

McAnaney, K. D. (1989). Single parenting: The hardest thing I've ever done. *Exceptional Parent*, *19*(5), 28-33.

McCubbin, H., Comeau, J., & Harkins, J. (1981). *FIRM: Family inventory of resources for management.* Madison: University of Wisconsin.

McCubbin, H., McCubbin, M., Nevin, R., & Cauble, A. E. (1983). *CHIP: Coping health inventory for parents.* Madison: University of Wisconsin.

McCubbin, H., Patterson, J., & Wilson, L. (1983). *FILE: Family inventory of life events.* Madison: University of Wisconsin.

McCubbin, M. A. (1989). Family stress and family strengths: A comparison of single- and two-parent families with handicapped children. *Research in Nursing and Health*, *12*, 101-110.

McCubbin, M., & Patterson, J. (1983). Family transitions: Adaptation to stress. In H. I. McCubbin, & C. R. Figley (Eds.), *Stress and the family* (Vol. 1, pp. 5-25). New York: Brunner/Mazel.

Meyers, C. E., Mink, I. T., Nihira, K. (1981). *Home quality rating scale (HQRS): User's Manual.* Department of Psychiatry and Biobehavioral Sciences, University of California at Los Angeles.

National Center for Educational Statistics, (1992). *Digest of Educational Statistics.* Washington, DC: U.S. Government Printing Office.

Nelson, K. A. (1985). *On the frontier of adoption: A study of special needs adoptive families.* New York: Child Welfare League of America.

Olson, D., Bell, R., & Portner, J. (1978). *FACES I: Family adaptability and cohesion evaluation scales.* St. Paul: University of Minnesota Press.

Olson, D. H., McCubbin, H., Barnes, H., Larsen, A., Muxon, M., & Wilson, M. (1982). *Family inventories.* St. Paul: University of Minnesota.

Olson, D. H., Portner, J., & LaVee, Y. (1985). *Family adaptability and cohesion evaluation scales.* St. Paul: University of Minnesota.

Pederson, F. A., Anderson, B. J., & Caine, R. L. (1976, April). *A methodology for assessing parental perceptions of infant temperament.* Paper presented at the Fourth Biennial Southeast Conference on Human Development.

Roberts, C. S., & Feetham, S. L. (1982). Assessing family functioning across 3 areas of relationships. *Nursing Research, 31*, 231-235.

Roesel, R., & Lawlis, G. F. (1983). Divorce in families of genetically handicapped/ mentally retarded individuals. *The American Journal of Family Therapy, 11*, 45-50.

Rutter, M., Tizard, J., & Whitmore, K. (1970). *Education, health and behavior.* London: Longmans.

Salisbury, C. L. (1987). Stressors of parents with young handicapped and nonhandicapped children. *Journal of the Division for Early Childhood, 11*, 154-160.

Schilling, R. F., Kirkham, M. A., Snow, W. H., & Shinke, S. P. (1986). Single mothers with handicapped children: Different from their married counterparts? *Family Relations, 35*, 69-77.

Sherman, B. R. (1988). Predictors of the decision to place developmentally disabled family members in residential care. *American Journal on Mental Retardation, 92*, 344-351.

Simons, R. L., Beaman, J., Conger, R. D., Chao, W. (1993). Stress, support, and antisocial behavior trait as determinants of emotional well-being and parenting practices among single mothers. *Journal of Marriage and the Family, 55*, 389-398.

Shonkoff, J. P., Hauser-Cram, P., Krauss, M. W., Upshur, C. C. (1992). Development of infants with disabilities and their families. *Monographs of the Society for Research in Child Development, 57.*

Sullivan et al. (1976). *Utah Stress Scales.*

Telleen, S., Herzog, A., & Kilbane, T. L. (1989). Impact of a family support program on mothers' social support and parenting stress. *American Journal of Orthopsychiatry, 59*, 410-419.

U. S. Bureau of the Census (1991). Poverty in the United States: 1991. *Current Population Reports.* Washington, D.C.: U.S. Government Printing Office: Washington D.C.

White, K. R. (1991). *Final report for project period October 1, 1985-December 31, 1990 of the longitudinal studies of the effects and costs of early intervention for handicapped children* (Contract #300-85-0173). Logan: Early Intervention Research Institute, Utah State University.

Wikler, L., Haack, J., & Intagliata, J. (1984). Bearing the burden alone? Helping divorced mothers of children with developmental disabilities. *Family Therapy Collection, 11*, 44-62.

Chapter 19

Single Parent Widows: Stressors, Appraisal, Coping, Resources, Grieving Responses and Health

Kathleen A. Gass-Sternas

SUMMARY. This paper examines the stressors, appraisal of bereavement, coping, resources, grieving responses and health of four types of single widow parents: widows raising dependent children; widows raising a handicapped child; independent older widows with children; and dependent, ill, older widows with a child. A review of literature on single parent widow families and data from the author's research on single parent widows served as a basis for this paper. Major gaps in knowledge include: limited research on single parent widow families including longitudinal and theory-based research; findings which are based on small samples of single parent widows who are often mixed with other single parent types; little research on single parent widows from Black, Hispanic and other ethnic groups; and few studies on resources used by widows. A secondary analysis of data from the author's research indicated characteristics of high-risk, vulnerable, and healthy single parent widow families. High-risk single parent widow families are characterized by: presence of multiple stressors; intense grieving; appraisal of bereavement as a threat or harmful loss; use of less adaptive coping; limited use of resources;

Kathleen A. Gass-Sternas is affiliated with Rutgers-The State University of New Jersey, College of Nursing, 180 University Avenue, Newark, NJ 07102.

[Haworth co-indexing entry note]: "Single Parent Widows: Stressors, Appraisal, Coping, Resources, Grieving Responses and Health." Gass-Sternas, Kathleen A. Co-published simultaneously in *Marriage & Family Review* (The Haworth Press, Inc.) Vol. 20, No. 3/4, 1995, pp. 411-445; and: *Single Parent Families: Diversity, Myths and Realities* (ed: Shirley M. H. Hanson et al.) The Haworth Press, Inc., 1995, pp. 411-445. Multiple copies of this article/chapter may be purchased from The Haworth Document Delivery Center [1-800-3-HAWORTH; 9:00 a.m. - 5:00 p.m. (EST)].

and poor health. Characteristics of vulnerable single parent widow families include: presence of stressors including an unresolved grieving process; negative appraisals of bereavement with hope for a more positive appraisal in the future; limited coping abilities; use of some resources such as helpful social supports; and less than optimum health which can improve with intervention. Positive meanings of bereavement, use of adaptive ways of coping, a normal grieving process, use of many resources, and good health are characteristics which are prevalent in healthy single parent widow families. Themes in common to all four family types were: the grieving process; changes in roles and responsibilities; employment; loneliness; dating and remarriage; and caregiver stress. Directions for future research and implications for family professionals are discussed.

KEYWORDS. Single mothers, Widowhood, Single parent widows

INTRODUCTION

Single parent families are families in which one parent lives with children. A woman can become a single parent as a result of widowhood, divorce, separation, desertion, adoption, planned non-marital and premarital birth. Demographic data indicate increasing numbers of family households are headed by a female single parent (McLanahan & Booth, 1989). Every year, over 800,000 men and women in the U.S. experience the death of their spouse (Bruce, Kim, Leaf, & Jacobs, 1990). Greene and Feld (1989) point out that by age 65, more than 50% of American married women become widows. In the United States, approximately 5 to 15 % of children lose one or both parents by the age of 15 (Harris, 1991). However, there is little research on single parent widows reported in the literature (Simon, 1990; Weltner, 1982). The majority of all single parents are black (Eggebeen & Uhlenberg, 1989; Joe, 1986) and there are increasing numbers of Hispanic single parents. Gutierrez (1987) reports that for Hispanics, 23% of all families are single parent female-headed families.

In the past, widowhood was the most common form of single parenthood; however, since World War II divorce and premarital birth have become the major contributors to the growth of single parent families. There are differences among types of single parent families with respect to their access to economic and social resources. Widows often have much higher incomes and experience less social disapproval than do other groups (McLanahan, Garfinkel & Ooms, 1987). Another difference is that stressors, appraisal, coping, resources, grieving and health may also vary among different types of single parent families.

Single parent widows have different reactions to death of a spouse which may depend on their appraisal of bereavement, coping responses, and resources. Little work has been done on appraisal in relationship to single parent widow families. Researchers have begun to address appraisal as a key variable which influences persons outcome to bereavement. Several frameworks have focused on the appraisal and adaptation outcomes of single parent families. Using the Typology Model of Adjustment and Adaptation, McCubbin (1989) studied single and two-parent families' appraisal (meanings the family attaches to their situation), stressors and demands, family strengths and resources, and coping as factors which influence the family's adaptation over time. Mutran and Reitzes (1984) used exchange and symbolic interaction frameworks which recognize that individuals actively appraise and assess situations, and that expectations and benefits derive their meanings from the situation and past experiences.

Coping is another factor affecting grieving and health of single parent widows. Little research has focused on coping with single parenthood (Burke, 1987). Research has addressed coping responses of widows and children after the death of a father/spouse (Ide et al., 1990; Kaffman, Elizur & Gluckson, 1987; Rosen, 1991; Warmbrod, 1986). For example, Kaffman et al. (1987) found less adaptive coping by widowed mothers was related to emotional difficulties in their children.

Bereavement is a major transition. Widows may experience stress related to losses of income, emotional and social support and role changes. Bereavement may be especially difficult for widows with parenting responsibilities because they often have reduced resources and other stressors with which they must cope. Resources can affect the meaning of bereavement (appraisal), the intensity and duration of grieving, the degree of stress experienced by widows, and their ability to cope or adapt. Resources which are important following bereavement include: helpful social supports; practicing rituals and beliefs which facilitate the grieving process; possessing religious beliefs which foster an understanding of death; knowledge of the grieving process; opportunities for anticipatory grieving; good prior mental-emotional health; absence of additional losses with bereavement; history of a quality relationship with the spouse; an unpreventable death; ability to openly express grief; belief in control over stressors; and adequate finances (Gass, 1987a; Gass & Chang, 1989). The literature on single parent widows has primarily focused on the resources of social support, adequate finances and control over stressors (Greene & Feld, 1989; Hogan, Hao & Parish, 1990; Lindblad-Goldberg & Dukes, 1985).

The purposes of this article are to examine the stressors, appraisal of bereavement, ways of coping, resources, grieving responses and health of single parent widows in four types of families: widows who are raising dependent children; widows who are raising a physically or mentally handicapped child; independent older widows with one or more healthy children; and dependent, ill, older widows with a healthy child in the home. This paper is based on a literature review and on data from the author's research on widows who are single parents. Criteria for the literature included in the review were literature on single parent families and widowhood which focused on the stressors, grieving responses, appraisal, coping, resources and health of widows with children. Research studies and clinical reports by professionals investigating single parent families including widows with children were included in the review. Data on the stressors, appraisal, coping, resources, grieving responses and health of high risk, vulnerable, and healthy single parent widow families are presented and illustrated with case studies. Themes common to all four types of single parent widow families are discussed. It is important to note that there are variations on these single widow family types. This paper focuses on the single parent widow families most frequently encountered in the literature and in the author's research.

REVIEW OF LITERATURE

This review of literature focuses on four types of single parent widow families: widows who are raising dependent children; widows who are raising a physically or mentally handicapped child; independent older widows with one or more healthy children; and dependent, ill, older widows with a healthy child in the home. Each of these family types will be discussed in relation to their stressors, grieving responses, coping, resources, and health. Gaps in knowledge are identified.

TYPES OF SINGLE PARENT WIDOW FAMILIES

Widows Who Are Raising Dependent Children

Stressors. The literature on single parent widows raising children largely focuses on the effects of bereavement on the widow and her children. Widows undergo dramatic changes that place them at risk for stress. Taking on the roles of both mother and father requires additional responsibility and can lead to role overload (Bird, 1986; Weltner, 1982). This problem is made more difficult for single mothers who need to work outside the home. The multiple demands may result in a family life with little time and energy available to the widow for herself, homemaking, parenting, shared family activities, or for providing emotional support to children whose functioning and school performance have often declined after the death of the father (Amato & Partridge, 1987; Mietus Sanik & Mauldin, 1986; Weltner, 1982). The widow often feels isolated from friends and experiences guilt because she cannot respond to all demands (Weltner, 1982). Having children at home may make it difficult for the widow to date and have a social life (Kitson, Babri, Roach, & Placidi, 1989). Among low income mothers of young children, Hall, Gurley, Sachs, and Kryscio (1991) reported chronic stressors to include inadequate income and housing, unemployment, parenting worries, and problems with interpersonal relationships which were related to high depressive symptoms.

A major stressor which may affect all family types but is especially difficult for widows raising dependent children is economic problems (Amato & Partridge, 1987; Fulmer, 1983; Joe, 1986; Menaghan & Parcel, 1990; Morgan, 1989; McLanahan et al., 1987). The loss of a husband's salary following death is rarely compensated for by widows returning to work due to women's work being underpaid (McLanahan & Booth, 1989). Also, child care is expensive which often prevents women from returning to work. Some widows and their children may need to move after finding a job. Moving to another home may require adjustment to new neighborhoods and can mean the loss of important social networks. Economic problems may increase health risks for children (Angel & Worobey, 1988).

Another stressor which may affect all family types but has been discussed in relation to widows raising dependent children is grieving (Fulmer, 1983; Harmon et al., 1990). In order to detach from their relationship with the deceased spouse or father and develop new attachments, family members must grieve. Reactions to loss in childhood can include problems with eating and sleeping, withdrawal, dependency, regression, restlessness, school performance, strained peer relations, separation-anxiety, delinquency, truancy, drug abuse, increased smoking behavior, inability to form trusting relationships, poor self-esteem, loneliness, depression, alcoholism, and psychosis (Cheifetz, Stavrakakis & Lester, 1989; Covey & Tam, 1990; Fulmer, 1983, 1987; Harris, 1991; Kaffman et al., 1987; McIntyre, 1990; Murphy, 1986-1987). Parents can have difficulty explaining death and dying to children (Galloway, 1990) and parents grief affects their ability to help their children (Black & Urbanowicz, 1987; Harmon et al., 1990).

Unresolved grief may be a source of depression in single parent mothers, especially lower income women. Children can show symptoms in response to this depression which adds additional stress for these widows (Fulmer, 1987). There may be difficulty in maintaining generational boundaries (Fulmer, 1983; Rosen, 1991). Single parents often lack confidants who can provide support to them (Angel & Worobey, 1988). A single parent can become dependent on a child in an effort to replace the lost relationship with the spouse (Harris, 1991). The child assumes a confidant role with the mother and an older son may be asked to carry out the role of man in the home. Adolescents sometimes feel they must stay home and care for the mother rather than leave home to meet their own developmental needs. Finding time to develop appropriate outside contacts with peers, dates, membership in organizations is difficult for the widow (Weltner, 1982).

Coping and resources. Several researchers have addressed coping behaviors of children and widows following the death of the father/spouse. How successful a single parent widow is at coping with widowhood depends upon the resources available to her. The way the widow copes can have an impact on her children. Kaffman et al. (1987) found the mother's manifestations of helplessness, inability to express and share grief with the children were related to emotional difficulties in the child. When families are able to talk about the deceased father, there is more opportunity for the children to share their feelings as well. Other factors which affect coping reactions include: the child's previous emotional state; prolonged separations from parents; child's access to a surrogate father figure; the quality of the mother's relationship with the child; the child's understanding of death; and previous experiences with death (Kaffman et al., 1987; Rosen, 1991; Warmbrod, 1986). Stability and consistency of care of children after loss is crucial to a child's sense of control (Siegel, Mesagno, & Christ, 1990).

Harris (1991) found teenagers had little support or resources for their grief. The widowed mother was often preoccupied with her own grief and concerns. Other family members, relatives, clergy, social workers, and friends were rarely mentioned as helpful. Teenagers coped by remaining busy with peers and activities. Older teens spent less time at home and more time with peers while younger teens (ages 13-15) stayed at home with the widow parent or family. They tended to be more withdrawn, isolated, and less involved with peer activities.

Health. Depressive symptoms are high among mothers with young children (Hall & Farel, 1988). Hall et al. (1991) found high depressive symptoms occurred among 59.6% of the 225 mothers and were related to greater everyday stressors, fewer social resources, greater use of avoidance coping, and less use of active behavioral coping strategies. Brown and Harris (1978) found four factors contribute to women's vulnerability to depression: loss of their mother before the age of 11; lack of a job; lack of a confiding relationship; and three or more children under age 14 at home. Beckwith et al. (1990) found widows at high risk for complications following bereavement were younger, had more young children at home, had few available relationships, and were of lower socioeconomic status.

There is very little research concerning the physical health of children in single parent widow families. Jennings and Sheldon (1986) found that single-parent children may experience more ill health than two-parent children. Children in single parent families without fathers have poorer mental health and social maladjustment (Angel & Worobey, 1988).

Stresses and deprivations associated with living in poverty may negatively affect the health of children in lower-class single parent families (Hall et al., 1991). A single mother's stress may contribute to her viewing her child's health as poorer than it is (Angel & Worobey, 1988). Children and adolescents who lost a father or mother were studied by Weller, Weller, Fristad, and Bowes (1990) who found symptoms reported by children to include dysphoria, loss of interest, sleep and appetite disturbances, and morbid and suicidal ideation. Kaffman et al. (1987) in a study of 25 normal pre-adolescent kibbutz children who lost their fathers during the 1973 war in Israel found severe emotional and behavioral problems and poorer social functioning for over 40% of the children. These children were at risk for psychiatric disturbance, had intense grieving reactions, increased dependency on the mother, fears, aggressive behavior, discipline problems and restlessness. It is important to note that other researchers (Hanson, 1986; Loveland-Cherry, 1986), who have studied other kinds of single-parents and not widows per se, have reported single parenthood did not negatively effect children's physical or mental health. This finding suggests that children from different kinds of single parent families may have different health responses.

Widows Who Are Raising a Physically or Mentally Handicapped Child

Stressors, coping, resources and health. Research on single parent widows with handicapped children is scarce (Belcher, 1988; Jones, 1987; Schilling, Kirkham, Snow, & Schinke, 1986). Children with disabilities such as cerebral palsy, spina bifida, muscular dystrophy, mental retardation, schizophrenia and autism contribute to family stress. Single mothers with a young handicapped child report feeling more stressed than married mothers with such a child (Beckman-Bell, 1981; Holroyd, 1974). The stressors experienced by these single parent families include: grief from the loss of a normal child; child's handicap severity; dependency on the parent's care; the child's lack of social skills; parental fears for the health and safety of the child; hospitalization; cost of special equipment and transportation for medical care; fatigue from caring for the child; prospect of a child's lifelong dependence on the parent; change in family relationships and activities; and social isolation (Beckman, 1983; Jones, 1987; Kazak & Marvin, 1984; Koller, Richardson, Katz & McLaren, 1983; McCubbin, 1989).

Middle-aged or older widows who are caring for a physically or mentally handicapped child may also be at risk for stress and less adaptive coping. Belcher (1988) discusses the stress upon mothers who live alone and have to care for a chronically mentally ill adult child. Stressors encountered were: a reluctance to leave home; child's not taking psychotrophic medications; use of drugs or alcohol, and the child's acting out and inappropriate behaviors. Belcher (1988) found some mothers thought that eventually things would get better or the medication would help, while others coped by placing their faith in God or resigning themselves to a life of caring for a sick adult child. Inability to explain the illness and behaviors of the child contributed to friends withdrawing and isolation. Increased stress contributed to illness in the mother. Mothers reported being exhausted by their adult children's behavior.

Schilling et al. (1986) found that stress, appraisal and coping may differ for single and married parents of handicapped children because of differences in their resources. These researchers found single mothers spent less time with their other children and in leisure, and missed more work than married mothers. Single parents were less satisfied with their families, number of children, relationships with relatives, their own health, education, occupation, job security, and income. Single parents had lower financial well-being and were lower on mother's coping related to maintaining family integration, cooperation, and positive view of the situation. However, they were higher on family adaptability than two parent families, indicating more flexible family rules, power, and role relationships (McCubbin, 1989). Single-parent mothers of handicapped children reported using tranquilizers to cope with nerves (Burke, 1987). (Also see Boyce, White, Miller, & Godfrey in this volume.) Burns (1984) reports that single parent families often have fewer reserves for coping in times of crisis such as hospitalization of a handicapped child. Often lacking are social supports who can provide help to cope with the physical and emotional demands of handicapped children. Adaptive coping is fostered in single parent families by incorporating others into the supportive network of the widow.

Independent Older Widows with One or More Healthy Children

Stressors, coping and health. Older single women's experience of late-life singlehood has been studied infrequently (Hoeffer, 1987a). Often, older adults do not confront widowhood alone but have children aged 18 and older living at home. This family type is expected to increase due to the larger numbers of older adults who are living longer (U.S. Department of Health and Human Services, 1992) and who will remain living in the community with caregiver children because of choice or limited finances.

A major stressor identified by older widows is loneliness (Amato & Partridge, 1987). Hoeffer (1987b) studied a mixed group of single parents (n = 816) which included widows (82% of the sample), divorced, and separated women. Eighty percent or more of the widows and divorced or separated women reported having at least one grown child as a resource and confidant. However, widows reported being more lonely, less healthy and had a less positive life outlook than never married women. Hoeffer (1987b) points out that the discontinuity in social engagement and the isolation that widows experience may explain their loneliness and negative outlook on life. Rosenbaum (1981) found widows used medication to cope with loneliness.

Coping has been investigated in older independent widowed persons. Ide et al. (1990) conducted a longitudinal study on coping of Anglo and Mexican-American widows, 40 years of age and older, and found both ethnic groups preferred nonconfrontational strategies for widowhood problems, with Mexican-Americans using more confrontational strategies. Ways of coping with problems early in widowhood had significant long-term effects upon the widows health. The most effective coping methods over the first year involved combinations of independent action and emotional release. More effective strategies over a longer period, included being able to ignore problems, accept the situation, release tensions, and actively seek advice about problems. Findings for Mexican-Americans appear to be related to cultural patterns of familial support after a death occurs.

Resources. The studies which exist have focused on the interaction of adult children with their older parents with respect to social support, financial help or tasks provided by the single widow parent to the children and to the parent by the children. Children frequently provided economic, social, and emotional support to their widowed mother (Lopata, 1979). Depressed widows have been found not to have as many children living nearby as did widows who were not depressed (Bornstein, Clayton, Halikas, Maurice, & Robins, 1973; Clayton, Halikas, & Maurice, 1972). O'Bryant and Morgan (1990) studied 252 widowed women (87.7% white) aged 60-98 years with living children. Data suggested that widows are quite self-sufficient; however, in areas where support is needed, they largely depended on children. More children and greater perceived willingness of those children to help were positively related to children doing more of the tasks needed by their widowed mother. Higher income widows were more reliant on helpers other than children for support in meeting task needs.

Zautra, Reich and Guarnaccia (1990) studied persons experiencing the major stressors of conjugal bereavement or physical disability. The bereaved included widows between the ages of 60 and 80 years. The bereaved often showed less stability than persons with a physical disability in the areas of relations with children and other family members, social life, recreation, household management difficulties and work, and they had decreased mental health. In contrast, Ferraro and Barresi (1982) found stability in the frequency with which widows interacted with family members. Morgan (1983) found loss of a spouse did not reduce the support widows give to children, nor was the widowed woman less likely to continue to assist her children than a widowed man. Nonwhite parents were more likely to be poor and contributing to the support of children. Widows who reported a very close relationship with their children were less likely to need help following bereavement than widows who had no children or widows reporting a low level of closeness to their children (Goldberg et al., 1988).

Greene and Feld (1989) studied the relationship between social support and well-being in a national sample of women ages 50 and older which included recent widows, widows within the last five years, and widows for longer than five years. Recent widows experienced more stress and were less satisfied with their incomes, had experienced more life events, and had more negative emotions than did longer-term widows. Recent widows may gain support because they have problems and supporters may recognize and respond to these problems. Mutran and Reitzes' (1984) suggested that negative self-feeling of elderly widowed parents gather adult children's support. Those widows with the most distress may receive more social support than those with less distress. Talbott (1990) studied the intergenerational support to 55 older widowed mothers using exchange theory and found some mothers feel subordinant and unappreciated by their adult children. The mother provided services, help and money to children at great cost to herself. Forty-nine percent of the mothers commented on a negative side of their relationship with their children: they felt neglected, dissatisfied with amount of help received, emotionally dependent, and feared bothering or burdening their children.

Dependent, Ill, Older Widows with a Healthy Child In and/or Near the Home

Little research exists on dependent, ill, older widows with a healthy child in the home with respect to their stressors, coping, resources, and grieving responses and their health. This family type is expected to increase because of the increase in the number of elderly who will be living with caregiver children due to limited availability of nursing homes. Greene and Feld (1989) state that social support is important for many older persons because of declining health and other stressors related to aging. O'Bryant and Morgan (1990) found older and less healthy widows were performing fewer tasks for themselves and relied more on support for tasks from others.

Scott and Roberto (1987) studied the kinds of help white widowed parents aged 60 to 90 years received from children. The sample included 66 rural (38.6% widowed) and 135 urban females (22.0% widowed). Rural widows reported greater assistance from children in comparison to urban widows for illness, household repairs, yard work, and legal aid. Roberto and Scott (1986) found no significant differences between the young-old (ages 65-74) and old-old (ages 75+) rural elderly widowed in the help they were currently receiving from their children or in the amount of social activities with children. The researchers pointed out that widowhood may increase the older person's involvement with family and friends, and assuming responsibility for assistance to widowed parents could place children as well as parents under great stress. The child of a young widow may be in the helping role for a longer period of time, while the child of an old widow may be placed in a more demanding caregiver role due to widows' declining health and lack of help from others.

The interaction of adult children and their elderly parents was investigated by Mutran and Reitzes (1984) using a national sample of elderly widows and married parents. The sample was largely white and included 723 widowed of which 83% were widows. The elderly widowed were more likely to turn to family members to discuss the things that troubled them, and made confidants of their adult children which had a strong effect on the receiving of help for widows and reduced negative self-feelings. Poor health led to more assistance from adult children while contributing to negative self-feelings and reduced widows giving of help.

There is little known about the coping responses and concerns of young adults who live with their mothers after the death of a father. In one study,

Galloway (1990) investigated the reactions of 19 adults, aged 20-39 years, fourteen of whom had lost fathers. The adults expressed a need for support because grief was often profound and accompanied by somatic and psychological problems. Dealing with personal grief was complicated by responsibilities after the death and changes in relationships within the family, which occurred when the adult children were in the process of establishing an independent life, a career, and their own family. Often, there was a great change in the relationship with the surviving parent. The young adult assumed a "parental" role to a bereaved parent who became the "child." Resentment was expressed at this role change. Children were often overwhelmed by the parents' need for continual support and felt frustrated when parents were unable to make minor decisions independently. Two subjects reported an extended parent-child role reversal and felt drained from the stress caused by the dependent parent and began to emotionally withdraw to cope.

GAPS IN KNOWLEDGE

Review of the literature on single parent widows indicates that there are several significant gaps in current knowledge. The final section of the review of literature will focus on gaps in knowledge which family professionals will need to consider in their future research on single parent widow families.

Limited research studies exist on single parent families headed by widows. Many of the studies reported in the literature are based on very small samples of single parent widows (Bowen & Orthner, 1986; Burden, 1986; Gladow & Ray, 1986; Harris, 1991; Lindblad-Goldberg & Dukes, 1985; Schilling et al., 1986). Widows are often mixed with other single parent types (Angel & Worobey, 1988; Hall et al., 1991; McCubbin, 1989; Risman & Park, 1988) including divorced, separated and never married (Burden, 1986; Fulmer, 1983; Covey & Tam, 1990; Hoeffer, 1987a; Scott & Roberto, 1987; Mueller & Cooper, 1986; Hogan et al., 1990) or with widowers in the category of widowed (Mutran & Reitzes, 1984; Roberto & Scott, 1986). When studying the effects of death of family members on single parents and their children, data on spousal loss has been grouped with data on sibling loss (Cheifetz et al., 1989; Lehman et al., 1989) and children who have lost a father have been grouped with children who have lost a mother (Black & Urbanowicz, 1987; Harris, 1991). Also, widows who live alone have been grouped with widows who live with children (Angel & Worobey, 1988). Data on mixed samples may be biased. Several researchers have emphasized the need not to mix samples but to examine similarities and differences between the types of single parent families since they are not a homogeneous group and differences exist (Amato & Partridge, 1987; Burns, 1984; Fulmer, 1983; Gove & Shin, 1989; Jones, 1987; Kitson et al., 1989). Fulmer (1983) points out that we can expect different responses to loss in both mother and children based on whether the single parenthood occurs as a result of the death of the spouse, divorce, separation, desertion, accidental pregnancy, or adoption. Types of stressors, appraisal, coping, resources and grieving responses may differ for these different family types. Thus, it is important to analyze data separately on the different family types rather than combine data in research studies investigating single parent families.

Lack of knowledge is all the more evident in relation to single parent widows from Black, Hispanic and other ethnic groups. The majority of the research has focused on largely white single parent samples (Harris, 1991; Risman & Park, 1988; Lehman et al., 1989; Mutran & Reitzes, 1984; O'Bryant & Morgan, 1990; Schilling et al., 1986; Morgan, 1986). This is a serious limitation given that single parents are of different ethnic backgrounds and there may be cultural differences in stressors, appraisal, coping, resources, grieving processes and health among ethnic groups (Angel & Worobey, 1988; Wojkiewicz, McLanahan & Garfinkel, 1990). The studies which do focus on ethnic groups often have a small number of ethnic subjects (Sable, 1989; Lindblad-Goldberg & Dukes, 1985) and are limited to examining economic and/or social support within the family (Morgan, 1983; O'Bryant & Morgan, 1990; Hogan et al., 1990). In addition, there is a lack of research on health and coping among ethnic groups (Ide et al., 1990).

Most prior research has not employed suitable control or comparison groups against which stressors, appraisal, coping, resources, grieving and health reported by single parent widows can be evaluated. Limited longitudinal studies have been done and few have been guided by theoretical frameworks or theory. There is a need for theory-based research on single parent families. Some researchers and practitioners have addressed theory or theoretical frameworks in their work but few have tested or evaluated theory. The most frequently used theories and frameworks have included: Bowlby's attachment theory (Kitson et al., 1989; Sable, 1989); object relations theory (Murphy, 1986-87); exchange (Talbott, 1990) and symbolic interaction theories (Mutran & Reitzes, 1984); structural theory (Weltner, 1982); Folkman and Lazarus' stress-appraisal-coping framework (Kirschling & Barron McBride, 1989; Schilling et al., 1986); and the Typology Model of Adjustment and Adaptation (McCubbin, 1989).

SINGLE PARENT WIDOW FAMILY TYPES: STRESSORS, APPRAISAL, COPING, RESOURCES, GRIEVING RESPONSES AND HEALTH

The next section of this paper focuses on the methodology and results from a secondary analysis of data from the author's research on stressors, appraisal of bereavement, coping, resources, grieving responses and health of single parent widows. Characteristics of high-risk, vulnerable, and healthy single parent widow families are described and three case studies are presented. Themes in common to the four family types are identified.

Methodology

Reanalysis of data from bereavement studies on widows (Gass, 1987a; 1987b; Gass & Chang, 1989) and data from two additional studies, one which tested a new appraisal of bereavement scale (Gass, 1991), and another which focused on the evaluation of a bereavement intervention program (Gass-Sternas, 1993) were utilized for this paper. Original questionnaires from these studies were reviewed to obtain data on widows with parenting responsibilities. Widows bereaved within one year were interviewed in terms of their stressors, appraisal (meaning) of bereavement, ways of coping, resources and physical and psychosocial health functioning. Methodology is reported in Gass (1987a, 1987b) and Gass and Chang (1989). For the 1991 study, 59 widows whose names were obtained from church burial records, completed the Appraisal of Bereavement Scale, Ways of Coping Revised, Profile of Mood States and Ratings of Physical Health. Criteria for inclusion was a widow whose spouse died between 1 and 16 months prior to participation in the study, who was aged 50 or older and not remarried. For the bereavement intervention study (Gass-Sternas, 1993), Black, Hispanic and White bereaved persons including widows were identified from churches, community agencies and obituary column information. Those who perceived their bereavement to be stressful were interviewed using the Appraisal of Bereavement Scale, Ways of Coping Revised, Assessment of Resources Revised, Texas Revised Inventory of Grief (Part II), Social Support of Adults, Profile of Mood States and the list of Physical Health Conditions and Problems before and after intervention.[1] Focus group and case study data on widows were collected. Data from 40 subjects were utilized for this paper. Lazarus' and Folkman's (1984) stress-appraisal-coping theoretical framework guided all investigations including development or selection of questionnaires, and content for the intervention program. A limitation is that findings are based on the widows' perspective since only widows and not children were studied. Data on children is based on single parent widows' perceptions of how their children are managing following the death of their father.

RESULTS

Four types of single parent widow families were identified: widows who are raising dependent children (n = 10); widows who are raising a physically or mentally handicapped child (n = 10); independent older widows with one or more healthy children (n = 10); and dependent, ill, older widows with a healthy child in the home (n = 10). All women became single parents as the result of spouse's death. Widows who were raising dependent children were aged 46 to 75 ($\bar{x}$ = 62.7 years) and bereaved for a period ranging from 106 days to 510 days ($\bar{x}$ = 248.7 days). Number of children ranged from 1 to 7 ($\bar{x}$ = 3.3). Seven of these subjects were White, two were Black and one was Hispanic. Nine widows were Catholic and one was a Jehovah Witness. Five subjects had less than a high school education, four completed high school or a higher level of education and one had completed college. Four of these widows were currently working, four had worked in the past, and two never worked. Incomes ranged from under $5,000 a year to over $34,999, with 60% of the subjects reporting a yearly income of under $11,000.

Widows who were raising a physically or mentally handicapped child ranged in age from 64 to 84 ($\bar{x}$ age = 72.8) and were bereaved from 128 days to 355 days ($\bar{x}$ days = 283.3). Nine of these widows were White and one was Black. Nine subjects were Catholic and one was Lutheran. Level of education ranged from less than high school (n = 1) to completion of high school or more education (n = 7) to completion of college (n = 2). Number of children ranged from 1 to 5 ($\bar{x}$ = 2.1) with only one handicapped child in each family. Type of handicap included: severe arthritis (n = 1); weakness of muscles and legs (n = 1); mental retardation (n = 3); Down Syndrome (n = 2); manic depression (n = 1); depression with suicidal thoughts (n = 1); and schizophrenia (n = 1). None of these widows were currently working. Eight widows had a prior history of working and two persons never worked. Yearly incomes ranged from under $5,000 to $19,999 with 80% of the subjects reporting a yearly income of under $11,000.

Independent widows with healthy children ranged in age from 56 to 74 years ($\bar{x}$ age = 67.8) and were bereaved from 87 days to 730 days ($\bar{x}$ = 244.6 days). Number of children ranged from 1 to 3 ($\bar{x}$ = 1.7). Eight subjects were White and two were Black. Six widows were Catholic, three were Lutheran and one was Baptist. Two subjects had less than a high school education, six completed high school, and two had more education. Four widows were currently working and six had worked in the past. Incomes ranged from $5,000 a year to over $50,000, with 60% reporting a yearly income of under $14,999 and 40% reporting an income of over $20,000.

Dependent ill widows ranged in age from 60 to 83 ($\bar{x}$ = 73.8 years) and were bereaved from 52 days to 730 days ($\bar{x}$ = 249.6 days). All subjects were White. Eight were Catholic, one was Baptist and one was Lutheran. Six of the subjects had less than a high school education, two completed high school and two had a higher level of education. Seven widows had worked in the past, two widows never worked and one depressed widow was currently working. Yearly incomes ranged from under $5,000 to $34,999, with 70% reporting yearly incomes under $14,999 and 30% reporting an income of $15,000 and over. Number of children ranged from 1 to 4 ($\bar{x}$ = 2.1). Most widows had multiple chronic health problems. The major illnesses which contributed to dependency were: severe arthritis (n = 3); asthma (n = 1); heart disease (n = 2); fracture (n = 1); weakness due to frail health (n = 1); depression and loneliness (n = 2).

Viewing family types on a continuum ranging from high risk single parent widow families to healthy single parent widow families was considered helpful. Three case examples for levels of risk for different family types are presented below to illustrate stressors, appraisal, coping, resources, grief and health adaptation of widows.

High-risk single parent widow families. These include families in which there are multiple stressors in addition to the death of the father. Stressors include other losses at the time of bereavement such as death of other relatives, relocation to a new home, health problems and financial losses. These widows appraised their bereavement as a threat or harmful loss. They used less adaptive ways of coping such as escape-avoidance, wishful thinking, and self-blame. Taking medications or drinking alcohol, sleeping more, avoiding or getting mad at people including their children, and using fantasy were specific ways of coping used by high-risk single parent widows. There were limited resources available to these families such as little or no social supports, lack of knowledge of the grieving process, presence of additional losses or stressors with bereavement and inadequate finances. Family members may demonstrate pathological grieving. High-risk widows had poor psychological-emotional health and poor physical health and reported higher amounts of tension-anxiety, depression-dejection, anger-hostility, fatigue-inertia, confusion-bewilderment and little vigor. The following case study illustrates these characteristics.

Case Study 1: Independent Widow with Healthy Children

Mrs. R, a white widow of 56 years, was referred to the bereavement program because of her intense grieving over the death of her spouse. A friend at work mailed her name to the group leader. Assessment indicated that she appraised her bereavement as a threat. Major stressors in her life included: intense grieving over her spouse for a long period of time which prevented her from functioning effectively; death of a mother about a year before her spouse's death; severe loneliness; a difficult work situation with a demanding boss and threat of job loss; problems with an alcoholic son; birth of a new grandchild to a daughter who had drug dependency problems; and two best friends who had serious health problems. Mrs. R reported having never lived on her own, living first with mother, and then her husband, and now with a daughter. She moved in with her daughter because of severe loneliness but did not feel she was receiving the support she needed. Mrs. R described her husband as wonderful and stated that she had a very close relationship with him. She was dependent on her spouse and seldom went anywhere on her own. She reported experiencing severe anxiety and fear when going out by herself. The spouse's death had been so stressful that Mrs. R had a heart attack from the stress. Initially, Mrs. R used less adaptive ways of coping such as escape-avoidance, self-blame, crying, taking Valium for her anxiety, sleeping all day, and avoiding her children so as not to have to deal with their problems. Mrs. R reported having few resources, namely, previous experiences with loss through death and practicing rituals which eased grieving. She had little family support and reported her social supports as minimally helpful. She had become less close with God after the death of her spouse and her religious beliefs were not helpful to her understanding the death. Her relationship was characterized by being overly close, very dependent, and she expressed limited belief in her control over bereavement. She reported her physical and mental health had gotten worse after the spouse's death. Her ratings on tension-anxiety, depression-dejection, anger-hostility, fatigue, confusion-bewilderment were high.

Mrs. R attended a bereavement intervention program. After participation in the bereavement support program, her appraisal of bereavement was more positive, that is, she appraised her situation more as a challenge and beneficial-positive experience rather than a threat. Mrs. R increased her use of adaptive coping strategies including seeking social support, planful problem-solving, positive reappraisal, and self-controlling coping, and decreased her use of escape-avoidance coping. She increased her use of informational, emotional, and integration support. The helpful support she received from her daughter and family increased. Her psychological-emotional health improved, in that she had less tension-anxiety, depression-dejection, anger-hostility, fatigue, confusion-bewilderment and more vigor. She was going out on her own without anxiety attacks, spending more time with her children, and reported less intense grieving and loneliness. This demonstrates that high-risk single parent widows can have positive outcomes with intervention.

Vulnerable single parent widow families. These are families in which stressors and problems exist and the grieving process is unresolved. Sometimes there are problems in the mother-child relationship such as a son may be required to assume some of the spouse's responsibilities for which he feels unprepared. Widows hold negative meanings of bereavement and perceive their bereavement to be a harmful loss, but feel hopeful that they will view this loss in a positive way in the future once problems are resolved. Widows' coping abilities are limited and may include the use of less adaptive strategies such as escape-avoidance, with some adaptive strategies such as distancing and planful problem-solving. The widow usually has sufficient strength to maintain family functioning because she has available some key resources such as strong religious beliefs, helpful social supports and practicing rituals and beliefs that ease grieving. The widow usually does not seek help for problems; however, with the death of a family member, problems may develop in the family for which she seeks help. Psychological-emotional health of these widows is not optimum. Widows report high tension-anxiety, depression-dejection, anger-hostility, confusion-bewilderment, and fatigue and low vigor. The following case study illustrates these characteristics.

Case Study 2: The Single Parent Widow Raising Dependent Children

Mrs. L, a Black female of 46 years, came to the bereavement support program because she had recently lost a son. She lost her husband through death about a year prior to her son's death. She described a poor quality relationship with her spouse before his death because of problems with family alcoholism and wife abuse. She reported that her four adolescent children had become unmanageable after their brother's death. Cause of his death was under investigation. Mrs. L stated her son had fallen down 26 steps and he laid in a coma in a hospital for months before dying. He had no identification on him so they were not able to contact Mrs. L regarding the location of her son. Mrs. L had contacted the missing persons bureau because she had not heard from her son. When the missing persons bureau found her son, the widow had to identify his body in a city morgue. Mrs. L was in need of understanding her grief and ways to manage her rebellious children. Her health had become poor and she reported feeling depressed, worried, unable to sleep and fatigued. The children were grieving the father's death and doing fairly well in spite of financial problems. When the son died the family situation became extremely difficult. Her children started using drugs, stealing money from her, and selling family possessions to maintain their drug habit. One adolescent dropped out of school and refused to go for drug rehabilitation. A daughter became pregnant without marriage and had wanted her boyfriend to move in with the family. She could not leave the children home alone. When she returned possessions would be missing. She made them leave the house when she left. Mrs. L verbalized poor self-esteem, feelings of no control over her family situation, and loneliness. Her children blamed her for the son's death since she made him leave home and go for help for his drug problem. The widow experienced extreme guilt and sorrow for having sent her son away. Additional stressors included limited finances, no job, and a brother who was very ill from AIDS. Through all the blame and anger, and in spite of all the pain, the widow was able to identify some strengths. Her resources included her strong religious background, her church congregation who were a major source of support, and a good previous mental health history. Although not currently working when she came to the bereavement intervention program, she had a goal to better herself and get a job. Initially, she appraised her bereavement as a threat and harmful loss. After the bereavement program, these negative appraisals decreased and she appraised her bereavement primarily as a challenge. Initially, she used high amounts of escape-avoidance and accepting responsibility coping. After the program, she used more adaptive strategies including positive reappraisal, increased planful problem-solving, more seeking social support, distancing and confrontive coping. Specific coping strategies included: praying; turning to God and her religion (Jehovah Witness) to help her cope; taking care of her health; keeping busy by going to church meetings and reading the Bible; and talking to friends who had lost a child. After completion of the program her resources increased. With some guidance she obtained training as a home health aide and began working in this capacity. Her financial situation approved. She now had some money which allowed her to go places such as church outings and movies. Mrs. L learned to reassume her role as parent and to be assertive and set limits for the adolescent children. For example, she had decided that the daughter's boyfriend could not move in with the family. She would help them with child care if he went to school to obtain an education and job so the daughter and he could afford to marry and live on their own. She was working toward placement of her son in a treatment center for drug abuse problems and met regularly with community social workers to plan placement. Her helpful social supports increased. Her health improved and she was advancing through the grieving process. Mrs. L had learned about the grieving process and strategies to manage grief. She had come to understand the blame and anger of her children from the bereavement program. There was a decrease in the intensity of her grieving and in her tension-anxiety, depression, anger-hostility, fatigue, confusion-bewilderment and an improvement in her sleeping. She planned to follow up on the cause of her son's death. She believed that she would come to better accept his death once she understood whether the fall was an accident or due to other reasons.

Healthy single parent widow families. These widows express positive meanings of bereavement. That is, they appraised their bereavement as a challenge or beneficial-positive experience. Adaptive ways of coping are used including distancing, planful problem-solving, positive reappraisal coping, growth and problem-focused coping. They cope by keeping busy, participating in social groups, learning new skills, using religion and prayer, recalling happy memories, and maintaining ties with the deceased spouse. Healthy single parent widows have resources and use those available to them. Resources have included helpful social supports, religious beliefs about death, belief in control over bereavement, good prior mental health and no additional losses at the time of bereavement. These resources have been associated with less psychosocial dysfunction following bereavement. Practicing death and mourning rituals, belief in control over bereavement, and no other losses with bereavement have been related to less physical dysfunction in widows. Adaptive responses to their situation is reflected in their health which is characterized by low tension-anxiety, low depression, low anger and confusion, low fatigue and high vigor. These widows welcome the challenges of bereavement and single parenthood and are able to take on new roles and responsibilities like employment. They seek out professional help such as a bereavement program so that they can be in control of their bereavement and family situation. They respond to suggestions shared by other widows for managing their problems. These widows believe that they will cope with their bereavement and share this with their children. They have begun the grieving process and understand their emotions and feelings as well as encourage expression of grief among the children. These characteristics are illustrated by the following case study.

Case Study 3: The Single Parent Widow Raising a Mentally or Emotionally Handicapped Child

Mrs. C was 64 when her husband died of lung cancer. She had been widowed for 8 months when she participated in an interview. She had 5 children: four healthy adults and one male child aged 28 with a diagnosis of manic depression. She maintained open communication about the father's death with her children. Mrs. C had the support of her family who listened to her talk during her grieving process. She was able to continue with all family functions, assume her spouse's responsibilities, and help her children with their grieving process. Mrs. C appraised her bereavement as a challenge and used adaptive coping strategies which included problem-focused and growth coping, religion and prayers, keeping busy, and learning new skills like writing checks and maintaining a budget. Resources which were available to this widow included good finances, stable social support from all children in helping to care for their emotionally handicapped brother, use of hospice services while the father was dying, and strong religious beliefs which helped her to accept the death. Practicing rituals which ease grieving, an opportunity for anticipatory grieving, absence of other losses at the time of bereavement, ability of the family to openly discuss grief, belief in control over the situation and a quality relationship with the spouse before death were also resources which gave her strength to deal with her loss. Her major stressor was caring for her emotionally handicapped son who went through periods of depression and manic states with no sleeping for several days. The son was maintained on medication but there were times when he refused to take his medication. This resulted in a crisis period with the son being verbally abusive, aggressive, and unable to sleep. With the help of a supportive psychiatrist and her other children, Mrs. C managed to get through these crisis. The widow had excellent health and was grieving normally. The family was able to talk about the deceased father in a positive manner but reported that they missed him particularly on special occasions like birthdays and anniversaries.

THEMES

Several themes emerged from the secondary analysis of the data which may be worthy of further investigation by family researchers and practitioners who are caring for single parent widows and their children. These themes include: the grieving process; roles and responsibilities in the family; employment; loneliness; dating and remarriage; and caregiver stress. These themes in relation to the four different family types are discussed below.

Grieving process. In general, widows who are raising dependent children or a handicapped child have expressed a difficult grieving process. Often there was intense grieving over death of the spouse because of his young age. Some children became overly close to the widow. There was limited time for the widow to grieve since she was so busy caring for her children. Widows often found it hard to grieve in front of the children, and felt they had to be strong for them or the family would fall apart. If the widow could not help her children grieve, they often developed health and behavioral problems which needed professional intervention. Widows with a handicapped child reported that the child needed special attention after the death of the father. The child may be very upset and the widow's grief may make the child more upset. In some cases the handicapped child did not understand the loss and showed little concern.

Adult children either encouraged the grieving process of the widow or tried to protect her by not talking about the death. When feelings were permitted to be expressed the grief process progressed in a normal way. Often children were a major source of support to the widow. In other cases, the adult child was uncomfortable with death or was afraid of upsetting the ill widow so the death was not discussed openly. Problems arose when the widow needed support herself but had to support the adult child who was grieving intensely over the father's death.

Roles and responsibilities in the family. Changes in roles and responsibilities in the family contributed to role stress for the younger widow. The single mothers often reported that they had to assume the responsibilities of the deceased father in addition to taking on new roles such as working mother. When other children were present, they often helped the widow in the care of the handicapped child.

Independent older widows often had one or more healthy children living at home who were single or divorced and had returned to their parental home when their marriage ended. Adult children were busy with their own lives so they often had little time for the widowed mother. Time was spent together on holidays and special occasions. Some widows found it difficult because they were helping their adult children but felt they received little in return. Independent older widows valued their independence and health and managed by themselves for the most part. Generally, there was a good relationship between the widow parent and child.

Roles and responsibilities in the family changed when the adult child assumed responsibility for the care of the dependent, ill, older mother. These widows often had a healthy child, usually a daughter, living in the home who moved in with the mother or the mother moved in with her child after the husband's death. The widow usually had many physical or mental health problems and was dependent on the spouse for care before his death. For example, one spouse administered insulin to his diabetic wife and gave her physical care because of her severe arthritis. Another widow moved in with the child because of severe depression and loneliness following the husband's death. The child took over the roles and responsibilities of the now deceased spouse. If adolescent grandchildren lived in the home they often helped in the care of the dependent widow. When possible, the widow had responsibilities to her adult child. The widow provided financial help or bought clothes for the child or grandchildren in exchange for care.

Employment. Often the widow raising dependent children had to work because of financial problems. Widows reported employment as stressful on top of raising children. Several widows were working two jobs in order to pay their mortgage to keep their homes. Widows had work-related expenses including transportation which added to their financial stress. Some widows did not have supportive family who could help them with child care. For some widows, employment was not possible because of the care demands of the handicapped child who often received benefits such as SSI which helped with financial costs of his/her care.

Independent older widows were often employed out of financial need or for enjoyment. Those who appraised widowhood as a challenge saw widowhood as an opportunity to do the things they never did before, including taking a job. The caregiver child of the dependent, ill widow usually was unable to work because she had to stay at home to care for the widow.

Loneliness. Loneliness was not reported to be a major stressor for younger widows because they were so busy with children and work that they had little time to feel lonely. Some widows reported receiving companionship from the handicapped child. Yet, younger widows felt isolated since they had no time to socialize with other adults. Older independent widows expressed some problems with loneliness due to missing the spouse. Older healthy widows coped in adaptive ways such as by keeping busy. Less adaptive coping occurred when the widow sat at home feeling isolated and self-absorbed or taking medication. If the relationship between the dependent, ill widow and child was a good one, the widow was happy to have family nearby and loneliness was not a problem. On the other hand, children of dependent widows reported experiencing loneliness in having to let go of friends, activities, and dating to care for the widow.

Dating and remarriage. There was an interest in dating by younger widows, but their major concern was whether the children would like or accept the man. A few experienced feelings of guilt. Some widows with a handicapped child did not see remarriage as a future possibility. They felt that no man wants the burden of caring for a handicapped child. Older widows said they married their husbands for life, and thus there were no plans for another marriage. Some widows still maintained ties with their deceased spouse whom they said was in heaven. They asked the spouse to guide them in the management of their difficult situation. Some widows in their forties and early fifties thought about remarrying while others were not sure because they thought they were too old. There was concern over having to care for "another sick man" and several widows decided not to take this risk. Several expressed that they enjoyed time for themselves and were now taking trips and doing things they had never done before. In general, the dependent widow saw herself as too ill to date or remarry.

Caregiver stress. Caregiver stress was seldom mentioned as a concern by younger widows or independent older widows except if the widow had to assume the major caregiver role for a family member. However, some middle aged widows realized they may have to care for an ill parent later in life. Caregiver stress was expressed by widows with a handicapped child. Some felt it was not easy to care for a child with behavior problems who cannot be left at home alone. In spite of the difficulties, no widow spoke of wanting to place the handicapped child in an alternative living facility. Widows saw the care of the child as their responsibility.

Caring for a widowed mother with health problems can lead to caregiver stress and burden. Adult children reported how they were made to feel guilty if they wanted to go out: "I'm old and sick, how can you go out and leave me with a stranger." Caregiving was very stressful, especially if one adult child assumed all of the care of the widow parent. There was stress among the children due to splitting up the tasks related to taking care of mother. If the situation does not work out, arrangements are often made to place the widow in a nursing home. No widows reported a family decision regarding nursing home placement. Families that were fortunate to have the finances to purchase respite care seemed to manage much better.

DIRECTIONS FOR FUTURE RESEARCH

More research is needed on the four types of single parent widow families. Single parent widows will continue to care for large numbers of children in the next decade. The stressors they experience, the ways they cope, their resources and grieving process are important to consider because they influence health. Widows are at risk for bereavement overload due to the stressors of single parenthood superimposed on the stressor of spousal loss.

A major problem with earlier research is that widows are mixed with other types of single parent families and single parent families are treated as a homogeneous group. Yet, long term effects are likely to be influenced by the type of single parent family situation, that is, whether loss of a father is due to death, divorce, separation or another reason. Types of stressors, appraisal of the situation, ways of coping, resources and grieving may differ for these different family types. Research which includes separate analyses of data on single parent widows from the other types of single parent families is needed. Also, larger samples of single parent widows need to be studied. The small sample size of single parent widows in most studies makes findings tentative until larger samples have been investigated.

Most research has focused on Caucasian persons with little attention to other ethnic groups. Future research must examine single parent widows of different ethnic and cultural backgrounds including Black and Hispanic individuals. Also needed is research on how supportive functions are different among ethnic groups.

Future research should examine the role of children in single parent widow families and the kinds of social supports available to widows of the different family types. Research on the reasons under which older widows help their children and vice versa is of great interest given the increase in the number of elderly for the future. More needs to be learned about the types of social support that are most useful to single widow parents with dependent and handicapped children, and the informal and formal social supports that are used by these single widow parent families to help them to cope with bereavement and single parenthood. Also, only widows with children were examined in this paper. Widows who never had children may present different stressors, coping, resources, grieving and health. Research on remarriage in widowhood and how this affects children in single parent families is also needed (Kitson et al., 1989). Single parent widows who are living with grandchildren is another area for study (Talbott, 1990).

Further research is needed on the process and outcome of bereavement for single parent widows and their children. Risk factors contributing to morbidity following death of a father need to be investigated to plan ways to prevent health problems. More research is needed which generates data that help identify those single parent widows and children at risk for poor outcomes following conjugal bereavement.

Researchers have usually focused on the grief reactions of one surviving family member, usually the widow or a child. However death of a father is a shared stressor. The surviving family members must deal with their grief both as individuals and as a family. Individual family members as well as the family as a unit need to be studied. Only as we come to understand the process of grieving following bereavement within single parent widow families can we better help widows and children adapt to two major transitions, namely, bereavement and single parenthood.

Longitudinal research which investigates changes in stressors, appraisal, coping, resources, grieving processes and health after the spouse's death for the different family types is needed. Following family members over time to investigate how these variables change and impact on family relationships is worthwhile. The impact of widowhood and single parenthood continues long after the death of a spouse. By investigating changes over time, we can better understand the influence of widowhood and single parenthood and their impact upon widows and the family's health and adaptation processes.

Family researchers must continue to investigate factors that affect the different family types so that they will have a strong knowledge base on which to develop intervention programs and policies. Research suggests that positive meanings of bereavement need to be studied further because they are related to the use of adaptive ways of coping and healthy outcomes to bereavement. More research on the meaning of single parenthood and how single parent widows cope with the stressors of family life needs to be done. To date, most research has focused on the resources of social support and adequacy of finances for the widow. Research on other resources such as rituals and beliefs which facilitate grieving, types of information considered helpful, and opportunity for anticipatory grieving, which can help widows cope following bereavement is needed.

Research is needed to evaluate the effectiveness of intervention strategies including counseling programs for single parent widows and their children. Interventions which are worthy of further study focus on: increasing parents' understanding of the nature and range of bereavement reactions in themselves and their children; and addressing factors that can influence adaptation to the loss such as quality of parenting after the loss, stability of the family environment, and helping children express feelings about the loss (Buchsbaum, 1990; Kaffman et al., 1987; McIntyre, 1990; Warmbrod, 1986). Effectiveness of programs in reducing stress, promoting normal grieving, and improving adaptive coping, use of resources and health need to be addressed. Evaluation of the effectiveness of specific interventions should be investigated using experimental designs. There is a need to modify frameworks and create new interventions that are specific to the different types of single parent widow families.

Researchers and clinicians need to determine which theories, frameworks and models are useful in guiding research and the care of single parent widows and their children. Frameworks and theories which hold promise and which should be tested and further evaluated are Lazarus and Folkman's stress-appraisal-coping framework, the Typology Model of Adjustment and Adaptation, Bowlby's attachment theory, exchange and symbolic interaction theories, object relations and structural theories. Ihinger-Tallman (1986) suggests that studies on single parent families provide concepts and relationships among variables which can be used in the development of theory. They can serve as a beginning for theory generation which will help family practitioners, educators and researchers positively influence single parent family's coping and adaptation to stressors.

IMPLICATIONS

The present review and findings have implications for practice, education and social policy. Assessing and identifying stressors for the different family types, promoting positive appraisals or meanings of bereavement, and educating widows and their children about adaptive coping strategies will strengthen single parent widow families. Helping widows identify and utilize resources which promote a healthy outcome to bereavement is an important task for family professionals. The best way known to date to reduce single parent widows stress is to increase their resources including social supports. Use of extended family and community resources can help. Greene and Feld (1989) suggest that clinicians might assist widows to learn ways to develop support systems. Widows might be encouraged to participate in support groups in which participants learn to provide support to one another. Development of support programs which teach widows social interactional skills and provide information on available resources may help reduce the stress and loneliness that single parent widows identify. Loneliness was a problem particularly of older widows. Amato and Partridge (1987) and Gladow and Ray (1986) found that the frequency of close contacts with friends was the best predictor of happiness for single mothers suggesting that interventions aimed at increasing the number of close friends of bereaved mothers may be beneficial. Community outreach programs for managing loneliness in single parent widows are needed. The single parent widow may need counseling on dating and remarriage issues, financial problems, job difficulties, childcare, role changes and providing support to children.

Because widows may utilize a variety of resources after the death of a spouse, it is necessary that family professionals educate single parent widows about other resources in addition to supports which impact on adaptation to bereavement and single parent widowhood. Other resources may include obtaining strength from one's religion and belief in one's control over stressors. Interventions should strengthen areas with which the single parent widow has had previous success, and introduce new resources that they may not have considered.

In trying to meet the demands of their job and raising their children, many single widow parents are so busy that they make no or little time to meet their own needs. Educational programs which emphasize time for self in contributing to better health are needed. Mothers may need to learn skills in how to be more assertive and effective with their children. Involving children to assist the single-parent mother with family functions, and promoting a clear definition of mother and child roles by letting children know their responsibilities will help promote the maintenance of family functions, roles and routines.

Family professionals can help develop programs for prevention and treatment of unhealthy outcomes to bereavement in single parent widows and their children. As limited programs exist, efforts also need to focus on the development of educational and intervention programs which can help single parent widows and children identify and strengthen their use of adaptive coping strategies. More community based bereavement programs should be made available to widows which address issues of single parent widows that are culturally sensitive to Black, Hispanic and other ethnic groups. Churches are an excellent place for community bereavement and single parent widow support groups. Churches provide a source of volunteers who can be trained to conduct bereavement programs, and their members know the cultural and ethnic practices, beliefs and values of their community. Increased budgets for support groups to provide education on bereavement and single parenthood will likely reduce stress.

Grief often does not resolve itself after a year. Therefore single parent widows, especially those identified as being at high risk, may need to be followed up for at least two years after bereavement. Multidisciplinary family professionals can help develop educational programs for single parent widows at high risk for pathological grieving. Anticipatory guidance could focus on helping widows and children understand the normal grieving process following bereavement. The widow and children may benefit from information about usual responses to death such as loneliness, fatigue, guilt, anger and difficulty concentrating.

Young adults can anticipate that the existing relationship with the mother may change. Extensive grief in the surviving widow may precipitate the adult child to withdraw emotional support. Thus, policy and services should strengthen existing support networks of adult children. Support programs need to be developed and made available to caregivers. Involving children in the planning and delivery of care to dependent, ill widowed, encouraging friends assistance with care, and providing services that add to the support system of the widow and her children will increase family strength.

Economic problems of single parent widows can be addressed at the level of social policy. Government policy which increases benefits available to single parent widows in the form of health care coverage and higher salaries for employment would help reduce the negative effects of lower income on the health of single parent widows and their children. Individual practitioners can also help by teaching single parent widows strategies for managing financial problems such as budgeting and strategies to enhance the mother's opportunities for employment. More job training programs to prepare widows for employment as well as more child care centers for employed single-mothers are needed. Burden (1986) discusses implications for employers who need to recognize that they must provide support to single parent employees who have job and family responsibilities. Support benefits might include greater flexibility in work schedules, availability of child care programs at the workplace, and programs on work/family issues to reduce stress. Child care policy needs to be developed which includes affordable government supported child care. McLanahan et al. (1987) state that many social institutions important to mothers such as schools and medical clinics operate on schedules that make no allowance for single parent mothers who must work. The consideration of the needs for flexibility in scheduling of appointments is useful when developing policies and programs. Galloway (1990) points out that support policies need to be developed which give widows who are having problems with bereavement or child care time off to manage problems. Young adults may need time off from work to care for an ill, dependent, widowed mother. Community mental health centers should be allocated more monies to increase their caretaking potential so that single parent widows can have access to respite to reduce stress related to caring for a handicapped child. Similarly, these services should also be available to adult children caring for a dependent, ill, widow parent.

CONCLUSIONS

In summary, this paper has focused on describing the stressors, appraisal of bereavement, ways of coping, resources, grieving responses and health of four types of single widow parents: widows who are raising dependent children; widows who are raising a physically or mentally handicapped child; independent older widows with one or more healthy children; and dependent, ill, older widows with a healthy child in the home. Gaps in knowledge were addressed. An investigation of single parent widow family types which focused on stressors, appraisal, coping, resources, grieving responses and health of high-risk, vulnerable, and healthy single parent widows was presented. Themes common to all four types of single parent widow families included: the grieving process; changes in roles and responsibilities in the family; employment; loneliness; dating and remarriage; and caregiver stress. Directions for future research and implications for practice, education and social policy for family professionals were discussed.

Finally, families with single mother widows can cope more adaptively if family professionals will evaluate their strengths and weaknesses, provide support and interventions which reduce or eliminate stressors and educate widows and children about helpful appraisals, coping strategies and resources. Single parent widows will discover new resources within themselves, their families, and within their communities that can be used to improve their health and strengthen their families.

AUTHOR NOTE

The author wishes to thank Susan Haas for her assistance with the literature review. Shirley Hanson, Marsha Heims, Doris Julian, and Barbara Gagliardi, are acknowledged for their helpful feedback on an earlier version of this manuscript.

NOTE

1. Information on the instruments used in these studies, including a description of the instrument and reliability and validity, are available from the author. Please address all correspondence to: Dr. Kathleen Gass-Sternas, Ph.D., R.N., Rutgers, The State University of New Jersey College of Nursing, 180 University Avenue, Newark, New Jersey 07102.

REFERENCES

Amato, P. R., & Partridge, S. (1987). Widows and divorcees with dependent children: Material, personal, family and social well-being. *Family Relations*, *36* (3), 316-320.

Angel, R. & Worobey, J. L. (1988). Single motherhood and children's health. *Journal of Health and Social Behavior*, *29*, 38-52.

Beckman, P. (1983). Characteristics of handicapped infants: A study of the relationship between child characteristics and stress as reported by mothers. *American Journal of Mental Deficiency, 88*, 150-156.

Beckman-Bell, P. (1981). Child-related stress in families of handicapped children. *Topics in Early Childhood Special Education, 1* (3), 45-53.

Beckwith, B. E., Beckwith, S. K., Gray, T. L., Micsko, M. M., Holm, J. E., Plummer, V. H., & Flaa, S. L. (1990). Identification of spouses at high risk during bereavement: A preliminary assessment of Parkes and Weiss' Risk Index. *The Hospice Journal, 6* (3), 35-46.

Belcher, J. R. (1988). Mothers alone and supporting chronically mentally ill adult children: A greater vulnerability to illness. *Women & Health, 14*(2), 61-80.

Bird, G. W. (1986). Contemporary family and human development materials. *Family Relations, 35*, 222-224.

Black, D., & Urbanowicz, M. A. (1987). Family intervention with bereaved children. *Journal of Child Psychology and Psychiatry, 28* (3), 467-476.

Bornstein, P. E., Clayton, P. J., Halikas, J. A., Maurice, W. L., & Robins, E. (1973). The depression of widowhood after thirteen months. *British Journal of Psychiatry, 122*, 561-566.

Bowen, G. L., & Orthner, D. K. (1986). Single parents in the U.S. Air Force. *Family Relations, 35* (1), 45-52.

Boyce, G. C., Miller, B. C., White, K. R., & Godfrey, M. K. (1995). Single Parenting in families of children with disabilities. *Marriage & Family Review, 20* (3/4), 389-409.

Bruce, M. L., Kim, K., Leaf, P. J., & Jacobs, S. (1990). Depressive episodes and dysphoria resulting from conjugal bereavement in a prospective community sample. *American Journal of Psychiatry, 147* (5), 608-611.

Buchsbaum, B. C. (1990). An agenda for treating widowed parents. *Psychotherapy Patient, 6* (3-4), 113-130.

Burden, D. S. (1986). Single parents and the work setting: The impact of multiple job and homelife responsibilities. *Family Relations, 35*, 37-43.

Burke, S. (1987). Assessing single parent families with physically disabled children. In L. Wright & M. Leahey (Eds.), *Families and chronic illness* (pp. 147-167). Springhouse, Pa.: Springhouse.

Burns, C. (1984). The hospitalization experience and single-parent families: A time of special vulnerability. *Nursing Clinics of North America, 19* (2), 285-293.

Cheifetz, P. N., Stavrakakis, G., & Lester, E. P. (1989). Studies of the affective state in bereaved children. *Canadian Journal of Psychiatry, 34* (7), 688-692.

Clayton, P. J., Halikas, J. A., & Maurice, W. L. (1972). The depression of widowhood. *British Journal of Psychiatry, 120*, 71-78.

Covey, L. S., & Tam, D. (1990). Depressive mood, the single-parent home, and adolescent cigarette smoking. *American Journal of Public Health, 80* (11), 1330-1333.

Eggebeen, D. J., & Uhlenberg, P. (1989). Changes in the age distribution of parents 1940-1980. *Journal of Family Issues, 10* (2), 169-188.

Ferraro, K., & Barresi, C. (1982). The impact of widowhood on the social relations of older persons. *Research on Aging, 4*, 227-248.

Fulmer, R. (1983). A structural approach to unresolved mourning in single parent family systems. *Journal of Marital and Family Therapy, 9* (3), 259-269.

Fulmer, R. H. (1987). Special problems of mourning in low-income single-parent families. In J. C. Hansen & M. Lindblad-Goldberg (Eds.), *Clinical Issues in Single-Parent Households*, (pp. 19-38). Rockville, Maryland: Aspen Publishers, Inc.

Galloway, S. C. (1990). Young adults' reactions to the death of a parent. *Oncology Nursing Forum, 17* (6), 899-904.

Gass, K. A. (1987a). The health of conjugally bereaved older widows: The role of appraisal, coping and resources. *Research in Nursing and Health, 10*, 39-47.

Gass, K. A. (1987b). Coping strategies of widows. *Journal of Gerontological Nursing, 13* (8), 29-33.

Gass, K. A. (1991). *Measuring appraisal of bereavement and its prediction of coping and health.* Symposium presentation, Stress and Coping Research Section, 15th Annual Midwest Nursing Research Society Conference, Oklahoma City.

Gass, K. A. & Chang, A. S. (1989). Appraisals of bereavement, coping, resources, and psychosocial health dysfunction in widows and widowers. *Nursing Research, 38* (1), 31-36.

Gass-Sternas, K. A. (1993). *Test of a bereavement intervention program: A pilot study.* Presentation at the 17th Annual Midwest Nursing Research Society Conference, Cleveland, Ohio.

Gladow, N. W., & Ray, M. P. (1986). The impact of informal support systems on the well being of low income single parents. *Family Relations, 35* (1), 113-123.

Goldberg, E. L., Comstock, G. W., & Harlow, S. D. (1988). Emotional problems and widowhood. *Journal of Gerontology, 43* (6), 206-208.

Gove, W. R., & Shin, H. (1989). The psychological well-being of divorced and widowed men and women: An empirical analysis. *Journal of Family Issues, 10* (1), 122-144.

Greene, R.W., & Feld, S. (1989). Social support coverage and the well-being of elderly widows and married women. *Journal of Family Issues, 10* (1), 33-51.

Gutierrez, M. J. (1987). Teenage pregnancy and the Puerto Rican family. In J. C. Hansen & M. Lindblad-Goldberg (Eds.), *Clinical Issues in Single-Parent Households*, (pp. 73-84). Rockville, Maryland: Aspen Publishers, Inc.

Hall, L., Gurley, D., Sachs, B., & Kryscio, R. (1991). Psychosocial predictors of maternal depressive symptoms, parenting attitudes, and child behavior in single-parent families, *Nursing Research, 40* (4), 214-220.

Hall, L. A., & Farel, A. M. (1988). Maternal stresses and depressive symptoms: Correlates of behavior problems in young children. *Nursing Research, 37*, 156-161.

Hanson, S. M. (1986). Healthy single parent families. *Family Relations, 35* (1), 125-132.

Harris, E. S. (1991). Adolescent bereavement following the death of a parent: An exploratory study. *Child Psychiatry and Human Development, 21* (4), 267-281.

Harmon, R. J., Stall, P. J., Emde, R. N., Siegel, C., Kempe, R. S., Margolin, M. H.,

Mc Gehee, R., & Frederick, S. R. (1990). Infant Psychiatry Grand Rounds. Unresolved grief: A two-year old brings her mother for treatment. *Infant Mental Health Journal, 11* (2), 97-112.

Hoeffer, B. (1987a). Predictors of life outlook of older single women. *Research in Nursing and Health, 10* (2), 111-117.

Hoeffer, B. (1987b). A causal model of loneliness among older single women. *Archives of Psychiatric Nursing, 1* (5), 366-373.

Holroyd, J. (1974). The questionnaire on resources and stress: An instrument to measure family response to a handicapped member. *Journal of Community Psychology, 2*, 92-94.

Hogan, D. P., Hao, L., & Parish, W. L. (1990). Race, kin, networks, and assistance to mother-headed families. *Social Forces, 68* (3), 797-812.

Ide, B. A., Tobias, C., Kay, M., Monk, J., & Guernsey de Zapien, J. (1990). A comparison of coping strategies used effectively by older Anglo and Mexican-American widows: A longitudinal study. *Health Care for Women International, 11*, 237-249.

Ihinger-Tallman, M. (1986). Member adjustment in single parent families: Theory building. *Family Relations, 35* (1), 215-221.

Jennings, A., & Sheldon, M. (1986). The health of pre-school children and the response to illness of single-parent families. *Health Visitor, 59* (November), 337-339.

Joe, T. (1986). The economic status of black men and its affect on the black family structure. *Journal of the National Black Nurses' Association, 1*(1), 66-71.

Jones, C. W. (1987). Coping with the young handicapped child in the single-parent family: An ecosystemic perspective. In J. C. Hansen & M. Lindblad-Goldberg (Eds.), *Clinical Issues in Single-Parent Households*, (pp. 85-100). Rockville, Maryland: Aspen Publishers, Inc.

Kaffman, M., Elizur, E., & Gluckson, L. (1987). Bereavement reactions in children: Therapeutic implications. *Israel Journal of Psychiatry and Related Sciences, 24* (1-2), 65-76.

Kazak, A., & Marvin, R. (1984). Differences, difficulties, and adaptation: Stress and social networks in families with a handicapped child. *Family Relations, 33*, 67-77.

Kirschling, J. M., & Barron McBride, A. (1989). Effects of age and sex on the experience of widowhood. *Western Journal of Nursing Research, 11* (2), 207-218.

Kitson, G. C., Babri, K. B., Roach, M. J., & Placidi, K. S. (1989). Adjustment to widowhood and divorce: A review. *Journal of Family Issues, 10* (1), 5-32.

Koller, H., Richardson, S. A., Katz, M., & McLaren, J. (1983). Behavior disturbance since childhood among a 5-year birth cohort of all mentally retarded young adults in a city. *American Journal of Mental Deficiency, 87*, 386-395.

Lazarus, R., & Folkman, S. (1984). *Stress, appraisal, and coping.* New York: Springer Publishing Company.

Lehman, D. R., Lang, E. L., Wortman, C. B., & Sorenson, S. B. (1989). Long-term effects of sudden bereavement: Marital and parent-child relationships and children's reactions. *Journal of Family Psychology, 2* (3), 344-367.

Lindblad-Goldberg, M., & Dukes, J. L. (1985). Social support in black, low-income, single-parent families: Normative and dysfunctional patterns. *American Journal of Orthopsychiatry, 55* (1), 42-58.
Lopata, H. Z. (1979). *Women as widows: Support systems.* New York: Elsevier.
Loveland-Cherry, C. (1986). Personal health practices in single parent and two parent families. *Family Relations, 35* (1), 133-139.
McCubbin, M. A. (1989). Family stress and family strengths: A comparison of single- and two-parent families with handicapped children. *Research in Nursing and Health, 12,* 101-110.
McIntyre, B. B. (1990). Art therapy with bereaved youth. *Journal of Palliative Care, 6* (1), 16-25.
McLanahan, S., & Booth, K. (1989). Mother-only families: Problems, prospects and politics. *Journal of Marriage and the Family, 51,* 557-580.
McLanahan, S. S., Garfinkel, I., & Ooms, T. (1987). Female-headed families and economic policy: Expanding the clinician's focus. In J. C. Hansen & M. Lindblad-Goldberg (Eds.), *Clinical Issues in Single-Parent Households,* (pp. 1-18). Rockville, Maryland: Aspen Publishers, Inc.
Menaghan, E. G., & Parcel, T. L. (1990). Parental employment and family life: Research in the 1980s. *Journal of Marriage and the Family, 52,* 1079-1098.
Mietus Sanik, M., & Mauldin, T. (1986). Single versus two parent families: A comparison of mothers' time. *Family Relations, 35* (1), 53-56.
Morgan, L. A. (1989). Economic well-being following marital termination: A comparison of widowed and divorced women. *Journal of Family Issues, 10* (1), 86-101.
Morgan, L. A. (1983). Intergenerational economic assistance to children: The case of widows and widowers. *Journal of Gerontology, 38* (6), 725-731.
Morgan, L. A. (1986). The financial experience of widowed women: Evidence from the LRHS. *The Gerontologist, 26* (6), 663-668.
Mueller, D. P., & Cooper, P. W. (1986). Children of single parent families: How they fare as young adults. *Family Relations, 35,* 169-176.
Murphy, P. A. (1986-1987). Parental death in childhood and loneliness in young adults. *OMEGA Journal of Death and Dying, 17* (3), 219-228.
Mutran, E., & Reitzes, D. (1984). Intergenerational support activities and well-being among the elderly: A convergence of exchange and symbolic interaction perspectives. *American Sociological Review, 49* (1), 117-130.
O'Bryant, S. L., & Morgan, L. A. (1990). Recent widows' kin support and orientations to self-sufficiency. *The Gerontologist, 30* (3), 391-398.
Risman, B. J., & Park, K. (1988). Just the two of us: Parent-child relationships in single-parent homes. *Journal of Marriage and the Family, 50,* 1049-1062.
Roberto, K. A., & Scott, J. P. (1986). Confronting widowhood: The influence of informal supports. *American Behavioral Scientist, 29* (4), 497-511.
Rosen, H. (1991). Child and adolescent bereavement. *Child and Adolescent Social Work Journal, 8* (1), 5-16.
Rosenbaum, J. (1981). Widows and widowers and their medication use: Nursing implications, *JPN and Mental Health Services,* (January), 17-19.

Sable, P. (1989). Attachment, anxiety, and loss of a husband. *American Journal of Orthopsychiatry, 59* (4), 550-556.

Schilling, R. F., Kirkham, M. A., Snow, W. H., & Schinke, S. P. (1986). Single mothers with handicapped children: Different from their married counterparts? *Family Relations, 35* (1), 69-77.

Scott, J. P., & Roberto, K. A. (1987). Informal supports of older adults: A rural-urban comparison. *Family Relations, 36* (4), 444-449.

Siegel, K., Mesagno, F. P., & Christ, G. (1990). A prevention program for bereaved children. *American Journal of Orthopsychiatry, 60* (2), 168-175.

Simon, J. (1990). The single parent: Power and the integrity of parenting. *The American Journal of Psychoanalysis, 50* (2), 187-198.

Talbott, M. M. (1990). The negative side of the relationship between older widows and their adult children: The mothers' perspective. *The Gerontologist, 30* (5), 595-603.

U.S. Department of Health and Human Services (1992). *Healthy People 2000: National Health Promotion and Disease Prevention Objectives*. Boston: Jones & Bartlett.

Warmbrod, M. T. (1986). Counseling bereaved children: Stages in the process. *Social Casework: The Journal of Contemporary Social Work, 67* (6), 351-358.

Weller, E. B., Weller, R. A., Fristad, M. A., & Bowes, J. M. (1990). Dexamethasone suppression test and depressive symptoms in bereaved children: A preliminary report. *Journal of Neuropsychiatry and Clinical Neurosciences, 2* (4), 418-421.

Weltner, J. S. (1982). A structural approach to the single-parent family. *Family Process, 21*, 203-210.

Wojkiewicz, R. A., McLanahan, S. S., & Garfinkel, I. (1990). The growth of families headed by women: 1950-1980. *Demography, 27* (1), 19-30.

Zautra, A. J., Reich, J. W., & Guarnaccia, C. A. (1990). Some everyday life consequences of disability and bereavement for older adults. *Journal of Personality and Social Psychology, 59* (3), 550-561.

Chapter 20

Widowers as Single Fathers

Jane K. Burgess

SUMMARY. This paper suggests that widowed fathers while continuing to fill the traditional family role of provider, are also capable of providing tender, loving care for the emotional and physical needs of their children. Role theory will be used to examine the processes widowers go through as they adapt to their new parenting role and how they cope with their own feelings. Three facets of the parental role that may enhance the widowed father's relationship with their children will be discussed. Their therapeutic role is to provide continuity and sensitivity to help their grieving children cope with the loss of their mother. Their child socialization role relates to the teaching of family values to their children. The child-care role involves the physical well being of their children. The ecological perspective will be used to examine how they adapt to changes occurring in systems outside the family, such as the workplace. Implications for professionals and recommendations for further study of the widower as custodial parent will be discussed.

KEYWORDS. Single fathers, Widowers, Father-child relationships

INTRODUCTION

The purpose of this paper is to describe the interactions of the newly widowed man and his children as both adjust to the reality of their new

---

Jane K. Burgess is Professor Emeritus, Sociology, University of Wisconsin, Waukesha.

[Haworth co-indexing entry note]: "Widowers as Single Fathers." Burgess, Jane K. Co-published simultaneously in *Marriage & Family Review* (The Haworth Press, Inc.) Vol. 20, No. 3/4, 1995, pp. 447-461; and: *Single Parent Families: Diversity, Myths and Realities* (ed: Shirley M. H. Hanson et al.) The Haworth Press, Inc., 1995, pp. 447-461. Multiple copies of this article/chapter may be purchased from The Haworth Document Delivery Center [1-800-3-HAWORTH; 9:00 a.m. - 5:00 p.m. (EST)].

lives. Theoretical perspectives are used to examine (1) how the widower handles new stresses, seeks guidance, and adapts to his new parenting roles, (2) how he copes with his own feelings and needs, and (3) how he adapts to changes occurring in systems outside the family, such as the workplace. A final section discusses implications for professionals and recommendations for further study.

Until very recently most American fathers have been on the periphery of the family as far as parenting is concerned. This is in part because of the way young women are socialized. Little Sarah receives a doll and begins to practice being a mother. She may also receive trucks, planes, cars, and computer games, giving her the perception that there are a wide variety of roles she may fill. There has been no counterpart to this in terms of socialization for the male child. Little Tommy's toys, such as trucks, tools, and electrical games, suggest to him that he will grow up and eventually become a provider, his primary role in life.

It is important to note that recent studies suggest that men, while continuing to fill the traditional family role of provider, are also capably providing tender, loving care for the emotional and physical needs of their children (Burgess, 1988). Although many men report finding little support or guidance for their new role as a single parent, many do an admirable job, especially in explaining death and reassuring their children that they are loved and will always be cared for. When given the opportunity, men can become parents in the fullest sense of the word. In general, fathers who share the nurturing role before their wife's death tend to be more successful in fulfilling the physical, social, and emotional needs of their children afterward (Burgess, 1988).

THEORETICAL PERSPECTIVES

The widowed father is defined as a man who assumes custody and primary care of his children following the death of his wife. Role theory will be used to examine the processes a widower goes through as he adapts to his new role as single father (Hanson, 1991). The ecological perspective will be used to examine how external systems affect those processes.

The Role Theory Perspective

Roles are the prescriptions and expectations of the self and others for the behaviors that are required in any particular situation. When the widower becomes the primary caregiver, he must usually redefine his parental role. Role clarification is important in order for him to do this. While he may find it difficult at first to recognize that he can be a tender, loving, caring person with full responsibility for his children, he generally will succeed in accepting this change in his identity. To do so, however, he must have knowledge of the specific information and cues needed to perform his role as primary caregiver. Whatever the circumstances of a wife's death, the sense of loss and isolation and the fears about caring for his children alone are overwhelming for most widowers (Burgess, 1988).

If the widower fails to identify with his new role, that of a parent with full responsibility for his children, he may require role supplementation. Role supplementation is the process whereby reasons for his failure to assume the new role are identified and strategies are developed to increase role clarification for him. For example, the widower may seek information and encouragement from support groups in order to develop greater awareness of any problems existing in his relationships with his children and to learn effective communication skills that may enhance his relationship with them.

This next section discusses three facets of the parental role that may enhance the widowed father's relationship with his children: the therapeutic role, the child socialization role, and the child care role (Burgess, 1985).

The Therapeutic Role

The therapeutic role of the widowed father is to provide continuity and sensitivity to help a grieving child cope with the loss of a mother. Yet the father is in the early stages of grief himself, and it may be difficult for him to counsel his children. Regardless of how well a widower works through his own feelings of grief, anger, abandonment, sadness, and guilt, he may have difficulty helping his children face the reality of death and cope with their sense of loss (Burgess, 1988).

Whether a wife dies suddenly or after a lingering illness, the pain is there, and the widower must work through his feelings alone. Guilt, anger, and self-pity must be vented before he can find inner peace. A widower will recover from grief when he recognizes his emotions and finds ways to work through them. In the early stages of grief, counseling is often needed. Parent education programs such as those offered by child and family centers can assist a bereaved parent in his efforts to provide continuity and sensitivity to help his grieving children cope with emotional pain. Psychotherapy for both father and children may be necessary when their emotional problems or defensive reactions impede the mourning process (Buchsbaum, 1990).

Children's Feelings: Anger and Fears of Death. Many widowers do not know what their children are feeling about the death of their mother. These men may be so consumed by their own grief that they are unable to give their children the kind of help needed to handle their feelings. Depending on factors such as age, personality, and the type of relationship they had with their mother, children respond in various ways to death. As a result, the trauma they suffer will differ in intensity. If not handled well by the surviving parent, the child who has lost a parent may suffer emotional and behavioral disturbances in adulthood.

For the widower to effectively help his children cope, it is necessary that he explain the facts and circumstances of the death in a realistic, clear manner so that the child comprehends death and can go on with the process of mourning. For example, at the age of six, Jean was unable to grasp the finality of her mother's death. She was able to understand the fact of physical death but not its permanence. As a result, she was very distressed by separation from her mother, but no one understood the deep feelings she had about her mother's death. As many adults mistakenly do, the adults in her family assumed she was too young to comprehend what was going on (Burgess, 1988).

In another example, Tom's wife died after a long illness, leaving him with three-year-old Sarah. He told Sarah that she would never see her mother again but that "Mother" could always be in her thoughts. Sarah talked frequently about "Mommy," but she did not seem to expect to see her again, "because," she would say, "Mommy is dead." Adults should realize that young children are able to grasp the truth about death if they are told the truth with gentleness.

Although older children may have more coping skills than younger children, they must still deal with feelings of anger, guilt, abandonment, and sadness. In order to help his children face the reality of death and cope with grief, the widower must first recognize that children at all ages will have some sort of reaction to death. Scott, who was ten when his mother died, said, "At first I was angry with her for dying and leaving me. I wondered why she hadn't lived through her illness. I wondered if she died because she didn't care about us anymore. Next I blamed the doctor, and finally I felt it was God's fault. Why did he have to take her? I was angry at myself, remembering the times she asked me to do something and I didn't. I even became angry at my two best friends because they still had their mothers. For a while I experienced a feeling of guilt that I had done something wrong, and God was using my mom's death as punishment. I had a hard time dealing with this guilt, and I can't truly explain how I resolved it." It is important for children to be allowed to express angry feelings. Boisterous behavior and noisy expressions of anger are signs that they are getting their feelings out in the open where they can be dealt with and finally left behind (Burgess, 1988).

From a common-sense point of view, a child's anger or other emotions may seem unreasonable. However, as Burgess (1988) and Hanson (1985) found in their research, it is important for parents to recognize that their children can and do have such feelings. It is equally important, according to Burgess (1988), for parents to point out to a child ridden with guilt and anger that no one succeeds in being good and loving all of the time. A child should be told, "It is all right to get angry sometimes. What is important for you to believe is that you did the best you could and that we love you and understand how you feel." Children should never be allowed to associate illness and death with sin and punishment (Burgess, 1988).

Just as an adult needs to grasp reality and to find ways to express emotions in order to cope with grief, so children must be allowed some means for expressing their feelings. They should be free to feel sorrow in their own time and manner. They should not be rushed or pushed into communicating feelings, and, most important, they should not be brushed aside in the mistaken belief that they are too young to understand or that someday they will understand.

Burgess (1988) found that adults must tell a child the truth yet at the same time understand that a child may not be willing to accept it. Twelve-year-old Ruth was nine when her mother died. "She had cancer, and they told me that it was better for her to die instead of living in misery. I felt like they were lying, and I didn't want to believe them. I couldn't sleep nights, and I didn't care whether I ate or not I kept confusing death with sleeping."

The Parental Role in Helping Children Cope with Death. When caught up in their own problems, it is easy for adults to overlook the real feelings of their children. One widower said, "You have to tell people to lay off their clichés about boys not crying. I told my kids, 'It's rough on us. Losing Mother really hurts a lot.' I cry with my children and tell my eighteen-year-old son that it takes a man to cry." Adults cannot be reminded too often that children must be allowed to express honest emotions, whatever they are (Burgess, 1988).

In addition to the suggestions discussed in the previous section, there are other ways a widowed father can enhance his therapeutic role. He should assure the children of his presence and love, particularly in the early periods of grief. He should try to get them to talk about their dead mother and give them every opportunity to review their memories. Referring to past experiences makes it easier for children to reminisce. And he should not be afraid to cry with his children. For them to see that Dad hurts, too, will make them feel freer to express themselves. It is more frightening to children to be sent away than to see an adult cry (Burgess, 1988).

It is also important not to convey to children that deep sorrow is something fearful or bad. Rather, point out that sorrow is mainly feeling sorry for themselves because they miss the person who has died. In keeping with his religious beliefs, the widower may want to assure his child that the dead person is safe in God's care.

There are many ways to help a child cope with grief. But no matter how a widower chooses to help his children face the death of their mother, it is very important that they be allowed to share in the family's grief. They should not be sent away to a neighbor or a friend during preparation and mourning. This might intensify their feelings of loneliness and increase the difficulty of their adjustment (Burgess, 1988). This happened to thirteen-year-old Bobby. "I really didn't know that my mother was dying," he recalled. No one really told me. I wanted to catch up on all the time we had been missing since she got sick, but I was constantly told to go to someone else's house. I felt in the way and left out, and for a long time, I couldn't believe that my mom was gone."

Buchsbaum (1990) sums up five specific parental functions as essential in helping a bereaved child cope with the death of a parent:

1. Providing a stable environment for the family.
2. Explaining the facts and circumstances of the parent's death in a realistic, clear manner.
3. Understanding the child's developmental capacities in both the behavioral and emotional aspects for mourning.
4. Modulating tension and mood stages; encouraging the child to experience the effects of grief as well as fostering progressive development.
5. Assisting the child in dealing with new romantic relationships that the father may develop at the end of the mourning period.

The surviving parent's ability to perform these parental functions profoundly affects the child's ability to comprehend, adapt to, and grieve for the dead parent (Buschbaum, 1990).

Another problem for the widowed father is to protect his children from stimulation that can negatively affect their grieving process such as urging them to display unfelt sorrow. An earlier section of this paper discussed how a child can become fearful of losing the surviving parent and how important it is that the child be assured that dad is healthy and will be around for a long time. In many families there seems to be an emotional barrier that prevents parents and children from communicating with each other about intimate and sensitive areas of their lives. Each may be afraid to open the wound for the other, so they all avoid the topic. At this point seeing a therapist would be helpful for opening up conversation between the father and his children (Buchsbaum, 1990).

The fifth parental function considered essential by Buchsbaum (1990), helping the child deal with the father's new relationships, can be especially challenging for the widower. Unless there is frequent communication between the widower and his children, the children may have varying degrees of readiness for dad's new relationships. He may be sufficiently disengaged from his dead wife to be ready for dating and may even be thinking of remarriage. The children, however, may be still in a deep process of mourning, and the thought of a stepmother in their home can be very threatening.

For example, Mary was ten when her mother died and fifteen when her father remarried. She said, "I am an only child, and was very close to my Mom. I still miss her so much. Dad was usually considerate of my feelings, but he could not understand my resistance to his dating. When he told me he was going to ask the lady he had been dating for a year or so to marry him, I was completely devastated. I did not really dislike Anne, but I did not want another woman in our home. I resented anyone taking my mother's place." This newly constituted family sought advice from a therapist who was able to help Mary understand why her father wanted to remarry. The stepmother began to understand how her attitudes and behaviors affected Mary's behavior. With counseling, this family was able to improve the quality of the stepmother-child relationship and the family bond grew stronger.

The Child Socialization Role–Teaching Family Values

Success in fulfilling the therapeutic role is relevant to success in performing the child care and child socialization roles. A father's communication skills have a direct bearing on his ability to teach basic family values to his children. The family, more than any other institution, is where basic values are taught and learned–where children develop their own identity. It is within the family circle that parents pass on to children the basic traits of character and citizenship that are essential to individual and societal well-being (Blankenhorn, 1990). Generally, women do most of the teaching of children, helping them develop a sense of responsibility and showing them how to get along with others. Of necessity, this socialization function is assumed by the widower after the death of his wife.

When the widower becomes the chief caregiver of his children, he must now redefine his normative role from that of provider to that of a nurturing parent, one willing to socialize his children and to be totally responsible for their care. The children in this "new" family must also accept the changes and reciprocate in such a way as to sustain the new interaction. If the father feels incapable of performing his new roles, he may require professional counseling, as has been noted previously. Parent training classes may be helpful for improving his skills in communication, discipline, affective listening, and other parenting skills.

According to Burgess (1988), widowers with children find that they become more actively involved in doing things with their children than before their wife died. As one father said, "I must confess that I used to let my many outside activities take me away from home too often. Now I spend more time at home, and I am finally getting to know something about our children. I am becoming more involved in their religious training, whereas before my wife's death, I left that up to her."

Most widowers say their children have become more independent, and the older children more supportive (Burgess, 1988). Typically, the widowers say, "My children have taken more responsibility for making decisions that concern themselves, seem more reliable in carrying out my wishes, and are assuming more responsibility for our everyday living together."

Widowers usually find that their children are more willing to help around the house. The father of a seventeen-year-old daughter says, "She is really something special. From a little scatterbrain, she is now assuming much of the responsibility of keeping our household together." Just as the problem of getting the children to help around the house often proves to be minor for most widowers, so does discipline. The father and the children have suffered a similar loss and share similar pain. Thus, children seem to sense the importance of cooperation. Actually, most widowers express great satisfaction with how well they and their children become socialized into their new lifestyles. These men enjoy looking after the well-being of their children and are proud of their children's behavior (Burgess, 1988).

The Child Care Role

The above discussion indicates that widowers can be successful in socializing their children into age-appropriate lifestyles and behavior patterns. Similarly, providing child care does not pose an insurmountable problem for those fathers who have previously been involved in it. Widowed fathers usually find they must cut back on activities as part of the adjustment to their new situation. Bob, a young father with three children ages eight, nine, and eleven, was panic-stricken when his wife died suddenly. He said, "Actually, when my immediate grief subsided, caring for the children was not that difficult because I had always been involved in feeding and bathing them, helping them with their schoolwork, and seeing to their discipline. So I was more fortunate than some men who have never done any of the child caring before."

Finding the right child care facility at an affordable cost is a problem for many men with young children. However, many single fathers receive offers of child care from parents or other family members. See manuscript by Gass-Sternas for widowed mothers experiences (Gass-Sternas, 1995). Widowers with older children report a minimum of problems. School-age children often are cared for by friends, neighbors or relatives after school until the fathers come home from work. A typical response from widowers is, "Taking on the responsibility for my children's care has given me a sense of growth as a person. I feel good about myself."

There is little question that widowers can fill the parenting roles–therapeutic, child socialization, and child care–very effectively. While men may find it difficult at first to recognize that they can be tender, loving, caring people with full responsibility for their children, they generally succeed in accepting their role transition.

The Ecological Perspective

The preceding discussion has concentrated primarily on the role theory perspective. This section uses the ecological perspective for a greater understanding of how conditions surrounding the family affect both parental roles and the relationship between parent and child.

Ecological factors affect the widower's ability to maintain family stability. A father's need to move to another community or his need to change the composition of a household, such as by bringing in a housekeeper, may undermine a child's sense of security. Research shows that the mourning process of a young child may become more difficult when changes are made in his or her situation. When a move is necessary, a full explanation should be given to the child and connections with family and other familiar people, places, and events should be kept constant whenever possible (Buchsbaum, 1990).

In many cases, widowers left with very young children and minimal economic resources face a crisis. For example, Bill said, "The problem of finding babysitters was a nightmare. When my wife died, my children were fourteen months, and three and five years old. My solution was to accept my sister's offer to take the baby into her home, and to send my older children to live with their maternal grandmother. These changes in living quarters were difficult for the children, and the regression in behavior by the three- and five-year-old was difficult to handle. At the suggestion of a therapist, I united my children by accepting my mother's offer to move into my home to care for them. In a short time, the older children's behavior returned to normal and life generally became orderly for all of us."

In the ecological framework, what happens outside the family unit may have as much of an influence on what happens within it. This perspective views fathers and their environments as mutually shaping systems, each changing over time, and adapting to changes in each other. It is important for the therapist to understand and ask questions about the family's milieu–neighborhood, extended family and friends, employment, larger community, and legal situation. Each of these social contexts has implications for clinicians, educators, researchers and social policy makers. To further elaborate on the ecological perspective, it is helpful to review the work of Bronfenbrenner (1990) and Hanson (1985). They identify four different levels of systems that affect the family: microsystems, mesosystems, ecosystems, and macrosystems.

Microsystems. Microsystems are settings in which individuals experience and create day-to-day reality. The family is a microsystem within which the widower and children interact together. In order for children to develop into emotionally secure social beings, they must develop through interaction with parents (or other adults) with whom they form a strong mutually emotional attachment. The widowed father, then, has extra responsibility for being committed to the children in his care with lifelong attention to their well-being and development.

The widowed father should select programs outside the family that accelerate the child's psychological development. Programs that enhance curiosity or create imaginative activity are preferable. For example, a father who communicates his interest in nature to a young child and interacts with the child in a wildlife program can establish a reciprocal emotional bond. As this bond continues to grow, the child's psychological development will grow.

Mesosystems. Mesosystems are the relationships between several microsystems, including extended family members and friends. It has been noted in the discussion of the widower's child care role that quite often these fathers turned to family members for assistance. When the single parent receives support from relatives and friends, children are much less likely to develop behavior or educational problems, such as impaired academic achievement, dropping out of school, sexual promiscuity, and criminal acts (Bronfenbrenner, 1990).

Ecosystems. Ecosystems involve ongoing patterns of interaction between settings that include home, child care programs, the school, and the parents' place of work (between family and outside) (Bronfenbrenner, 1990). Widowed fathers, for example, are unable to escape the demands of their work because they are the sole support of their children. The business world generally is not sympathetic to a man's role as parent, contrasted with the consideration a working mother may receive. When a working mother calls to report that her child is ill, for example, it is usually expected that she will stay home and tend to the child. A man, on the other hand, is usually expected to arrange for a female substitute to care for his child during times of emergency. In fact, he himself may expect that he cannot remain at home, so indoctrinated are most men to the role of worker.

Bronfenbrenner (1990) suggests that the following accommodations can be made between the two domains of family and work: flexible work schedules, availability of part-time jobs for both men and women without loss of job benefits and opportunities for advancement, and establishment at the work place of a family resources office to serve as an advocate on family-work issues. He indicates that such measures are economically sound for industry. They reduce absenteeism and job turnover and enhance employee morale and quality of work performance (Bronfenbrenner, 1990).

Widowed fathers should be encouraged to become involved in their children's education (Burgess, 1988). Contact between the parent and teachers can help teachers better understand any unusual behavior on the part of the children and make it more comfortable for them to discuss it with the parent. Through contact with teachers, widowed fathers can be better prepared to assist their children with homework and to understand any problems they may be having in school.

Macrosystems. According to Bronfenbrenner (1990), the systems are the broad, ideological and institutional settings of our culture such as religion, that protect the sanctity of the family. Microsystems, mesosystems, and ecosystems are set within the macrosystem. Widowers with children require support from caregivers, teachers, and other professionals as well as from relatives, neighbors, co-workers, the community-at-large, and the major social, economic, and political institutions of a society. These social institutions must provide stability, status, belief systems, customs, and actions to aid in developing and sustaining strong family systems (Bronfenbrenner, 1990).

IMPLICATIONS FOR PROFESSIONALS

The increasing interest in widowers as fathers, among social scientists as well as among the lay public, has many implications for professionals–educators, researchers, clinicians, and those who establish social policy.

Educators and Researchers

The prevailing stereotype holds that most men have neither the talent nor the inclination to perform the fathering role. Historically, cultural values and expectations have determined parental roles. Recently, changing expectations about the role of women has created concomitant changes in the role of men, with men increasingly participating in parenting their children. Men have always cared for children under certain circumstances. Indeed, because of high maternal mortality in past centuries, widowed fathers were the original single (custodial) fathers. However, in more recent times, when a man gets sole custody of his children, he has been seen as not being capable of providing care for them. Many have been pressured into remarriage to provide a mother for their children. Sometimes a relative became a substitute mother. In either case, men seldom identified with the nurturing aspects of the parenting role.

This paper on widowers as fathers refutes some myths and negative notions about the values, attitudes, and behaviors of men who have custodial care of their children. Although men may find it difficult to add the nurturing parent role to work role that is the primary source of their male identity, research shows that widowers as fathers generally succeed at parenting. They may be unable to escape the demands of their work, but they can and do change many of their outside activities in order to have more time with their children. Studies on the influence of family demands on the work role has focused on women but not on men. It is important that researchers and educators, particularly family life educators, learn more about how men balance the demands of work and family (Burgess, 1988).

The major task for educators and researchers is to inform the public–professionals and lay persons alike–of the importance of rearing children in such a manner as to free them from the negative myths regarding the nurturing parent role for fathers. The same socialization assimilated by women may provide men with a basis for freeing themselves from this stigma of gender. This in turn, would make them function better should they ever become widowed (Burgess, 1985).

Clinicians

The implications described for educators and researchers apply as well to clinicians. Clinicians may be unaware of the terrible pain men feel when they lose a spouse. Society in general, and men in particular, have identified with the comment frequently expressed to the author, "Why study men? They don't have any problems they can't handle by themselves!"

Thus, men learn to keep their emotions to themselves, and the people may assume that a man without a spouse is coping.

According to Burgess (1988), a man's only confidante is likely to be his wife. When she dies, he is alone. He may cry in private, but he finds it very difficult to discuss his feelings with anyone. In fact, many widowers find that most other people avoid discussions of their wife's death. Without someone to share his feelings with, a widower's recovery is slow. Before a man can help his children with their emotional needs, he must first begin to cope with his own feelings of anger, guilt, fear, and loneliness. Therefore, it is important that the therapist from whom a widower seeks counsel is sympathetic and has a full understanding of the pain he may be suffering.

Social Policymakers

In today's society, the fact that there is no valid research demonstrating that being male is a barrier to parenting has special relevance for professionals such as lawyers, judges and social workers. Yet female parental competence has been reinforced by our cultural norms as well as by our legal system, which strongly favors maternal custody rights. However, recent research is showing that gender is not an exclusive determinant of a parent's ability to nurture, socialize, and provide physical care to a child. It substantiates the fact that many men are capable of playing the "mother" role in the most basic sense (Burgess, 1985).

Social policymakers need to be reminded that men as well as women can fill the parenting role as described in this paper. This is particularly relevant for father headed single parent families when child custody is being considered. Social policymakers must also become aware of the need of single parents for assistance with childcare. Our political system must provide a family leave program that will protect the jobs of all parents and will provide financial aid to obtain good home care for children when needed.

RECOMMENDATIONS FOR FURTHER STUDY

Of the 64,216,000 children under the age of 18 living in the United States in 1990, 218,000 live with custodial fathers. Of these 165,000 live with widowed fathers (U.S. Bureau of Census, March, 1992). Because of the availability of larger samples, most of the research on single parent families and child custody has concerned mothers and their children.

Research on single-parent fathering has focused on small, nonrandom samples of white middle and upper-middle-class divorced men. This limited approach creates a bias because of notable differences in the attitudes and behavior of men and women and because a widowed father's experience and emotions may differ in several aspects from those of a divorced custodial father. For example, there is the finality of death that does not exist in divorce (Burgess, 1985). Consideration of these factors suggests a need to include widowers and their children in the studies on fathering.

Longitudinal studies should follow widowers and their children over time as they develop their new relationships in a single parent family. Multiple research methods, using large, randomly selected samples . . . broad ethnic and social class basis, are needed to determine the multidimensional, complex variables that impinge on the widower, his children, and his family as a social unit (Burgess, 1985).

CONCLUSIONS

The use of role theory to discuss the performance of the widower as parent delineates the many factors involved in the widowed father's successful transition from the role of provider only to fulfilling therapeutic, child socialization and child care roles as well. For widowers who have assisted their wives with childrearing, assuming full responsibility is less difficult. Widowers who receive voluntary assistance with child care from family, friends, or neighbors find less stress in performing their roles as fully responsible parents. As stated previously, for the development of mutual interaction, there must be attentiveness and persistence on the part of both adults and children. This is more likely to occur in families where there is a strong, mutual emotional attachment, and where parents find time to spend with their children (Mellman, 1990).

The ecological framework has been used to examine the role of the widower as parent in terms of how he and his family relate to the basic institutions of society. As discussed in this paper, what happens outside the family unit as well as inside it has important implications for social policymakers, educators, researchers, and clinicians. It is crucial that these professionals apply social scientific findings to promote the social acceptance of fathers as capable and successful custodial parents. So doing would benefit all of society in terms of opening wider the horizons of parenting (Burgess, 1985).

REFERENCES

Blankenhorn, D. (1990). American family dilemmas. In D. Blankenhorn, A. Bayme, & J. B. Elshtain (Eds.), *Rebuilding the nest.* Milwaukee, WI: Family Service of America.

Bozett, F. W., & Hanson, S. M. H. (1991) (Eds.). *Fatherhood and families in cultural context.* NY: Springer.

Bronfenbrenner, J. (1990). Discovering what families do. In D. Blankenhorn, A. Bayme, & J. B. Elshtain (Eds.), *Rebuilding the nest.* Milwaukee, WI: Family Service of America.

Buchsbaum, B. C. (1990). An agenda for treating widowed parents, *Psychotherapy Patient. 6,* 114-120.

Burgess, J. K. (1985). Widowers as fathers. In S. M. H. Hanson & F. W. Bozett (Eds.), *Dimensions of fatherhood.* Beverly Hills: Sage Publications.

Burgess, J. K. (1988). *The single-again man.* Lexington: Lexington Books.

Fuchs, V. R. (1990). Are Americans underinvesting in children?" In D. Blankenhorn, A. Bayme, & J. B. Elshtain (Eds.), *Rebuilding the nest.* Milwaukee, WI: Family Service of America.

Gass-Sternas, K. A. (1995). Single parent widows: Stressors, appraisal, coping, resources, grieving responses and health. *Marriage & Family Review, 20* (3/4), 411-445.

Hanson, S. (1985). Single custodial fathers. In S. M. H. Hanson & F. W. Bozett (Eds.), *Dimensions of fatherhood.* Beverly Hills: Sage Publications.

Hanson, S. M. H. (1985). Fatherhood: Contextual variations. *American Behavioral Scientist. 29,* 55-77.

Mellman, M., Lazarus, E., & Rivlin, A. (1990). Family time, family values. In D. Blankenhorn, A. Bayme, & J. B. Elshtain (Eds.), *Rebuilding the nest.* Milwaukee, WI: Family Service of America.

U. S. Bureau of Census, Dept. of Commerce. Marital status & living arrangements of the population. March 1992, Table 6 Current Population Report, Series pp. 20-468.

Chapter 21

Single Parent Families: A Bookshelf

Benjamin Schlesinger

SUMMARY. The purpose of this single parent families bookshelf is to provide potential users with a sampling of recent books that deal with various aspects of single parenting. Books are focused on the time period of 1980 to 1993. Resources include primarily North American and Canadian entries. The titles are presented in the following categories: children and one-parent families, cross-cultural references, divorced single parents, ethnicity and single parent families, frameworks for examining single parent families, never-married biological teen mother headed families, practical guides to single parent family living, single fathers with custody following separation and divorce, and special issues of journals focused on single parent families.

KEYWORDS. Books, Single parents, American, Cross-cultural

INTRODUCTION

The purpose of this chapter is to provide an annotated bibliography of books and monographs on single parents and single parent families.

Benjamin Schlesinger is Professor, Faculty of Social Work, University of Toronto.

[Haworth co-indexing entry note]: "Single Parent Families: A Bookshelf." Schlesinger, Benjamin. Co-published simultaneously in *Marriage & Family Review* (The Haworth Press, Inc.) Vol. 20, No. 3/4, 1995, pp. 463-482; and: *Single Parent Families: Diversity, Myths and Realities* (ed: Shirley M. H. Hanson et al.) The Haworth Press, Inc., 1995, pp. 463-482. Multiple copies of this article/chapter may be purchased from The Haworth Document Delivery Center [1-800-3-HAWORTH; 9:00 a.m. - 5:00 p.m. (EST)].

The bookshelf is arranged according to major issues discussed in the existing literature related to the topics of this special volume of *Marriage & Family Review.* Topics are arranged in alphabetical order. The section dealing with cross-cultural entries omits the United States. There are 125 entries.

The author has been involved in examining the issue of single parents for the past thirty years; however, in preparation of this bookshelf, I decided to focus on the 1980-1993 period. For entries of articles and books prior to this period consult the books by Schlesinger (1978, 1985), which contain annotated bibliographies dating back to the 1960s.

For the present search, the *Social Work Abstracts, Psyclit* and *Sociofile* were found to be most helpful. They are all available on CD Rom. These resources include primarily American and Canadian entries. Another comprehensive reference is the annual *Inventory of Marriage and Family Literature* (Touliatos and Czaplewski, 1991) which includes items on single parent families. These inventories began publishing in 1967, and are still available.

The entries in the first volume cover the 1900-1964 period. The inventories are sponsored by the National Council on Family Relations. This bookshelf also includes listings related to cross-cultural content on single parents. In our "global village" it is important to move away from our own ethnocentric boundaries, and to examine single parents on a cross-cultural basis. The addresses for selected international entries have been included to enable the reader to obtain the items under review. The cross-cultural entries can not be found in most American data banks. The bookshelf also includes special issues of journals which contain content related to single parents and single parent families.

The advantage of these special issues is that one finds under one cover a comprehensive review of a specific topic (divorce and family life, children and divorce, etc. . . .). At the same time the papers in these journals all have references which bring the topics up-to-date.

Review and use of the literature on the family, including the single parent and single parent family will hopefully be guided by this focused bookshelf. Readers are encouraged to continue the critique and revision of their own focused annotated bibliographies.

CHILDREN IN ONE-PARENT FAMILIES

Cantor, D.W. and Drake, E.A. (1983). *Divorced Parents and Their Children: A Guide for Mental Health Professionals.* New York: Springer Publishing Co.

A source of information for professionals working with divorced parents and their children. Case examples illustrate the text.

Dolmetsch, P. and Shih, A. (Eds.) (1985). *The Kids' Book About Single Parent Families*. Garden City, N.Y.: Doubleday and Co.

Written by children aged 11-15, for other children. The children give guidance to others who are living in one-parent families.

Emery, R.E. (1988). *Marriage, Divorce and Children's Adjustment*. Newbury Park: Sage.

A discussion on how children cope with divorce. Evidence from research and clinical experience is integrated in this monograph.

Furstenberg, F.F. and Cherlin, A.J. (1991). *Divided Families*. Cambridge, MA: Harvard University Press.

First in a series on family and public policy. Uses interdisciplinary research findings to show how children are affected by divorce.

Gardner, R.A. (1983). *The Boys and Girls Book About One-Parent Families*. New York: Bantam Books.

A guide to the many questions asked about one parent families by children.

Hutcherson, T.W. (Ed.) (1985). Child support enforcement. *Juvenile and Family Court Journal*, 36:3.

Fourteen papers discuss varied aspects of child support; child custody, non-support, and enforcement.

Rofes, E. (Ed.) (1981). *The Kids' Book of Divorce*. Lexington, MA: Lewis Publishing Co.

Twenty children aged 11-14 wrote this book "For and about kids" on divorce.

Stuart, I.R. and Abt, L.E., (Eds.) (1981). *Children of Separation and Divorce: Management and Treatment*. New York: Van Nostrand Reinhold.

Fifteen papers examine the legal, social, and emotional consequences of marital breakdown. Many of the contributions focus on the effects on children of separation and divorce. The authors come from a multi-disciplinary background.

Teyber, E. (1992). *Helping Children Cope with Divorce.* Lexington, Mass.: Lexington Books.

Guidelines to help parents handle the problems that emerge at each stage of the divorce process.

CROSS-CULTURAL REFERENCES

Ambert, A.M. (1980). *Divorce in Canada.* Toronto: Academic Press.

The first monograph on divorce in Canada. It contains an overview of the topic, focusing on the Canadian scene.

Ambert, A.M. (1989). *Ex-Spouses and New Spouses: A Study of Relationships.* Brooklyn: JAI Press.

This study explores the relationship that ex-spouses develop after their separation, divorce, and remarriage. A Canadian sample was used for the study.

Brown, J.C. (1986). *In Search of a Policy: The Rationale for Social Security Provision for One-Parent Families.* London: National Council for One-Parent Families. (255 Kentish Town Rd., London, NW5 2LX).

There are now one million one parent families in the United Kingdom and the majority live in poverty. This book examines the British social security system towards one-parent families.

Canada, Dept. of Justice (1986). *Divorce Law for Counsellors.* Ottawa: Communication and Public Affairs, Dept. of Justice.

The major changes in Canada's divorce law, which is under federal jurisdiction are described. Geared to counsellors and mediators, written in plain language.

Deven, F. and Cliquet, R.L. (Eds.) (1986). *One-Parent Families in Europe.* Brussels: Population and Family Study Centre.

The proceedings of an international workshop on one-parent families. Twelve European papers review the topic at hand.

Dumas, J. and Péron, Y. (1992). *Marriage and Conjugal Life in Canada: Current Demographic Analysis.* Ottawa: Statistics Canada.

A historical analysis of marriage, divorce, and remarriage in Canada, which includes data until 1990.

Edgar, D. and Headlam, F. (1982). *One-Parent Families and Educational Disadvantage*. Melbourne: Institute of Family Studies. (Working Paper #4).

A discussion of the educational setting and one-parent families in Australia.

Family Policy Studies Centre. (1990). *One-Parent Families*. London: Family Policy Studies Centre. (231 Baker St. London, England NW1 6XE).

A comprehensive presentation of facts and trends related to one-parent families in Britain, which constitute one in seven of all families. This Centre has other publications on family policy.

Handelman-Shamgar, L. (1986). *Israeli War Widows: Beyond the Glory of Heroism*. South Hadley, Mass.: Bergin and Garvey.

A study of the adjustment of war widows of soldiers killed in five major wars in Israel. Personnel profiles of 71 widows are included in this study.

Handelman-Shamgar, L. and Palomba, R. (Eds.) (1987). *Alternative Patterns of Family Life in Modern Societies*. Rome: Collana Monografie; Istituto di Ricerche Sulla Popolazione. (Viale Beethoven, 56, 00144, Roma, Italy).

Seven of the papers deal with varied topics dealing with one-parent families. The countries include Israel, Italy, Holland, Sweden, and Europe.

Hardey, M. and Crow, G. (Eds.) (1991). *Lone Parenthood*. Toronto: University of Toronto Press.

Nine papers discuss one-parent families in Great Britain. The topics include housing, health and illness, day care, family policy, transitions to lone parenthood, and demographic changes.

Hudson, J. and Galaway, B. (Eds.) (1993). *Single Parent Families: Canadian Research and Policy Implications*. Torumlsi Wall and Thompson (6 O'Connor Drive, Toronto, Ontario, Canada, M4K 2K1).

Twenty-two papers discuss Canadian and some international research related to single parent families. The editors are social work professors.

Kilmartin, C., Booth, S., Spencer, C., Longmuir, B., Mulholland, T., and Khoo, S.E. (1988). *Families in Focus in Western Australia*. Perth: Office of the Family, Government of Western Australia. (197 St. Georges Terrace, Perth, Western Australia, 6000).

A comprehensive report on families and family life in Western Australia including divorce and one-parent families. (available from 32 St. George's Terrace, Perth, W.A., 6000).

Kwong, L.C. (1991). *Needs of Single Parent Families: A Comparative Study*. Hong Kong: Family Welfare Society.

A study of the needs of one-parent families in Hong Kong, which comprise about 8 percent of families.

Lero, D.S. (1981). *A Different Understanding: Divorce, A Family Crisis*. Toronto: TV Ontario.

This small book discusses the effects of divorce on the four members of a family. This was part of a T.V. series on family life.

McKie, C. and Thompson, K. (1990). *Canadian Social Trends*. Toronto: Thompson Educational Publishing.

Articles which deal with social trends including family and marriage. Eight of the contributions are related to one-parent families.

Moors, H. and van Nimwegen, N. (1990). *Social and Demographic Effects of Changing Household Structures on Children and Young People*. The Hague: Netherlands Interdisciplinary Demographic Institute (P.O.Box 11650, 2502 AR The Hague, Netherlands).

This report describes changes in the household structure of the European population of member states of the Council of Europe. One-parent families are included in this analysis (pp. 31-56).

National Council for One-Parent Families. (1990). *Annual Report 1989-90*. London: National Council for One-Parent Families. (255 Kentish Town Rd., London, England, NW5 2LX).

A good summary of the situation of one-parent families in Britain. The data includes key facts, problems, and resources for researchers.

National Council for One-Parent Families. (1991). *We Don't All Live with Mum and Dad.* London: National Council for One-Parent Families.

A guide to books for children and young adults living in one-parent families. The Council has other publications related to one-parent families.

Office of the Family, Western Australia. (1988). *Families in Focus in Western Australia.* Perth, Western Australia.

A complete discussion and demographic data about families in the State of Western Australia, including one-parent families.

Ram, B. (1990). *New Trends in the Family.* Ottawa: Statistics Canada.

A discussion of the changing trends in Canadian family life, including the lives of one-parent families.

Roll, J. (1992). *Lone Parent Families in the European Community.* London: Family Policy Studies Centre. (231 Baker Street, London, England, NW1 6XE).

This report is an overview of the numbers, characteristics and economic situation of one-parent families in the European community.

Schlesinger, B. and Schlesinger, R. (1989). *Canadian Families: A Resource Guide.* Toronto: The Ontario Institute for Studies in Education Press.

An annotated bibliography, which contains entries related to Canadian families including single parent families.

Sev'er, A. (1992). *Women and Divorce in Canada: A Sociological Analysis.* Toronto: Canadian Scholars' Press.

Traces the causes and consequences of divorce for women, children, and men. Special focus is placed on the resilience of children to cope with divorce.

Statistics Canada (1992 July). *Age, Sex and Marital Status: The Nation, the 1991 Census.* Ottawa: Statistics Canada.

The 1991 Census data points out the increasing number of Canadian one-parent families.

Van Gelder, K. (1985). *One Parent Families in the Netherlands: Their Number and Type.* The Hague: NIMAWO (Willem de Zwijgerlaan 66, 2582 ES's Gravenhage, Netherlands).

This report summarizes the situation of Dutch one-parent families.

Vayda, E.J. and Satterfield, M.T. (1984). *Law for Social Workers: A Canadian Guide*. Toronto: Carswell.

A guide to family law in Canada including divorce issues.

DIVORCED SINGLE PARENTS

Aarons, C.R. and Rodgers, R.H. (1987). *Divorced Families: A Multidisciplinary Developmental View*. New York: W.W. Norton and Co.

Families do not cease to exist because a divorce occurs. They reorganize into a binuclear family. Divorce is a normative developmental process that can contribute to growth. The authors are family life educators.

Berger, S. (1983). *Divorce Without Victims*. New York: Houghton-Mifflin.

A psychiatrist looks at divorce from the child's perspective and suggests how parents can help their children.

Bulka, R.P. (1992). *Jewish Divorce Ethics*. Ogdensburg, N.Y.: Ivy League Press. (P.O. Box 1192, Ogdensburg, N.Y. 13669).

This volume discusses the root causes of divorce, and examines the biblical interpretations related to Jewish divorce.

Cantor, D.W. and Drake, E.A. (1983). *Divorced Parents and Their Children*. New York: Springer Publishing.

A guide for mental health professionals related to counselling and treating divorced parents and their children.

Folberg, J. (Ed.) (1991). *Joint Custody and Shared Parenting* (2nd Edition). New York: The Guilford Press.

Deals comprehensively with the research and legal aspects of joint custody.

Furstenberg, F.F. and Spanier, G.B. (1984). *Recycling the Family: Remarriage After Divorce*. Beverly Hills: Sage.

An eight-year study of the social, psychological and economic aspects of the divorce to remarriage transition.

Goldstein, S. (1982). *Divorced Parenting: How To Make It Work*. Toronto: McGraw Hill-Ryerson.

A child psychiatrist talks about divorce and its impact on children. Based on cases seen by the author.

Halem, L.C. (1982). *Separated and Divorced Women*. Westport, CT: Greenwood Press.

The author describes the economic and psychological vulnerability of the population of separated and divorced women, looking at their community to see if the needed resources are there, and finding large gaps. She concludes that middle-class women who are separated or divorced may be the real victims of the social service system, falling between the cracks because they are unable to afford private services, yet are ineligible for public ones.

Irving, H.H. and Benjamin, M. (1987). *Family Mediation: Theory and Practice of Dispute Resolution*. Toronto: Carswell.

A resource book for practitioners and others in the field of mediation. It offers practical help to understand the divorce process.

Jacob, H. (1988). *Silent Revolution: The Transformation of Divorce Law in the United States*. Chicago: The University of Chicago Press.

This book focuses on divorce law reform law in the United States. The reform is discussed in three areas: no fault divorce, marital property rights and joint custody.

Levinger, G. and Moles, O.C. (Eds.) (1979). *Divorce and Separation: Context, Causes and Consequences*. New York: Basic Books.

Nineteen contributors discuss marital dissolution and the consequences for family members.

Little, M. (1982). *Family Breakup*. San Francisco: Jossey-Bass.

This book studies the causes, patterns, and effects of family breakup on families.

Luepnitz, D.A. (1982). *Child Custody: A Study of Families After Divorce*. Lexington, MA: Lexington Books.

The author compares the post divorce experiences of families in three custody patterns. The sample consists of 43 families.

Myers, M.F. (1989). *Men and Divorce*. New York: The Guilford Press.

Using findings from the literature, the author examines men's reactions to divorce, including the process of separation.

Nadelson, C.C. and Polonsky, D.C. (Eds.) (1984). *Marriage and Divorce: A Contemporary Perspective*. New York: Guilford Press.

An analysis of how changes in the family impinge upon the clinical practices of marital and family therapists.

Price, S.J. and McKenry, P.C. (1988). *Divorce*. Newbury Park: Sage.

This monograph summarizes the existing research and demographic trends related to American divorces.

Ricci, I. (1980). *Mom's House, Dad's House: Making Shared Custody Work*. New York: Collier Books.

A practical and systematic guide for parents, which focuses on making joint custody work.

Riley, G. (1991). *Divorce: An American Tradition*. New York: Oxford University Press.

A history of marital breakdown in America from Colonial Times to the present.

Sell, K.D. (1981). *Divorce in the 70s: A Subject Bibliography*. Phoenix: The Oryx Press.

This bibliography lists the majority of materials, excluding fiction written on divorce in the United States during the 1970-1979 period.

Spanier, G.B. and Thompson, L. (1984). *Parting: The Aftermath of Separation and Divorce*. Beverly Hills: Sage Publications.

The authors unravel the process of marital breakup, presenting one of the most rigorous and comprehensive longitudinal studies of separation and divorce. Why do marriages fail? How does divorce affect a person?

Textor, M.R. (Ed.) (1989). *The Divorce and Divorce Therapy Handbook*. Northvale, N.J.: Jason Aronson.

Contains chapters in single parent families as viable family systems. Divorce therapy is also discussed.

Vaughan, D. (1986). *Uncoupling*. New York: Oxford University Press.

Through the use of research and case histories the author examines the underlying patterns related to disintegrating relationships.

Wallerstein, J.S. and Kelly, J.B. (1980). *Surviving the Breakup*. New York: Basic Books.

The results of a 5-year study of 60 families in their post-divorce stage. The study focuses especially on the children ranging in age from 3 to 16 years.

Wallerstein, J.S. and Blakesloe, S. (1989). *Second Chances*. New York: Ticknor and Fields.

A follow-up of a study of 60 middle class families in the midst of divorce, begun in 1971. The complexities of divorce are explored.

Weitzman, L.J. (1988). *The Divorce Revolution*. New York: The Free Press.

A ten-year study about the consequences of divorce. Women are disadvantaged in the divorce process.

Willison, M.M. (1981). *Diary of a Divorced Mother*. New York: Bantam Books.

The diary of a 27-year-old woman left to raise two sons on her own.

ETHNICITY AND SINGLE PARENT FAMILIES

Billingsley, A. (1992). *Climbing Jacob's Ladder: The Enduring Legacy of African-American Families*. New York: Simon and Schuster.

A professor of sociology and social work reviews the African-American family, with emphasis on the strengths of these families.

Boyd-Franklin, N. (1989). *Black Families in Therapy: A Multisystems Approach*. New York: Guilford Press.

Contains specific chapters on single parent families.

Coll, C.T.G. and Mattei, M.L. (Eds.) (1989). *The Psychosocial Development of Puerto Rican Women*. New York: Praeger.

Contains chapters dealing with single parent Puerto Rican families.

Combrinck, G.L. (Ed.) (1989). *Children in Family Contexts: Perspectives on Treatment*. New York: Guilford Press.

A chapter on successful minority single parent families by Marion Lindblad-Goldberg is helpful in balancing the stereotype of this family pattern.

Heatherington, E.M. and Arusteh, J.D. (Eds.) (1988). *Impact of Divorce, Single Parenting and Step-Parenting on Children*. Hillsdale, N.J.: Lawrence Erlbaum.

Contains chapters on Black single parent families, ethnicity and single parenting, children of divorce, and custody.

Logan, S.M.L., Freeman, E.M. and McRoy, R.G. (Eds.) (1990). *Social Work Practice with Black Families: A Culturally Specific Perspective*. New York: Longman.

The primary purpose of this book is to bridge the gap between the sociological literature about black family life and practice principles. Edited by social work professors.

McGoldrick, M., Pearce, J.K. and Giardane, J. (Eds.) (1982). *Ethnicity and Family Therapy*. New York: Guilford Press.

A resource book for American ethnic families. The topic of single parents is included in some of the 26 papers.

Williams, C.W. (1991). *Black Teenage Mothers: Pregnancy and Child Rearing from Their Perspective*. Lexington, MA: Lexington Books.

A study of Black teenage mothers which examines the experiences of motherhood.

FRAMEWORKS FOR EXAMINING SINGLE PARENT FAMILIES

Booth, A. (Ed.) (1991). *Contemporary Families: Looking Forward, Looking Back*. Minneapolis: National Council on Family Relations.

Four contributions deal with divorce, and mother-only families. In the mother-only families paper the authors examine the economic and social well-being, their long term consequences for children, and their role in the politics of gender, race, and social class.

Bozett, F.W. (Ed.) (1987). *Gay and Lesbian Parents*. New York: Praeger.

A nursing professor edits this volume of 13 papers with the focus on the possibility of becoming a single parent family. This content will help to understand homosexual parenthood.

Cherlin, A.J. (1992). *Marriage, Divorce, Remarriage* (2nd ed.). Cambridge, MA: Harvard University Press.

An examination of the course of family life in America from the end of the Second World War through the early 1990s.

Dornbusch, S.M. and Strober, M.M. (Eds.) (1988). *Feminism, Children and the New Families*. New York: Guilford Press.

Contains chapters on divorce law reform, divorce and children, and single parent families.

Gangla, P. and Thompson, E.H. (1987). Single parent families. In M.B. Sussman and S.K. Steinmetz (Eds.), *Handbook of Marriage and the Family* (pp. 397-418). New York: Plenum Press.

A comprehensive review of research related to the one-parent family in the United States.

Greif, G.L. and Pabst, M.S. (1988). *Mothers Without Custody*. Lexington: Lexington Books.

An in-depth look at the growing number of mothers who by choice or decree live apart from their children.

Kissman, K. and Allen, J. A. (1993). *Single-Parent Families*. Newbury Park: Sage.

Special treatment methods based on gender, head of the household, ethnicity, age, and sexual orientation are discussed by two social work professors.

Levine, S.D. (1981). *The Singular Problems of the Single Jewish Parent*. New York: United Synagogue Commission on Jewish Education.

A 39 page booklet which examines the growing rate of one-parent families in the Jewish community.

Little, M. (1982). *Family Breakup*. San Francisco: Jossey-Bass.

A review of the causes and patterns which effect family dissolution.

Macklin, E.D. and Rubin, P.H. (Eds.) (1983). *Contemporary Families and Alternative Lifestyles: Handbook on Research and Theory.* Beverly Hills: Sage.

Two chapters review existing research dealing with single parent families and divorce.

Morawetz, A. and Walker, G. (1983). *Brief Therapy with Single-Parent Families*. New York: Brunner-Mazel.

Provides a theoretical and practical framework by examining every aspect of this family constellation. Based on a three-year project conducted at the Ackerman Institute for Family Therapy, it covers basics in theory and practice, presents detailed cases illustrating successful treatment strategies for working with families at different stages of separation, and discusses desertion, marriage, divorce, and death.

Morgan, L.A. (1991). *After Marriage Ends: Economic Consequences for Midlife Women*. Newbury Park, California: Sage Publications.

A study of the differential consequences of divorce, separation, and widowhood for women, ages 35-39. The author examines the economic changes women experience following marital disruption.

Orthner, D.K. (1980). *Families in Blue: A Study of Married and Single Parent Families in the U.S. Air Force*. Washington, DC: Office of the Chief of Chaplains, USAF, Bolling Air Force Base.

An examination of one-parent families in the Air Force which comprise 1% of the total American Air Force.

Sadler, J.D. (1988). *Families in Transition: An Annotated Bibliography.* Hamden, CT: Archon Books/Shoe String Press.

This bibliography contains items on one-parent families, divorce, teen parenthood and widows.

Schlesinger, B. (Ed.) (1978). *The One Parent Family: Perspectives and Annotated Bibliography* (4th ed.). Toronto: University of Toronto Press.

Six papers discuss motherless and fatherless families, divorce, widowhood, and never-married mothers. The annotated bibliography contains 750 items.

Schlesinger, B. (Ed.) (1985). *The One-Parent Family in the 1980s: Perspectives and Annotated Bibliography 1978-1984*. Toronto: University of Toronto Press.

Five essays review the literature on the subject from a wide range of perspectives. The annotated bibliography contains 490 annotations published between 1978-1984.

Schlesinger, B. (Ed.) (1987). *Jewish Family Issues: A Resource Guide*. New York: Garland Publishing.

An essay on Jewish one-parent families, and an annotated bibliography which includes items on divorce and one-parent families are part of this volume.

Sussman, M.B. and Steinmetz, S.K. (Eds.) (1987). *Handbook of Marriage and the Family*. New York: Plenum Press.

This handbook contains 30 reviews of existing literature on various family topics. Patricia Gangla and Edward Thompson discuss single parent families. Helen Raschke writes on divorce.

Touliatos, J. and Czaplewski, M.J. (Eds.) (1991). *Inventory of Marriage and Family Literature Volume 17–1990/91*. Anoka, MN: Data Traq International.

The inventory includes entries on varied topics related to one-parent families. Previous yearly editions cover the 1900-1989 period.

Weiss, R.S. (1979). *Going It Alone*. New York: Basic Books.

A classic book which examines the life of persons who are left to care for children on their own.

NEVER-MARRIED BIOLOGICAL TEEN MOTHER HEADED FAMILIES

Bedger, J.E. (1980). *Teenage Pregnancy: Research Related to Clients and Services*. Springfield, IL: Charles C Thomas.

A report of a comprehensive day care program for pregnant teenagers in Chicago.

Bolton, F.G. (1980). *The Pregnant Adolescent: Problems of Premature Parenthood*. Beverly Hills, CA: Sage.

A discussion of the existing literature on adolescent pregnancy.

Committee on Adolescence of the Group for the Advancement of Psychiatry. (1986). *Crises of Adolescence–Teenage Pregnancy: Impact on Adolescent Development*. New York: Brunner-Mazel.

Adolescent psychiatrists discuss the consequences of teenage pregnancies.

Chilman, C.S. (1980). *Adolescent Pregnancy and Childbearing: Findings from Research*. Washington, DC: U.S. Department of Health and Human Services.

This book includes the papers given at the Conference on Determinants of Adolescent Pregnancy and Childbearing in 1975 and 1976.

Furstenburg, F.F., Lincoln, R. and Menken, J. (Eds.) (1981). *Teenage Sexuality, Pregnancy and Childbearing*. Philadelphia: University of Pennsylvania Press.

Twenty-eight papers reprinted from "Family Planning Perspectives" discuss the varied issues dealing with teenage mothers in America.

Furstenberg, F., Brooke-Gunn, J. and Morgan, S.P. (1987). *Adolescent Mothers in Later Life*. New York: Cambridge University Press.

A twenty-year study of 300 young mothers, their children, the fathers, and the extended families. The study documents how the mothers cope.

Merritt, S. and Steiner, L. (1984). *And Baby Makes Two: Motherhood Without Marriage*. New York: Franklin Watts.

Single women in their thirties are becoming mothers. This is a nationwide survey of 100 women who decided to have a child while single.

Miller, S.H. (1983). *Children as Parents: Final Report*. New York: Child Welfare League of America.

The final report on a study of childbearing and childrearing among 12-15 year olds.

Renvoize, J. (1985). *Going Solo: Single Mothers by Choice*. London: Routledge and Kegan Paul.

The book focuses on women who have deliberately chosen to have children outside a permanent relationship.

Stuart, I.R. and Wells, C.F. (Eds.) (1982). *Pregnancy in Adolescence: Needs, Problems and Management*. New York: Van Nostrand and Reinhold.

A multi-disciplinary discussion in nineteen papers on the topic of teenage pregnancy and parenthood.

PRACTICAL GUIDES TO SINGLE PARENT FAMILY LIVING

Atlas, S.L. (1981). *Single Parenting: A Practical Resource Guide*. Englewood Cliffs, NJ: Prentice Hall.

Practical advice, based on personal experiences and insights are presented in this book.

Barnes, B.C. and Coplon, J. (1980). *The Single Parent Experience a Time for Growth*. New York: Family Service Association of America.

The advantages and demands of being the sole custodial parent are discussed in this manual. The workshops help participants to recognize and deal with resentment, anger, and loneliness; provide practical information concerning such matters as taxes, wills, obtaining credit, and finding good child care services; and offer important perspectives on the parent's relationship with his or her children.

Barnett, P., Gaudio, C.P. and Sumner, M.G. (1980). *Parenting Children of Divorce*. New York: Family Service Association of America.

This model grew out of the need of divorced parents for help in dealing with the effects of divorce on their children. The sessions include material to facilitate discussion of feelings about divorce and of communication problems and stresses that affect both parents and children.

Besson, C.C. (1982). *Picking Up the Pieces*. New York: Ballantine Books.

A Christian minister offers comfort and guidance to the recently divorced.

Cantor, D.W. and Drake, E.A. (1983). *Divorced Parents and Their Children*. New York: Springer Publishing Co.

This book is a guide to mental health professionals, who are involved in counselling and treating divorced parents and their children.

DeFrain, J., Fricke, J. and Elman, J. (1987). *On Our Own: A Single Parents Survival Guide.* Lexington: Lexington Books.

A "how to" raise your children alone guide. The stresses related to divorce and custody are explored, and suggestions of dealing with these stresses are made.

Knight, B.M. (1980). *Enjoying Single Parenthood.* New York: Van Nostrand Reinhold.

Written by a single father, this guide gives information on many social and personal areas of single parenthood.

Murdock, C.V. (1980). *Single Parents Are People Too.* New York: Butterick.

A single parent herself, the author includes in her book pointers from various helping professions on living as a single parent.

SINGLE FATHERS WITH CUSTODY FOLLOWING SEPARATION AND DIVORCE

Greif, G.L. (1985). *Single Fathers.* Lexington: Lexington Books.

A study of almost all-white, Protestant/Catholic single fathers, who were members of Parents Without Partners in 1982.

Klinman, D.G., Kohl, R. (1984). *Fatherhood U.S.A.* New York: Garland Publishing.

A national guide to programs, services and resources for and about fathers, including single fathers.

Knight, B.M. (1980). *Enjoying Single Parenthood.* New York: Van Nostrand Reinhold.

Written by a single father, it is a guide to social and personal issues facing single fathers.

Oakland, T. (1983). *Divorced Fathers: Reconstructing a Viable Life.* New York: Human Sciences Press.

Practical advice is offered to divorced fathers. The psychological impact of divorce on the entire family and the father's role adjustments are also reviewed.

Rosenthal, K.M. and Keshet, H.F. (1981). *Fathers Without Partners*. Totowa, NJ: Rowman and Littlefield.

This study describes the lives of fathers with custody, joint custody, and men who visit their children.

Wilson, J. (1990). *Single Fathers: Australian Men Take On a New Role*. Melbourne: Sun Books.

A discussion of single fathers in Australia. Based on a study by the author.

SPECIAL ISSUES OF JOURNALS

Anderson, C.L. (Ed.) (1988). Single parents and their children (Special issue). *Human Ecology Forum, 17* (1). (Cornell University, The New York State College of Human Ecology).

Five papers discuss single mothers, and their children including clothing expenditures.

Bonham-Price, S. and Balswick, J.O. (Eds.) (1980). The noninstitutions: divorce, desertion, and remarriage (Special issue). *Journal of Marriage and the Family, 42* (4).

This special November issue is a decade review of the 1970s. The authors review selected research and theoretical writings of the decade.

Brubaker, T.H. (Ed.) (1991). Adolescent pregnancy and parenting. (Special issue). *Family Relations, 40* (4).

Fourteen selections cover programs, social support and stress among adolescent mothers.

Everett, C.A. (Ed.) (1988/89). Children of divorce. Developmental and clinical issues (Special issue). *Journal of Divorce, 12* (2/3).

A collection of 18 articles which examine developmental, structural and interactional issues related to children in divorcing families.

Everett, C.A. (Ed.) (1991). Marital instability and divorce outcomes: Issues for therapists and educators (Special issue). *Journal of Divorce & Remarriage, 15* (1/2).

Eleven contributions discuss a wide variety of issues related to theoretical, empirical, and clinical patterns related to post-diverse adjustment.

Family Relations (1989). Child care and the family (Special issue). *Family Relations, 38* (4).

This special issue includes four papers on single parents and child care (pp. 390-417).

Fisher, E.O. (Ed.) (1981). Impact of divorce on the extended family (Special issue). *Journal of Divorce, 5* (Fall and Winter).

Eleven papers written by psychologists, sociologists, lawyers, and clinicians focus on the extended family and divorce.

Hanson, S.M.H. and Sporakowski, M.J. (Eds.) (1986). The single parent family (Special issue). *Family Relations, 35* (1).

Twenty-eight papers in this special issue cover the topic of the single parent family. Demography, single mothers and fathers, economic and health issues, children, and community are topics in this volume.

Pett, M.A. (Ed.) (1992). Consequences of later life divorce (Special issue). *Family Perspective, 26* (1).

Seven papers deal with a topic which has not had much exposure in the one-parent literature. The contributors write about social support networks, life satisfaction, self-esteem, and coping with later life divorce.

Theilheimer, I. (Ed.) (1989, March). Multiple issues for single parent families. *Transition, 19* (1).

The Vanier Institute of the Family in Ottawa, Canada publishes *Transition*. This issue contains five short papers on Canadian one-parent families (120 Holland Ave., Ottawa, K1Y 0X6).

Trost, J. (Ed.) (1980). One parent family (Special issue). *Journal of Comparative Family Studies, 11* (Winter).

Eight papers discuss one-parent families on a cross-cultural basis.

Chapter 22

Video/Filmography on Single Parenting

Lee C. Kimmons

SUMMARY. The purpose of this video/filmography is to provide potential users with a sampling of recent videotapes that deal with various aspects of single parenting. Titles were gleaned from film and video directories, distributor catalogues, and video review publications which are identified in Appendix A. Date of release, running time in minutes, address and telephone number of distributors are given with each title along with purchase/rental prices. The titles presented are organized into the following five categories: (1) The Single Parent Experience, (2) The Child's Experience, (3) Teenage Single Parenting, (4) General Interest, and (5) Feature-Length Television and Film Releases. Awards received are noted at the end of each synopsis and intended audience levels are provided.

KEYWORDS. Film, Video, Single parents

The purpose of this video/filmography is to present a sampling of film and videotape titles that deal with significant aspects of single parenting released since Kimmons and Gaston (1986). Most of the titles selected are relatively short (less than 60 minutes) educational films, but ten feature-

---

Lee C. Kimmons is affiliated with the Department of Human Resources, University of Hawaii.

[Haworth co-indexing entry note]: "Video/Filmography on Single Parenting." Kimmons, Lee C. Co-published simultaneously in *Marriage & Family Review* (The Haworth Press, Inc.) Vol. 20, No. 3/4, 1995, pp. 483-498; and: *Single Parent Families: Diversity, Myths and Realities* (ed: Shirley M. H. Hanson et al.) The Haworth Press, Inc., 1995, pp. 483-498. Multiple copies of this article/chapter may be purchased from The Haworth Document Delivery Center [1-800-3-HAWORTH; 9:00 a.m. - 5:00 p.m. (EST)].

length television and motion picture releases are also included. The use of the videotapes listed in this article, whether for instruction, enlightenment or entertainment, should reflect the realities as well as influence positively the attitudes about single parents in society.

Some of the titles selected were National Council on Family Relations (NCFR) Media Award winners, and several received high ratings (e.g., 3 Star–*Good*; 4 Star–*Highly Recommended*; and 5 Star–*Excellent*) in the *Video Rating Guide for Libraries* (VRG). Most of the titles were chosen on the basis of information provided by the producer/distributor in film/video directories, distributor catalogues and educational media review publications (see Appendix). The reviews in *Video Librarian* and *Video Rating Guide for Libraries* were particularly useful in determining respective merit when deciding which titles to include. (The author is greatly indebted to Randy Pittman, editor and publisher of *Video Librarian* and *Video Movies*, for his suggestions on titles to include in the feature-length section.)

Since most filmstrip and 16mm film titles are available on videotape, all of the titles listed here are on videotape. In recent years, videotape appears to have prevailed in the film/video purchase and rental market. One feature-length video (*Dark Horse*) and one educational film (*How Families Differ*) are *made-for-video movies*, i.e., they were produced for the video purchase/rental market. Of 108 total entries in the 1992 NCFR Media Awards Competition, only one film and two filmstrips are included here (Pocs et al., 1933).

Other formats such as 1/4 inch compact videocassette, beta, super-VHS, 3/4 inch U-matic cassette, 16mm film, 8mm videocassette, filmstrips, laser videodisks and PAL or SECAM (for use in foreign countries) may be available from some distributors. Many programs on videocassette have been Closed-Captioned (CC) for the hearing impaired. Format, rent/lease, loan, purchase, trade-in, off-air-record, subscription, and duplication options vary according to title and distributor. Purchase/rental prices are those listed by the distributor for VHS (1/2 inch) videotapes.

Although some companies are producing bilingual versions (usually Spanish, e.g., Sunburst Communications), few of the producers of the videos listed here appear to do so. Film makers also appear to pay little attention to the single parenting experience in different ethnic and cultural groups. Videos listed here that do include different ethnic groups are *Stories of Change* (Asian and Latino) and *Always Roses* (Hispanic). A world-wide perspective is offered in *Teenage Mothers: A Global Crisis*.

The influence of television (TV) and the videocassette recorder (VCR) upon individuals and families can hardly be ignored. There is at least one video rental outlet in virtually every community, along with retailers such as Wal-Mart, K-Mart, Target, even McDonald's, selling prerecorded videotapes ("McDonald's," 1993). The five-year study by the American Psychological Association's (APA) Task Force on Television and Society reports that most of the nation's households have two or more TV sets, a VCR, and subscribe to a cable system (Huston, Donnerstein, Fairchild, Feshbach, Katz, Murry, Rubinstein, Wilcox & Zuckerman, 1992). In addition, the role and influence of television worldwide is documented by Lull (1988).

Although researchers have analyzed how American families, including single parents, are portrayed on television (Cantor, 1991; Cantor & Cantor, 1992; Spigel, 1992; Tichi, 1991) and in film (Levy, 1991), it does not appear that marriage and family researchers have studied the effects of TV and film upon family relations to any great extent (Fabes, Wilson & Christopher, 1989). Fabes et al. (1989) report that only 22 articles pertaining to television appeared in the NCFR journals after 1950, and that most of these articles (14) appeared in journals published since 1980. (Seven of these appeared in the special issue of the *Journal of Family Issues*, 1983, Vol. 4, devoted to television and families.)

The 54 titles are organized into the following categories: (1) The Single Parent Experience, (2) The Child's Experience, (3) Teenage Single Parenting, (4) General Interest, and (5) Feature-Length Television and Film Releases. Titles in each category are listed by date, beginning with the most recent releases. (Sometimes a different date will be given in various catalogue and directory listings. This is due to either a difference between the production date and the date of release, or the year in which a distributor obtains the rights to a particular title.) The date of titles given in this video/filmography is the date given by the distributor.

Information about the titles named in this article includes date, length in minutes, producer (if different from distributor)/distributor, distributor address and telephone number (including toll free 800 number, if available (in U.S., dial 1-800-etc., outside U.S. dial country and city codes)), and purchase/rental price (in U.S. dollars, USD) at the time of this writing. (If rentals are not available from the distributor given, only the purchase price is given.) For most companies, the purchase price includes postage, and the reader should keep in mind that not only do film and video prices frequently change, but that more than one distributor may exist for a title. Also, many public and/or university libraries may have some of the titles listed here in their collections.

Virtually all video rental outlets have *Videolog*, a loose-leaf index listing of all currently available videotapes (Appendix). Although this index has an Educational/Special Interest section, the listings are not comprehensive. All of the feature-length titles in this video/filmography, however, are listed in *Videolog* and can be ordered by any video store, if not already in stock.

Intended audience levels are designated by the following: p–primary; i–intermediate; j–junior high; s–senior high; c–college; a–adult; and g–general (for a wide variety of audiences). An exception to the preceding audience levels is in the category of Feature-Length Releases. Since most of these titles were theatrical releases, the Motion Picture Association of America (MPAA) ratings are given instead, i.e., G, PG, PG-13, R, and NC-17.

VIDEOS AND FILMS

The Single Parent Experience

Stories of Change (1991–57 minutes). Theresa Tollini. Future Educational Films./New Day Films, 121 W. 27th St. #902, New York, NY 10001. (212)645-8210. $250/$100 USD.

Sponsored by the Ford Foundation and the California Council for the Humanities, this award-winning documentary film profiles the lives of four ethnically diverse young women (Anna, Angelina, Mink-Floa, Anitra) who surmount incredible odds that include divorce, poverty, substance abuse, solo parenting, discrimination and cultural barriers. Each tells of overcoming difficult times to emerge stronger, more self-reliant and independent with a "renewed sense of life's purpose." The four segments can be viewed independently as each portrays the human condition and celebrates women who have coped with life–and triumphed! (4 Star, VRG). ca

The Ticket Back (1991–49 minutes). National Film Board of Canada./The Media Guild, 11722 Sorrento Valley Rd., Suite E, San Diego, CA 92121. (619)755-9191. $345.

This film is a realistic portrayal of one woman's experience as she tries to free herself from an abusive ex-husband. In this case, Linda Morris attempts to provide a normal, stable environment for her children despite the attempts of her violent ex-husband Bill to remain in control. sca

Single Mothers: Living on the Edge (1989, film transfer to video–29 minutes). Megan Siler./Churchill Films, 12210 Nebraska Ave., Los Angeles, CA 90025. (310)207-6600. $250/$60 USD.

This documentary portrays the stark realities of life for three single mothers. Each talks about their individual situations, including their education, jobs, living conditions and finances. The first is divorced with two young girls, trying to get child support payments through the U.S. judicial system. The second is a teenage mother, high school dropout living at home with her own divorced mother. The third holds two jobs, receives no child support and has experienced discrimination as an ethnic minority in the work force. (4 Star, VRG). sca

Single Parenting (1989–30 minutes). Kathy Barr. JVM Productions./Video-11, P.O. Box 1429, Durango, CO 81302. (303)259-3172, (800)843-3611. $150/$50.

This program explores the joys and difficulties of single parenting. Both single mothers and fathers, interviewed by Psychoanalyst Veryl Rosenbaum, give advice from their own experiences as to what works and what to avoid. Children of single parents reveal their true feelings about their families by discussing pictures they have drawn with Jean Rosenbaum, MD. An excellent guide through the complexities of single parenting. (4 Star, VRG). ca

Single Parenting: A New Page in America's Family Album (1989–25 minutes). NEWIST/CESA # 7./Centre Communications, 1800 30th St., Boulder, CO 80301. (303)444-1166, (800)886-1166. $285/$50.

This video presents a positive overview of changes in parenting. It looks not only at the divorced single mother who often ends up in poverty, but also case histories of the single parent father, women who have chosen to have children without marriage, and co-parenting, the joint responsibility of rearing children outside of the nuclear family. sca

Empowering Single Parent Families (1988–22 minutes). University of Illinois Cooperative Extension Service./c/o Bob Hughes, 1105 W. Nevada, Urbana, IL 61801. (217)244-6673. $20.

This program begins with statistics on single parent families and includes interviews with both male and female single parents, custodial as well as non-custodial. ca

The Family in Transition: Single Head of Household (1988–30 minutes). PORTRAIT OF A FAMILY Series. RMI Media Productions, Box 123, Shawnee Mission, KS 66205. (913)262-3974, (800)745-5480. $99.

This episode in the series deals with the single parent family that comes as a result of divorce, separation or death. sca

The Child's Experience

A Kid's Guide to Families (1992–35 minutes). Words./Learning Tree Publishing, P.O. Box 4116, Englewood, CO 80155. (303)740-9777. $125.

Aimed at children from kindergarten to third grade, this program is intended to show that families can take many forms, and that regardless of the combinations a non-traditional family assumes, it is still a family needing to meet the needs of its members. Important family basics are examined in terms meaningful to young children. (Winner, NCFR Media Awards). pi

We're a Family (1992–15 minutes). Sunburst Communications, P.O. Box 40, 39 Washington Ave., Pleasantville, NY 10570-0040. (800)431-1934. $89.

Introduces young children to the idea that families come in many different forms, from nuclear to blended to step to single parent. The film shows that no matter what its structure, a family is the people who care for and about you and offer security and love. Worksheets, guide. pi

Always Roses (1991–29 minutes). George Figueroa. National Hispanic Media Coalition & Columbia College Universal Television (1990)./Direct Cinema, P.O. Box 10003, Santa Monica, CA 90410. (310)396-4774, (800)525-0000. $195.

Mike Rutledge, a young teen of Hispanic heritage, is the son of upper, middle-class parents in Los Angeles. His parents are separated and divorce seems inevitable. Trying to cope with the emotional strain, his mother sends Mike to live with her parents in Arizona for the summer. His grandparents are hardworking, bilingual farmers and live a very simple lifestyle. At first Mike rejects the lifestyle and his heritage, but comes to appreciate both. In subtle ways, the film shows that an appreciation of the past enhances one's ability to deal with the present. (4 Star, VGR). g

Decisions (1991–15 minutes). YOUR CHOICE . . . OUR CHANCE Series. Agency for Instructional Technology (AIT), 1111 West 17th St., Box A, Bloomington, IN 47402-0120. (812)339-2203, (800)457-4509. $180/$25.

Twelve-year-old James is under stress because of his parents' recent divorce, his mother's long work hours, his father's departure from town and responsibilities for his younger brother. ij

The First Steps: Helping Young Children Cope with Divorce (1991–25 minutes). Baltimore County Schools./Chip Taylor Communications, 15 Spollett Dr., Derry, NH 03038. (800)876-CHIP. $169.95/$89.95.

Divided into segments of interviews with a clinical social worker, a lawyer, a divorced mother, and a stepmother, this video is narrated and facilitated by Dr. Frances Bond. (4 Star, VGR). ca

Wanted: The Perfect Guy (1990–45 minutes). AIMS Media, 9710 DeSoto Ave., Chatsworth, CA 91311-4409. (818)773-4300, (800)367-2467. $99.95.
Danny and Melanie try to find Mister Right for their divorced Mom (Madeline Kahn). This is an Emmy Award winner about single parents and their children. g

No Fault Kids: A Focus on Kids with Divorced Parents (1989–27 minutes). RMI Media Productions./United Learning, 6633 W. Howard, Niles, IL 60648. (708)647-0600, (800)647-0600. $95.
This documentary focuses on the problems facing kids with divorced parents. The kids themselves tell about the isolation, embarrassment, anger and guilt that they feel as they talk about the ordeal of their parents' divorces. Helpful advice on how to deal with the stress is offered. g

The Red Wagon (1989–30 minutes). Jones & Jones Films./AIMS Media, 9710 DeSoto Ave., Chatsworth, CA 91311-4409. (818)773-4300, (800) 367-2467. $295/$50.
Ten-year-old Peter, becomes quiet and withdrawn after his parent's divorce. One day Peter finds he is being followed by a small red wagon that communicates with him through its horn. Feeling ignored by his father and his mother, he begins to see the wagon as his only friend. g

Robert (1989–15 minutes). National Film Board of Canada./The Media Guild, 11722 Sorrento Valley Rd., Suite E, San Diego, CA 92121. (619)755-9191. $210.
With a dad that walked out years earlier, a bleak future, various hassles at school, and discomfort with a newly discovered interest in girls, Robert is suddenly confronted with the fact that his mother has a serious boyfriend. He attempts to hide his feelings behind a glib, sarcastic demeanor, but his security at home and his own self-esteem are seriously threatened. jsa

When Your Parents Divorce–The Storm's Inside (1989–21 minutes). Peter Babakitis & Rick Santangelo./Encyclopedia Britannica Educational Corp., 310 S. Michigan Ave., Chicago, IL 60604. (312)347-7956, (800)554-9862. $89.
Using puppets to demonstrate the problems children have during a divorce, this program offers children the assurance and coping skills they

need. A boy named Jolly is awakened in the night by his parents' argument about divorce and is convinced that he is the cause of the problem. He is consoled by a funny creature called the "Big Kahooney," who helps him gain valuable insight into the feelings he is experiencing. (4 Star, VRG). p

A Kid's Guide to Divorce (1988, Enhanced filmstrip transfer–36 minutes). Learning Tree Publishers, P.O. Box 4116, 7108 S. Alton Way, Englewood, CO 80155. (303)740-9777.
This program emphasizes the importance of helping children cope with family situations such as those in the process of parental separation and divorce. The video is divided into four segments: "Where's Daddy?", "Do They Still Love Me?", "Who Can I Talk To?", and "Am I Still Me?" (4 Star, VRG). ij

Tender Places (1987–25 minutes). Group W Television./Coronet/MTI Film & Video, 108 Wilmot Rd., Deerfield, IL 60015. (708)940-1260, (800)621-2131. $540.
Adapted from the play written by thirteen-year-old Jason Brown, this film shows how one boy deals with a custody fight during his parents divorce. Jason's story can help children understand why divorce occurs, that it is not their fault, and to come to grips with their conflicting feelings. (1st Runner-up, NCFR Media Awards). js

When Mom and Dad Break Up (1986–32 minutes). Paramount Home Video, 5555 Melrose Ave., San Mateo, CA 94403. (415)362-2520. $24.95.
Hosted by Alan Thicke, this video introduces the concept of divorce to children ages four to twelve and offers methods of coping. (4 Star, VGR). pij

Teenage Single Parenting

Teenage Mother: Looking Back . . . Moving Ahead (1992–30 minutes). Menninger Video Productions, P.O. Box 829, Topeka, KS 66601-0829. (800)345-6036. $99/$45.
This program profiles three young women over a five-year period who represent positive role models for teenage mothers. Each tells her own story of facing the challenges of teenage pregnancy, which inspires others to keep fighting for a better life for themselves and their children. ca

Playing for Keeps (1991–44 minutes). Silva Basmajian./John Sirabella, National Film Board of Canada, 1251 Avenue of the Americas, 16th Floor, New York, NY 10020. (212)596-1770, (800)542-2164. $200/$70.

The realities of life as a teenage mother are revealed in this gritty documentary which presents portraits of three young women; Debbie, Karen, and Tracy; each a single parent. Their stories will help other young women to think about the lifelong consequences of teenage motherhood. (Winner, NCFR Media Awards). sca

Project Future: Teenage Pregnancy, Childbirth, and Parenting (1991–145 minutes). Adriene Miesmer./Vida Health Communications, 6 Bigelow St., Cambridge, MA 02139. (617)864-4334. $595.
Filmed over one year, Project Future is spun off of the experiences of twelve young men and women whom we meet during the third trimester of pregnancy and follow through the first three months postpartum. In conversations both before and after their babies are born, the teens tackle the issues that confront adolescent parents. (Winner, NCFR Media Awards). jsc

Real People: Meet a Teenage Mother (1989–18 minutes). Sunburst Communications, 39 Washington Avenue, P.O. Box 40, Pleasantville, NY 10570-9971. (914)769-2109, (800)431-1934. $250/$75.
Seventeen-year-old Lauri became a mother at 15. Live-action video documents her story to give viewers a revealing look at the problems faced by a teenage single mother. js

Teen Father (1989–34 minutes). ABC Video Enterprises./Cornet-MTI Film & Video, 108 Wilmont Rd., Deerfield, IL 60015. (707)940-1260, (800)621-2131. $250/$75.
This ABC afterschool special tries not to trivialize the plight of a teenage unwed couple with a baby on the way. It generally succeeds. js

Teenage Father (1989–38 minutes). Sunburst Communications, 39 Washington Ave., Pleasantville, NY 10570-9971. (914)769-2109, (800)431-1934. $250/$75.
Demonstrates that an unplanned pregnancy can have long-range implications for a teenage father as well as a teenage mother. Helps viewers understand that two people share the responsibility for an unplanned pregnancy, and that both need to be involved in the solution. (4-Star, VRG). js

Teens With Tiny Strangers (1989–29 minutes). NEWIST/CESA #7, IS 1110, University of Wisconsin-Green Bay, Green Bay, WI 54301. (414)465-2599. $195/$50.
This program emphasizes the importance of learning parenting skills by teenage parents and examines several model parenting programs. One program is the nationally acclaimed Beethoven Project in Chicago, where

young parents learn more about their babies, parenting, and themselves. (4 Star, VGA; Winner, NCFR Media Awards). sca

Teenage Mothers: Beyond the Baby Shower (1988–27 minutes). Planned Parenthood of Northern New York./Perennial Education, 1560 Sherman Ave., Suite 100, Evanston, IL 60201. (708)328-6700, (800)323-9084. $295/$50.
Three women serve as examples of what happens to teenage mothers. js

What Should a Guy Do? (1988–29 minutes). NEWIST/CESA, IS 1110, University of Wisconsin, Green Bay, WI 54311. (414)465-2576. $395/$50.
Richard has just discovered that his girlfriend is pregnant. As he thinks through the problem, the candid statements of other teens and experts help clarify the many issues involved in male responsibility. js

And Baby Makes Two: A Look at Teenage Single Parents (1987–25 minutes). Centre Productions./Centre Communications, 1800 30th St., Suite 207, Boulder, CO 80301. (303)444-1166, (800)886-1166. $260/$50.
This video looks at sex education, peer pressure, the teen father's responsibilities, and an array of programs designed to give teen parents ways of becoming successful, productive adults. (1st Runner-up, NCFR Media Awards). sca

Four Pregnant Teenagers, Four Different Decisions (1987–51 minutes). Sunburst Communications, P.O. Box 40, 39 Washington Ave., Pleasantville, NY 10570. (914)769-2109, (800)431-1934. $249.
True-to-life vignettes dramatize the difficult decisions faced by unwed pregnant teenagers. Will help students weigh the emotional, ethical and financial problems involved in the four options: adoption, marriage, single parenthood, abortion. (Winner, NCFR Media Awards). scag

Teenage Parents: Their Lives Have Changed (1986–23 minutes). Alfred Higgins Productions, 6350 Laurel Canyon Blvd., North Hollywood, CA 91606. (818)762-3300, (800)766-5353. $295.
Teenage parents share their experiences and relate what it's like to raise a baby alone, to be unable to enjoy the usual activities of teenage life, and to modify or give up their long term goals. (1st Runner-up, NCFR Media Awards). sca

General Interest

Working Parents: Balancing Kids and Careers (1992–25 minutes). Louise Welsh Shrank. The Learning Seed, 330 Telser Rd., Lake Zurich, IL 60047. (708)540-8855, (800)634-4941. $89.

This video interweaves the life of a fictional television reporter and single parent with interviews with family life specialists who work in government and industry. Viewers meet single parents as well as married couples who suggest ways to successfully combine family and work. Benefits that employers can offer are explored. The film concludes with some personal advice for coping with the pressure of combining a job, housework, and parenthood. Excellent program. cag

How Families Differ (1991, Made-for-Video Movie–15 minutes). Conrad Communications./Meridian Education Corp., 236 E. Front St., Bloomington, IL 61701. (309) 827-5455. $45.
This video examines the nature of the contemporary American family, noting how and why it differs from families of the past. Several types of nontraditional families are described through interviews with individuals living in such situations. (3 Star, VRG). jsc

Shattered Dishes: Picking up the Pieces of Our Parents' Divorce (1991–28 minutes). Deborah Ellman./Fanlight Productions, 47 Halifax St., Boston, MA 02130. (617) 524-0980, (800)937-4113. $195.
This video is a poignant look at the reminiscences of three young adults, two white males and one black female, concerning the effect of divorce on their adult selves. Extremely well done, technically and philosophically. (4 Star, VRG; Honorable Mention, NCFR Media Awards). ca

A Single Regret (1990–29 minutes). National Film Board of Canada, 1251 Avenue of the Americas, 16th Fl., New York, NY 10020-1173. (212)586-5131, (800)542-2164. $350.
This is the true story of a married man who fathered an illegitimate son and how he coped with the secret for 20 years. Not allowed any contact with his son by the boy's mother, he makes a video will for the boy, revealing his thoughts and fears. ca

Teenage Mothers: A Global Crisis (1990–55 minutes). Better World Society./The Cinema Guild, 1697 Broadway, No. 802, New York, NY 10019. (212)246-5522. $295/$90.
This documentary examines the worldwide crisis in teenage pregnancies through four case studies of teenage women in Ghana, England, Cuba, and the United States. In addition to interviews with the four young women and their families, the video features commentary from professionals on ways to cope with the problem (e.g., education, increased employment opportunities, contraception and job training). (Honorable Mention, NCFR Media Awards). scag

Divorced Parents and Children (1989–75 minutes). Virginia Satir./NLP Comprehensive, 2897 Valmont Rd., Boulder, CO 80301. (800)233-1NLP (-1657). $85/$15 + membership.
This program is a live demonstration of Satir's family therapy method of working with parents and their children in a group, helping them develop positive bonds and stronger relationships. ca

Families in the Balance (1989–23 minutes). David Gluck. PhotoSynthesis Productions./Cornell University A-V Center, 8 Business & Technology Park, Ithaca, NY 14850. (607)255-2091. $36.
This program is a tool for discussion of the important child-care issues with legislators and business and community leaders. Narrated by actress Ellen Burstyn, the story is told through the daily struggles of four American families trying to cope with the demands of work and parenting. One of the families is a Boston police officer who happens to be a single parent. (5 Star, VRG; Winner, NCFR Media Awards). cag

For Richer, for Poorer (1989–30 minutes). Ariadne Ochrymorych./National Film Board of Canada, 1251 Avenue of the Americas, 16th Floor, New York, NY 10020-1173. (212)586-5131, (800)542-2164. $550/$60.
This program is an indictment of a legal system which has failed to address the needs of single mothers and their children, and of a society which leads women to have false expectations about their economic futures. ca

Single-Parent & Blended Families: How the Schools Can Help (1988–28 minutes). Iowa State University Cooperative Extension Service./Media Resources Center, Film & Video Booking, 121 Pearson Hall, Ames, IA 50011. (515)294-8022, (800)447-0060. $37/$14.
An excellent production using interviews with teachers, a school counselor, and children (teens and preteens). Feelings about the absent parent, child's attitude toward school, and how teachers can recognize that there may be a problem at home are addressed. ca

Single Parenting (1988–20 minutes). THE PRACTICAL PARENTING VIDEO Series. United Learning, 6633 W. Howard St., Niles, IL 60648. (800)424-0362. $95 (30 day approval).
This program is intended to help single parents learn how to deal with the unique challenges that are a part of single-parent life. It focuses on ways to minimize the adverse effects that a divorce or death in the family may have on children. sca

Problems of Working Women (1987–24 minutes). Films for the Humanities, Box 2053, Princeton, NJ 08540. (609)452-1128, (609)275-1400, (800)257-5126. $149/$75.

The first half of this video deals with four divorced women, raising such post-divorce problems as loneliness, child care expense, and fatigue from working in the labor market and at home. The second half is a debate about women's economic position in the labor market and the supports needed. ca

A Family to Me: Redefining the American Family (1986–28 minutes). Linda Harness./New Day Films, 121 W. 27th St., Suite 902, New York, NY 10001. (212)645-8210. $199/$50.
This video looks at two brothers who discover new identities as househusbands; a Black single parent and her philosophy of child rearing and "going it alone"; a lesbian couple mothering twin boys; and a divorced couple who have created a joint custody arrangement congruent with their Jewish values. (Honorable Mention, NCFR Media Awards). ca

Feature-Length Television and Film Releases

Crisscross (1992–101 minutes). MGM/UA Home Video, 10,000 W. Washington Blvd., Culver City, CA 90832-2728. (310)280-6000. $19.98.
After being abandoned by her shell-shocked Vietnam-veteran husband, Tracy Cross (Goldie Hawn) struggles to bring up her twelve-year-old son and recreate the happy home life they once had together. R

Dark Horse (1992, Made-for-Video-Movie–98 minutes). Live Home Video, Box 10124, Van Nuys, CA 91410-0124. (800)752-9483. $89.98.
Young Allie is devastated when her father relocates them to a small town after her mother's death. Missing her friends, she quickly makes new ones whose bad influence results in her getting into trouble. This results in doing community service on a horse ranch where she befriends a beautiful championship horse. PG

Gas, Food, Lodging (1992–101 minutes). Columbia/TriStar Home Video, 3400 Riverside Dr., Burbank, CA 91505. (818)972-0937. $34.
Based on Richard Peck's novel *Don't Look and It Won't Hurt*, this first feature film by Allison Anders traces the complex relationship between a single mother (Brooke Adams) and her two teenage daughters who, after the father walks out, try to live as normal a life as possible. R

Kiss Shot (1992–88 minutes). Embassy Entertainment, 9250 Wilshire Blvd., Suite 303, Beverly Hills, CA 90212. (310)276-2196. $89.95.
Whoopie Goldberg plays a struggling single Mom, with an unpaid mortgage and a precocious daughter, who falls back on her pool playing skills in order to pay her debts. As soon as she gets into a big-money tourna-

ment, a globe-trotting ladies' man appears and threatens to disrupt their lives. In the end, everything rides on a single shot. PG

This Is My Life (1992–94 minutes) CBS/Fox Video, P.O. Box 900, Beverly Hills, CA 90213. (213)236-1336. $94.98.
Directed by Nora Ephron, this is a story of a working mother (Julie Kavner) torn between her skyrocketing career as a stand-up comic and her two daughters. PG-13

Little Man Tate (1991–99 minutes). Orion Home Video, 1325 Avenue of the Americas, New York, NY 10019. (212)956-3800. $92.98.
A seven-year-old genius is the prize in a tug of war between his mother, who wants him to lead a normal life, and a domineering school director who loves him for his intellect. An acclaimed directorial debut for Jodie Foster, with overtones of her own extraordinary life as a child prodigy. PG

Sarah, Plain and Tall (1991–98 minutes). Hallmark Hall of Fame./Republic Pictures Home Video, PO Box 66930, 12636 Beatrice St., Los Angeles, CA 90066-0930. (310)306-4040. $89.98.
Adapted from Patricia MacLachian's novel, Glenn Close stars as a New England school teacher who travels to 1910 Kansas to care for the two children of a widowed farmer who has advertised for a wife. Superior entertainment for the whole family. G

Men Don't Leave (1989–115 minutes). Warner Home Video, 4000 Warner Blvd., Burbank, CA 91522. (818)954-6000. $19.98.
A recent widow tries to raise her kids single-handedly after moving from a small town to the big city. PG-13

Parenthood (1989–124 minutes). Imagine Entertainment/MCA/Universal Home Video, 70 Universal City Plaza, #435, Culver City, CA 91608. (818)777-6419. $19.98.
Four grown siblings and their parents struggle with various levels of parenthood: From the college drop-out, to the nervous single mother (Diane Wiest), to the yuppie couple raising an overachiever, every possibility is explored, including the perspective of the older generation. PG-13

The Good Mother (1988–104 minutes, CC). Touchstone Home. Video, 500 S. Buena Vista St., Burbank, CA. 91521. (818)562-3883. $36.95.
A divorced single mother (Diane Keaton) tries to create a fulfilling life for herself and her eight-year-old daughter that includes an honest and open

education about every subject, including sex. Her ex-husband decides to fight for custody of their daughter after allegations of sexual impropriety on the part of the mother's new lover. R

REFERENCES

Cantor, M.G. (1991). The American family on television: From Molly Goldberg to Bill Cosby. *Journal of Comparative Family, 22*(2), 205-216.

Cantor, M. G., & Cantor, J. M. (1992). Prime-time television: Content and control (2nd Ed.). Newbury Park, CA: Sage Publications.

Fabes, R. A., Wilson, P., & Christopher, F. S. (1989). A time to reexamine the role of television in family life. *Family Relations, 38*(3), 337-341.

Huston, A. C., Donnerstein, E., Fairchild, H., Feshbach, N. D., Katz, P. A., Murry, J. P., Rubinstein, E. A., Wilcox, B. L., & Zuckerman, D. (1992). Big World, small screen: The role of television in American society. Lincoln, NE: University of Nebraska Press.

Kimmons, L., & Gaston, J. A. (1986). Single parenting: A filmography. *Family Relations, 35*(1), 205-211.

Levy, E. (1991). The American dream of family in film. From decline to a comeback. *Journal of Comparative Family, 22*(2), 187-204.

Lull, J. (Ed.). (1988). World families watch television. Newbury Park, CA: Sage Publications.

McDonald's turns into video giant. (June 1, 1993). Honolulu Star-Bulletin, p. C-5.

Pocs, O., Gentry, D., Walsh, R., Fearson, J., & Scott, J. (1993). Twenty-fourth annual National Council on Family Relations media awards competition. *Family Relations, 42*(1), 99-105.

Spigel, L. (1992). Make room for TV: Television and the family ideal in postwar America. Chicago: The University of Chicago Press.

Tichi, C. (1991). Electronic hearth: Creating an American television culture. New York: Oxford University Press.

APPENDIX

Bowker's Complete Video Finder. (1993). New Providence, NJ: R.R. Bowker. (908)464-6800, (800)521-8110.

The Educational Film & Video Locator. (1991). New Providence, NJ: R.R. Bowker. (908)464-6800, (800)521-8110.

Film & Video Finder (3rd Ed.). (1991). Medford, NJ: Plexus Publishing. (609)654-6500. Published for the National Information Center for Educational Media (NICEM), Box 40130, Albuquerque, NM 87196. (505)265-3591, (800)468-3453.

Media Review Digest (Vol. 21). (1992). Ann Arbor, MI: The Pierian Press. (313)434-5530, (800)678-2435.

Video Librarian. Bremerton, WA: Randy Pitman. (206)377-2231.

Videolog. (1993). San Diego: Trade Service Corporation. (619)457-5920, (800)854-1527.

Video Rating Guide for Libraries. Santa Barbara, CA: ABC-CLIO. (805)968-1911, (800)422-2546.

The Video Source Book (14th Ed.). (1993). Detroit: Gale Research. (313)961-2242, (800)877-4253.

Chapter 23

Resources for Single Parent Families

Doris J. Julian

SUMMARY. Single and primary parents can benefit from external resources which support their parenting activities. This paper identifies examples of supportive organizations which are currently available. These resources offer information, advocacy, peer-support and options for professional services. When possible, national headquarters are listed as a primary source of information. Informal resources for locating local organizations are also described. These organizations are also of value to the general population of parents and grandparents.

KEYWORDS. Community resources, Support groups, Self-help organizations

INTRODUCTION

Families, when confronted with significant transition events, such as divorce, death, or disability of a parent or child, can benefit from supportive services. Such services can provide practical information, contacts

Doris J. Julian is affiliated with Oregon Health Sciences University, Portland, OR 97201.

[Haworth co-indexing entry note]: "Resources for Single Parent Families." Julian, Doris J. Co-published simultaneously in *Marriage & Family Review* (The Haworth Press, Inc.) Vol. 20, No. 3/4, 1995, pp. 499-512; and: *Single Parent Families: Diversity, Myths and Realities* (ed: Shirley M. H. Hanson et al.) The Haworth Press, Inc., 1995, pp. 499-512. Multiple copies of this article/chapter may be purchased from The Haworth Document Delivery Center [1-800-3-HAWORTH; 9:00 a.m. - 5:00 p.m. (EST)].

for assistance and counseling resources. Useful services to be shared with others can also be generated by families who are experiencing a specific transition. Self-help support groups focusing on a particular family issue, such as parenting by single individuals, can be an important resource.

This paper will list and describe selected examples of organizational resources of value to individuals who have primary responsibility for parenting one or more children. Many of these resources will also be of value to parents in general and to professionals who provide services for families.

The selected resources will emphasize a national headquarters if one is available. Although resources in the United States may predominate, selected organizations from other countries are included. Information is current as of this publication but readers are reminded of the potential mobility of many of these resources and will need to verify addresses, telephone numbers, and availability of services. Toll-free numbers in the United States have a prefix of 1-*800*.

Resources are grouped by categories or types of parents, distinctive needs of children and by broad areas of potential concern such as financial resources and legal issues. The final category describes multi-issue organizations and lists selected national resource directories. Many excellent resources not included in this inventory will be found in the directories. Space limitations precluded additional entries.

GENERAL SINGLE PARENT ORGANIZATIONS

Parents Without Partners, Inc.
8807 Colesville Road, Silver Springs, MD 20910
Tel: 1(301)588-9354
Tel: (for prospective members) 1(800)637-7974

This is an international non-profit member organization. It offers support through educational activities, family activities, and parent social/recreational activities. Single parents may join chapters in the United States or Canada. The official publication is *The Single Parent*.

National Council for Adoption, Inc.
1930 17th Street, N.W., Washington, D.C. 20009-6207
Tel: 1(202)328-1260

The council provides information for adoptive families, single parents, or prospective adopters. It's also a resource for public policy, legal advocacy and public education.

Resources for Adoptive Parents, Inc. (RAP)
P.O. Box 27373, Minneapolis, MN 55427
Tel: 1(612)926-6959, 1(800)944-5230

RAP is an independent, non-profit organization founded and directed by adoptive parents. Its services include education, support groups, parent networking, speakers' bureau for schools and groups and legislative advocacy. The official newsletter is *The Adoption Post*.

Widowed Persons Service
American Association of Retired Persons (AARP)
1909 K Street, N.W.
Washington, D.C. 20049
Tel: 1(202)872-4700

The AARP provides information on resources for widowed individuals including peer support opportunities.

Theos Foundation
The Penn Hills Mall Office Bldg., Rm. 306
Pittsburgh, PA 15235
Tel: Not available

This foundation offers resources for widowed individuals and their families. Peer support groups are available.

Mothers Without Custody
P.O. Box 27418, Houston, TX 77227-7418
Tel: 1(800)457-6962

This is a non-profit, self-directed, national support group with a primary purpose of enhancing the quality of life of children by strengthening the role of non-custodial mothers in regard to custody, child support, visitation and parenting. Services include public education, liaison between organizations, and networking for parents.

The National Congress for Men and Children
2020 Pennsylvania Ave., N.W., Suite 277
Washington, D.C. 20006
Tel: 1(202)328-4377

This national, non-profit organization provides information and advocacy supporting the participation of non-residential parents in issues related to their children's emotional, financial and educational needs. The organization works to reduce gender discrimination in society and in family courts. It serves members in the United States and Canada. A quarterly newsletter, *NetWork*, provides information. An additional quarterly newsletter, *OUR VIEW*, is designed for children.

Families Need Fathers (FNF)
134 Curtain Road, London, England EC2A3AR
Tel: 071-613-5060

FNF is a voluntary self-help society with registered charity status. The organization offers practical assistance to non-custodial parents, particularly fathers, and to grandparents, to enhance and safeguard contacts with their children. Peer support groups, publications, resources and limited legal advice are a part of the services offered.

Young Nonresident Fathers
American Association for Marriage and Family Therapy, Research and Education Foundation
1100 Seventeenth St., N.W., The Tenth Floor, Washington, D.C. 20036
Tel: 1(202)467-5114

The foundation will provide a report by Family Impact Seminar (1990): *Background Briefing Report* which has information on such issues as: paternity establishment, child support and job strategies.

National Organization of Adolescent Pregnancy and Parenting
4421 A East-West Hwy., Bethesda, MD 20814
Tel: 1(301)913-0378

This organization promotes comprehensive services for adolescents related to pregnancy and parenting through advocacy, information, conferences and publications including a *Directory of Adolescent Pregnancy and Parenting Programs*.

Grandparents Raising Grandchildren
P.O. Box 104, Colleyville, TX 76034
Tel: 1(817)577-0435

This organization's mission is providing support and legal assistance for grandparents who are primary caregivers. Specific activities include advocating for legislative changes and for policy changes with health insurance companies, health care providers, public educational systems and social security regulations.

Grandparents as Parents (GAP)
11260 Overland Avenue, 17-D, Culver City, CA 90230
Tel: 1(310)839-2548

Founder and Director: Sylvie de Toledo, LCSW

GAP is a non-profit corporation initiated as a Long Beach, CA based charity in 1987 with the purposes of offering psychological assistance and case by case financial assistance. The organization is currently involved in helping with the formation of similar support groups in other states and a National Coalition of Grandparents. See organization listed below.

Grandparents United for Children's Rights, Inc.
Executive Headquarters: 137 Larkin St., Madison, WI 53705
Tel: 1(608)238-8751

Executive Director: Ethel Dunn

This organization focuses on supporting and developing services which enhance and secure the rights of grandparents/step-grandparents and kinship providers to access and protect children. The organization is concerned with legislative reform, education of public and private agencies and education of grandparents, step-grandparents and kinship care providers.

Stepfamily Association of America, Inc.
215 Centennial Mall S., Suite 212, Lincoln, NE 68508
Tel: 1(402)477-7837

Executive Director: Bill Munn

This is a national advocacy organization which has 50 chapters in the United States offering self-help and education. The *Stepfamily Bulletin* is published quarterly. An annual national Stepfamily Conference provides educational and networking opportunities.

Gay and Lesbian Parents Coalition International
(Formerly Gay Father's Coalition), P.O. Box 50360
Washington, D.C. 20091
Tel: 1(202)583-8029

This organization serves as a clearinghouse for information concerning gay and lesbian parenting. In addition, it coordinates the establishment of support groups for parents and children and conducts public educational outreach programs.

Institute for the Advanced Study of Black Family Life and Culture
175 Filbert St., Suite 202, Oakland, CA 94607
Tel: 1(510)836-3245

This organization's focus is on revitalizing African-American culture through work with agencies, school systems, and the juvenile justice system. A training curricula for teen parents has been developed.

Black Women Organized for Educational Development
518 17th St., Suite 202, Oakland, CA 94612
Tel: 1(510)763-9501

The goal of this non-profit organization is to encourage empowerment of low-income, socially disadvantaged women through a variety of services including: support groups, educational seminars and workshops. In addition, a mentoring program links junior high school girls with professional women to provide career and personal guidance, addressing concerns of teen pregnancy, school drop-outs, substance abuse and potential for violence.

Native American Community Board
P.O. Box 572, Lake Andes, SD 57356-0572
Tel: 1(605)487-7072

This organization is concerned with the educational, social, and economic advancement of American Indians. It maintains a Native American Womens' Health Education Resource Center which offers self-help programs and workshops related to family issues.

CHILD CUSTODY, SUPPORT, AND PAY EQUITY

Association for Children for Enforcement of Support, Inc. (ACES)
723 Phillips Avenue, Suite J, Toledo, OH 43612
Tel: 1(800)537-7072; 1(419)476-2511

ACES is a non-profit organization with a primary purpose of assisting disadvantaged children affected by parents who do not meet legal and moral child support and/or visitation obligations. The organization provides educational programs and counseling for families about those issues. In addition, representatives advocate for children through participation on governmental commissions and task forces. ACES has chapters in 49 states.

National Child Support Advocacy Coalition
Box 420, Hendersonville, TN 37077-0421
Tel: 1(615)264-0151

This organization serves as an advocacy and information group for enforcement of financial child support.

Department of Health & Human Services
Family Support Administration, Office of Child Support Enforcement
370 L'Enfant Promenade, S.W., Washington, D.C. 20447
Tel: 1(301)401-5524

This organization, housed within the Department of Health and Human Services, is responsible for the establishment of national policy and the collection of child support monies. It coordinates all 50 state's child support enforcement agencies. In addition, funding is available for demonstration and research projects to support child access and visitation demonstration grants by private and public groups.

Custody Action for Lesbian Mothers
P.O. Box 281, Narberth, PA 19072
Tel: 1(215)667-7508

This organization provides free legal and counseling services for lesbian mothers seeking child custody. It offers support for litigation addressing constitutional rights on the basis of sexual preference. It assists in providing nationwide contacts for lesbian mother groups.

National Committee on Pay Equity (NCPE)
1126 16th St. N.W., Suite 411, Washington, D.C. 22036
Tel: 1(202)331-7343

NCPE is a national coalition of labor, women's and civil rights organizations, professional associations and religious organizations concerned with the elimination of sex and race-based wage discrimination. The organization serves as a central, national clearinghouse on pay equity information, including the provision of child care and family leave.

LEGAL

American Bar Association
Center on Children and the Law, 1800 M St., N.W., Suite 200 South,

Washington, D.C. 20036-5802
Tel: 1(202)331-2250

Director: Howard Davidson

This association offers legal and technical support to professionals and attorneys who work with children on abuse and neglect cases, parental abduction, and financial child support.

National Women's Law Center
1616 P Street, N.W., Suite 100, Washington, D.C. 20036
Tel: 1(202)328-5160

This center is a national resource to advance the status of women through law. This includes litigation of key cases, advocacy of women's rights, consultation with state and federal policy makers about issues such as women's rights, consultations with state and federal policy makers about issues such as women's employment, child care, and child support. The center's special focus in on women who are most disadvantaged, including women of color, low-income women and women in prison.

PARENTING SUPPORT: FOCUS ON THE CHILD

The ARC, Formerly: Association for Retarded Citizens of the United States
P.O. Box 104, Arlington, TX 76004
Tel: 1(817)261-6003

The ARC is a national parent organization on mental retardation. It is concerned with supporting individuals with mental retardation through education, research, advocacy and supporting families and friends. Information about state chapters is available.

Attachment Center at Evergreen
28000 Meadow Drive, P.O. Box 2764, Evergreen, CO 80439
Tel: 1(303)674-1910

This organization provides information about the Attachment Disorder Parent's Network, a support group for parents and families of children with attachment disorders. Their information brochure notes that the majority of unattached children are adopted, but the disorder can also be found in other children.

March of Dimes Birth Defects Foundation
1275 Manaroneck Avenue, White Plains, NY 10605
Tel: 1(914)428-7100

This organization provides information about birth defects; and a listing of state or local chapters as resources for parents or professionals.

National Clearinghouse on Family Support and Children's Mental Health
Portland State University, P.O. Box 751, Portland, OR 97207-0751
Tel: 1(503)725-4040; 1(800)628-1696

Services of this organization include: (1) Computerized data bank; (2) Fact sheets on issues related to children with emotional disabilities and their families; (3) A state-by-state resource file; and (4) Access to a family resource coordinator on staff.

Parents Anonymous, Inc.
520 S. LaFayette Park Place, Suite 316, Los Angeles, CA 90057
Tel: 1(800)421-0353

This is a non-profit organization offering parent led, professionally facilitated, self-help groups and services to parents under stress. The goal is to keep families together and empower parents by increasing their self-esteem and parenting abilities.

School-Age Child Care Project
Wellesley College Center for Research on Women
Wellesley, MA 02181
Tel: 1(617)235-0320, ext. 2500; 1(617)431-1453

This project provides research-based information on the "latchkey" child as a basis for action by policy makers and child-care professionals. It also provides information on characteristics of a quality school-age program including school-age children with special needs.

The Society of Special Needs Adoptive Parents (SNAP)
1150-409 Granville Street, Vancouver, British Columbia V63 1T2, Canada
Tel: 1(604)687-3114 or 1(800)663-7627

This organization is mandated to provide post-adoption support groups and one-to-one community contacts, information services, beginning referral services, and public education. Single parents are welcome, but are not specifically targeted.

National Association for the Education of Young Children
1509 16th Street, N.W., Washington, D.C. 20036-1426
Tel: 1(202)232-8777; 1(800)424-2460

This is a non-profit professional organization with the goals of: (1) providing educational opportunities and resources to promote the professional development of those working for and with young children and (2) working to increase public knowledge and support for high quality early childhood programs. Print and video resource materials are provided. It also offers a voluntary, national accreditation system for early childhood programs.

GENERAL INFORMATION AND RESOURCES

American Self-Help Clearinghouse
St. Clares-Riverside Medical Center, Denville, NJ 07834
Tel: 1(201)625-7101 or TDD 1(201)625-9053

The Clearinghouse provides information and contacts for self-help groups including information on model groups. It also publishes a directory, the *Self-Help Sourcebook*, biannually.

Center for Family Resources
384 Clinton Street, Hempstead, NY 11550
Tel: 1(516)489-3716

This organization serves as a resource clearinghouse, training center, and provider of model programs for professionals working with families. It publishes *In Touch* two times yearly, with periodic inclusions of a *Single Parent Supplement* which updates resources, programs, and services for family professionals.

Children's Defense Fund
25 E Street, N.W., Washington, D.C. 20001
Tel: 1(202)628-8787

This organization provides national child advocacy including on-going lobbying for a legislative agenda supporting children. Its annual publication is *The State of America's Children*.

Children's Rights Council (also known as the National Council for Children's Rights)
220 I Street, N.E., Suite 230, Washington, D.C. 20002-4362
Tel: 1(202)547-0227

This is a non-profit national organization with local chapters. Its goals are advocacy, public information. It offers a resource directory and a publication, *Speak Out For Children*.

Child Welfare League of America
440 First St. N.W., Suite 310, Washington, D.C. 20001-2085
Tel: 1(202)638-2952

Executive Director: David Liederman

This organization provides information and advocacy supporting the well-being of children, youth and families. Specific examples include issues related to foster care, adoption, teen pregnancy, and day care.

Family Resource Coalition–National Resource Center for Family Support Programs
200 South Michigan Avenue, Suite 1520, Chicago, IL 60604
Tel: 1(313)341-0900

This is a non-profit organization which operates a national resource center for family support programs, and provides technical assistance for programs. It also offers information to policy makers and professionals and links family support to other services.

Family Service America, Inc.
11700 West Lake Drive, Park Place, Milwaukee, WI 53224
Tel: 1(414)359-1040

This is an international non-profit association with member agencies in the United States and Canada. It offers community-based family counseling and support services, and technical assistance to support innovative program development at the local level. The Severson National Information Center serves as a clearinghouse on family issues and also presents national programs on family issues.

National Information Center for Children and Youth with Disabilities
P.O. Box 1492, Washington, D.C. 20013-1492
Tel: 1(800)999-5599 (Toll Free)(V-Voice)
1(703)893-8614 (TT-Text Telephone)

This center provides a selected list of toll-free numbers for national organizations concerned with disability and children's issues. Some telephone numbers are available in both voice or text and some are also available in Spanish.

United States Department of Agriculture Extension Service
Tel: 1(800)726-4995 (Federal Information Service Number)

Ask for Human Development, Family Relationships Services, *or* locate *State* offices through the states' land grant universities. This official organization provides a variety of services and materials including topics such as parent education, family resource management, family relationships, family nutrition and youth development.

DIRECTORIES

A Parent's Guide to Accessing Programs for Infants, Toddlers, and Preschoolers with Handicaps (1989)
Available from National Information Center for Children and Youth with Handicaps, P.O. Box 1492, Washington D.C. 20013

This guide identifies resources for parents and guardians of young children with special needs. It has a specific focus on early intervention services for children, birth through two years old and special education services for children ages three through five years old.

Children's Health Resource Guide. Flower, J. (1992)
Let's form a circle in *Healthcare Forum Journal*, Nov./Dec.

This guide lists health, social service, policy-making and resource organizations, as well as their publications.

Directory of Fathers Rights Organizations (1993)
Available from Fathers for Equal Rights, Inc., 3623 Douglas Ave., Des Moines, IA 50310-5345
Tel: 1(515)277-8789

This directory lists organizations, agencies and the names of activists who offer a variety of services aimed at supporting the relationship between parents and their children after divorce or separation. These services include child access counseling, lawyer referral, support groups, information, education and self advocacy.

Encyclopedia of Associations (1993) 27th Edition
Edited by Deborah M. Burek, Published by Gale Research, Inc. of Detroit and London

This publication is available in many metropolitan libraries. It provides an annotated directory of over 23,000 national and international organizations. Current contact people are listed when possible. It is updated on a yearly basis.

International Parenting Directory of Organizations
Available from the Children's Rights Council (CRC)

220 I Street, N.E., Washington, D.C. 20002-4362
Tel: 1(202)547-6227, Fax: (202)546-6272

This directory lists approximately 1,200 organizations by state, province, or country which provide child and family related services. A list of chapters is provided. It is published annually.

National Organization of Single Mothers Membership Directory (1993)
Available from National Organization of Single Mothers, P.O. Box 68, Midland, NC 28107-0068
Tel: 1(704)888-2337, Fax: 1(704)888-1752, or 24-hour information message: 1(704)888-5437

The directory lists members by state and province. Its purpose is networking for mutual support.

National Organizations Concerned with Mental Health, Housing, and Homelessness (1993)
Available from National Resource Center on Homelessness and Mental Illness, Delmar, NY
Tel: 1(800)444-7415, Fax: 1(518)439-7612

This publication provides a resource list of Federal agencies and national organizations with concerns related to housing, mental health treatment, and other service needs of both homeless individuals and homeless families. The list is updated on a regular basis.

Selected Child Abuse Information and Resources Directory (1992)
Available from the National Committee for Prevention of Child Abuse (NCPCA)
Publication Sales, P.O. Box 94824, Chicago, IL 60690
Tel: 1(312)663-3520

The directory provides general information including reporting, hot-lines, and a literature search. Its wide variety of resources include: legal, medical and culture-specific organizations.

CONCLUSION

This listing of organizations represents an introduction to a few resources which can be of value to parents and professionals. Directories will provide a broader spectrum of existing organizations. The reader is also directed to useful local resources which will vary by locality. These may be located through the community services section of telephone books, community-based information and referral services (such as United Way) and through official health and social services agencies. Informal resources such as churches are of value. Public libraries and local media services can also be helpful. The concept of networking is a crucial element as parents and professionals share with each other the resources that *are* available and those that need to be developed. Resource creation will remain an on-going issue.

Chapter 24

Quality of Life and Well-Being of Single Parent Families: Disparate Voices or a Long Overdue Chorus?

Marilyn Ihinger-Tallman

SUMMARY. This discussion brings together the multiple factors that impact single parent families and effect their overall quality of life and well-being. Influential variables were identified and organized at three levels–institutional, interpersonal, and individual. A model was developed that included the most salient determinants of single parent family well-being. These included cultural norms and values, health of family members, social and demographic factors, individual personal characteristics, social support networks, and social institutions such as the law, the economy, the polity (represented in the formation of public policy) and education. Variables associated with the noncustodial (nonresidential) parent also were identified as affecting the quality of life of single parent family members. In combination these factors help establish, maintain, and change the environment within which single parents raise their families.

KEYWORDS. Single parent family well-being, Theoretical development

---

Marilyn Ihinger-Tallman is affiliated with the Department of Sociology, Washington State University, Pullman, WA 99164-4020.

[Haworth co-indexing entry note]: "Quality of Life and Well-Being of Single Parent Families: Disparate Voices or a Long Overdue Chorus?" Ihinger-Tallman, Marilyn. Co-published simultaneously in *Marriage & Family Review* (The Haworth Press, Inc.) Vol. 20, No. 3/4, 1995, pp. 513-532; and: *Single Parent Families: Diversity, Myths and Realities* (ed: Shirley M. H. Hanson et al.) The Haworth Press, Inc., 1995, pp. 513-532. Multiple copies of this article/chapter may be purchased from The Haworth Document Delivery Center [1-800-3-HAWORTH; 9:00 a.m. - 5:00 p.m. (EST)].

INTRODUCTION

Webster (1972) defines the verb "integrate" as meaning to form into a whole; to incorporate into a larger unit. In 1985 this author was invited to write an integrative epilogue to a special issue on the single parent family for the journal, *Family Relations* (Ihinger-Tallman, 1986). The assignment synthesized the research findings that were reported in that volume and a model was developed that included family formation, dissolution, and re-formation variables. In 1992 another invitation was offered–this time the task involved reviewing and integrating the information contained in four volumes of a special issue of *Marriage & Family Review.* Who could refuse such a challenge?

The chapters in these volumes constitute a rich source of information about single parenting. The identification of key variables and processes, the most recent demographic information, and the few available explanations of single parenting behavior are collected there. The intent of this chapter, reflected in the title, is to ask if this information can be best characterized as a collection of literature reviews and miscellaneous findings, with each chapter (or voice) offering a set of generalizations that are isolated and independent of those in other chapters. Or can the collected information be viewed as a chorus, in the sense of the ancient Greek chorus, which was a company whose narration provided explanation and elaboration of action. This chapter creates the "chorus" by attempting to synthesize the material into a coherent whole to reveal a framework that ties together the disparate information found in the literature that is summarized in those chapters. This is done in order to better understand and explain single parent family phenomenon. The goal is to move beyond description toward conceptualization and ultimately theory building.

The method used was to abstract the key variables and relationships discussed in each chapter, thus reducing the amount of material, avoiding redundancies, and synthesizing the vast array of information. While the ideal goal would be the development of a theoretical synthesis involving the derivation of fundamental principles, propositions, and hypotheses, that task is beyond the scope of time and space available for this chapter. However, an effort will be made to provide the groundwork for such a formulation that might be constructed by family scholars in the future.

All but three of the 19 chapters in the volume are condensed in this way. The three that are omitted are the filmography (Kimmons, 1995), the bookshelf (Schlesinger, 1995), and the resource guide to community agencies (Julian, 1995). The editors of this special volume (Hanson, Heims, Julian, & Sussman, 1995) were thorough in selecting chapters that covered the many diverse topics related to single parent families. These included one chapter that reviewed the demographic and socioeconomic characteristics of single parent families (Bianchi, 1995); another showed the benefits of expanding the definition of family by putting the single parent family in a wider (beyond kin) relationship context (Donati, 1995); others focused on economics (Lino, 1995; Bowen, Desimone, & McKay, 1995); the legal system (Walters & Abshire, 1995); parenting issues (Horowitz, 1995); living arrangements (Steinbock, 1995); noncustodial (nonresidential) parenting (Herrerías, 1995; Fox & Blanton, 1995; & Arditti, 1995); parenting disabled children (Boyce, White, Miller, & Godfrey, 1995); teen parents (Prater, 1995; Marsiglio, 1995); parenting that results from divorce (Ladd & Zvonkovic, 1995; Greif, 1995), death (Gass-Sternas, 1995; Burgess, 1995), and adoption (Shireman, 1995); and grandparent custody due to adult children's failure to parent (Burton, Merriwether-deVries, & Dilworth-Anderson, 1995).

As soon as the key variables were identified and empirical generalizations were summarized, it became clear that the recurring theme in most chapters (whether explicit or implicit) was the quality of life and well-being of single parents and their children. It thus was identified as the dependent variable of this chapter's analysis. After reading an earlier version of this paper, Jenness (1993) observed that this present chapter pulled together a variety of independent variables and rendered them predictors of an outcome that the chapters themselves may or may not have demonstrated.

This is an accurate interpretation, and therefore, it is emphasized again that the quality of life and family well-being was implied more often than it was clearly specified in the chapters of this special volume. For example, in Herrerías' (1995) chapter on noncustodial mothers, the focus of the article was on (a) the factors that influenced mothers to relinquish custody of their children after divorce; (b) the process that led to the decision; and (c) the mother-child relationship after relinquishment. Implicit in most of the reasons for relinquishing custody was the well-being of the children. (Well-being of children was an explicit reason for relinquishing custody in most of the literature that was reviewed in that chapter as well.) Financial well-being and the emotional well-being of the mother herself were other principle reasons for giving up custody. Thus the quality of life and the well-being of family members were latent variables in this chapter. In other chapters the well-being of family members was clearly specified as the dependent variable (Gass-Sternas, 1995; Boyce, White, Miller, & Godfrey, 1995).

Because disparate information was subsumed under the concepts identified as quality of life and family well-being, definitions of these concepts are offered in order to prevent conceptual confusion. Trotter's (1989) definition of child well-being is borrowed and modified to incorporate all family members. Thus, family well-being is defined as the degree to which family members are able to engage successfully and appropriately in interpersonal relationships and in work or play activities with relative freedom from noxious social behavior, burdensome emotions, and poor physical health. Having a good quality of life means living in an environment and under circumstances in which the greatest degree of well-being is fostered for all family members.

All articles in the special volume (Hanson et al., 1995) identified variables that can be described as being antecedent to, having an influence on, or be said to contribute to the quality of life and well-being of members of single parent families. Examples of these variables include the emotional and physical health of parents and children; the educational level of parents; the availability of jobs that provide adequate pay, benefits, and promotional opportunities; and the availability of quality day care. All of these factors influence single parent family well-being. Variables such as these were characterized as the independent variables in this chapter. The task, then, was to identify the most salient variables and show how they interrelate and influence one another in order to develop a model that incorporates variables important to an explanation of well-being in single parent families.

An example of the process through which the variables in the various articles were synthesized is presented using the material in Kathleen Gass-Sternas' (1995) chapter on widowhood. These variables are presented in Figure 1 to illustrate one parsimonious way the most salient variables in this paper are interrelated.

While reading these chapters the information seemed to be best summarized by utilizing three separate levels of analysis. That is, there were important variables and variable relationships found at the societal (institutional) level, the social psychological (interpersonal) level, and the personal (individual) level. In addition, the temporal dimension contained in so many of the chapters suggested that it too must be incorporated into any conceptualization that attempts to explain single parent family life. These are discussed as follows.

A FRAMEWORK FOR INTEGRATION: INSTITUTIONAL, INTERPERSONAL, INDIVIDUAL, AND TEMPORAL

The information in the special volume on single parenting (Hanson et al., 1995) provides a thorough depiction of the circumstances of over 10

FIGURE 1. Variables Included in Chapter on Single Parent Widows

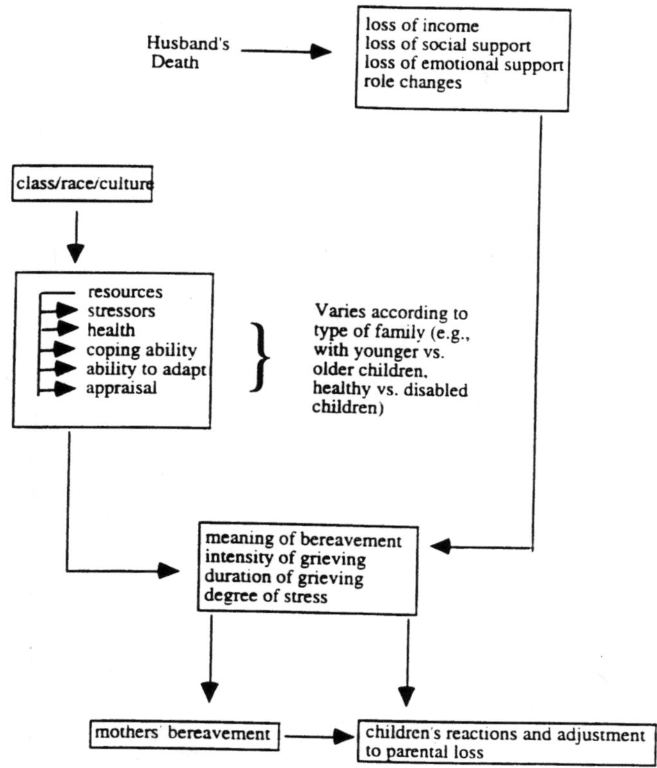

million families in America headed by single parents. The description is complete because it incorporates information on the social environment in which single parent families are embedded and the institutions which impact them; on how ex-spouse, relatives, friends, and other significant persons in a parent's interpersonal network foster or hinder the family's well-being; and on how individual characteristics, such as age, race or ethnic identity, level of education, state of health, etc., help or inhibit family well-being. It is not possible nor desirable to summarize all the relevant information contained in the various chapters that clustered into the categories of social institutions, interpersonal relationships, individual characteristics, and time. Only selected information that helps illustrate why these dimensions are important will be reviewed. It should be acknowledged that the analysis will not extend beyond the specific information presented in the papers included in the special volume. That is, while there may be influential institutions (e.g., religious institutions) that play important roles in the lives of single parent families, if they were not discussed in the special volume, they were not included in the analysis. The same caveat applies to interpersonal relationships and individual characteristics.

Social Institutions

Several social institutions are identified in the special volume (Hanson et al., 1995) that have a direct impact upon single parents and their children. The first of these is the legal system, as discussed by Herrerías (1995), Greif (1995), Marsiglio (1995), Walters and Abshire (1995), and Fox and Blanton (1995). If the transition event that initiates single parenting occurs through separation or divorce, then custody arrangements and child support awards/payments must be negotiated. Hostility and conflict between former spouses makes negotiation difficult. Support awards may not be honored and visitation may cease or be sabotaged by one or the other parent when the former spouse relationship is conflictual. However, if conflict and hostility are contained enough for parents to cooperate, increased well-being for all family members is the outcome. The chapters in this volume are consistent in their conclusion about the emotional importance to children of visitation by non-residential parents and of the economic importance of child support payments for the residential parent. Custody, visitation, and child support (or lack thereof) are the three most important aspects of the law that impact parents and children after marital dissolution. However, other aspects of the law, discussed by Walters and Abshire (1995), profoundly effect the behavior of single parents. Two of these are court restrictions on the mobility of a residential parent, and restrictions on a residential parent's sexual behavior (e.g., cohabitation, or gay or lesbian unions). Unconventional sexual behavior may threaten or lose legal custody. The importance of the law and its impact upon single parents' lives cannot be minimized.

A second social institution discussed in the special volume (Hanson et al., 1995) is the economic institution. It is the focus for attention in chapters by Bianchi (1995), Lino (1995), Bowen et al. (1995), Desimone and McKay (1995), Steinbock (1995), and Herrerías (1995). Bianchi reports that children who grow up in single parent families often are economically disadvantaged compared to children in two-parent families. The income of many single mothers and their children falls below the poverty line because of the loss of economic resources postdivorce. Dependence on one income that is insufficient to support a family leaves few opportunities for a family to have a satisfactory standard of living. When the labor force from which that income derives has (a) a shortage of jobs, (b) few benefits associated with those that are available, and (c) small potential for training or further education that allows for promotion and advancement, then the quality of life of these earners and their children suffers.

Third, schools and community agencies are part of the institutional environment within which single families are embedded, as discussed by Burgess and Prater (1995). Burgess reviewed Bronfenbrenner's (1990) ecological perspective and emphasizes the importance of school, work, child care programs, etc., for widowed fathers who become single parents. Burgess noted that fathers who become involved with their children's education help the children attain greater emotional and mental stability. The focus of Prater's chapter is never-married teen mothers. The curtailment of teen mothers' education is the most far-reaching consequence of teen pregnancy, for both mothers and children.

Fourth, the political institution, in the form of government decisions and social policy (local as well as national), is discussed in the special volume (Hanson et al., 1995) by Donati (1995), Walters (1995), Prater (1995), Bowen et al. (1995), and Steinbock (1995). Prater calls for more responsiveness, greater innovativeness, more comprehensive aid, a more positive attitude toward clients on the part of employees in service agencies, and nonpunitive policies toward clients who better themselves. This means, for example, making changes in the current policy that deprives benefits to a teen mother who completes a high school education and becomes employed but whose wages still cannot adequately support the family and pay for benefits (health care, food supplements, etc.). Donati (1995) recognizes that traditional family support behavior is not always forthcoming and suggests that social policy-makers recognize the concept of "wider family." One of the benefits of a wider family is that it is responsive to institutional change, dislocation, and it helps overcome normative stigmas (such as illegitimate status of children born to unwed mothers). Wider families represent an adaptive response to family needs that are not met through the traditional family system.

Interpersonal Relationships

Several authors in the special volume (Hanson et al., 1995) call attention to the importance of interpersonal networks for single parents, including relationships with extended kin and support provided by friends, relatives, ex-spouse, and new partners. (See especially the chapters by Ladd & Zvonkovic, 1995; Arditti, 1995; Horowitz, 1995; Donati, 1995;

& Gass-Sternas, 1995.) Prater (1995) elaborates the social support variable by differentiating three categories of support, including social embeddedness, perceived social support, and enacted social support. Data indicate that after divorce, social interaction significantly decreases. Often friends withdraw in order to avoid "taking sides" after marital disruption (Donati, 1995). This effects the degree of social embeddedness of a divorced individual. The result of such a decrease is often increased vulnerability and poor psychological adjustment. In contrast, a positive adjustment to singlehood, and single-parenthood, is more likely when individuals are integrated into social networks. The benefits of a support network include less distress, more responsiveness and attentiveness to children, and increased interest in children's development.

Widowhood often decreases interpersonal interaction when young mothers who suddenly must assume two parental roles find themselves too busy to be lonely but feel isolated from other adults because there is no time for socialization (Gass-Sternas, 1995). Donati (1995) suggests that "wider family" networks are formed to substitute for parents and kin who are emotionally and socially distant. She observes that these networks which are currently being created by many single parents, especially women, closely resemble the long-time use of fictive kin in African-American communities.

The interpersonal relationship between nonresidential parents and children is discussed by Walters and Abshire (1995). These authors pointed out the legal connection between a financial support award and visitation by the nonresidential parent. They note that "When support and visitation are linked, the child and the custodial parent's need for financial support may be subordinated to the noncustodial parent's need for a relationship with his or her child" (1995, p. 175). Again, in terms of parent-child relationships, residential parents are important "gatekeepers" to the relationship between nonresidential parents and children (Arditti, 1995). To ensure that quality time and attention are available to children from the absent parent, coparental cooperation between divorced spouses is necessary. Arditti (1995) claims that the coparental relationship may be the most important socio-emotional variable that mitigates the relationship noncustodial fathers have with their children postdivorce (1995, p. 289). Much clinical research suggests that such time and attention is necessary for children to thrive.

Individual Characteristics

The importance of individual personality characteristics for the adjustment and well-being of single parents is noted by Gass-Sternas (1995),

Herrerías (1995), Boyce et al. (1995), as well as Horowitz (1995). These authors emphasize the importance of parents' mental, emotional, and physical health, their ability to adapt, their coping ability (to handle divorce, desertion, unwed motherhood, bereavement, etc.), and an ability to assess and appraise circumstances and experiences. Strength of purpose and a sense of control over one's life also are personal qualities that foster parental well-being and promote successful family functioning. Age of a parent is a contributor that affects the quality of life and family member well-being. For example, Gass-Sternas (1995) reports research that indicates younger widows with dependent children at home, who have few available relationships, and whose socioeconomic status is low are more at risk for complications following bereavement. Teenage mothers are more likely to have fewer resources (in the form of finances, education, and emotional maturity), have shorter spacing between births, and more than one non-marital birth (Prater, 1995). In addition, their children tend to have more difficulty in school.

Race may seem to be an important personal characteristic that effects quality of life and single parent family well-being but one must consider the interactive effects of race and class. African-American single parent mothers are more likely to be poor than single parent mothers of other racial groups. Steinbock (1995) reports that the greatest incidence of poverty in the United States in 1990 is among African-American female-headed households with children under 18 years of age. Considering other aspects of race, Gass-Sternas (1995) found very little information on Black, Hispanic, or single parent widows of other ethnic groups, but suggested "there might be cultural differences in stressors, appraisal, coping, resources, grieving processes, and health among ethnic groups" (1995, p. 423). To the degree that social structural variables such as access to institutional resources and opportunities are held constant, then, all else being equal, one can expect cultural and subcultural norms and values to differentially impact the quality of life and family well-being of family members with different racial or ethnic characteristics. For example, there appears to be a slight tendency among children of minority mothers (compared to Anglo mothers) to relinquish their children to a relative other than the biological father (Herrerías, 1995). When Hispanic mothers relinquish custody of children there is a tendency for these children to return to live with their mothers, more so than when Black or Anglo mothers relinquish custody. Further, census figures indicate that while the number of single parent families has increased for both blacks and whites, racial differences remain extremely large. Single parenting is much higher among blacks than whites; in 1990 only one-quarter of black children were living with both parents compared to two-thirds of white children (Bianchi, 1995). Perhaps Arditti (1995) summed up the state of knowledge about this important variable best when she wrote, "Race and ethnicity have been all but ignored in the literature and must be included in research on parenting postdivorce. Given what we know about diversity in racial and cultural attitudes about parenting, children, and close relationships . . . such an omission probably means that existing research obscures or misrepresents the experiences of minorities" (1995, p. 295).

Time

As mentioned earlier, a temporal dimension was identified in a number of articles included in the special volume (Hanson et al., 1995). Whether conceived as stage in the family life cycle, as changing life experiences (i.e., a longitudinal focus), or as a resource to be spent, time is a relevant variable when analyzing and interpreting the processes and factors associated with single parenting. Considering the processual nature of time, the initial way it might be referenced when conceptualizing single parent family life is to classify the status of the family according to the marital status of the mother: single parenting may begin with a married or unmarried mother. As we begin to formulate a synthesis of all the information in the special volume, *marital status* is conceptualized as marking the first point in time (T1), prior to assuming a single parent status.

One of five *transition events* must occur before a person can hold the status of single parent–and move the family to the second point in time (T2). These events are: separation/desertion, divorce, widowhood, premarital birth (either planned or unplanned), and/or the adoption of a child by an unmarried person. Once one of these events occurs and the assumption of single/primary parent status begins, *family life is carried on under the leadership of only one parent*. This time period is represented as (T3). Finally, only two events can change the structure of the family and alter single parent status: remarriage/repartnering or the loss of the child (through adoption, foster care, move to other parent or other kin, or the child's death). Time four (T4) is when *single/primary parent status is relinquished.*

The authors of the chapters in this special volume (Hanson et al., 1995) focus attention on one or another of these time periods. In the following section the variables that are discussed in these chapters and designated as having an effect on the well-being of single parent families in one or another of these time periods are delineated. The time frames and the key variables that will be discussed as predictors of quality of life and single family well-being are presented in Figure 2.

MODELING THE FRAMEWORK: FACTORS THAT INFLUENCE SINGLE PARENTING

The Method

The strategy that was adopted when synthesizing chapter content (i.e., clustering it into levels of analysis) loses its value when the goal is to model the key variables into a framework that is organized temporally. This is because macro (institutional) and micro (interactional and individual) variables are interactive. For example, a relationship exists between a person's degree of physical health (an individual characteristic) and the social resources, determined by social policy, (institutional characteristics) available to that individual. These influence the degree to which medical help is present in the environment and the degree to which it is available to that person. The individual and institutional levels of analysis cannot be separated when attempting to disentangle the complexities of social behavior. Thus the variables discussed below will not be categorized according to different analytical levels. Rather, they will be organized along a time dimension, with the expectation that (a) the individual characteristics of people living in single parent families will influence their social interactions with others, including interactions with institutional organizations in the environment, (b) social support networks and the degree of social embeddedness will influence individual characteristics as well as overall quality of life and well-being; and (c) social institutions in the environment will influence family members' individual development as well as members' interactions within an interpersonal network. Further, (d) if social institutions are effective in providing opportunities and resources to assist family members in times of crisis, then individual development, interpersonal networks, a sense of well-being, and a higher quality of life in single parent families will be facilitated.

The Variables

The process of identifying the most salient variables that impact the quality of single family life begins prior to the event that marks the start of the single parenting process. Ladd and Zvonkovic (1995) delineate several decisions and behaviors that precede divorce: the decision to divorce, the public announcement, discussions about material matters (money, property settlement, etc.) and discussions about legal matters (custody, support, visitation). However, divorce is not the only way a person becomes a single parent. According to Lino (1995), other transition events through

FIGURE 2. Variables Important to Establishing Quality of Life and Well-Being in Single Parent Families

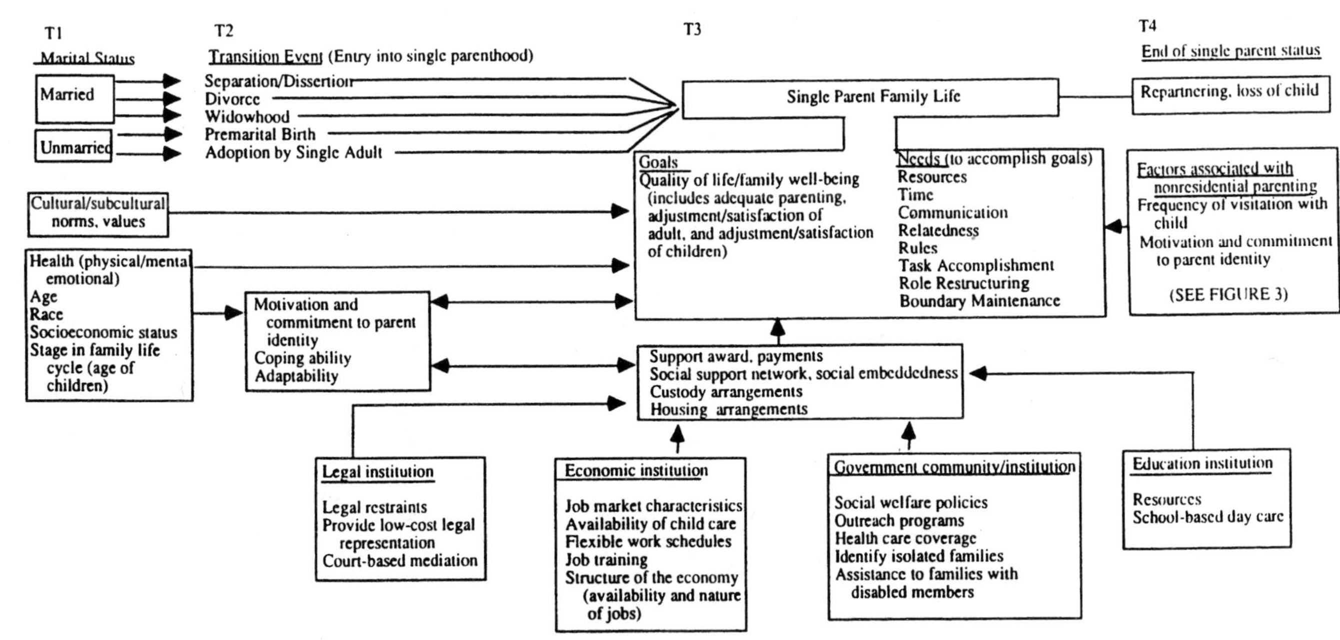

which a man or woman becomes a single parent are widowhood, separation/desertion, adoption, or premarital birth. Regardless of the transition event, once one assumes single parenthood status multiple factors influence family well-being.

Of particular import are the sex, age, socioeconomic status (including education, income, and occupation), and race of the parent. These all help to determine the standard of living and quality of life of single parent family members. Two other factors are important–the state of health of family members and stage in the family life cycle. When a member of the family is depressed, disabled, or mentally unstable, (e.g., mentally or physically disadvantaged) the quality of family life is affected. When single parents assume leadership of a family with a dependent and/or disabled child, they face different challenges than if the child is an adolescent or adult, and healthy (see Boyce et al., 1995). Whether the family contains infants or preschoolers, adolescents or young adults determines the type and number of social institutions with which the family interacts and/or looks to for assistance. These variables serve to collectively define the parameters within which single parenthood is enacted.

A critical factor that contributes to the well-being of family members is the motivation and commitment of residential parents to fulfill parenting roles with as much skill as possible given their particular individual characteristics and socialization. Other characteristics important to parents who are experiencing role strain, emotional hardship (including bereavement), and economic stress (often associated with single parenting) are adaptability, appraisal, and coping ability (Gass-Sternas, 1995).

Motivation to perform parenting roles is reinforced through the support network a parent develops. Support in the form of aid or assistance from relatives (e.g., child care, car and home maintenance and repairs), and financial support in the form of child support awards/payments from the child's father are part of this support. It also includes assistance from neighbors, friends, and those who make up a "wider family." It includes help from institutional sources, such as community outreach programs, counseling programs, Aid to Families with Dependent Children, legal aid, school-based child care programs, etc. The degree to which single parents are embedded in a social support network and have access to support from the community affects how successfully they are able to meet family goals.

Steinbock (1995) points out the economic factors that put a single parent on a trajectory towards homelessness. Inability to pay for adequate housing is a consequence of having few economic resources. This situation often results from the lack of support award/payments from the father (in the case of residential mothers) and/or unemployment. Several factors affect both opportunity and the decision to enter the work force. These include the availability of jobs and adequacy of wages, the nature or type of jobs available, whether there is job security, health and retirement benefits, and the opportunity for promotion and potential for training or further education. Provisions for child care preclude any decision regarding labor force participation. Other economic factors include the degree to which court ordered child support (or equally important, informal arrangements for support) is paid, and local and state policies regarding aid to families with dependent children. These all affect the life quality of non-employed single parents. Too often the consequence of a lack of adequate economic resources is eviction, homelessness, and foster care for children. Lino (1995) discusses the factors associated with poverty, such as being unmarried, and the unavailability and inadequacy of transfer payments and public assistant programs in the community. He also points to the critical nature of the availability of child care services, which in turn depend upon such factors as single parents' earnings, availability of social security, the structure of the divorce settlement, and, if the single parent is a mother, the circumstances of the father (including his economic and health status and his responsiveness to and identification with parenting roles).

The Role of Nonresidential Parent

The special circumstances of fathers as non-residential parents is discussed by Fox and Blanton (1995). These authors delineate a series of variables that influence the nature of postdivorce fathering, e.g., father's educational level, proximity to child's residence, time since divorce. However, these variables would appear to pertain to parenting by mothers as well as fathers who do not live with their children. While there are distinct and recognized differences in behavioral expectations and norms between women and men as parents, the list of variables–as variables–are not expected to differ by gender. That is, the variables that are hypothesized to influence the nonresidential parent-child relationship are similarly measured, although the conditions under which they are enacted may differ for men and women. Further, variable outcomes can be expected to differ because of different normative expectations for men and women. Because of their social roles, mothers may develop different parent-child relationships than fathers. Nevertheless, the parent-child relationship (as an example) is an identifiable, measurable variable that is expected to be an important factor influencing noncustodial parenting by mothers and fathers. The variables in Fox and Blanton's chapter are so salient that they are identified and listed in Figure 3.

A final part of the model that has not yet been discussed includes a set of needs that must be met if single parent families are to accomplish the goal of achieving a satisfactory degree of well-being and life quality. This list is derived from Horowitz (1995) who wrote about the parenting process in general; her discussion was not tied to a particular family structure. However, these variables are included in the model because it is believed that factors related to parenting are essential to any explanation of family well-being. Horowitz indicates the necessity of having (a) adequate resources (e.g., financial resources, social support); (b) adequate amounts of time to spend with children; (c) maintaining effective communication

FIGURE 3. Factors That Affect Noncustodial Parenting

Educational level of parent

Proximity to child's residence

Time since divorce

Remarriage

Legal mandates

- visitation privileges
- support award, payments
- custody disposition (solo, joint, split): includes physical (residential) and legal (decision-making); includes formal (de jure) and informal (de facto) custody

The parent-child relationship

Degree and type of contact with child

Communication pattern between parent and child

Involvement in decision-making

Relationship (autonomy versus connectedness) with former spouse; includes post-separation conflict

Power shift between parents; personal versus positional power

Alternative sources of support and social contact

Personal characteristics

Motivation to pay support and to assume parent roles

Degree of distress associated with attachment and separation

Psychological state, including stress, anger, depression, grief between family members; (d) developing and fostering attachments and trust among family members; (e) establishing rules that are clear and consistently yet flexibly enforced (taking into consideration special circumstances or changing conditions); (f) fulfilling parental tasks (including providing safety, meeting physical needs, assisting children to reach developmental milestones, modeling problem solving and coping strategies, teaching survival skills such as academic and occupational achievement, promoting self-esteem and a positive identity, and encouraging the development of a sense of personal values, life-meaning, and altruism); and (g) fulfilling the multiple roles associated with parenthood, including maintaining role boundaries.

Summary

The factors identified by Fox and Blanton (1995) are variables associated with the noncustodial parent, and are expected to influence the well-being of single parent family members. Next, attention is centered on summarizing the totality of variables that directly or indirectly impact the single/primary parent and his or her family. Many of these have already been discussed; they are only summarized here to show their mutual influence and interconnections, and to place them in a logical timeframe which begins with a time prior to the single parent family formation and ends with the loss of single-parent status. As mentioned earlier, these are institutional, interactional, and individual variables that are now placed within a temporal framework. It is stressed again that families cannot be separated from the environment in which they are embedded when well-being and quality of life is what is being explained.

Within any social system that constitutes an environment for a single parent family are a number of key institutions. These institutions are important elements of the network of relationships within which family members live and carry out their daily lives. Based upon the information provided in the chapters in this volume, there are several that are central to the well-being of single parent families. These were mentioned earlier in this chapter, and include the legal, economic, community (including government in the form of state and federal policy decisions), and educational institutions. The power of these institutions within the total social system, and the degree to which personnel serving in them are cognizant of and sensitive to the needs of single parent families affects the goals and outcomes of such families. These goals and outcomes are the ability to parent successfully and to have a high quality family life that produces well-adjusted adults and healthy, well-functioning children. Several factors that have already been mentioned impede or facilitate these goals and outcomes, including: cultural or subcultural norms and values, age and race of family members, socioeconomic standing within the community (influenced but not entirely determined by income, education, and occupation of the primary adult), mental and physical health of family members, and stage in the family life cycle. The individual factors already discussed (such as adaptability, coping ability, motivation and commitment to parent, and salience of parent role identity) are influenced and affected by these variables.

Nonresidential parents cannot be excluded from this process. Mothers and fathers who relinquish residential custody continue to influence the quality of life for those who live in single parent families. They are important because of their place in family history, because the residential parent often continues to be dependent upon them, at least financially, (especially if the nonresidential parent is a father), and because children continue to be mentally and emotionally tied to their parents, whether present or absent from the household.

Finally, those who work in the social institutions that serve American families have the power to heal or harm families, to ameliorate problems or exacerbate them. Institutional forces can affect a single parent's economic situation, social status, social support network, housing or living arrangements, and custody arrangements.

CONCLUSION

Before concluding this chapter, it seems advisable to recall the earlier attempt at synthesizing a body of empirical research on single parent families. In 1986, Hanson and Sporakowski edited a special issue on the single parent family for the journal *Family Relations*. In an epilogue to that issue, this author attempted to synthesize the empirical findings reported in that issue that explained the process whereby family members restructure their household (and the roles, norms, values, and status changes that accompany such restructuring) after becoming a single parent family. Variables that were deemed critical to the adjustment of single parent family members were identified by the authors in that volume. The dependent variable in that article was the adjustment of individual members, and the restructuring process more generally. Transition events, time, aspects of interpersonal relationships (e.g., communication, conflict) and community factors were the basic elements of analysis in the model that was developed. Variables were limited to those investigated in the empirical studies reported in the issue. Three core variables were identified as influencing the restructuring process–social support, economic resources, and psychological attributes. One can see that these variables also emerged as important determinants of the quality of family life and family well-being, the dependent variable in the present chapter. However, a key difference between the two articles is that most of the chapters in the present special volume were not based on empirical studies (thus empirical generalizations could not be generated). Rather most authors reviewed the literature pertinent to the many types of single parent families. This focus enlarged the scope of influential variables. As a result the present synthesis is broader and more inclusive. When considered jointly, the two pieces provide a comprehensive overview of single parenting.

On that basis the question formulated by the title of this chapter is raised again. Shall we speak of disparate voices that address the issues surrounding this particular family type? Or, rather, can this literature be viewed as a totality, with information on key variables and variable relationships collected and laid as the foundation upon which we now can begin to build a better understanding and more explicit explanations? From these efforts can we conclude we hear a long overdue chorus? This company of authors set out to discover and describe the many forms of single parent families. They delineated the multiple variables that affect the quality of life and well-being of members of these families. They did this for the purpose of explanation and elaboration. This chapter has attempted to show that they were not "going it alone." This information can indeed be said to constitute a chorus, one with a growing voice and in need of a methodological and theoretical orchestration.

AUTHOR NOTE

The author wishes to thank the editors of this special volume for their patience and helpful feedback on earlier versions of this paper. She is especially grateful to Valerie Jenness whose creativity helped break the inevitable writer's block.

REFERENCES

Arditti, J. A. (1995). Noncustodial parents: Emergent issues of diversity and process. In S. M. H. Hanson, M. L. Heims, D. J. Julian, & M. B. Sussman (Eds.), *Single parent families: Diversity, myths and realities. Marriage & Family Review, 20*, (1/2), 283-304.

Bianchi, S. M. (1995). The changing demographic and socioeconomic characteristics of single parent families. In S. M. H. Hanson, M. L. Heims, D. J. Julian, & M. B. Sussman (Eds.), *Single parent families: Diversity, myths and realities. Marriage & Family Review, 20*, (1/2), 71-97.

Bowen, G. L., Desimone, L. M. & McKay, J. K. (1995). Poverty and the single mother family: A macroeconomic perspective. In S. M. H. Hanson, M. L. Heims, D. J. Julian, & M. B. Sussman (Eds.), *Single parent families: Diversity, myths and realities. Marriage & Family Review, 20*, (1/2), 115-142.

Boyce, G. C., Miller, B. C., White, K., & Godfrey, M. K. (1995). Single parenting in families of children with disabilities. In S. M. H. Hanson, M. L. Heims, D. J. Julian, & M. B. Sussman (Eds.), *Single parent families: Diversity, myths and realities. Marriage & Family Review, 20*, (3/4), 389-409.

Bronfenbrenner, J. (1990). Discovering what families do. In D. Blankenhorn, A. Bayme, & J. B. Elshtain (Eds.), *Rebuilding the nest*. Milwaukee, WI: Family Service of America.

Burgess, J. (1995). Widowers as single fathers. In S. M. H. Hanson, M. L. Heims, D. J. Julian, & M. B. Sussman (Eds.), *Single parent families: Diversity, myths and realities. Marriage & Family Review, 20*, (3/4), 447-461.

Burton, L. M., Dilworth-Anderson, P., & Merriwether-deVries, C. (1995). Context and Surrogate Parenting Among Contemporary Grandparents. In S. M. H. Hanson, M. L. Heims, D. J. Julian, & M. B. Sussman (Eds.), *Single parent families: Diversity, myths and realities. Marriage & Family Review, 20*, (3/4), 349-366.

Donati, T. (1995). Single parents and wider families in the new context of legitimacy. In S. M. H. Hanson, M. L. Heims, D. J. Julian, & M. B. Sussman (Eds.), *Single parent families: Diversity, myths and realities. Marriage & Family Review, 20*, (1/2), 27-42.

Fox, G. L., & Blanton, P. W. (1995). Noncustodial fathers following divorce. In S. M. H. Hanson, M. L. Heims, D. J. Julian, & M. B. Sussman (Eds.), *Single parent families: Diversity, myths and realities. Marriage & Family Review, 20*, (1/2), 257-282.

Gass-Sternas, K. A. (1995). Single parent widows: Stressors, appraisal, coping, resources, grieving responses, and health. In S. M. H. Hanson, M. L. Heims, D. J. Julian, & M. B. Sussman (Eds.), *Single parent families: Diversity, myths and realities. Marriage & Family Review, 20*, (3/4), 411-445.

Greif, G. L. (1995). Single fathers with custody following separation and divorce. In S. M. H. Hanson, M. L. Heims, D. J. Julian, & M. B. Sussman (Eds.), *Single parent families: Diversity, myths and realities. Marriage & Family Review, 20*, (1/2), 213-231.

Hanson, S. M. H., Heims, M. L., Julian, D. J., & Sussman, M. B. (1995). Single Parent Families: Present and Future Perspectives. In S. M. H. Hanson, M. L. Heims, D. J. Julian, & M. B. Sussman (Eds.), *Single parent families: Diversity, myths and realities. Marriage & Family Review, 20*, (1/2), 1-25.

Herrerías, C. (1995). Noncustodial mothers following divorce. In S. M. H. Hanson, M. L. Heims, D. J. Julian, & M. B. Sussman (Eds.), *Single parent families: Diversity, myths and realities. Marriage & Family Review, 20* (1/2), 233-255.

Horowitz, J. A. (1995). A conceptualization of parenting: Examining the single parent family. In S. M. H. Hanson, M. L. Heims, D. J. Julian, & M. B. Sussman (Eds.), *Single parent families: Diversity, myths and realities. Marriage & Family Review, 20*, (1/2), 43-70.

Ihinger-Tallman, M. (1986). Member adjustment in single parent families: Theory building. *Family Relations, 35*(1), 215-221.

Jenness, V. (1993). Personal communication.

Julian, D. (1995). Resources for single parent families. In S. M. H. Hanson, M. L. Heims, D. J. Julian, & M. B. Sussman (Eds.), *Single parent families: Diversity, myths and realities. Marriage & Family Review, 20*, (3/4), 499-512.

Kimmons, L. C. (1995). Video/filmography on single parenting. In S. M. H. Hanson, M. L. Heims, D. J. Julian, & M. B. Sussman (Eds.), *Single parent families: Diversity, myths and realities. Marriage & Family Review, 20*, (3/4), 483-498.

Ladd, L. D., & Zvonkovic, A. (1995). Single mothers with custody following divorce. In S. M. H. Hanson, M. L. Heims, D. J. Julian, & M. B. Sussman (Eds.), *Single parent families: Diversity, myths and realities. Marriage & Family Review, 20*, (1/2), 189-211.

Lino, M. (1995). The economics of single parenthood: Past research and future directions. In S. M. H. Hanson, M. L. Heims, D. J. Julian, & M. B. Sussman (Eds.), *Single parent families: Diversity, myths and realities. Marriage & Family Review, 20*, (1/2), 99-114.

Marsiglio, W. (1995). Young nonresident biological fathers. In S. M. H. Hanson, M. L. Heims, D. J. Julian, & M. B. Sussman (Eds.), *Single parent families: Diversity, myths and realities. Marriage & Family Review, 20*, (3/4), 325-348.

Prater, L. (1995). Never married/biological teen mother headed household. In S. M. H. Hanson, M. L. Heims, D. J. Julian, & M. B. Sussman (Eds.), *Single parent families: Diversity, myths and realities. Marriage & Family Review, 20*, (3/4), 305-324.

Schlesinger, B. (1995). Single parent families: A bookshelf. In S. M. H. Hanson, M. L. Heims, D. J. Julian, & M. B. Sussman (Eds.), *Single parent families: Diversity, myths and realities. Marriage & Family Review, 20*, (3/4), 463-482.

Shireman, J. F. (1995). Adoptions by single parents. In S. M. H. Hanson, M. L. Heims, D. J. Julian, & M. B. Sussman (Eds.), *Single parent families: Diversity, myths and realities. Marriage & Family Review, 20*, (3/4), 367-388.

Steinbock, M. R. (1995). Homeless female-headed families: Relationships at risk. In S. M. H. Hanson, M. L. Heims, D. J. Julian, & M. B. Sussman (Eds.), *Single parent families: Diversity, myths and realities. Marriage & Family Review, 20*, (1/2), 143-159.

Trotter, B. B. (1989). *Coparental conflict, competition, and cooperation and parents' perception of their children's social-emotional well-being following marital separation.* Unpublished Doctoral dissertation, University of Tennessee, Knoxville.

Walters, L. H., & Abshire, C. R. (1995). Single parenthood and the law. In S. M. H. Hanson, M. L. Heims, D. J. Julian, & M. B. Sussman (Eds.), *Single parent families: Diversity, myths and realities. Marriage & Family Review, 20*, (1/2), 161-188.

Webster, A. M. (1972). Webster's Seventh New Collegiate Dictionary. Springfield, MA: G. & C. Merriam Company.

Chapter 25

From Stereotype to Archetype: Single Parent Families

Kris Jeter

KEYWORDS. Single parent families, Stereotypes, Greek Mythology, Christianity, Judaism, Archetype

When I was a child growing up in a small community in Colorado, there were a number of families with one parent. One friend and her siblings were being reared by her father because her mother had died in childbirth. The father expected my eleven-year-old friend to assume the mother role in entirety; she soon became pregnant by him.

Parents of a classmate divorced and he lived with his mother and three brothers. On the sly, the boys would visit their father. Years later, on my friend's wedding day, the mother refused to attend the ceremony because the father was invited.

Then, there was the scandal caused by the older sister of another classmate. Not only did she have a baby, but she then proceeded to rear the child without the benefit of marriage. With her head held high, she made no apologies or explanations. The town buzzed with gossip. Why didn't her father use a not-so-gentle persuasion to facilitate a "shot gun wedding?" Why didn't she marry just anyone, so "at least the child would have a name?"

Kris Jeter is a Principal in Beacon Associates Ltd., Inc., Newark, DE.

[Haworth co-indexing entry note]: "From Stereotype to Archetype: Single Parent Families." Jeter, Kris. Co-published simultaneously in *Marriage & Family Review* (The Haworth Press, Inc.) Vol. 20, No. 3/4, 1995, pp. 533-550; and: *Single Parent Families: Diversity, Myths and Realities* (ed: Shirley M. H. Hanson et al.) The Haworth Press, Inc., 1995, pp. 533-550. Multiple copies of this article/chapter may be purchased from The Haworth Document Delivery Center [1-800-3-HAWORTH; 9:00 a.m. - 5:00 p.m. (EST)].

Today, a generation later, these stories which were sensational at the time seem tame. Families headed by single parents are no longer just caused by death, divorce, or unplanned pregnancy. In western society, single parenthood is often now a conscious choice, indeed, a cognizant decision.

The media presents many sensational stories about the single parent. For instance, a thirty-five year old virgin chose to utilize artificial insemination to have two children. The already great popularity of Murphy Brown, a television character portrayed by Candace Bergen, increased because of Vice President Dan Quayle's insensitive comments. Quayle said that the character's choice to rear a child without a husband set an example of a "poverty of values" (Horyn, 1992).

Meanwhile in real life, Monaco's Princess Stephanie, the beautiful, glamorous, headstrong, and rich daughter of Princess Grace Kelley and Prince Rainier has had a son out of wedlock. The father is a former worker at the local fish market who had recently become the princess' bodyguard.

Today, my friends who are single parents live stories reflecting the contemporary times. One female corporate executive adopted a child in India. A divorced male physician rears three young children; his former wife felt uncomfortable with the role of both mother and wife. I feel greatly saddened for my woman friend, a high level bureaucrat, who married a man who already had children from a previous marriage. Her husband said bluntly that she could also have children, but not to expect anything from him. They all live together and he has kept up his side of the agreement. Although, he provided the sperm, he sits in his arm chair; being physically present, he is actually an absent father.

However, conscious choice regarding single parenthood is a luxury. The interplay of economics, famine, hatred, overpopulation, religion, politics, prejudice, science, technology, warfare is facilitating the increase of single parent families in at least three areas of the world. For instance, in Somalia, "warlords" steal food that is targeted for adults. Food intended for children does not please the tastes of the illegal market merchants. Thus, more adults are starving to death than children, leaving many children to live, if they are lucky, in families with one parent.

The Bosnian government has reported that in the first nine months of their war with Serbia, more than 30,000 Muslim women, aged twelve up, have been raped by Serbian soldiers. The women, many sexually inexperienced and single, are allegedly restrained in camps, humiliated and raped until they are visibly pregnant. The generation of children, many born to unmarried women, will tax the strength of mother love and familial pride (Maass, 1982).

In India, it is now common practice for pregnant women to undergo a sonagram in order to determine the sex of the fetus. Should the fetus be female and the woman be unable to pay $40 for an abortion, she risks alienation and exile. It is not uncommon for the mother and child to be murdered. Many mothers are abandoned to rear their girl child the best way they can.

When we are enthralled by a story it becomes a model for our life. We tell the story, we live the story. Faith, defined by Miller (1973) as "being gripped by the story," invariably searches for import, intent, significance, and substance. To recite poetry, weave stories, compose art is to express faith in the universe. To play music, perform in a play, to play with children is to recreate, to enjoy the cosmos. To rear a child–especially alone–in spite of unknown difficulties, expresses ultimate confidence in the future, the uttermost communion with humankind.

Possessing all the Kaiser's treasure
Could not add much to my pleasure.
You're my joy, my treasure fine,
Having you, the world is mine!
Sleep, my child,
Rest in your sleep,
Grow strong.
No diamonds and no precious things
Could stir my heart until it sings
You're my love, my treasure fine,
Having you, the world is mine!

–Jewish Ukrainian Lullaby
Israel Goldfarb

PURPOSE

Is there something or someone vitally missing in a single parent family? Stereotypical labels often describe the single parent as being irresponsible and negligent with an uncertain future. It is often deficiency instead of sufficiency which becomes the focus of the one parent family.

Historically, although inconsistent in itself, the family unit has always been under challenge; each loss, each death, each divorce or each gain, each birth, each marriage presents an opportunity for the family to reconstitute itself. Throughout it all, there is ideally a continuity of care that emerges from each family's life story.

In this analytic essay, I tell the stories of two ancient lineages, one based on Hesiod and one based on the Hebrew and Christian scriptures. These lineages are examined within the context of history plus societal and kinship norms. I then propose a schematic that may elevate our view of the single parent family from that of a stereotype of victimization to one of responsible archetype.

Lineage, predicated on mythology and delineated by heritage, tells us about the spiritual and historical foundation of a human group along with all family and social relationships. Lineages are often pictured as living trees with ever expanding branches, such as the Tree of Jesse, a popular theme of art in the Middle Ages. Rituals elicit and re-vitalize memories of ancestors. Kin strength is available at any time, by recitation, recollecting the past glories.

Stories in Greek mythology as well as the Hebrew and Christian scriptures provide varied characters, role models, and prototype options for living. Immersed in the depths of the human psyche is the universal, primordial, collective unconscious inhabited by archetypes, internal forces of energy which seek to organize the psyche's varied interactions and to sustain the ego consciousness. These archetypes are spontaneously expressed cross-culturally as vital life forces and archetypal images in art, fantasies, dreams, fairy tales, and myths. It is through the archetypal images that the human being reveals profound unconscious longings and yearnings (Jung, 1969).

A LINEAGE IN GREEK MYTHOLOGY

Around 730-700 BCE, one of the earliest known Greek poets, Hesiod recorded the lineage of Greek deities in "Theogony" and to a lesser extent in "Works and Days." Hesiod refers to three hundred gods and goddesses plus innumerable abstract concepts and environmental entities. The source of much of his genealogy is Babylonian and Hittite mythology. I invite you to read about this lineage, noting the single mothers and their progeny.

> Once upon a time, Uranus, the King of the Mountains, and Ge, Mother Earth, bore Titan children, a pre-Greek pantheon of nature deities. Uranus was afraid that his children would overthrow him and so shoved them back into Ge's womb. Ge persuaded her son, Cronus, the Crow, to fight his father. With a sickle, Cronus castrated Uranus.

Cronus was challenged by his sons, Hades, Poseidon, and Zeus. The three brothers easily defeated Cronus. The brothers drew lots to determine their respected domains. Hades ruled the underworld, Poseidon the waters, and Zeus the sky. Earth, especially Mt. Olympus, was a shared sphere. The sky, surrounding the underworld and waters was the most advantageous property and provided Zeus with innumerable opportunities to mate with anyone he desired.

Zeus' first wife was Metis, Wisdom. When Metis was pregnant with her second child, Zeus swallowed her whole, knowing that, as were his father and grandfather, he was in a prime position to be overthrown by his children. Metis' first born, Hephaestus split open Zeus' forehead from which Athena emerged in full armor. Thus, Greek mythology provided us with three generations of parent-child conflict and physical violence.

The second wife of Zeus was Themis or Divine Justice. They became the parents of the Fates, Human Justice, Peace, the Seasons, and Wise Laws.

Eurynome, a nymph of the ocean, was Zeus' third wife. The three Graces were their children.

Then, Zeus lusted after his sister, Demeter. She denied his advances. Zeus, in the form of a bull, raped Demeter. A daughter, Persephone was born from this sexual violation.

Zeus married Mnemosyne, Memory. The nine Muses were their children.

Zeus' wife of longest duration is Hera, the Protectress. At first, Hera was unimpressed by Zeus. So, Zeus transformed himself into a unkempt cuckoo bird. Hera sympathized with the bird and provided her breast as a sanctuary. Immediately, the bird reverted back into Zeus who had intercourse with Hera. To hide her condition, Hera married Zeus. The union was combative and long suffering because of Zeus' sexual appetite and Hera's resentment of Zeus' continuing affairs.

Zeus had an extramarital affair with Leto. Despite Hera's tormenting of Leto, two love children, Artemis and Apollo, were born.

One night, while Hera slept, Zeus had a sexual relationship with Maia. The result was Hermes, the messenger and trickster god. Still another affair was with Dione, who afterwards bore Aphrodite.

Another night, Zeus visited the mortal Theban Princess Semele. When Semele learned of her pregnancy, she bragged that Zeus was the father. Hera, disguised as a nurse, asks Semele how she knew that Zeus was the father and recommended asking him to show himself to her. Zeus had promised Semele any wish, and heavyheartedly fulfilled her request. The brilliance of his true self torched Semele to death. Zeus sewed her fetus in his thigh and in time Dionysus was born.

Other women with whom Zeus had extramarital affairs include Leda, Io, Europa. He also lusted after boys, such as Ganymede.

THE LINEAGE OF JESUS

In chapter one of Matthew, the first book of the Christian scripture, the lineage of Jesus is set forth. Forty-two generations of male progenitors from Abraham in the Hebrew scripture to Joseph in the Christian scripture are listed. Only four women are named. The biographies of three of the women indicate that they were single parents, at least for a portion of their lives. Moreover, the behavior of each of these women is less than conventional and exemplifies the virgin archetype. I invite you to read a story of the lineage of Jesus, noting the attributes of his female ancestors.

> Once upon a time, approximately 3000 years ago, when the Philistines had stolen the sacred Ark of the Covenant, the charismatic Judge Samuel facilitated the unification and self-defense of Israel under King David. Since then, Jews have long awaited the coming of the Messiah, a savior who will attain for Israel the blessings of the prophets. This Messiah will teach the Torah, defeat enemies, restore the land, promote spiritual bliss.
>
> A thousand years ago, Yeshua ben Yussef was born to Mary and Joseph. Jesus lived 32 years, told spellbinding parables about a loving, practical lifestyle, performed miracles, spoke against the foreign Roman rulers, and ultimately was crucified by them. Jews still await the coming of the Messiah who will stimulate the observance of the old laws and, thereby, save the world-at-large.
>
> Meanwhile, a major world religion developed, recognizing Jesus as the Messiah who had brought a new law to override the old law. Isaiah, Samuel, and other books of the Hebrew scripture were utilized to construct the genealogy of Jesus from Abraham to Joseph. Four women are designated.
>
> Tamar was named. Tamar was the wife of the Er and Onan, Judah's elder sons. Er and Onan died prematurely, before Tamar could conceive a child. Judah refused to provide her with a child. So, Tamar camouflaged herself as a professional harlot so that she could lure Judah into a sexual relationship which produced the twins

Phares and Zerah. Phares and his parents were honored as ancestors of Jesus (Genesis 38:6, 11, 13-30; Ruth 4:12; 1 Chr. 2:4).

Rahab, the most conspicuous prostitute in the Hebrew scripture, was named. Rahab lived with her family on Jericho's city wall. She was instrumental in providing the intelligence information required for the capture of Jericho by the Israelites. After the fall of Jericho, Rahab and her family were invited to live in the safety of the nation of Israel. She and Salmon were the parents of Boaz. They were honored as ancestors of Jesus (Josh. 2:1-21; 6-22-23, 25).

Ruth from Moab was named. Ruth traveled with her mother-in-law Naomi to Bethlehem. There, Ruth, followed Naomi's instructions, gleaning the leftover barley and wheat of the fields of her dead husband's well-to-do kinsman, Boaz. During a harvest celebration, Ruth lay down at the feet of Boaz as he slept on the threshing floor. When Boaz awoke, he was astonished to find Ruth. She declared to him, "spread your skirt over your maidservant, for you are next to kin" (Ruth 3:9). Boaz recommended that they enact the proper procedure for the redeeming of her dead husband's lineage. After conducting this legal ceremony, they married and became the parents of Jesse (Book of Ruth). They were honored as ancestors of Jesus.

Bathsheba was named. Bathsheba was the wife of a Hittite officer, Uriah. One night King David looked down from his palace on the hill upon the community. There he saw the beautiful Bathsheba bathing upon the roof of her house. While Uriah was on campaign, King David invited Bathsheba to the palace. They fell in love and she became pregnant. King David arranged leave for Uriah; Uriah refused to sleep with Bathsheba because it would be a luxury not afforded his troops on the battlefield. Thus, King David ordered a military maneuver which would insure the death of Uriah. The first child of Bathsheba and David died; however, their second son Solomon lived to be king (2 Sam. 11:3, 12:24; 1 Kings 1-2; 1 Chro. 3:5; Ps. 51 title). They were honored as ancestors of Jesus.

CONTEXTUAL BACKGROUND

Ancients would listen to stories, look upon art, participate in rituals within the context of the time and place. We can develop an empathy with and sensibility about varied cultures which can facilitate our reading of these lineages with the eyes of the original beholders. This enhanced knowledge base can assist us to contemplate the virgin as an archetype for single parent families.

Joseph Campbell (1964) has proposed that the age of heroes for both the ancient Greeks and Jews were concurrent. Between 1250 and 1150 BCE, established subsistence farmers were met by waves of animal herders. Accounts of the era were recorded around 850 BCE as the *Iliad* in Greek literature and the Yahwist (J) text of the Book of Judges of the Hebrew scripture. Around one hundred years later, the *Odyssey* and the Elohim (E) text were written. It is interesting to note the differences in remembering and recording of the heroic past when humans could communicate with their deity; the Greeks utilized poetry and the Jews developed a code of laws.

GREEK POETRY

In Greek poetry, Zeus is actually the Thunder God of the Zagros mountains who with each Aryan invasion sweeps westward across Asia and the Mediterranean Sea. The history of the invasions of animal herders with a Thunder God becomes incorporated into the poetic mythology. The invader's mythology was intermixed with the indigenous mythology through Zeus' mating with the local goddess of each geographic site.

Mythologically, Zeus was considered the powerful chair of the board with headquarters on Mt. Olympus. The ancient Greeks preferred to think of Zeus as being the legal husband of Hera and the entertainer of a multitude of mistresses as well as young men.

Historically, human kinships began to mirror the Dorian military invasions and Zeus' sexual conquests. There was a change from matrilineal to patrilineal succession. Males become concerned, if not obsessed with knowing which children were biologically theirs so that land, rights, and privileges could be appropriated as they saw fit.

Chastity became an attribute of womanhood which male relatives by birth (and later by marriage) jealously insisted upon and assiduously guarded. For the unrelated males, the chaste female became wild game to tame, the animal to pursue, the instinct to chase, the blossom to deflower, a prize to own–if only to possess once for the fleeting moment of her initial coitus. Indeed, the Greek word for wife, *damar*, has as its root meaning, "to subdue, to tame" (Keuls, 1985, 6).

Keuls (1985) has analyzed the relationship between male social power, enactment of violent acts, and fear of women that prevailed in Athens until 430 BCE, the end of the age of Pericles. A favorite theme in the arts, the slaughter of female Amazons by Greek men, illustrates the predominant male psyche of the time.

Early in the sixth century BCE, Solon established the city of Athens upon the concept of democracy–for free-born males, that is. Laws were codified which suppressed female sexuality for the benefit of the male and his family. Unchaste, unmarried girls could be sold by their fathers into slavery. Prostitutes were organized into state-run brothels and prices were determined by the state. Prostitutes were used by men for occasional diversion, concubines for regular satisfaction of physical needs, and wives for bearing legitimate children and caring for possessions. There was a police force for women and another police force for children.

JEWISH LAW

Six hundred and thirteen laws were written within the literature of the Hebrew scripture. Savina J. Teubal (1984, 1990) has analyzed these laws in light of archaeological and linguistic evidence and identified five characteristics of the matriarchal social environment in Genesis, circa eighteenth to sixteenth centuries BCE.

1. Rigorous ordinances prescribed family membership. Primary families consisted of uterine siblings.

2. Because ancestry was determined by matrilineal descent, endogamy or marriage of a woman to a brother by her father could occur.

3. Ultimogeniture has been noted as a pattern in both the literature of Genesis and in the ethnography of matrilineal descent; the youngest received the legacy.

4. In this matrilocal society, the man when married relocated from his home to live with his wife in an extended family of kindred women and their spouses.

5. Sororal polygyny occurred in matrilocal families with a limited number of progeny. To compensate for small family size, two or more sisters married one man. Thus, he was charged by a number of marriage contracts to support this kinship network and future born children.

Carol Meyers (1988), through in-depth studies of anthropology, archaeology, Hebrew scripture, and sociology, has reconstructed the social organization and familial roles of pre-monarchy Israel and Judah, the Iron I period dating twelfth and eleventh century BCE. The twelve tribes of Jacob were the larger, political-social units. Each tribe was composed of fifty clans. The clan (*mispahah or 'eleph*) was the social and political unit which addressed such issues as land allocation, grants, and defense. This was also the group from which endogamous mates were selected for marriage.

The household (*bayit*) or extended family (*bet'ab or bet'em*) was a self-sufficient co-residential social unit consisting of a dozen familial and non-familial members. Intermarriage was common in early Israel. The talents of each member of the family were valued. Moreover, the worship of a wide variety of deities was allowed by the foreign-born wives. Divine assistance from any realm was welcomed.

Meyers proposes that tasks were delegated according to age and season. Each job was essential to the survival of the household. Thus, members were interdependent upon each other. Women were active and valued in generating, apportioning, and processing foodstuffs. They also produced for their own personal use, as well as for sale and trade, fabric, clothing, perfume, and perhaps, pottery.

In Proverbs, the roles of both the father and the mother are delineated; the primary task for each parent is to educate their children. Hebrew was the first language in the Near East to have an alphabet with a reduced number of letters. Thus, reading and writing an alphabet of only 22 letters was a skill any person could acquire.

The word for husband (*ba'al*) also means owner. Descent was patrilineal. An estate of rocky, hilly land required a particular knowledge base of how to survive utilizing to best advantage the available water supply while adapting to each change of temperature, wind force and direction. This specific information was passed from father to son.

Exogamy encouraged women to be autonomous, yet adaptable; independent while interdependent. Women were responsible for the future generations of the household, family, tribe, and nation. The inclusion of stories about prophetesses and wise women in the Hebrew scripture indicates that they did indeed live and were valued. Wisdom (*hokma*) was depicted as a woman, a colleague of God, source of education, enlightenment, morality, and veracity.

Intermarriage and acceptance of the foreign partner's religion was a tradition through many centuries. *Teraphim* were female statues used by the Babylonians and Israelites for divination (Ezek. 21:21; Judges 17:5; 18:14-20). Rachel and Micah felt it important to keep *teraphim* within their possession (Genesis 31; Judges 17:1-13; 18:1-31). It was only in 658 BCE that King Josiah destroyed all profane altars and cult objects from the Temple and outlawed heathen shrines (2 Kings 23).

By 538 BCE, intermarriage was decreed illegal. Jews returning from exile in Babylon were ordered by Ezra, the Hebrew priest and scribe, to divorce "foreign wives" (Ezra 10:10-11).

To this day, the 613 laws plus commentaries are studied. Day-to-day living by the laws was a desirable goal of behavior. Lineal descent is considered through the mother.

I was recently reminded of the matrilineal tradition. One cool spring night in 1992, I stood dressed very warmly, thus conservatively, in line at a bank of outdoor public telephones in Jerusalem. A gentleman clothed as a Hassidic Jew with long curls and a hat framing his face began to converse with me. He questioned me about my life and seemed pleased with the answers; I was in Israel studying ritual pilgrimages. He then asked if my mother was Jewish. I shall always wonder if the gentleman was simply being hospitable to the traveler, if he were curious and practicing his English, or if he was matchmaking for himself or another man!

The genealogy of Jesus set forth in Matthew is male-oriented. It is not matrilineal. Women are mentioned in less than one-tenth of the generations listed. Moreover, the more favored feminine archetypes of the Hebrew scripture, often utilized as positive role models, such as Sarah, Leah, Rachel, and Rebecca are neglected. Rather, archetypal renegade women are presented.

Tamar, Rahab, Ruth, and Bathsheba each do what they believe to be correct for themselves and family members. Tamar and Ruth are concerned with the lineage of their dead husbands. Rahab becomes a spy and insures a safe home for her family. Bathsheba follows her heart, knowing that public stoning could well result. Rahab is a prostitute and Tamar pretends to be a prostitute–which may well attest to the popularity of this way of life. All four women could well be non-Israelites.

Authorship of the Book of Matthew is attributed to Matthew, a tax collector and one of the twelve disciples. Today, a large number of Biblical scholars indicate that the Book of Matthew was not written by a contemporary of Jesus. The author's prime intentions were concurrent with Greek Christian theologians of second century CE–to indicate that Jesus plus the Christian faith and law was a fulfillment of prophecies in the Hebrew scripture. Thus, Greek traditions of patrilineage and interest in parthenogenesis were woven with the texts of the Hebrew scripture and information from the Book of Mark to create the Book of Matthew.

The lineages in Greek mythology and the Book of Matthew were read by ancients within the context of their lives. Joseph Campbell (1964) proposed that both the Greeks and the Jews experienced their age of heroes during the same time span, from 1250 to 1150 BCE. Greeks responded with poetry and Jews responded with laws.

Between 1250 BCE and 300 CE, Greece lived through the Dark Age, the Aristocratic Age, the Persian Wars, the Classical Age, the Peloponnesian War, the Macedonian Age, and Roman occupation. Meanwhile, Israel experienced the Period of the Judges, Philistine invasions, the united monarchy, the destruction of the First Temple, exile in Babylon, the building of the Second Temple, the Hellenistic and Maccabean Period, and the Roman occupation. With each interaction with the outside world, social expression broadens. Greek law and Jewish poetry are inevitable outcomes.

Throughout it all, the primordial wonderment about the creation of the human, the respect and even (for the Greeks) *fear* of the mother who was able to conceive and rear a child no matter what the obstacles, was safeguarded as a precious memory not to be disturbed in the human psyche. The etymological roots of the Greek word for wife, *damar*, to subjugate and the Hebrew word for husband, *ba'al*, to own, give us significant information about the single mother; she would not be subjugated or owned! Her independence was admired and even revered. Sacred lineages retained references to the archetypes of the virgin and parthenogenesis and were read within the context of awe.

ACCURATE TRANSLATION OF TERMINOLOGY

Since childhood, I have been curious about the survival over the past two thousand years of the Greek cosmogony and the genealogy of Jesus. Not only have these stories continued through time, but they are classics known to almost every person. The Greek cosmogony clearly stars Zeus, a man who not only has lust in his heart, but satisfied his every passion through incest, rape, shapeshifting, and in other possible ways. The genealogy of Jesus in the Book of Matthew clearly acknowledges four women whose biographies in today's culture might have been sanitized by cultural sensitivity.

I propose that the deep memory of the archetypes of the virgin and parthenogenesis appear to have kept these lineages intact. Humans have long had a deep need to know that they had a very strong mother and were born despite all odds. Ancients entertained and welcomed the potential and even probable appearance of the polymorphous virgin, especially when called upon in time of need. Later translators narrowed and restricted, and moreover befuddled and confounded the role of the virgin.

Children have often been perplexed with the concept of the virgin birth. "How is it possible?", the genuinely naïve or the class clowns ask. Teachers without a background in cross-cultural mythology or Greek and Hebrew linguistics attempt to answer questions the best way they know how, often emphasizing moral values of chastity.

The Hebrew word, *almah*, and the Greek word, *parthenos*, are accurately translated as an unmarried female who may or may not be sexually chaste. The Hebrew word for sexually chaste female is *basala* (when pronounced by Ashkenazi) or *btula'* (when pronounced by Sephardi).

Isaiah 7:14 was incorporated into Matthew 1:23 to be a cornerstone verse in Christianity: "Behold! a virgin shall conceive, and bear a son, and shall call his name Emmanuel: God with us." In the King James Version of 1610 CE, the word *almah* in Isaiah 7:14 was interpreted to mean virgin. Centuries of commentary and art repeated the error. For instance, George F. Handel popularized the verse in a recitative for alto in his oratorio, *The Messiah.* In 1901, scholars translating The Revised Standard Version correctly defined *almah* as young woman.

Parthenogenesis is a word derived from the Greek words *parthenos* meaning unmarried woman and *genesis* meaning birth. Major world religions such as Buddhism, Christianity, Hinduism, and Zoroastrianism, base a significant portion of their doctrine on parthenogenesis. Egyptian and Orphic myths, and much of the world's folklore, contain stories of parthenogenesis. Parthenogenesis speaks to the beholder of the possibilities of new beginnings. The virgin archetype is the independent core, the original essence, the free spirit who animates the wind, the breath, and lets flow the beginning of a new world where anything is possible.

THE VIRGIN ARCHETYPE

> What then do we mean by "virgin?" It may help us to examine those ways in which we use the word which are not directly concerned with sex. We speak of a "virgin forest" as being one in which the powers of nature are untrammelled and untouched by man.
>
> –John Layard
> *The Incest Taboo and the Virgin Archetype*

The word virgin, means a woman who does not allow herself to be the possession of any man. She regenerates by yielding and surrendering to the summons of instinct. She is private and solitary, comfortable within herself, responding to the alternate creative and chaotic challenges of nature. By being hospitable to every stranger, treating every unknown person as a god-in-hiding, she receives their precious gifts of life and constantly renews her spirit.

The virgin goddess is a goddess because of her own actions, not because of her relationship with a man. She may elect to entertain and present herself to a number of lovers; she never allows herself to be mastered or possessed. Thus, the virgin goddesses of the Greek pantheon and Mary, mother of Jesus are all unmarried women. The identity of the virgin is associated with biological instinct rather than the legal state of matrimony. Divinely created nature, not human decreed law is important to the archetypal virgin.

Women call upon the virgin archetype, for instance, Artemis and Mary, to open wombs, to facilitate fertility and safe childbirths. Fecundity, not marriage, is the virgin's domain. Their primary goal is autonomous independence, rather than domestic mergers.

Virgins are often mothers. Pregnancy and the mother role are actually an induction ritual for the virgin. She must egress before she can bloom. Only when one chooses to experience the option of being impeded, encumbered, obstructed, can one fully experience ease, exposure, and openness. Only when a woman has held two souls within her body and felt the ultimate separation, can a woman be fully integral.

The major concern is not about paternity. The body of the virgin is the sacred temple for the worship of the numinous. Herein, the soul meets nature, instinct is transmuted into spirit. The virgin mother is whole unto herself; the virgin born child is likewise a complete organism.

Rejection and renouncement are required for emancipation and freedom. Inspiration and creativity grow because the virgin recognizes and accepts personal strengths. Attributes of the virgin may well be a key for unlocking the single parent from its restrictive, negative stereotype.

CONCLUSION

Is there something or someone vitally missing in a single parent family? Stereotypical labels often describe the single parent as being irresponsible and negligent with an uncertain future. It is often deficiency instead of sufficiency which becomes the focus of the one parent family.

More and more humans in the nineteenth and twentieth centuries are choosing or are forced by economic and social forces to parent a family alone, at least for an unknown period of time. During the Industrial Revolution in England, social critics noted the increased number of single parents. They declared that the phenomenon was one example of the assault of mass industrialization upon the fragility of community and humankind.

Until the last decade, South Korea was an adoption haven for Western parents. Young girls would travel from the countryside to work in Seoul's factories, become pregnant, receive excellent prenatal health care, and then present their baby for adoption. When the nation was under the scrutiny of the international press core gathered for the Olympics, Korean officials simply decided to prohibit international adoption. Young single mothers cope the best they can.

In the United States, the number of inner city teen pregnancies keeps rising. Children are having children, often without the support of a kin network. Is modernity causing an increase of unwed mothers? Could adolescent pregnancy be an unconscious fulfillment, albeit the darkened shadow side, of the ancient virgin archetype (Benedict)? I believe that lineages presented in ancient literature and contemporary life stories provide an archetype with positive attributes, a reference point of strength for single parents.

We live in the family concurrently as a social group and a mythological story. We can face the unknown future with archetypal images, re-create our own lineage, tell our stories to transform fear into love. One exemplary program of social artistry for inner city teen parents utilizes the sharing of recent lineages of the archetypal virgin and parthenogenesis to facilitate the elevation of the quality of life for the women with whom they work. This program is called *Mama Said* and was founded and is administered by Helen Finner (1991).

Helen Finner raised six children and currently is rearing her five-year old granddaughter in an apartment in a public housing complex in Chicago, Illinois. One day when Finner was walking outside her apartment house, she saw a young mother with two crying children. Finner listened to the adolescent's problems, comforted her, told her stories of her own personal life as a single mother. It occurred to Finner that in the small towns in rural America, there is a sense of community; aunts and grandmothers tell girls how to be autonomously independent and young mothers how to be a mother.

In the city, there are mixed signals. The teenage girl is told to be dynamic, to get straight A's by her mother. Often, the mother is working long hours and under great pressure to make ends meet. The adolescent girl is alone and gets attention from a young man, often leading to pregnancy.

In 1991, Finner founded *Mama Said*, a social action program for adolescent mothers housed in ground floor office space in five public housings facilities in Chicago. She sees young mothers and young grandmothers who have not benefited from hearing their kinfolk tell stories of the independent woman and the self-sufficient mother. Finner believes that child abandonment, abuse, and infant deaths are due to the frustration of being alone physically, and moreover without the stories of familial lineages. Finner's message is, "I had no one to help me as a single mother and I succeeded. You can succeed. Make up your mind that you want the best for your children."

Social worker and mother, Tanya Stewart, has joined and expanded *Mama Said*. Girls participate in rap sessions and life skills classes. *Mama Said* is a form of initiation; a focus point is created and questions of "Where are you now?" and "Where do you want to be?" are asked. The wisdom and love of the virgin archetype across the ages is transmitted to this generation of women living out the millennia old story, transforming the mothers, their children, and society. *Mama Said* is providing a context for the adolescent pregnancy, presiding over an ancient archetypal induction ritual for the virgin.

Admittedly, the virgin archetype is confusing to us today. (The self-publicizing rock and movie star, Madonna, has done nothing to heal the chasm.) The virgin archetype is chaste *and* pregnant. She isolates herself and welcomes the unknown. She is secure in herself, following her biological nature, ignoring human written law. Within her, spirit is constantly being manifested from instinct.

Academic contemplation leading to social action on the issues of single parenthood is a fertile area for research. Single parenthood can be uplifted to the level of archetype; indeed, it need not be viewed as a stereotype. Social artists may wish to frame programs for pregnant adolescents and teen mothers within the time-honored lessons of the virgin archetype and parthenogenesis. Social commentators may do well to recognize that choice by responsible adults to bear and rear children alone is an ancient tradition and worthy of praise today in the light of its time-honored integrity.

> Is a family like an island?
>
> I wonder, as I hang the sea green curtains my mother chose 30 years ago, and which still seem fresh. No, a family keeps on growing, controlling new points of land and experience, stretching out to lives no one–even one who can read the weather from a flagpole–could ever predict. And yet, a family is like an island; a sustaining place of return nestled in the wide blue world where one is at home with what one knows and celebrates.
>
> – Kim Waller
>
> *Thoughts of Home: A Family, An Island*

REFERENCES

Benedict, Elizabeth. (6 February 1993). Personal communication. Port Jervis, NY: Foundation for Mind Research.

The Bible, (1901, 1971). Revised Standard Version. London, England: The British and Foreign Bible Society.

Campbell, Joseph. (1964). *The Masks of God: Occidental Mythology.* Volume III. New York, NY: The Viking Press, 146 in 1984 edition.

Finner, Helen and Tanya Stewart. (Thursday 14 November 1991). *CBS News Nightwatch on Mama Said.* Interview by Christopher Matthews. Washington, D.C.: CBS News Division.

Goldfarb, Israel. (1934). The Jewish lullaby. *The Jewish Woman: Background, Foreground, Prospects*. The Jewish Library. Third Series. Leo Jung (Ed.). New York, NY: The Jewish Library Publishing Company. Chapter XII, 313-325.

Goldstein, Sidney. (9 August 1992). Classical sources. *The Jewish Idea of the Messiah: 5752 Tisha B'Ab Program*. Philadelphia, PA: Congregation Mikveh Israel.

Gottwald, Norman K. (1979). *The Tribes of Yahweh: A Sociology of the Religion of Liberated Israel, 1250-1050 BCE*. Maryknoll, NY: Orbis Books.

Hall, Nor. (1980). *The Moon and the Virgin: Reflections of the Archetypal Feminine*. New York, NY: Harper and Row.

Handel, George F. (1912). Number 8–Recitative for Alto: 'Behold! A virgin shall conceive.' *The Messiah*. T. Tertius Noble (Ed.). New York, NY: G. Schirmer, Inc.

Harding, M. Esther. (1971). *Woman's Mysteries: Ancient and Modern, A Psychological Interpretation of the Feminine Principle as Portrayed in Myth, Story, and Dreams*. New York, NY: Harper and Row.

Hesiod. (1967). "Theogony." *The Homeric Hymns and Homerica*. Evelyn-White, Hugh G., (Translator). Cambridge, MA: University Press.

Hesiod. (1967). "Works and Days." *The Homeric Hymns and Homerica*. Evelyn-White, Hugh G. (Translator). Cambridge, MA: University Press.

The Holy Bible. King James Version. Cleveland, OH: The World Publishing Company.

Horyn, Cathy. (28 September-4 October 1992). Single parenthood: The best choice I ever made: Why is my life being reduced to a stereotype? *The Washington Post National Weekly Edition*. (9:48) 25.

Jeter, Kris. (1992). The spirit of home. *The Journal of Couple Therapy*. (3:1).

Jeter, Kris. (1993). The heart of the story: Mythology in service of the past, contemporary, and future family. *Families Look Toward the Future: Planning for Challenge and Change. Marriage & Family Review*. (18:3,4).

Jung, Carl G. (1969). *The Archetypes and the Collective Unconscious*. Second Edition. R. F. C. Hull (Translator). Princeton, NJ: Princeton University Press.

Ladwig, Michael. (6 February 1993). Personal communication. Port Jervis, NY: Foundation for Mind Research.

Layard, John. (1972). The incest taboo and the virgin archetype. *The Virgin Archetype*. New York, NY: Spring Publication. 290.

Maass, Peter. (4-10 January 1993). In Bosnia's dirty war, rape is a weapon. A Muslim schoolgirl, 17, describes how she was assaulted by a Serbian warlord. *The Washington Post National Weekly Edition*. (10:10) 17.

McGrory, Mary. (15-21 February 1993). What to do about parents of illegitimate children: To begin with, stop legitimatizing their behavior. *The Washington Post National Weekly Edition*. (10:16) 25.

Mendelsohn, I. (1948). The Family in the ancient near east. *The Biblical Archaeologist*. (XI: 2) 24-40.

Meyers, Carol (1988). *Discovering Eve: Ancient Israelite Women in Context*. New York, NY: Oxford University Press.

Miller, David L. (1973). *Gods and Games: Toward a Theology of Play.* NY: Harper and Row, Colophon Books. 164 ff.

Patai, Raphael. (1979). *The Messiah Texts.* Detroit, MI: Wayne State University Press.

Stroud, Joanne and Gail Thomas (Eds.). (1982). *Images of the Untouched.* Dallas, TX: Spring Publications, Inc.

Teubal, Savina J. (1990). *Hagar the Egyptian: The Lost Tradition of the Matriarchs.* San Francisco, CA: Harper and Row.

Teubal, Savina J. (1984). *Sarah the Priestess: The First Matriarch of Genesis.* Athens, OH: Swallow Press.

Waller, Kim. (September 1992). Thoughts of home: A family, an island. *House Beautiful.* 12, 16.

Woodman, Marion. (1985). *The Pregnant Virgin: A Process of Psychological Transformation.* Toronto, Canada: Inner City Press, p. 24.

Index

Page numbers in *italics* indicate figures; page numbers followed by t indicate tables.

Biographical Sketch of Authors

Carla Rae Abshire, BS

Carla Rae Abshire is a graduate student in the Department of Child and Family Development at The University of Georgia in Athens, GA. She received training as a legal assistant at the National Center for Paralegal Training in Atlanta, Georgia in 1988 and a Bachelor of Science degree at the University of Georgia in 1991. Her research interests include sexual abuse, cognitive development, legal requirements for competence to testify, and children and families and the law.

Joyce A. Arditti, PhD

Joyce A. Arditti is an Assistant Professor in the Department of Family and Child Development at Virginia Polytechnic Institute and State University in Blacksburg, Virginia. She received a Doctorate in Family Studies (University of North Carolina, Greensboro, 1988). Her research interests include noncustodial parents, patterns of father involvement, postdivorce, and divorced mothers' adjustment and parenting. Dr. Arditti is a member of the National Council on Family Relations and the International Society of the Study of Personal Relationships. She is on the editorial board for *Family Relations*. She has authored articles about divorced parents in *Family Relations*, *Journal of Marriage and the Family*, *American Journal of Orthopsychiatry*, *Journal of Divorce & Remarriage*, and *Conciliation Courts Review*.

Suzanne M. Bianchi, PhD

Suzanne M. Bianchi is a Demographer in the Housing and Household Economic Statistics Division of the U.S. Bureau of the Census. She received her Ph.D. in Sociology from the University of Michigan in 1978. Her current research focuses on the educational progress and economic well-being of children, gender inequality, and family compositional change. She is a member of the Population Association of America, the American Sociological Association, and the National Council on Family Relations. Her publications include: *Household Composition and Racial Inequality*, 1981, Rutgers University Press; *American Women in Transition*

(Bianchi and Spain), 1986, Russell Sage; *Family Disruption and Economic Hardship*; "The Short-Run Picture for Children" (Bianchi and McArthur), 1991, *Current Population Reports*; and "America's Children: Mixed Prospects," 1990, *Population Bulletin.*

Priscilla White Blanton, EdD

Priscilla White Blanton, Ed.D. is a Professor in the Department of Child and Family Studies at The University of Tennessee in Knoxville, TN where she received her Doctorate in Counseling Psychology. In 1992 she received the Arch of Achievement award from The College of Human Ecology for her outstanding contributions to teaching, research, and the direction of doctoral students. Her research interests include issues of families and stress. Of particular interest have been the ways in which families experience work-related stressors. She recently completed a national study of clergy families and work related stressors. She is currently initiating a study of power and marital relationships.

Gary L. Bowen, PhD, ACSW

Gary L. Bowen, PhD, ACSW is the William R. Kenan Distinguished Professor and Co-Chair of the Ph.D. Program in the School of Social Work at the University of North Carolina at Chapel Hill. He received his Ph.D. in Child Development and Family Relations from the University of North Carolina at Greensboro, and his MSW from the University of North Carolina at Chapel Hill. Under contract with the U.S. Department of Health and Human Services, he recently completed an investigation of the influence of the availability of subsidized daycare on the welfare independency of low-income parents with preschool children. Dr. Bowen, with colleagues, has designed a self-report instrument to monitor and assess the social context of middle school and high school students who have been identified as "at risk" for school dropout. His books include *Navigating the Marital Journey*, published by Praeger in 1991, his published articles appear in *Marriage & Family Review, Family Relations, Journal of Marriage and the Family,* and *Journal of Family and Economic Issues.*

Glenna C. Boyce, PhD

Glenna C. Boyce is a Research Associate at the University Affiliated Center for Persons with Disabilities and an Adjunct Professor in the Department of Family and Human Development at Utah State University in Logan, Utah. She received her Doctorate degree in Family and Human Development from Utah State University in 1990. Her professional associations include the National Council on Family Relations, the National Association for the Education of Young Children, and the Society for Research in Child Development. Her research interests are parent-child interaction and sibling relationships, particularly in families of children with disabilities. She is also involved in research concerning early intervention services for children with disabilities and medically fragile infants.

Jane K. Burgess, PhD

Jane K. Burgess is Professor Emeritus of Sociology at the University of Wisconsin-Waukesha, where she has taught since 1967. She received her Ph.D. in 1972 from the University of Illinois at Champaign-Urbana. She has authored "The widower as father," in *Dimensions of Fatherhood* (1985); "Widowers," in *Variant Family Forms* (1988); *The Widower* (1978), *Straight Talk About Love and Sex for Teenagers* (1979); and *The Single-Again Man* (1988). Her research interests include the single parent family, widowhood, divorce, the effects of death and/or divorce on the emotional development of children, and family relationships as they contribute to obesity. She has been a long-time member of the National Council on Family Relations, and a member of the board of directors of the Wisconsin Council on Family Relations since 1975.

Linda M. Burton, PhD

Linda M. Burton is Professor of Human Development and Sociology at The Pennsylvania State University. She is a former Brookdale Fellow, National Institutes of Mental Health (NIMH) Fellow, and a Fellow at the Center for Advanced Study in the Behavioral Sciences at Stanford University. Her Research focuses on studying the effects of adolescent childbearing on multigenerational African-American families.

Laura Desimone, MPA

Laura Desimone received a Master's of Public Administration, 1991 from American University. While in Washington, D.C., she worked for the National Association of Housing and Redevelopment Officials (NAHRO), a national program designed to remove public housing residents from the welfare rolls and provide them with education and training in order to become self-sufficient. In 1991, she entered the Ph.D. Public Policy Analysis Curriculum at the University of North Carolina at Chapel Hill. Her research interests focus on national and local policies regarding school success of socioeconomically disadvantaged minority students.

Peggye Dilworth-Anderson, PhD

Peggye Dilworth-Anderson, Ph.D., is a Professor of Human Development and Family Studies at the University of North Carolina at Greensboro. She received her undergraduate degree in sociology from Tuskegee Institute in 1970, her Master's and Doctorate degrees from Northwestern University in 1975. She received additional training in family therapy at Northwestern in 1985 from the Institute of Psychiatry. Her recent studies in aging and Alzheimer's disease were done at the Harvard University Geriatric Center in 1990.

Dr. Dilworth-Anderson's research focus is on aging and Black family functioning and intergenerational relations in Black families. She received funding for her research from the March of Dimes Birth Defect Foundation and the Administration on Aging (AOA). She recently completed an AOA funded project on Black intergenerational support in a daycare setting involving at risk Black children and socially isolated elderly Blacks. Her research agenda involves studying the structure, process and outcome of caregiving to the elderly in Black families.

Dr. Dilworth-Anderson has served in numerous consulting capacities including among them her current membership on the Human Development and Aging Review Panel for NIA and as a consultant on several research projects on aging and elderly Blacks. She is also on the editorial board of two journals.

Teresa Donati, PhD

Teresa Donati is a Professor of Sociology at Fairleigh Dickinson University at Teaneck. She has been active in the development of the all-university Core Curriculum. She has served as Department Chair of the Sociology Department. Her educational background includes a Doctorate and Master's degrees from Columbia University. Research interests include cultural change and curricular issues in higher education, family and religious changes as outcomes of cultural change. Dr. Donati was the recipient of the New Jersey Fellowship on the Academic Profession, and Fairleigh Dickinson University teaching award.

Greer Litton Fox, PhD

Greer Litton Fox, Ph.D., is University of Tennessee in Knoxville Distinguished Service Professor in the Department of Child and Family Studies at The University of Tennessee in Knoxville, Tennessee. She received her Doctorate in population sociology from the University of Michigan. A Danforth Fellow, she has maintained a commitment to undergraduate instruction and teaches family diversity by race, ethnicity, gender and class. Her research interests have included adolescent sexual socialization and behavior and parent-adolescent relationships; antecedents and consequences of divorce; and issues of violence and justice within and outside families. She is a member of the American Sociological Association, National Council on Family Relations, Population Association of America, and Sociologists for Women in Society. She serves on the editorial board of *Family Perspectives*, *Journal of Family Issues*, and the *Journal of Marriage and Family.*

Kathleen Gass-Sternas, PhD, RN

Kathleen Gass-Sternas is an Assistant Professor of Nursing at Rutgers, The State University of New Jersey. She has been a Henry Rutgers Research Fellow; and consultant on loss, grieving; engaged in health promotion for the bereaved and of bereavement support groups. Her educational background includes: a Ph.D. in nursing from Case Western Reserve University; Master's in nursing from Pennsylvania State University; and Baccalaureate in nursing from Rutgers University. Professional activities include participation in: Sigma Theta Tau International Honor Society in Nursing; Midwest Nursing Research Society; The Gerontological Society of America; and the American Society on Aging. She has published research in the area of stress and coping with a focus on the stressors, coping process, resources and health of widowed persons.

Michael K. Godfrey, PhC

Michael K. Godfrey is a Doctoral student in Family and Human Development at Utah State University and Research Associate at the Early Intervention Research Institute. His professional associations include the Society for Research in Child Development and the National Association for the Education of Young Children. He has served on committees overseeing the development or implementation of key services for children. He has made presentations at national, state, and local conferences and co-authored papers on topics relating to children and their families. His research interests include child care, parenting, and children's socialization.

Geoffrey L. Greif, DSW, ACSW, LCSW

Geoffrey L. Greif is Associate Professor at the School of Social Work, University of Maryland at Baltimore. He received his Doctorate at the Columbia University School Social Work in 1983. His research interests include single parent families, parental kidnapping, fathering, AIDS, group work and family therapy with low-income families. He has authored or co-authored more than fifty articles and book chapters as well as four books, *Single Fathers* (Lexington, 1985), *Mothers Without Custody* (Lexington, 1988), *The Daddy Track and the Single Father* (Lexington, 1990), and *When Parents Kidnap* (Free Press, 1993). He is contributing editor to *The Single Parent* magazine and a reviewer for professional journals.

Shirley M. H. Hanson, RN, PMHNP, PhD, FAAN

Shirley M. H. Hanson is a Professor in the Department of Family Nursing at Oregon Health Sciences University in Portland, Oregon. She received her Doctorate at the University of Washington in 1979. Her research interests include families and health, single parent families, fatherhood, and child/adolescent/family mental health and therapy. She is a member of the American Nurses Association, Sigma Theta Tau, American Association of Marriage and Family Therapy (Supervisor), and the National Council on Family Relations (Certified Family Life Educator). Dr. Hanson also practices as a child, marriage, and family therapist. She has authored/coedited many articles and chapters in books and journals including *Dimensions Of Fatherhood* (1985), *Fatherhood and Families in Cultural Context* (1991), and *Family Assessment and Intervention* (1991). She is on the editorial board/reviewer for *Nursing Research, Western Journal of Nursing Research,* and *Advances in Nursing Science*. Dr. Hanson is a Fellow of the American Academy of Nursing.

Marsha L. Heims, EdD

Marsha L. Heims is an Associate Professor in the Department of Family Nursing at Oregon Health Sciences University in Portland, Oregon. She is a Registered Nurse with a Master of Science in child health and health education (University of Arizona, 1974) and a Doctorate in Educational Leadership, and Postsecondary Education from Portland State University (1991). The focus of her career has been the health of children and families, and the education of the nurses. Her research interests include family nursing and nursing education. Dr. Heims is a member of the American Nurses Association, Sigma Theta Tau International Honor Society of Nursing, the National League for Nursing including the Council for Research in Nursing Education, the National Council on Family Relations, the American Association for Higher Education, and the American Educational Research Association. She has coauthored articles on nursing education and family nursing in the *Journal of Nursing Education* and *Family Relations*.

Catalina Herrerías, PhD

Catalina Herrerías is Regional Director for the Philadelphia Office of Lutheran Children and Family Service of Eastern Pennsylvania, a private, nonprofit social service agency affiliated with the Evangelical Lutheran Church of America. She is a licensed social worker with a Master of Social Work in administration and planning (University of Oklahoma, 1981) and a Ph.D. (Social Work) specializing in child and family relationships (University of Texas at Austin, 1984). Her career has focused on child welfare services (foster care and protective services) and ethnic sensitive practice with Latino populations. Her research interests include maternal noncustody, ethnic sensitive practice with Latino populations, and child sexual abuse prevention. Dr. Herrerías is a member of the Society for the Psychological Study of Social Issues, American Association for the Protection of Children, and the International Society of Child Abuse and Neglect. She has authored articles on child abuse prevention and research methodology. Her safety guides in child sexual abuse prevention ("For Kids Only," "Teen to Teen," and "Parent Talk") are used throughout the U.S.

June Andrews Horowitz, PhD

June Andrews Horowitz is an Associate Professor and Chairperson of the Department of Psychiatric-Mental Health Nursing, Boston College School of Nursing, in Chestnut Hill, Massachusetts. She is a Registered Nurse with a Master of Science in Psychiatric-Mental Health Nursing (Rutgers-The State University of New Jersey, 1975) and a Doctor of Philosophy in Nursing Research and Theory Development from New York University (1982). Her clinical and scholarly efforts have focused on family mental health. Family structure and patterns of development, members' functioning, postpartum adjustment, couples' negotiation processes, and parenting have been areas of particular interest. Dr. Horowitz is a member of the American Nurses Association; Sigma Theta Tau International, Honor Society of Nursing; The Society for Education and Research in Psychiatric-Mental Health Nursing (SERPN), Nurses United for Responsible Services (NURS), and the American Orthopsychiatric Association. She has written articles and book chapters concerning her clinical and scholarly interests and nursing education, and has coauthored a book on parenting.

Marilyn Ihinger-Tallman, PhD

Marilyn Ihinger-Tallman is Professor and Chair of the Department of Sociology at Washington State University. She received her B.A. and M.A. degrees from the University of California, Riverside, and her Ph.D. from the University of Minnesota. Ihinger-Tallman's research and writings focus on divorce, remarriage and stepfamilies. She has written numerous research articles and two books on the subject. A third book, *Stepparenting: Issues in Theory, Research and Practice* will be published in early 1994 by Greenwood Publishing Group.

Kris Jeter, PhD

Kris Jeter received a Ph.D. in Human Development from Texas Women's University, 1975. Currently she is a Principal in Beacon Associates Ltd., Inc., Newark, Delaware, a research and consulting firm. She is the Analytic Assay Editor for the international journal, *Marriage & Family Review.* She has authored over 60 publications and produced over 60 photo essays, illustrated lectures, and multimedia events. Her scholarly writing is on the family over the life cycle; utilizing the family as a unit of analysis in research; and examining its important linkages with archetypal psychology and studies. Her scholarly audiovisual production work is on cross-cultural whole systems transitions, the individual and community developing consciously, choosing appropriate changes which restore and expand the mythic story. The most popular photo essay is "Guiding Lights: Hearing Messages, Seeing Angels." She is a collector and cataloger of a research image archive and a library of 35,000 cross-cultural slides.

Doris Moor Julian, EdD

Doris Moor Julian (Doris J. Julian) is an Associate Professor of Family Nursing, Department of Family Nursing, the Oregon Health Sciences University, Portland, Oregon. Past experiences include: Training Director of Nursing, University-affiliated Program, Portland and Instructor and Research Associate, Mental Retardation Nurse Training Project, Seattle, Washington. She received a Doctorate in Higher Education from the University of Oregon, and Baccalaureate and Master's degrees in Nursing from the University of Washington. Research interests, include family nursing, disability, single or primary parenting and adult learning. She was elected Fellow in the American Association on Mental Retardation in 1990 for contributions to the field.

Lee Kimmons, PhD

Lee Kimmons is a Marriage and Family Therapist who holds a M.A. in counseling, Wake Forest University and a Ph.D. in Family Relations from Florida State University. He has taught at the University of Nebraska in the Department of Human Development and the Family and served as a coordinator for the National Symposiums on Building Family Strengths. More recently, he taught in the Department of Human Resources, University of

Hawaii Cooperative Extension Service. He is a member of the National Council on Family Relations and the American Association of Marriage & Family Therapists. His research interests include work and family issues, sex roles, media and family relations. He has previously co-authored articles on rural, midlife single adults and filmography on single parenting in Family Relations.

Linda Darmer Ladd, PhD

Linda Darmer Ladd is an Assistant Professor in the Extension Home Economics Department of Oregon State University. She received her Doctorate in Human Development and Family Studies from Oregon State University, Corvallis, Oregon; and a Master's degree in Psychology from Portland State University. Research interests include parenting, family systems, and communication.

Mark Lino, PhD

Mark Lino is an Economist with the Family Economics Research Group of the U.S. Department of Agriculture. His educational background includes a Doctorate and Master's degree in Consumer Economics from Cornell University. Research interests include the economic status of single parent families, expenditures on children, and changes in the economic status of American families.

William Marsiglio, PhD

William Marsiglio is an Associate Professor of Sociology, Department of Sociology, University of Florida. He was formerly an Instructor and Assistant Professor, Oberlin College, Oberlin, Ohio. He received a Doctorate and Master's degrees in Sociology from the Ohio State University. Theory and research interests include: sexuality, procreation, parenting, and primary relationship issues relevant to men of varying ages. He is currently serving as guest editor for two forthcoming volumes of *Journal of Family Issues* devoted to fatherhood issues.

Cynthia Merriwether-deVries, PhD

Cynthia Merriwether-deVries is a Ph.D. candidate in Human Development and Family Studies at the Pennsylvania State University. Her research interests include two major areas: evaluating the role of context on intergenerational family process, and the role of sibling relationships in promoting African-American family strength and resiliency. Her master's thesis explored the association between the reported level of depressive symptoms and neighborhood quality among urban resident adolescents. Ms. Merriwether-deVries is a member of the Golden Key Honor Society and the Association of Black Psychologists. She has coauthored an article on surrogate grandparenting among African-Americans, and is coauthor of a forthcoming book chapter on intergenerational relationships among adolescent African-American parents.

Jennifer K. McKay, MPA

Jennifer K. McKay, a 1993 recipient of the Presidential Management Internship, currently is employed as a Research Assistant for the Cities in Schools Evaluation Project, University of North Carolina School of Social Work. She is a 1993 graduate of the Master of Public Administration Program at the University of North Carolina at Chapel Hill where she specialized in education and labor policy analysis. She has worked for the Fiscal Research Division of the North Carolina General Assembly and the Division of Youth Services, North Carolina Department of Human Resources.

Brent C. Miller, PhD

Brent C. Miller is a Professor in the Department of Family and Human Development at Utah State University. He has been the Publications Vice President and Program Vice President for the National Council on Family Relations, and in 1991-92 was President of NCFR. His other professional affiliations include the American Sociological Association, the Society for Research on Adolescence, and the Population Association of America. He has been a member and chair of several national peer review and advisory panels for the National Institute of Child Health and Human Development and for the Office of Adolescent Pregnancy Programs. He is widely published on marriage and family topics, and adolescent pregnancy-related issues. His most recent book is *Preventing Adolescent Pregnancy: Model Programs and Evaluations* (1992).

Loretta Pinkard Prater, PhD

Loretta Pinkard Prater is an Assistant Professor of Human Ecology, School of Education, the University of Tennessee at Chattanooga. She has been a secondary school Home Economics classroom teacher and school district level administrator of Drug Free Schools. Her educational background includes: (1) a Doctorate in Child and Family Studies from the University of Tennessee at Knoxville; (2) Baccalaureate and Master's degrees from the University of Tennessee at Chattanooga in Secondary Education and Guidance Counseling, respectively; and she received vocational teacher certification from the University of Georgia at Athens. Research interests include adolescent pregnancy, parenting and social issues affecting minorities. She was selected as the C.C. Bond Professor of Education in 1992.

Benjamin Schlesinger, MSW, PhD

Benjamin Schlesinger is a Professor in the Faculty of Social Work, University of Toronto, Canada. He has been on staff since 1960. He received a M.S.W. from the University of Toronto and a Ph.D. in Family Relationships from Cornell (1961). He is the author and editor of twenty-two books in the area of family life and human sexuality; five of which relate to one-parent families. His research interests include remarriage, grandparenthood, one-parent families, lasting marriages, and the sandwich generation. He is a member of the National Council on Family Relations, Vanier Institute of Family, and the Association for Canadian Studies. He spent his sabbatical years in India, Jamaica, Australia, New Zealand, and Israel. His articles have appeared in North American and International Journals. He is a Fellow of the Royal Society of Canada.

Joan Foster Shireman, PhD

Joan Foster Shireman is a Professor at the Graduate School of Social Work at Portland State University and the Director of the Ph.D. program at that school. Past academic positions include Associate Professor at the Jane Addams College of Social Work, University of Illinois, Director of Research at the Chicago Child Care Society, Chicago, Illinois. Her Ph.D. and M.A. degrees are from the School of Social Service Administration at the University of Chicago. Her research and writing has focused on issues of protective services, foster care, and adoption. She is the author of numerous journal articles and book chapters, and co-author of one book.

Marcia R. Steinbock, JD

Marcia R. Steinbock is an Assistant Professor of Criminal Justice at Richard Stockton College of New Jersey. She is a licensed social worker and attorney with a Master's of Social Work (State University of New York at Albany, 1977) and a Juris Doctor (Rutgers University School of Law, 1982). The focus of her career has been counseling and representing indigent individuals in the criminal justice system and the education of students who will be working with this population. Her research interests include poverty and homelessness. She is a member of the National Association of Social Workers, the New Jersey State Bar Association, the Academy of Criminal Justice Sciences and the National Society of Experiential Education. She has authored articles on homelessness and experiential education.

Marvin B. Sussman, PhD

Marvin B. Sussman is UNIDEL Professor of Human Behavior Emeritus at the College of Human Resources, University of Delaware; and Member of the CORE Faculty, Union Graduate School, Union Institute, Cincinnati, Ohio. A member of many professional organizations, he was awarded the 1980 Ernest W. Burgess Award of the National Council on Family Relations. In 1983, he was elected to the prestigious academy of Groves for scholarly contributions to the field, as well as awarded a life-long membership for services to the Groves Conference on Marriage and the Family in 1984. Dr. Sussman received the Distinguished Family Scholar Award of the Society for the Study of Social Problems (1985) and the Lee Founders Award (1992). He has over 275 publications.

Lynda Henley Walters, PhD

Lynda Henley Walters, Ph.D., is a Professor in the Department of Child and Family Development at The University of Georgia in Athens, GA. Her research interests include families and law, cross-cultural comparisons of families, and issues in adolescent development. She is past president of the National Council on Family Relations, and a member of the Society for Research on Adolescents, Society for Research in Child Development, and the American Home Economics Association. She has authored/coauthored articles and chapters in books including *Fatherhood and Families in Cultural Context* (Springer, 1991), *Journal of Marriage and the Family, Family Relations, American Behavioral Scientist,* and *Educational and Psychological Measurement.* She is a reviewer for *Journal of Marriage and the Family, Journal of Family Issues, Journal of Adolescent Research,* and *Journal of Early Adolescence.*

Karl R. White, PhD

Karl R. White is a Professor of Psychology and Special Education at Utah State University. He has been extensively involved in research on the effects and costs of early intervention programs during the past 15 years. He has directed numerous research projects funded by federal agencies, state government, and private foundations and has served as a consultant to the U.S. Department of Education, the Bureau of Maternal and Child Health, the Administration on Children, Youth, and Families, the National Institutes of Health, and numerous state and local agencies. He has written extensively on issues related to provision of early intervention services with over 50 articles or book chapters and more than 100 presentations made at professional meetings.

Anisa Mary Zvonkovic, PhD

Anisa Mary Zvonkovic is an Assistant Professor of Human Development and Family Sciences, College of Home Economics, Oregon State University. Her advanced degrees (Doctorate and Master's) are in Human Development and Family Studies from the Pennsylvania State University. She has previously published on the topic of divorce in the *Journal of Divorce & Remarriage* and *Contemporary Psychology*. Her other major research interests are work and family.

Glossary of Terms

Adoptive parent support group: A group of parents who have adopted, usually in similar circumstances, and who meet regularly to discuss their experiences as adoptive parents.

Adoption subsidies: Payments made by the state to adopting families, based on the child's needs and the family's economic status. The purpose is to remove barriers to adoption of children for whom adoptive homes are difficult to find, and for whom expensive care may be needed.

Age of majority: Age at which, by law, one is entitled to the management of personal affairs and to the enjoyment of civic rights; the opposite of minority. Age of majority differs according to state and issue.

Agency placements: Placements made by a licensed child welfare agency. Such agencies usually work with the birth mother around her decision for her child, conduct an adoption study, make placements, and provide supervision and sometimes support services after the adoption.

Anticipatory socialization: Having been prepared to expect certain patterns of behavior which conform to social or cultural norms.

Before-tax income: Total income from major sources such as salary or earnings, alimony and child support, public assistance, Social Security, pensions, and other sources.

Best interest of the child: A principle used by courts to make decisions about child custody.

Capital-intensive productions: Method of production that uses proportionately more capital (machinery, tools, and facilities) relative to other factors of production (labor, land).

Case law: Law that is the result of an aggregation of cases or evolves from judgments in a series of cases on a particular subject.

Child care role: The child care role of the widowed father includes becoming father involved in feeding and bathing the children, helping them with their school work and seeing to their discipline.

Child custody: The care, control, and maintenance of a child which is awarded by a court to a parent or other person.

Child socialization role: The child socialization role of the widowed father is to pass on to children the basic traits of character and citizenship that are essential to individual and societal well-being.

Child support: A legal obligation to provide economic resources for living.

Conjugal bereavement: Loss of a spouse through death.

Custodial status: Refers to the court-ordered relationship of the parent and child wherein the parent's responsibilities for the child are changed from those of a residential parent.

Decision-making model: The theoretical process by which one identifies a problem, lists alternatives, considers the pros and cons of each alternative, selects a path, and accepts responsibility for a decision.

Debt: Home mortgage, investment real estate, home equity lines of credit, credit cards, car loans, and other.

De facto relationship: A relationship that is actually existing.

Deficit model: The theoretical structure which views behavior in terms of negative consequences.

De jure relationship: A relationship that is ordered by the court; irrespective of what is actually occurring.

Developmental delay: Each state decides its own definition of developmental delay and designates the levels of functioning that determine eligibility for services. Generally, children need to exhibit a delay in one or more developmental areas, e.g., cognitive, physical (vision and hearing), language, psychosocial, and self-help). Standardized diagnostic instruments and procedures are used to assess development.

Disability: Includes developmental delay or diagnosed physical or mental condition that has a high probability of resulting in developmental delay (Down syndrome). These conditions may be due to congenital abnormality, trauma, deprivation, or disease.

Domino effect: An incident occurs which triggers a series of other related happenings.

Due process: Judicial processes in which a person must be notified and have an opportunity to be heard before the federal or state government can deprive that person of life, liberty or property, as interpreted by courts regarding the 5th and the 14th Amendments to the United States.

Early intervention services: Services that are designed to meet the developmental needs of each child (up through age 5) who meet the disability eligibility requirements, and the needs of the family related to enhancing the child's development. Services are selected in collaboration with parents and are provided by a multidisciplinary team. Assessment, education (i.e., instruction in all the developmental areas), therapy (e.g., speech, physical, occupational therapies) and health services are among the services provided.

Ecological perspective: In the ecological perspective, what happens outside the family unit may have as much of an influence on what happens inside it. Outside family influences include neighborhood, extended family and friends, employment, the larger community, and the legal milieu that surrounds each family.

Emancipation: To be set free; often equated with reaching the age of majority.

Empowerment: The ability to use resources to take charge of one's own destiny and future well-being.

Ex parte: A court proceeding in which, because of the emergency nature of the action, only one side is present.

Family: A family is a group of two persons or more related by birth, marriage, or adoption and residing together.

Family group: A family group is any two or more persons residing together, and related by birth, marriage, or adoption.

Family household: A family household is a household maintained by a family, and any unrelated persons who may be residing there are included.

Family of origin: The family in which a person is reared as a child.

Federalism: A philosophy which promotes the rights of each state to make law and policy for its citizens with a minimal amount of interference from the federal government.

Financial assets: Checking, savings, money market, and retirement accounts; certificates of deposit; stocks; bonds; trusts; and other.

Head of household: The person in charge of the provision and management of resources to care for the needs of family members.

Housed children or families: Those persons who have housing, as opposed to those who do not, who are considered homeless.

Household: A household consists of all the persons who occupy a housing unit. A household includes the related family members and all the unrelated persons who share the housing unit.

Householder: The householder refers to the person in whose name the housing unit is maintained.

Human capital: Skills, abilities, ideals, health, etc., that result from expenditures on education, on-the-job training programs, and medical care. These characteristics, which usually require an initial investment, give rise to greater personal productivity.

Independent adoption: Adoptive placements arranged directly with birth parents, or through a doctor or attorney who acts as intermediary. All but six states permit independent adoptions, but laws regulating them vary.

Joint custody: An assignment of physical custody to one or both parents and legal custody to both parents.

Jurisdiction: The authority by which courts and judicial officers hear and decide cases.

Labor-intensive production: Method of production that uses proportionately more labor (people) relative to other factors of production (capital, land).

Long-arm statutes: State legislative acts that make it possible for a state to have jurisdiction over a person in another state.

Macroeconomics: Study of the overall aspects and workings of a national economy, such as income, output, and the interrelationship among diverse economic sectors.

Manufacturing sector: The sector of the economy which specializes in the processing of agricultural products, the extraction of raw materials, and the production of man-made goods.

Marital presumption: Assumption that the integrity of the marital unit is of primary importance. A presumption is stronger than a mere assumption in that the party against whom it is directed must present evidence to rebut.

Marital status: The marital status classification identifies four major categories; never married, married, widowed, and divorced.

Married couple: A married couple is a husband and wife enumerated as members of the same household.

Noncustodial father: Men whose parental rights and obligations are redefined through judicial action.

Noncustodial parent: A situation wherein the parent and child are not in residence with each other. This situation is paradoxical as biological in-residence parenting is that standard against which all other parenting arrangements are measured.

Nonfinancial assets: Principal residence, vehicles, business, investment real estate, and other.

Nonresidential parent: A parent who does not share a primary residence with their child.

Own children and related children: "Own" children in a family are sons and daughters, including stepchildren and adopted children, of the householder.

Parenting: A dynamic process that is in continual development over the life course, subject to change as parent's circumstances, preferences, and children's developmental needs change. Parenting includes a contextual feature of the parent and child being in some type of residence with each other.

Per se: In and of itself, alone.

Persons of Hispanic origin: Persons of Hispanic origin were those who indicated that their origin was Mexican, Puerto Rican, Cuban, Central or South American, or some other Hispanic origin.

Poverty: The absence of sufficient economic resources to adequately meet basic needs. Families or individuals with income below a particular threshold are classified as below the poverty level. The poverty thresholds are updated every year to reflect changes in the Consumer Price Index.

Precedent: A decision of a court that serves as an example or authority for a similar case arising later on a similar question of law.

Prima facie: At first view.

Principle of legitimacy: Bronislaw Malinowski's term describing the child's need for a socially recognized father, in order for the child to obtain status placement in that society.

Productivity growth: A change in the efficiency with which output is produced.

Protective order: A court order which defines behavioral limits, i.e., in a domestic violence case the violator can be subjected to contempt proceedings.

Putative father: The alleged father of an illegitimate child.

Race: The population is divided into three groups on the basis of race; White, Black, and other races. The last category includes Indians, Japanese, Chinese, and any other race except White and Black.

Real wages: Wages measured in terms of the quantity of goods that can be purchased. Because it controls for inflation, the use of real wages allows for comparisons in wage rates across time.

Reference groups: Groups of which we need not be members; comprised of persons of similar status, against whom we measure our progress in a given status.

Related subfamily: A related subfamily is a married couple with or without children, or one parent with one or more own never-married children under 18 years old, living in a household and related to, but not including, the person or couple who maintains the household.

Remand: To send back, specifically when an appellate court sends a case back to the original court in which it was heard to have some further action taken on it there.

Role: The pattern of behavior expected of a person in a group.

Role theory perspective: According to role theory, roles are the prescriptions and expectations of self and others for the behaviors that are required in a particular situation.

Safety net: The minimal level of social services which prevent people from becoming destitute.

Service providers: Generic term for the multidisciplinary personnel who provide any intervention services.

Service sector: The sector of the economy which specializes in the provision of business and personal services, such as retail trade, real estate, and banking. It is distinguishable from the manufacturing sector because no goods are produced.

Significant others: Persons who are perceived by an individual as important and influential figures in their life.

Single fatherhood: A father having sole custody the vast majority of the time, i.e., a minimum of five days and nights a week on average. In these arrangements, the fathers are performing the bulk of the childrearing and are seen as having to adjust accordingly.

Single parent adoption: Adoption of a child by a person who is not in a marital relationship and who plans, at the time of the adoption, to raise the child without a partner. Single parent adopters make a conscious decision to become single parents.

Single-parent families: Single parents and their children who reside in housing units they own or rent.

Single-parent situations: Single-parents and their children who reside in housing units they own or rent, as well as single parents and their children who share others' homes.

Sole custody: An assignment of legal rights, duties and obligations for children to one parent only; residential (physical) and legal (decision-making) custody are two major components of sole custody.

Special needs children: Older children, physically handicapped children, children of color, children who are members of sibling groups, and children with serious emotional and behavioral problems.

Split custody: In most jurisdictions split custody refers to the division of siblings between parents.

Statute: A law enacted by a legislative body of a nation or a state.

Statutory law: Law created by acts of a legislature as contrasted with law generated by judicial opinions (case law) or administrative regulations.

Statutory presumption: A presumption in a statute that if certain facts are provided, then other facts are presumed to be true.

Subjective utilities model: The theoretical framework which proposes that persons and/or institutions within the environment surrounding the individual impacts behavior.

Therapeutic role: The therapeutic role of the widowed father is to provide continuity and sensitivity to help grieving children cope with the loss of a mother.

Total expenditures: Expenses on housing, food (at home and away from home), transportation, clothing, personal insurance and pensions (including Social Security taxes), entertainment, health care, education, personal care items, and miscellaneous goods and services.

Unrelated subfamily: An unrelated subfamily is a married couple with or without children, or a single parent with one or more own never-married children under 18 years old living in a household.

Wider families: Families which emerge from lifestyle, and which go beyond the bounds of kin or marriage. They arise out of needs which change as lifestyles change, and vary in duration; they are noncoercive, noncontractual, and are only incidentally (if at all) connected to the presence of children.

Years of school completed: Education of parent refers to the years of school completed by the parent.

COSTS: Please figure your cost to order quality copies of an article.

1. Set-up charge per article: $8.00
   ($8.00 × number of separate articles) __________
2. Photocopying charge for each article:
   - 1-10 pages: $1.00 __________
   - 11-19 pages: $3.00 __________
   - 20-29 pages: $5.00 __________
   - 30+ pages: $2.00/10 pages __________
3. Flexicover (optional): $2.00/article __________
4. Postage & Handling: US: $1.00 for the first article/
   $.50 each additional article __________
   Federal Express: $25.00 __________
   Outside US: $2.00 for first article/
   $.50 each additional article __________
5. Same-day FAX service: $.35 per page __________
6. Local Photocopying Royalty Payment: should you wish to copy the article yourself. Not intended for photocopies made for resale. $1.50 per article per copy
   (i.e. 10 articles x $1.50 each = $15.00) __________

GRAND TOTAL: __________

METHOD OF PAYMENT: (please check one)

❑ Check enclosed ❑ Please ship and bill. PO # ________________
(sorry we can ship and bill to bookstores only! All others must pre-pay)

❑ Charge to my credit card: ❑ Visa; ❑ MasterCard; ❑ American Express;

Account Number: ________________ Expiration date: __________

Signature: ✗ ________________ Name: ________________

Institution: ________________ Address: ________________

City: ________________ State: __________ Zip: __________

Phone Number: ________________ FAX Number: ________________

MAIL or *FAX* THIS ENTIRE ORDER FORM TO:

Attn: **Marianne Arnold**
Haworth Document Delivery Service
The Haworth Press, Inc.
10 Alice Street
Binghamton, NY 13904-1580

or FAX: (607) 722-1424
or CALL: 1-800-3-HAWORTH
(1-800-342-9678; 9am-5pm EST)